RESEARCH AND STATISTICS FOR SOCIAL WORKERS

Using real social work examples written specifically to allay student fears, *Research and Statistics for Social Workers* brings research and statistics together, bridging the gap to practice. This book covers conceptualization, ethics, cultural competence, design, qualitative research, individual and program evaluation as well as nonparametric and parametric statistical tests. The tests are explained narratively, mathematically, as well as with a comprehensive step-by-step, fully illustrated SPSS computer analysis of social work data.

Tom R. Lawson, PhD, is Professor and Director of the International Studies Program at the Kent School of Social Work at the University of Louisville. He consults globally with scientific academies, universities, governmental agencies and international organizations with regard to social work education, and issues concerning social and health policy. He serves as a scientific reviewer for publications of the Institute for Political Science of the Hungarian Academy of Science. He holds honorary doctorates and professorships from universities in China, Russia and Hungary, is a Fellow of the University of Applied Sciences, Munich, Germany and was awarded the Order of Merit Knight's Cross by the President of Hungary. Dr. Lawson teaches Comparative International Social Policy at the MSSW and BSW level, and doctoral classes in research, statistics and theory. Dr. Lawson is a retired Army Social Work Officer who developed and is the coordinator of the Military Social Work Specialization.

Anna C. Faul, PhD, is Professor and Associate Dean for Academic Affairs at the Kent School of Social Work at the University of Louisville. Dr. Faul is a Hartford Faculty Scholar, and she has published numerous articles and book chapters on various research topics over the years, ranging from child welfare, measurement issues in social work, women and diversity issues, gerontology and health disparities. During Dr. Faul's time at the University of Louisville she has received various awards, namely Outstanding Faculty Award, Provost Award for Faculty Advising and the Distinguished Educator Achievement Award from the Kentucky Association for Gerontology.

A.N. Verbist, MSSW, completed his doctoral studies at the University of Louisville in the fall of 2018. His practice background is in foster care and residential treatment. His research interests are centered on child welfare; he is currently investigating the role of standardized assessments in evidence-based treatment decision-making.

RESEARCH AND STATISTICS FOR SOCIAL WORKERS

Tom R. Lawson, Anna C. Faul, and A.N. Verbist

NEW YORK AND LONDON

First published 2019
by Routledge
52 Vanderbilt Avenue, New York, NY 10017

and by Routledge
2 Park Square, Milton Park, Abingdon, Oxon, OX14 4RN

Routledge is an imprint of the Taylor & Francis Group, an informa business

Library of Congress Cataloging-in-Publication Data
Names: Lawson, Thomas R., author. | Faul, A. C. (Anna Catharina), author. | Verbist, A.N. (Alton Nathaniel), author.
Title: Research and statistics for social workers / Thomas Lawson, Anna Faul, and A.N. Verbist.
Description: New York, NY : Routledge, 2019. | Includes bibliographical references and index. |
Identifiers: LCCN 2018040429 (print) | LCCN 2018041976 (ebook) | ISBN 9781315640495 (Master Ebook) | ISBN 9781317277187 (Web pdf) | ISBN 9781317277170 (ePub) | ISBN 9781317277163 (Mobipocket) | ISBN 9781138191020 (hardback) | ISBN 9781138191037 (pbk.)
Subjects: LCSH: Social service—Research—Methodology. | Social service—Statistical methods. | Social service—Practice.
Classification: LCC HV11 (ebook) | LCC HV11 .L294 2019 (print) | DDC 001.4—dc23
LC record available at https://lccn.loc.gov/2018040429

ISBN: 978-1-138-19102-0 (hbk)
ISBN: 978-1-138-19103-7 (pbk)
ISBN: 978-1-315-64049-5 (ebk)

Typeset in Times New Roman
by Apex CoVantage, LLC

Printed and bound by CPI Group (UK) Ltd, Croydon, CR0 4YY

Visit the eResources: www.routledge.com/9781138191037

We dedicate this book
To our families who have supported us
To our colleagues world-wide who have encouraged us
To our students who have inspired us and for whom it has been written

CONTENTS

Section 1

FOUNDATIONS OF RESEARCH

Chapter 1

INTRODUCTION—FEAR, RULES, LIGHT BULBS

The main function of this book is to assist students in learning how to get answers to questions that are important to the practice of social work. This may sound *simplistic* but it is not an easy task to get sound and usable answers to the important questions that social workers pose. It is our hope that this book will provide knowledge, methods and techniques that will assist you in obtaining those sound and usable answers to critical questions facing you as a social worker and those facing our profession.

In developing this book we assumed that (1) you want answers, (2) you might have zero knowledge and/or skills to obtain those answers and (3) (most likely the biggest assumption of all) you may have a mortal fear of research and statistics. We also assume there is one question you always ask when there is something that can improve your social work knowledge and skills—"How do I do it?" Throughout your journey using this book, you will see that it is a step-by-step, logical process of "How can I get answers to important questions for my practice and profession, and how can I get over my fear and become a better-informed social worker?"

Other research textbooks for social work have tried to explain the process of research by categorizing designs utilizing terms like descriptive, exploratory or experimental research, discussing in-depth how to collect data and how to read reports but typically not addressing statistics at all. It is our belief from teaching this material for many years that using a different approach fosters in students a greater interest, even enthusiasm, and more importantly, a much better understanding of the concepts and greater ability to use research and statistics as professional social workers. Furthermore, we also know that understanding how to do it as well as the ability to do it makes better practitioners who, in turn, provide much better services to those in need.

You will see as you continue through the chapters that the question(s) you pose, the amount of knowledge you have about the area, how you measure things to answer the question, and the importance of gathering clean, reliable and valid information become critically important to get the best possible answer to your question. These topics are presented in such a way that you will be able to understand and utilize appropriate methods and skills to obtain the answer. We know that many of you might not conduct a study yourself, but most of you in the future as a practicing social worker will be involved in a study. Even if you are not involved directly in getting the answer to a social work question, it is important for you to be able to accurately access the answer someone else provides.

RULE 1: DON'T IMMEDIATELY ASSUME YOU CAN'T DO THIS

Learning research and statistics is much like learning a language. As social workers you have already learned or started to learn many new languages—the language of social work, the language of mental health, the language of oppression. Now, it is important that you learn the language of research. You will first learn a few words that you are not able to put into a sentence, and, at this point, a paragraph would be out of the question. But slowly words are learned and simple sentences can be constructed; even if the grammar and pronunciation or gender is not absolutely correct, you will be able to converse. Give yourself time. Remember as a social worker you would not expect a client to be able to do something immediately—give yourself the same consideration.

RULE 2: TRUST US—WE KNOW THAT IT IS NOT SOMETHING YOU WILL BE ABLE TO DO OVERNIGHT

Remember the light bulb! The light bulb will go on for you as a flicker and go off for a while. It will continue to go on again and off again. This is normal! It will take a while for the bulb to remain on for longer periods of time and even for those of us who have taught this for years—YES—our light bulbs can also go on and off.

RULE 3: JUST KEEP PUTTING ENERGY INTO THAT LIGHT BULB

As an overview of how the book is organized we will take just a few pages to orient you to the process of how to obtain answers through the research and statistical process. If you start with a very basic question, have minimal knowledge to answer that question and there is no literature to provide a good answer, the question is likely to be, "Does it exist and if so how much is there?" An example of this type of question might be: "What reasons do clients give for not getting to their appointment in my agency?" If there is no data already collected by your agency ("literature") that can give you the answer, then this becomes an important unanswered question for you and your agency; important because you need to know what hampers clients from getting to the agency to receive much-needed services. The answer to this question is one that can be obtained by designing a small research study, gathering and then analyzing data. However, if there is data already collected by the agency and the information is available, then you do not need to do research to get the answer; simply refer to the answer already provided. The research process is one that is ever evolving from the basic to the more complex. The same is true of the process of learning research and statistics. The key to research and the key to your understanding of research and statistics is to maintain energy, to press on, and to always keep putting energy into the light bulb.

RULE 4: DO NOT CREATE A STUDY AND COLLECT DATA BEFORE DETERMINING IF THE ANSWER IS AVAILABLE IN THE LITERATURE

For a social worker, it is important to conduct research on **unanswered questions** that impact the well-being of individuals, families, groups, communities and the world. Whether the question is a very basic one of trying to determine if something exists or a more complex question of determining the cause of a problem or the effectiveness of an intervention, **there is no difference in importance. Value should be placed on the need for an answer that is accurate** and not on being a question of causation involving complicated and high-level statistical computations. ***The assessment of the value of research should be based upon the lack of an answer and the ability to utilize the answer.*** Answering the question, "Does it exist and, if so, how much?" does not constitute poor or low-level research. Many years ago, documenting the existence and prevalence of domestic violence certainly was highly valued and important research and was influential in shaping our profession's programs. The initial research on HIV/AIDS focused on documenting the incidence and not on a cure. These two examples demonstrate that the importance and value of research is related to the ability of that research to provide a good answer to an important and unanswered question and not that it is a highly sophisticated causal design. **Clearly, if the question of existence and amount has been answered, then it would not be of benefit to do this study again.** Rather, research should move on to determining the conditions under which domestic violence or HIV/AIDS occurs as the next question to be answered and would be the appropriate level and sequence of research. Some insist that there is a hierarchy of good and bad, more important or less important research, depending upon the type of question or the level of statistical knowledge required to answer a question. Such thinking is elitist and stifles research into new and uncharted areas that are so critical to social work practice. From finding out the availability of drinkable water in a refugee camp to determining the success of a new and totally different intervention for single mothers in poverty, if that question has not been answered, then it is important and one for social work research to answer.

RULE 5: USE THE eRESOURCES: THEY ARE YOUR LEARNING FRIEND AND GUIDE

The special Chart of Statistical Tests has been designed to help you to select the appropriate test given in the number of samples and the level of measurement. It is an invaluable and easy-to-use tool. The set of problem exercises gives you the opportunity to practice your abilities. These exercises like those in the book have the answers provided. The **eResources** has been specifically constructed for social work students like yourself to "ease the pain and improve the gain". **USE IT!**

In this book you will also learn about and be able to calculate statistics. You will learn a lot more about it throughout this book and, again, remember **Rules 1, 2, 3, 4 and 5**. There are many different statistics and different ones are used with different types of research designs; you will learn that both the research design and statistics are combined to provide the answer to the question. Indeed, everything in research is driven by the question, with the research design and statistical analysis being specifically selected to provide the best possible answer.

So, if one looks at the types of research questions, the most basic would be, "Does it exist and, if so, how much exists?" The next level would be the question, "Is there a difference?" For example, "Is there a difference in the number of African Americans and Caucasians living in a particular county since the last census?" You can see this question compares two groups over time to determine the amount of change or difference. After obtaining the answer to that question, you might then move on to a question that would try to find what this difference might be attributed to. Can you find a relationship between something else and the change in the percent of African Americans living in the county? The answer to these questions can be very useful in your practice of social work and would provide direction to the delivery of better services to clients and the community. If a change has occurred—a difference in the percent of Caucasians and African Americans in a given county between the 2000 census and the 2010 census—then we would pose the question, "To what can we attribute this change?" We are now looking at relationships between certain variables (predictor/causal/independent variables) and the change in the number of African Americans in the county (predicted/outcome/dependent variable). We will have much more to say about types of variables, research designs, causal and correlational relationships and various statistical analyses, but, for now, just follow the train of research questions and logical thought process.

Often, in social work, we observe changes and seek to find relationships that might be highly related to that change and operate as if **the variable caused the change.** We always have to be very aware that we **cannot assume causality when there is a relationship** but can use these relationships that are highly correlated to seek to improve social work practice. So, if there is a change in the percent of African Americans and Caucasians in a given county, the social worker might begin to examine other things that occurred in that county during that ten-year time period. Has there been a change in employment or transportation? Has there been an economic downturn? Has there been a change in acceptance of African Americans in the community?

But since we are looking back into the past we have no way of knowing if any of those things "caused" the change. We simply do not know but are supposing that this is the result of those things. Finally, after investigating differences and finding relationships, we can begin to talk about experimenting and trying to create differences. So, if you look at our initial questions, you can begin to see the differences that occur with the types of questions we ask. Now the question becomes, "Can I create a difference? Can I do something that will make a difference? Can I do something that will make a difference occur?" There are many things you as a social work practitioner with questions you want answered can begin to investigate, and it is the function of this book to assist you to be able to find the answers to questions important to the field of social work.

WHAT ARE RESEARCH, STATISTICS AND SCIENCE?

As we told you in the previous section, you have to learn a new language; however, not only must you learn a new language, you will have to understand and be able to apply the scientific approach to problem solving. While you may have some knowledge of this approach, and indeed use it in your practice, we will become much more precise and specific as we delve into social work research.

What is the difference between the scientific method and ***untested*** practice wisdom (note that the word "untested" is critical to this definition of practice wisdom)? First, simply relying on ***untested*** practice wisdom that utilizes a conceptual scheme that cannot be scientifically tested can lead to very poor and potentially dangerous social work practice. But this is important and critical to the practice of our profession; ***practice wisdom can be scientifically framed and tested! That is why this book has been written—so that you, a social worker, can both utilize tested practice wisdom and also be able yourself to test that practice wisdom.*** The scientific way of thinking builds a theoretical structure based upon observation, makes sure that the theory is consistent, and continuously tests it empirically and revises theory based upon these empirical findings. Furthermore, scientists realize that concepts are created by people and therefore have to be defined and tested, not just accepted.

Second, the scientific method requires testing of theory and hypotheses. Common sense too often is used to test hypotheses; however, using common sense is selective and, because it is "your" common sense and not someone else's common sense, it is selective and biased to gather evidence in support of your position. We selectively perceive those events that support our hypotheses and selectively fail to perceive those events that do not support our position. The scientific method is an attempt to remove as much selectivity and subjectivity as possible.

Third, in the scientific method there is the need to control. As a social work scientist you, very carefully, mindfully and systematically, try to rule out variables that could potentially affect the outcome with the ultimate goal of keeping only those variables/things that cause or are related to the thing in which you are interested. For example, you have a question: "What causes/is related to a parent abusing their child?" The rule in/rule out process and notion of control would start with many ideas about what is related to parental abuse—gender, age, use of drugs, age of child, education, poverty and many more. The scientific method would lead you to start to test these variables to see the relationship.

Fourth, the scientist consistently pursues relationships between variables. With science, multiple and repetitive relationships are viewed as supporting the relationship between two variables. So the method stresses many observations of the same relationship occurring in the same way as a means to support the validity of that relationship before it can be introduced into good social work practice.

Finally, as professional social workers, there is a major difference in how we explain things. We do not accept explanations that cannot be tested. Certainly we have values that we do not test (e.g. social justice and the worth of all people), but these are values and not explanations. In social work we do not accept explanations or relationships without them being tested. Because a proposition cannot be tested does not mean that it may not be true or that the proposition is not important. In social work it is imperative for us as professionals to create policy, programs and interventions that have been tested and shown to be effective.

As social workers we have an interesting professional situation much like that of a physician. We have to utilize theory and interventions that apply for most people, but, at the same time, we also have to be concerned with and respond to individuals and their unique differences. That is why we have to be able to integrate into our profession and into our own personal world view the science of the group and general explanations as well as the science of the individual and idiosyncratic explanations. This book will primarily focus on the science of the group, but the authors equally value the science of the individual as developed in single subject/individual designs (Chapter 6) and in qualitative research (Chapter 7).

The scientific method is a special type of thinking and investigation. First we identify that we have difficulty in understanding something, or wonder why something happens the way it does. The first step is then to put this lack of understanding into a question. Thus, we now have a specific question that we are going to try to answer. For example, as a social worker you may have observed that there appears to be a group of clients who do not return for follow-up appointments in the clinic. You wonder about why some clients return and some do not. Is there something about those clients who do not return that is different from those who do return? Your question then is "What is the difference between clients who return for their appointments and those who do not return?" You observe those clients who return and who do not, and you go to the literature and read about which clients return and which do not. Following this, you have an idea about what the answer might be. You want to find out if this answer is correct. In order to find out if your proposed answer is correct, you have to put that answer into a particular format that is called a **hypothesis**. The hypothesis is basically your best guess about the relationship between two things (variables).

Now comes a very important step—critical thinking, reasoning and deduction. As social workers you now seriously examine the hypothesis you have formulated. In doing this you might end up with a very different hypothesis than you started with. For instance, in the example stated, you may, after some critical thinking and reading more about this situation in the literature, come to the conclusion that it may not be a question of what client characteristics are related to returning for services; it might be that it is the services that determine which clients return to the agency. Indeed, you may think that both aspects are important to be answered, and you may have to conduct studies into both client characteristics and program characteristics with respect to those who return and those who do not.

Another example might be that there is going to be a new program developed in your community living center for the elderly. There will be a 30-minute daily stretching and easy exercise program tailored for each person. Here the question might be, "Will the people who take part in the activity be able to do certain basic activities, like walking a specific distance, with less pain and faster than before the program?" The hypothesis would be that individuals who take part in the program will be faster in walking a specific distance and will report less pain after taking part in the program than before the program.

You will see that ideas, concepts, methods and analyses are presented and, sometimes, presented again in a different chapter or section. There are reasons for this repetition. First, it is difficult to present material in a sequential linear way when the material tends to require simultaneous presentation. For example, you cannot talk about a variable without the concept of measurement, and it is difficult to talk about the concept of measurement without a variable. Thus, in these situations, material is presented twice in two different sections in order to present the concepts. Second, we know that repetition results in better understanding and clarity for the reader as well as the ability to apply and utilize the concepts in practice.

Already you have started on your research journey. Research and social work are intertwined and inseparable. Why are they inseparable? They are inseparable because we want to help people. In order to make positive changes in the world and not create more problems, we have to be critical of our practice. We have to test what we do. We have to be accountable to those we are serving, and we want to make sure that we are not making the problem worse or doing harm. Research is what helps us to stay on that path—to improve what we do and to improve the lives of those we work with.

Chapter 2

RESEARCH THINKING, QUESTIONS AND PROBLEMS

Often there is too much polarization and "my way or the highway" in research thinking today. This polarization results in arguments and segregation, polarizations of practice vs. research, individual vs. group, qualitative vs. quantitative, positivism vs. post-modern, parametric vs. nonparametric or descriptive vs. explanatory and inhibits development of better social work methods and the resolution of problems we encounter. We should be concerned with "reality" and understanding problems and finding the best possible solutions to utilize in social work practice. It is inclusive rather than an exclusive thinking, encouraging knowledge development and problem solution over theoretical and territorial protection.

Evidence-Based Practice (EBP) is viewed as a tripartite system of (1) client, (2) social worker and (3) research. In EBP the method, intervention or approach selected for use in any practice situation should stem from evidence found in ALL THREE of these areas. All too frequently, a gap (distance) exists between those who are "researchers" and engage in very little practice and those who are "practitioners" and do very little research. This gap creates a lack of mutual understanding and respect and results in poor information exchange. Some researchers may say practitioners rely on intuition and what they do is not based on empirical findings and they never read research. Practitioners on the other hand may assert that researchers are so far removed from practice they have no idea what a "real client" is like and the research they do has no application to actual social work practice.

Practitioners and researchers often disagree on what is important in the EBP system, with each giving significantly more weight to the part of the system where they "work". Question(s) requiring answers that improve conditions for those we serve should provide the impetus for investigation. Answers are needed and all areas of the EBP system are equally important in finding those answers. It is time to focus on questions, to equip all social workers with skills to find answers to them, and to engage all parts of the EBP system in finding those answers. It is time to provide you with the ability and tools to be "question developers" and "answer finders". For it is when ***all social workers are involved in the process of creating questions and supplying answers that we, as a profession, are fulfilling our mandate to assist and to improve our society***.

IDEOLOGY, PARADIGMS AND THEORIES

Our understanding of the world—that is the way that each of us views the world—is seasoned by our experiences (i.e. what we have been exposed to both in life experiences and learning experiences). Our ***belief system can be rigidly fixed in the case of an ideology*** in which we so ardently believe that we will not, nor cannot, change unless there is a huge event that forces us to change. On the other hand, our beliefs can be well constructed, but not so rigid that they prevent us from changing. And when informed by credible evidence, we are able to adapt and make changes in our belief system.

Belief systems that are unbendable and not amenable to change are often encountered in religion, ethnicity, race, culture and politics and, indeed, these areas often overlap. Some individuals, no matter what evidence is presented, remain rigid and will not change their beliefs. From a systems point of view, it can be said that the boundaries of their beliefs are impermeable and do not allow any new competing ideas to enter the system. Thus, there is no opportunity for new information to induce change. You are likely to hear from individuals who hold very strong ideological belief system statements like the following:

"I am right and nothing you can say will ever change me".
"I believe in ________ and it is the only way!"
"There is only one answer and it is ________".

Paradigms are similar to ideologies in that they help us to organize and make sense out of the world, but their boundaries are more open. Paradigms, therefore, are more open to new information and to accepting ideas that compete with ones in the paradigm. Allowing competing ideas in can result in a paradigm alteration, shift or change.

Well then, what is a paradigm? **A paradigm can best be described as a world view.** It organizes the world in such a way that it provides an understanding of very complex and often divergent circumstances for that person. Many people have never really looked closely at their own belief systems or questioned their own assumptions concerning their belief systems in a way that includes paradigms. Do you believe that there is a "reality" or ultimate "truth" that exists in the world and it is the same for everyone? Or do you believe that there is no "ultimate reality" and that the world is seen completely differently by each individual? Granted, these are extremes in points of view and many do not espouse either of these extremes, but have you thought about where you stand? Many pondering this question decide that neither of these extreme paradigms fit, and come to the conclusion that both are necessary and useful in understanding of the world. You may conclude an "ultimate reality" exists but it cannot be seen and each person sees that ultimate reality differently. As individuals, we can still work together to understand. As individuals, we have our own perceptions of the world that differ; but even so, the world is seen as being basically the same for most of us. If we have a similar life and experiential history, our perceptions may be more similar to those with the same life and history than those with very different lives and experiential histories and even when they are different we can work toward understanding and acceptance of the other viewpoint.

Paradigms help us to organize and evaluate the world of experiences in a systematic way. Paradigms that are often discussed in the world of social work are those of positivism and constructivism, which can be seen in the above examples. These paradigms form the poles for understanding the world from a philosophical and fundamental basis. That is, there is a unitary reality (positivism) or there is only subjective reality (constructivism). Research and science have used these two starting points to develop different explanations concerning social and psychological life.

More recently, another paradigm has emerged in the social work literature that can be viewed as deriving more from a value base than from the base of universal or individual reality. Although this value base has long been associated with social work, it is only in more recent years that it has been elucidated as a paradigm for the profession. It has been variously labeled "empowerment", "strengths-based", "advocacy" or "feminism". This paradigm has to do with the purpose of research, based upon the values of the profession. The authors of this book prefer to label this paradigm "humanism", a belief system that sees all people as having dignity, worth and the capability of self-fulfillment, and that barriers hindering any individual from achieving their potential should be removed.

One must always remember that ideologies, paradigms and theories are all conceived within a context, an environment and a historical frame that is reflected in each ideology, paradigm or theory. The paradigm of humanism has been the subject of philosophical debate and thought for hundreds of years and was reflected in both individual and social beliefs and actions. Even so, it was not labeled a paradigm until the 1960s and 1970s equal rights movement.

In social work research, "humanism" can operate as a value base. Once this underlying value is established for most of us, the choice of a paradigm (world view) is not a matter of either/or; rather, the chosen paradigm combines elements of both positivism and constructivism. In fact, many operate along a paradigm—the continuum between positivism and constructivism with the place on the continuum at any given time being determined by the question and the type of research one is undertaking. If the question is related to determining the characteristics of a particular individual or their response, then it is more on the constructivist end of the continuum. It is exploring in-depth and not trying to determine a more universal explanation or relationship. However, if the research is trying to establish general characteristics of a group or attempting to determine causation or relationships between variables across a large number of individuals, it is toward the positivist end.

As you can see, both viewpoints have validity and importance and where they are on the paradigm continuum is based upon the question and situation, and they are able to move toward either end based upon the question and the situation. This is the "reality" of research and, in particular, social work research, as we have to operate in a "real world". Indeed, we know that everyone is different and unique and we have to be able to some extent to "tailor" interventions, programs and our relationships to each individual. We also know that there are some basic and general characteristics that help to guide us and allow for application across large numbers of individuals. We have to develop programs and interventions recognizing that we cannot have a specific program for every person. ***Social work as a practice profession must be general and tailored, and our approach to research must be the same.***

Theories are much more specific than paradigms. As noted, paradigms (positivist–constructivist) focus our belief system about how we view the world. However, theories start with some clearly specified assumptions and then combine definitive statements in an attempt to explain or predict phenomena. In social work, we can group theory into two types: (1) basic theory, which we will label explanatory theories of individual and social behavior, and (2) intervention theory, which has much more to do with the utilization and application of theory to practice.

Theories that apply to a myriad of situations, exhibiting a breadth to explain individual or social interactions can be identified as basic theories. Examples of basic theories found in social work are general systems and behavioral theory. These theories also have depth as they allow one to explain specific situations under the umbrella of an overarching theory. At the most fundamental level, basic theories typically compete with each other as overarching explanations. However, over time, many have recognized that there is not a singular explanation for everything and combining basic theories and operating on a continuum of theoretical explanations (as discussed concerning paradigms) is more realistic and likely to lead to more useful practice applications. Today there are very few ardent proponents who maintain use of only one explanatory theory; rather, most adapt and combine theories to develop the best and most fitting explanation.

Intervention theories are more applicable to practice situations and can also be referred to as practice theories. Intervention theories often incorporate various parts of different basic explanatory theories to shape and refine explanations of personal and social conditions so that they are more applicable to interventions in social work practice. While ideologies and paradigms provide the foundation for what we believe and underlie our approach to the world (our world view), both basic theory and intervention theory are most utilized to test out or attempt to explain in testable ways how and why people act or interact, how social systems operate, and most importantly, how to intervene as social workers to solve problems and create more just social conditions.

This book is divided into three major sections: (1) foundations of research, (2) finding differences, which is the basis for testing explanations (if experimental conditions are built into the design) and (3) finding relationships and making predictions, which is concerned with determining relationships between things and if knowing one thing helps you to better predict another thing. It is critical that you understand that simply finding a relationship does not establish causality. Establishing that when y occurs x also occurs only establishes a very strong relationship but does not demonstrate causation. Yes, if you know that y has occurred then x is very likely to occur, but you cannot say that y caused x.

For example, every day when you leave class and drive home you come to a railroad track and there is a train passing. This is a situation where two things are occurring at the same time; that is, there is a relationship between you arriving at the track and the train going in front of you each time. Now certainly, if you are there at the same time every day, you could predict with a lot of certainty that the train would pass each day as well. However, your presence at the crossing did not cause the train to pass in front of you. You could certainly predict that if you are there at a particular time the train will come and be right most of the time. So, if you were to make a bet with someone that you can tell when the train will arrive based upon you being at the crossing at a certain time, you will win that bet. However, in order to test if your being at the crossing caused the train to arrive, you would have to come to the track at different times and see if the train arrives. This may sound like a stupid example, but in other situations some do make the leap from relationship to causation. Another example might be "being on welfare ***causes*** women to not want to work and get a job". Do we need to even begin to question this leap from a relationship to causation?

DIFFERENT WAYS OF REASONING—INDUCTIVE AND DEDUCTIVE

There are two different types of reasoning (deductive and inductive), and both are used in research.

Inductive reasoning starts with observations of specifics in the world. Research utilizing this reasoning is most often associated with practice. The research process starts with specifics and ends with generalizations. This form of reasoning/research is used extensively by those conducting qualitative research and is often associated with "theory development".

Deductive reasoning/research starts with generalizations and ends up at specifics. This type of reasoning is most frequently found in quantitative research and is associated with "theory testing".

If you start with a theory, develop hypotheses (best guesses) based upon that theory and then test those hypotheses, you are using deductive reasoning. We will discuss this process in detail in later chapters, but now it is important for you to recognize the two types of reasoning/processes. We then conclude that what we thought (based upon the theory) and defined in our hypotheses are indeed "true" (based upon a high degree of probability), or we conclude that what we thought (based upon the theory) and defined in our hypothesis is not "true" (based upon probability).

There is no best method (of reasoning), only the most appropriate method. You cannot test theory without developing it. If you do not test the theory you developed, how can you determine the validity of the theory?

It is important to recognize that both inductive reasoning and deductive reasoning flow seamlessly back and forth as we weave our understanding and ability to improve practice.

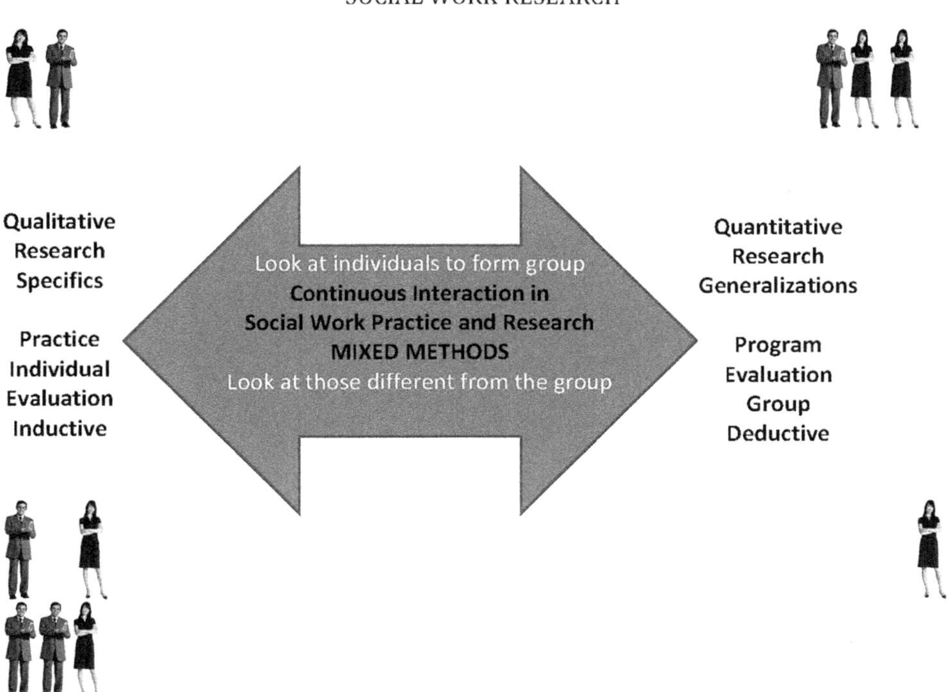

The historical categorizations of social work research into qualitative, quantitative and program evaluation is sometimes very difficult to understand. The difficulty seems to arise from the categorization resting on definitions based upon methodology, measurement and exclusivity. Although these categories have been developed for ease of classification, they are by no means exclusive or independent.

Broadly, we can speak ***about qualitative research as a way of trying to answer questions about a person, group or culture more in-depth***. This approach has roots in anthropology and rests on the foundation that each person, group or culture is highly unique—a tenant of social work since the inception of the profession. This methodology is not aimed at being able to generalize from findings to a population, but rather on gaining a greater and much more definitive understanding about specific individuals, groups or situations. For social workers, this carries into practice the recognition that we have to be attuned to each individual as unique. ***The intent is to single out and to determine individuation rather than to find some general characteristics that apply to groups*** (Chapters 6, 7).

The next type has been labeled ***quantitative research, where the aim is to select a sample from a population and gather evidence from the sample with the intent to generalize results back to that population***. (See Chapters 15–21.) Categorization of group similarities, differences between groups, and predictions estimated from group probabilities are goals of this method. Quantitative research usually implies the collection of information in a way that can be measured with numbers, even if those numbers are nothing more exotic than counting the individuals on welfare in your county. It is related to a sociological approach since understanding the individual starts with an understanding of the group to which they belong. It is seen in practice when we use some general characteristics as a way to start programs or begin our initial work with an individual client. For example, we have a general understanding and methods to approach to a person who is facing poverty, oppression or discrimination. This general understanding is the way we start to interact with individuals who are in this situation. Remember, evidence about the overall characteristics as well as individual characteristics of the client are necessary for social workers in working with clients.

The third category is program/outcome evaluation, which can be divided into two subtypes: "Individual/Practice" discussed in Chapter 7 and "Program/Practice" discussed in Chapter 8. Both types of evaluation may and frequently do use both quantitative and qualitative methodology in the same evaluation study. The process of measuring effectiveness and efficiency of an intervention flows across both forms of outcome measurement from (1) determining needs to (2) planning and implementing the intervention and finally (3) evaluating the outcome. This third overarching area of research should be near and dear to the heart of any social worker as we want to make sure that we are providing the best possible services and outcomes for all of the people we are serving.

For most social workers, the research process consists of recognizing something (practice that sparks a question requiring an answer), moving to more questions that relate to the answer found, trying to find the cause or being able to predict and finally developing a theory model or practice model.

The following definitions and examples are necessary to begin the journey—the first of the flickers of the light bulb in your path to becoming a social work practitioner/researcher.

What Is a Researchable Question?

A researchable question is a specific type of question that asks about the existence, amount of or characteristics of a variable or about the relationship between two or more variables and is stated in such a way that it can be tested with empirical research.

What Is a Concept?

A concept is an abstract idea that has been created by putting numerous individual observations together. A concept often used in social work is "marginalized". It is an abstraction formed from observations about situations that occur to certain people. The term marginalized is used to define an individual who has been set outside of the normative group for various characteristics. In this case, marginalized means outside the normal range. Thus, we have developed a concept that we can apply to situations when racial or religious groups are not included within the circle, when disabled or women are excluded or set aside, when immigrants are not included, and so on. We have taken many different situations and created an abstraction "marginalization" formed by the observation of numerous cases of exclusion. It is important to note that marginalization is measured or conceived as being below the average, whereas "advantaged" is the opposite of marginalized as individuals or groups are above the average or norm. Recognize that concepts are culture bound and what the concept of marginalized is in the United States is likely very different from the concept of marginalized in Somalia or Norway. Concepts are developed before and underlie constructs.

What Is a Construct?

A construct is a concept that has properties such that it can be measured and used in science to develop questions. Constructs are developed to create a way to measure abstract ideas (concepts). For example, we have a concept or abstract idea of poverty. Not only do we have a concept of poverty, we have a construct of poverty because we can measure it, and utilize it in theory and in practice.

What Is an Operational Definition?

An operational definition of a construct is defining that construct by its measurement. For example, poverty can be defined as the amount of dollars below the established poverty line with the poverty line set at a specific amount of dollars. However, there are some concepts for which we really have no ability to create a construct or have general agreement about so that we can scientifically measure it. An example might be post-death experiences.

What Is a Variable?

A variable is a construct that we can assign values/attributes to and use in research (it is a construct that can vary). Some examples of important variables that are studied in social work are: income, social class, depression, poverty, physical child abuse and conformity. Values can be assigned to variables in order to study them. For example, the variables just discussed might be assigned the following values:

Income = 0 dollars to billions of dollars
Social class = high, middle and low

Depression = score on the Beck Depression Inventory
Poverty = the amount below the established poverty line

Physical child abuse = the number of injuries found on the child that are determined to not be accidental

What Is a Hypothesis?

A hypothesis is a statement/declarative sentence about the relationship between two or more variables. This statement is made in such a way that it is clear, specific and can be tested. Examples of hypotheses are provided throughout the book and you will practice developing and testing hypotheses.

Conceptual thinking: It is very important to understand the types of questions, research designs, statistical analysis and potential answers you would be able to obtain from your research study before you proceed. If you are trying to describe or determine the existence of something that has not been clearly described before, you would be conducting **descriptive/exploratory research**. If you are trying to find out if two groups differ or if you want to know if there is an association between two variables, then you are conducting **difference/association research**. Finally, if you are trying to explain why something is happening or using one variable to predict another variable it is **explanatory/predictive research**.

These categorizations are slightly different from those used in other texts, but you will see how useful and helpful these classifications are in developing designs and appropriate statistical tests. Let's use Hurricane Katrina as an example of how to understand this research categorization.

Examples of Questions Resulting in Descriptive/ Exploratory Research

What are the life experiences of the survivors of Katrina?
How much depression did people in the 9th Ward have one week post Katrina?
What were the attitudes of the people in the 8th Ward toward FEMA 12 months after the hurricane?

Examples of Questions Resulting in Difference/ Association Research

Are the life experiences different between survivors of Katrina and those of Hurricane Sandy?
Is there a relationship between attitude toward FEMA and depression for Katrina survivors?

Examples of Questions Resulting in Explanatory/Predictive Research

Is there a difference in level of depression between Katrina survivors who received crisis intervention support in the first three days after the hurricane and those who did not?

Can level of family support, social support, church support and financial stability predict the amount of depression Katrina survivors experienced?

The cycle of social work research depicted in the diagram on page 10 as well as the three types of research designs can be shown by a series of studies by one of the authors, a practicing social worker in the 1970s. A lot of soldiers seen in the clinic were using drugs (both legal and illegal). There had been no prior documentation of the problem in the military. The first step was to ***determine the type and amount of use (exploratory/descriptive)*** and the next step was to determine if differences existed between different types of illegal users as well as those who were prescribed legal drugs by physicians (difference/associative). Finally, an evaluation was conducted on programs designed to reduce use in one group compared to another as well as using various tests to predict type and amount of drug used ***(explanatory/predictive)***.

Start with the question that needs to be answered. Let the need to find those answers be your guide—the guide that will assist you in using research and statistics to better understand, better assist and provide solutions for practice.

Discussion Articles

Discuss the following articles as representing the interaction and progression that occurs from observation of a problem in practice to exploring it, finding differences, creating a potential theory, evaluating an intervention (program) and providing guidelines for physicians.

Rardin, D. R., Lawson, T. R., & Rush, J. A. (1973). Drug use by American soldiers in Europe. *Social Work*, *18*, 34–41. Retrieved from www.jstor.org/stable/23712513?seq=1page_scan_tab_contents

Rardin, D. R., Lawson, T. R., & Kruzich, D. J. (1974). Opiates, amphetamines, alcohol: A comparative study of American soldiers. *International Journal of Addictions*, *9*, 891–898. doi:10.3109/10826087409022184

Silsby, H. D., Lawson, T. R., & Hazelhurst, C. D. (1975). Drug abuse prevention in the military: A punitive/administrative action approach. *Military Medicine*, *140*(7), 486–487. doi:10.1093/milmed/140.7.486

Winstead, D. K., Lawson, T. R., & Abbott, D. (1976). Diazepam use in military sick call. *Military Medicine*, *141*, 3, 180–181. doi:10.1093/milmed/141.3.180

Lawson, T. R., & Winstead, D. K. (1978). Toward a theory of drug use. *British Journal of Addiction*, *73*(2), 149–155. doi:10.1111/j.1360-0443.1978.tb00135.x

Winstead, D. K., Blackwell, B., & Lawson, T. R. (1979). Psychotropic drugs: A biopsychosocial approach. *American Family Physician, 19*(1), 109–114. Retrieved from www.ncbi.nlm.nih.gov/pubmed/760420

Winstead, D. K., Whitworth, H., & Lawson, T. R. (1981). Life changes, personality patterns, and drug abuse. *The International Journal of Addictions, 16*(1), 25–31. doi:10.3109/10826088109038807

Chapter 3

USING LITERATURE— HOW TO USE EXISTING KNOWLEDGE TO HELP YOU FORMULATE YOUR QUESTION

There are four primary purposes for using literature in social work:

(1) To obtain knowledge and information relative to practice specifically to be an evidence-based practitioner
(2) To find out more about a problem or situation you want to research
(3) To determine gaps in knowledge with respect to a problem or situation you want to research
(4) To provide background, information and support research for research ideas and hypotheses that you develop.

The first purpose is not addressed in this book since our focus is to understand and conduct social work research. In some cases, literature can be used for more than one purpose—it might provide evidence for practice while at the same time provide information about a problem or situation you want to study.

EXAMPLES OF LITERATURE SOURCES

Basic Information and Data (Often Found on the Internet)

(1) Abstracts that offer a quick method to narrow and focus the search
(2) Facts and statistics (census data, CDC, Eurostat, health departments, cabinets for human services, etc.).

Books

Books provide greater depth, broader scope and application to practice on a topic or subject, for example, motivational interviewing, cognitive behavioral interventions, linear regression, prejudice in the US, community centers and proposed solutions to inner city youth problems. However, just because a book is in print does not mean that it is totally factual or presented in an unbiased manner. Authors have particular points of view and that point of view will develop the focus, material included and the outcome of arguments presented in that book. Always evaluate books, like everything else, critically. Actively search for competing points of view so that you can determine your own position using all available information.

Journals

Most journals present detailed research articles. However, some journals have a different focus; they may analyze policy, provide overviews, critique theoretical positions or offer narratives and discussions. Journals can be divided into those that are peer reviewed and not peer reviewed, those that are strictly online, those that are printed and may also be online and those where the author pays a fee to publish. Journals tend to be topic specific and you will find that journals follow a particular research theme or theoretical point of view or they publish findings that will attract readership. In fact, some journals may not publish articles that differ from the particular point of view of that journal and/or their editors or a journal may not publish results that contradict findings the journal previously published. Results that run counter to traditional thought may be presumed to be erroneous or politically incorrect or simply "weird" and therefore do not see the light of paper. Some of this is to be expected as many journals are aimed at particular segments of the profession, for example behavioral interventions, drugs and alcohol, child welfare, etc. You would not expect to see psychodynamic papers published in a behavioral journal or analysis of immigration policy in a clinical journal.

There has been a proliferation of journals in all professions, and social work is no exception. There are a huge number of journals spanning the gamut of social work. In some cases, the editors of those journals and authors publishing in those journals are often the same individuals. Indeed, you may detect a tendency in some journals where articles seem to be written in a circumscribed fashion, appearing that the authors are writing to each other in the journal.

Journals as well as authors are often rated in terms of the impact they have on other authors and the profession. Most impact factors are based upon the number of times articles from a particular journal are cited in other articles. These measures can be somewhat difficult to understand and erroneous; for example a journal with a small readership is not as likely to be cited frequently in a lot of other journals. However, there might be many citations within the group of authors who write on the particular topic of the journal, thus increasing the number of citations. There is also the perception within the profession about the "validity" and "worthiness" of journals that may have little to do with the quality of the work presented. I am sure you know from your own experience that some people would say without any evaluation "if X said it" then it is a great idea, or if you went to "X university" you have the best education or if you read "X journal" you are getting the best information.

It is up to you to search the spectrum of journal information and to critically evaluate every article for relevance, validity and reliability.

Other Sources

Experts, Conferences, Newspapers, Media (TV, Radio, Blogs, etc.) and Magazines

Information from these sources are generally more suspect than information contained in journals or books. Although newspapers provide quick and usually reliable information about facts (the number of individuals dead as a result of a hurricane), the information they present is time sensitive and these "facts" can change from day to day simply due to a "true" change. You must remember that newspapers are owned by individuals and/or corporations that have a particular viewpoint that can slant the interpretation of information toward the understanding of the fact or to match the political expectations of their clientele.

Experts have their own interpretation of the information and facts, and while one expert may report on positive aspects the next expert may report on the negative aspects. The same can be said for most of the "media" outlets like TV, radio, social media and magazines. All are designed to attract followers (listeners and readers) and thus their content is usually designed to appeal to a certain genre of readers/listeners. Are you right or left? What do you listen to and read? Do you already have a firm idea and then listen or read those that support your pre-conceived idea? Recognizing most forms of media have a viewpoint to present, these forms of information are typically not used very much in research. The other reason they are not used is because they offer shortened versions of the information and that does not provide the reader with a complete enough picture of the situation to be able to critically evaluate it.

CONDUCTING A LITERATURE SEARCH

Unless you have been working in a particular area of research for a period of time you are unlikely to know the names of authors writing on the topic. But should you have been interested and reading about a particular topic you may have already encountered authors who are particularly interested in and publish in this area. If you begin your search with authors, it will be more specific earlier and typically take you down the same path the author has taken. If you start your search with the topic, it will be broader and likely to branch out into more related areas.

We suggest that you perform a literature search using both methods. If you start with a topic, you then can identify authors writing in this area and search for other materials written by them. If you start with an author you proceed to the topic, enlarge your search to related topics and other authors, and read what is written by those authors creating a more comprehensive understanding. However, as budding researchers you are more likely to start your search based upon the question you have and the topics that are related to your question; just be sure to also follow the author's path. Later in the chapter we will use the following questions that emanated from social work practice as examples in conducting a literature search: (1) "What refugee characteristics are related to accepting and following through with a mental health referral and what characteristics are related to them not accepting a referral?" (2) "What are the characteristics and social support systems of migrant Hungarian Female prostitutes who travel to another country to engage in legal sex work?"

Most researchers start with abstracts and overarching databases. A recent survey found that a representative university had over 300 databases covering a wide array of subjects. These databases are accessible to faculty and students at no cost and provide a wealth of information to start a literature search. Along with the Internet search engines that also provide a method to find literature, you can remotely access a plethora of related materials. Remember that sites generated by search engines usually are presented in order of the most frequently accessed and it is important to look beyond those first sites in order to appropriately address literature that may be less frequently opened but potentially more informative. The chart below lists some of the most accepted and frequently used sites and databases.

General Academic Databases
EBSCO Academic Search Complete
JSTOR
ProQuest Direct
General Social Work and Social Sciences Databases
Social Sciences Abstracts
Social Sciences Citation Index
Social Services Abstracts
Social Work Abstracts Plus

Sociological Abstracts
Sociological Collection
Subject-Specific Databases
AgeLine (Gerontology)
CINAHL (Nursing and Allied Health)
Criminal Justice Abstracts (Criminology/Criminal Justice)
Embase (Health Sciences)
ETS Testlink (Educational and Psychological Testing)
Health and Psychosocial Instruments—EBSCO (Health Sciences and Psychology)
MEDLINE—EBSCO (Health Sciences)
MEDLINE—Ovid (Health Sciences)
Mental Measurements Yearbook (Educational and Psychological Testing)
PsycINFO—EBSCO (Behavioral Science and Mental Health)
Race Relations Abstracts (Ethnic Studies and Immigration Studies)
Public Domain Sites
Agency for Healthcare Research and Quality—Guideline Clearinghouse (www.guideline.gov)
Campbell Collaboration (www.campbellcollaboration.org)
Cochrane Library (www.cochranelibrary.com)
Community Guide (CDC) (www.thecommunityguide.org)
European Union Statistics (ec.europa.eu/Eurostat)
Education Resources Information Center (ERIC) (https://eric.ed.gov)
Google Scholar (https://scholar.google.com)
Institute of Education Sciences—What Works Clearinghouse (http://ies.ed.gov/ncee/wwc/)
National Implementation Research Network (http://nirn.fpg.unc.edu)
SAMSHA National Registry of Evidence-Based Programs and Practices (www.nrepp.samhsa.gov)
Social Security Programs Around the World—US Social Security Administration (http://ssa.gov/policy/docs/progdesc/ssptw)
US Department of Veteran Affairs Evidence-Based Synthesis Program (www.hsrd.research.va.gov)

Another way your literature search can start is by (1) using evidence/information previously compiled by other authors or by (2) gathering evidence yourself and not relying on judgments made by others concerning relevance and importance. Compilations made by others take the form of a meta-analysis or a literature review whereby the author has determined the value of information retrieved, excluded those of little value and placed a relative value on the information included. The major problem in using compilations created by others is not the value placed on the literature presented (you can evaluate this yourself) but on the literature not included because you have no idea what was excluded and it may be of importance. If you collect material yourself it requires you to be critical, thorough and unbiased in determining quality and relevance of the literature to your question and hypotheses. If you rely on material collected by others, you have to be critical, thorough and able to see biases in their valuation criteria and to still look at what is written to determine what they may have excluded.

Extensive, in-depth literature reviews require time and investment. Using previously completed analyses or reviews saves a lot of time. Such analyses can also be the means by which you delimit your search into more specific areas directly related to your question, hypotheses, model or research design. You should look for commonalities, similar and consistent findings, contradictory findings and gaps in understanding that have not been explored. Therefore, we recommend using both approaches because they are complementary and provide a more comprehensive and reliable search.

In all searches and subsequent writing, you should include "classic" theory and research findings to underpin the subject and then recent theory and research flowing from them that demonstrates the present "state of knowledge". Both are highly important to show readers your understanding of the topic. Whether you are using the literature to inform practice or to develop research you have to be able to critically evaluate the material (1) in terms of intent and bias, (2) assumptions made, (3) theory used, (4) type and appropriateness of the design, and statistical analyses and (5) validity of conclusions. **This book has been written with that in mind, to provide you with the tools you need to critically evaluate the research designs, statistical analysis and conclusions found in professional articles. It has been designed to assist you to become an evidenced-based social worker *and even more to help you to design and complete research studies yourself!***

ANNOTATED BIBLIOGRAPHY

An annotated bibliography is a very useful method to catalogue your literature search. It has four important parts: (1) specific bibliographic information (author, title, etc.), (2) a summary of what was written, (3) a critical evaluation of what was written and (4) how the material can be utilized in your research or practice. Why create an annotated bibliography? By developing this type of bibliography, you not only list entries but it also makes you focus on and evaluate what was written. Too often bibliographies containing any and all types of information are gathered with no evaluation, with the hope these entries will find a place in a paper. The process utilized in annotation is quite different in that you must sift through a large amount of literature, select those references that are germane to your work, summarize, analyze and consider how they can effectively be used in your work. The annotated bibliography provides a perspective on the depth and breadth of writing on the topic, helps to elucidate gaps in knowledge and thereby provides a foundation for your research question(s) and hypotheses.

The specific bibliographic reference material to include title of the work, author and date of publication is written in American Psychological Association (APA) format. The summary of the content is written in paragraph form but the length is always related to how much is necessary for a summary and how important this material might be in your research. If there is a lot of information that is pertinent to your work, then you will have more but if there is only one point the annotation can be rather short. The detail you include rests again on how it will fit into your work. The annotation must include the main focus or goal of the article (book, etc.) and how the author presents the material to support their position.

The following is an example of one entry that could be found in an annotated bibliography.

Ballard-Kang, J., Lawson, T., Evans, J. (2017, June). Reaching Out for Help: An Analysis of the Differences Between Refugees Who Accept and Those Who Decline Community Mental Health Services. *Journal of Immigrant and Minority Health*, 1–6.

Definition of refugee indicating history of violence and trauma. Unique population of immigrant in terms of acculturation and marginalization. Literature on refugee mental health, preflight, flight and post flight. Coping mechanisms used and complex stress. Mental health symptoms and screening procedures—Refugee Health Screener -15. Data on the test. Possible reasons for not following through on mental health referrals—age, gender, stigma, lack of knowledge of mental health, culture, referral source. Study looked at those factors and specifically the factors of regional background as defined by country of origin (Middle East, Cuba, Southeast Asia and Africa) and time in the US.A sample of 414 refugees in large Midwest city. Time in US, country of origin and referral source were significant predictors of following through on a mental health referral; the other factors were not significant. Suggested further concerning alternatives to mental health services, and to explore the gap expressed by refugees in their need for services and the utilization of services.

In social work research, most of the questions requiring some form of research to provide an answer arise during practice. We will continue to use the example of refugees and mental health referrals from the annotated bibliography to show areas and topics to be examined in a literature search. While working with the refugees, the social worker recognized that some refugees did not follow through and go to a mental health service provider when she referred them. This resulted in her question, "What are some factors that might lead to not following through on a mental health referral?"

You might start with a literature search concerning refugees and specifically refugee mental health with Google or Google Scholar. A search starting from those initial sources will broaden as well as become more specific as articles and books from this initial list provide threads to follow. Some of those themes are outlined below. The articles in those themes you found important would then be included in an annotated bibliography.

REFUGEE

Definition of refugee
Numbers (world and US resettlement)

REFUGEE MENTAL HEALTH

Victims of torture triple trauma paradigm
Preflight, flight and post-flight stressors trauma
Post-flight adaptation and integration

USE OF PERSONAL AND COMMUNITY STRENGTH TO FACE ADVERSITY

Protective factors
community and family support
spirituality
education,
language skill
employment

REFUGEE MENTAL HEALTH
COMMON MENTAL HEALTH PROBLEMS

PTSD
Anxiety
Depression
Prolonged trauma
complex post-traumatic stress
substance abuse
family problems
domestic violence
somatic problems

OTHER PROBLEMS AND SYMPTOMS

sleep phobias
panic attacks
hyper vigilance
aggression, psychosis

ACCULTURATION PROBLEMS
AMERICAN SOCIETY PROBLEMS
MARGINALIZATION
MENTAL HEALTH SCREENING

Policy of connecting to services
Office of Refugee Resettlement

SYMPTOM CHECKLIST
HARVARD TRAUMA QUESTIONNAIRE
REFUGEE HEALTH SCREENER 15

Populations tested
Reliability and validity
Use of the screening instrument and ability of instruments to screen

SPECIFIC VARIABLES RELATED TO MENTAL HEALTH PROBLEMS

age
gender
Females

PREVALENCE by country of origin
USE SERVICES by ethnic background
COUNTRY

ethnic background
need for services
seek services
understand services

TIME IN THE US—RELATED TO AMOUNT OF SYMPTOMS
REFERRAL SOURCE

Mental health professional
Self-referred
Family and friends
Another example of a reduced literature search with themes from the following article:
Fabian, G., Huse, L., Szoboszlai, K., Lawson, T., Toldi, A. (Dec. 2017) Hungarian Female sex workers: social support and vulnerability at home and abroad. *International Social Work, 1–13*. DOI: 10.1177/0020872817742692

PROSTITUTION IN EUROPE

Countries
Migrants and locals
European stats (Eurostat) foundations

PROSTITUTION IN HUNGARY

Statistics and practice (laws and regulations)

AMOUNT OF MONEY IN THE INDUSTRY
LEGAL IN SOME COUNTRIES

Individual right to business
Victims of human trafficking

PROSTITUTION ABROAD
WHY

Earn money vs. risk
Money for kids
Better way of life

SITUATION

No knowledge of rules and regulations
Life abroad isolated

COLLABORATION OF SOCIAL WORKERS ON PROBLEMS

How to collaborate cross-culturally

MENTAL HEALTH AND PSYCHOLOGICAL PROBLEMS
FAMILY PROBLEMS
SOCIAL SUPPORT

Measuring social support

METHODS TO CONDUCT RESEARCH WITH PROSTITUTES

The keys to literature searches are being (1) thorough and (2) unbiased. If you remember and follow these key points then you would investigate all of the relevant literature, accepting materials that support your position/research/hypotheses/practice **AND** accepting materials that **DO NOT** support your position/research/hypotheses/practice. Research like social work is founded on getting rid of as much bias as possible, being non-judgmental and "going" with the evidence and facts. Literature searches are not confined to developing research proposals; they underpin evidence-based practice. As a social worker, you have to critically appraise what is written across the spectrum of theoretical positions and research findings both from qualitative and quantitative studies. The purpose of research is to improve practice. Without practitioners evaluating and implementing findings, without practitioners learning how to and conducting research, we will not fulfill our mandate as a profession.

Chapter 4

ETHICS—MAKING SURE IN SEARCHING FOR THE ANSWER YOU DO NO HARM

The Nürnberg Code was developed following the Nürnberg trials for Nazi war criminals which included Nazi physicians who performed unethical research on humans prior to and during WW II. These "research studies" involved experiments on prisoners in concentration camps who were forced to be in the study. "Participants" were subjected to some of the most terrible conditions you can imagine—surgical mutilation, oxygen depletion, exposure to chemical weapons and untried/bizarre medications that frequently resulted in death. One of the authors previously lived in Nürnberg and he has taken numerous social work student groups to Nürnberg as well as to the concentration camp at Dachau. Here the students see firsthand what occurred and can better understand what can happen with the loss of freedom, oppression and the horror that results from unethical and unregulated human experimentation.

THE NÜRNBERG CODE

1. ***The voluntary consent of the human subject is absolutely essential.***
   This means that the person involved should have legal capacity to give consent; should be so situated as to be able to exercise free power of choice, without the intervention of any element of force, fraud, deceit, duress, over-reaching, or other ulterior form of constraint or coercion; and should have sufficient knowledge and comprehension of the elements of the subject matter involved, as to enable him

to make an understanding and enlightened decision. This latter element requires that, before the acceptance of an affirmative decision by the experimental subject, there should be made known to him the nature, duration, and purpose of the experiment; the method and means by which it is to be conducted; all inconveniences and hazards reasonably to be expected; and the effects upon his health or person, which may possibly come from his participation in the experiment. The duty and responsibility for ascertaining the quality of the consent rests upon each individual who initiates, directs or engages in the experiment. It is a personal duty and responsibility which may not be delegated to another with impunity.

2. The experiment should be such as to yield fruitful results for the good of society, unprocurable by other methods or means of study, and not random and unnecessary in nature.
3. The experiment should be so designed and based on the results of animal experimentation and a knowledge of the natural history of the disease or other problem under study, that the anticipated results will justify the performance of the experiment.
4. The experiment should be so conducted as to avoid all unnecessary physical and mental suffering and injury.
5. No experiment should be conducted, where there is an a priori reason to believe that death or disabling injury will occur; except, perhaps, in those experiments where the experimental physicians also serve as subjects.
6. The degree of risk to be taken should never exceed that determined by the humanitarian importance of the problem to be solved by the experiment.
7. Proper preparations should be made and adequate facilities provided to protect the experimental subject against even remote possibilities of injury, disability, or death.
8. The experiment should be conducted only by scientifically qualified persons. The highest degree of skill and care should be required through all stages of the experiment of those who conduct or engage in the experiment.
9. During the course of the experiment, the human subject should be at liberty to bring the experiment to an end, if he has reached the physical or mental state, where continuation of the experiment seemed to him to be impossible.
10. During the course of the experiment, the scientist in charge must be prepared to terminate the experiment at any stage, if he has probable cause to believe, in the exercise of the good faith, superior skill and careful judgement required of him, that a continuation of the experiment is likely to result in injury, disability, or death to the experimental subject.

["Trials of War Criminals before the Nuremberg Military Tribunals under Control Council Law No. 10", Vol. 2, pp. 181–182. Washington, D.C.: U.S. Government Printing Office, 1949.]

The Helsinki Declaration, signed in 1964, was the first international agreement regulating human research officially endorsed by the medical profession. It was based upon and included the principles of the Nürnberg Code as well as other agreements/declarations concerning research. The major emphasis of the Helsinki Declaration was making the health and welfare of the research participant more important than the requirement of science or the desires of the society. Over time the declaration has been changed with a very important addition being independent and external reviews that most often are conducted by Institutional Review Boards (IRBs). Other significant additions were ensuring that minors (through adult representatives) and other persons who have less power (prisoners, etc.) have an opportunity to dissent to engaging in research with no negative consequences. Procedures for protecting these specified groups is a part of the review process of the IRBs and not simply left up to the researcher to implement. More recently other requirements have been added that include provisions that research provides benefit to the community in which it is conducted and that there is protection against exploitation of poor and vulnerable populations.

One of the most insidious studies conducted in the United States was the Tuskegee Syphilis Study initiated in the 1930s and continued for over 40 years. It was initiated to study the progression of syphilis by recruiting poor Black Males living in and around Tuskegee, Alabama, who were given only very marginal benefits to participate. Some did not have syphilis and were used as a control group while the others had previously contracted syphilis but were not told they had the disease. Some years after the research began, a new drug, penicillin, was found to be an effective treatment for the disease; however, it was not provided to the participants—a clear violation of the ethics codes. This violation of both the Nürnberg Code and the Helsinki Accord led to the development of the Belmont Report in 1978, which has two basic principles: (1) beneficence (respect for the person) and (2) justice.

The Belmont Report specifically enumerated that a person upon whom research is being performed must be protected from both psychological and physical harm (***beneficence principle***). This means the researcher must conduct research in such a way that does not harm the person. While research should attempt to achieve the greatest gain in knowledge, it must at the same time provide the least possible risk to the individual. There always is a balance in research—the balance between benefitting others and the potential harm to the individual. Decisions concerning society benefit and participant risk are relatively easy where there is great discrepancy between benefit and risk, but when the benefit and risk are relatively equal they are much more difficult. Think about a person who is terminal with stage 4 cancer. The risk of harm from an untried and potentially deadly drug which may have a small chance of saving the participant's life, compared to not providing the drug and certain death can make this decision for the participant relatively easy. Compare this to a situation where a very strict behavior code is enforced in a classroom (no movement in class, no bathroom breaks, making students sit in uncomfortable positions, etc.) with the projected result of the intervention being to improve the student's scores by five points on the upcoming 100-point exam. The balance is always between the risk and harm to the participant vs. the benefit to society.

One of social work's most important values is social justice, and the ***justice principle*** is a cornerstone of research as well. In a research context, the value of justice is applicable in two ways: (1) that all participants in the study are treated equally and (2) that those benefits from the research will be equal to all. Let's look at the first aspect of justice—equal treatment of participants. Clearly participants in research are often placed into groups, some of whom receive certain interventions, and some who receive other interventions or no intervention at all. Adherence to the principle of justice comes about when participants are randomly selected into groups and not "handpicked" into those groups. In this type of selection process the risk or benefit during the study of any participant is not based upon any specific selection criteria imposed by the researcher. The value of justice is also evident when the study does not use vulnerable and oppressed participants to find results that would only be available to non-vulnerable and non-oppressed groups. The best way to describe this "justice" principle would be equality in picking and treating participants and equality in terms of benefit from the results. The authors recognize that this might be difficult to grasp, so here are examples of both parts of the justice principle. Assume that you are trying to find out which of three interventions works best in helping individuals who are on welfare to get a job. You have three types of interventions you want to test out—video training, personal coaching from a business recruiter and tips from a person who is working but was previously on welfare. Everyone in the study is on welfare (no difference in the participants) and the participants are randomly assigned in the groups. At present, you have no idea which of these methods is superior. You will only find out following a predetermined length of time which is the "best" method in terms of those who were able to get a job and those who were not. Each of the participants is randomly assigned and all methods are deemed to be equal in their ability to assist in obtaining a job (participant justice)—a very clear example of equality of treatment. Using this same example, the results would be made available after the study was completed and it was determined which was the best method, to all welfare recipients (equality of benefits—benefit justice). The outcome, how each method effects the participant in obtaining a job, would benefit all welfare recipients and not a select few.

For social work, it is important to distinguish between practice and research. The definition as promulgated by the Department of Health and Human Services makes the following distinction:

For the most part, the term "practice" refers to interventions that are designed solely ***to enhance the well-being of an individual patient or client and that have a reasonable expectation of success. The purpose of medical or behavioral practice is to provide diagnosis, preventive treatment or therapy to particular individuals [2]. By contrast, the term "research" designates an activity designed to test a hypothesis, permit conclusions to be drawn, and thereby to develop or contribute to generalizable knowledge (expressed, for example, in theories, principles, and statements of relationships). Research is usually described in a formal protocol that sets forth an objective and a set of procedures designed to reach that objective***.

www.hhs.gov/ohrp/regulations-and-policy/belmont-report/index.html

IRBs review research at universities on human subjects irrespective of the discipline. It not only includes faculty research but research that is conducted by undergraduate and graduate social work students (typically co-Principal Investigators—PI—with a faculty member as the PI). The Federal Policy for the Protection of Human Rights is used as the definition of research: "a systematic investigation including research, development, testing, and evaluation designed to develop or contribute to generalizable knowledge". This is a very broad definition of research and we will not try to determine what may be included or excluded. The best approach is to always develop and design your research proposal to meet the principles of ethical consideration and to always submit your proposals to the IRB at your institution. Major exceptions to the IRB not having oversight of research protocols you might be involved in are (1) educational research that is carried out in the normal process of the institution—comparing different courses of study, examinations, internships or preparation of graduates and (2) agency research, developed and carried out by an agency. We recommend that you check with the IRB every time you are involved in a research project to make sure you are following the appropriate guidelines.

A key component of all research is to inform the participant of what is to happen—**informed consent**. **Informed consent** means that the researcher must provide the potential participant with the following information: what the research is about, what will happen to them in the study, if there is any risk or harm that might happen to them, any benefits to them or others because of the study and that finally they can drop out of the study at any time with no negative results.

Ethics and concern for the participant may often conflict with the goal of science to be unbiased and to ensure results are not by prior knowledge. One of the most common situations when this problem is encountered occurs when informed consent information and prior knowledge obtained in this information biases a person's performance in the study.

If a client knows that they are receiving the new and specialized interventions that are likely to be highly effective in solving their problem and the other clients are being informed that they will not receive any interventionc, it may be likely that their responses will be very different and prejudice the outcome. However, we have to provide all of the participants (clients) with full information about what they are involved in, agree to and the potential outcomes. This dilemma often confronts social work researchers.

As practitioners and researchers, we want to make sure participation in treatment and research activities is always voluntary and that individuals are informed of potential outcomes. There is also the possibility of what is thought to be voluntary consent is in effect not so "voluntary". Frequently the person conducting the research is in a position of "power" over the participant and therefore consent while nominally voluntary is not voluntary. Consider the student who is asked by the faculty member to complete a questionnaire or a survey. Of course, the faculty member can say you can fill it out or not but since this is a "power" position, most students would not decline to answer the survey provided by the faculty member. There are many more of these types of situations where participation has only the appearance of being voluntary. Consider research conducted by social workers on prisoners or children who have almost no power. Given potentially great disparity in power and ability to consent, federal guidelines specifically identify prisoners and children as being in special "powerless" situations. Studies with such groups must be considered even more carefully with respect to consent, the ability of the participant to fully understand the study and to freely decline to participate. Research involving these groups as well as others that are highly vulnerable must be addressed by the researcher in the protocol.

In obtaining voluntary participation the IRB most likely will require you to create and obtain signatures on a consent form. This form will provide the participant with all the information needed to make an informed decision about voluntarily agreeing to be in the study. It explains in detail to the participant what the study is about, what they will be asked to do, risks to them and how their participation will be guarded in terms of anonymity and confidentiality. Information includes the possible risks and the possible benefit they can obtain from participation. For example, you are conducting a study to try to determine the best intervention with children who have attention problems in school and you are surveying all children in the system. However, if the intervention will only be available in certain schools in the city then you are not providing equal justice with respect to everyone involved in the research and are violating the principle of justice. If the plan is to implement the best method to everyone after the study then everyone will benefit from the study.

Many of the studies in social work involve asking the participants about their past activities which may have been illegal or considered unacceptable or shameful. By revealing their past, it might cause the person to be upset, to become depressed or to have other deleterious psychological effects. We must be concerned and address these types of problems in the research design by clearly stating both to the individual and to the IRB the potential for this to happen and to provide the participant with avenues to address such situations if they arise—access to treatment and leaving the study immediately with no consequences.

The profession stresses confidentiality with the client and that anonymity be maintained. How are these terms defined in research? ***Anonymity*—the *researcher* cannot identify the response as coming from a specific respondent.** Anonymity is almost impossible in most social work research. We interview individuals, and collect data that is specific to that individual. Thus, in most cases we cannot guarantee anonymity. One way we attempt to provide anonymity is by separating identifying information from other data to reduce the possibility of linking responses to a particular person. In addition, we also try to design our studies in such a way that there is not a large group of identifying variables that could potentially identify a specific individual. That is, there could only be one person in the study with that particular and unique combination of identifying variables (age 25, race W, gender F, school attended Top University, major primate biology, internship Congo Institute for Ape Studies), then this identification could be linked to the data about this person, for example drug use.

***Confidentiality*—when the research participant can be identified by the researcher but they are guaranteed that their identity will not be made public.** Confidentiality is most often accomplished by identifiers being removed from data (names, specific characteristics, case file, etc.) and only a non-identifiable number is used. For both confidentiality and anonymity, it is almost impossible to identify any specific individual after the data has been aggregated. The exception to this is when one of the aggregated groups has only one or two individuals then individuals may be recognizable. In this situation, researchers recognize identification is possible even after aggregating. There is another problem with very small numbers in group-related analysis which is addressed in later chapters. Therefore, confronted with two problems (identification of participants and analysis), researchers simultaneously solve both problems by combining the very small group with a larger group or deleting those few individuals from the study.

IRBs require that records be secured, locked, often encrypted and only available to the researcher, the research team and the IRB. Following a specified length of time, the data is destroyed, further protecting the respondent's identity. Most potential participants agree to participate when there is a promise of confidentiality, when the methods to ensure confidentiality are explained and subsequently demonstrated. Social workers, in practice classes and practicum, have learned about, been trained on and are already practicing confidentiality. Thus, there can easily be a transfer of maintaining confidentiality into research. In research, as in practice, we are bound to report situations where there is potential for harm or there is illegal activity. We also must inform participants of our responsibility to report these situations to the appropriate authorities. The exception to the policy of reporting these situations can only be granted by the National Institute for Health (NIH) under provisions of the Public Health Service Act. These exceptions are rarely given and occur when the overall risk to society is much greater than risk posed by not reporting individuals. Any research study that promises "full" identity protection of participants to include forced disclosure to legal authorities by the researchers must first be approved by the IRB then forwarded to NIH for final approval and granting of the exemption.

In a recent study conducted by one of the authors with individuals in treatment for using illegal substances in five different treatment centers, obtaining "true" and accurate data while at the same time maintaining anonymity and confidentiality was very difficult. As a method to create anonymity and confidentiality the survey instrument was taken to those five centers, each of which had over 100 clients. In these centers, a member of the research team who is a recovering "user" but who did not know the participants in the treatment centers, explained the research during a group meeting. The survey (with no identifying numbers or names) was then left with the participants who could fill it out whenever they wanted during the day and evening and then place it into a sealed box to be picked up the following day. The raw data from the individual response sheets was encoded into the database using only a number. In this way both anonymity and confidentially were achieved. Since the size of the sample was large (over 500) with no small groups, it was not possible to identify any specific individual. Not only was confidentiality and anonymity maintained, the research participants recognized that this method precluded them from being identified, resulting in over a 90% response rate.

Below is an example of a consent form and the information provided to potential research participants about a social work research study. The information was read by potential participants prior to completing a consent form.

CONSENT FORM PARTICIPANTS SIGNED

Standing in the Intersection: ***Using Photovoice to Understand the Lived Experiences of African American Gay and Lesbian College Students Attending Predominantly White Postsecondary Institutions***

Research Subject's Rights, Questions, Concerns, and Complaints

If you have any concerns or complaints about the study or the study staff, you have three options. You may contact the principal investigator at the phone number below.

If you have any questions about your rights as a study subject, questions, concerns or complaints, you may call (XXX XXX XXXX) the Human Subjects Protection Program Office (HSPPO). You may discuss any questions about your rights as a subject, in secret, with a member of the Institutional Review Board (IRB) or the HSPPO staff. The IRB is an independent committee composed of members of the University community, staff of the institutions, as well as lay members of the community not connected with these institutions. The IRB has reviewed this study.

If you want to speak to a person outside the University, you may call (XXX XXX XXXX). You will be given the chance to talk about any questions, concerns or complaints in secret. This is a 24-hour hotline answered by people who do not work at the University.

This paper (EXPLANATION OF THE STUDY provided below) ***tells you what will happen during the study if you choose to take part. Your signature means that this study has been discussed with you, that your questions have been answered, and that you will take part in the study. This informed consent document is not a contract. You are not giving up any legal rights by signing this informed consent document. You will be given a signed copy of this paper to keep for your records.***

___________________________________ ***Signature of Subject/Legal Representative***
___________________________________ ***Date Signed***

____ ***Signature of Investigator***
___________________________________ ***Date Signed***

___________________________________ ***Signature of Person Explaining the Consent Form (if other than the Investigator)***
___________________________________ ***Date Signed***

INVESTIGATORS AND THEIR PHONE NUMBERS

INVESTIGATOR (PI) NAME DR. ____________ ***PHONE NUMBER*** __________

INVESTIGATOR (CO—PI) NAME ________________ ***MSW, PHD STUDENT PHONE NUMBER*** ________________________

EXPLANATION OF THE STUDY

Standing in the Intersection: Using Photovoice to Understand the Lived Experiences of African American Gay and Lesbian College Students Attending Predominantly White Postsecondary Institutions

Investigator(s) name and address

Dr. ________________________________ (Principal Investigator PI)
Address ____
Email ___________________________ Phone ___________________

_________________ MSW doctoral candidate (Co-Principal Investigator CO-PI)
Address ____
Email_____________________________ Phone _________________

Introduction and Background Information

You are invited to participate in a research study. Dr. ______ and ______ MSW, Doctoral Candidate, will conduct the study. The study will take place at the University of _______ on locations throughout the campuses. Approximately 25 subjects will be invited to participate.

Purpose

The purpose of this study is to understand the lived experiences of African American gay and lesbian college students as well as explore how students understand and balance their racial and sexual identities.

Procedures

In this study, you will be asked to document using photographs and video your daily experiences on and off campus. In group photo selection sessions, you and other study participants will critically analyze the photos/videos with the goal of creating a cumulative list of images that best represent your community experience. During this process, you will also be asked to participate in a 1–2 hour individual interview conducted by the researcher. All photo selection sessions and interviews will be audio recorded. You have the right to decline to answer any questions asked during the group photo selection sessions or individual interview that may make you uncomfortable. Finally, you will be asked to plan and participate in a campus exhibit of the selected photos/videos for campus and community officials.

Potential Risks

There are no foreseeable risks other than possible discomfort in answering personal questions; however, there may be unforeseen risks.

Benefits

The possible benefits of this study include the opportunity to participate in a social action project whose goal is to raise the level of awareness of the needs of students at the university and in the local community. The information learned in this study may also be helpful to students at other colleges and universities.

Compensation

Standing in the Intersection: Using Photovoice to Understand the Lived Experiences of African American Gay and Lesbian College Students Attending Predominantly White Postsecondary Institutions

You will be paid $50, in the form of a gift card for your time, inconvenience or expenses while you are in this study. Because you will be paid to be in this study the University must collect your name, address, social security number, ask you to sign a W-9 form, and keep records of how much you are paid. You may or may not be sent a Form 1099 by the University. This will only happen if you are paid $600 or more in one year by the University. We are required by the Internal Revenue Service to collect this information and you may need to report the payment as income on your taxes.

This information will be protected and kept secure in the same way that we protect your other private information. If you do not agree to give us this information, we can't pay you for being in this study. You can still be in the study even if you don't want to be paid.

Confidentiality

Total privacy cannot be guaranteed. Your privacy will be protected to the extent permitted by law. If the results from this study are published, your name will not be made public. While unlikely, the following may look at the study records:

University Institutional Review Board, Human Subjects Protection Program, Office for Human Research Protections.

Additionally, study participants will have the option to have their image and or their photographs and or videos included in a web-based exhibit. A separate written consent/media release will be required to participate in this portion of the project. Without written consent from the study participant no images/videos or likenesses of study participants will be released.

All photographs, videos, recordings of photo selection sessions, interview recordings and accompanying transcripts will be housed on a password-protected computer in a locked cabinet within a locked office. Only the principal researcher and co-investigator will know the password and have key access to said location.

Conflict of Interest

This study does not involve a conflict of interest because no payment or other benefit will be made to the institution or the investigator.

Voluntary Participation

Taking part in this study is voluntary. You may choose not to take part at all. If you decide to be in this study you may stop taking part at any time. If you decide not to be in this study or if you stop taking part at any time, you will not lose any benefits for which you may qualify.

You will be told about any changes that may affect your decision to continue in the study.

Another aspect of research ethics is related to what the profession determines is important as evidence or is not important. The authors will point out in subsequent chapters how critical it is to provide information not only on what works (is significant) but also what does not work. We find that professional research publications almost always publish research studies that show a significant difference between things—this intervention is better than no intervention or this group is significantly different from this group. The exception to this in social work is when we can present evidence that oppressed minority or those who are "othered" can be shown to not be different and publication of such findings is crucial to our society. However, we believe that it is very important the profession be made aware of interventions that do not make a difference (do not work) so we do not provide ineffective services. In addition to the lack of publication of studies that do not find significant differences, a great amount of evidence is available that demonstrates radical or new ideas and changes in the status quo both in science and practice are not acknowledged, published or accepted—the earth is round, Blacks are intelligent, behavior can be shaped, practice can be based upon research.

Another problem encountered in the ethics of research is journals not publishing replications of research. The assumption is if there is an intervention or difference found in a study this same result will always or almost always be found in other groups and/or in other situations—that the finding is basically "generalizable to all". Do the results found in the following groups: Males, Hispanics, university students, middle income, inner city, apply to the following groups: Females, bi-racial, high school graduates, very low income, or rural? Replication is important to provide a firm foundation for practice and studies should be replicated with diverse groups in diverse situations to provide the best evidence for practice. Replication does not need to continue "ad infinitum" but rather to the point where evidence is built for the finding to be more broadly applicable. You will learn in later chapters that the outcome (model) is determined by the sample and replication with a different sample is imperative to determine the validity of the model. We have to recognize these problems in dissemination of findings and not be disregard research with negative or non-significant results. Such studies are important to increasing knowledge, improving practice and, with more replication of studies, improving our ability to determine if findings are applicable in a broader context.

In the chapters that discuss experimental design you will see how important it is to be able to compare a group who does not receive an intervention (service) to a group that does receive the intervention (service) to determine if the intervention (service) is effective. Critics of these designs see it as an ethical problem since some clients receive services and some clients do not. The dilemma posed is to either deny services to a group of clients who are in need or to provide services that may be ineffective.

Researchers have developed some methods to try to overcome this dilemma. One is to not deny services but rather to provide services to the "no service" group later—in effect place them on a waiting list. This method does not create great ethical problems since often there are waiting lists where not everyone can receive services at the same time—a waiting list is normal. The problem with this method is the assignment of clients to either the no immediate treatment "waiting list" group or treatment group. In evaluation of intervention it is important that clients be assigned randomly to the group receiving the intervention (service) and to those not receiving the intervention (service). Assigning clients with the most severe problems to the waiting list where they do not receive services increases the potential for the problem to become worse. The alternative is to bias the study by assigning those with the most severe problems into the treatment group. Neither alternative is satisfactory. If the problem is not likely to become a lot worse by randomly assigning that participant to a waiting list, then this is a good strategy.

Another method we discussed briefly earlier can be utilized when there is more than one intervention available. For example, you have clients who are below the poverty line and want to become employed. You may have three different methods to prepare the clients for employment: (1) on-the-job training, (2) classroom training and

(3) computer-assisted training (comparing alternative interventions). In this scenario, all clients would receive services (interventions), thus no one is without services and a comparison can be made of the intervention that produces the best employment outcome. This type of design helps practitioners determine which intervention produces the best outcome and to not continue to use those that are less effective.

In some studies, there has been a lack of awareness and attention to bias particularly in the areas of gender, culture, race and sexual identity. Conducting research that is biased toward one group or another can occur either when researchers are aware of their bias and when they are not aware of their bias. **When there is awareness of the bias then it becomes an ethical problem because there is an intention to obtain certain desired results.** When there is **no awareness there is still bias but is not an ethical problem because there was no intention to obtain desired results (but it is always a problem resulting in a high potential for bias in the outcome)**.

An example of intentional manipulation based on a bias occurs when the design and implementation of the study exclusively and consistently support results/outcomes the researcher wanted to obtain before conducting the study. Advertisers have used this type of research when wanting to influence people to buy their product, and it has also been used by organizations that want to get donations. Manipulative research is designed and employed so that one group consistently was found to be "better" than another group, and places one group above or below another. For example, creating research or using previously conducted research that shows how changes in the national budget will be better for everyone or better for the rich or for the poor—depending on which ideology is to be supported.

As you can see some individuals conducting research are not above prejudice and using manipulation. It frequently occurs in the media and advertisement where research results are selected, edited and used to support a product or political position. Unfortunately, today too many individuals do not critically evaluate all the evidence relating to the situation and consider only the evidence that supports their already held position. As a researcher, it is important to recognize your own bias, the bias of others and research results and to employ critical thinking and analysis in all research endeavors. This is the foundation of ethical scientific research.

The lack of cultural awareness and its impact on research will be addressed in the following chapter as it pertains to ethical research. Frequently, those starting into research and even into social work are unaware of their own biases, that discrimination, prejudice and oppression are culturally bound and depending on the cultural context anyone can be subject to these conditions. Becoming aware of and effectively dealing with bias both as a practitioner and as a researcher is imperative. Remember that bias takes two forms—bias against and bias for and when a person has a bias they tend to find what they are looking for.

Conducting research requires funding/resources (time, money, etc.) and sometimes it requires significant amounts. When resources for research come from private or even non-profit organizations, they determine what they want studied and the questions they want answered. Often the researcher is faced with trying to answer questions and find solutions for problems deemed important to the funder and not necessarily important to the researcher. Even governmental entities resource studies that are of specific interest to those governmental agencies. Over time trends can be observed in research that are not only derived from identified problems but also where funding streams are directed. Sometimes it is almost as if there is a problem of the year or problem of the decade resulting in research agenda trends. There has been a "war on poverty", a "war on teen pregnancy", a "war on drugs", a "war on AIDS", and recently a "war on opioids" has begun with money being focused on these areas and taken away from other research. This can cause both ideological and ethical problems for researchers who are concerned about finding funds to conduct research, focusing efforts on other critical problems and remaining objective during the process.

Researchers themselves must always be reminded that in any research they conduct they are part of that research and as such their own subjectivity is part of the process. No one can be completely objective including social work researchers! Being aware of your subjectivity is critical to not only ethical, but also to valid research. Practitioner-researchers should review regularly the NASW Code of Ethics, especially the section on Evaluation and Research to undergird and reinforce their commitment to evidence-based practice.

In Chapter 2 we presented the interactive model of qualitative and quantitative research. Those who have championed qualitative research have long shown and are acutely aware of the subjective impact on the research process and subsequent outcomes. In fact, qualitative research, as you will see in Chapter 6, requires researchers to specifically identify their own points of view, their own biases and their influence on the research process and outcomes. As more interaction between qualitative and quantitative methods occurs (see Mixed Methods in Chapter 6), delineation of the researcher, the methods, the funding sources and many others factors that can subjectively affect research are being identified and addressed.

Ethics, social work and research are inextricably intertwined. As social workers, it is fundamental to both practice and research that the principles of social justice, the Nürnberg Code, Helsinki Accord, Belmont Report and the continuing quest for knowledge and solutions to society's problems be ethically conducted.

Discussion Articles

Discuss the following article as it summarizes four main areas of concern in qualitative research.

Peled, E., & Leichtentritt, R. (2002). The ethics of qualitative social work research. *Qualitative Social Work*, *1*(2), 145–169. doi:10.1177/147332500200100203

Each student should select an area from the NASW article to present and discuss in class.

NASW Social Work Ethics Resources and Research. Retrieved from www.socialworkers.org/News/Research-Data/Social-Work-Policy-Research/Ethics-Resources-Research-Articles

Discuss the following article with respect to specific and different conditions facing refugees and why the authors argue "do no harm" is not enough.

Hugman, R., Pittaway, E., & Bartolomei, L. (2011). When 'Do No Harm' is not enough: The ethics of research with refugees and other vulnerable groups. *The British Journal of Social Work*, *41*(7), 1271–1287. Retrieved from www.jstor.org/stable/43771515

Chapter 5

RESEARCH IN A CULTURAL CONTEXT—MAKING SURE YOUR QUESTION AND METHODS OF OBTAINING AN ANSWER ARE ATTENTIVE TO CULTURE

Each of us is embedded in different cultures and subcultures, and the research we propose and conduct will flow from our own cultural context and take place in the cultural context of the participants. A lack of cultural awareness in research is insensitive, can be harmful, and certainly results in potentially unsupportable results. The emphasis on cultural competence in practice is equally important in research. Cultural competence is never fully achieved, it is a continuing process of striving to more fully understand, to use research methods and pose questions that are appropriate to the culture. The process of improving cultural competence in research is similar to the one you employ in practice. In practice, you are always working to better understand the client and their situation. Additionally, the relationship between you and the client has its own cultural context, and in research the same occurs with respect to the interface of the researcher and participant particularly with respect to asking and answering questions.

Every situation has its own cultural context. Think about yourself. There are probably many situations you can identify where you have been exposed to or became part of a different culture. Moving from one neighborhood to another in the same part of town; moving from grade school to high school to college; becoming a social work major and not an English, engineering or music major; traveling to or living in a different region, state, country; or being with a different age group all involved experiencing cultural differences. With all of those changes you had to learn a different culture and how to function in it.

In many ways entering into a culture and becoming functional is similar to learning a new language or any new skill. Initially you know very little and might be considered a total beginner stumbling and making many mistakes, but over time as you progress up the cultural ladder you acquire more knowledge of the culture and can begin to successfully integrate. What about social work? With each semester and each year, you are becoming more and more a part of that culture with greater skill in understanding and better able to be a part of it. You are obtaining knowledge about being a social worker, what they believe, what they know and the language they speak. As this process unfolds, you become more accepted and more comfortable in what you are doing. You recognize the difference between those who are new to the profession and those who have been part of the profession for a long time. You begin to see subcultures within the profession—child welfare, mental health, drug and alcohol—each with its own language, interactions and acceptances.

It is also extremely important when engaging in research to recognize that each individual is different, even different from the norms of their own cultural background. If you do not recognize and incorporate both the overarching cultural background and the individual background, the likelihood of inaccurate results is high.

Two major types of problems can occur when cultural differences exist between the researcher and participants in the study: (1) ***lack of awareness***—assuming participants will react/respond the same as the person developing the research, and thus not incorporating cultural differences into the research process; (2) ***ethnocentrism***—recognizing differences but **evaluating results based upon the cultural background of the researcher**. Both require the researcher to continuously work to address their own awareness of and/or prejudice toward those who are different. Even with your social work training, you cannot assume that upon engaging in research you will automatically be culturally objective. The key to moving toward more objectivity is a twofold awareness, awareness of one's own biases and preferences and awareness of the culture of the participant.

The following example depicts becoming more aware of one's self within a cultural context. A social work student was participating in an exchange program in Germany. In her practicum at the university prior to the program she worked with individuals who were not able to read. After one day in Germany the student told the professor,

"I have always had empathy for the clients I work with in their inability to read but now here in Germany where I am not able to even read a street sign or menu, I truly know what it is like". Another situation depicting cultural differences and problems in understanding those differences occurred in Argentina. An American social work student spent the day engaged in activities with a 10-year-old boy who was very ill and living with a parent and other families with sick children in a facility close to a rural hospital. At the end of the day, as the student was leaving the young boy brought out a piece of gold jewelry and gave it to the student. The student said on "No, I cannot accept it", but the boy said it was his mother's ring and was a "love gift". The student became even more adamant that she must keep the jewelry and again she said, "No". Then the boy went and brought his mother who told the student it was a "love gift" and she had to have it because "you have shown so much love for my son and made him happier than he has been for a long time". The student finally accepted the gift with tears. She told the boy and his mother she would wear it on a chain around her neck for the rest of her life to remind her of this time and she would dedicate her life to helping others like him. Both of these examples clearly demonstrate the need for cultural awareness and how it can affect a situation. Even though these examples occurred with American social work students in a foreign country, cultural differences and the need to attend to them are equally salient in America.

An example of the need to include the cultural situation in research involved a cross-cultural comparison of prostitution. In some countries prostitution is legal and individuals can be registered as sex workers. If the researcher does not recognize and account for cultural and legal differences concerning prostitution, it will likely result in poor research and unusable results. Even if the cultural and legal differences are known, the analysis of results can be ethnocentric and this too can result in biased and non-valid results.

One of the most important assets a researcher can bring to the process of working with participants in another culture or subculture is the willingness to learn as much as they can about the culture and then employ it in their research. A good way to find out about the cultural history of the individuals you are studying is to try to find commonalities between yourself and the participants. Sometimes this is done by study and sometime it can be done through focus groups. Working with researchers and participants from Hungary, a researcher from Kentucky was able to relate that the oldest royal crown of Hungary—the crown of St. Stephen—was kept in the gold vault at Ft. Knox, Kentucky during WW II. Being able to discuss this historical fact with the Hungarians showed there was a common background, an interest in Hungarian culture/history that went beyond just participating in research. You may find that you have more in common with other researchers and research participants than you could have imagined.

When you are interacting with individuals who have a different first language you should always try to learn a few words of their language even if there are translators because it shows your respect for them, their language and their cultural background. As you have learned in social work, the ability to find commonalities that assist in developing relationships—food, sport, leisure-time activities, dreams, family, clothing, music and art—help to bridge the culture gap and improve your cultural competence.

In conducting research in another culture/subculture, recognize you are often the one who is different, the one who is the intruder and the one who will have to wait to be accepted. One of the authors worked in South Africa with a tribal community helping to improve their social, health and economic condition. The researcher spent almost two years working with the chief and the council, speaking to the chief on a regular basis in those councils. For two years the chief never responded to the author directly, only through his assistant who sat beside him. Finally, after two years the chief looked at the author and said "I see you", indicating that the social worker was now being **recognized as a person** by the chief. Time and patience are required to improve your cultural awareness and competence and we have to be aware of and willing to wait for acceptance.

Mutual concerns can be the bridge between known adversaries. In the 1980s the Surgeon Generals of the Russian Army, Navy and Air Force as well as the Surgeon Generals of the People's Republic of China came to the United States for long talks/demonstrations/exercises about how the military of any nation can respond to natural disasters like floods and earthquakes. Even adversaries can find ways to work together if there are concerns of importance to both groups that require cooperation. Common problems and potential research to solve these common problems can override and help to assuage a lack of cultural competence. Greater acceptance is provided when there is an acknowledgement of professional expertise and willingness to share and work on common research.

In a recent research study published in Europe about Hungarian prostitutes traveling to Switzerland to be legal sex workers, the collaboration between social workers from Hungary and Switzerland was critical to obtaining reliable and valid information. Without the combined knowledge and the interaction of social workers from both countries, a very incomplete picture of the social supports for prostitutes at home and abroad in Switzerland would not have been possible. The ability to understand and incorporate the cultural context of "both" lives increased the knowledge of migrant sex work and improved the ability of practicing social workers in both countries to offer services to these women. Understanding and sharing of the two cultures made is possible for the sex workers (prostitutes) to trust and "open up" to the researchers, thereby providing previously unknown facets about their lives.

Often researchers themselves misjudge the ability of research assistants to interact with respondents and obtain information required by the study. One situation occurred when university researchers assumed that a doctoral student who was not from the area (the university was located near the waterfront with international docks) would not be able to work with and interview dock workers (seen as a very different and hardened group) about their illegal drug use even though they knew that the student had previously worked successfully and researched drug users in other situations. Since no one else was available they decided to go ahead and use the student to interview participants. The directors of the project were amazed that the student was very successful in obtaining the information needed. The point of this example is that researchers themselves often make judgments about cultural differences and even the ability of co-workers in culturally different situations that are not valid. Substantive knowledge and knowledge of a particular subculture (drug users) may transcend other differences like work place or region that may appear initially very important. One has to assess all aspects of the differences and similarities in the situation in order to arrive at what is needed in terms of "cultural knowledge" to successfully conduct a research study.

Some investigators who develop a research proposal believe they are not sufficiently competent (difference in culture, ethnicity, gender, age, etc.) to be able to develop the research, and they often rely on other social work researchers who are from or well acquainted with those groups. For example, a non-Hispanic researcher who is researching both non-Hispanic and Hispanic attitudes toward being a foster parent may include a Hispanic social work researcher. The non-Hispanic researcher also needs to recognize that the Hispanic social work researcher may have general knowledge about Hispanic culture but not have knowledge of a specific Hispanic group that could be the target of the study. Often the researcher assumes that having a researcher on the team who is part of some group automatically resolves all of the problems that might arise based upon cultural differences—a bad assumption. It might well be that a person who has been a foster parent may have more substantive input into the design of the study than either the non-Hispanic or Hispanic researcher.

HOW TO GET AND KEEP PARTICIPANTS WHERE THERE ARE CULTURAL DIFFERENCES

A researcher looking to enroll participants from a different culture or subculture must first understand them. Where they reside, what they watch on TV, what they read, who they talk to, who they keep contact with, what social media they use, where they frequently go—markets, shops, restaurants, bars, public parks, community centers. Each answer provides an opportunity for recruitment. If there is a place where those who you want to be in the study congregate, then you need to be there. If they read the neighborhood paper, you put information about how to participate in your study in that paper. The more you know about the target population for your study, the better able you will be to recruit individuals for the study. First, you need to become aware of the cultural differences, and admit to those you are recruiting for the study where you lack awareness, indicate how much you respect their culture and how willing you are to learn more about their culture.

Geographic recruitment seems so simple but is often forgotten. Social work researchers are better at understanding cultural differences and the interaction of the person in their environment because our practices are often in those environments. Examples are: research with the elderly—churches, retirement centers, programs that are specifically designed to serve elderly, community centers with meals or medical services. To access elderly, potential media includes: neighborhood newspapers, church bulletins, specific time slots on TV (during programs most watched by elderly), social media sites frequently used, and materials already distributed to the elderly across neighborhoods by the municipality. Of course, pre-developed lists of elderly are available from programs and city resource centers already serving elders. Consider the difference in the situation if you want to conduct research on teenagers, college students, welfare clients or poor individuals in specific neighborhoods; census data can be a good place to start to identify specific groups by where they reside.

You can also utilize non-random sampling methods (Chapter 10) as a way to find potential participants that are hard to reach and might be termed "fugitive participants". Fugitive participants include those groups that are unwilling to meet with or participate in research because there is a lack of trust concerning the researcher or the aims of the study. In these situations, the snowball method of sampling is invaluable. Snowball sampling occurs when you get one person to participate who trusts you and believes in the research and they become the person who recruits others from the culture to participate. "Snowballing" proceeds until you have a sample large enough to conduct the research. This methodology has been particularly successful with oppressed individuals/groups, those who do not like research or those who are fearful of legal conditions—for example, women who have been harassed and/or raped, individuals who use drugs, elderly who are fearful of disclosing information, individuals who have health problems they do not want to disclose and many others.

Community leaders are invaluable to assist in implementing and maintaining a research project. If you are planning to conduct research in a community that has a particular contextual/cultural identity (all neighborhoods or communities have such an identity), trust and subsequent sanctioning by local leaders are vital to gaining entrance into the community. Formal leaders (elected or officially designated to represent the community) are not always the best avenue into that community. Often the informal leader (a person who is trusted by the community and turned to for opinions and advice but not officially elected) is the one you have to engage and receive "the OK" from in order to begin a study in that community. Frequently a woman is the informal leader or possibly a small group of individuals who are seen as the ones who protect the community.

Using both formal and informal leaders, having them understand, support and assist you in the research will go a long way in helping you to recruit and sustain your project.

Providing appropriate compensation can assist in obtaining participants. Compensation may be necessary for individuals to even be able to participate—for example child care for mothers. Compensation must be relevant to the person and also fit the requirements for the research. You must find out what is important to participants and what they view as appropriate compensation, for example, candy, time to play video games, money, supermarket or restaurant certificates, free pizza, paid babysitting; whatever it is must be rewarding enough to warrant participation. Most of the time it is not possible to provide incentives for participation. In addition, incentives must be culturally appropriate. Finally, the use of incentives for participation may "skew" the sample to include only those individuals who want the reward. Remember that any incentive that is chosen may be important for some and not important for others—coupons to a particular restaurant that is liked by some and not liked at all by others. In such cases you would get a sample that does not represent the population. Also, participants who receive rewards for participation may have a tendency to try to figure out the answers they think you want and then provide that answer rather than their "normal" answer. If the reward/incentive is delivered, then the respondent may no longer feel the need to continue to participate. They may drop out of the study or if they remain their involvement/response is "blown off".

Participation rates are improved it you conduct the research in a place where participants are comfortable. Some participants may not want to be seen with the researcher, and you may need to conduct the research away from their "home". For others, a familiar surrounding is best—often close to where they live—for example, a restaurant, coffee shop, park, local community center, church or school. Conducting research in a more formal setting, university lab, hospital, etc. may not be conducive to participation for certain groups or for certain research, but for others who have health problems it may be the most appropriate and "best" place. Some individuals prefer to be interviewed in their home while it is not acceptable for others. Most participants prefer a setting that is familiar, offers comfort and has easy access. Providing a setting that incorporates these aspects will increase participation rates.

Differences occur not only in culture but also in variables like age and gender and sexual orientation, so be attuned to all types of differences and account for them in your research endeavors. Confidentiality is paramount in all research and potential breaches of confidentiality and anonymity of respondents is doubly critical when there are cultural differences. In a recent study of refugees and immigrants, findings showed that refugees with a particular geographical and cultural background were more likely than refugees from another geographical and cultural background to accept mental health referrals. If you were considering a study with refugees who are receiving mental health services, you would have to look at the background of those individuals because certain groups of refugees and immigrants (geographical and cultural) do not accept referrals. Thus, those refugees and immigrants who are receiving mental health services may not be representative of the total refugee and immigrant population. The greater your knowledge of the group studied, their cultural background and history has a major impact on the subsequent reliability and validity of your study.

In some cultures or groups, participation in research might lower the status of the person within their group. In situations like this it is very difficult to get that person to participate. The key would be to demonstrate how participation might actually be able to improve their status. For example, if there can be compensation for participation, then you might give money to the community for every individual who participates in the research, for example $10 is donated to improve a small park in the neighborhood.

Sometimes there are natural or recognizable cultural reference points important to be aware of in conducting research. Churches, synagogues, mosques and other religious and spiritual connecting points for individuals can become places/sources to initiate research. There are also places where cultural heritage offers potential to support your research efforts. By your participation at events and talking about your research in these venues, for example, art and music festivals, concerned citizen programs, neighborhood association meetings, city park activities, community center services and programs and locales, all provide an opportunity to improve your competence, your visibility and are an excellent portal for research.

In order to effectively represent any population, the sample must represent the proportions found in that population (Chapters 10, 15). In fact, for over 20 years most research funding requires the researcher to have adequate representation of minorities and women in the sample unless the focus of the study provides a strong scientific reason they should not be included. In a study of gay men with HIV, women could be excluded but minority gay men should be included in the sample based upon the proportion in the general population of minority gay men. Look at these variables and think about differences and how you might have to account for them in your research: average age, number of children, religious affiliation, social status, years of education, income, English language capability.

Who is the majority and who is the minority as well as who has power and who has little power is contextual. Look at different groups, neighborhoods, cities, regions, states and you will see how the context determines positions and also how those positions might change over time. Who is powerful in one context might not be powerful in another context. Furthermore, within a minority or oppressed group there will be subgroups and certain individuals who are even more oppressed and have much less power within that minority, oppressed group. This has been referred to as "double oppression or multiple oppression", i.e. a Black Female who is lesbian. **In all situations, and at all levels be mindful of context and always seek to improve your competence and understanding of that context and those in it.**

LANGUAGE

Differences in language can create many problems in developing and conducting research. Even within the same language, words carry different meanings in different places as well as phrases and idioms can vary greatly. Everyone may not be aware that a lorry (UK) is a truck (US) or that a biscuit (UK) can be a cookie (US). A Female server in the south calling a customer in a restaurant "honey" would be responded to very differently in Vermont. In other countries, the same type of difficulty exists; for example, "Guten Tag" is the standard German greeting of good day but in Bavaria it is more likely to be "Grüß Gott" (greetings from God). So, for the American researcher who is trying to do cross-cultural studies it is not only the "official language" but the language used in the local daily life that one must recognize and use. While American social workers study social policy, most European social workers study the same topics but it is called "social law". General differences in language are highly visible with the term "that's sick" to an 18-year-old skateboarder or a 75-year-old resident in an elderly home. One of the classic language problems is illustrated in a speech given in Berlin by John F. Kennedy. He spoke one sentence in German and said "Ich bin ein Berliner" which can mean "I am a donut" because a Berliner is also a type of pastry. Be aware of words and dialects if you attempt to communicate in a different language.

In later chapters (Chapter 9), you will see that in measuring many things we create and rely on an operational definition (Chapter 2) of something, for example homelessness. Defining this concept rests upon what the researcher views as homelessness. Research in another country introduced a new and different concept of homelessness based upon cultural "rooflessness". "Rooflessness" is when the person is living "rough" in the streets with no shelter at all. "Homelessness" was defined as occurring when a person is living in a place that is not listed as an apartment, in a place that is not provided by the government or living in an apartment that is not possessed by the person living there, so this person lives in the risk of homelessness—you do not have your "own home". You can see how these definitions differ a lot from the ones used in the US. Although this exemplifies differences in the cultural context, you can see how a researcher creating definitions of a problem or concept can subjectively influence how things can be measured and counted and thereby influence the outcome of the study. It is also important to be aware that sometimes government and non-profit agencies serving the homeless population may define homelessness differently with the result that outcomes and results may be quite different.

Researchers frequently fall into the "**jargon trap**". Falling into the jargon trap occurs when words or phrases that only have meaning inside the profession or maybe with other closely aligned professionals are used. **For others, these words and phrases are not understood, create a lack of understanding (especially for participants) who may "tune out", and ultimately effect the validity and reliability of results.**

Often bi-lingual interviewers/researchers are an essential part of the research team. They are invaluable in developing the research protocol, but become more important during the data gathering phase. The level of linguistic ability varies considerably among those who are bi-lingual. Researchers, including social work researchers, are not highly trained linguists who are extremely proficient in the second language and should not be automatically seen as experts in the other language. Even when a person is highly proficient in a language, as demonstrated earlier they may not be fully able to understand vocalization or meanings found in various dialects or regional differences within that language.

Differences in language become pronounced if you are using existing measurement scales. There are three areas of importance in determining if you can use a scale developed in one culture/language and use it in another culture/language. There is a ***linguistic equivalent***—using the same words in another culture, ***conceptual equivalence***—measuring the same constructs in another culture and ***measurement equivalence***—only possible when the first two are achieved and thus, you can compare culturally different groups because you are measuring the same thing in both groups using a common metric. The scales have been normed (standards against which respondents are evaluated) in a particular language and with particular respondents, for example, the constructs of scales of depression, self-efficacy, anxiety and prejudice. What is "normal" anxiety may not be normal anxiety in another culture. Words used for anxiety may not be used for anxiety in another culture. What is "normal" sorrow in one culture may be extreme grief in another culture. Scales have to be translated into the language of the culture then **back translated** into the original language. The process is to translate from the original language into the second language, then have a different person translate from the second language back into the original language. The question is "when the back translation" is compared to the original, is it the same? So now that the words are the same—the translation is correct—there is still the issue to determine if these words convey the same meaning. This analysis requires additional evaluation to ensure validity and reliability of the scale and is beyond the scope of this book. Not only do scales need to be "back translated", any interaction between respondents who speak a different language must also be "back translated"—instructions, information, forms and questions.

COMMON GROUND

Common ground may be found without having to use words. Words are not always necessary to share and enjoy food, sport or games; non-verbal actions and reactions form an international language with no words. In many cultures soccer (football) is the primary sport but more recently we have seen the proliferation of other sports across the world, offering the opportunity for cultural exchange and the opportunity to improve cultural competence. Likewise, globalization of cuisines from a plethora of regions and cultures provides another opportunity to connect, show interest in their "world" and increase your cultural competence. Global concerns like climate, women's rights and peace often require no language to be understood. The emergence of computers, graphic art, emojis and other visual representations allow for communication without words.

There are many other areas of common ground which could be explored—likes and dislikes, family, children, events in the past, dreams for the future, what we can do and not do. All too often we think of cultural competence as related to nationality, race or ethnic background, but cultural competence can be gained in other ways and through common ground through work and pastimes, gardening, seeing new things, hobbies, craft, music, art, all of which can provide entry to people in another culture.

PERSPECTIVES

An interesting situation can occur between social workers from different backgrounds. Assume you are from one culture (culture 1) and there is a social worker who is from a different culture (culture 2). You are both providing services to homeless individuals. Let's take a situation where you and the other social worker are providing exactly the same type of services (day care) to the same type of people (elderly) but are from totally different cultures and language backgrounds. Even with minimal communication skills or with translation you can communicate and discuss services fairly well because you are providing the same thing (common professional ground). But the culture, policies, form of government and method of financing services is very different, making understanding and communication difficult (uncommon ground). Now assume that you are from very similar cultures and speak the same language (common ground) but your programs are totally different (uncommon ground). In this situation, it might be difficult to understand the differences in services because the programs are different. Even when cultures are different, sometimes problems and approaches to problems are similar and pose less a problem in cultural competence, whereas competence within the overall culture may be problematic.

We are suggesting the perspective approach to cultural competence—to assess where you are most competent in a different culture—where do you need the most assistance, where do you need to improve the most and where can you move forward with a better understanding? The perspective approach does not mean that you are competent in any area of the culture; rather it leads to an assessment of your capability in different facets of the culture. Remember that within a different culture as we noted earlier there are areas of common ground and it is in those that you can first engage while working on the other areas that require improvement.

Many years ago, a social work researcher was hosting some social workers from China. The American social worker bought nice table clocks to present as departing gifts. Later the social worker found out that giving a clock as a gift to someone from China is seen as a reminder of the shortness of life and the future of death. An apology was immediately sent indicating that this meaning was not known. The Chinese were most gracious and replied that there were no bad feelings at all and said that no one can know all of the various and many customs of any culture. What is to be gained from this example is in that conducting research in different settings with people different from you, you will make cultural mistakes. Just remember:

(1) ***Do your best to avoid mistakes by improving your ability to understand the population and groups in your research***
(2) ***You improve your competence by spending time within the culture. If you expect to conduct research and if you want that research to be reliable and valid you must continuously engage as possible with the culture***
(3) ***Be honest about your mistakes, admit them, be natural, be yourself and be respectful.***

Discussion Articles

Discuss how the teaching activities presented in the article might be transplanted to your program of social work.

Conley, C. L., Deck, S. M., Miller, J. J., & Borders, K. (2017). Improving the cultural competency of social work students with a social privilege activity. *Journal of Teaching in Social Work*, *37*(3), 234–248. doi:10.1080/08841233.2017.1313804

Discuss problems encountered in working cross-culturally, how this was resolved in this study and how it might have affected the outcome.

Fabian, G., Huse, L., Szoboszlai, K., Lawson, T., & Toldi, A. (2017). Hungarian Female migrant sex workers: Social support and vulnerability at home and abroad. *International Social Work*, 1–13. doi:10.1177/0020872817742692

Discuss how cultural differences can affect obtaining help and how it can be addressed in other research studies.

Ballard-Kang, J., Lawson, T., & Evans, J. (2018). Reaching out for help: An analysis of the differences between refugees who accept and those who decline community mental health services. *Journal of Immigrant and Minority Health*, *20*(2), 345–350. doi:10.1007/s10903-017-0612-6

Chapter 6

QUALITATIVE RESEARCH—IN-DEPTH AND UP-CLOSE ANSWERS

From materials presented in your social work practice classes and participation in practicum you are probably familiar with methods that are more closely related more to qualitative than quantitative research. As depicted in the research diagram (Chapter 2) qualitative studies are aimed at (1) exploring unexplored areas, (2) "digging deeper" into phenomena and (3) investigating individuals/smaller subgroups and/or situations that differ from the norms that have been found/established in larger groups. Qualitative research does not look at larger groups in order to generalize findings to a population, its methodology places emphasis on the inherent subjectivity in research studies, incorporates that subjectivity into its designs and systematically evaluates it.

Qualitative studies are often precursors to quantitative studies and in addition frequently conducted following a quantitative study to develop an in-depth investigation of some of the findings or those cases that are "outliers" (those individuals within the group that are a lot different from the norm [average] of the group). More recently it is becoming more common to include both qualitative and quantitative methods in tandem as an integrated approach to create more holistic and better research studies. In this chapter, different ways or approaches to conducting qualitative research will be discussed including examples of the methodology used in those approaches.

CASE STUDY

Social work students are most familiar with the case study approach as it is similar to a psychosocial assessment of a client over time in a "real" situation during a field placement. In that psychosocial assessment, multiple sources of information are utilized: client interviews, observations, records, documents and information from others within the client system, family members, co-workers and friends. While you might also include from other sources not related to that specific client what is drawn from other similar cases, the information gained from that specific client is the most important and an example of understanding the person in their environment. The case study approach is used in other disciplines including sociology, psychology, business, law, medicine and engineering. Each of these disciplines assumes a different case focus—social work (individual, family, group), sociology (institution, organization), business (development of a product) and law (specific legal case). In each discipline, however, the case is delineated (circumscribed) to a specific occurrence at a specific time in a specific place. Another way of stating this feature is each individual case study is bound by people, place, time and situation.

Case studies can be broadly categorized into two groups: ***those that are focused on the person (intrinsic) and those that are focused on the phenomenon (instrumental)***. If we look at social work practice there are different types of case studies: (1) to examine and understand the unique and individual characteristics of that particular situation for that particular person—to resolve the individual's problems—intrinsic, (2) to examine and understand the overarching problem (for example, opiod use) and situation and not a specific individual by characterizing the context or to understand a particular issue or situation related to a human service organization—instrumental. Irrespective of the discipline or which type of case study is used, multiple in-depth data sources are compiled into a detailed and comprehensive report. As part of that description, themes, problems and patterns are identified and explicated that relate to that specific case. A corollary to the case study found in qualitative research is the aforementioned psychosocial assessment that is directed at gathering a complete description of a person or persons (e.g. family) and provides an in-depth perspective of that person or group of individuals. However, there is no intent in case study research to find a solution to a problem; rather it is to provide information about how something happened to provide a complete picture of the situation—to offer a full description. The case study does provide the materials that could be used to develop potential solutions. The same is true in practice—that from a full description and assessment you can then proceed to proposed solutions.

Another type of case study is aimed at a problem, or issue and uses a case or cases to more fully elucidate it. The study can be directed toward a problem occurring at the individual, family, group or organization level but the nexus of the study is to illuminate a problem or issue and not the person or persons. We frequently see case studies conducted to acutely portray problems—deportation of refugees, access to abortion and child sexual abuse. To bring the problem/issue into greater awareness the researcher may select several cases that are different but are illustrative of the problem in order to provide perspective on that particular problem. For example, a case study of the problem of human trafficking may include children, teenagers, adults, Males and Females, origins and destinations, and potential uses for those trafficked. In these types of studies, common themes are identified that relate to the case or all of the cases. Finally, meaning is made from the research that results in understanding through the description of the individual or an issue/problem that can be applicable to practice about the individual in a descriptive case study or an issue or problem that can be utilized. ***The purpose of a case study is to investigate in-depth a person or problem using a circumscribed case(s) that occurred during a specific period of time and context that can lead to analysis and ultimately application in practice.***

There are four different types of case studies, illustrative, exploratory, critical instance and cumulative. An ***illustrative case study is one that is highly descriptive and selected to vividly portray a situation.*** An illustrative case study makes known what is unknown and additionally is often used to develop action stemming from knowledge obtained from that case. A recent basketball game at a major university was dedicated to increasing awareness and obtaining donations for breast cancer. To vividly show that breast cancer can affect anyone, a visually impaired girl who was 6 years old, wearing a breast cancer awareness pink t-shirt, sang the national anthem at center court in front of more than 15,000 spectators while over 75 breast cancer survivors representing different ages, races and gender gathered on the court to depict how breast cancer affects everyone.

An ***exploratory case study*** is conducted as a precursor to large-scale studies and might be considered a pilot study. In an ***exploratory study the researcher conducts a small-scale investigation to identify and/or refine research questions, determine who and where to sample, as well as the best type of design for the following more extensive study***. In practice this occurs informally, for example, when a social worker recognizes that over the past three–four months there has been an increase in clients not returning for follow-up appointments. The social worker wonders why they are not returning and decides to call or email a few of those who have not returned to ask why with the purpose of using this information to create a survey that could be sent to all clients. In this small exploratory study, the social worker would be able to refine the initial question and develop additional questions to be used in a more extensive qualitative study with more clients. In another example, a social worker observes that some of the refugees who are receiving services in the center do not want to go to one specific health care provider, but will follow-up on a referral to all other health care providers. An exploratory case study, interviewing a very small number of refugees to determine the reason for not going to that particular provider, was instituted prior to a more extensive study.

Critical incident case studies provide a thorough investigation into one specific instance of a phenomenon—the critical incident. It attempts to offer a reason for the incident, that is, a causal explanation for the incident—"Why did it happen?" Since a critical incident is rather unique it is very unlikely to have more than one case or at most a very few examples to be investigated. Critical incident analyses are frequently conducted following a mishap, accident or disaster to try to determine the cause and if the incident could have been prevented. This method can be used to test hypotheses about the cause of the incident, but not to generalize all other situations; however, it may be used to identify relationships that could be tested when similar incidents occur. For example, a critical incident case study on the implementation of FEMA following Katrina to try to determine why the response was not what was expected. The results can then be disseminated and used to generate additional hypotheses and form the foundation for studies of similar incidents—hurricanes Harvey, Irma and Maria.

The cumulative case study much like meta-analysis in quantitative research ***compiles and aggregates information from several case studies of a single phenomenon occurring at different sites and different times that have previously been conducted.*** It is not a cross-sectional design since it does not look at many studies at a single point in time, nor it is longitudinal because it does not follow the same case over time; rather it ***follows many different cases over a period of time***. Because cumulative case studies use previously collected data (secondary data), it can reduce both the time and cost to study the phenomena. Even more importantly, by using multiple cases across various situations and different times, it creates greater diversity and an increased number of cases offering the potential for initial generalization of findings. As research moves from a single case (instance) to multiple cases (instances) whether focused on a person or on an issue, the design begins to move in the direction of larger samples and a more quantitative design (see the diagram in Chapter 2). One can see how they can merge from one into the other, starting with a qualitative study merging into quantitative research or starting with a quantitative study that merges into a qualitative design.

The case study approach provides not only a description but a thorough analysis of a case or series of similar cases on the same topic. Case analysis is not confined to an individual(s) but may include an event (the Women's March in Washington), or an activity/program (enrolling for the first time in "Obamacare") or be restricted to a specific type of information. Most researchers conducting case studies will triangulate findings by using interviews from multiple individuals, as well as documents and tangible objects (for the Women's March, videos, posters, etc.) in order to obtain a more valid and reliable case study.

NARRATIVE

The narrative approach uses the lived story (narrative) as the basis of inquiry for an individual using a written or spoken account of what happened in chronological order. Stories come directly from the individual or from just a few interacting individuals (person and partner, family) providing the meaning of those experiences through their life-stage narrative. The narrative becomes the medium to understand the individual and their identity. While the story emanates from the lived experiences of the person, it should be remembered the research process itself and the interaction of the researcher and the individual can influence the story as it unfolds. For the narrative researcher, the frame (place/context) in which the story happened is extremely important to understanding the text (person/environment). The analysis can be focused on what the person is saying, the way they are saying it or the purpose for telling the story. Social work practice is also built on the narrative in much the same manner as the narrative approach—what is being said, how it is being said and why it is said are all critical to understanding.

Stories can be obtained and developed in different ways and for different purposes. First, a story can be categorized on the basis of who developed it. If it is developed, and constructed solely by the individual, it is autobiographical and may be created in different formats, written, audio or audiovisual. Another form is biographical where the researcher becomes the person to record the lived experiences, again in any of the formats. Narratives can also be categorized by time and by number of narratives. The time dimension can range from a life history, a portion of the life or simply an experience. A researcher can also choose to obtain more than one life story/experience that are all related. A defining feature of inquiry is the understanding of how the story is told with emphasis on ascribed meanings of the experiences rather than an oral history of the event. With that in mind look at the following examples of experiences and differentiate how each would be studied using both the narrative approach and an oral history approach.

The life of Anne Frank
The day the Gestapo found Anne Frank
The lives of five individuals who survived the Holocaust
The time spent living in the same concentration camp for five different individuals.

All of these situations are excellent examples of narratives of Holocaust victim(s) that graphically depict the lived experiences and the environment. In looking at these examples, it becomes clear that the narrative is designed to obtain great detail and ascribed meaning whether it is from one person or a small group. In much the same way that a documentary might put together a person's or persons' recollection(s) of their experience in concentration camps into the correct sequence and order, a researcher might have to "re-story" the narrative into the proper sequence—a distinguishing characteristic of the narrative approach compared to the other qualitative approaches. Also, like a documentary there is a beginning, middle and end all flowing into and containing a central theme. The process of obtaining a person's story usually through interviews, and then placing them in chronological order, the theme or themes that emerge becomes that person's "life story narrative".

ETHNOGRAPHIC

This ethnographic approach to qualitative research is characterized by its focus on and examination of the shared culture of a group. Ethnography has been used in anthropology and sociology for over 100 years to document similarities and differences in cultures and subcultures. Initially used to study "primitive cultures", more recently it has been used to study various subcultures, for example "gangs" and neo-Nazis. It is not within the scope of this book to discuss all of the positions, theories and subtypes found in the ethnographic approach; however, two different forms are briefly presented. We have noted in an earlier chapter that research can flow from a particular value stance or political purpose. Critical ethnography is based upon the proposition/concern that present society is one where power resides in a few due to their having a certain class, gender, religion or race with the marginalization of all others. Critical ethnographic research is conducted to support this proposition and to use the finding to advocate and make the public aware of the issues of inequality and power.

In contrast to critical ethnography is what has been termed "realist", the method used by most ethnographic researchers. This approach is aimed at trying to portray the culture and situation as objectively as possible. Groups/cultures/subcultures are assumed to not be "pre-judged" by the researcher (although subjectivity is always present) in an effort to portray the "pure" traditional aspects of a culture, family, social groups, work, status, religion as close as possible to "reality" from a "third person view". The ethnographic approach is particularly useful in finding patterns within a cultural group when that group has not been adequately described, is very different from the general population, and there is a need to describe the interactions, functioning, beliefs and problems within that group/culture. The ultimate goal of the ethnographic research is to develop a holistic view of a particular cultural group.

As in all qualitative approaches the amount of time to complete research is a major concern but it is even more salient in ethnographic research where the person conducting the research has to be in the field and "inside" the group for an extended period of time. Therefore, prior to an ethnographic study the researcher must very carefully plan the amount of resources required to include time necessary for successful completion of the project. The outcome is to provide detailed descriptions and interpretations (deep and rich) of behavioral patterns, beliefs and norms occurring in a particular cultural group. It requires conducting interviews (with members as well as key informants) and field observations with detailed notes of the members to be able to adequately and accurately describe that group and how it functions.

PHENOMENOLOGICAL

As the name suggests this approach is to obtain the lived experience(s) of a particular situation/phenomenon usually from a small number of individuals. The researcher collects data from individuals who have all ***experienced this particular situation, assembles a description of the phenomenon and then proceeds to provide an understanding of that experience***. It differs from the narrative approach which focuses more on the life story of individuals and the essence of the individual whereas ***this approach emphasizes a description of the phenomenon itself and not the individual and tries to uncover a common meaning to the phenomenon*** (not to the individual) across individuals. The goal of phenomenological qualitative research is capturing the ***commonality of experience from a small heterogeneous group with respect to the phenomena and not the individual's experience of it***. It might be viewed as obtaining many reports of the same phenomena. For example, painting verbal pictures based upon the experience of trying visual reality glasses for the first time, having to sign up for food stamps or seeing a video of young children being trafficked. ***The hallmark of phenomenology is that descriptions of experience are viewed as conscious experiences and reality is an interactive, inseparable process between the individual and what the individual is experiencing. The purpose of the research study is to provide vivid descriptions and not analyses of those experiences.*** The researcher attempts to remove their view, their experience of the phenomena, from the process by what is known as ***"bracketing" their experience***. This means that ***the researcher's experience is acknowledged, presented and then as much as possible excluded from the "combined experienced description" provided by the participants***. The combined experience description is a result of integrating all of the participants' reflections concerning the experience itself ("what happened") and those things that have shaped the experience ("influences"). ***It is directed at the commonality or common core of the experience (a particular phenomenon) and not on the individual who experienced it and is reached by interviewing a few individuals who have "lived" that same experience.*** Other sources of information related to the experience may be used as well—the expression of the experience through various art forms (music, visual art, etc.) or written materials.

GROUNDED THEORY

The object of grounded theory is to ***discover/uncover/reveal theory that is generated from the experiences of those who have experienced it/lived it***. Theory is built from experiences (inductive) rather than starting with a theory and testing it through research (deductive). Grounded theory is a very systematic and continuous method of obtaining information (data) and at the same time processing and finding themes, concepts or processes within that information. There is not a clear point where the gathering process ends and the analysis process starts (iterative). A major activity that is a characteristic of this approach is the use of memos. Memos are notes of the researcher's ideas written during the process of collecting and analyzing information in an attempt to delineate what is emerging in the research. ***"Memoing" is the continuing documentation of the research process that allows the researcher to track ideas and begin to tease out those categories that could ultimately form the basis for a proposed theory.***

Grounded research has two different primary methods of inquiry, ***objectivist grounded theory (more structured and positivistic) and constructivist grounded theory (less structured and post-modern)***. Even with these fundamental differences in their philosophical base, both methods strive to obtain diversity in representation with respect to reality. The structured (objectivist) method makes use of sequential coding wherein the information is first placed into major categories (open coding) followed by another series of categories (axial coding) that can be viewed as surrounding and related to the open-coded major categories. You might envision describing a planet as ***open coding***, and describing the moons, suns and other planets that have influence on it and interact with each other as ***axial coding***.

The amount of data collected in the field will depend on the data itself. When the information reaches ***the point where little or no new information is provided and when it becomes repetitious (the point of saturation)*** data collection is ended. The point at which saturation is achieved is based upon how saturation is defined. There are four different ways to define when saturation has been reached: (1) based upon developing new theory—when there are no more new properties or concepts emerging from the data, (2) based upon previous theory—when the themes or codes emanating from that theory have been found in the data, (3) based upon theme saturation—when there are no more new codes or themes arising in the data and (4) based upon the data itself—when there is overall information redundancy.

Researchers using the structured approach collect data and analyze, collect data and analyze, again and again until saturation occurs. After reaching saturation, a model of the phenomena is constructed that includes "causal" factors, the response to those factors and the surrounding/contextual factors that influence the response and the outcomes. Theory developed from this method is seen as having more general applicability across different situations.

The constructivist method emanates from a more post-modern view than the structural method. Rather than using a structured coding method, it uses implicit meanings to undergird theory development. Meaning is to be found through the myriad worlds, realities and in the overall complexity. It is incumbent on the researcher to bring their own view, existing theoretical concepts and pragmatism to the process, to blend their own experiences into the situation, to learn about the experience and to uncover what is hidden within the situation. Experiences to be studied occur more in the values, beliefs and ideology of the individuals than other aspects of the individual's experience. Clearly this approach emphasizes the role of the researcher in what is studied, how it is studied and the perspective from which grounded theory is applied. The constructivist, in contrast to the objectivist, views the developed theory as not able to be applied generally across time with individuals or groups, but as located in a specific situation in time and space, representing multiple realities.

When do you select grounded theory as an approach to qualitative analysis? Since its goal is to derive theory, it would be the approach of choice when there is minimal knowledge or when no theory has been postulated. Another instance to use grounded theory is when current theory does not include or adequately address other aspects (variables). Often the lack of inclusion or an inadequate theory becomes recognized in practice and selecting grounded theory becomes the appropriate approach to find out if it can improve theory.

Grounded theory aims at developing the nexus of a theory from the participant's perspective originating in the field. The goal of analysis is to reveal the properties and dimensions of a category or categories, or the description of transitions of a social process. It involves more participants than the other qualitative approaches except the ethnographic approach which is not aimed at theory development. The primary method for gathering information is to conduct a rather large number of interviews and then process them using various methods of coding into an integrated "field" theory.

DATA COLLECTION

You are already probably familiar with many of the qualitative sampling and data collection methods. Two sampling methods frequently used ***are purposive and snowball sampling***. Neither of these methods utilize randomization that would allow for generalization to the whole population, but this is not the intent of qualitative research. ***Purposive sampling is the method where the researcher specifically selects certain individuals to be in the research that provide the best and most extensive information with regard to the question to be answered and the direction of the research (Chapter 10).*** In this method, for example investigating social work burn-out, the researcher selects a small number of practitioners who have had clients that severely abused their children and conducts interviews about the effects of that experience on their ability to continue to work with abuse cases. ***A snowball sample*** is the method in which the ***researcher finds the first individual to be included as a participant in the study and this first participant makes referrals to the researcher about other potential participants who have had the same experience*** (Chapter 10).

Qualitative research utilizes three data collection methods: ***(1) individual (one-on-one) interviews, (2) focus groups and (3) observation***. Individual interviews or observation are the most common. ***Interviews can range from highly structured to unstructured; however, most researchers use a semi-structured interview*** that has some structure but allows the researcher or participant to step outside the structure provided. ***A completely structured interview is one in which every question is scripted and the interviewer is not allowed to deviate from that script to obtain answers to those specified questions.*** Positive aspects of a completely structured interview are: (1) it helps to ensure consistency across interviewers if more than one interviewer is involved, (2) it ensures that each participant is asked to provide information about the target questions in the study and (3) when multiple interviews are conducted with the same person over a period of time (longitudinal study) the consistency of the questions with no deviation allows for comparison of data gathered from that person at all of the different points in time.

An unstructured interview allows the participant to recall and describe the experience in their own terms without the requirement of fitting their answers into a series of predetermined questions. An unstructured interview might start with a single question that asks a person to describe their feelings when they were told they had cancer. This very open-ended single question allows the participant to guide the narrative and bring forth their experience, emphasizing what was salient for them. An unstructured interview is a good method to use when (1) there is very little known about the experience or (2) you want to obtain a particular individual's life story.

A ***semi-structured interview*** has predetermined questions like the structured interview provided in a protocol but differs from it in some aspects. ***A semi-structured interview allows the interviewer to clarify and to explain questions for the participant.*** In addition, the interviewer can follow up to ***obtain more detailed information or pursue leads into other areas/topics*** that are voiced by the participant (Chapter 12).

Focus groups are a variant of an interview. A focus group consists of a small number of participants who are asked to respond to a specified set of questions while in a group setting. Individuals respond to the question themselves, but also interact with others to help to clarify and expand their narrative. Typically, small groups (usually not more than 15) are organized to address the particular experience to be investigated. Focus groups can be used in a very different way (non-qualitative research), to obtain the in-depth responses from the community, for example their attitude toward building a new community center or hospital. In this case multiple focus groups are created representing diverse parts of the population so that the attitudes generated are reflective of the community (generalization is not the goal of qualitative research). Typically, a single focus group is formed to obtain information about a specific experience.

There are ***two different types of observation: non-participant observation and participant observation. In non-participant observation, the researcher only observes and tries to remain outside the situation as possible.*** The researcher does not become involved in any of the activities of the person or persons being studied. Non-participant observation occurs when a social work student sits outside the circle of a mutual support group and only observes the interaction of the members or when a social worker observes the interaction of a mother and her child when the child is playing in the waiting room of the agency. In both, the person observing is not involved at all in the activities of those being observed. In participant observation, the observer is actually taking part in the experience. It can be exemplified by reporters who are embedded in military units and writing/speaking about the experience of members of the unit as well as their experience during military missions or a social work student who takes part in a protest march in an effort to observe and report on what is happening to those marching as well as their own experience of the march.

If the researcher is planning on observing participants as part of the research study, it is required that participants be informed that you are conducting research and that you are observing them (Chapter 4). While informing individuals that they are being observed is ethically responsible and required by the IRBs, at the same time it creates a problem with the validity of the observations. When participants know they are being observed, their behavior is likely to be altered. Consequently, in both the collection and analysis of observational data recognize that what is being observed is different from what would happen if the researcher was not there.

Observation is never conducted without a pre-conceived plan of what to observe. In that sense, all observation research has some structure concerning the focus of the observation. However, there is a continuum in the amount of structure. One may choose to only focus on one out of all of the potential activities the person exhibits (structured observation) or observe and record everything that happens (unstructured observation). The more that is already known about what is to be observed and studied, the more specific the protocol can become about what to observe. In the example of observing the mother and child in the waiting room, the protocol may be very structured with the observer told to observe and record only instances where the mother demonstrates anger toward the child, or the observer may be told to write down all of the interactions between the mother and child—highly unstructured. When observation is used as a data collection method in quantitative research, it is usually highly structured.

If a highly structured observation instrument for recording observations has not been developed, then field notes become even more important. It is impossible for any observer to remember exactly all of the behaviors and interactions individuals have during the period of observation. Therefore, some record other than memory should be employed to capture and document the observations. For over a century, field notes have been the primary method to document and preserve qualitative data and still play a critical role in data gathering. For the participant, field notes usually are less intrusive and create less anxiety than other methods to record results, i.e. audio/video. Audio recordings preserve the exact words and intonation of the participant but miss all of the non-verbal aspects of the interview. If only audio is used then it should be supplemented by field notes that include the non-verbal behaviors that accompanied the verbal behavior. Even if video is used, field notes are still important to clarify and amplify ***through the lens of the researcher/observer*** what is on that video.

Often incorporated into qualitative studies is having an individual other than the researcher perform a check on the collected information. If data has been recorded (audio/video) and subsequently transcribed into written form, ***the "outside" person can compare the transcription with the original recording to identify mistakes (transcription checking)***. In the objective grounded theory approach, if the information has been coded (open and axial) the reliability and validity of the coding can be checked by another coder or set of coders who start with the original material and code it without seeing the first coding results. These coding efforts can then be compared (inter-observer agreement in coding) to see where there is consistency (agreements) and lack of consistency (disagreements). Standard practice is to resolve disagreements by coming to consensus about the proper coding or if no consensus can be reached then discarding that particular item.

Studies frequently will engage an external social work researcher skilled in qualitative methodology as well as highly knowledgeable in the topic being studied to perform a peer review of the study. Upon reviewing the protocol, how the information was gathered, the data and the proposed results, the external expert will give feedback and a review of the study to clarify and reduce errors that might have occurred. Another option is to include ***member checking*** in the research protocol. ***Member checking is when the collected information is given to the participants and they are to provide feedback on its accuracy.*** When participants perform member checking, they must be informed at the very beginning of the study as part of the consent process (Chapter 4). The ability of the participant to remember exactly what was said or done will vary from participant to participant influencing the reliability and validity of the study.

Concern about reliable and valid data exists in both qualitative and quantitative research. In qualitative research rigor and trustworthiness are related to internal validity, external validity and reliability in quantitative research (Chapter 9). ***Internal validity in quantitative research reflects how well you are measuring what you say you are measuring. Credibility encompasses the same idea for qualitative research. To establish credibility the researcher, at a minimum, must use well-established research methods, random sampling, triangulation (multiple methods to check on information) and have experts and/or participants check the materials.***

Generalizability in quantitative research is the ability of the results to extend beyond the sample of participants to the population. Qualitative research uses the term "transferability" to indicate the same concept. Qualitative research always uses a small number of participants and therefore the ability to generalize is difficult to achieve; however, there is ***greater transferability when (1) there is a larger number of participants, (2) the small number of participants is taken from a broader cross-section of the overall population, (3) there are a number of sessions to collect the data or (4) the data is collected over an extended period of time***. The inclusion of any or all of these processes will improve the ability of the qualitative results to be transferred (generalizable) to other situations.

Dependability encapsulates the same concept as reliability in quantitative research—if we do the research study exactly the same way again and again will we get the same results? The way to achieve ***dependability in qualitative research has much to do with very clear and precise recounting of all of the research processes, definitions, selection of participants, recording of responses and reporting results, so that another person would be able to replicate the study and see if the same results would be replicated as well.***

One of the ***problems associated with qualitative research (and also to some extent in quantitative research) is determining objectivity vs. subjectivity*** in what information is to be identified, collected and used in the results. ***Confirmability refers to the need for objectivity in qualitative research.*** Is any researcher totally objective or completely subjective? While this problem of total objectivity can never be resolved for either research method, ***one of the best ways to try to manage subjectivity in any research study is to be reflexive***. Reflection has long been a basic part of social work training where students are taught to reflect on situations with clients and to try to unravel the interaction between themselves and the client in an effort to determine within the context of the relationship how their own participation has altered, changed and influenced the responses of the client. In research and especially in qualitative research building reflection into the study makes ***the researcher look at and try to understand how their values, perceptions and behaviors affect the research***. Other methods to increase awareness of and to attempt to diminish subjectivity in research are: (1) having others check the process and (2) employing triangulation.

MIXED METHOD

The current and most accepted definition of mixed method design is ***one in which the research includes a minimum of one qualitative and one quantitative research component in the design***. You have been introduced to qualitative approaches (narrative, case study, etc.) and to the basic quantitative categories—exploratory/descriptive, difference/association and explanatory/predictive (see Chapter 2, Chapter 11 for detailed descriptions). A mixed methods design can be any combination of one of the quantitative and one of the qualitative types of designs. It might be a research project to study the effects of a new motivational treatment with depressed clients. The quantitative portion of the study may evaluate how much the level of depression was reduced using standardized scales for measuring depression while the qualitative portion might be collecting verbal descriptions from selected clients about their experience during the treatment process.

A major reason to conduct a mixed method design is to provide complementary information to answer the research question. Let's look at some research questions through the lens of a mixed method "qualitative–quantitative" (QQ) study. "How does bussing students out of a 'segregated' neighborhood to schools with diverse classrooms affect student prejudice and acts of discrimination?" The quantitative part of the study may measure (1) prejudice using an attitude scale administered to the students before and after bussing and (2) the number of times a student sits next to a person of a different color at lunch. The qualitative part of the study may obtain the student's story about the experience to include details about how they felt—fear, anger, anxiety, etc. as well as interaction experiences with students of a different color. Using both methods provides a more complete and complex picture of the effect of bussing across a large group of students (quantitative) as well as some of the specific effects (qualitative) on the individuals themselves.

"Is there a relationship between domestic violence perpetrated by a man on a woman and the number of deployments overseas for members of the US Military?" In a quantitative study to answer this question the researcher may (1) gather data on the number of deployments and the number and severity of domestic violence incidents and also (2) measure the anger level of the military member following each individual deployment. The qualitative portion of the research might include interviewing the military member and the victim of abuse, detailing the circumstances surrounding each of the violent episodes for both the victim and perpetrator to form a graphic picture of the situation before, during and after the incident of domestic violence. ***When both qualitative and quantitative research methods are included in a mixed method design, each method is referred to as a "strand".*** There is a qualitative strand and a quantitative strand in this mixed method design that offers a more complete picture than if both were not included in the protocol.

These examples demonstrate the usefulness of both research methods in compiling an in-depth picture as well as data that could be used for potential explanations and generalizations. In many instances, when there is little known, the question will lead to exploration, whether that be quantitatively (exploratory/descriptive—does it exist and if so how much), and/or qualitatively (describe in much greater detail the essence from the perspective of the individual involved). In the following examples of quantitative ***exploratory/descriptive*** design studies, what would you include in a mixed method as the qualitative strand?

The initial identification of AIDS patients in clinics.
Suicide in soldiers returning from Afghanistan and Iraq.
Uncertainty, anxiety and depression among "DREAMERS" in 2017, 2018.

In the quantitative ***difference/association*** questions, think about what could be gained by inclusion of qualitative research.

Is there a relationship between the caseload of a child welfare worker and "burn-out" resulting in quitting their job?
Is there a difference between elderly Males and Females and their attitude toward following a discharge plan from a social worker in a hospital?
Is there a difference between refugees from different countries and their willingness to accept mental health referrals?

Consider what you might develop qualitatively to go with the following ***predictive/explanatory*** questions:

Does being molested as a child predict if a girl will not graduate from high school?
Will the number of calories elderly individuals living in a group home consume per meal increase if fish are placed in an aquarium in the dining room and fed at the same time as the residents?
Does training social workers to recognize human trafficking increase the reporting of incidents, the rescue of individuals and the apprehension and conviction of traffickers?

When contemplating the development of a mixed method study, the researcher must be mindful of three factors that are associated with this type of design. The first is cost. Adding a second method to any design compared to a single method will increase cost irrespective of which method is added. Second, because there are two methods, the researcher must be facile in both to successfully develop, implement, transpose and translate the protocol to others who might carry out the research "on the ground". Finally, mixed method is more time consuming for the researchers as well as the participants. Therefore, the decision to conduct a mixed method research study requires the researcher to carefully weigh the benefits compared to the cost to see if it is worthwhile to conduct research using two rather than a single method. Is it better to conduct a study using one method first and see if the other method is needed after reviewing the results of the first method?

Three reasons to use a mixed method design:

(1) To ***describe in detail*** using qualitative methods ***and*** to ***generalize*** those findings using quantitative methods
(2) To ***investigate specific individuals/subgroups from a larger population*** and to ***more fully discuss*** those who are ***different from the norm*** in the quantitative findings
(3) To ***view the question*** and to be able to ***look at the explanations through multiple lenses***.

A mixed methods design is not just a parallel implementation of two separate studies focusing on the same question; it is an integrated research design that infuses, integrates the inquiry and in so doing augments the process of discovery.

Discussion Articles

Discuss the article's analysis of mixed method research in social work to include the focus, analytical methods and implications for social work.

Chaumba, J. (2013). The use and value of mixed method research in social work. *Advances in Social Work*, *14*(2), 307–333.

Discuss how the authors used a mixed method design to test an intervention in a program evaluation.

Bender, K., Begun, S., DePrince, A., Haffejee, B., Brown, S., Hathaway, J., & Schau, N. (2015). Mindfulness intervention with homeless youth. *Journal of the Society for Social Work Research*, *6*(4), 491–513. Retrieved from www.journals.uchicago.edu/doi/10.1086/684107

Chapter 7

"N OF 1" INDIVIDUAL RESEARCH DESIGNS—FINDING ANSWERS ABOUT THE OUTCOME OF AN INTERVENTION WITH ONE CLIENT, ONE COUPLE, ONE FAMILY

Practitioners have been doing individual research for decades. However, you have not called it research and have not seen it as a basic individual research design. Usually individual outcome evaluation has not been systematic and rigorous using clearly defined measurement. Most of our evaluations are called a B design because there is no formal measurement of the amount of the problem prior to the intervention. A sort of informal baseline for the amount, or number of occurrences of the problem, is often established in the initial interview(s) but not measured except in terms of the verbal reports by the client. Following the informal establishment of the baseline of the problem, the intervention process begins and the client reports what change may or may not have occurred with respect to the problem. Social workers have always employed some form of feedback mechanism to monitor client progress. A single subject design is a more precise way to (1) define the outcome and (2) obtain measured feedback about client progress and the efficacy of the intervention.

Social workers can use single subject/single unit designs to evaluate their practice. These designs are aimed at answering the question, "Is the intervention creating the desired change in a particular client, a couple, a family?" Evaluation of a neighborhood or community (mezzo/macro practice) utilizes other designs that are found in the program evaluation chapter (Chapter 8) and in the analysis chapters (Chapters 15–21).

Single subject designs used to evaluate practice ***have two important limitations: (1) you are only looking at results from one individual, couple, family that was not randomly selected from the population—you cannot generalize the outcome to the population and (2) you cannot conclude that the invention was the cause of the outcome since you did not exclude (control for) other variables that might affect the outcome***.

Using single subject research methods to evaluate practice can be considered the start of the interactive research process presented in Chapter 2 where measurement of a positive outcome of the method of intervention with an individual, couple or family can then be used with other clients, aggregated then ultimately to larger groups of clients in a program with the potential to generalize.

As a practitioner, you might use this same intervention again with a similar client collecting more outcome data and when you have a larger number of clients and there has been change resulting from the intervention across most of the clients, you begin to formulate that this type of intervention appears to be successful with certain problems in certain types of clients. The next step might be to utilize this intervention with these types of clients in explanatory/experimental group designs that can be generalized to larger populations with the ability to control for potential competing explanatory variables. Single subject (single case) designs are an accepted method of measuring interventions; consequently using this method and diffusing results throughout the profession is a way to improve practice and help to form one part of evidence-based practice to track and promulgate interventions that work.

Chapter 11 focuses on group research designs where you will find that a panel design studies a group of respondents similar to the way an individual is studied in a single subject design. In both the outcome is measured for a specific individual, multiple times. The primary difference between the panel design and a single subject design is that a panel design measures many individuals over time and aggregates those measurements.

Single subject designs were developed to more critically assess outcomes and have been borrowed/adapted from those used by other professions. Typically, the outcome is operationally defined in terms of a specific behavior or attitude although the method is not limited to these types of dependent variables. Examples of operational measurements of behavior might be (1) a reduction in the number of arguments, (2) increasing the number of positive comments to another person or (3) increasing acceptance of minorities as measured on a minority acceptance scale. Operational definitions of the DVs measure directly or are aggregated as interval or ratio levels of measurement (Chapter 9).

In recent years this methodology has become more useful and more frequently applied in practice with the greater focus on EBP. Practitioners are recognizing the benefits of the method to improve their ability to deliver more successful services. In all types of research, and especially in determining the effectiveness of an intervention with a single client, it is imperative that there is a clear definition of the outcome and that the design used is one that can demonstrate the outcome was a result of the intervention.

All single subject designs are based upon (1) the introduction of an ***intervention*** and (2) a ***longitudinal design*** (over time) with many sequential measurements preferably in all three stages of the intervention process: (1) the pre-intervention, (2) intervention and (3) post intervention. The practitioner/researcher evaluates the relationship between the rate/amount of the behavior and the presence or absence of the intervention. This will become quite evident as we present the various single subject/case study designs.

Frequent measurements prior to the intervention are taken to establish a baseline of the typical amount/rate of the defined target (problem, behavior) of the intervention. A baseline is established so that the amount of the defined target post intervention can be compared to the amount pre-intervention. There can be a lot of variation in the amount over time; thus it is important to have multiple measurements because one measurement might be the time when the problem/behavior/target was happening a lot (too high) or infrequently (too low) compared to the average or normal amount. In later chapters, you will recognize that baseline measurement is like a "control" group in that it measures the target of change (DV, dependent variable) as it is naturally occurring (the regular occurrence of something on average over time). In a group design, we can use the average of the group receiving no intervention as the "baseline/average for the population" and for an individual/couple/family (N = 1) their own average prior to an intervention as their baseline.

All longitudinal designs should, if possible, include multiple pre-intervention measurements to establish a valid and reliable measurement of the dependent variable (DV, target of intervention). **The period prior to initiation of an intervention *(A phase)* where the practitioner collects data on the typical (average) rate/amount of the variable that is the object of the intervention and change is called *baseline.*** Sometimes it is not possible for practitioners to collect data prior to starting an intervention/

change; when the target of change is very disruptive/harmful and the social worker is called upon to immediately begin the intervention—for example, acting out in a classroom. Even though there was no formal baseline measurement, the worker may be able to establish a baseline from school records or teacher reports. You should always try to establish a baseline that would record the presence of the target of change from which one could determine if the target behavior/problem changed or did not change. In all situations where the intervention has to be started immediately with no opportunity for an actual measurement of the A phase (baseline measurement), a social worker should always try to gather data in another manner that could help to support an analysis that could determine if change occurred and if it occurred with respect to the introduction of the intervention.

What is a reliable, valid baseline? It is one that is consistent and representative of the average/range of the target of change. The more measurements the more reliable and valid is the baseline. A rule of thumb is that a minimum of five periods of time are recommended but more is always better. In order to establish a **stable baseline** you should collect enough measurements to see on a graph that the target of change falls between upper limits and lower limits that are easily seen and that the target of change is occurring relatively consistently with no large fluctuations. The practitioner must be mindful of how differences occur and what might create changes in the baseline measurement. For example, if a person's self-rated measurement of stress occurs at 8 PM daily and you only had recordings from the five-day work week, it would not include the "potentially less stressful" weekend days and would be inaccurate for a total week—include the weekends. If anger is the target and if it is greater in the presence of a specific person, then knowing when the baseline measurements were taken (absence or presence of this individual) becomes vitally important to baseline accuracy.

These types of designs are used with a single unit of analysis and no comparison is made to other persons/groups, etc. The target/object of change/intervention can be measured in different ways. You could ***measure how often something happens***—with an individual client the number of anger bursts in a one hour, length of time using a computer game, number of interruptions in a community meeting. You can also ***measure how long something occurs***—minutes spent exercising per day for an obese individual, minutes spent in department meetings on administration vs. client care; ***measure time between something happening***—days between panic attacks, days since an automobile fatality; ***or measure how much***—calories consumed per day by an elderly client who is not eating properly, money spent for education.

Let's look at some of the various pre-intervention baselines.

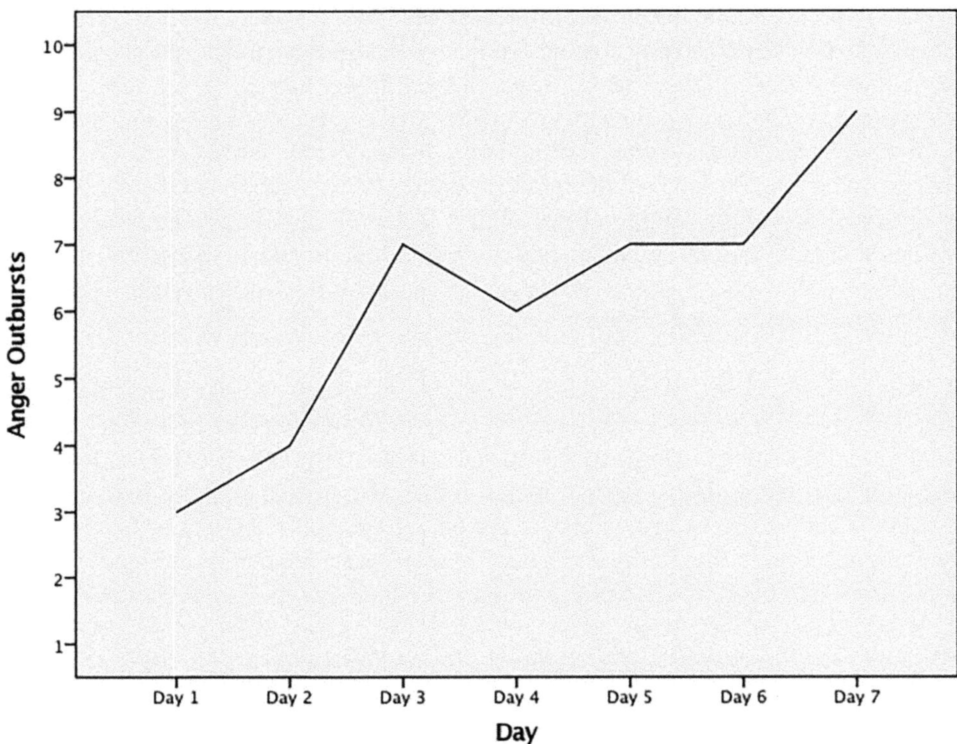

The first baseline is one where the target of the intervention is basically increasing. You might encounter this type of baseline retrospectively when you are called in for an emergency intervention—for example with an acting out child in school. The teacher reports that the child's in-class behavior has been getting worse every day and you must intervene immediately with no formal measurement of the baseline. Another scenario could occur when you have been working with a client for a while and now they begin to report in the weekly meetings that they are eating more often every day. In both cases you have an increasing baseline with your client. While the baseline is increasing it is also stable in that it is increasing and would be expected to increase in the future if the intervention is not successful in "stopping or slowing" the increasing baseline. While this is not the most preferred baseline to work with, it is stable in that there is a continuous pattern of the target of the intervention and it can be used to measure the success of the intervention.

A decreasing baseline is also stable but in the opposite direction. Like an increasing baseline, a decreasing baseline is not the most preferable baseline but it can be used to measure the success of the intervention. Examples of decreasing baselines might be a decrease each night in the amount of sleep, or a decrease in an older adult's memory.

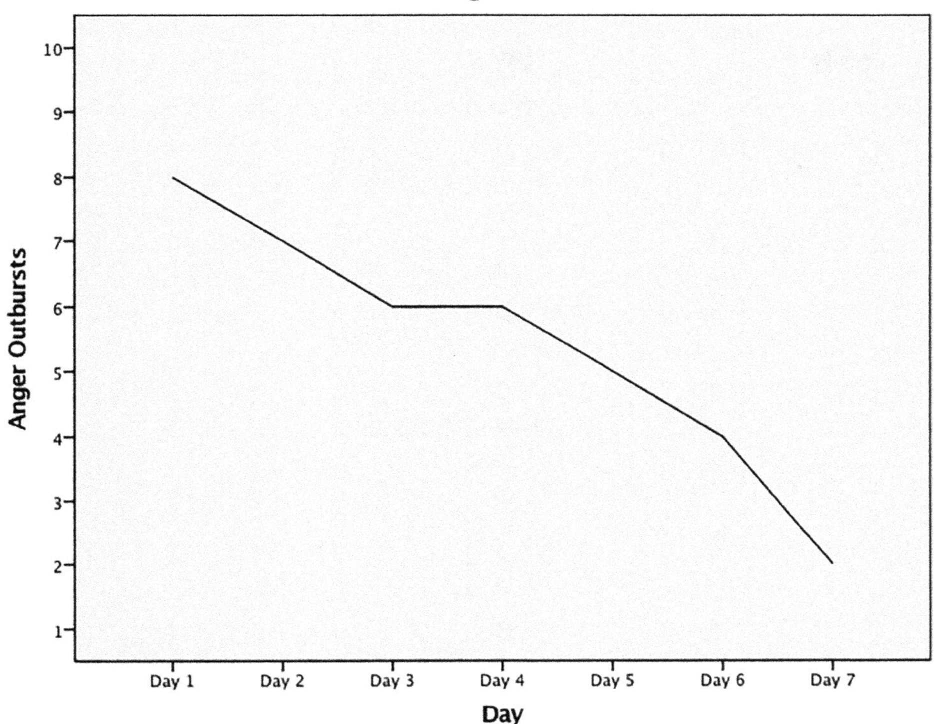
Decreasing Baseline
Anger Outbursts
10
9
8
7
6
5
4
3
2
1
Day 1
Day 2
Day 3
Day 4
Day 5
Day 6
Day 7
Day

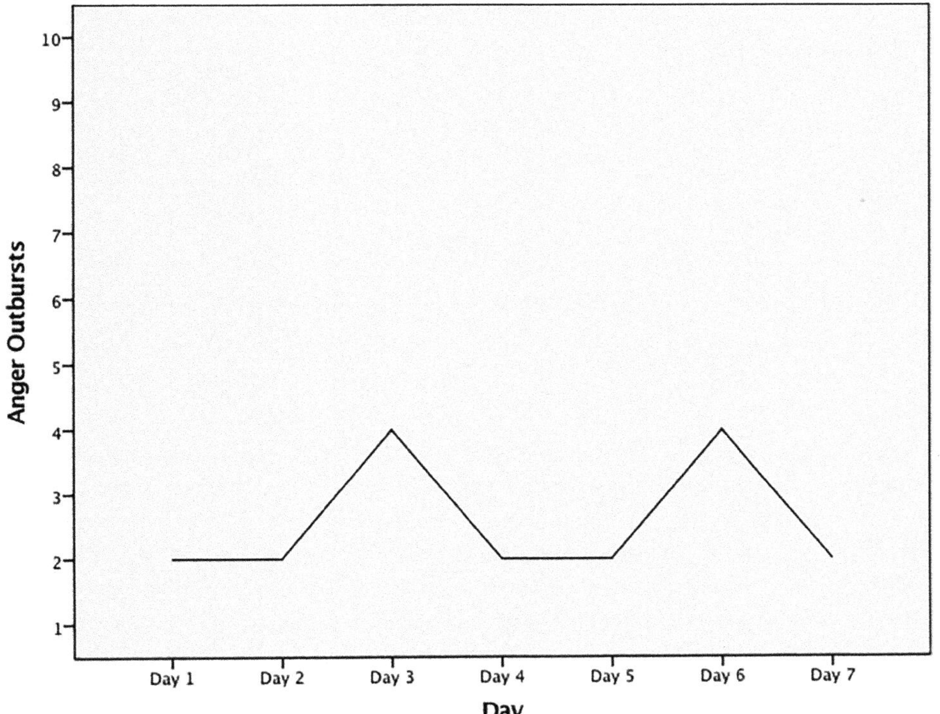
Cyclic Baseline
Anger Outbursts
10
9
8
7
6
5
4
3
2
1
Day 1
Day 2
Day 3
Day 4
Day 5
Day 6
Day 7
Day

A cyclic baseline has an observable and repetitive target pattern (DV). For many college students, this might be their level of frustration on Tuesday and Thursday afternoons when they have their social work research and statistics class. Cyclic patterns of targets are often observed in a specific context (work, family, individual). Consider the following targets—stress five days and not on two days each week, family dinners, interactions with a particular person, time in the morning to go to school—as representing cyclic baselines. When determining what is the intervention, how to implement the recognition and integration of the cyclic nature of the target must be built into the intervention and measurement plan.

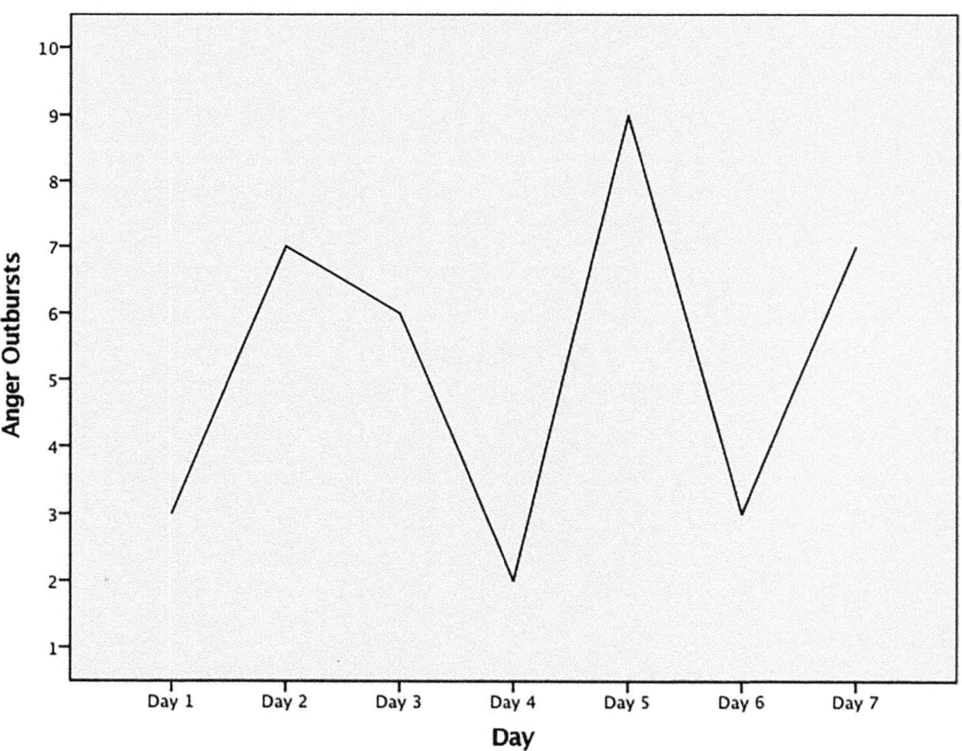

The baseline that creates the most problems in measuring the effect of the intervention is an unstable baseline. Since the target of the intervention is not consistent, the worker does not know how or when to intervene, and measurement even after intervention it is difficult to compare to the pre-intervention period because you do not know which period to compare to the post-intervention measurement. Imagine working with parents who have a child who has "temper tantrums" but there is no consistency "in what triggers them" or any way to determine when they might occur. How to develop an intervention under these conditions is very difficult and trying to measure it even more difficult. The best option is to attempt to stabilize the baseline. In mental health situations, this is often accomplished by use of medication. In other situations, it might be accomplished by stabilizing interpersonal relationships or living conditions (providing shelter, food and other basic needs). If these cannot be developed or if they are not appropriate to the client situation, then the only option for the worker is to initiate an intervention that is aimed at the target outcome without stabilization, to compare the overall post-intervention value of the target to the overall pre-intervention value of the target.

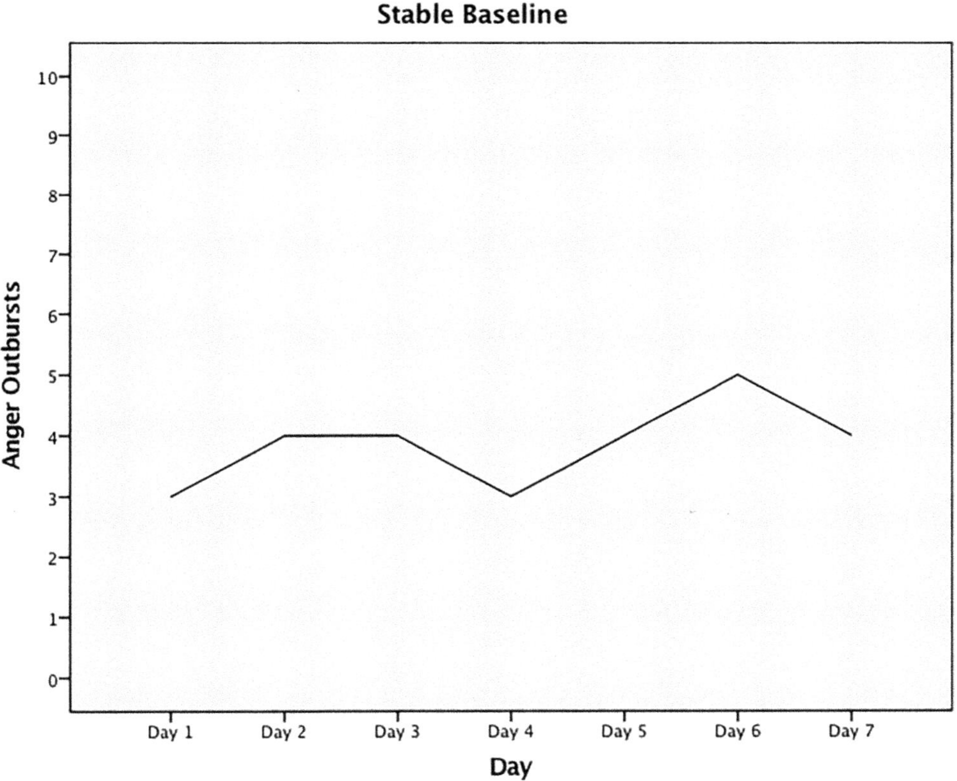

What everyone hopes for is the baseline depicted above—a stable baseline. A stable baseline does not have wide fluctuations, and is consistent under different circumstances. A stable baseline in target behavior (DV) is the easiest to develop a longitudinal plan for the intervention and the easiest to compare the target pre-intervention to the post intervention.

Once you have established the baseline you implement the intervention while continuing to monitor the target outcome (DV) over time (longitudinally). If you were measuring the target outcome (DV) daily during the baseline phase, then you would continue to measure it daily during the intervention phase; that is you use the same longitudinal time period for both pre- and post-intervention measurement.

SINGLE SUBJECT (SINGLE CASE) DESIGNS

The **AB design** is the most basic design with a baseline/pre-intervention phase **(A)** followed by the intervention phase **(B)**. This design becomes a B design if there was no measurement prior to intervention. As a practitioner, you should always measure the outcome of the intervention even if there is no baseline so that you can determine if there is a desired change occurring in the outcome. If you only have the B phase then you would want to see a steady increase or steady decrease (depending on the direction you were trying to create change) in the targeted outcome (DV) variable.

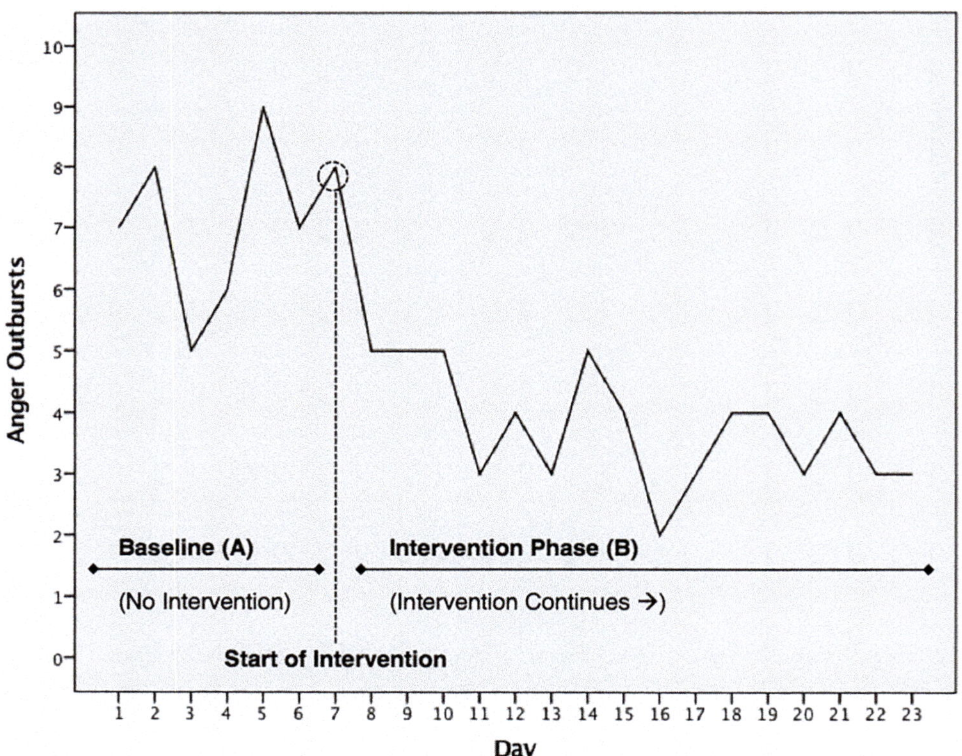

One of the concerns in using the AB design is the B phase is one of continual intervention. You do not know if the desired outcome will continue following the stoppage of the intervention. If during phase B the anger outbursts of the child diminish, the question remains "Will this lowered level continue if you stop seeing the child?" An initial way to try to answer this question is to create another A phase (no intervention) after the B (treatment) phase which creates an ABA design.

There has been concern within the profession that if you stop the intervention "for research" purposes, it is not ethical. However, this same situation occurs in practice when no intervention takes place in the form of a "vacation" or "testing out the success of the intervention" but the client continues to monitor the target outcome (DV). It is common practice to determine the extent of the problem (A phase), institute an intervention (B phase), measure the success of the intervention and then have the client go out and practice it on "their own" and report back about the outcome. In the post-intervention phase the client may simply phone/email with a status report or they may keep a diary of the target outcome and after a specified time return to see you. Standard social work practice is to have an evaluation phase following termination of the intervention.

We often work with multi-problem situations and the specific problem—the one you have designated for intervention in the SS design—may be only one of the problems to be addressed. In these practice situations, you could stop the intervention on one problem—continue to measure it in an A phase—while you start to work on another problem. In these types of multiple interventions, you cannot discount the "bleed over" of one intervention into another.

In practice, there are some other naturally occurring sequences that can be developed into a ABA, BAB or even a ABAB or BABA design. There can be a natural A time when there is no intervention or where it is built into the plan that interventions occur at specified intervals and measurement occurs continuously—school breaks for children or planned breaks with clients because of work schedules. One might see these periods of non-intervention phases in terms of recurring training sessions, re-inoculation sessions, "booster sessions", etc. In any case the social work researcher/practitioner in conjunction with the client can use such naturally occurring situations as ways to implement these designs into practice and to improve the evaluation of outcomes.

As you can see, the ABAB design is one that occurs naturally in practice. The sequence of phases can start with the AB series or with a BA series and both include an intervention phase and a non-intervention phase. Should this alternating series continue, the result is an ABAB or BABA design with more periods to measure the target outcome in during both intervention and non-intervention. In practice, we often refer to these sequences as periods when the client is testing their own ability to "go it on their own" so that the client can maintain the outcome achieved with no continuing intervention from the social worker.

Work schedules of both the client and social worker provide an excellent opportunity for A phases (no interventions periods) to be placed into the intervention plan. Recognize that the A phase "follows intervention" where we plan for the client to continue successfully and achieve the outcome without any continued assistance or intervention from the worker. Examples of outcomes are: being self-sufficient economically, having positive self-esteem, being "drug free", being able to hold a job, being "off the street", increasing positive comments to your child.

Many social workers look at a design that ends in the no intervention (A) phase and see it as not a "poor" practice model. If you really look at what social work is attempting to accomplish, it is exactly that—for the client to function without our assistance. This is a good practice model. This method requires specification of what is to be changed and how to measure that change and to develop an agreement between the client and social worker when to end the intervention activity. Remember that during the client's first visit you start to plan for termination with the client but at termination you have the option to tell the client to return/call in the future should they need more assistance. The other is to have the client call back after a certain period of time to report on how they are doing. Thus, the concern of the social worker about abandoning the client and not providing assistance is addressed as well as the concern of the client that they are being deserted.

From the point of view of research, the alternation of AB phases can lead to the discovery of a relationship between the intervention and the outcome in the target (DV). We prefer to focus on the "success" in the social work intervention and less on making the case for causal determination with a single case. Clearly none of these single subject designs can isolate the "causal" factor for an outcome; rather it is usually a "coming together" of different variables/factors that result in the change and the desired outcome. In daily practice, social workers should focus on the outcome, the clients' functioning and well-being and recognize that trying to isolate the "causal" factor is not primary. Practitioners focus on "what works" and if it works then with my next client (who has the same problem and in somewhat similar circumstances as this client), I will use the same intervention or tweak it because it has been successful—using EBP. The important aspect of practice is for social workers to develop some very well-defined intervention techniques, and specific and well-defined outcomes so that measurement of the intervention and the measurement of the outcome can be accurately assessed to determine if there is a relationship. Using single subject designs allows the social worker to have tested interventions that can be applied to similar client situations in the future. Additionally, "case studies" can be disseminated to other professionals to utilize in their cases.

ABCD DESIGNS

We find that in practice we have to create interventions that are aimed at multiple targets of change (DVs) that are parts of an overall outcome and is more common than utilizing a single intervention and target outcome. Let's say that you are working with a client who is attempting to lose weight (overall target outcome). The client has trouble following routines, instructions, eating properly and has low self-esteem. In working with this client, you plan to utilize different interventions, each of which is aimed at a specific target outcome. For example, you want the client to (1) eat certain foods that are nutritious and provide a rounded diet, (2) consume less fat and calories, (3) eat regularly rather than not eat and later have a huge meal and finally (4) improve their self-image. Each of these target outcomes will have a different intervention but all are combined to affect the overall outcome of weight loss.

The interventions might be:

(1) Have the client keep a "weight" journal of everything they eat
(2) Create a list of certain foods the client is to select from to develop a well-rounded diet that provides the requisite nutrients for better health. The client is to consume only items on this list and maintain a record keeps of all items consumed in a journal
(3) Have the client record the time they eat, the number of calories consumed in each meal and totaled for the day
(4) Attend weekly sessions that are designed to improve self-image.

The A phase (pre-intervention—not shown) determines the baseline of the individual's weight. During the (B) intervention phases the client (Phase B1) keeps a journal of everything they eat, (Phase B2) eats only those foods that are on the approved list and keeps track of all items consumed in the journal, (Phase B3) records in the journal everything they eat and drink and the time they eat and (Phase B4) attends weekly self-improvement sessions.

The design would look like the one shown below with data to indicate the effectiveness of the different (Phases B1–4) multi-intervention approach.

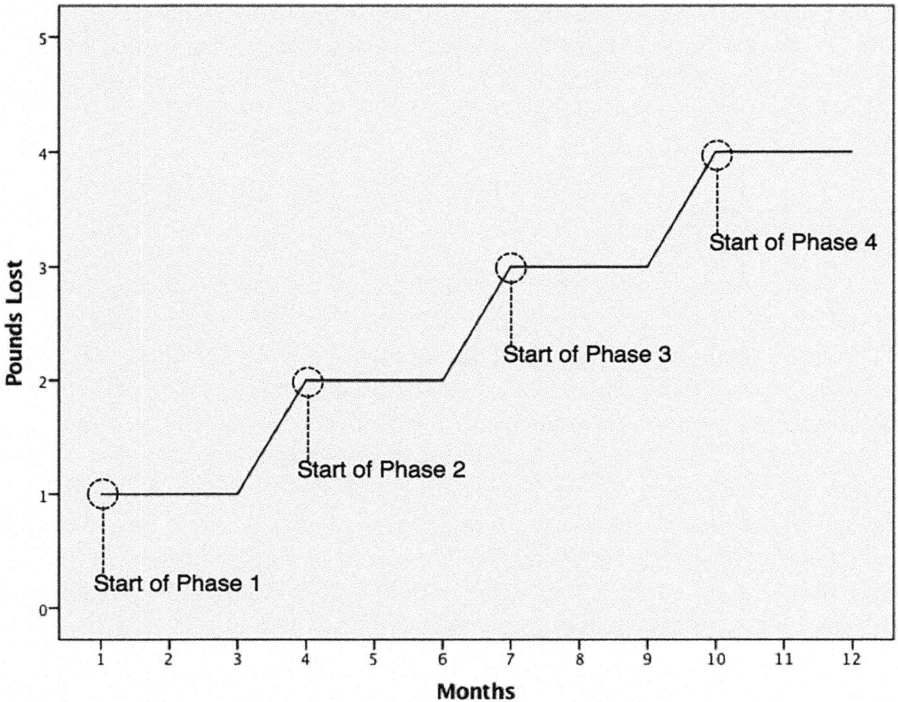

The graph of the ABCDE design shows with the introduction of succeeding interventions there was an increase in the loss of pounds per month. In the first three months (Phase B1), the person lost 1 pound per month with the intervention of keeping a journal of eating. In the second three months (Phase B2) keeping the journal of eating and adding the selected list of foods that can be eaten, weight loss increased to 2 pounds per month. Keeping a count of calories and time of eating (Phase B3) while retaining the first two interventions weight loss increased to 3 pounds per month. Finally, with the introduction of interventions to improve self-image (Phase B4) along with the continuing use of the previous interventions, 4 pounds per month were lost. It is difficult to determine the exact contribution of each intervention after the first one due to the contribution of preceding interventions carrying over to subsequent interventions. To try to reduce the amount of carryover from one phase B to another phase B and to accurately determine the contribution from each intervention you could insert an A phase between each of the B phases. Of course, there will still be carryover but A phases would reduce it and provide better measurements of the interventions. From the results, you might conclude that it is important in working with clients who have weight management difficulties to utilize all four interventions. As a practitioner/researcher you cannot determine what sequence of interventions might work best as you have not tried other sequences. Changing the sequence of the ABCDE design, for example ABDCE, can help the practitioner determine how best to sequence interventions to provide optimal benefits.

MULTIPLE BASELINE

So far, we have been talking about only one "problem" or target outcome (DV), although it may consist of sub-problems that are parts of the larger problem as in the previous example. However, we typically work with clients/situations where we try to resolve more than one problem at a time. In these cases, some of the ***target outcomes are related*** and we might develop a single intervention that would be successful in changing all of the target outcomes simultaneously. ***There was only one problem, loss of weight in the previous example,*** and was the only outcome measured even when utilizing multiple interventions. ***Where there are multiple problems that are the object of the intervention you should employ a multiple baseline design.***

Let's use anger as an example. A Male client has anger management problems that occur with co-workers, his spouse and children. There are three related target outcomes: (1) anger outbursts at work, (2) anger outbursts with the spouse and (3) anger outbursts with the children. The client identified that the most serious (acknowledging that all were related and had to change) were with the spouse and children. It was decided to initially focus the intervention on anger outbursts at home.

In a multiple baseline design, the A phase should still precede the B phase (intervention). The client and spouse estimated that approximately eight anger outbursts toward either the spouse or children occurred per week. In this case because of the severity of the problem there was no formal A phase, but the estimate of eight per week was accepted as an estimate of the non-intervention amount. The severity and need for immediate intervention at the work situation was less. At the same time as the initiation of intervention for anger at home (B phase), the client was instructed to write down each day the number of anger outbursts he had at work (a baseline A phase for work; see the graph below).

When the intervention (B phase for home) was started (Day 1 home only until Day 8) there was an immediate improvement in anger outbursts at home. You can also see what appears to be a slight drop occurring in outbursts at work even though there was no intervention aimed directly at work. What often happens with target outcomes that are related is that there is an "intervention effect" that will influence or "spill over" to the other target prior to an intervention specifically directed at the second target (work).

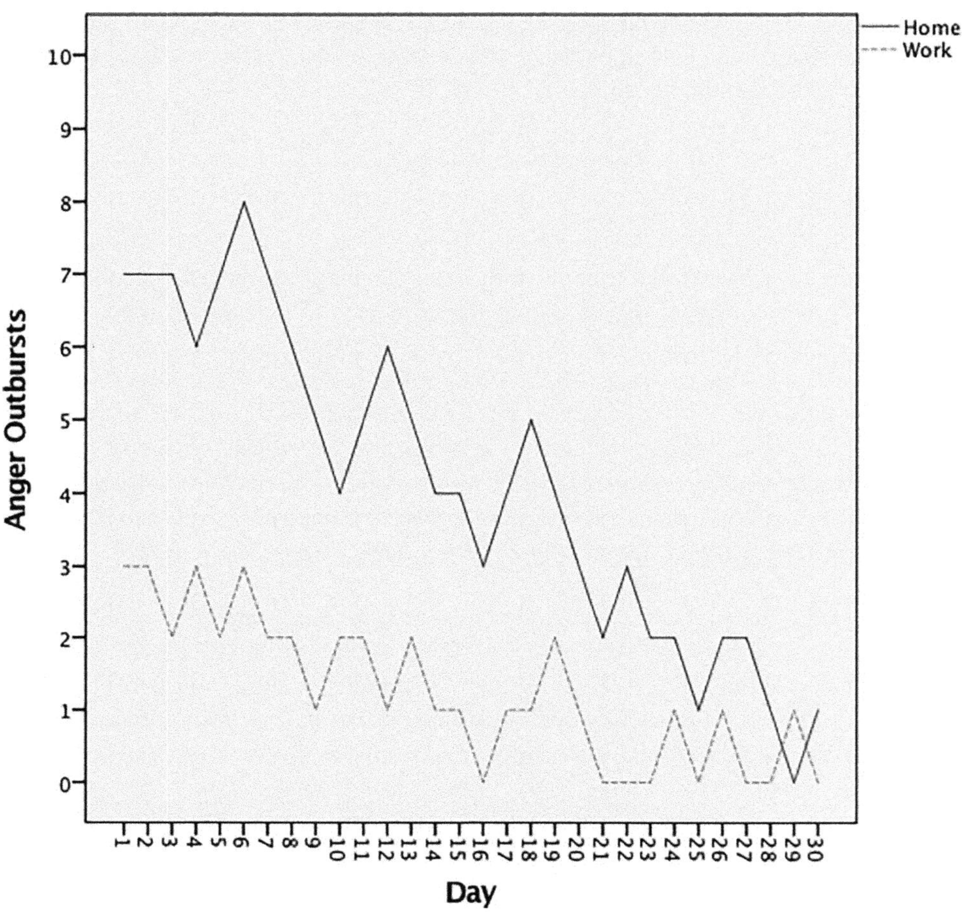

When a specific intervention was directed at anger outbursts at work (Day 8), there was an even greater drop at work indicating the effectiveness of the intervention directed specifically at work. We also see again the "spill-over effect" from work to home even after the intervention had already been initiated before the one at work. This indicated that both anger situations are related and that intervention in one will affect the outcome in the other. In essence, "boosters" in both directions.

Many of the N = 1 designs rely on the client reporting effects on the target outcomes occurring in the "outside and real world". To that extent, we cannot directly observe or measure the outcome and must rely on the memory and veracity of the client and must always be conscious of the validity of that assessment. Even if the client is trying to be very accurate and unbiased, measurements based upon verbal accounts are not always precise. There are better methods to measure than a weekly verbal report.

Some methods that provide potentially more accurate measurements are recording by smart phone, tablet or even keeping a journal each time the target outcome occurs. The shorter the time period between occurrence of the outcome and recording the greater the precision.

There is ever increasing importance of multiple baseline methods. Up to this point, we have been talking about an N of 1 or intervention with a single client. But now let's begin to see the "tie in" with group designs or even program evaluation. Envision you are working in a setting where you have many clients coming for basically the same problem. We can continue to use the anger management problem discussed above, and let's assume you would utilize the same basic intervention with these clients. In effect, you have many similar clients with similar interventions or many N = 1s. Indeed, these clients form a "group" with similar problems/circumstances where similar interventions are used to address these problems. The diagram in Chapter 2 shows the relationship between individuals and groups in research and practice, and you can see that you are developing a set of individuals that move across the arrow into the group model. Subsequent research that could evolve from the aggregation of many N = 1s could evolve into a program evaluation (Chapter 8).

What about the relationship between research, practice, good services, replication, generalizability and program evaluation? These questions are often posed with respect to single subject N = 1 designs. First, the method is one that can be easily infused into a social worker's practice and should be embraced to improve what we do, and to provide the best possible services and interventions that will result in the best outcomes. We are professionally remiss if we do not measure ourselves and our services to clearly demonstrate meeting goals for clients. This methodology fits our mission of social justice well because we need to ensure we are providing effective and efficient services equally to all.

Replication is the foundation to test support for continued use of methods and approaches. By using the same methods and approaches with multiple clients we can begin to codify through replication across many individual clients, methods that are more broadly applicable. Certainly, interventions have to be tailored to meet individual needs but without a generalized intervention method, we would have to develop a completely new approach for each client resulting in delays to initiate interventions and assistance.

We are not proposing everyone is the same; we are saying that over time a practitioner, using N = 1 single subject designs with numerous clients, develops a set of interventions/methods as a base to work with certain problems. In the past, this set of interventions/methods was often called "practice wisdom" and was used by some as a derogative term to "put down" what was labeled a "lack of research" in practice settings. We believe that this "practice wisdom" is knowledge gained from many N = 1 research designs that had not formalized beyond the level of the individual practitioner or a circle of practitioners. It is important to formalize and disseminate this practice wisdom so that all within the profession can better measure interventions and outcomes that ultimately can be aggregated into group designs for program evaluation and generalization to populations. Again, have a look at the research diagram in Chapter 2—there is a continuous back and forth path from individuals to groups. Recognize that outliers from the group (those different from the norm) can become the basis for N = 1 study to determine what those differences are and how to understand and work with those individuals. ***You might view this continuous interchange between individuals and groups as a form of social justice embedded into social work practice and research.***

N = 1 methods are not intended to determine causality. In many cases a strong relationship is shown and we conduct more N = 1 interventions research in practice "AS IF" there was causality. That is, we operate "**as if** it was causal" and knowing that it is likely to happen in a certain way much of the time, we practice and function on "the probability of the evidence that shows if I do this then that will happen". Such is social work practice. Such is social work research.

Working with clients using these methods requires more time. Sometimes we are forced to choose between seeing more clients or seeing fewer clients and taking the time to measure and determine outcomes in an N = 1 design. As a practitioner, you may be torn between spending the time to measure outcome on a certain number of clients or using that time to see more clients. A difficult decision for sure. In many agencies, there is a similar "double bind" where the agency must demonstrate effectiveness to funding sources as well as seeing a greater number of clients that can increase funding. It is a delicate balance and one to be negotiated in a manner that effectiveness is measured but not at the expense of a large reduction in client count and/or limiting services. Effective services can be developed/improved using N = 1 designs or through program evaluation (Chapter 8). Improving effectiveness can ultimately reduce time spent as clients have problems resolved and fewer of them return for the same problem.

Often when practitioners use N = 1 design they do not see it as "doing research"; rather it is measuring client progress and informing their practice and is not called research because it does not fit the classical experimental causal explanation group design. However, many agencies and universities (when a student is using this method to monitor outcomes) consider it a form of research, and policies and regulations discussed in Chapter 4 are required to be followed. Find out if you are starting to initiate

N = 1 designs if they are considered research by the agency and/or university. In developing the intervention plan and measurement of target outcomes, the client must be an integral part of the process whether considered research or not. The ethics of this professional relationship dictate full disclosure about methods, processes and outcomes and the client must understand and agree to the N = 1 design and how it is being utilized in the intervention.

Over the years other methods have been created to determine effective of social workers in their practice. Agencies have relied on feedback from clients which has taken the form of satisfaction surveys. However, satisfaction does not always equal success. You can imagine that clients who return satisfaction surveys are ones who feel passionate about their response and have an important reason to reply. This important reason usually is that they either had a great experience or had a terrible experience reflecting the ends of the satisfaction continuum. What about you; do you take the time to answer surveys about how much you liked something if it was a neutral experience? Satisfaction surveys are not known for accurately measuring the outcome of an intervention and responses frequently reflect how much they liked the worker and not how much they benefitted from the service.

Reviews of case records is another method to try to evaluate successful completion of the goal/outcome but it relies on what is entered into the record and entries may not be consistent across all cases, all workers and all clients. Information in case records is usually difficult to aggregate because it is based upon different situations and clients and might result in adding clients, problems, outcomes that do not belong together. Finally, remember case records are only as good as they are maintained.

N = 1 research, no matter which design, improves outcome measurement and provides the practitioner with their own database about the efficacy of their interventions—"what works" and "what does not work". This assessment is supported by sound methodology, and critical testing of various treatment modalities for problems we as social workers are expected to help resolve. This methodology provides a way to monitor practice and improve services and therefore assist our clients more effectively and efficiently using evidence-based practice. We believe that we can and must show how we as a profession are making a difference in lives, in the world and in seeking social justice. Showing this difference is not always accurately found in case records and certainly not in satisfaction surveys, annual evaluation or supervisory records. We feel that this can be best captured at the individual level in clearly explicated and carried out N = 1 designs where the target outcome (DV) is specifically designated, the intervention to address that problem is clearly defined and followed, and where measurement is precise, consistently recoded and ultimately evaluated.

Discussion Articles

Discuss the pros and cons of different designs presented and how they are applicable to social work practice. Do you think that they would improve practice and be used?

Wong, S. L. (2010). Single-case evaluations designs for practitioners. *Journal of Social Service Research*, *36*(3), 248–259. Retrieved from https://doi.org/10.1080/01488371003707654

Discuss how single subject design studies are used or can be used in behavioral change. Do you believe they are optimal and should include statistical analysis in social work practice? Give the rational for your opinion.

Dallery, J., & Raiff, B. (2014). Optimizing behavioral health interventions with single-case designs: From development to D. *Translational Behavioral Medicine*, *4*(3), 290–303. doi:10.1007/s13142-014-0258-z

Chapter 8

PROGRAM EVALUATION—FINDING ANSWERS ABOUT THE PROCESS OF IMPLEMENTATION AND THE OUTCOME OF A PROGRAM

The social work profession, based upon its mission and code of ethics, has an imperative to evaluate all the services it provides whether to a person, group, neighborhood or community. We have previously written about evaluation of services (interventions) for individuals and families (Chapter 7). In this chapter, the focus is on evaluating services (programs) to groups. Program evaluations provide an empirical evaluation of services to three important stakeholder groups (1) those receiving services, (2) those funding services, and (3) those providing services.

Research evaluating social work programs can be categorized into four areas, all of which may include components of qualitative and quantitative methodology. Those four areas are:

(1) **Needs Evaluation (Assessment)**—"What are the needs?"
(2) **Program Development Evaluation**—"What program can best meet those needs?"
(3) **Implementation Evaluation**—(A) "How is the initiation of the program progressing?" (B) "How is the program functioning after implementation?"
(4) **Outcome Evaluation**—"How well did the program resolve the need and at what cost?"

These four areas tend to occur sequentially and will be addressed separately although evaluation of implementation and outcome may overlap and are frequently continuous and concurrently occurring processes during the life of any program.

Needs Assessment Evaluation—Phase 1

Identification and Elucidation of the Problem

Program Development and Implementation Evaluations—Phase 2

Selection, Creation, Developing Delivery Systems, Monitoring and Assessing Delivery Systems and Making Changes to Improve the Program

Outcome Evaluation—Phase 3

Determining the Program Impact on the Need (Problem) and the Level of Effectiveness and Efficiency of the Program.

Phase 1 is the **needs assessment** where the needs/problem is determined and the program to resolve them is selected
Phase 2 is a **formative evaluation** where the critical function is to evaluate how the program is developing toward "rolling out" the program
Phase 3 is a **summative evaluation** where it is determined how well the program is achieving the defined outcome(s).

As an example of how this process occurs in everyday life, we will use a Thanksgiving meal. In the needs assessment, you determined that there was a need for your family to have a Thanksgiving meal provided on a specific day to 12 people. Next, you have to develop and implement the program, which is the delivery of the meal. The development phase would include obtaining all of the ingredients for the meal, planning what different dishes would be included, what days to prepare certain parts of the meal, when to start cooking each part, how long it will take, etc. In the functioning and management phase you would evaluate if you are on time, if all of the component parts are ready to be served and ultimately how the meal is served and consumed (management function). Finally, the outcome evaluation would be to determine from the guests if the meal was "good", if there was enough and if they were satisfied.

Program evaluations use both qualitative and quantitative methods and different types of designs. Interviews and group discussions reflect qualitative methodology while utilization of previously collected data, like a census or a survey of the population, reflect quantitative methodology. Historically, program evaluation has been seen as a linear process starting with a needs assessment to evaluation of the outcome. The process is not truly linear and although there is a beginning and an end, the process is more likely to be a series of moving forward and looping back, always progressing, utilizing feedback to make corrections throughout the development and delivery processes.

NEEDS ASSESSMENT

Seldom is a needs assessment conducted without something to trigger it—something that initiates evaluation of the conditions/problems. That trigger is the recognition of a critical problem(s) that has been identified by the group/community, etc. itself or by an external entity which leads to the determination a needs assessment should be conducted. The problem(s) can range from very broad (a section of a city that is very poor with a myriad of problems) to very specific (no day care in a ten-block radius).

An exploratory/descriptive design (Chapter 2) is most often used in assessing need, and includes the situation, magnitude and impacting factors. Questions in this phase include: Is there a problem? What are its characteristics? What is its extent? Are there certain groups within the population more affected than others? If there is provision for the need will it be used? What seems to make it change for the better or worse? What are the proposed solutions to the problem? What can inhibit the solution of the problem? This part of the process is very similar to conducting a psychosocial assessment of an individual but in this case, you are conducting the assessment on a group of individuals and obtaining a larger and broader array of data (information) that requires analysis to answer questions related to the need(s).

There are various ways to obtain information about the "need(s)". Most social workers use a multifaceted approach or multiple sources of information/data to provide reliable and valid assessment answers. One source of information includes ***previously collected and available data on the population under consideration***: census, health, school and economic factors related to the need. Reliability and validity of this data may vary depending on the source and how it was collected (census, neighborhoods, associations, agencies, etc.) and they must be critically evaluated for reliability and validity as well as applicability prior to inclusion into the needs assessment.

Key informants are another source of information (Chapters 6, 12). **Key informants are individuals who by virtue of the position they have in the community or with the defined problem can provide specific and detailed information and are typically interviewed individually by the researcher.** Key informants may be service providers (social workers or others) who have been trying to deal with the problem, community leaders who have publicly discussed the problem, informal leaders who are living in the context of the problem, elected or appointed officials who are familiar with the problem. Researchers have to decide who the key informants are and which ones to interview in order to obtain a complete and accurate representation of the problem and potential solutions.

TOWN HALL MEETINGS OR COMMUNITY FORUMS

Town hall meetings are a popular method in politics to provide an open venue for anyone to attend and voice opinions—usually about any subject. This same process—**town hall meeting/community forum** can be adopted and used in a needs assessment where **the community is invited to attend a meeting to discuss problems confronting the community (often it is delimited to a specific set of problems or one specific problem already identified)**.

SURVEYS

Surveys or questionnaires are another way to obtain information for completion of a needs assessment (Chapter 12). **Surveying individuals has two components: (1) development of a questionnaire that addresses salient aspects of the problem and (2) utilizing appropriate sampling techniques that provide a valid reflection of the community's view.** Developing and conducting a survey requires research skills in both questionnaire development and sampling methodology (Chapters 10 and 12). They rely on sampling techniques that select individuals who represent and provide information from the population affected and often provide information which differs from and supplements that obtained from key informants and focus groups.

FOCUS GROUPS

Focus groups, while a separate method of gathering information, can also be seen as combining elements of the other three methods. Participants for a focus group are ***specifically selected because of their greater knowledge of the problem in question*** and thus, are different from the town hall group meeting. Focus groups interact with each other concerning specific and directed questions provided to the group for discussion and answers. It is a discussion guided by the researcher toward obtaining answers to questions posed by the researcher. Finally, it is similar to a survey because the **researcher has a set of prepared questions that are directed to this specific group for discussion, interaction and answers**. In both interviews and focus groups you should (1) determine the existence, magnitude and the characteristics of the need (problem) and (2) seek potential solutions envisioned by those you sample.

In the same way, you get information about a client, from significant others and the context in which they function (work, social, etc.). A similar process occurs in conducting a needs assessment where you obtain information from numerous perspectives and points of view. This reduces bias and offers multiple ways to look at the problem/needs. For example, you may have been asked to find out about the need/problem of public transportation in a particular part of the city where the majority of the population have incomes below the poverty line. Different perspectives might be given by elderly and young, those with cars and those without, those working and not working, those whose jobs are in the area and those who jobs are not, those needing medical care and those not, and those attending school and those not. Officials who run the transportation system as well as those who own businesses in the area may have a very different perspective. Data about past, current and potential public transportation routes, usage and costs should be obtained. You have to determine what information you need, the sources of that information, where to obtain it and the likelihood of actually getting it.

Information can be obtained in a multitude of methods but it is typical to start with qualitative methods like interviewing specific individuals from the groups you feel have important positions or views about the problem. Then proceed to develop a questionnaire using that information to be distributed to a much larger sample to determine the amount of support for different points of view. Secondary data is also extremely important in formulating the needs assessment; for example, census reports might show demographic and population changes in the area, historical records would show changes in public transportation routes to include utilization of public transportation and route changes related to usage can be used in focus groups or questionnaire development.

Another important aspect that must take place at the very start of any program is support from the community—(1) to help define the needs, (2) to determine potential solutions, (3) to select the solution, (4) to implement it, (5) to provide resources and (6) to assist in the evaluation. This phase provides an opportunity not only to collect data but also to analyze that data using the statistical methods provided in the later chapters of this book. Comparisons can be made between various segments of the population concerning their perception (Chapter 20) and potential solutions, between previous conditions and current ones, as well as an evaluation of previous attempts to resolve the need.

Once characteristics and seriousness of the need(s) has been determined, the next step is to develop potential solutions for the need. Finally, program selection becomes the solution for that need/problem. But what is the solution? If the needs assessment simply states that there is not enough public transportation in the neighborhood, it begs the question what is not enough? Who does not have enough transportation? Is there a period of time when more is needed and a period when less is needed? What type of public transportation would be the best? If transportation is provided, will it be used? Who will pay for the transportation if provided? Such questions must be addressed in the needs assessment and program development phase. While assessing the needs locally, you should also find out if a similar need existed elsewhere, its characteristics, solutions utilized and the outcome. In fact, you might begin to make an assessment of the feasibility of adopting a solution developed elsewhere to the need in your community. Even if the program cannot be adopted, even if modified, the information gained will provide valuable assistance in framing, shaping and focusing your analysis.

A good way to begin to evaluate potential solutions is to utilize a "solution matrix".

SOLUTION MATRIX

		OUTCOMES		
	Riders Approve	Low Cost	Reduced Complaints	Business Approval
PROGRAMS				
Route A, schedule 1, large vehicle				
Route A, schedule 1, small vehicle				
Route A schedule 2, large vehicle				
Route A schedule 2, small vehicle				
Route B, schedule 1, large vehicle				
Route B, schedule 1, small vehicle				
Route B, schedule 2, large vehicle				
Route B, schedule 2, small vehicle				

The above is a very simple example of a solution matrix with the columns representing the outcomes of the program that are envisioned and the rows indicating potential programmatic solutions that might address the problem.

Let's look at another example. Assume the community concern (need) is that children are playing in the streets, being loud, causing problems and generally posing a "nuisance" during the summer when there is no school. This resulted in many complaints and numerous visits by the police. The needs assessment determined that **the goal of the program would be to reduce the number of complaints to police about children in the neighborhood during the summer "out of school months"**. Again, let's look at a "solution matrix".

	Number of Complaints Reduced	Cost	Personnel Available for the Program	Community Acceptance and Support	Planning Time Needed	Duplication with Other Programs
Program A						
Program B						
Program C						

The solution matrix ***clearly does not represent all of the potential solutions (programs) and certainly not all of the potential factors needed to evaluate the solutions,*** but it does demonstrate a systematic review comparing potential solutions of important factors.

During the needs assessment, consideration of programs that have already been developed for similar problems and might be adapted for use in your community should be evaluated. If programs like this exist, assess the similarities and differences between the program that already exists (origin) and the conditions you have (destination—your community). ***The amount of similarity/difference evaluated a priori (before the adoption of any externally developed program) including factors like culture, clients to those delivering the program will help you to determine the potential success or failure of transplanting the program to your community.***

Prior to initiating the program, a detailed plan should be developed in order to successfully achieve the outcome goals selected. ***A logic model is the method most frequently***

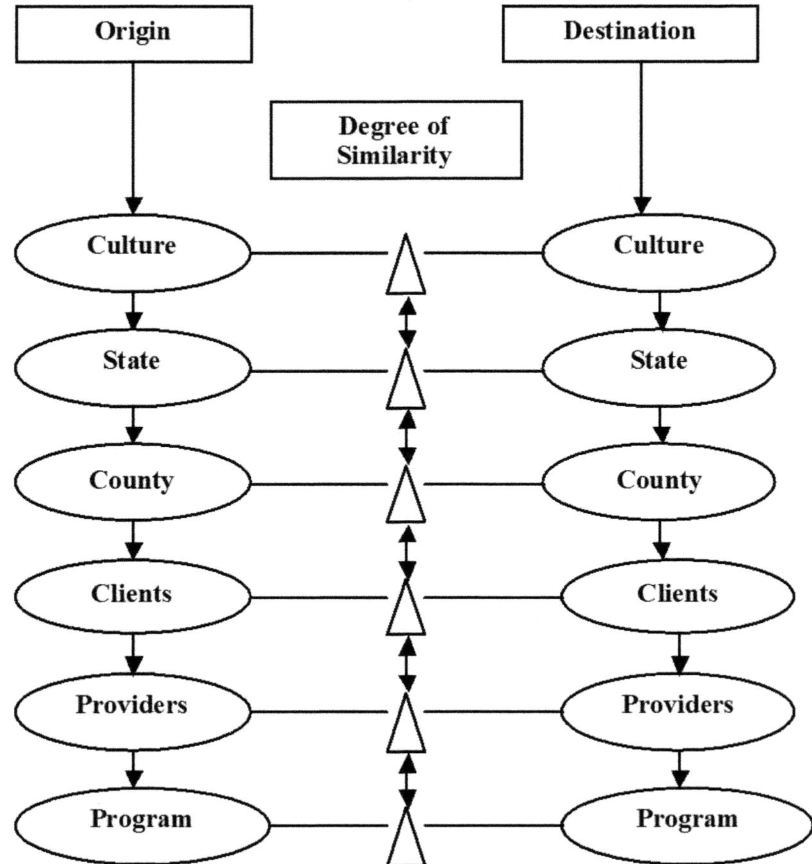

used to ensure the successful "roll out" of a program and one that will achieve its goals. A logic model lists step by step the assumptions, materials, processes and objectives from inception to the outcome. Any program can be visualized and developed starting at the end point (the outcome) and working backward, utilizing the outcome to determine assumptions and initial material, processes and objectives, or one can start from the assumptions and work forward to the outcomes. The logic model, while appearing linear in practice, is not. The guiding force during the development process is the outcome ***(start at the end point using backward planning)***. Recognize there is always a continuous back and forth movement, between initial assumptions and requirements, to outcomes with stops along the way. The logic model should be formalized and provided to all participants so that everyone is "on the same page" from design to outcome measurement.

After selecting the program to meet the need the implementation process begins. During the implementation phase, additional evaluation takes place. This evaluation is not to measure outcome(s); rather it is to measure and evaluate the development and subsequently how well the program is running and if it is running as designed. This part of the evaluation has two phases, (1) ***development of what occurs from program selection until the "roll out" of the program***—that is, all the various steps and activities that have to be completed in order to deliver the program to include changes made during development and (2) if the ***program is functioning as envisioned*** during operation to include difficulties in delivery and unexpected outcomes.

One of the most frequently overlooked areas of program evaluation is this development phase. Active involvement by the researcher (using consultation and evaluation) with program developers and providers is critical to success. It is during this phase that changes may be needed to correct the course of implementation. Changes—***midcourse corrections***—are often required due to unexpected factors: a reduction in funding, loss of key personnel or the inability to obtain equipment or facilities. All of these must be evaluated concerning the effect they will have on the final program and the impact on outcomes.

We will first look at the development phase. During this phase, a major consideration is securing and mobilizing resources—to include money, personnel, building and equipment. There is a timeline and a logistical implementation plan developed whereby each component—desks, computers, buildings, Internet connections, specific personnel, forms and files, etc. are needed. From the day that work starts on program development to the day of the "roll out", there should be a plan with milestones that are evaluated to see if progress is as planned. If not, what should be changed or done? Not starting a program on time, not having the materials and personnel in place and trained at the proper time, not having the equipment and not meeting expectations of opening provided to clients and community results in loss of credibility and poor service when the program does open.

The next area of the ***formative evaluation is evaluation of the ongoing operation and management of the program***. Much of this phase involves evaluating data collected by or for the program by other agencies—auditing how long clients wait to receive services, how complete client records are, cost for equipment and personnel and length of time in the program are just a few examples. Are policies and practices explicit? Explicit and complete policies, sets of operating procedures and records that are complete do not automatically make for positive outcomes, but they are important in reaching them. Without good records from inception through implementation to provision of services, it becomes very difficult to conduct a good outcome evaluation.

Part of the evaluation process, whether considered within the formative-implementation phase or the outcome evaluation phase, is to gather additional information that is happening as the program is implemented and carried out. The specific outcome might be improving the nutritional value of free meals provided to the homeless by the local community center and the additional information could be: Who is not being served by this program? What is the outreach to others in the community? Are the individuals coming to the program learning about better nutrition? Which are the best sources to obtain nutritious food at the lowest cost, and are there others that might be developed? Answers to these and other questions are important to the program providers, funders and community.

Now let's return to the previous problem of complaints about children during the summer and the number of "runs" made by the police to the neighborhood for those complaints and develop a **basic logic model for a program using the backward planning approach**.

A VERY SIMPLIFIED BACKWARD LOGIC MODEL

Outcomes (1) Reduce Complaints
(2) Reduce Police "Runs"

BACKWARD PLANNING ASKS WHAT IS NEEDED TO ACHIEVE THESE OUTCOMES

THEN

DEVELOPS THE REQUISITE MATERIALS AND PROGRAMS.

Many other objectives and processes would be included before, during and after the ones listed below. The one outlined here is a very basic example of a logic model and only used to demonstrate the process.

Develop schedules of programs; volunteers put materials needed into the correct area for programming and sequence of programming.

Keep all stakeholders in the loop as you go through the development and implementation process. Utilize their expertise in planning and programming as well as their ability to publicize the program. Re-evaluate programmatic decisions and staffing as you receive input from stakeholders (including the children).

If equipment is needed for programs, determine cost of materials and see if they can be supplied free or if you can get donations to purchase this equipment. If equipment cannot be obtained, re-evaluate programs and drop those you cannot equip and add those you can equip and staff.

Determine the availability and secure a place or places to offer these programs.

Select programs that interest children and determine availability of volunteers to staff these programs. Keep those that are of interest to children and those you can staff.

Recruit experts in programming for children and youth. Use them to identify potential programs and ask children what they would like to put these two points of view together.

Develop and start to use basic program implementation and outcome evaluation plans to include data collection and input from all involved in the program phases.

Programs must be interesting and ones that children will engage in.

Facts:	Complaints are most frequent between 1–5 and 6–9 PM.
	Complaints are about children ages 6–16.
Assumption:	Programming during those hours for children 6–16 will reduce complaints.

The example of complaints about children causing problems during the summer will be used to demonstrate outcome measurement. The police had to make frequent calls to the neighborhood to try to keep the children from being loud, playing in the streets and generally causing problems. The program developed and implemented for the neighborhood was intensive, multifaceted and comprehensive for the 300 children in the neighborhood. The age range of the children was 1 to 18, but the complaints centered on children aged 6 to 16. The program offered a wide range of activities including athletics, learning to swim in the pool in a nearby park, books and reading programs, craft activities, learning about local flora and fauna, and excursions to local museums, fire and police stations. The "Best Neighborhood Association" developed and implemented the summer activities for children. It received a lot of donated products, volunteers donated time to teach and run sports programs, Red Cross volunteers taught swimming, and other volunteers offered craft activities. Local community college students held reading assistance classes in the park every day. There was a significant amount of publicity for the "Best Neighborhood Association" in the local paper and on TV. The association was awarded the most outstanding summer program in the state.

There are three major ways to measure the outcome of a program:

(1) Effectiveness—the amount of change from the previous level
(2) Efficiency—the amount of change related to the amount of cost to produce that change
(3) Cost benefit—the cost of the program compared to the total monetary value of all benefits accrued as a result of the program.

The goal of the program was to reduce the number of complaints and police runs to the neighborhood during the three summer months. Data from the previous year showed that there were 87 complaints and 33 police runs during June, July and August. This year there were 9 complaints and only 1 police run. If you look at the number of complaints last year, 87 per 300 children, and then the number this year, 9 per 300 children, you are looking at the first of the two basic outcome measures for the program. Last year 33 police responses per 300 children and this year 1 per 300 children. They both appear to be highly significant and can be statistically tested (Chapter 15). In both of these outcome measures there is no mention of the cost, rather a measure of the outcome of the intervention compared to the previous amount. (Note: statistical tests covered in the last chapters of this book provide you with the ability to evaluate all of these metrics.)

COST EFFECTIVENESS

In conducting a cost-effective analysis, you have to determine the cost of the program and divide it by the number of positive outcomes achieved. In this case there were two outcomes—complaints and police runs. **Police runs to the neighborhood were estimated by the local department to be $375 each. For the previous year, the total would be $9,075 compared to $375 for this year. The cost for police responses was reduced by $8,700. The *total cost of the program was $3,600* with a lot of donated materials and time and training provided by volunteers.**

Cost Effectiveness

Police responses: ***The cost to reduce each police run was $3,600 / 32 = approximately $113 per response.***
Complaints: ***The cost per complaint $3,600 / by 88 complaints reduced = approximately $41 per complaint.***

This is a really inexpensive method of reducing complaints and police runs. Cost effectiveness calculations should be compared to another method/program that might have been employed to reduce police response and neighbor complaints. Unfortunately, we do not have any comparison programs in our neighborhood that would provide appropriate comparisons. However, you could search to find programs in other neighborhoods that have tried to reduce summer complaints and police responses and see how this program compares to them in cost per unit of positive outcome.

Cost Benefit Analysis

A cost benefit analysis takes into account not only the defined outcomes (police responses and complaints reduced), it will also include any other benefits that can be attributed to the program and attach a monetary value to those benefits. In this example, there was a reduction in police responses with a value of $8,700. Now to include other benefits that can be attributed to the program. The reading program increased the reading grade level for 38 children by one year. The local school system estimated that it would cost (teacher time and books, etc. to improve one year level) $265 × 38 children for a total benefit of $10,070. Over the summer 124 non-swimmers were able to learn how to swim using volunteers. The cost to enroll each child in an external swimming program was $25 per child × 124 children for a benefit of $3,100. There was excellent publicity estimated to be worth $650 for the "Best Neighborhood Association" with an increase in donations to the association of $2,700 over the previous year during the summer months.

The total benefit (there were others but for this example we will not continue to evaluate them) **was $25,620**. Even when subtracting the cost of the program **$25,620 – $3,600 = $22,020** the total accrued benefits from the program were large.

It is imperative that social workers do all of these types of analyses because we often "sell short" the impact of our programs by limiting it to simple outcome evaluations of the designated goal(s)/outcome(s). One of the most important aspects of such analysis is that it becomes a huge marketing point for our programs to the community when we can demonstrate not only the desired specific and singular outcome but the breadth and impact of our programs by **"putting money values on what we do in order to show in a very tangible way the value we add to our society"**.

There is a classic example from the mental health field demonstrating a terrible program evaluation resulting from poor definition of goals. An evaluation of program outcomes at numerous mental health clinics all in the same system was undertaken. In one mental health clinic, the director provided data showing that over the past six months, visits to the clinic declined significantly. As an explanation for the decreased patient visits, the director said, "we do such a good therapeutic job they do not have to come back". At the next clinic, the director produced data indicating over the past six months there had been a great increase in the number of patient visits. As an explanation of increased patient visits the director said, "we do such a great job of outreach here that it has significantly increased the visits". Since outcome goals had not been defined across the system for all clinics, each clinic could then define the goal in such a way to fit the data and therefore all outcomes are acceptable.

DESIGNS FOR PROGRAM IMPLEMENTATION

Research designs will be covered in great detail in Chapter 11, but three of the most basic ones will be briefly introduced here. Research designs are utilized to attempt to control for variables that could influence the outcome other than the variable the researcher introduces. The operative word here is control—of other explanatory variables. We are always trying to exert more control over the research situation so that we can be more confident in our ability to state that the variable under consideration was the "cause" of the outcome. Of course, we know that this is only calculated with a probability but we want to be able to say with greater probability that we think it was caused by the variable we are studying. In the children complaint example, there was very little control of other variables that might explain the changes. We do not know if the children who were causing complaints last summer were here this summer, we are not aware if there are other programs in the area that are attracting children and we don't know if there may be fewer police or if there are the same number of police if are they responding to more serious calls for assistance that could provide alternative reasons for the change.

One-Shot Post-Implementation Design

Our summer program basically used this design with the addition of historical data from the summer before. ***In a one-shot post-implementation design, there is no data directly collected on the identified participants (each child) prior to the implementation of the program and there is no data collected on them following the program.*** There was, however, data available from the past summer and of course data was collected on complaints and police runs during the program in the summer. There was no group of children who did not receive the program (comparison group) that could be measured for neighborhood complaints and police runs to compare to those who were in the program. There was no measurement after the program to see if the impact of the program continued into the following months or into the next summer. Our summer program has the basic characteristics of a one-shot post-implementation study.

One Group Pre–Post Design

In this design, you ***measure the variable you expect to change (outcome) with each participant prior to being in the program and then measure the same participants after experiencing the program***. The participant has some level prior to the program; it is measured and then measured again after the program to determine the amount of change. For example, in a program for elderly the goal was to get them to be more active. You measure the level of activity prior to the program for each elderly person and then you implement the program and after they have participated you measure their activity level again to see if there has been an increase in activity level. You are measuring each individual before and after the program and comparing their pre-program level of activity to the post-program activity.

In the summer program example, we do not measure the participants themselves before the program and after the program BUT you do have the data from the previous summer to use as a comparison. If we make the assumption that the individuals this summer are very similar to the individuals who were creating the complaints last summer, although we cannot measure the effect of the program on the individuals, we can compare this year to last year recognizing that other factors might have changed that could "cause" the change in the number of complaints this year.

Two Group Pre–Post Control Design

The design is the same as the one group pre–post one group design (measure before and after the program) but you add another group that does not receive the program. In the elderly example, there would be a group that does not get the program and they would be measured pre-program at the same time as the group getting the program and measured post-program at the same time as the group who had received the program (Chapter 11).

If you do not have a "non-program" group in the study you might be fortunate and have ***a group similar*** to the non-program group (control group) available for comparison, even though they were not selected randomly from the population and randomly placed into a control group. In most program evaluations, it is the case you will not be able to randomly assign into groups. In a study by one of the authors, a program was provided to one group while another group was basically identical (similar in both demographic and major variable characteristics) to the program group that did not receive the program. In this case the non-program group was a good comparison to the program group due to great similarity, not receiving the program, but the design did not reach the "experimental" random assignment level of control (Chapter 11).

POLITICAL AND VALUE CONSIDERATIONS IN PROGRAM EVALUATION

The final product of a program evaluation is frequently a formal report to government officials, a manager/director, a board, the recipients of the program and through the media to the public. In essence, the report is prepared for those who have a vested interest in the outcome. There are some important elements to address in the report. What is the aim of the evaluation? Who is requiring the evaluation? Is the purpose of the evaluation to ensure good services are delivered and the outcome is achieved or is it to change a program or move funds into certain directions? Is it motivated for reasons other than measuring the process and outcome with respect to the stated goals of the program? Is it being used to change the agency or focus that agency into another direction that may have no relationship to the declared program goals?

The evaluation should not be conducted to answer what is frequently a political question, "do we continue the program or not?" that may arise from program providers, program participants, program funders or other stakeholders. Rather, the evaluator should find out if the outcome was achieved, what resources were required to get the outcome and could the same outcome be produced with less cost so that those resources can be used elsewhere.

One should be mindful that an outcome that was specified at the outset of the program may not be achieved but other important outcomes may be achieved and should be documented; for example, providing pets to elderly in nursing homes with the outcome measure being to increase elderly activity. In measuring variables other than activity level it was found that when there were pets, residents (1) were much happier, (2) made fewer calls to the staff for services, thus freeing staff to spend more time with residents who had more serious medical needs, (3) were healthier overall with improved eating, (4) made fewer complaints. (5) Relationships with family members increased and improved, and (6) there was a cost benefit when pets were available to the residents.

Evaluation reports basically follow the same format found in journal articles, but the sections usually have different names. The first section is much the same as an abstract; it provides a summary of the overall report. Instead of being called an abstract this section is typically referred to as a "Summary" or "Executive Summary". It provides the reader with the salient findings from the other sections. In a journal article the author provides the theory and research to support the development of the research design, and in the second part of the evaluation report reasons for the program are presented. This section summarizes aspects of the development of the program that was discussed in the **Needs, Program and Implementation** section of the report and provides the reader with information about the assessment to include the findings, how these findings led to development of this particular program of services and then all of the data concerning the implementation of the program, specifically identifying factors that slowed or changed the objectives and goals. It includes information on staffing, training, facilities and other areas related to the initiation of the program and states clearly the goals and specific outcomes of the program.

The next section presents the research design used to measure program outcomes. ***Only when you put into place the evaluation design at the very beginning will you***

be able to collect the data required to appropriately evaluate your program. Outcome measures reported must relate to identified need (from the assessment) and the development of a particular programmatic solution.

The Results section is where findings are presented with no interpretation or discussion; they are simply presented utilizing appropriate statistical analysis (Chapters 15–21). In this part, the unidentified and unexpected outcomes are reported, like those from the pets in the nursing home. Discussion is the last section which points out possible reasons for the results, implications of these results and recommendations about future programming that is reflective of the last section of a journal article.

Program evaluation is always related to the mission and goals; however, over time the goals of an organization may change due to changes in program leadership or in external circumstances. Such a situation arose for the "March of Dimes" which had been a program to find a cure for polio. When the vaccine for polio was developed and polio was successfully eradicated, the March of Dimes as a viable and well-known program across America changed its goals to "working together for stronger and healthier babies". In such situations evaluations become very important in helping to re-focus the direction of the program by measuring once again the needs of a community to shape the program to meet those needs.

Discussion Articles

Discuss how "serendipity" can be important in finding a comparison group. Do you think that this was a "strong enough" evaluation to demonstrate that the program did not work?

Silsby, H. D., Lawson, T. R., & Hazelhurst, C. D. (1975). Drug abuse prevention in the military: A punitive/administrative action approach. *Military Medicine*, *140*(7), 486–487. doi:10.1093/milmed/140.7.486

Discuss how the authors developed different approaches to program evaluation. What aspects of those approaches are important to you and how would you see them being used in your agency?

Joly, B. M., Williamson, M. E., Bernard, K. P., Mittal, P., & Pratt, J. (2012). Evaluating community outreach efforts: A framework and approach based on a national mental health demonstration project. *Journal of MultiDisciplinary Evaluation, 8*(17), 46–56.

Chapter 9

MEASUREMENT—CREATING CONDITIONS TO OBTAIN A VALID, RELIABLE AND USABLE ANSWER

What do we mean by measurement? We are talking about how you can determine difference and the amount of difference between things or the amount of similarity between things. In the research literature two different positions have been posited—that the selection of measurement must come before selection of the sample, and the other that the selection of the sample must come before selection of the measurement. As in most aspects of research, we believe that the process is not linear (one occurring before the other), but that it is really a combined process where both are evaluated and addressed interactively with each informing the other in order to achieve the best combination of sample and measurement to answer the question posed.

Another area of disagreement in social work is whether all variables can be made quantifiable. Researchers who primarily conduct qualitative studies might say that not all variables can be measured with the currently available measurement scales. While those who conduct quantitative studies might argue that all things can be measured. As we have said before concerning other quantitative/qualitative disagreements, it is not a yes/no answer; it is the question that will determine the type of investigation or "measurement" and the level of measurement used. An old phrase was "to take the measure of a person" which meant to "understand and see the person" for who they were. It was not to find the weight and height of a person; rather, it was to determine "what that person was like". Today we would be more inclined to talk about qualitative understanding related to quality and not quantity.

OPERATIONALIZATION

In much of social work research we have tried to quantify many attributes by creating operational definitions. An operational definition defines the attribute in terms of the way it is measured—the measurement itself. For example, the quality of kindness is measured by "the number of acts of providing assistance to another person in a group setting within a one-hour period". A person on welfare is operationally defined as "a person receiving food stamps at the time of the study". The operational definition must be justifiable to others and follow a logical path from construct to measurement. If these criteria are followed, then one can argue about whether the logical path has been followed or not from construct to the operational definition. But if the operational definition is clear and measurable for everyone to follow, then the definition itself provides an unambiguous measurement that everyone taking measurements of the same individuals would arrive at the same number of individuals on welfare. One might argue that the definition for being on welfare—using food stamps—is not the best way to measure being on welfare. Indeed, that criteria for defining welfare might be challenged, but the measurement itself—receiving food stamps—is very clear and easily counted. Operational definitions are critical to how social work measures constructs important to policy and practice.

LEVELS OF MEASUREMENT

When we conduct research in social work, we have to be concerned with how we are measuring variables. There are two properties that affect how we measure variables: (1) the variable may be more appropriately measured or can only be measured using a specific level of measurement and (2) the precision afforded by the measurement technique. Let us take a look at the four major levels of measurement.

NOMINAL LEVEL

As the title implies this level of measurement places things into groups and by name where measurement is based upon inclusion into mutually exclusive categories. For example, with the variable fruit you could have categories of pears, plums, oranges, limes, pineapple and so on and you can count how many are within each category. In social work we are often counting things in categories—gender, sexual identity, race, welfare status, school attendance, state of residence. As you can see, these variables can only be measured at the nominal level. This level of measurement provides the least precision but one must realize that this should not be a criticism since these variables cannot be measured with more precision. In Chapters 15–21, nominal level variables will have a number assigned to them, but that number is simply a way for the computer to be able to **count the values on the variable**. Remember, the computer will use numbers simply to represent the category so 1 might be "on welfare" and 2 might be "off welfare" and the computer would simply count up the number of times a 1 appeared and the number of times a 2 appeared and provide the total amount of 1s in the data and the total amount of 2s in the data. The criteria for creating the values (categories) within a nominal level variable are (1) **they must be mutually exclusive**—something cannot have two different values (be in two categories —you cannot be off welfare and on welfare at the same time) and (2) **they must be exhaustive**—you must create a value (category) for every possible/potential value of the variable. If race is the variable and you have the categories Black, White, Hispanic then you must create another value/category OTHER so that any value or in this case any individual who is not Black, White or Hispanic would be included and could be measured and placed into a category. With a nominal level variable, you can be more or less specific, for example, (less specific) married or not married, other or (more specific) married, widowed, never married, divorced, other. ***Statistics to analyze nominal variables may be the only appropriate ones given the variable can only be measured at the nominal level and many of the important variables in social work are nominal level.*** Below is an illustration of nominal level measurement of race using three categories.

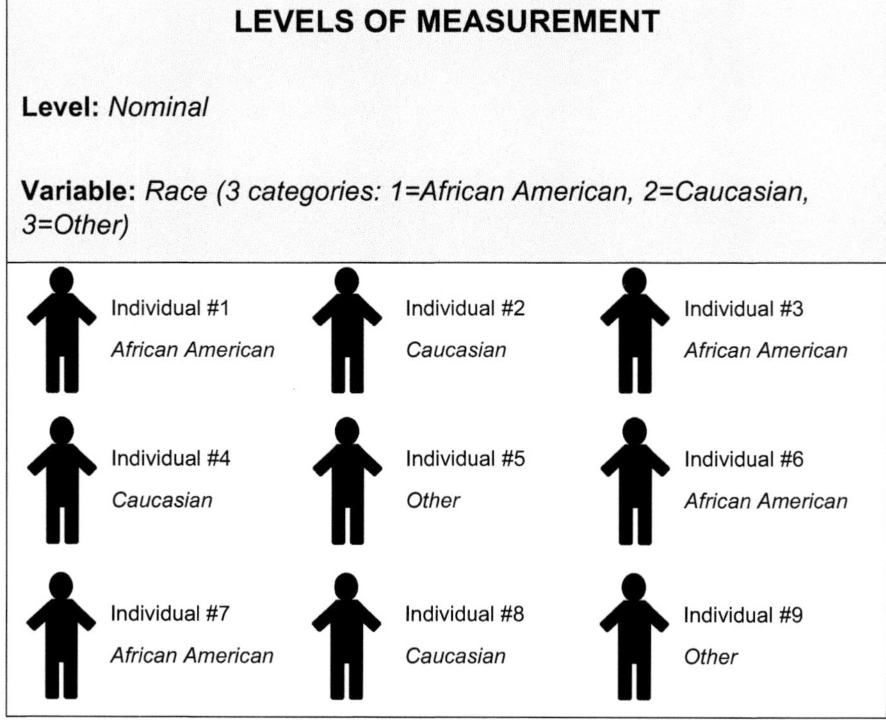

ORDINAL LEVEL

The word to always remember with ordinal level of measurement is ***rank***. Ordinal measurement results in ranking things (people, attitudes, pain, events) with respect to some particular quality. One of the classic examples of ranking is: 1 = totally disagree, 2 = disagree, 3 = neutral, 4 = agree and 5 = totally agree. This ranking system you recognize immediately and you have more than likely responded to such an ordinal measurement—"What is your position on. . . ?"

With ordinal scaling we can recognize that there is a difference in the ranks of 1, 2, 3, 4 and 5 ***BUT WE DO NOT KNOW HOW MUCH DISTANCE IS THERE BETWEEN THE VALUES***. Is there the same distance between 1 and 2 as there is between 4 and 5? Is it the same for everyone? A classic example of an ordinal scale is to place students in a class from shortest to tallest, and you can then say that a particular person is shorter than another person BUT you do not have any precise measurement like the person is 5 inches taller than the other person. **With an ordinal scale you do not know the magnitude of the difference between the ranks.** When you start to measure in inches then you have moved to the next levels of measurement that has more precision.

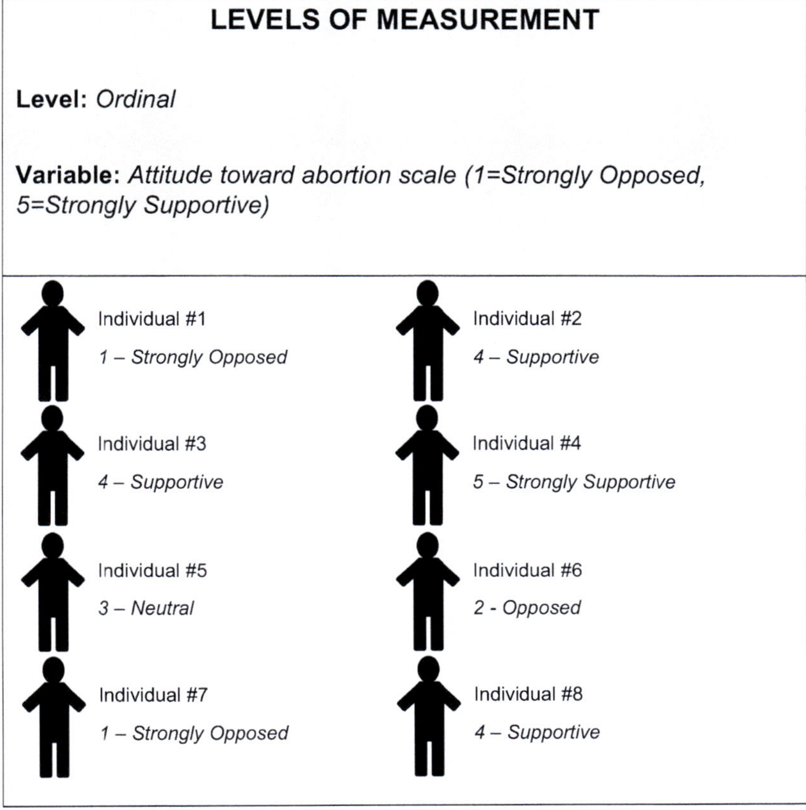

INTERVAL LEVEL

With interval measurement we enter the realm of a common unit of measurement. Now we have measurement where there is an equal distance between each of the adjacent numbers. It is an ***equal-interval scale***. Classic interval measurements you are well aware of are IQ, self-esteem scales, depression scales, prejudice scales and many many more. (It is not within the realm of this text to address the adequacy, validity and reliability of these scales rather to simply note that they are examples of interval level of measurement.) **One of the most important characteristics of interval scales is that there is no known zero.** *We do not know what zero intelligence is and thus we cannot use this level of measurement to say, for example, if you have a score on depression of 15 and someone else has a score of 30 they are twice as depressed because you do not have a zero point.*

Interval scales cannot be used to create ratios!

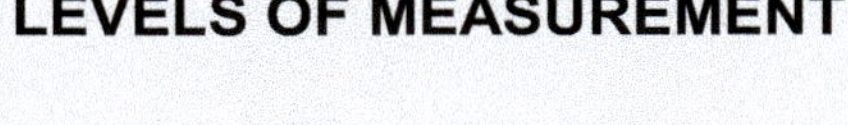

Level: *Interval*

Variable: *Beck's Depression Inventory (Range = 0–63)*

Method: *The BDI is administered to a random sample of 20 individuals.*

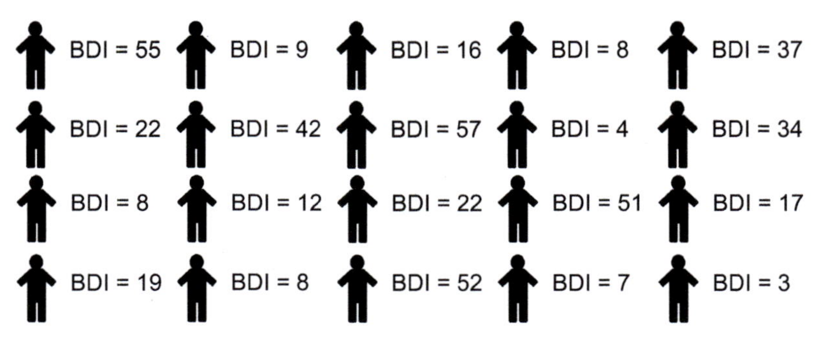

RATIO LEVEL

The most precise level of measurement is ratio. For many of the variables we study in social work, this level of precision is often not attainable. In ratio level of measurement all values (points) on the variable are equidistant from each other and **there is**

a known zero point. Some examples of variables from social work that have known zero points are income, behaviors, number of visits, number of years' education and number of years of practice experience. Since ratio level variables have a known zero we can state differences in terms of ratios and percents. For example, we can say that a person has twice as much income as another person; that the client exhibits 50% less aggression than they did a month ago or that a person has 3 times more years of practice experience than the average. We certainly could have defined practice experience differently and then measured it based upon that definition—the number of client intakes the person has, the number of children placed in foster care.

LOWERING THE LEVEL OF MEASUREMENT

Each level of measurement must have the attributes of all levels of measurement that are below it. For example, a ratio level measurement must have the attribute of being exhaustive and independent—the criteria for the nominal level of measurement. To illustrate how all higher levels of measurement include the characteristics of the lower level of measurement consider a person who weighs 150 pounds is in the 150-pound category and not the 149- or 151-pound categories showing ***independence of each point in the scale***. Additionally, the scale starts at zero pounds and increases to infinity showing that it includes the characteristic of being ***exhaustive***. A ratio level variable may be changed to a less precise level of measurement if it is appropriate for gathering and analyzing data. For example,

Variable = Income

Ratio:	Dollars	
	Income of $2,010 per month.	
Ordinal:	High, Above Average, Average, Below Average, Very Low	
	High	Over $10,000 per month
	Above Average	$5,000—$9,999 per month
	Average	$3,000—$4,999 per month
	Below Average	$1,500—$2,999 per month
	Very Low	Below $1,500 per month
Nominal:	Has Income	
	Does Not Have Income	

In this example a person with $2,010 on the ratio level scale can be placed in the Below Average rank of income at the Ordinal level and in the category of Has Income at the Nominal level. Lowering a ratio level variable to a less precise level of measurement depends on the question you are asking and the willingness and the ability of the person to answer. If you are only concerned about whether the person has income or not, then you would not ask individuals to specify the exact amount of their income. There is also the consideration that (1) the individual might not want to report their income in an exact amount or (2) that they cannot remember the exact amount. When developing measurement for questions you really need to know the population well that you are going to study. For example, some can easily provide income per hour, some per day, some per week, some per month and some per year. You need to know when designing questions and the level of measurement used to specify the values on that variable how specific the data need to be and how well the respondents can provide that level of specificity and precision. **The rule is to collect data at the highest level possible but consider the amount of difficulty in gathering it. That choice rests with you as the social work researcher.**

VALIDITY

What is validity? Validity is the term used to indicate that when you have the results of your research they are (1) representative of the group you have measured and (2) have really measured the variable you are studying. In other words, did your measurement of the group (sample) you measured reflect the population and did you measure the right thing.

The first type of validity—representing the population—is referred to as external validity, and the validity of the findings depends on how well you sampled the population.

The second type—internal validity—addresses the problems in measuring what you say you are measuring.

Validity, both external and internal validity, must be considered relative measures because we are never totally sure that the measurement we obtain is an absolutely perfect measurement—totally valid. Does the sample **perfectly reflect the population** and are we **perfectly measuring what we say we are measuring?** External validity will be considered in-depth with random sampling in Chapter 10.

Even with the most precise measurement instruments in the physical sciences, the measurement is likely to be a "little off"—not absolutely perfect. Therefore, we need to remember that valid is a relative term. We want to always improve validity and would not use measures that have low validity. Another aspect is the context of validity; a measurement might have high validity for one purpose but not be high for another purpose. There are scales that measure anxiety with many of them measuring specific types of anxiety but also to some extent measuring overall anxiety. We can say that all such scales have some validity in measuring overall anxiety, but that each of them has a higher validity in measuring a specific type of anxiety—designed for that anxiety. For example, one scale has higher validity in measuring anxiety related to test taking while the other scale has higher validity in measuring anxiety related to being in large crowds. For measuring anxiety, they both might measure it fairly well but both have been created to measure a certain type of anxiety. There are more valid scales to measure overall anxiety; however, each of these measures are more valid and "better" at measuring the specific types of anxiety for which they were developed.

METHODS TO DETERMINE INTERNAL VALIDITY

Typically, in determining the validity of a measure (scale/test) different methods are used to assess the validity of the measurement. Often in developing the validity of a measure these methods are sequential but not always. The first form of assessing validity is ***face validity***.

FACE VALIDITY

Face validity is exactly what the term implies; when you look at the statement or scale it has the appearance of measuring what you want to measure. The following statements would have face validity with what it is purported to measure: "I am depressed"—depression, "I use opiates"—opiate user, "I am a certified social worker"—certified social worker. What is important to note is that many statements that would have face validity may be statements that a person is not willing to admit or agree with. Unless you have already developed a relationship with the participants, you might be given answers that are not "truthful", hence face validity—measuring what it is supposed to measure will not occur; for example, most people would not openly admit to using opiates, and some might not be willing to admit to depression. Face validity is typically seen as the lowest or weakest form of validity because (1) many items that "on the face of them" are directly associated with what is to be measured are items that individuals may likely not answer "truthfully" and (2) some items that have face validity in reflecting or measuring what you want to measure may have validity for some individuals and not for others or may relate to the measurement you want for some and not for others—"I have trouble sleeping" might indicate depression for some respondents and anxiety for others.

CONTENT/CONSTRUCT VALIDITY

Whereas face validity referred to the "initial appearance of the measure" with respect to what is being measured, content validity refers to the ability of the measure to capture all of the aspects (content) of the variable to be measured. Let's assume that you are wanting to measure depression. The first thing you have to do is determine what are the various aspects or content of the construct depression. From your experience as a social worker you know that some of the aspects of depression are behaviors, feelings, emotions, interactions with others and attitudes to be part of the construct called depression. Some of the items you might include to measure depression relate to disturbances in sleeping—I have trouble sleeping, I wake up in the middle of the night and cannot go back to sleep, I sleep all of the time. Another aspect of depression is disturbance in emotions—I feel down all the time, I am sad, I am unhappy. Another is interaction with others—I want to be left alone, I don't like to do things with people anymore. And another is being active, I have no energy, I do not feel like doing anything, I cannot work. You could now put all of these aspects of depression (ways to measure the content of depression) and have experts make a judgment concerning if these items adequately and accurately measure depression.

These first two types of validity are very helpful in developing measurements for variables. Social work researchers start with face validity and then proceed to content validity to develop a set of items (questions) that might ultimately be turned into a scale to measure that particular variable. For example, in developing a set of questions to measure the ability of social work students to perform successfully in their field practice, items might include knowledge of policy, skills of interaction with people, knowledge of the agency, years of prior practice in working with people, etc.

Researchers have found ways to measure construct validity is to determine how a variable may fit into one construct and not into another construct—those items that are part of one construct should not be part of another construct. If we are measuring the construct of depression, then that measurement should not be measuring intelligence. We recognize that the performance on an IQ test is affected by the mental mood of the person taking the test, but there should not be a high correlation between depression and intelligence. This would demonstrate that measurement of a construct should not include measurement of other constructs. This does create problems when we recognize that there are some behaviors, attitudes, feelings and emotions that overlap and this is what makes it difficult to create scales and questionnaires—to determine the difference between depression and grief, or between symptoms for depression and some symptoms of anxiety.

Once a set of questions has been developed that is purported to measure the ability of the social work student to perform in practice then it becomes important to see if this measure (set of measures) test/scale really does measure that ability. This leads us to the next type of validity—**criterion validity**.

CRITERION VALIDITY

Criterion validity means that the measure is compared to other measures to test the assumption that the measurement is actually measuring the construct it is said to be measuring. You have a criterion that you use as a standard to determine if the measure is indeed the measurement of the specific construct. There are two types of criterion validity: concurrent validity and predictive validity.

CRITERION VALIDITY—CONCURRENT

Concurrent validity is when the new measurement is tested against other known measures at the same time. There are two ways to test the measurement. First to compare it to existing measures of the same construct where a high positive relationship should exist because they should be measuring the same thing. The second is to compare the measurement to existing measurements that are not measuring the same construct in which case there should be a minimal relationship because they should not be measuring the same thing. Often these two are combined to improve the assessment of validity between the measures since they are measuring the same construct. A scale to measure ability to work with clients in the field (a series of questions that relates to all of the domains/aspects of that ability) could be compared to existing measures of the same construct that are occurring at the same time such as grades in practice class, skills classes, etc. The measurement of scale of ability to work with clients in the field might also be compared to a scale that is not designed to measure that construct at all; it could be compared to a "quality of life scale" (a different construct) where very little relationship would be expected. Thus, you might expect that the new scale to measure ability to work with clients in the field would have high concurrent validity with the grades in practice and skill classes and rather low relationship to the quality of life scale.

CRITERION VALIDITY—PREDICTIVE

Predictive validity means that the measure should be able to predict an external criterion that is used later to measure the same construct. An example of this would be: does the scale developed to measure ability to work with clients in the field correlate or match with the ratings or evaluations of the field supervisors of these students when they are later in field practicum? That is, do social work students who score high on their ability to work with people on the ability to work with clients scale also score high on field supervisor's evaluations of their practice skills? There should be a relationship between the score of students and their field evaluation if the scale is actually and accurately measuring the ability of students to perform in the field. We know that this match or correlation will not be perfect but at least there should be a relatively good positive relationship between the measure and the evaluation. Even when the validity of a measure has been established there are threats to the validity of the results that can occur from two processes (1) external—selection of the sample or group to be measured not being representative of the population from which they were drawn (2) internal—situations and activities during the research process itself that could affect the validity of the results. Threats will be discussed in greater depth in Chapters 10 and 11.

RELIABILITY

Reliability of a measure means that you get the same results/score/outcome again and again. A reliable measure is one that is consistent—one that under different conditions would provide the same result. It is important to remember the critical distinction between reliability and validity. ***Validity refers to the measurement measuring what it is supposed to measure and reliability refers to getting the same result time after time.***

We need to discuss the interrelated aspects of reliability and validity prior to discussing how we can attempt to determine reliability. With any measurement it is critical that it be both valid and reliable. However, we can realize that there can be a reliable measurement but not a valid one. This situation occurs when you have a measurement that provides the same results over and over again but it is not measuring the concept you think that it is measuring. Assume that you are working in a program that is trying to help individuals reduce their body fat. The measurement being used is the weight of a person. This measurement is reliable only if the scales were accurate and did not change from one weight session to another and if the person always had on the exact same clothes and shoes each time. While it is a valid measurement of the weight, it is not a valid measurement of body fat. The time-worn example of reliability utilizes target shooting. If you are consistently hitting the target in the very top right not near the bull's eye but at the outer edge again and again almost right on top of each other, this result would be reliable but not accurate (valid) in that it is not "on target" and hitting the bull's eye which is where it should be to be valid.

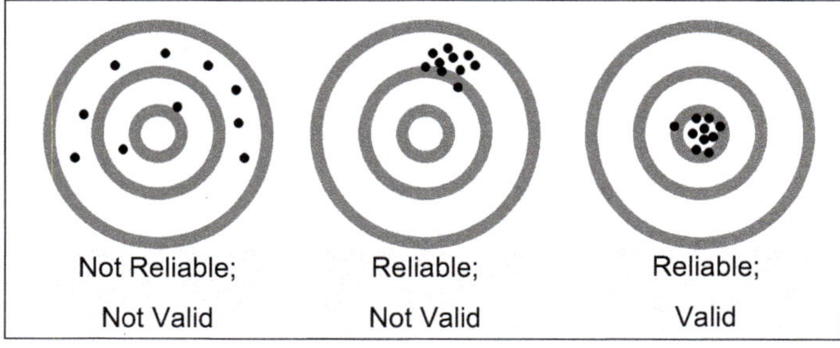

Situations in the measuring environment itself often affects the reliability. You might have a highly valid measurement but conditions render it not reliable. Think about yourself. What about if you have slept or not slept before the exam or if you have two or three other exams earlier on that same day. The test could be a very valid measurement of your knowledge but not reliable because the conditions under which it is conducted affect the outcome and make it not reliable.

To show how reliability and validity of a measurement affect social work practice and research, assume you are interviewing individuals who are known users of drugs and you are asking if they are using drugs. Everyone answers repeatedly during the interviews they are NOT using drugs when in fact they ARE using drugs. The answers would be reliable but certainly not valid. Now assume the same situation but one in which you have a very good relationship with these same clients and they trust you. Now they might be more forthcoming and answer yes which would be both reliable and valid. You can see how validity and reliability can be affected by the situation.

DETERMINATION OF RELIABILITY MEASURES

Inter-Observer Reliability

In social work we very often use observers to measure results. We might have observers (following training about what constitutes an angry interaction between a mother and child in a play situation) record the number of angry interactions for the mother and child in a 30-minute play session. We could then perform mathematical calculations (correlation coefficient) to see how well the observers agreed on the number of angry interactions. (You will learn how to calculate such correlations later in the book.) If the correlation was high, then you are very certain that the number reported was very close to the actual number of angry interactions that occurred. The better the training of the observers, the clearer the definition so that distinctions are easily made between occurrence and nonoccurrence, the more precise the measurement.

Test-Retest Reliability

This method to test for reliability involves administering the measure once and then administering it again with only a short lapse of time. The reliability is obtained by determining the amount of correlation between the scores from the two administrations. There are problems associated with this type of reliability because individuals remember their responses from the first time they respond to the second time and this memory can influence the second measurement. Another factor is the person may look up potential responses between the first measurement and the second and use this knowledge in the second answer. Finally, if there is a delay (time is definitely to be considered as an issue in this form of reliability—too long or too short) between the measurements because what happened between the times, this could change the relationship.

Parallel Forms of the Measure

Many standardized scales (measures) have more than one form of the measure—SAT, GRE, etc. You might be involved in using these measurement instruments but it is unlikely that you would be involved in developing such scales as they require very specific expertise, significant amount of resources to develop and time to complete the parallel forms.

Split Half Reliability and Chronbach's Alpha

Split half reliability occurs when you take all items in a measurement scale and divide them into two parts and then compare the answers on one half to the other half. If the measurement scale is reliable, then all items in the scale which are to measure the same construct will be correlated with other items in the scale, and therefore if you compare the answers from each individual on one half to the other half of their response to the scale, it should be highly correlated as the same person is answering items about the same construct. The items could be split in many different ways: first half to second half, every other item and so on. The measurement of a single construct is the key to split half reliability. If all items are measuring the same construct, then all items should be highly correlated and no matter how you split the items they will be highly correlated.

Cronbach's alpha makes use of the multiple ways to split the scale by obtaining the average of all possible split half-reliability correlation coefficients. This is a very strong method to determine reliability and the most commonly used today in determining the reliability of a scale. This method looks at the internal consistency of all items in the scale—no matter how we split and arrange the items in all potential pairings there is high internal consistency (a high correlation coefficient averaged across all of the possible splits).

Discussion Articles

Discuss how the authors used snowball sampling and why they used it.

Browne, K. (2002). Snowball sampling: Using social networks to research non-heterosexual women. *International Journal of Social Research Methodology*, *8*(1), 47–60. doi:10.1080/1364557032000081663

Chapter 10

SAMPLING

How Do I Select People/Things That Provide a Representative and Valid Answer to My Question?

The method to get the best answer to your question would be to have all individuals in the population included because then you do not have to estimate the answer for all of them based upon the answer from a representative group. If you want to know how residents in your city feel about social justice, the best answer would be if everyone in the city answered because you would know exactly and precisely the attitude of everyone. However, if you do not have the time or money to obtain answers from all residents, you must take **a sample of the residents** and then use the sample to **estimate how the population** feels about social justice. There is a single selection process involved in taking a sample from the population if you are not measuring the effect of an intervention (non-experimental design) and a two-selection process if you are measuring the effect of an intervention (experimental design). The first selection which is included in both experimental and non-experimental designs is to select a representative sample, possibly from the population as those you will study. After you have drawn a random sample from the population, a second selection process occurs in experimental designs. From the individuals selected in the first, another random selection is conducted to assign individuals into the groups you will use to measure the effect of the intervention (control and intervention groups).

Let's talk about the process of how to select a sample to obtain information that is intended to accurately reflect the population. A population is the group of things/

elements/people that is being studied. The population is defined in the research design indicating very specifically what is to be included in the population. For example, the question may be "Do Females have a greater number of days receiving welfare than Males?" The population might then be defined in the research design as: Males and Females over the age of 21 receiving welfare benefits in Hardship County. The results of the research are then limited to Males and Females over the age of 21 receiving welfare in Hardship County.

Another example might be, "Does CBT work better than other interventions for refugees?" The definition of the population in the research design would clearly state who are refugees and where they are residing. The definition might be: Male and Female refugees between the ages of 18 and 65 from the continent of Africa currently living in Accepting City during the years 2010 and 2016. In addition, you would have to define refugees with respect to the appropriate legal definition at the time of their entry into the country.

The population may not always consist of individuals; it could be records in a child welfare agency. Consider the following question, "Are all the items required to be completed actually completed in the social work case files?" Once again the population would have to be specified: all social work case files opened between January 1, 2015 and December 31, 2015 in the Assist Agency in Helpville. Once the population is defined, then the sample of records from the population of files could be drawn.

There is a difference between the population and the sampling frame. ***The sampling frame is what the population becomes after it is reduced by the ability to actually be included in the sample.*** Let's look at the previous examples as a way to understand sampling frames.

In the first example the population might be reduced to only those records where gender is included. It might be reduced because the record indicates that the family received benefits and you cannot determine if it was provided to a Male or Female. Finally, a case may be open but the record is incomplete with respect to benefits provided although it does specify gender. All of these factors limit the individuals who can be selected from the population into the sample, hence the reduction factors result in a sample frame that is only a part of the complete population.

For the second example the sample frame might be reduced by only being able to obtain records for certain years or months, definitions of refugee may have changed, only asylum seekers were referred or only individuals referred who had transportation to go to the service.

The "required" items in the third example to be closed are not defined and may vary from supervisor to supervisor or worker to worker. The researcher must very clearly define which items in the record are expected to be completed. Another limiting factor may be that items required to be completed are not required to be completed until the case is closed. In effect, the sample frame is now reduced to only those records closed between those dates.

We will use the concept of "sample frame" as a way to make sure that the population is very cleanly and clearly defined by what can "actually be sampled". Once this has been done ***we suggest that (1) you clearly redefine the population in terms of the sample frame and use that as the population from which the study develops OR (2) you can identify in your research report the reduction of the population to a specific sample frame as a limitation to generalizing the results to the original "total" population***. Using either one of these approaches addresses the reduction caused by the sample frame and makes absolutely clear to those reading the research the origin of the final sample and that the results refer to the redefined population (sample frame) and not the larger original population.

The sample is that group (subset) of items (individuals-scores-records, etc.) that can be accessed and selected from a population and upon which you conduct the research. It is important to try to "come as close as possible" to make the sample accurately reflect the population. In research, we are always concerned with "representativeness", that is, does the sample represent the population or stated another way, how similar is it to the population? Ultimate representation is to use the whole population which is almost always not feasible. The next best way to obtain representativeness of the population is to ensure that every person in the population has an equal chance (opportunity) to be in the sample, but it is very difficult to accomplish. In most social work research, we are never able to "mirror" exactly the population in the sample but we try make it representative with respect to important variables (ones that might have impact on the answers we obtain).

Many of the variables we want to study are affected by other variables such as race, gender, age, etc.; therefore, we are very conscious about trying to draw our sample that is representative of the population with respect to these variables. We have to be aware of these types of variables and incorporate them into the design and study. In effect, all variables that are found in the population should be equally represented in the sample and then subsequently represented in all of the subgroups created by the researcher to investigate differences or relationships so that the variable would not affect or have uneven influence on the results. If income is equally reflected across the selection process in the research, then income should not have an influence on the results. Another way to deal with the impact of other variables on the results of the study is to include that variable in the study and determine its impact on the results.

The total population is reduced when every element does not have an equal opportunity to be selected into the sample. A very real problem today in research is that certain groups might be excluded or included in research based upon computer access, land lines or cell phones. Using one of these methods of communication would clearly result in a reduction of individuals available for research in the general population. In social work, our focus is often on marginalized or oppressed groups, those who are under-represented in the population and individuals who are often reticent to be included in research, so in our studies it is frequently very difficult to obtain representative samples.

Another critical aspect of sampling is obtaining **an adequate size sample**. If the sample size is too small, it is unlikely to be representative. If you sample only 10 people from a population of 1,000 you might get 10 individuals who really do not represent those 1,000 individuals. For example, let's assume that there are 500 Males and 500 Females in those 1,000 individuals and that by selecting 10 you might get 10 Females by chance. Those 10 Females do not adequately represent the population in terms of gender. If you increase the sample to 100 you are much more likely to have closer to 50% Males and 50% Females than if you only sampled 10 people. While a sample can be too small it can also be too big. If you have a very large sample, a significant difference may be found simply because it is a large sample and is called ***power—the power* to see difference between groups is related to sample size** (Chapter 13). The larger the group the more you can detect small differences. Another factor influencing if you can see difference between groups is ***effect size***. **Effect size is how great an effect or change was brought about by the intervention.** If the intervention created a big change (effect size) then the difference is so large that it can be detected even with a very small sample (Chapter 13).

SAMPLING BIAS

Sampling bias occurs when you do not account for the possibility of obtaining a non-representative sample. A non-representative (biased) sample is the result of getting too much or too little of a variable than the amount in the population. Assume that a researcher is standing outside a grocery store in an affluent part of the city and is asking individuals about their attitude toward migration. The neighborhood is 97% White with no immigrants. The city is only 78% White and has resettled thousands of immigrants over the past 20 years. This is a classic example of a researcher collecting a biased non-random sample based upon a poorly conducted convenience sample.

Many studies are biased because it includes only volunteers and the biased would is a result of characteristics that would distinguish between those who volunteer and those who do not. Volunteering itself reduces the overall population to only those who volunteer. What are the characteristics of those who are volunteering and what are the characteristics of those who are declining? In social work, we strongly support self-determination and the choice individuals have to be included in a research study, but we must remember to include the reduction of representativeness in the sample based upon those who agree to be studied.

PROBABILITY SAMPLING

SIMPLE RANDOM SAMPLING

Sampling Type: *Probability Sampling*

Method: *Units are selected at random from the target population with each unit having an equal probability of selection.*

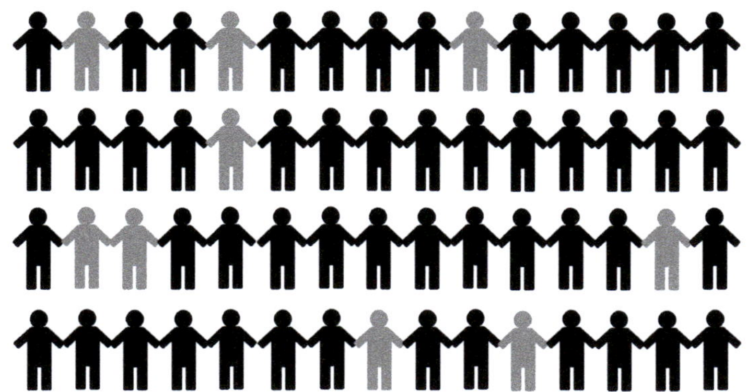

Probability sampling occurs when every member of the population has an equal chance of being selected into the sample. The reason to collect a random sample from the population is to attempt to ensure using the most accurate selection method and that the sample reflects the population. Of course, the accuracy of representativeness is tempered by the size of that sample but in general if the sample size is large enough then it accurately reflects the population (methods to test if the sample in fact accurately reflects the population are in Chapter 15). While simple random samples are always preferred, in many cases it is not possible nor feasible to use this method. To sample randomly you have to have a full and accurate list of every person/element in the population so that each one has an equal chance of being selected for the study. Such a list may not be available precluding simple random sampling. Another reason that you may not be able to random sample might be cost—cost in terms of money and/or time, and random sampling is time consuming and typically more expensive.

If the study is to determine if an intervention works, ethical problems may arise when random sampling. Assigning individuals who need intervention to the non-intervention group can pose an ethical problem. Even if you provide two different interventions to alleviate the problem, another ethical problem may arise by randomly assigning individuals who have the greatest need to a low-level intervention group and individuals who have the least need to the high-level intervention group through simple random sampling (Chapter 11).

Systematic Random Sampling

SYSTEMATIC RANDOM SAMPLING

Sampling Type: *Probability Sampling*

Method: *Beginning at a random position, every nth unit from the population is selected for inclusion in the sample.*

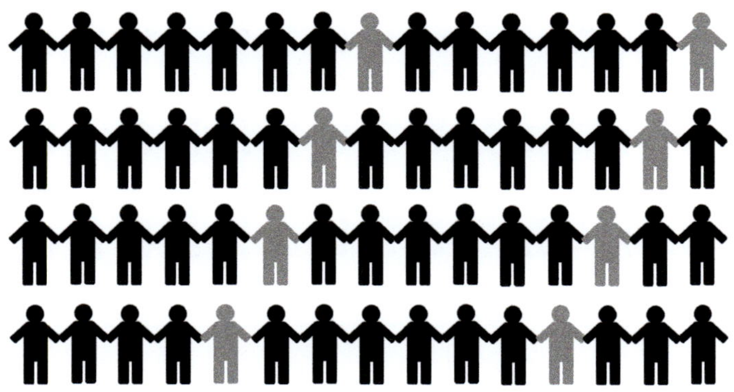

Systematic random sampling is frequently selected as the sampling method when conducting research using social work case files. Let's assume you want to conduct a survey about the attitudes of foster parents to proposed changes in the payment system for fostering children. There are over 300 foster parents registered in the county system and because of cost and time you cannot include everyone in the research. You have determined that 20% (60 foster families) would be an adequate sample of the population of 300. Systematic random sampling method was selected as the best method to obtain the sample. The method to select the foster families to be included in the sample might be as follows:

(1) Place the name of all of the foster families in a list alphabetically and assign a sequential number to each family starting with the first family as 1 and proceeding to the end with the last family having number 300
(2) In a list of random numbers go through the numbers until you reach the first number that is between 1 and 300 (example = 47).
    Go to the family that is number 47 on the list and they will be the first family selected for the study
(3) Select every 5th family in the list and when you get to the 300th family move to the 1st family in the list and continue the process for every 5th family until you have the 60 families.

This procedure works very well to obtain a random sample unless the list itself has a sequential bias as a result of people being placed in a specific order on the list.

Stratified Random Sampling

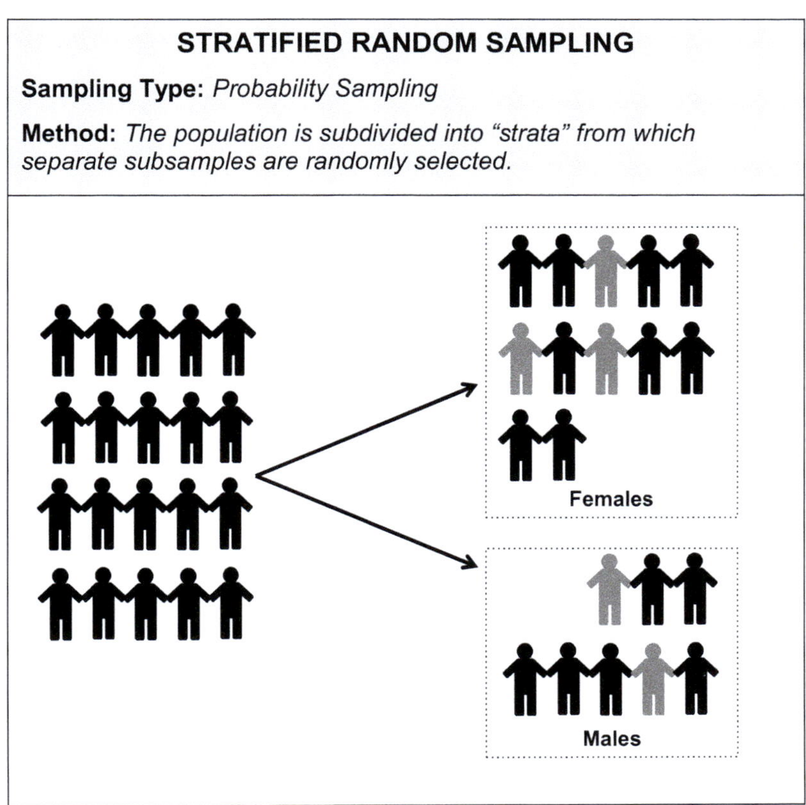

Stratified random sampling has two important features and is an important sampling method. ***Stratified random sampling (1) reduces the error of sampling and (2) ensures that all the values on the variable are represented proportionally.*** What is stratified random sampling? ***It is a method where the values on the variable are listed and the sample is selected proportionally from the population with regards to those values.*** Stratified random sampling is used in many social work studies to achieve appropriate representation of all of the subgroups of an important variable. Remember in simple random sampling there is a possibility that some of the subgroups might not be selected by chance and therefore not be studied. Stratified random sampling solves this problem by stratifying the population into the appropriate subgroups of a variable and then the selection of the sample is based upon selecting individuals randomly from those subgroups. The selection from those subgroups can either be proportional to their percent in the population or not in proportion to the percent in the population. When drawing the sample proportionally from the strata in the population, the results are reflective and can be generalized to the population. However, if the researcher wants to compare the subgroups, then disproportional sampling from the strata may be employed because some of the subgroups may be small compared to the other subgroups and due to the size differential cannot be statistically compared. Using disproportional sampling allows for more reliable and valid comparisons of subgroups but is not as reflective of the population.

The use of **proportional stratification** can be seen in the following example. A researcher wanted to assess the attitude of all social work students toward statistics at the university. In the university 85% of social work students are Female and 15% are Male. The sample to be drawn was to reflect the attitude of all social work students, and the researcher was concerned that a **simple random sample might result in very few or no Males and this would not represent the population**. Thus, the researcher collected a stratified random sample by placing all the Males in one list and all Females in another list and then drew 85% of the required sample from the Female list and 15% from the Male list.

If the researcher wanted to **compare the attitude toward statistics of Male social work students to Female social work students, then the research would use a disproportional stratified random sample** and collect data on equal numbers of Males and Females.

Stratification from the population to the sample can be based upon two variables (or more). In the example above the population was stratified on the basis of gender. The researcher might also want to find out if previously having a statistics course would affect the attitude toward the statistics course in social work. The population could then be stratified as follows: Females with a prior statistics course, Females with no prior course, Males with a previous course and Males with no previous course.

Then a stratified random sample could be drawn by selecting the appropriate percent in the sample to match the percent in the population for these four groups. Examples of variables that are often stratified in social work research are: age (10-year age groups for adults), gender, race and income level ($5,000 income level increments).

Cluster Sampling

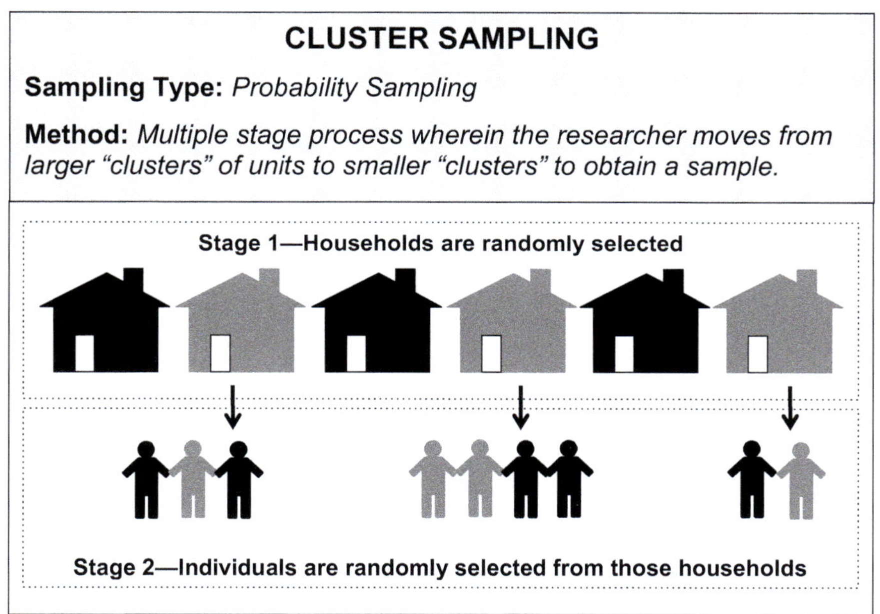

Cluster sampling is a random sampling method that is frequently used when the population is (1) very large, (2) it is difficult to obtain a complete list of the individuals and/or when (3) the population is spread geographically. A researcher wanted to determine across the state how seniors attending senior service centers felt about proposed changes to Obamacare. There was no state-wide list of seniors attending the centers. However, the state is divided into seven regions and within each region there are a number of senior centers. The centers within each region could each be considered a cluster of seniors fitting the definition of the individuals needed for the research. The researcher would then randomly select a previously determined number of centers until obtaining the sample size required for the study. Once the clusters have been randomly assigned, the researcher can then include all of the individuals in the center (a cluster) or randomly select individuals from the selected clusters. Using all of the individuals from the cluster or only a random selection from the cluster typically is a result of the amount of individuals in the cluster. If the clusters are very large then random selection within the cluster usually occurs; if they are small then typically everyone is included.

A combination of stratified and cluster sampling might actually be the method to obtain the most representative sample. Let's say that we know the number of seniors in each of the seven regional areas. Then we could stratify on the basis of regions and proportionally sample from the centers (clusters) that have been randomly chosen in the region to obtain our sample. This would be an excellent example of a method to obtain representativeness across the state. Remember, using only the cluster you might end up with many clusters from one region of the state and few from another part of the state. By stratifying (regions) prior to cluster sampling and then sampling proportionally you have reduced the sampling error that might arise from a poor distribution of respondents from throughout the state.

NON-PROBABILITY SAMPLING

These sampling methods are most often used to (1) obtain information that ultimately can be a foundation for theory (2) when the researcher is not conducting an experimental study, (3) is determining differences or associations (non-experimental) and/or when it is an initial attempt (pilot) to demonstrate the effect of an intervention and there is little control used in the experimental design. In all studies, random samples are always preferable but due to cost, feasibility and access to respondents, non-probability sampling methods may have to be used. Non-probability sampling should not be used if generalization to the population is intended.

Convenience Sampling

A convenience sample is one that the researcher can readily and easily obtain. There is no selection based on any criteria other than the respondents are accessible. The use of a convenience sample may be done to get a quick response to a question that could then be followed by more rigorous sampling procedures. This method often appears in the evening news reports. A reporter stands on a busy street corner and asks those who pass by if they are in favor of the death sentence. A representative of the university standing outside a lecture hall at the start of the semester asks first-year students about their impression of the university. Both are examples of convenience sampling.

Let's assume you want to obtain information about a proposed grocery in a high-poverty neighborhood where there is no store. You might go to the community center in that neighborhood one evening and ask everyone who comes into the center their attitude about a store opening in the neighborhood. This sample is limited to only those who come to the center, and only those who are there on that particular evening and excludes everyone else. It is convenient for you to get this information but it certainly does not provide a representative answer of all the people in the neighborhood about the store. However, this little study using a convenience sample

CONVENIENCE SAMPLING

Sampling Type: *Non-probability Sampling*

Method: *Units are selected because they are readily available.*

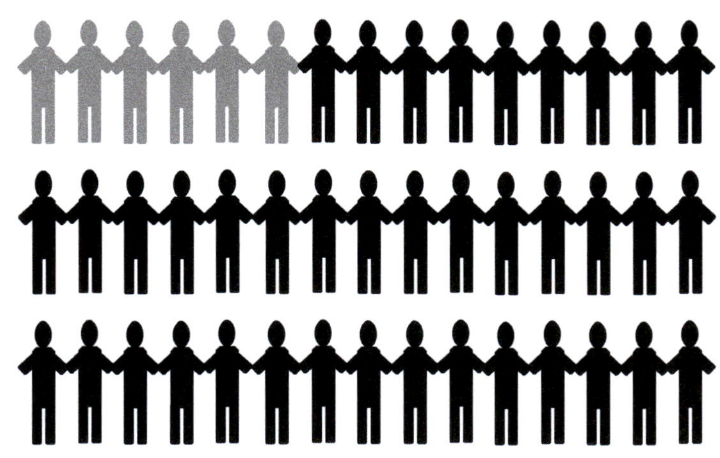

can help to frame a more rigorous study, developing better and more comprehensive questions and using a sampling method that can be more reflective of the population in that neighborhood. **Convenience sampling is the least representative; however, it is cost effective and quick and is best used to gain basic information prior to a more definitive study.**

Purposive Sampling

Purposive sampling is a non-probability method used to select a very specific sample. The researcher has a definite purpose or goal in mind in terms of the individuals that are to be the focus of the research. In addition, the researcher knows the characteristics of the population very well and has determined which individuals in the population can best provide the information needed. Frequently, the purposive sampling method is used to get information from key informants, experts on the subject being studied or individuals who have specific experience with what is being studied. **Purposive sampling specifies particular individuals to sample for information.**

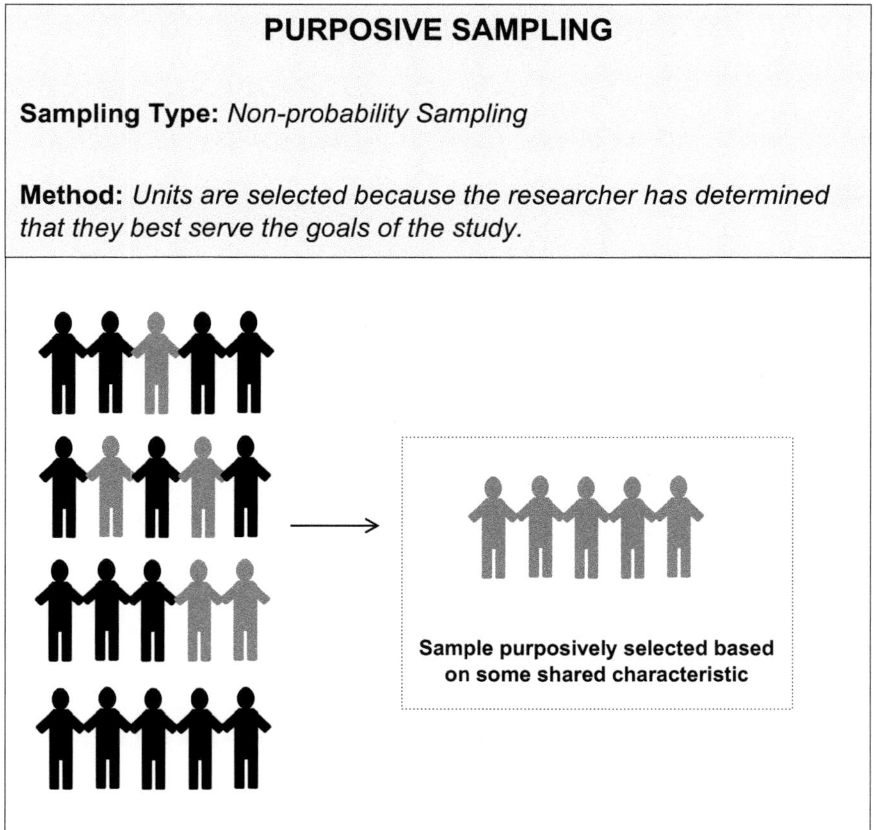

A classic example of purposive sampling found in both quantitative and qualitative research is the use of ***key informants***. Let's see how key informants might be used in the previous example about attitudes toward the new grocery store. To find out how key leaders in the community felt about the grocery store opening, you could make a list of individuals representing some of the important segments in the community, for example, business owners, various levels of government, religious leaders, community activists, informal leaders, school representatives, heads of organizations in the area.

Another way to use purposive sampling is to obtain answers from individuals who represent the both ends ***(extremes) of the population***. Social work frequently compares extremes—the attitudes of the top 5% income bracket to the lowest 5% income bracket, the academic achievement of the best-funded local school to the poorest-funded local school. We frequently want to have a sample that represents the extremes in the population in order to answer a question about differences between the polar opposites in order to understand the attitudes and concerns of individuals at both ends of the continuum.

Another way to use purposive sampling is ***not selecting a heterogeneous group that is representative of the population but rather to select a homogenous group that represents a subgroup of the population***. Assume that the population is everyone enrolled at your university, but you want to find out about the attitude toward abortion from only social work majors. When you sample only social work majors, you have selected a homogenous group (social work students) from the general heterogeneous population of university students. However, the results you obtain only reflect the attitude of social work majors and not the university.

The last example of purposive sampling and one that is very typical of social work research is ***sampling a single extreme group***. Many examples can be found in social work research—those in abject poverty, victims of human trafficking, raped women, asylum seekers. While extreme with respect to the population, the oppressed and marginalized are the ones we have the most concern for, those we need to study and find answers for, thus we frequently use this sampling method.

There are different ways that purposive sampling can be utilized to select a specific subgroup(s) to answer a question that can best be answered by those groups. ***Except for sampling using key informants, when conducting purposive sampling (selecting a particular subgroup from the large population) you could still collect a random sample of that particular subgroup.*** Remember, the key is the definition of the population you select from and then you can generalize your findings. A purposive sample that is collected on a particular subgroup without randomization restricts the researcher's ability to generalize even to the subgroup and any generalization must be approached with caution. However, if you randomly select from a particular subgroup then the particular subgroup in fact becomes a population and you can then generalize to that subgroup. This form of purposive sampling is highly recommended in social work research where we are most often sampling extreme cases within the population as we are committed to equality, social justice and alleviation of oppression.

Snowball Sampling

Snowball sampling is a method where you ***start with a few individuals in the sample and allow those individuals to identify others who may become participants*** in the research. In effect when you start to collect data for your sample you do not have a large group of individuals (population) to sample from so you allow those who

SNOWBALL SAMPLING

Sampling Type: *Non-probability Sampling*

Method: *Initial units lead to the identification of more units, which lead to more units, until an adequate sample size is obtained.*

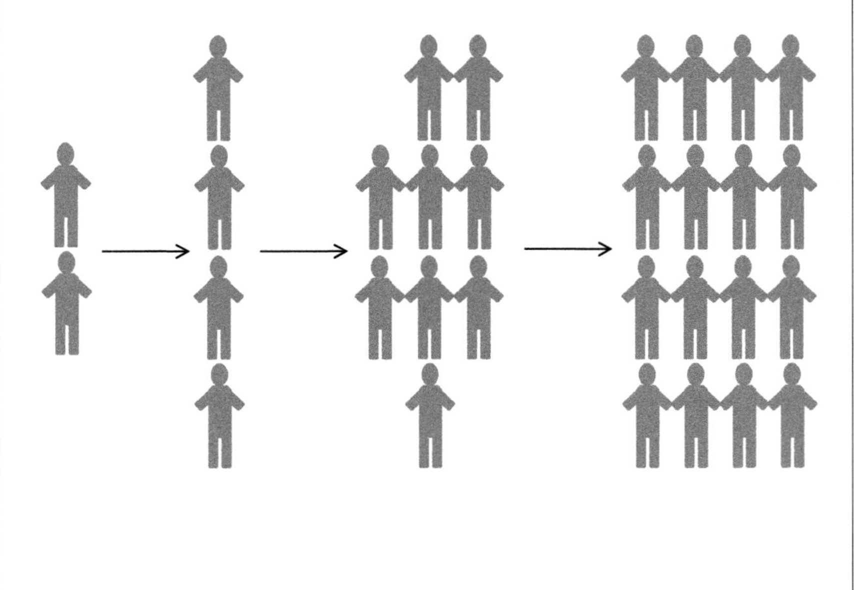

participate in the research to become recruiters to help you to enroll others in the research study. The snowball method is an excellent way to obtain participants that are difficult to access or when there is an initial lack of trust in the research or researcher. These situations happen frequently in conducting social work research on individuals using drugs, those who have been incarcerated, women who have been raped, those who are homeless. If the researcher can establish trust with just a few individuals, it can open up access to others that would not be possible with other sampling methods. One of the authors of this book was studying drug use among dock workers in a port city. Trust was established with one individual who then took the author to meet other drug users working on the docks who then were willing to provide information about their drug use. The use of a snowball sampling method was the only way the research could be completed.

Quota Sampling

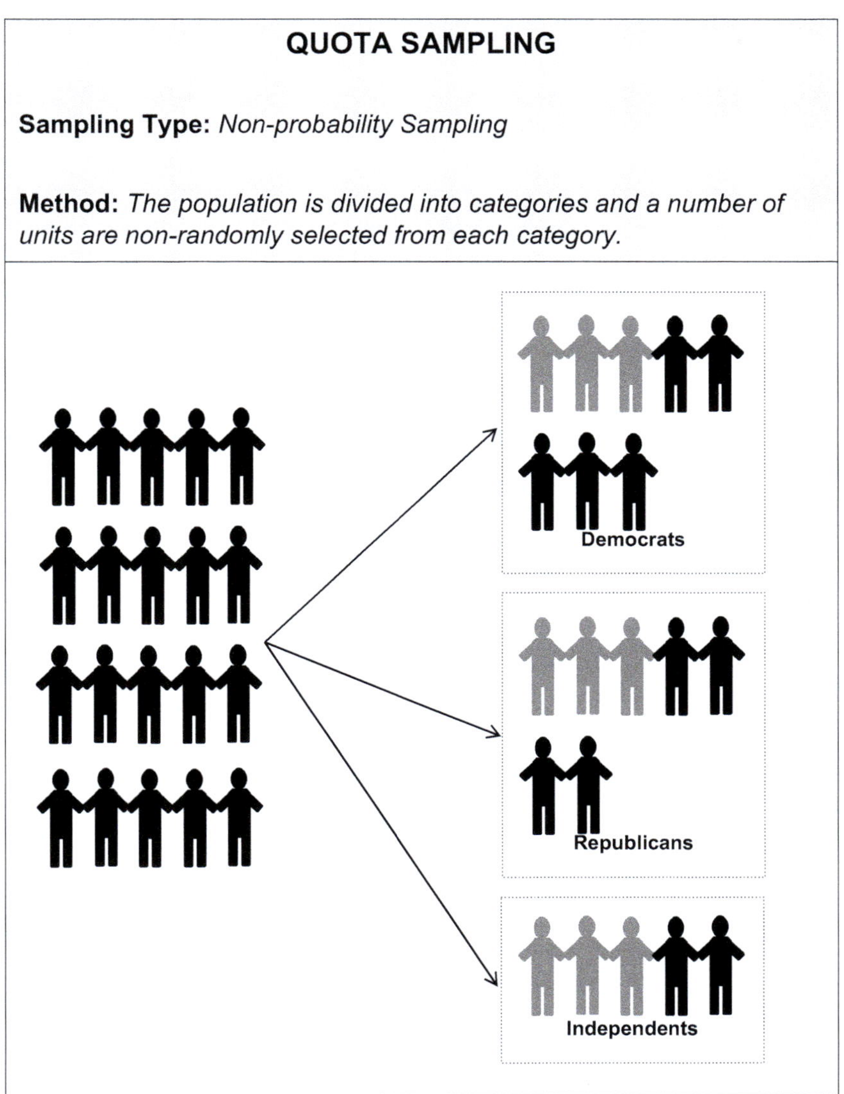

Quota sampling can be utilized when you know the characteristics of the population sampled and want to make sure you **sample all levels of a specific characteristic (variable) but you do not sample randomly within the characteristic**. This method is used to try to ensure that variables like gender, race and income level are appropriately sampled with respect to the population. If you know the percent of Females and

Males in the population, you can draw a sample that has the same percent of Males and Females as the population. If you want a sample of 100 individuals who are receiving welfare at your agency and you know that 85% of the recipients of welfare at the agency are Female and 15% are Males, then you select participants for the sample until you have 85 Females and 15 Males. Thus, you have the same percent (quota) in the sample as the population; that is, you have matched the quota for the variable gender. An example using race as a variable might be the racial percentage in the city: 28% is African American, 19% Hispanic, 6% Asian, 1% Native American or other and 46% White. ***To collect a quota sample, you sample from the population until you matched the sample percent to the percent in the population of these groups; however, within each subgroup you have not sampled randomly.***

In order to collect a sample using the quota sampling method you have to have an accurate accounting of the percent of each value on the variable in the population that you want to match. For certain variables, this is rather easy because records are kept (census, agency) that are accessible for variables like race, gender, age and income but for other variable quota sampling may be more difficult due to the lack of data on the percent of that variable in the population. In social work agencies, you might have data on many variables of interest like income, race, marital status, mental status, drug use, number of children and many others. Thus, research that is within an agency might have the population data available for quota sampling to be conducted. ***Quota sampling is a method that attempts to ensure that for the particular variable the results of the study will reflect the population from which it was drawn, but it is not randomly selected.***

Sometimes a researcher will **oversample a certain portion of the population**. ***Oversample means that you collect additional data on a part of the population that is small with respect to the percent of that group in the population.*** Assume that in the city population there is only 2% African Americans. If you randomly select, you are not likely to obtain many African Americans in your sample. Oversampling this group would mean you continue to sample African Americans until you get more African Americans—say 20 out of 200 or 10% so that a good response (representative response) from this group could be obtained. However, you cannot use the additional data from those “oversampled” individuals to generalize to the population because the addition of those in that specific subgroup does not represent the population. When there are important groups but ones that have a small percent in the population, researchers frequently oversample the low percentage group in order to hear their voice.

There are two methods that can be employed to try to match the percent of the variable after the sample has been collected. The percent of the values on the variable in the population must be known to use either of these methods. The first method is performing a statistical test to determine if there is a significant difference between the sample and the population on the variable in question (Chapter 15). If there is not a significant difference, then the analysis of the results may proceed on the assumption that the sample reflects the population on this variable. The other method is to weight the sample on the basis of the percent in the population. For instance, if 30% in the sample have low income but 40% of the population have low income, then the number of responses from the low-income group are adjusted (weighted) and increased from 30% to 40% before analysis.

In summary, during the process of sampling from the population there are some characteristics of the research that often will influence the method and the type of sample you select. The first is the type of design you are going to use. If you want to generalize to the population from an experimental design (Chapter 11), then random sampling from the population to the sample and then random assignment into the experimental and control groups is critical. If, however, you are conducting a pilot study or exploring a phenomenon, then a non-probability sample may be more appropriate. It is always better to have a random sample, but for initial investigations, the time and expense to obtain a random sample might be prohibitive and a non-probability a better choice. Time, money and personnel become constraints. Finally, as you will see in the statistical analysis chapters (Chapters 15–21), the method of analysis also influences the type and size of the sample.

As a final caveat to sampling, always collect demographic data in your studies. Even if you are not collecting a probability sample, you need to be able to show that the basic demographic characteristics of the sample are similar to the population.

Chapter 11

FOCUSING RESEARCH—DESIGN AND CONCEPTUALIZATION—CREATING THE CONDITIONS TO OBTAIN A CORRECT AND USABLE ANSWER

A crucial first step is to accurately and clearly determine what you are trying to investigate. Trying to sort out what you are trying to investigate (often called the unit of measurement) is frequently a problem. For example, in looking at the relationship of mothers and their children the unit of analysis might be the child, the mother or the pair. Often researchers assume they are gathering information representing the whole household when they really only get information from a particular person. An example occurred when a researcher planned to obtain information about households in an Arabic country. The plan was to use the information from whoever happened to open the door as representing the household. This presented a problem in determining the unit of analysis (person vs. household) and there was also another problem: gender differences affecting the answer that occurs in all cultures but was magnified in this culture. These problems were rectified prior to the initiation of the study.

You must clearly define what you are selecting to study, and what the question is designed to answer. If the question is "Do women differ from men on their attitude toward poverty?", the unit of analysis is the individual, the individual woman and individual man that represents the group of women and the group of men. If you study the ***interaction of a mother with her child by observing their actions together then the unit of analysis is the dyad*** (mother and child) and the documentation of the interactive patterns. However, if you study the interaction of the mother with her child by asking her about her interaction with the child then the unit of analysis would be only the mother and you are studying her perception of the interaction. The unit of analysis becomes clear when the question is clear and then specify in your design, methodology and measurement the conditions that will answer the question reliably and validly.

CONTINUOUS VS. DISCRETE VARIABLES

Variables are defined as either continuous or discrete. A **continuous variable** is one that can assume any value in a ***set of values that are ordered***. Ordered means that the values are placed sequentially from high to low or low to high and there is no gap/break in the values (points) making up the sequence. Ordinal, interval and ratio scales can all be developed as continuous variables. A **discrete variable** is one where the values are ***categorized*** by their attribute or characteristic and the characteristics do not have a sequence of values and cannot be placed from high to low or low to high. For example, gender, religious affiliation, race or political affiliation are discrete in that each category is separate from the others but there is no ordering from high to low. A critical aspect of discrete variables is that the definition of the variable and those categories that make up the variable have to be very carefully and specifically defined so that placement into a category is unambiguous and a value cannot assume two different categories.

PARAMETRIC AND NONPARAMETRIC STATISTICS

Before attempting to perform any statistical analysis, it is important to define parametric and nonparametric statistics. **Parametric statistics** are analytical methods based upon continuous data where certain types of calculations can be made, like an average, and the variation of values around that average. In order to make these calculations, interval or ratio level data is needed (or ordinal level data in some specific cases as you will see in later chapters). In these statistics, the researcher is concerned about the distributions being normal and the relationship of the variables (you will learn how to determine these statistical relationships in later chapters).

Nonparametric statistics are a group of statistical methods that are used when you have nominal or ordinal level dependent variables. They are also used when you have a very small sample or cannot meet the assumptions required for parametric statistical analysis. ***It is better to analyze with more precision if possible using parametric statistics. However, it is equally important if you do not meet the assumptions for parametric statistics, do NOT USE them; USE the appropriate nonparametric statistic.***

INDEPENDENT AND DEPENDENT VARIABLES

Independent/Predictor variables are variables that (1) can be used to account for or deemed to cause a change in a dependent variable, (2) occur chronologically before another variable (dependent variable) or (3) are predictors of another variable (predicted variable).

Dependent/Predicted variables are variables (1) in which changes can be accounted for or deemed caused by an independent variable, (2) that occur chronologically after another variable or (independent variable) and (3) that are predicted from a predictor variable. A distinction is made between the pairing of an independent and dependent variable and the pairing of predictor and predicted variable. In experimental/causal studies where causality is to be determined (independent/dependent variables), the researcher actively manipulates/changes/moves the independent variable and measures the result in the dependent variable. In these types of studies the researcher has control of the independent variable and to measure the resulting change in the dependent variable. For example, providing additional money (independent variable) and measuring if more money results in a change in the purchase of more nutritious food (this is a very basic example and does not include all of the important aspects of controlling for effects of other variables). There are many situations where you as a social work researcher cannot manipulate or move the independent variable and other situations where it is not ethical and would be completely outside the standards of social work to manipulate that variable (Chapter 4). Examples of variables a researcher cannot change are race and country of birth. When you cannot manipulate the variable, you can still look at relationships between variables by looking at differences in the dependent variable in relationship to the independent variable—whether is there a difference in prejudice (dependent variable) in different racial groups. However, you cannot use race as a cause (explanation) for difference in prejudice because you did not manipulate the variable. Race is framing the study as a predictor variable and you are using it to predict another variable, the predicted variable of prejudice, without attempting to determine causality or explanation. Thus, you are using the results you obtain to predict amount of prejudice a person might have based upon on their race. This type of study does allow you to determine the ability to place a value on how well you can determine the value of the predicted variable based upon the predictor variable. Another study could be to use the score on a standardized math test to predict the test taker's final exam score in statistics—since you did not manipulate their math ability you did not cause the score on the final exam. A classic example of the difference between the independent (causal) relationship and the predictor/predicted relationship pair is: Every morning the rooster crows and the sun comes up. The rooster crowing always happens prior to the sun coming up. One would not use the causal relationship explanation because we know that the rooster does not cause the sun to come up; however, we know that the rooster is a very good predictor of the sun coming up and in fact might almost be 100% accurate. Thus, we would want to use the rooster (predictor) to predict the sunrise (predicted variable). We have so many situations in social work where the variable is already present and we cannot control it—child abuse, poverty, domestic violence, drug use, lack of education, prejudice and cannot determine in the causality. **We should not fall into *the trap of saying it is causal when the situation is one of high predictability and should be used only "AS IF" it was causal in terms of practical application.***

Social workers who make a causality assertion when it is a predictive situation leave themselves vulnerable to refutation of causality due to lack of experimental procedure and hence lose credibility and the usefulness of prediction.

Throughout this book we will rely on **graphic representations** that will help you to visualize, understand and provide organization for the **overall research process**. These graphic representations ("Tom's boxes") are divided into two basic types, **DESIGN BOXES** and **VARIABLES BOXES**. We will use these boxes and their accompanying shorthand method to depict, easily identify and conceptualize research. They will provide a solid foundation for selecting and utilizing the various statistical tests provided in this book.

DESIGN BOXES

Design Box Abbreviations:

M = Measurement. **The measurement of a dependent variable with the subscript indicating the specific variable being measured.**

$\mathbf{M_1}$ = Measurement of Variable 1

$\mathbf{M_2}$ = Measurement of Variable 2

$\mathbf{M_{...}}$ Measurement of other variables

T = Time. **The point in time when the measurement is taken with the subscript indicating a specific point in time. If there is more than one measurement of time, then Time may become an independent variable (discussed in later chapters).**

$\mathbf{T_1}$ = Time period number 1

$\mathbf{T_2}$ = Time period number 2
$\mathbf{T_{...}}$ = Additional time periods

P = Person. **The person identifier (P_1, etc.) is used to identify a specific person in a design (1) that is measuring the value on two variables for the same person OR (2) that is measuring the value on a variable for the same person at one time and the measurement of that same variable on the same person at a later time period.**

$\mathbf{P_1}$ = Person number 1
$\mathbf{P_2}$ = Person number 2
$\mathbf{P_{...}}$ = Additional persons

We will use income as the single dependent variable to be measured and gender as the independent variable. The question is, "Is there a difference in the income of Males and Females?" The measurement will take place at a single point in time. Since we are not concerned with identifying persons (specific individuals), we will not use the person identifier. The **notation inside the design box would be**:

$$\mathbf{M_1T_1}$$

indicating that you are measuring income at a particular point in time. Later we will depict two groups.

The next example is a design with two different time periods and in this design now Time becomes the Independent Variable. Income remains the single dependent variable to be measured but we will use January 1, 2015 and June 30, 2015 as the two different time periods. We are only interested in the change in group income and not in how much each individual's income changed between these time periods so we do not identify specific persons with the P_1, P_2, $P_{...}$

$\mathbf{M_1}$ = Income
$\mathbf{T_1}$ = January 1, 2000
$\mathbf{T_2}$ = January 1, 2010
$\mathbf{M_1T_1}$ = Measurement of Variable 1 at Time 1
Income on January 1, 2000
$\mathbf{M_1T_2}$ = Measurement of Variable 1 at Time 2
Income on June 30, 2010

It would be shown in design format as:

$$\mathbf{M_1T_1} \qquad \mathbf{M_1T_2}$$

In this example time has become an independent variable because we are measuring to see if there is a difference in income between two different points in time. There was no intervention. The study was only measuring the variable (income) at two different times. For example, census data was used for the average income of people living in Louisville in 2000 to 2010. The designation and relationship of a dependent variable and an independent variable will become clear when you see the design box. The next example is a very basic intervention design.

INV = INTERVENTION

An intervention design is one in which there is an introduction of a variable to determine if that variable causes a change in another variable. For example, providing free child care to one group of mothers on welfare and not to another group and measuring the number of those who become employed in both groups. **The symbol INV will be shown when there it is an intervention design, with the independent variable manipulated by the researcher in an attempt to create a change in the dependent variable. It will not appear when there is no attempt to manipulate the IV to create a change in the DV.** ***The important aspect of intervention designs is the amount of control (the ability to rule out a change in the DV resulting from variables that you are not manipulating) you have.*** **We will discuss and show different designs to indicate the amount of control the design has to rule out competing explanations.**

The following is the most basic intervention design and possesses the least amount of control for competing explanations.

Assume that you are starting a referral program to mental health facilities for refugees. You have no mental health data on the referral group and no other comparison group. You provide the referral and measure the refugee's self-described mental health after eight weeks.

$\mathbf{M_1T_1}$ = Measurement of self-described mental health at time 1

(Note here that it is not a strong experimental design because it does not control for other variables that could create any change you find.) For example, becoming more accustomed to their new community, being away from the trauma situation, finding others from their home country that are supportive of their situation.

The design is:

$$\textbf{INT} \longrightarrow \mathbf{M_1T_1}$$

PRED = PREDICTIVE

If the design is a predictive one rather than an intervention one where a predictor variable is used to predict a predictor variable, it will be shown as follows:

$$\mathbf{PRED} \longrightarrow \mathbf{M_1T_1}$$

One other symbol will be used in the design abbreviations that will indicate the level of measurement. An additional subscript indicates the level of measurement of dependent variable. (nominal, ordinal, interval and ratio).

N = nominal
O = ordinal
I = interval
R = ratio

$\mathbf{M_{1\,(N)}}$ = Measurement of variable one that is a nominal level variable
$\mathbf{M_{1\,(O)}}$ = Measurement of a variable that is an ordinal level variable
$\mathbf{M_{1\,(I)}}$ = Measurement of a variable that is an interval level variable
$\mathbf{M_{1\,(R)}}$ = Measurement of a variable that is a ratio level variable.

CATEGORIZATION OF RESEARCH DESIGNS

Research designs can be categorized based upon:

(1) ***Individual/in-depth or group/generalization***

In-depth and individual (in-depth = qualitative [Chapter 6]; Individual N = 1 [Chapter 7])
Group/generalization (program evaluation [Chapter 8]; Generalization [Chapters 16–21])

(2) ***Time***
(3) ***Type of question*** (purpose of the study)
(4) **Amount of control of the variables** (attempting to determine causation).

These are not exclusive categories. You can have a group design that has a time dimension and is developed to answer a question concerning if an intervention was effective. While we are discussing these designs separately, later we will develop designs and methods to obtain and evaluate answers that are combinations of these various categories.

The concept of these designs was introduced briefly in Chapter 2. Individual/in-depth designs and group designs have a major difference in the number of people studied as well as the intended outcome of the study. Individual/in-depth designs look at an individual or a very small number of people and attempt to provide a very complete and highly specific picture of characteristics and variables. Group designs on the other hand look at large numbers of people and attempt to determine an overall picture that would fit most of those in that group.

TIME

There are two types of designs that reflect the time continuum, ***cross-sectional designs and longitudinal designs***. Longitudinal designs are further subdivided into three distinct subtypes. ***Time is an important control factor to be included in a design if you are attempting to determine causation. In most experimental designs, you measure the dependent variable in one group (intervention/experimental group) and another group (no intervention/control group) prior to and after the intervention to determine if differences occurred.***

CROSS-SECTIONAL

A cross-sectional study is one where the dependent variable is ***measured only at a single point***. This design is called a "cross-sectional design" because you are simply taking a "slice in time" measurement and not looking at the variable across (over) time. The question might be "What is the attitude of foster children toward school when they go to high school on the first day?" *You measure their attitude using a questionnaire administered on the day they enter high school—a single point in time—a cross-sectional design.* It is the appropriate design because it provides the answer to your question. You are only concerned about their attitude on that single point in time—the first day of high school. Since you just learned about individual and group designs, you recognize that this is not only a cross-sectional design it also is a group design and would be classified as a cross-sectional group design. Below is the first of many design boxes that are utilized to conceptually depict research designs.

$$M_1T_1$$

Another example might be a spending two days living in the home of refugee family to get an in-depth perspective of their daily life. Even though this is a period of two days it is a cross-sectional design because it is a "slice in time of their lives" **and does not include a second measurement and therefore is not longitudinal**. This particular research design represents an **in-depth cross-sectional design**.

LONGITUDINAL DESIGNS

Longitudinal designs measure a variable(s) periodically over time. For the in-depth design above, the inclusion of a longitudinal aspect might be to live with the same refugee family two days each month for a period of one year. You would have in-depth information about the family but it would be over a 12-month period so that you could observe how it changes over time. Hence there would be 12 measurements (T_1, T_2, T_3, to T_{12}).

For a group design, you might measure the attitude of foster children on their first day in 2019 and then measure their attitude every month until the end of the school year. **The measurement of change might simply be seeing if a change occurred without any attempt to include an intervention or prediction.** Longitudinal designs provide a method to answer questions that include a time element. ***The different longitudinal designs discussed is related to the way participants are selected and studied.*** A specific longitudinal design is selected because it will determine the population and sample that answers your particular question.

Trend Design

A ***trend design*** is when a sample is taken from a population but that ***population the sample is selected from is always changing over the time of data collection***. An example of a trend study might be that you want to find out the attitude of elderly in your community about services provided for them and you want to see if that attitude changes over time. You develop a questionnaire and sample randomly from the population of elderly in your community defining elderly as anyone over the age of 65. You conduct this study every decade between 1980 and 2010. The population of elderly in the community changes every year based upon those leaving the community, those who died, those who move into the community and those who turned 65. Therefore, **the population of elderly that you select the sample from changes every year**. In this study, your question would be "Does the attitude of elderly in my community toward services for the elderly change over time?" You are not trying to follow a particular group of elderly over time or particular individuals over time; you simply want to find out if the attitude has changed for those who are defined as being elderly over that period of time. You are not trying to get the attitude measurement from a specific subgroup of the population or from the same people each time you do the study; you simply want to sample elderly individuals. ***Sampling participants from a larger population of individuals at different points in time characterizes a trend study. The design is one that would provide a good answer to the question***

"Does _______ change over time in the population (not a particular subgroup of that population)?" Another question might be "What was the favorite toy of pre-school children in 1980, 1990, 2000, 2010?" Note that the population of pre-school children changes every decade.

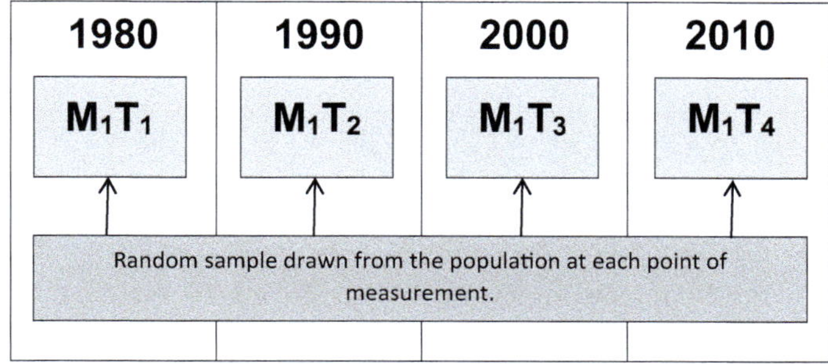

Cohort Design/Study

A ***cohort*** design is one in which the ***population (the potential group or*** pool ***of participants in the study)*** does not ***change but the individuals within the pool of participants can change. Each time you measure the dependent variable you do not specifically select the same individuals to measure but you always select from the same pool/group of individuals.***

You can imagine this group as marching through time together. People may drop out (death for example or cannot be reached) but the defining characteristic is specific and a person is in this group or out based on a definition that is created at the start of the study and excludes anyone else from entering the group over the course of the study. Suppose that your social work program wants to find out if the attitude of graduates toward the program change over time. They realize that it is not a good research plan to put graduates from all years together because students are very different. If you combine those graduating in 2000 with those graduating in 2012 they may have had different professors, taken different courses and the problems facing social work can change. Thus, their research plan was to survey their attitude toward the program using graduates of 2000, 2004, 2008 and 2010. The groups remain the same—2000 graduates, 2004 graduates, 2008 graduates and 2010 graduates—but the individuals that receive the survey can change within each of the year groups. They are not selecting a particular individual but are selecting from a particular group. Each time they select a person they do not know who that person is only that they graduated in that specific year. In this study there are four populations: the population of students who graduated in 2000, the population of those who graduated in 2004, the population who graduated in 2008 and the population who graduated in 2010. ***A cohort design***

is used to answer the question "Does __ change over time for this specific population?" The exact* SAME *population is sampled every time a sample is selected compared to a trend study where the population changes each time a sample is selected.

A cohort study shows how the same specified group changes over time.

Cohort Design

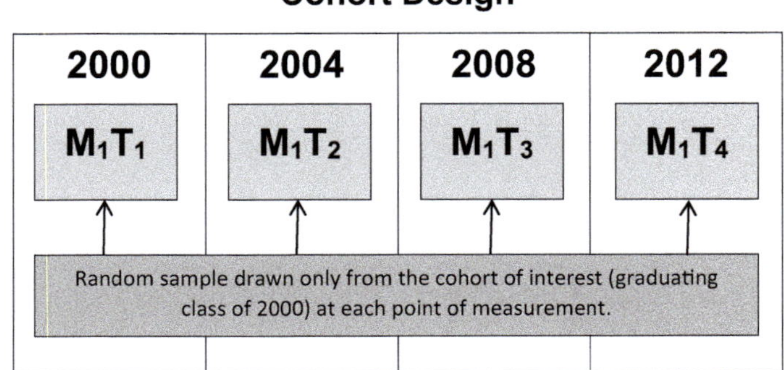

Cohort studies are common when comparing different age groups—Boomers, Gen X, Millennials, etc.—or when studying a particular group over time. How did voters who became 21 in 1980 vote in the 1980, 1990, 2008 and in the 2010 elections? The question might be "Do voters become more liberal or more conservative as they get older?"

Panel Study Longitudinal Design

Panel studies are designs where the exact same people ***are measured over time.***

At time 1 (T_1) a measurement (M_1) of a variable takes place for a specific person (P_1), then that same measurement is taken with the same person at a later time, T_2. The simplest of the panel designs is when there are only two measurements of the exact same people, which would have the notation (M_1 P_1T_1) indicating that there is a measurement of a specific variable (variable 1) for a specific person (person 1) at a specific time 1, then after a period of time a measurement of the same variable (variable 1) for that same person (person 1) takes place at time 2, with a notation of ($M_1P_1T_2$). This measurement takes place for every person in the group from P_1 to the last person $P_{\ldots}$ in the group. ***This very simple panel design is often used as a foundation for explanatory designs when there is an introduction of an intervention between Time 1 (T_1) and Time 2 (T_2).***

Classic examples of panel studies have been conducted with children over their developing years, elderly individuals as they age and to study the development of illnesses and diseases and how it affects individuals directly because there is a need to have individual specific information and analysis. A panel study would be used with children who have Type I diabetes over their lifetime with the same children followed year after year. You can see that this is an integration of what we discussed earlier as characterizing individual/in-depth research and compiling it for numerous individuals over time into a larger group. A similar study might be to follow a group of young girls who were sexually abused through their teen and adult years to look at specific variables, for example, depression, school achievement and anxiety. In panel studies the question is "Does the **characteristic within the person change over time for a specific group of people**?"

Panel Design

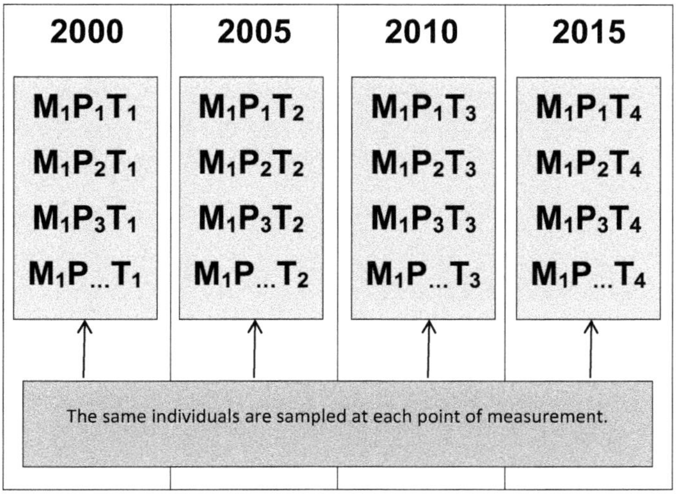

2000	2005	2010	2015
$M_1P_1T_1$	$M_1P_1T_2$	$M_1P_1T_3$	$M_1P_1T_4$
$M_1P_2T_1$	$M_1P_2T_2$	$M_1P_2T_3$	$M_1P_2T_4$
$M_1P_3T_1$	$M_1P_3T_2$	$M_1P_3T_3$	$M_1P_3T_4$
$M_1P_{...}T_1$	$M_1P_{...}T_2$	$M_1P_{...}T_3$	$M_1P_{...}T_4$

The same individuals are sampled at each point of measurement.

One form of panel study is utilized for a pre-post intervention/experimental design as noted earlier. This is shown below as the most basic experimental pre-post design.

Experimental Pre—Post Design

PRETEST		POSTTEST
Experimental Group M_1T_1	INT →	Experimental Group M_1T_2
Control Group M_1T_1	No INT →	Control Group M_1T_2

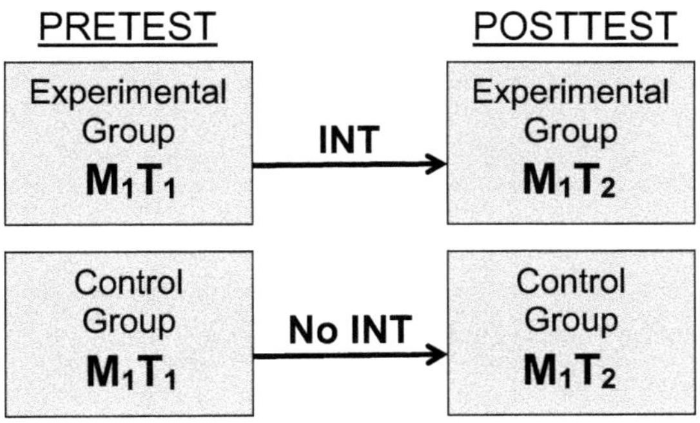

A form of longitudinal design is used to evaluate outcomes with a single person by using measurement at multiple time periods and is a foundation of individual intervention designs (Chapter 7). Some serious problems can arise when conducting longitudinal studies with groups; they typically are more expensive to complete than cross-sectional studies, there is often attrition of the participants, especially for studies that are carried out over months or years (dropping out, moving, inability to reach subjects and death).

To sum up, the longitudinal research designs attempt to answer the following questions: (1) trend studies—does the object/attitude, etc. change over time (favorite toy); (2) cohort studies—does the specified sub-group's characteristics change over time (voting preference); (3) panel studies—does the characteristic of an individual change over time (diabetes) for a group of people with the characteristic.

Types of designs have been developed to conduct research based upon (1) the question asked, (2) amount of information you have and (3) amount of control. It is important to remember that these categories while separated in this text are not totally distinct.

EXPLORATORY/DESCRIPTIVE

When you have very little information, are faced with minimal understanding and cannot find a good answer in the literature, it is likely that you will conduct exploratory research. You may find yourself asking the question "Does something exist?" Many of the problems that social workers are actively working with today had to be identified and shown to exist—child labor, campus rape, drug use, feminization of poverty and HIV. Research using these designs are focused on exploring existence, amount and description.

The example about drug abuse in the military (Chapter 2) demonstrates how the authors were first trying to document that there was drug abuse in the military when previously only anecdotal information was available. ***When information and knowledge about the problem is already available, this design is not appropriate.***

Descriptive designs are ones that use measurement to describe phenomena, populations or samples. Summative measures (total, average, percent, etc.) are provided in an effort to convey what the group looks like. For example, in an agency that did not keep data, after a year of collecting information about clients, the agency could state that 74% of the clients were Female, average age was 34 years, average income was $16,000 and the average length of time receiving assistance was 8 months. ***An important aspect of Exploratory/Descriptive designs is that there is no attempt to***

use the measurements to compare the phenomena, population or sample to another phenomenon, population or sample. There is no formal (statistical) attempt to find differences or relationships.

Some examples of questions and answers with this type of design:

"What is the percent of Females seeking service in my agency?"

The percent is 68%.

"What is the percent of Hispanics using the Edenside Health Clinic?"

Thirty-five percent (35%) of those using the Clinic are Hispanic.

"How many clients in my agency are on welfare?"

In my agency, over 25% of the clients are on welfare.

"How many people filed for unemployment in my county last week?"

Last week, 179 people filed for unemployment in my county.

"How many people on my caseload last month at the VA had PTSD?"

Last month 23 people on my caseload at the VA had PTSD.

Frequency, amount, conditions under which they occur are paramount in exploratory/descriptive designs.

DIFFERENCE/ASSOCIATION

Difference/association designs go beyond descriptive designs by ***attempting to determine if differences or relationships exist and if so what is the amount of difference or relationship***. Here the researcher has to decide how willing they are to bet that the difference or relationship they find is the "truth". ***There is*** no ***attempt to introduce an intervention (variable) or a predictor (variable).*** Often the sampling method is random selection so that the results can be generalized to the population. In fact, one of the most important aspects of good difference/association research is to use random sampling procedures so that the differences or associations found can be accepted as validly representing the population. It is important to stress that results found using difference/association designs do not ***imply causation***. Difference/association designs are not intended and do not have the ability to evaluate the probability of causation or prediction. The following are examples of questions and results from difference/association designs.

"Is there a difference in the percent of women elected in Jefferson County than in the state of Kentucky?"

The percent of women in elected positions in Jefferson County (35%), Kentucky is greater than in the state of Kentucky (17%).

"Is there a difference in the number of days to placement for foster children in Boone County, Kentucky than in the state of Kentucky?"

There is no difference in the number of days to placement for foster children in Boone County, Kentucky (87 days) than in the state of Kentucky (89 days).

"Is there is a relationship between gender and political party affiliation?"

There is a relationship between gender and political party affiliation; 63% of Republicans are Males and 48% of Democrats are Males.

"Do women live longer than men in my city?"

Women live on average 8 years longer than men.

"Do people on welfare eat fewer vegetables?"

Individuals on welfare eat 75% fewer vegetables than individuals not on welfare.

These statements show differences or association/relationships that have been calculated, but at this time no statistical tests were conducted. You will learn in later chapters how to determine if statistical significances exist. Even if there are significant findings (differences, relationships) this design does not control for other competing explanations for causality or predictability.

EXPLANATORY/PREDICTIVE

Explanatory designs introduce an independent variable (***intervention***), manipulate it (vary the amount) and measure its effect on an outcome. The key aspect is that the researcher **introduces and manipulates the IV while measuring the outcome for explanatory designs and in a predictive design uses one or more variable to predict another variable. This is different from difference or association because in those designs there is no attempt to say what happened in one variable based upon another variable.** The most basic (with no control of other variables) explanatory design simply introduces the intervention and measures the outcome of a single group that was NOT randomly selected (often found in program evaluation). A stronger study to support the assertion that the IV was responsible for the change in the DV is to introduce the IV to one group and not to the other group, with both groups randomly selected. Testing the intervention with two groups that are randomly selected begins to more systematically control for the effects of variables other than the independent (intervention) creating the change in the dependent variable (***control of competing explanations from variables other than the one you are introducing***). To determine if computers improve language ability in 1st grade children, provide computers (intervention) to 1st grade children in one class and not to 1st grade children in another class in the same school and measure their language ability on a standard language ability test at the end of the fall semester if those children with computers had better language ability than those who did not receive computers.

The research could be improved by controlling other variables. ***What does control mean?*** Control means that the researcher would try reduce the number and effect of ***other variables that could influence the outcome***. Some of those variables that could influence the outcome might be language ability prior to getting the computers, age, gender, overall academic ability and access to computers outside of school. One way to control for the influence of other variables is by random selection from the population and then random assignment to the intervention group and the non-intervention group. By randomly selecting from the population and then randomly assigning individuals into the intervention and non-intervention groups the effects of any variable other than the IV ***should*** be equally present in both the intervention and non-intervention group. It is then assumed that any difference found between the intervention group and the non-intervention group is a result of the IV and not from other variables.

There are two other methods to control competing explanations. The first is to ***exclude the variable from the study***. You may exclude Males and study only Females thereby controlling for the variable gender. You then randomly select the two groups, the one getting the computers and the one not getting computers from a population of only Females. In this study (by controlling—excluding Males), gender cannot be an explanation for differences in any outcome resulting from the introduction of computers. The "trade-off" for this type of control is that you use the results you obtained from the sample and say the same result would happen in the population (***generalize***). You **reduced the whole population to a population of only Females**

from which you took the sample and it is only to **Females that you can generalize your findings**.

You can include the variable into the study and another IV and measure its effect on the DV which can be done in two different ways. The first is to include it as another IV. In the computer study, comparing 1st grade students, you think that another competing explanation for the difference in language ability might be if the student also has a computer at home. You can make it an IV in the study by having two additional groups which when combined with the other groups makes a total of four groups to compare (1) those who got computers and had no computer at home, (2) those who got computers and had computers at home, (3) those who did not get computers and had no computer at home and (4) those who did not get computer and had a computer at home. Now you can also look at differences related to having a computer at home as it effects language ability in addition to receiving a computer to use at school. Having a computer at home has been added into the study as an IV.

The other method is used when you cannot include the variable as a categorical variable. In the computer study the current language ability of the child could not be included as a categorical variable. You believe that the state of their language ability prior to receiving a computer would affect the amount of change in their language ability after the semester with the computers. One way to control for language ability is to measure language ability for all students prior to giving them the computer and then to statistically (using the student's language ability prior to getting the computer) subtract the initial language ability from language ability following the introduction of the computer. This method of controlling for the effect of a variable is to make the competing explanatory variable a **covariate (CV)** and subtract it out of the performance of everyone in the study. Thus, you are taking the variable's effect in the study (leveling the playing field for everyone in the study) with respect to prior language capability.

In explanatory designs the designs vary with respect to the amount of control they exert on competing explanations from other variables—to reduce the probability of variables other than the IV of interest to account for the change in the DV or to identify their interaction with the IV that may account for the change in the DV.

The variability (variance) in the DV by variables other than those that are part of the study **(1) excluding variance associated with gender by selecting only Females (2) including and testing the effect of another IV (addition of home computer) or (3) including a variable as a CV (prior language ability)** ***is unattributed variance and we will call "error"*** (Chapter 14). There are other variables—specifically those related to participation in the research process itself—that can also influence the results. These threats are ones that the researcher has to be aware of and design for in the research process.

INTERNAL VALIDITY

Internal validity refers to the confidence in the assertion that the independent variable was the "cause" of the change in the dependent variable. This is the classic definition of internal validity but we also must consider these "threats" to internal validity as affecting how much confidence we have in results of a "non-classical" experimental design. ***These threats are threats to any study.***

THREATS TO INTERNAL VALIDITY

Maturation

This threat that could change the outcome can be stated as "what amount of change can occur due to the 'passage of time'?". With a "common cold" over time a person will typically "get over the cold" and feel better. This would occur no matter what interventions were introduced to create an improvement. Introduction of drugs or other forms of treatment might not create any more difference than simply waiting for the cold to dissipate. The result of getting over the cold that might be have been attributed to medication (IV) was really the result of "time". One way to counter the passage of time explanation is to create a control group in the study where there is no intervention and simply a passage of time. You can measure the DV and compare it to the result of the intervention group and thus taking out passage of time as a possible explanation for change. Maturation is also a major concern when you are studying children longitudinally even if there is no intervention. They will change simply with the passage of time and this factor must be taken into account.

History

Rather than the naturally occurring changes reflected in the maturation threat, history is a factor that takes into account a significant event that occurred during the study that was not naturally occurring due to maturation and affects the whole group. Numerous examples of events that have affected social work research: attitude toward FEMA if measured before and after Hurricane Katrina, concerns about pollution if there happens to be an oil spill during the study, attitudes toward Muslims if there happens to be a terrorist attack and attitude toward health care following the ACA, or retention of child welfare workers if there is a change to retirement policy during the study.

Loss of Participants

Participant loss refers to number of individuals who started the study but were not in the study at the end of the study. Loss of participants is important to the outcome of the research in two ways: (1) Do you still have enough participants at the end that make your findings representative? (2) Is there some variable directly related to a certain group of participants that results in them not finishing the study? Do individuals from a particular race drop out and is what was representative of the population no longer representative? If you had the same percentage of Males and Females in the population at the start and you lost most of those from one gender, then do your results apply to both genders? What if those with the lowest income do not complete the study? What if only the ones with the greatest problems never return? In all of these instances, the results might not be a valid representation of the population you started with. A good research tries to minimize (1) any loss of individuals and (2) to ensure that any participants lost are distributed evenly across variables that may have influence on the DV.

Being Studied (Effects of Being Observed/Tested/ Looked At)

Simply knowing that you are in a research study or being observed changes the way you do things. If you are tested, you respond differently than if you are not being tested. You respond differently if you know the "test" counts than if it does not count. If you are tested on the same material two times in a row, the second test time will be related to how you performed on the first test. You might want to keep the responses and answer the same both times or you maybe have looked up answers and therefore change the way you respond the second time. A researcher has to be concerned with the effects of simply being studied and effects of multiple observations can influence the answers and the results of the study. These influences on the measurements of individuals in a study are often referred to as the "effects of testing".

Instruments

Administration of the instrument or the instrument itself might change from the first administration to the second administration. If there is more than one version of the instrument (and they are not precisely equal), if are they are administered in a different situation (classroom and Internet) then the validity of the study can be jeopardized. In social work research this may occur when different observers are used to judge a child's behavior, or different social workers read cases to determine the status.

Statistical Regression

In providing services or programs we frequently often provide these services to those individuals most in need or at the extreme end of the continuum of the measurement scale—we select those with the greatest poverty or those with the most depression. It is a fact in data analysis based upon sampling that over multiple measurements, extreme values on a variable tend to move closer to the center of all values (statistical regression). If the first time you measure the variable you obtain an extreme value it is likely that the second measurement of that variable will be not so extreme. It is simply a matter of measuring (sampling) that variable many times, resulting in obtaining more and more values you sample being closer to the center (the average) because most of the values on that variable are closer to the average. In the examples above, your first sample value might have been a person who was in the most extreme poverty but the next time you sample you will more than likely get a person who is not so extreme from the center of income. You can control for regression to the mean by creating two groups that both have extreme values on the variable. One group would receive the intervention, program or service and the other not. Since both groups were originally the same in terms of extreme values on the variable, statistical regression can be controlled by comparing these groups because the score on the variable (non-intervention group) could be used as the amount of statistical regression experienced when there is no intervention.

The following design boxes are used to conceptualize research that are used in difference/association research as well as in explanatory/predictive research.

DESIGN BOXES

Exploratory/Descriptive and Difference/Association Boxes

Explanatory/predictive designs are presented from the lowest to the highest with respect to control.

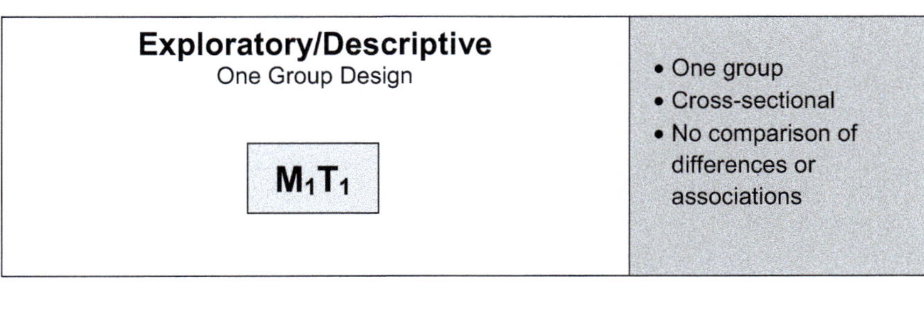

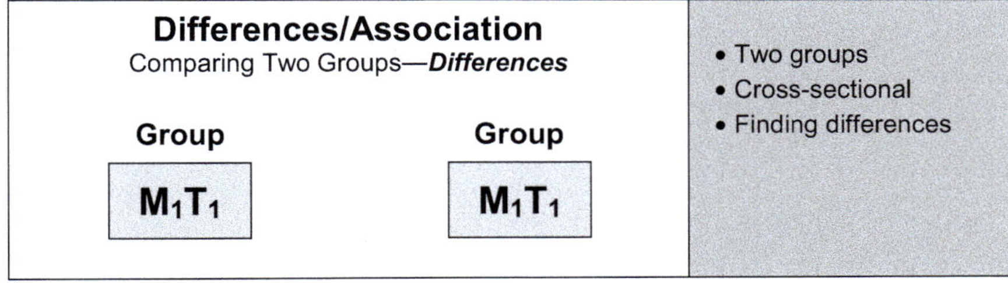

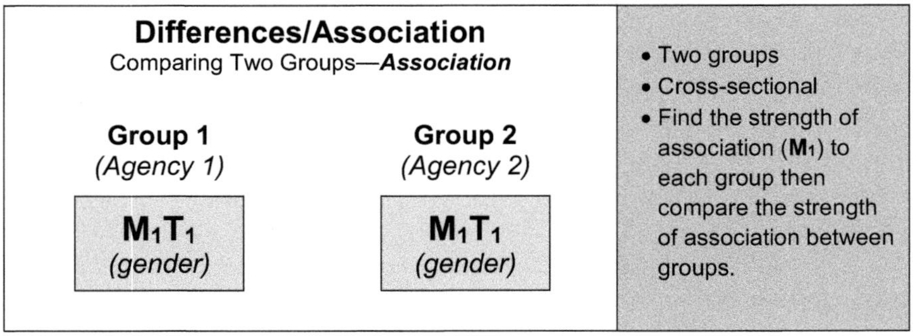

Differences/Association
Comparing Two Groups—***Association***

Group 1
(Agency 1)
M_1T_1
(gender)

Group 2
(Agency 2)
M_1T_1
(gender)

- Two groups
- Cross-sectional
- Find the strength of association (M_1) to each group then compare the strength of association between groups.

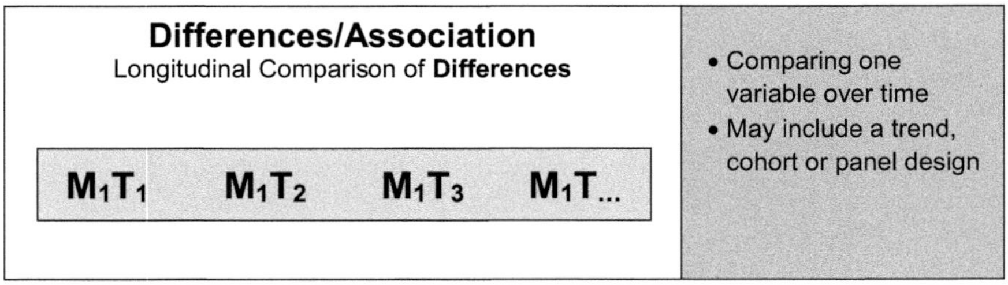

Differences/Association
Longitudinal Comparison of **Differences**

M_1T_1 M_1T_2 M_1T_3 $M_1T_{...}$

- Comparing one variable over time
- May include a trend, cohort or panel design

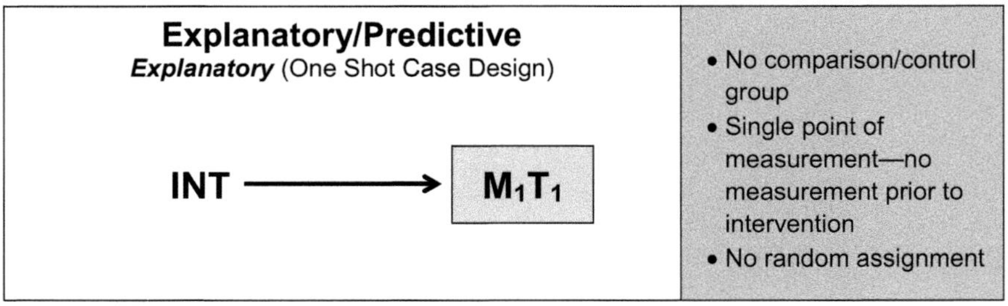

Explanatory/Predictive
Explanatory (One Shot Case Design)

INT ⟶ M_1T_1

- No comparison/control group
- Single point of measurement—no measurement prior to intervention
- No random assignment

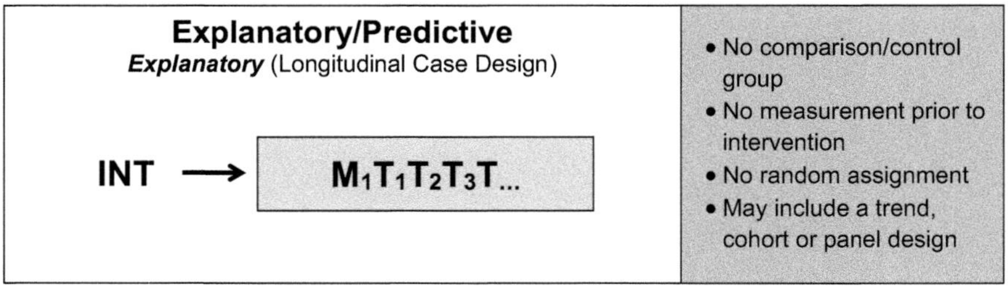

Explanatory/Predictive
Explanatory (Longitudinal Case Design)

INT ⟶ $M_1T_1T_2T_3T_{...}$

- No comparison/control group
- No measurement prior to intervention
- No random assignment
- May include a trend, cohort or panel design

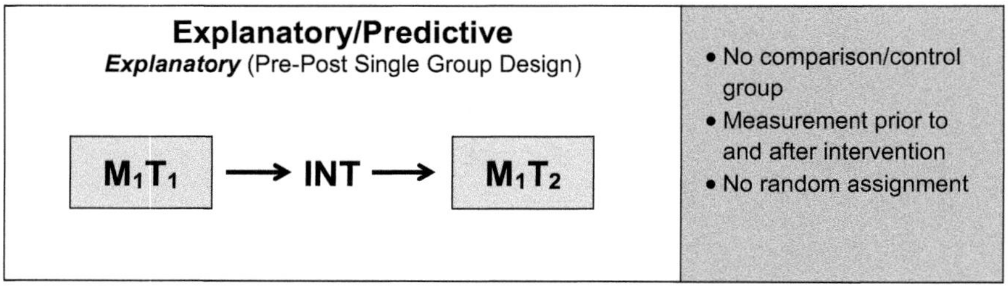

Explanatory/Predictive
Explanatory (Pre-Post Single Group Design)

M_1T_1 ⟶ INT ⟶ M_1T_2

- No comparison/control group
- Measurement prior to and after intervention
- No random assignment

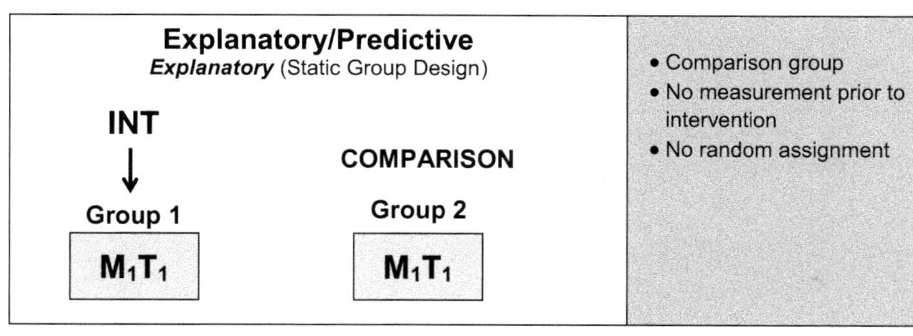
Explanatory/Predictive
Explanatory (Static Group Design)
INT
COMPARISON
Group 1
M_1T_1
Group 2
M_1T_1
• Comparison group
• No measurement prior to intervention
• No random assignment

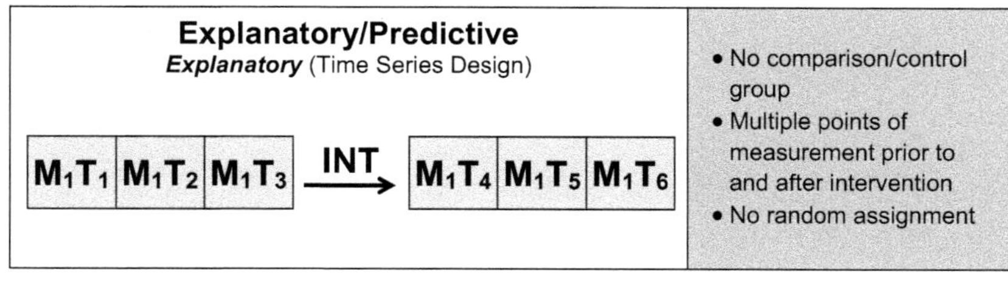
Explanatory/Predictive
Explanatory (Time Series Design)
M_1T_1 M_1T_2 M_1T_3
INT
M_1T_4 M_1T_5 M_1T_6
• No comparison/control group
• Multiple points of measurement prior to and after intervention
• No random assignment

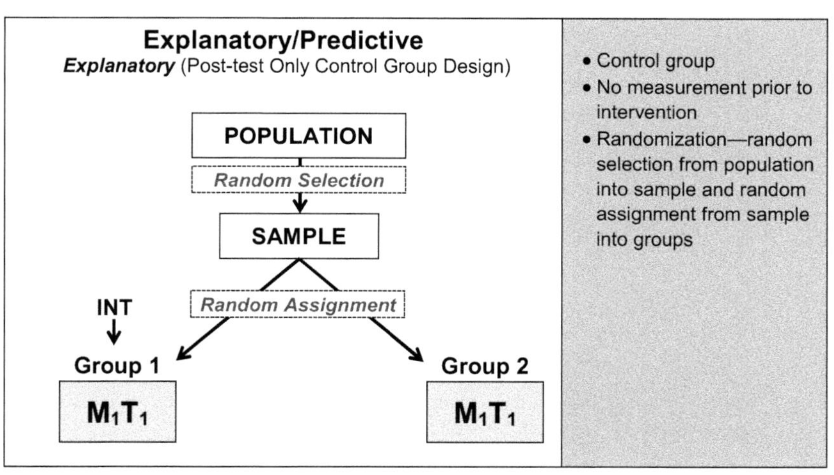
Explanatory/Predictive
Explanatory (Post-test Only Control Group Design)
POPULATION
Random Selection
SAMPLE
Random Assignment
INT
Group 1
M_1T_1
Group 2
M_1T_1
• Control group
• No measurement prior to intervention
• Randomization—random selection from population into sample and random assignment from sample into groups

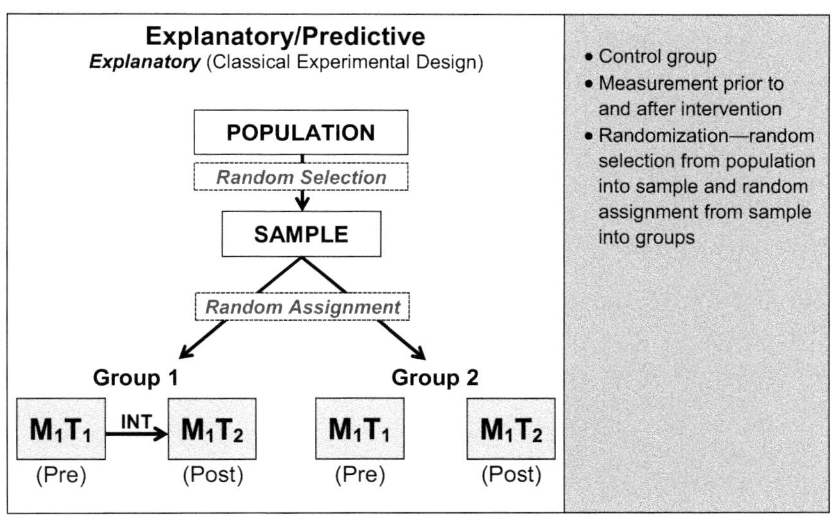
Explanatory/Predictive
Explanatory (Classical Experimental Design)
POPULATION
Random Selection
SAMPLE
Random Assignment
Group 1
Group 2
M_1T_1
INT
M_1T_2
M_1T_1
M_1T_2
(Pre)
(Post)
(Pre)
(Post)
• Control group
• Measurement prior to and after intervention
• Randomization—random selection from population into sample and random assignment from sample into groups

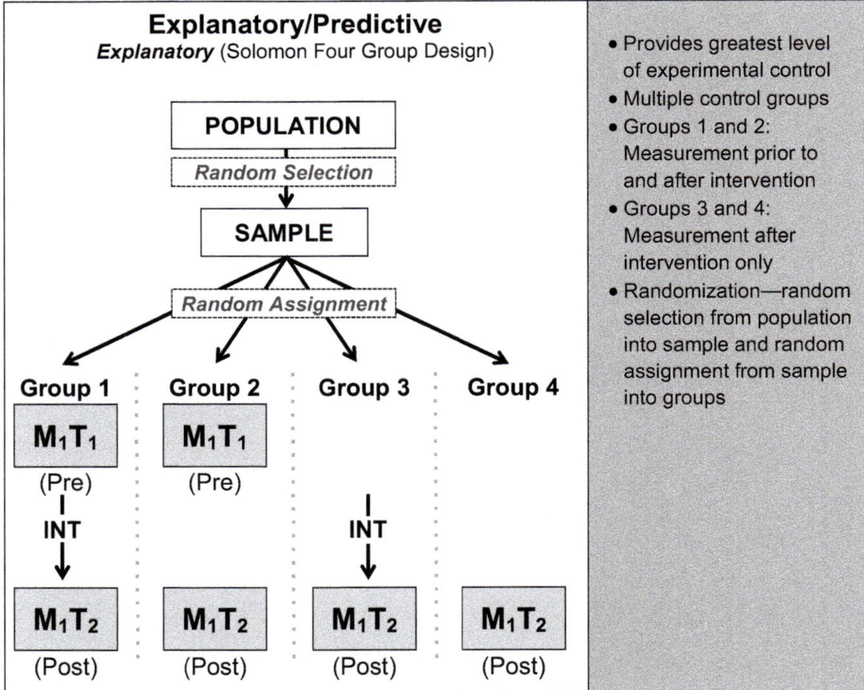

As shown, there is a continuum of explanatory designs from **"less control"** that have very minimal ability to rule out alternative explanations for causation to those that attempt to rule out many of the possible alternative explanations to those with "**more control**". In assessing how much one is willing to accept causation due to the influence of the IV, two conditions are always in play: (1) the amount of control limiting alternative explanations and (2) the significance (including power and effect size) which is discussed in detail in Chapter 13. There is always a trade-off between the amount of control you can create in a study and other factors—obtaining enough participants, having enough time or resources. In other words, there is a trade-off between what one wants for science and what is feasible in the real world.

Predictive Designs

Predictive designs are ones that show the amount of relationship/change in a variable(s) (predicted) that can be related/attributed to another variable(s) (predictor) when there is not an opportunity to introduce an IV into one group and not the

other. The variables already exist in the situation and the researcher cannot introduce or control these variables. The researcher can only measure the variables and try to determine the probability and amount of variance accounted for in the predicted variable (DV) by the predictor variable (IV).

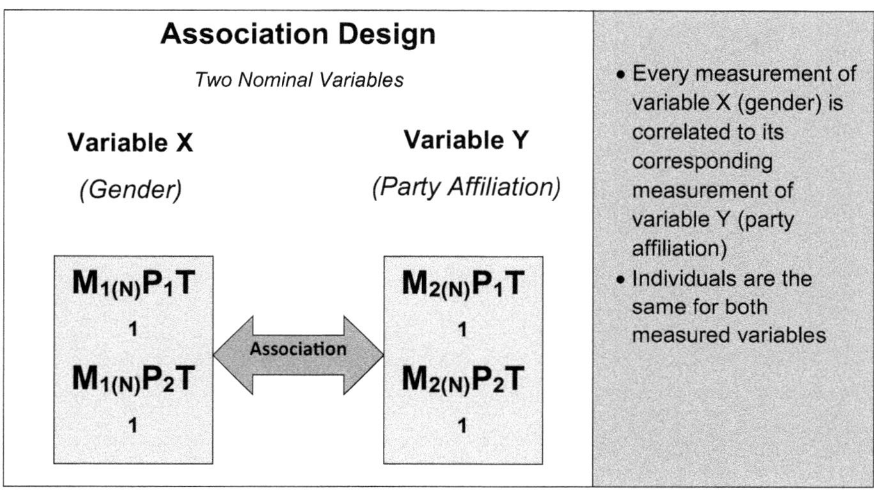

In the design above note the DOUBLE HEADED ARROW. This indicates ASSOCIATION in that the relationship is flowing both ways between the variables and not in only one direction and is not predictive from one to the other. If I know the value on one variable, I can reasonably assume the value on the other variable. There is no order or chronological order to the relationship of the variables.

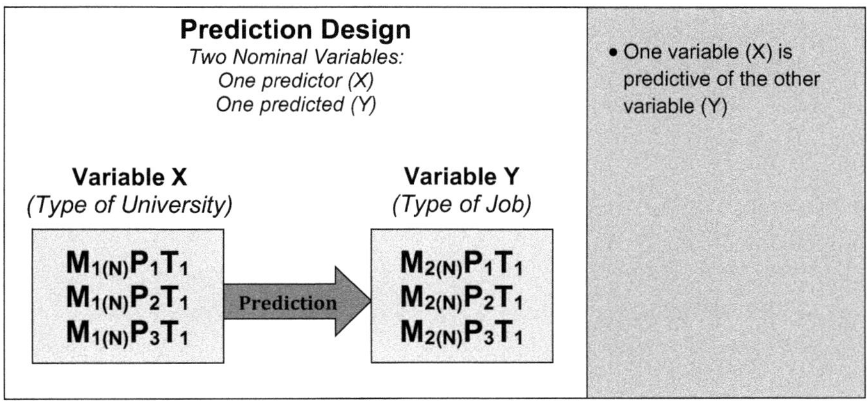

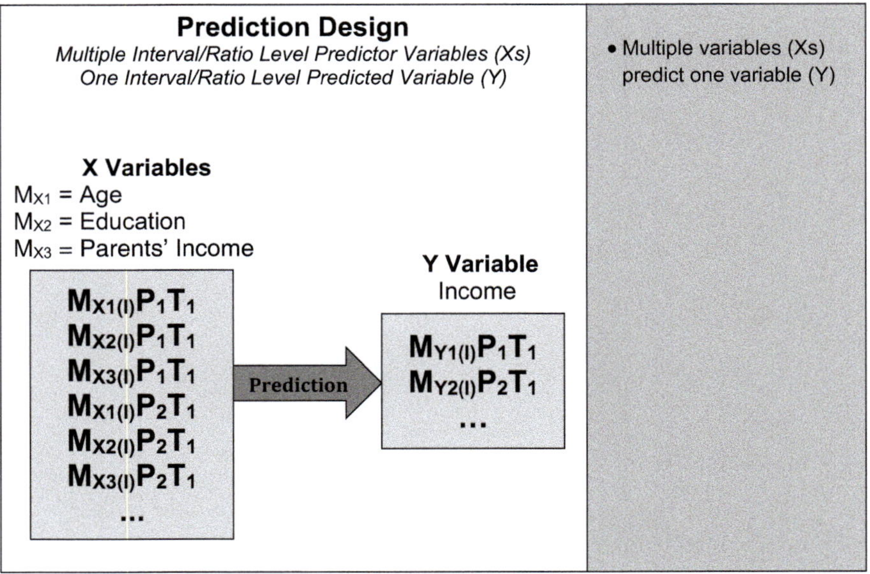

VARIABLE BOXES

From now on we will be working a lot with "boxes" and cells. These boxes and cells will provide you with a good visual representation and conceptualization of the variables under consideration in research design and also statistical analysis. Now look at the boxes on the next page. There are three (3) independent variables that are under study—

(1) Gender identified as variable A with two levels of gender—A1 Female and A2 Male
(2) Welfare Status identified as variable B with two levels of welfare—B1 on welfare and B2 not on welfare
(3) Homeless Status identified as variable C with two levels of homeless—C1 homeless and C2 not homeless.

Located within the overall block you can identify the various internal "cells" that would have values or scores for each individual under study. For example, assume that the dependent variable (DV) is a score on a scale that measures ability to obtain work hereafter referred to as AOW. In each of the smaller cells in the great box in the diagram there would be a group of scores that were specific to the variables that are related to that smaller cell.

Now let's take a closer look at this diagram. Let's assume that you want to look at only the difference between Males and Females (independent variable of gender)

VARIABLE BOX: A way to understand interaction between variables

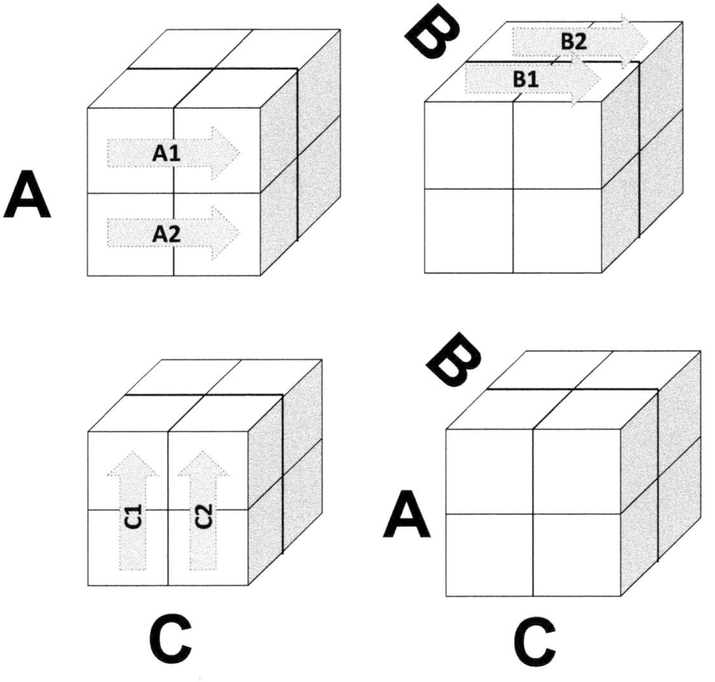

A = Gender: A1 = Women, A2 = Men
B = Welfare: B1 = On Welfare, B2 = Not on Welfare
C = Homeless: C1 = Homeless, C2 = Not Homeless

A1 $\cap$ B1 $\cap$ C1 = Women on Welfare and Homeless
A1 $\cap$ B1 $\cap$ C2 = Women on Welfare and Not Homeless
A1 $\cap$ B2 $\cap$ C1 = Women Not on Welfare and Homeless
A1 $\cap$ B2 $\cap$ C2 = Women Not on Welfare and Not Homeless
A2 $\cap$ B1 $\cap$ C1 = Men on Welfare and Homeless
A2 $\cap$ B1 $\cap$ C2 = Men on Welfare and Not Homeless
A2 $\cap$ B2 $\cap$ C1 = Men Not on Welfare and Homeless
A2 $\cap$ B2 $\cap$ C2 = Men Not on Welfare and Not Homeless

on the dependent variable AOW. In this instance, you are only looking at the A1 and A2 cells (horizontal division only) dividing the big box into a top half and bottom half or top half cell and bottom half cell. Later these divisions will become increasingly important as you design and statistically analyze the differences between groups or the relationship between variables. If you are looking at the variable of gender, then it is called looking at a "main effect"; you are specifically looking at the effect of gender (IV) on ability to work (DV). There are two other main effects, the Welfare Status, B main effect, and Homeless status, C main effect. Can you see how the big box would be divided if you only looked at the main effect of B on AOW? Can you see how the box is divided into the cells if you only looked at the main effect of C on AOW? Can you identify the cells in for the B main effect and the C main effect?

The next step is to look at what are called the "two-way interactions". Two-way interactions are when you are only looking at the relationship of two variables on the dependent variable. Thus, in this example you would have the following two-way interactions:

A × B the interaction of Gender AND Welfare Status on the AOW. What would be the groups in this case? Can you identify the cells?

There are the following interactions:

Females on Welfare
Females Not on Welfare
Males on Welfare
Males Not on Welfare

A × C the interaction of Gender and Homeless status on the AOW. What are the groups in this case? Can you identify the cells?

There are the following:

Females That are Homeless
Females That are Not Homeless
Males That are Homeless
Males That are Not Homeless

B × C the interaction of Welfare Status and Homeless Status on the AOW. What would be the groups in this case?

There are the following:

On Welfare and Homeless
On Welfare and Not Homeless
Not on Welfare and Homeless
Not on Welfare and Not Homeless

Finally, when you have three independent variables there is a three-way interaction.

That is, there is an A × B × C interaction. This results in the eight possibilities that are shown in the diagram above. Can you identify the cells? For example, homeless women on welfare.

This process can go on indefinitely with the addition of extra variables for example A × B × C × D and so on. As you will learn later in this book there are some major considerations associated with the addition of independent variables. As a precursor, there are two that are worth mentioning now and that you should make note of for your reading in the following chapters: (1) the number of scores in each cell should be no less than 10 and (2) if you have a large number of independent variables creating five- or six-way interactions they are very difficult to interpret.

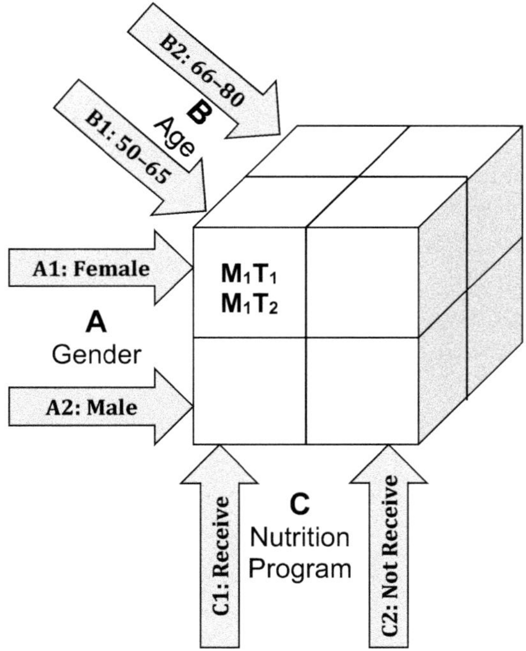

(IVs Outside the Boxes)

A = Independent variable Gender (with A1 = Female and A2 = Male)
B = Independent variable Age (with B1 = 50–65 and B2 = 66–80)
C = Independent variable Nutrition Program (with C1 = Receive and C2 = Not Receive)

(DV Inside the Boxes)

Dependent variable = Grams of Fat consumed. The measurement is Grams of Fat **(M1)** by each person **(P_1)** and is done at time 1 **(T1)** when they start the nutrition program.

Chapter 12

DATA GATHERING—HOW TO GET THE INFORMATION THAT WILL ANSWER YOUR QUESTION

Social work researchers have to formulate different types of questions, and know how to put them together to create surveys, interviews, questionnaíres, scales and indices. They have to know how they are validated and administered, as well as how to create situations where good responses are obtained. This chapter will address all of these fundamentals of data gathering.

TYPES OF QUESTIONS

There are two types of questions, **closed ended and open ended. A closed-ended question is one where the answers are provided to the respondent and no alternative response is allowed.** A closed-ended question frequently results in a nominal or ordinal level response in that the answers provided to the respondent have to be mutually exclusive (the respondent cannot select more than one category) and exhaustive (all possible answers are included). Closed-ended questions do not allow the respondent to answer in a way other than the options offered and thus may limit new and potentially very useful information. They do, however, allow the respondent to answer quickly, saving time which increases completion of items and higher return rates. The more that is known about the subject the better closed-ended questions are constructed. Examples of closed-ended questions are:

What is your current marital status? (Select only one)

(1) Single, never married
(2) Married
(3) Separated
(4) Divorced
(5) Widow, Widower.

What is your level of education? (Select only one)

(1) Did not graduate High School
(2) High School Graduate/GED
(3) Some College
(4) College Graduate
(5) Post-graduate studies.

What is your political party affiliation? (Select only one.)

(1) Democrat
(2) Republican
(3) Independent
(4) Other . . . Please specify ____________________

Open-ended questions are ones the respondent answers in their own words. They are found more frequently when interviews are part of the data-gathering method and where the researcher is able to obtain more information by probing to clarify an answer. Open-ended questions requiring long written answers if included in a questionnaire or survey are often not answered or only partially answered and non-understandable. Open-ended questions, however, are frequently used in pilot studies or initial interviews to gather preliminary data that can inform, be synthesized and reduced to closed-ended questions for specificity and ease of answering in a larger and more rigorous study. If open-ended questions are used in a quantitative study and statistically analyzed they have to be categorized and coded into specific groups that resemble the categories of a closed-ended question. Examples of open-ended questions are:

What is your opinion about the proposed changes in health care?
What do you think about the current war in Afghanistan?
What is your evaluation of the job the mayor is doing?
What do you think about the proposed changes to Obamacare?
There are some basic rules to follow when constructing questions.

RULE 1. THE QUESTION MUST BE TOTALLY CLEAR TO THE RESPONDENT

Remember that you may have a lot of information about a topic and this can lead to using jargon or being more specific than the respondent can comprehend. Try to answer these questions.

If you were building a bookcase would you use a 10d nail or 2 inch #8 screw?

What is your position with respect to the 19th Amendment?

RULE 2. THE QUESTION MUST NOT BE TOO LONG

Short questions are more easily answered and understood. The longer and more you have to explain the question the more likely (1) you have not been able to create a simple question around a complex concept, (2) the respondent will get "lost" in the question and (3) it needs to be split into more than one question.

Example: Provide your current and past as well as projected activities with respect to your outside-of-job activities that occur in the evening as well the weekends and holidays. A better way to state this question (although it could be more information than you need or that the respondent wants to answer) would be:

(1) Please list all the current outside the job activities (for example leisure, volunteer, religious, hobbies) you regularly engage in. Put E if you do it in the evening, W if on weekend and H if on holidays only:___________,___________,
___________,___________,___________,___________,___________

(2) Please list all the past outside the job activities (for example leisure, volunteer, religious, hobbies) you regularly engage in. Put E if you do it in the evening, W if on weekend and H if on holidays only:__,__,
___________,___________,___________,___________,___________

RULE 3. THE QUESTION MUST BE SOMETHING THAT THE RESPONDENT WILL ANSWER

Most people are willing to answer "public information" although given the number of scams and phishing there is a growing concern about providing even public information. Answers to questions that have been considered public information include: gender, age, race, education level and political party affiliation. There are questions that the respondent may view as sensitive subjects or as an "invasion" into their personal and private information. Inclusion of these types of questions may result in non-participation. If the researcher is able to first gain the individual's trust, then it may be possible to include more personal questions (Chapter 10). Trust and faith in the researcher and the research project are factors that improve obtaining personally sensitive data. As a social worker, you may have already established trust with some individuals or groups that will make it easier for you to get answers in studies. Social work agency may serve as a venue for trust, and an affiliation with a respected university also may open doors.

RULE 4. THE QUESTION MUST BE SENSITIVE TO THE CULTURE AND IDENTITY OF THE RESPONDENTS

As discussed in Chapter 5, all facets of study including the questions must respect the background of every potential respondent. Not only must the questionnaire, survey or research instrument be free of culturally negative items, it also must allow individuals to answer within their own cultural context. What a word means in one culture may not mean the same in another culture. Language is culturally specific and the researcher must be attuned to and use the language of those in the study. For example, in the past many researchers did not take into account the many subgroups within certain classifications. Hispanic is a linguistic category that includes many diverse cultures and the same word can take on many different meanings for different Spanish-speaking groups. Think about the difficulty a person might have whose parents were from Malaysia, was born in South Africa and now is an American citizen living in the United States when provided the following categories to check in a question:

_____ African American _______ Asian ____________ Caucasian

SCALES

A scale is a method to measure the attributes of a variable using aspects of that variable and consists of many questions or statements. For example, measuring prejudice:

I do not like to sit next to a person who is Black.
I think that this country has given too much to minorities.
The quota system for admissions and jobs should be abolished.
I think that people should be able to restrict who they sell their home to.

As you can see there are various facets of prejudice included in this set of statements. They could be used (with additional questions) as a scale. **Items in a scale all have to measure the construct, and the scale must be reliable and valid.** Most scales use a

Likert measurement method which allows the respondent to indicate the amount of agreement with each item in the scale. Using one of the statements above in a Likert scale:

The quota system for admissions and jobs should be abolished.

Strongly Agree				Strongly Disagree
1	2	3	4	5

Likert scales typically have a range of 5 or 7. By summing the scores from all items in the scale, a total value toward prejudice can be obtained so that each individual would have a prejudice score from low to high. Norms are developed for scales by having many individuals from across the population complete the scale and then an average for all those who have taken the scale is computed and used as the norm for the overall population. Norms can be calculated for different subgroups by taking only the scores on the scale from that subgroup and calculating the average score; for example, the prejudice norm for White Males over the age of 50.

A Likert measurement can be applied to a single statement with a ranking of 1–5 and then each statement can be individually analyzed and need not be included with other like statements to create a scale. For example, in a survey of a neighborhood the following questions that are not aggregated into a scale might be asked:

I like to walk in my neighborhood.

Strongly Agree				Strongly Disagree
1	2	3	4	5

I like to ride the bus to work.

Strongly Agree				Strongly Disagree
1	2	3	4	5

I would like to have an organic market in the neighborhood.

Strongly Agree				Strongly Disagree
1	2	3	4	5

A survey or surveying is the process of examining something—conducting a survey—surveying a neighborhood. A questionnaire is typically the object or

guideline that is used when surveying. Sometimes the words are interchangeably used but we will use the word questionnaire to mean the actual list of questions and statements that are to be answered. The person administering the questionnaire may use the term survey with a respondent because a word survey implies asking for their opinions, attitudes, feelings, etc. rather than answering a set of unimportant questions.

In constructing questionnaires, two procedures should be followed: (1) have experts on the subject and on questionnaire construction critique and suggest changes to improve it and (2) pilot the questionnaire with a few individuals from the population to see if it is clear and understandable, and to provide feedback for improvements. When obtaining feedback from the pilot study, inquire about the structure of the questionnaire, the length, which items were interesting to answer, which were difficult to answer and if there are items that should be deleted or added.

We will only cover some of the most important points to remember when creating questionnaires. No one likes to read fine print and in fact there is definitely a prejudice against it—think about contracts and insurance policies Not only is there a potential bias in terms of who is capable of reading a small font and who is not, there is also the potential that no one will be willing to complete such items. Construct the questionnaire in a readable font, and in the pilot study, ask about the ability to be able to not only understand but physically be able to read items. If you use a small font, there is a tendency to include more items using the same page limitation. This lengthens the amount of time required to read and answer, often resulting in a decreased return rate. Questionnaire construction should be about important items and not about the number of items. Include in the questionnaire only those questions and demographics that are important to adequately answer the study question(s), do not "fish" for other information that is only tangentially relevant or is "nice to know". "Fishing" increases the "work" for the respondent and is a source of lowered returns.

Attend to the format of questionnaire construction by arranging questions in such a manner that allows respondents to answer easily. Use check off boxes that are next to the answer and include the response.

☐ Totally Agree

☐ Agree

☐ No opinion

☐ Disagree

☐ Totally Agree

You probably have seen questionnaires where if you answer a question in a certain way it tells you to fill out the next set of questions, but if you answer a different way it tells you to skip those questions. These are contingency questions. You may think of them as moving forward step by step or jumping to the next group of questions on a different topic. You have probably answered them on medical history questionnaires

Q 14 Do you have allergies? Yes No
If Yes fill out Questions 15–17.
If No skip to question 18.
Q 18 Have you had any surgeries? Yes No

The order of questions is also important. We know from marketing how long you have to "hook" a person into an advertisement whether it is reading in the paper, watching it on TV, or on a mobile device, and that "hook" must happen very quickly. In the same manner, the questionnaire needs to be ordered in such a way that the respondent becomes interested in completing the questionnaire. Hopefully, you have interested the respondent enough with the cover letter to get them to look at the questionnaire; now the task becomes moving them from those first questions to completing the whole questionnaire. This is accomplished by providing questions that are interesting and arranged to carry the respondent with interest into the next question. Sometimes using only a few easy demographic questions, gender, etc. will ease respondents into answering, but other times it may be boring and cause them to throw it away. The pilot study can be a great help in finding out how individuals respond to the sequence of items. Specifically addressing the sequencing issue will pay invaluable benefits in ultimate response rates. **There is no perfect answer to ordering questions, only the best order for the particular questions asked, and the particular population to be studied. The best sequence pattern can be provided by the respondents themselves in a pilot study.**

In addition to the cover letter which addresses the need/reasons for the study, why they have been included as a respondent, the credentials of the researcher(s) and support from important people/agencies, you need to provide clear and concise instructions about how to complete the questionnaire. Some of these instructions are within the cover letter itself (how to mail back, etc.) and some are contained on the pages of the questionnaire itself. We have always felt that it is better to err on the side of being very concrete and specific than to assume respondents know what is expected. We call this method in our work as the "Jane, Bill and Spot" method as in "There is the little girl Jane and the little boy Bill with their dog Spot. Watch Spot run!" Simple language does not mean simple people are reading it, it means that we often create confusion by the way we state things. Adhering to very simple and common language solves many interpretation problems.

Timing is critical when you start the research. It is often very difficult to change timelines of pilot studies and the subsequent distribution of the survey. Planning for the "roll out" of research requires weeks and sometimes months and the return time for surveys may encompass weeks or longer. During that period, many things can affect responses to the questions (internal threat) and also the response rate. Think about if you were initiating a survey in Texas at the same time that Hurricane Harvey was devastating Houston and East Texas. If a survey had been planned for this area, it would not be possible for a long period of time. Some contingencies can be planned for—do not send out general population surveys during holidays and do not send out surveys of students and professors during the summer or finals. Always be "in tune" with what is happening or is potentially happening in the greater context of society that could affect responses and the return rate of your survey.

There are four primary methods to administer surveys: mail, online, telephone and face to face. Each of these methods has positive and negative attributes.

ONLINE SURVEYS

With the growth of the Internet a lot of social work research is moving toward collecting information via online surveys due to the reduced cost of data collection, the ability to collect large samples and increased opportunity for a variety of statistical analysis. As the Internet has developed so has software available to assist in development and administration. Online surveys provide the respondent anonymity which usually increases the rate of response to personal and sensitive questions. However, respondents are becoming wary of online surveys due to the potential of virus infection and intrusion into stored personal data which can lead to a decrease in the response rate. A major problem of online surveys is they reduce the population studied to those who have computers and have an Internet connection. Even though about 75% of the population has Internet access, as a social worker, you should readily recognize that lack of computer and Internet access may exclude groups we are most interested in—poor, oppressed, minorities and elderly. Finally, like a mail survey, it is easy to disregard and not answer an online survey.

MAIL SURVEYS

With the advent of the Internet, mail surveys are used less frequently. Compared to an online survey, mail surveys typically are more expensive per response due to cost of materials, mailing and follow-up letter. Like Internet surveys mail surveys are relatively easy for respondents to ignore. Since mail surveys are anonymous they have the same properties of an Internet survey in that personal and sensitive questions might have a greater chance of being answered. Also like the Internet survey a large sample is possible but is determined by the budget allocated for distribution of the mailed questionnaire. Response rate can be increased by (1) the inclusion of a cover letter that promotes a response (2) a return addressed and stamped envelope for the questionnaire and (3) a questionnaire that is well constructed.

A good cover letter not only describes the research, the credentials of the researcher and the support of the institutions for the research, it also provides the opportunity for the researcher to personally identify with the respondent. Phrases used by the researcher like: as a long-standing resident of the __, as a vet myself, as a graduate of, as a person concerned with the welfare of, as a graduate of, can help to elicit higher rates of response. A word of caution—test the cover letter with the pilot group to see how it appeals to them—does it elicit a heightened sense to respond or does it "turn them off", resulting in lower rates of return?

To generate a higher response rate, state in the cover letter if they would like results of the study you will make them available after the study is completed and ask them to provide their email or mailing address with the returned questionnaire. This no longer keeps the respondent anonymous, but you could maintain it by providing a postcard that requests the results totally separate from the questionnaire and cannot be traced to any particular respondent. Another method that maintains anonymity is to have a website address where the results will be posted in aggregate when the study is completed (for both online and mail studies).

Response rates of both mail and online surveys should be continually monitored to include the day they were returned and the total number each day. This tracking helps to determine when it is best to send a follow-up mailing or another call for participants in an online survey. While expensive, it is a good plan to send another questionnaire in a follow-up mailing. Many individuals may have discarded the first one and a repeat mailing with another questionnaire indicates the importance of completing the survey. The cover letter of course needs to be changed so that it will encourage completion. In mail surveys conducted by the authors we found that between two to four weeks is the period when the returns peaked. The day of the questionnaire was delivered affects the number of days until the drop off in responses (weekends, holidays affect the peak response rate). It is not good to have the questionnaires in the mail that results in a Friday or Saturday delivery, and certainly do not plan to have a mail survey delivered or expected to be completed during any holiday period.

Who typically responds to mail and online surveys? Respondents to these forms of surveys tend to be individuals who have an interest in the survey and those interested are those representing the ends of the continuum rather than the middle. Often you may obtain a bi-modal distribution with one group being centered negative and one positive, with those who do not have a strong position not responding.

Being a part of the group and knowing a lot about the respondents can significantly increase participation rates. A study conducted by one of the authors some years ago concerned attitudes and plans for early retirement among a certain group of individuals who were eligible for early retirement. The researcher was already known personally as a member of the group. The cover letter indicated the researcher's membership in the group, that results would be sent to them at the end of the study and how they might benefit. The rate of response was over 90%, indicating the importance of the cover letter but also the importance of shared background and interests. This method of shared group identity works well when there is a circumscribed group and one in which it is rather easy to be identified; however, we caution you not to say you are a member of a very large group because that is so often used it results in a "waste-basket" response—as a fellow American.

Some good ones might be: "Having worked in oncology social work for the past ten years myself I hope that you will take the time to answer this short survey about your practice in oncology social work". Another—"As a cancer survivor myself".

INTERVIEWS

Interviews are possible by three methods (1) face to face and (2) telephone (3) Internet. The commonalities and differences will be addressed in this section. In all three methods, a questionnaire is the foundation and guide and the interviewer is provided instructions to assist in explanation or probes for answers to open-ended questions if necessary. Interviewers conducting the survey must not deviate from the questions and instructions in order to obtain comparable results across all participants; therefore, training is a key component in collecting data using these methods. Because interviews are very a time-consuming method of surveying, a number of interviewers are used. Each interviewer must be trained how to conduct the interview and to follow the interview protocol exactly. When items require explanation, or are not understandable, trained interviewers already have experience in how to explain when to probe. Since the interviewer is able to provide explanations and ask for clarification of responses to open-ended questions, there is a reduction in the non-answered items and the "I do not know" answers often found on returned mailed surveys.

Interviewers themselves become a variable affecting responses. Ideally, we want responses uninfluenced by the interviewer. Training does help to reduce the difference between interviewers but we must recognize that in every interview (much more influential in face-to-face interviews) interviewer characteristics (gender, race, age, etc.) and the way the way they interact (types of explanations, probes for additional information or clarity) may affect responses. The effect of these "interviewer characteristics" are a source of bias, create error with respect to responses and are more prevalent in face-to-face interviews. Counterbalancing of interviewer characteristics with respect to sub-populations in the sample helps to alleviate some of this bias. For example, if there are four interviewers, two are Male and two are Female, and the study involves 20 elderly Males 65–75, 20 elderly Males 75+, 20 elderly Females 65–65 and 20 elderly Females 75+ the assignment of interviewers and stratification might be as follows:

Male 1 interviews 5 Males 65–75, 5 Females 65–75, 5 Males 75+ and 5 Females 75+
Male 2 interviews 5 Males 65–75, 5 Females 65–75, 5 Males 75+ and 5 Females 75+
Female 1 interviews 5 Males 65–75, 5 Females 65–75, 5 Males 75+ and 5 Females 75+
Female 2 interviews 5 Males 65–75, 5 Females 65–75, 5 Males 75+ and 5 Females 75+

With this assignment across the various subgroups the interviewer characteristics will be balanced out between the gender and age groups.

Interviewers may make recording errors in all three methods—face to face, telephone or Internet. During training interviewers should be coached and checked to ensure that responses to the questionnaire are recorded exactly—verbatim. Immediate recording of the answer to closed-ended questions must occur before moving to the next question. Open-ended questions must be recorded verbatim. Remember, open-ended questions will ultimately be grouped for analysis into categories and a full rendering of the response allows for increased reliability and validity.

Explanations about the content or thrust of a question by the interviewer need to be resolved prior to implementation of the survey. When explanations are needed and are developed is during the pilot (pretest) where questions that are difficult for respondents to understand can be (1) revised and asked again to improve understandability and (2) standard explanations are developed that can be used as necessary during the survey process. Standard explanations reduce variation in interpretations and in turn variation in responses.

Research involving interviewers should always heed the saying "Practice, Practice, Practice!" In both face-to-face and telephone surveys there is no substitute for the interviewers being required to conduct practice interviews under the supervision of the researchers. This is the time to make sure that all interviewers "are on the same page" and are as neutral in affecting responses during the survey process as possible.

FACE TO FACE (ACTUAL OR VIDEO CONFERENCING)

One aspect of a face-to-face (actual or video conferencing) interview that is not available in other methods is the interviewer is able to observe the reactions of the respondent and to provide contextual information. This includes the ability of the respondent to understand questions and to verbalize answers which is particularly important with, for example, individuals with challenges (hearing, sight movement, etc.), elderly and those whose primary language is not English. In face-to-face interviews the similarity of background between the respondent and the interviewer may help to improve responses or may impede responses. The goal is for all interview situations to be neutral with no other variables influencing agreeing to the interview or the response to questions. Of course, total neutrality is not possible. For example, elderly respondents are usually more open and forthcoming with their answers to older interviewers and younger respondents are more open to younger interviewers. When these pairings of interviewer and respondent occur, the respondent is likely to be more involved and try to answer each question thoughtfully and have fewer "I don't know" answers. When the pairings are reversed, the respondent is frequently less involved. Survey responses can simply be influenced by the pairing of interviewers and respondents. It should also be noted that when interviewer and respondent have commonalities, the interviewer must be mindful to "stay on script" with the survey protocol.

Although some characteristics of the interviewer the respondent cannot change (gender, race, age) there are some that can change. The first is knowledge of the research study and the questionnaire. The interviewer has to be able to answer questions that the respondent may have to include the aims, goals and ethical considerations of the project during the interview. Knowledge about what data the question(s) is trying to obtain and being "fluent" in voicing the question by reading it in a manner that is clear, understandable and almost conversational evokes much better responses.

What about interviewer attire? As an interviewer, you are automatically different from the respondent but you do not want to appear so different that you might be denied an interview or be given poor responses. How to find a balance? We believe that the best guideline is that you dress as a professional social worker would dress when working with this particular group of individuals. It might mean the attire you would wear when you visit an elderly person's home or what you would wear in your office, or what you might wear if you are at a camp with teenagers (just remember you are not a teenager so do not dress exactly like them). When you try to be exactly like the respondent in dress, or when you try to dress too much out of the "main-stream, neutral clothes of the general population", it can influence the interview situation. Clothes affect the initial impression and can open or close the door to an interview. Once that door is opened, the way the interviewer initiates the interview becomes paramount. Now the verbal and non-verbal behaviors of the interviewer become keys to a successful survey.

TELEPHONE

The same aspect of a face-to-face interview applies except visual cues are absent. However, the voice becomes more important and the research may be able to identify (certainly not perfectly) differences related to gender, age, ethnicity, race, origin—national/regional/local.

Telephone survey response rates can be increased significantly as noted earlier if there is an identified relationship between the caller and the respondent. Some years ago, in a city of with a population of 90,000 the mayor had a social worker develop and conduct a survey of what aspects of the city were the most important to the citizens. The survey consisted of questions related to highways/streets, parks, arts, schools, etc. A telephone survey was selected that included open-and closed-ended questions about those factors with a goal of obtaining 400 respondents. **Social work students from a small highly respected local university were specifically selected to be the interviewers.** When the respondent answered the phone, the student/interviewer **identified themselves as a student from that university and asked for their help in completing this survey which was very important to the future of their city**. The introductory sentence identifying the caller as a student from the highly respected university resulted in **over a 90% response rate**. Respect, identification, importance of the survey and the ability of the interviewer to interact with the respondent were the keys to obtaining high rates of response and complete surveys.

This survey was conducted before the tremendous growth of cell phones which has significantly changed the design of phone surveys. Today, 95% or more of the population has cell phones; over 50% have only cell phones and the percent of smart phone use grows significantly every year. The demographics of cell phone use—only cell users compared to land line only (6%) or land line and cell—are related to age, education and income. Thus, it is important when designing any phone survey to keep in the forefront the demographic characteristics of the population you want to sample and how using technology can bias your sample of the population.

Finally, we would like to report a slightly different and sort of combined method. In this survey, the researcher went to meetings of a group (drug and alcohol) of which they previously were a member. The researcher told the members of their past experience and asked if they would please complete the questionnaire. There were approximately 50 in each of these groups and the responses would be totally anonymous. The researcher then left and collected the completed questionnaires the next day. The response rate was very high. This is a situation where there was an explanation from the researcher to the group and one in which there was identity but then the questionnaire was completed without the researcher being present.

OBSERVATION

Falling somewhere between qualitative and quantitative research studies are those studies with a relatively small sample that is not sampled randomly and uses observers/

judges/raters that collect and measure the data. Studies of children playing and couple/family/group interactions are examples of this type. In these studies, the observer/rater may be either not seen by the respondent (behind a one-way mirror or otherwise concealed) or seen but not involved in the process (in the physical space like on a playground but not interacting with the child). The observed/rater has a list of actions/behaviors to record during a specified time (number of times the child was aggressive with a toy). Observers have specific training in how to recognize these events and to correctly record them. During these training sessions, the observers are exposed to examples of the same situation, record their observations and inter-judge reliability is calculated until all judges have a high degree of agreement when the behavior/action occurs and when it does not. Video vignettes as well as "live" situations are used to improve overall consistency between the raters. The sessions where the raters are recording the behaviors are often videoed to allow for additional consistency checks. Usually these types of studies where there is a small sample allow for both qualitative analysis as well as small sample quantitative analysis.

USING SECONDARY DATA

While most social workers will not be using secondary data in terms of large national data sets that are nationally collected, you are very likely to use smaller secondary data sets that have been compiled by agencies from their records. Some of you may be involved in developing research and implementing it, while others may analyze what has already been collected (typically in program evaluation research). Analyzing already existing data poses some unique and difficult problems for researchers. One problem is the person now doing the analysis was not the source of the question that drove the design that resulted in the data obtained. The one using secondary data is constrained by the limitations of another person's design. The questions you want to ask may not have data available in the database that could provide an answer. Even if some data is there it might not be in the form or the level of measurement you want. For example, if you want to know if races respond differently to the agency program and race was not collected as a variable you are constrained and cannot ask this question. If you think age is an important variable and you want to use it as a ratio variable but age was collected nominally as categorized as child, youth, adult or elderly you cannot analyze it using the level of measurement required to answer your question. The biggest frustration for most researchers when using existing data is that they do not have any control over the design, are constricted by what is available and which variables are included and the way they are measured, size of the sample, the characteristics of the sample and how the sample was drawn, resulting in limits being on what is available to investigate and the type of statistical analysis that can be conducted. Existing data can be an excellent source for research studies and provide the foundation (especially within a program) for you to work with the agency to analyze the existing data and then develop future research studies that answer questions of importance to the agency.

There are some clear advantages to using previously collected data sets for those who decide to use them: (1) minimal or no cost compared to original data collection, (2) large data sets that have been well funded have good designs, and excellent sample selection for representativeness (3) and have been developed by leaders in that particular area of research. Given the scope of well-funded national-level research they usually have a very have a large *n* and include a multitude of variables that may allow you to carve out and analyze a smaller subset of variables that has not been studied before. Another advantage is by using data previously collected you may not have to seek or have only minimal requirements for IRB approval to do the research since approval likely has previously been granted. If you are working for an agency and conducting research on their previously collected data, minimal permission by the IRB will be required. If you are working for another institution like a university, then the review process by the university will be specific to the way that the institution handles research using data previously collected by another source (Chapter 4).

There is a major difference in secondary analysis depending on whether you have access to the original data (the responses wherein you can do calculations before aggregations and statistics are done) or if you only have access to summary data. In the former you can manipulate the data and can analyze at the level the data was collected (often the individual level) while with the latter you are restricted to certain kinds of analysis. For example, US government data on how many individuals between the age of 21 and 30 are foreign born compared to how many individuals between the age of 21 and 30 in Germany are foreign born. With this type of data, you can compare aggregated descriptive statistics. You might not be able to look at the number of individuals who were Male between the ages of 21 and 30 and born in Guatemala because you do not have the individual data where you could select individuals with those particular characteristics. If you have the complete data set with all of the individual responses to every variable you can then revise, restructure, select certain parts of the data and use different levels of measurement, allowing you to use different statistical analyses. However, very large data sets that can be analyzed at the individual level require computer capability and statistical software large enough and powerful enough for storage and analysis.

You will see in the next two chapters that you have to know the data, know the data and know the data. You have to live it, breathe it and embrace it so that it is like a second skin, a companion you know so well that when asked about it you can always provide an answer. This is equally true of secondary data. In the literature chapter

(Chapter 3) you learned you have to know the literature that is related to and supports your research—now if you want to use secondary data you have to know and be able to use it as well as if it was your own. It is adopted data that has to be treated as if it was your creation. Secondly, since you did not collect it you have to be wary of the data itself. How was the variable defined? You are "stuck" with that definition and have to proceed with your research using that definition even if it does not fit your study, often requiring you to omit analysis of that variable. Another problem with using data you did not collect is that frequently you may not know what was omitted from the study and what was the criterion to be included.

For those interested in using large data sets that have been collected using sound research methods, many of which are updated continuously, the following are suggested:

Inter-University Consortium of Political and Social Research at the University of Michigan (www.icpsr.umich.edu) multi-topic data—from aging and substance abuse to health care

Annie E. Casey Foundation (http://datacenter.kidscount.org) well-being data from all states on children

Sources that are useful in providing excellent statistics:

Census Data (www.census.gov)

Center for Disease and Prevention (www.cdc.gov)

Health and Human Services (http://dhhs.gov)

Housing and Urban Development (www.hud.gov)

If you are interested in social policy and social programs in countries around the world you can access this information: www.ssa.gov/policy/docs/progdesc/ssptw/index.html

For European Statistics EUROSTAT is the best: ec.europa.eu/Eurostat

Chapter 13

DIFFERENT WAYS TO SUMMARIZE RESPONSES AND HOW TO DETERMINE THE IMPORTANCE OF YOUR ANSWER

In order to convey general characteristics of a sample and population we have to group data in order to present it—proportions, percentages, means, medians, modes, standard deviations and variance.

PROPORTION

A proportion is quite simply a fraction of a whole. For example, 1/3 is a proportion and may or may not also be used to create a percentage (33.3%) when considered as part of 1 (1.3 of 1 = 33.3%). Recall the definition of nominal measurement from Chapter 10—categories must be mutually exclusive (no measurement can be placed into more than one category) and exhaustive (every measurement can be placed into a category). The number in each category (n = category number of items) can be divided by the total number measured (N = the total number of items) to obtain the proportion for that category. Here is an example. There are only four agencies in your city providing elderly adult day care services (Seen Your Care—39, Good Old Tymes—27, Have a Great Day—23 and Come on Inn—57). The total number of seniors receiving adult day care in your city N = 146. The proportions are:

Seen Your Care	39/146
Good Old Tymes	27/146
Have a Great Day	23/146
Come on Inn	57/146

These proportions are interesting but difficult to understand, so they are typically converted to percentages.

PERCENTAGE

A percentage is a proportion (fraction) with the total number of values being equal to 100. This means that the total (N) becomes the denominator and the group value (*n*) becomes the numerator. The data above when converted to percentages is as follows:

Seen Your Care	39/146 = 26.7%
Good Old Tymes	27/146 = 18.5%
Have a Great Day	23/146 = 15.8%
Come on Inn	57/146 = 39%

Percentages work very well when the percentages are all from the same set—you are looking at subsets of a larger group. In the example above the total number of elders being served in the city (the denominator) and the relationships of each agency to the other agencies can be compared by that proportion because each agency would have the same denominator (N). Anyone looking at the values in the table can make a comparison between the agencies because they are all divided by the same number, the total in the city (N). Percentages become more difficult to interpret when you are comparing two different groups and talking about the percentages in those two groups as shown in the next example.

SPSS Commands

Open the data set ***Ch14 SummarizeAgency***.
Follow the steps below to produce a crosstabulation table.

(1) Click ***Analyze***.
(2) Scroll down and select ***Descriptive Statistics***.
(3) Select ***Crosstabs . . .***

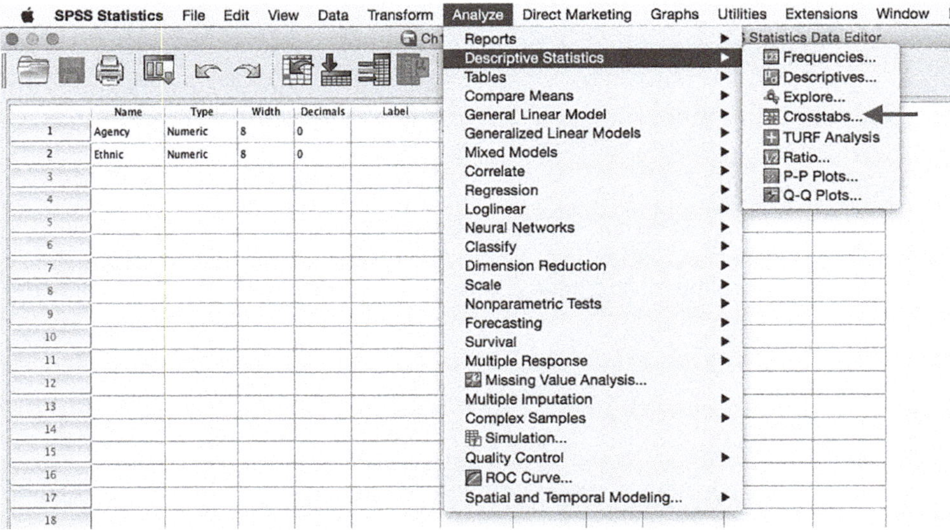

(4) Add the variable ***Ethnic*** to the ***Row(s)*** box; add the variable ***Agency*** to the ***Column(s)*** box.

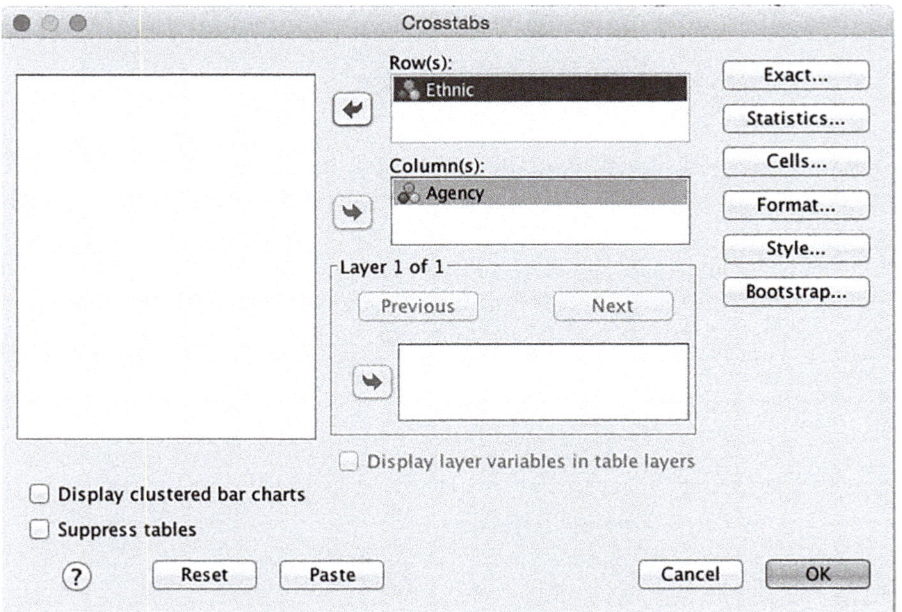

(5) Click on the ***Cells . . .*** button.

(6) In the ***Percentages*** box, check the boxes next to ***Row***, ***Column*** and ***Total***.

(7) Click ***Continue***.

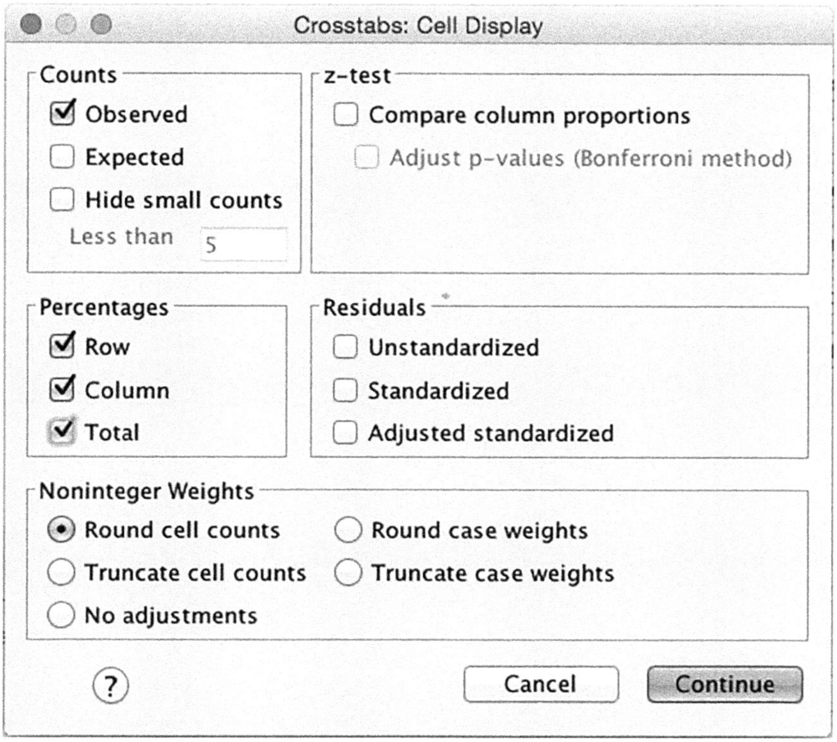

Crosstabs: Cell Display

Counts
- [x] Observed
- [ ] Expected
- [ ] Hide small counts

Less than 5

z-test
- [ ] Compare column proportions
- [ ] Adjust p-values (Bonferroni method)

Percentages
- [x] Row
- [x] Column
- [x] Total

Residuals
- [ ] Unstandardized
- [ ] Standardized
- [ ] Adjusted standardized

Noninteger Weights
- (•) Round cell counts
- ( ) Truncate cell counts
- ( ) No adjustments
- ( ) Round case weights
- ( ) Truncate case weights

? Cancel Continue

(8) Click ***OK*** to produce the crosstabulation table.

The crosstabulation output table presents counts and percentages with row (ethnicity), column (agency) and total.

Ethnic * Agency Crosstabulation

			Agency		Total
			Drop Inn	Stop By	
Ethnic	Black	Count	48	39	87
		% within Ethnic	55.2%	44.8%	100.0%
		% within Agency	48.0%	39.0%	43.5%
		% of Total	24.0%	19.5%	43.5%

(*Continued*)

			Agency		Total
			Drop Inn	Stop By	
	White	Count	28	32	60
		% within Ethnic	46.7%	53.3%	100.0%
		% within Agency	28.0%	32.0%	30.0%
		% of Total	14.0%	16.0%	30.0%
	Hispanic	Count	22	25	47
		% within Ethnic	46.8%	53.2%	100.0%
		% within Agency	22.0%	25.0%	23.5%
		% of Total	11.0%	12.5%	23.5%
	Asian	Count	1	3	4
		% within Ethnic	25.0%	75.0%	100.0%
		% within Agency	1.0%	3.0%	2.0%
		% of Total	0.5%	1.5%	2.0%
	other	Count	1	1	2
		% within Ethnic	50.0%	50.0%	100.0%
		% within Agency	1.0%	1.0%	1.0%
		% of Total	0.5%	0.5%	1.0%
Total		Count	100	100	200
		% within Ethnic	50.0%	50.0%	100.0%
		% within Agency	100.0%	100.0%	100.0%
		% of Total	50.0%	50.0%	100.0%

We might reduce this complex-looking table to present only those percentages of interest to our present inquiry.

Ethnicity of Clients at Selected Adult Day Care Center

	Drop Inn Center	Stop By Center	Total
Black	48%	39%	43.5%
White	28%	32%	30%
Hispanic	22%	25%	23.5%
Asian	1%	3%	2%
Other	1%	1%	1%
Total	100%	100%	100%

There appears to be little difference in the percentage of racial mix between centers. ***Drop Inn sees a greater percentage of Blacks than Stop By*** while ***Stop By sees a greater percentage of Whites, Hispanics and Asians than Drop Inn***. Putting percentages in the table has standardized the two centers using the percentages of the different races. Now we can compare if one has a greater percentage or different racial mix than the other. ***There are two key statistics in any data summary: (1) the total seen in percentage and also (2) the total count because both are needed to have a complete comparison.***

Ethnicity of Clients at Selected Adult Day Care Center

	Drop Inn Center	Stop By Center	Total
Black	48% (n = 64)	39% (n = 152)	43.5% (n = 216)
White	28% (n = 38)	32% (n = 124)	30% (n = 162)
Hispanic	22% (n = 30)	25% (n = 97)	23.5% (n = 127)
Asian	1% (n = 1)	3% (n = 12)	2% (n = 13)
Other	1% (n = 1)	1% (n = 4)	1% (n = 5)
Total	100% (n = 134)	100% (n = 389)	100% (n = 523)

While both agencies do not differ much in terms of racial percentages attending their program the total numbers are greatly different. We can say the two programs have basically the same percentage of Hispanics, 22% and 25%, but the **Stop By Center has over three times as many Hispanics visiting their center**. This example shows the need to provide both ways to evaluate summarized data: (1) the percentages to be able to compare them on a standard "yardstick" and (2) the actual numbers to be able to see the volume. Remember the importance of the question. If the question is focused on the sheer volume of people seen, then the numbers are absolutely critical; however, if it is focused on the distribution of racial mix, the yardstick percentages are very important. In either case the best method is to provide both for the reader.

RATIO

A ratio shows the relationship between two, such that one value is compared to the other value. While this sounds very complicated, an example will make it understandable. The question might be what is the ratio of PTSD for veterans who served in Operation Iraq Freedom (OIF) and Operation Enduring Freedom (OEF) compared to those who served in OIF and OEF but do not have PTSD? The ratio might be 1 returning veteran with PTSD compared to 6 returning without PTSD. Notice here we are not talking about percentages, simply the ratio.

We have to always look at the construction of the ratio. First the group or thing of interest—vets returning from Iraq with PTSD—becomes the numerator in the ratio and what it is compared to (the key here is ***COMPARED TO***) —vets returning from Iraq without PTSD. That ratio might be written as 1 to 6 or stated the way ratios are typically written 1:6. Ratios can also be an inverse, for example, the number of Blacks stopped for traffic violations (300) compared to Whites (100) with Blacks to Whites being stopped at a ratio of 3:1.

DISTRIBUTIONS

Distributions of Nominal Level Data

Distributions of nominally measured variables are distributions of groups where individual measurements are placed into a category. For example, if there are only two categories for the variable Gender—Female and Male, we would place all of the gender measurements from the sample into one of two categories: Female or Male. Females = 102, Males = 98.

Depending upon the variable, the number of categories reflecting the many attributes of the variable may change—country of origin, race, religion, welfare status, type of abuse and diagnosis. The characteristic of nominal level distributions is that the categories do not have any inherent rank (no lesser or greater) and many measurements can be placed into a single category (categories must be exhaustive and exclusive).

Distributions of Ordinal Level Data

Ordinal level data are the same as categorical level data except that the categories now have ranking with a hierarchy of the values on those categories. The distribution below depicts a distribution of an ordinal level of measurement. It is a distribution of 100 individuals' attitudes toward abortion ranked from 1 totally against to 5 totally for.

SPSS Commands

Open the data set ***Ch14 AbortionAttitude***.

Follow the steps below to produce a frequency table displaying the distribution of ordinal scores.

(1) Click ***Analyze***.
(2) Scroll down and select ***Descriptive Statistics***.
(3) Select ***Frequencies . . .***

(4) Move the variable ***AbortAtt*** to the ***Variable(s)*** box.
(5) Ensure the box next to ***Display frequency tables*** is checked.
(6) Click ***OK*** to produce the frequency table.

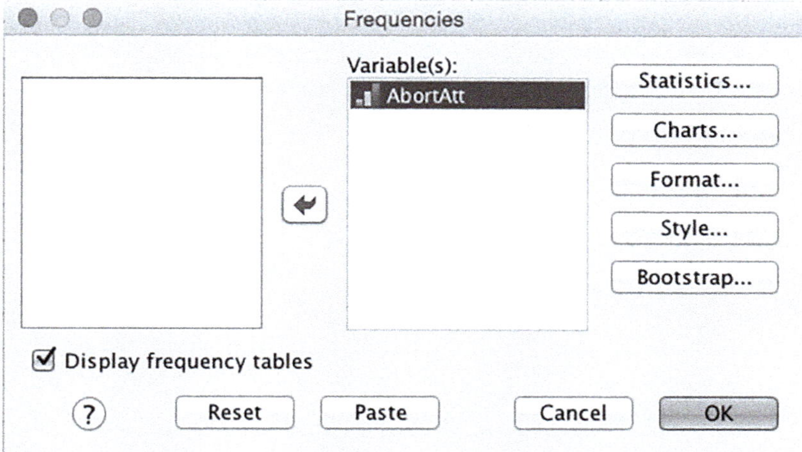

Attitude toward abortion

		Frequency	Percent	Valid Percent	Cumulative Percent
Valid	Totally against	12	12.0	12.0	12.0
	Against	16	16.0	16.0	28.0
	Undecided	22	22.0	22.0	50.0
	For	26	26.0	26.0	76.0
	Totally for	24	24.0	24.0	100.0
	Total	100	100.0	100.0	

Recall from the measurement chapter that a more specific level of measurement can be made less specific. For example, a frequency distribution of interval or ratio level data can be reduced to ordinal level or even categorical level distributions. You could create categories of income from very low to high or in increments of $10,000, or categories at a nominal level—have income, do not have income.

Distributions of Interval and Ratio Level Data

There are three key aspects of an interval or ratio distribution: (1) the shape, (2) the middle and (3) the width. A frequency distribution of interval and ratio level data will show all of the possible values on the variable starting with the lowest value obtained in the sample to the highest value obtained in the sample with equal intervals between the values. For statistical analysis, interval and ratio level data remain ungrouped; however, sometimes for ease of presentation and understanding, the data is grouped. When grouping, the convention is to not list all of the potential values because in many cases this would be a very long list, so first the list is truncated to include the values that occur between the lowest value and the highest contained in the data itself. To show how interval data is often grouped for presentation, assume you have ten people in your study of elderly at a senior center and the frequency distribution is as follows:

AGE	FREQUENCY
69	1
70	2
71	1
72	0
73	4
74	0
75	1
76	1

As you can see no age is reported below 69, which is the lowest value obtained in the sample, and no age is reported above 76, which is the highest age reported. Between the lowest and the highest all values on the variable are reported as this is a continuous ratio frequency distribution.

A problem arises when there are none or a very few values in a particular interval and the distribution is very spread out. The question is how to group this type of data into intervals that make sense but still represent the distribution of the data accurately. (Sacrificing precision—improving understanding.)

Incomes of Families Attending Your Agency for Services

Income	Frequency
13,100	1
13,190	1
13,830	1
14,200	1
14,360	1
14,374	1
15,450	1
15,675	1
15,895	1

Income	Frequency
15,900	1
15,910	1
16,020	1
16,370	1
16,420	1
16,370	1
17,145	1
17,190	1
17,200	1
18,380	1
18,470	1
18,800	1

This distribution does not provide visualization or understanding the incomes of your clients. A better representation can be created by grouping the data into intervals.

SPSS Commands

Open the data set ***Ch14 ClientIncomes***.

Follow the steps below to produce a frequency table displaying the distribution of ordinal scores.

(1) Click ***Analyze***.
(2) Scroll down and select ***Descriptive Statistics***.
(3) Select ***Frequencies . . .***
(4) Move the variable ***Income*** to the ***Variable(s)*** box.
(5) Ensure the box next to **Display frequency tables** is checked.
(6) Click ***OK*** to produce the frequency table.

Income

		Frequency	Percent	Valid Percent	Cumulative Percent
Valid	$13,000–$13,999	3	14.3	14.3	14.3
	$14,000–$14,999	3	14.3	14.3	28.6
	$15,000–$15,999	5	23.8	23.8	52.4
	$16,000–$16,999	4	19.0	19.0	71.4
	$17,000–$17,999	3	14.3	14.3	85.7
	$18,000–$18,999	3	14.3	14.3	100.0
	Total	21	100.0	100.0	

You will note that some basic principles were followed in developing the groupings. We first looked at the raw data and thought that maybe it would be good to **have groupings that were relatively equal in number of clients**. More importantly, that **the intervals be ones that are easily identifiable by the reader and ones that are in intervals that we typically use**. Thus, we looked at these criteria simultaneously but with the emphasis on easily understandable and usable intervals. We selected intervals of $1,000 which is a standard increment when reporting incomes. Next, if we started with the lowest income being the $13,000 grouping and created groups using $1,000 as the increment for each interval, we obtained six groups with almost the same number of families in each group. It should be recognized that $1,000 intervals for incomes in this low range indicate a greater percentage of difference than $1,000 increments for individuals whose income is over $100,000. For example, increasing income from $13,000 to $14,000 is an increase of approximately 12% but for a family making $130,000 income and increasing their income by $1,000 is less than 1%. Thus, selecting frequency intervals for ratio and interval data is also determined by the relative difference in the magnitude of the data itself. You can create a histogram of this type of data in SPSS like the example below.

SPSS Commands

To create a histogram of client income categories, make sure that ***Ch14 ClientIncomes*** data set is still active and follow these steps:

(1) Click ***Graphs***.
(2) Scroll down and select ***Legacy Dialogs***.
(3) Select ***Histogram . . .***
(4) Move ***Income*** in the ***Variable*** box.
(5) Click ***OK*** to produce the histogram.

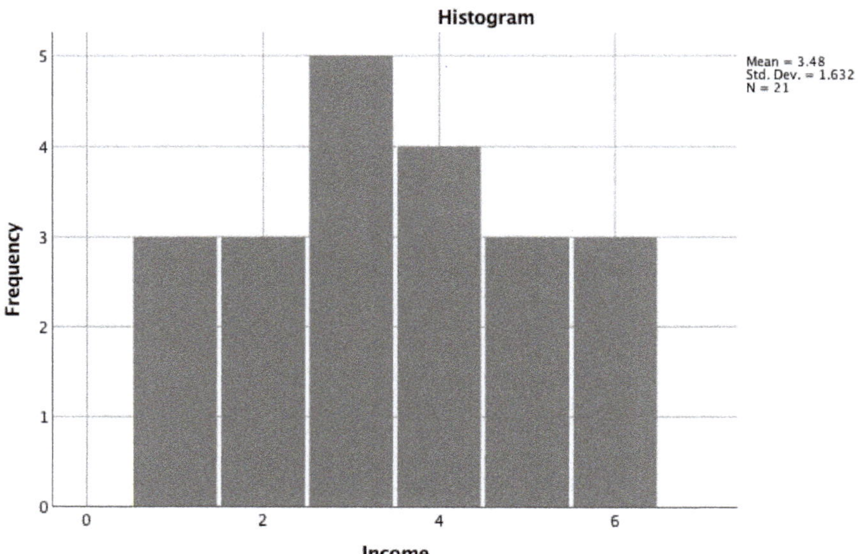

In constructing a graph, histograms are most appropriate for grouped data (nominal or ordinal level measurements) and a frequency polygon is most appropriate for interval or ratio level data that has not been grouped and is continuous. For instance, the following frequency polygon might represent the (ungrouped) income for all clients across an entire agency.

DISTRIBUTION SHAPES

The first way to describe a distribution of scores is to talk about it in terms of how many frequently occurring values there are in the distribution. The distribution is often calculated as if there is a single mountain or two mountains in the distribution.

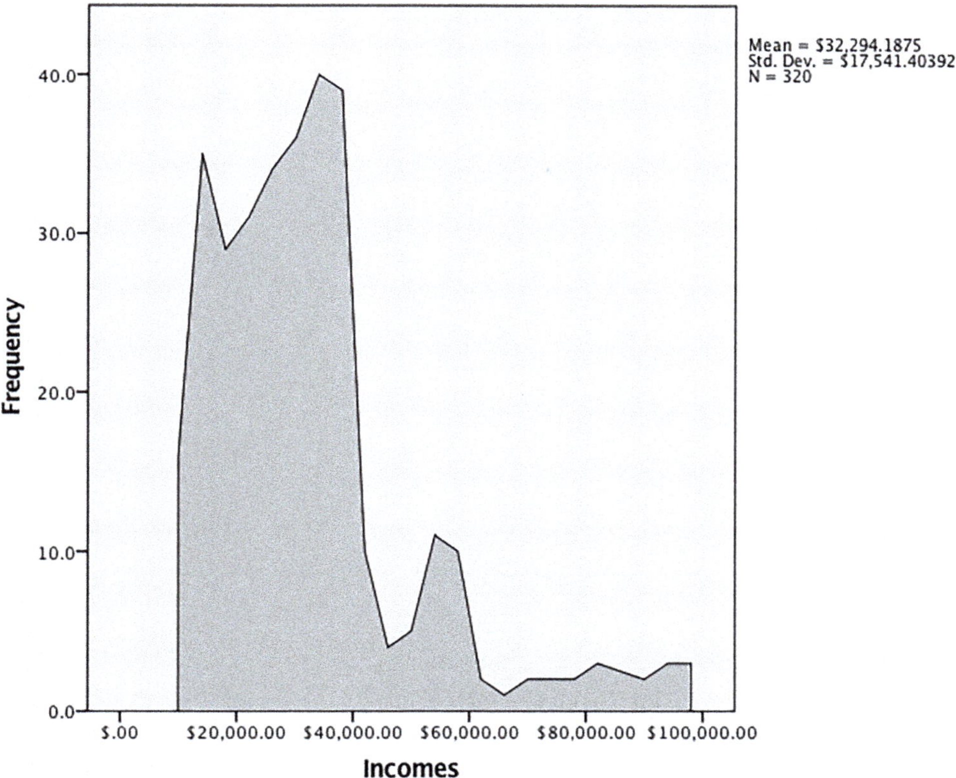

Unimodal Distribution

A unimodal distribution is a distribution with only a single value having the highest frequency.

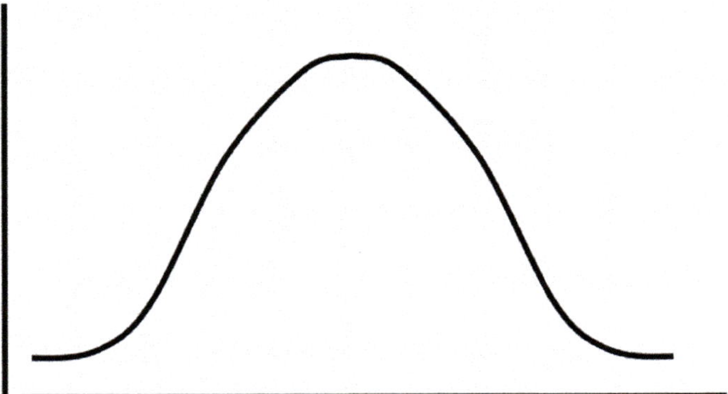

Bi-modal Distribution

It follows then that a bi-modal distribution is one that has two values that are the highest occurring and basically have the same frequency or nearly the same frequency and a multimodal one is a distribution that has more than two peaks.

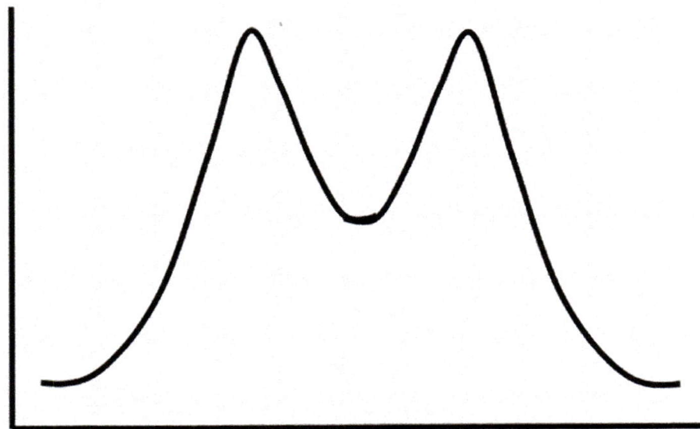

Another way to describe a distribution is to talk about it in terms of whether it appears to be equal on both sides. Is the **right half of the distribution basically a mirror image of the left side of the distribution**? We know in reality that it will **never be a totally perfect mirror image but is it basically similar**? If it is basically the same, we refer to the distribution as being **symmetric, that is, the sides are "the same"**.

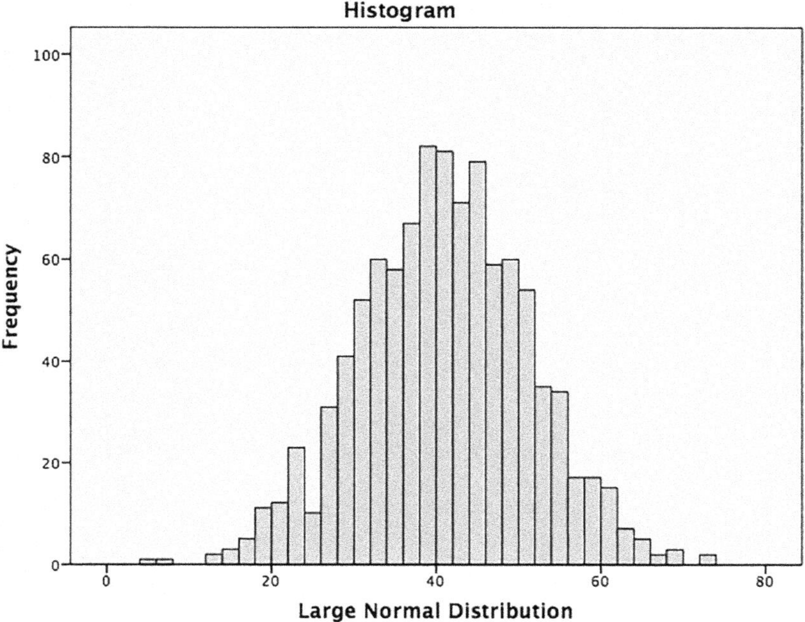

However, if one side (the tail of the distribution) is longer than the tail on the other side, then we talk about this distribution as a ***skewed*** distribution. If it is skewed to the right, we call it a positively skewed distribution.

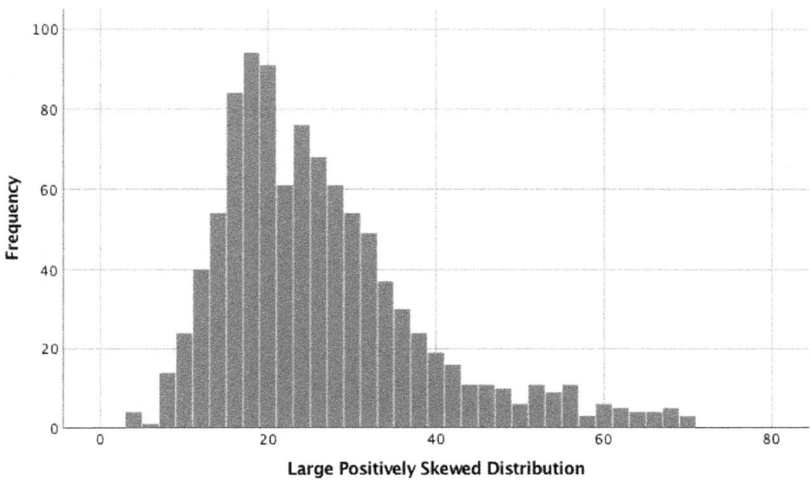

If it is skewed to the left, we call it a negatively skewed distribution.

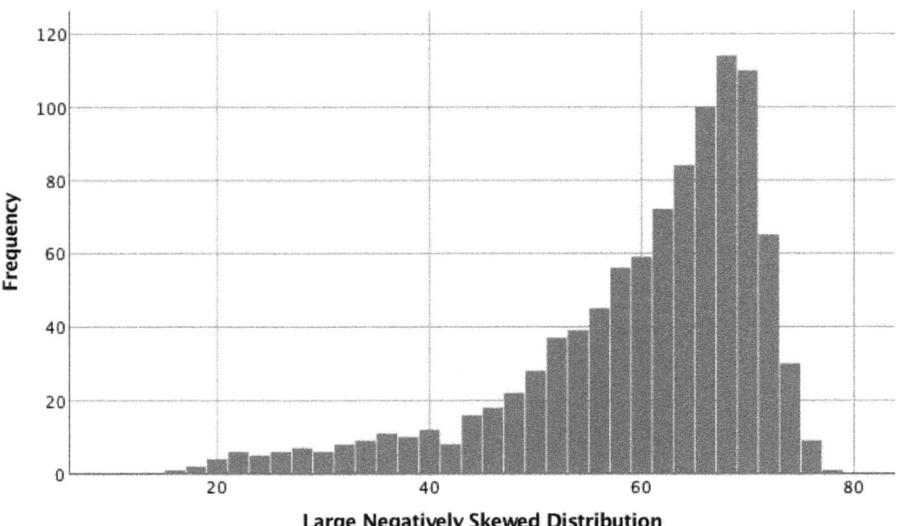

As a researcher you need to closely look at the distribution to see its shape.

Right tail longer = positive skew
Left tail longer = negative skew
Tails basically equal = symmetric

Remember in order to perform statistical tests to determine differences, the data have to be distributed normally or approximately normally. Curves that are either positively or negatively skewed too much impair the ability to analyze. We will show you later how to determine through a simple calculation if the skewness is so severe to preclude statistical analysis.

We not only have to be concerned with skewness—tailing off to the left or the right—we must also be concerned with (1) too much height in the middle and no tails or (2) no height in the middle and flat across the curve—the height and flatness of the curve is referred to as kurtosis.

The diagram below shows a curve that is too steep with no tails and represents what is called a **Leptokurtic distribution**.

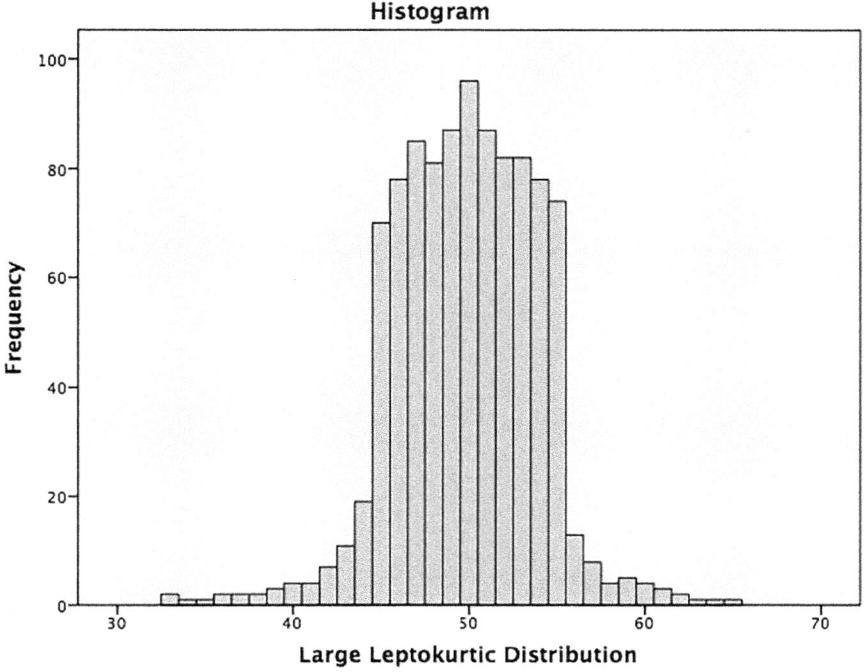

The next curve is very flat and is referred to as a **Platykurtic distribution**.

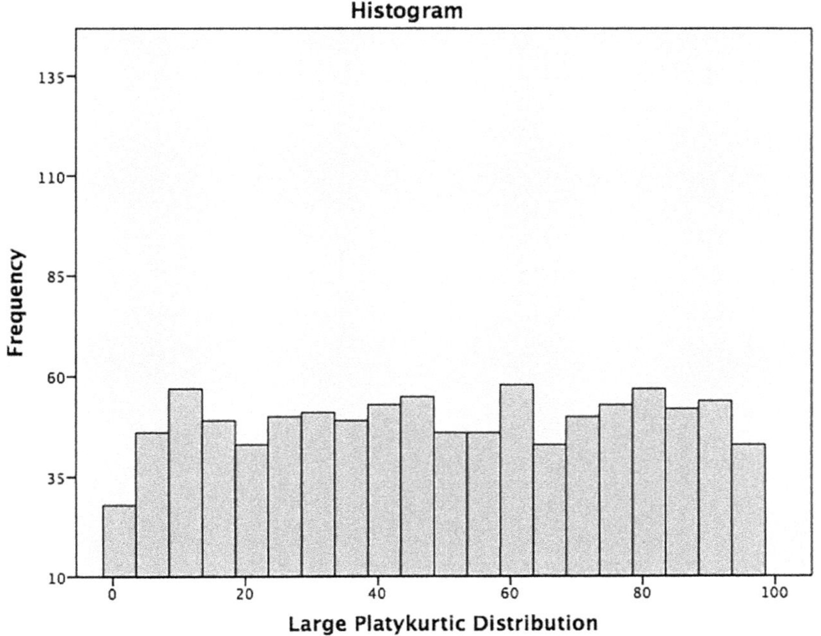

As with skewness, the amount of kurtosis can be a potential problem because normal distributions within limits (curves) are necessary for analysis. A rule of thumb to decide when these limits have been exceeded and you should not progress to analyze the data ***will be provided in the statistical chapters, but for now remember that the assumptions of a normal curve must be met and the distribution cannot have too much skewness or kurtosis!***

Finding the Center of a Distribution—Measures of Central Tendency

There are three ways we determine the **center of a distribution: (1) the mode, (2) the median and the (3) mean (average).** Each is based upon a different way to determine the central point of the distribution and all of them have different and specific uses depending on what question you are asking about the values of a variable and the distribution itself.

MEASURES OF CENTRAL TENDENCY

Mode

The mode is the most frequently occurring value in the distribution. This measurement of central tendency can be used for all measurement levels.

Nominal level of measurement—the greatest number of individuals are **Hispanic**

Ordinal level of measurement—the most frequent answer on an attitude toward abortion was (2) ***for abortion*** where the range was 1–5 with (5) being totally against and (1) being totally for

Interval/Ratio level of measurement—the most **frequently occurring age** of individuals attending the program **was 34.**

Of course, there can be more than one mode in a distribution if the highest (or ones are high and have very close to the same frequency) occurs more than once. In the previous examples, if there were the same number of Blacks and Hispanics, if there were an equal number of individuals having the "completely for" attitude as the "completely against" attitude and if there were the same number attending the program who were 34 years old and 29 years old, they would be bi-modal.

Median

The median is the value that is midway between the highest and lowest values. It is the value where exactly half of the values fall above it and exactly half of the values fall below it. With nominal data there is no ordering of the variable and hence there cannot be a median; therefore, a median can only be determined with respect to ordinal and interval/ratio level data. How do we determine the median? First, array all of the values from largest to smallest or smallest to largest with every value on the variable displayed. Then it is rather easy because there are only two rules that apply to finding the median. **The first rule is used when you have an *odd number of values* on the variable; then *the median will be the middle value in the list.***

A	B	C	D	E
	Case #	Age		
	1002	42		
	1013	42		
	1005	51		
	1014	53		
	1017	53		
	1016	54		
	1001	55		
	1004	66		
	1009	68		
	1010	70	Median Age = 70	
	1018	72		
	1012	74		
	1008	75		
	1006	78		
	1019	78		
	1007	79		
	1011	84		
	1003	86		
	1015	89		

However, if there is an even number of values on the variable, select the two values that are in the middle of the values and then divide the distance between the two values by 2.

Mean

The mean is the weighted center of the distribution. It is the place in the distribution where half of the "weight of the values" is to the right of the mean and half of the "weight of the values" is to the left of the mean. You most likely know the mean as an average—like the average income in your community.

Case #	Age	
1002	42	
1013	42	
1005	51	
1014	53	
1017	53	
1016	54	
1001	55	
1004	66	
1009	68	
1010	70	Median Age = (70 + 72)/2 = 71
1018	72	
1012	74	
1008	75	
1006	78	
1019	78	
1007	79	
1011	84	
1003	86	
1015	89	
1020	91	

The formula to compute the mean is shown below. The mean ($\bar{X}$) is obtained by summing (Σ) all of the scores/values (χ) in the sample and dividing by the number of scores (n). The ***n* below indicates the number in the sample not population.**

$$\bar{X} = \frac{\Sigma x}{n}$$

Client Number	Age (Years)
Client #1	22
Client #2	21
Client #3	26
Client #4	27
Client #5	30
Client #6	23
Client #7	22

Client Number	Age (Years)
Client #8	22
Client #9	23
Client #10	24
Total (Σx)	240
n	10
$\bar{X}$ ($\Sigma x/n$)	**24**

Using this formula, the calculated mean age among the individuals listed above is 24 years. This example can be extended to include more individuals whose ages are represented in the frequency table below.

Age

		Frequency	Percent	Valid Percent	Cumulative Percent
Valid	20	2	4.3	4.3	4.3
	21	4	8.5	8.5	12.8
	22	5	10.6	10.6	23.4
	23	6	12.8	12.8	36.2
	24	11	23.4	23.4	59.6
	25	9	19.1	19.1	78.7
	26	5	10.6	10.6	89.4
	27	3	6.4	6.4	95.7
	28	2	4.3	4.3	100.0
	Total	47	100.0	100.0	

Note that the mean age of these 47 individuals is also 24.

Statistics

Age		
N	Valid	47
	Missing	0
Mean		24.00
Median		24.00
Mode		24

Now, let us demonstrate the effect of extreme scores on a mean by making three individuals in the group much older. By examining the frequency table, you will notice that three 24-year-old individuals were removed from the group and three individuals in their 60s have been added in their place.

Age

		Frequency	Percent	Valid Percent	Cumulative Percent
Valid	20	2	4.3	4.3	4.3
	21	4	8.5	8.5	12.8
	22	5	10.6	10.6	23.4
	23	6	12.8	12.8	36.2
	24	8	17.0	17.0	53.2
	25	9	19.1	19.1	72.3
	26	5	10.6	10.6	83.0
	27	3	6.4	6.4	89.4
	28	2	4.3	4.3	93.6
	60	1	2.1	2.1	95.7
	63	1	2.1	2.1	97.9
	67	1	2.1	2.1	100.0
	Total	47	100.0	100.0	

What has happened to the mean? With the addition of only three extreme scores, the mean age has risen by more than 2.5 years!

Statistics

Age		
N	Valid	47
	Missing	0
Mean		26.51
Median		24.00
Mode		25

Extreme values—**outliers**—provide weight to one side of the distribution compared to the other side of the distribution. Remember earlier in the chapter we discussed skewness and now you can see how a **value that is extreme or values that are extreme at one end of the distribution can skew the distribution to that direction**. We will discuss methods to deal with outliers more specifically in later chapters but right now recognize that we can eliminate a few of them under certain circumstances and we can use tests that are based on ordinal or nominal level measurement rather than interval or ratio. ***Extreme values pull the mean of the distribution a lot in one direction and can create many problems for data analysis.***

NORMAL DISTRIBUTION

A normal distribution is one in which the mean, median and mode have the same values in the distribution. In practice the mean, median and mode should be relatively close to each other in order to use the values from the distribution as if they were from a perfectly normal distribution. In the analysis chapters, we will provide the limits we impose (how much we allow distributions to differ from a perfectly normal distribution) to use that data as if it was a normal distribution.

In the distribution of age without outliers you can see that the mean, median and mode are identical and suggest that it is a normal distribution.

Statistics

Age		
N	Valid	47
	Missing	0
Mean		24.00
Median		24.00
Mode		24

This can be readily visualized by looking at the histogram of the data with a normal curve superimposed on it.

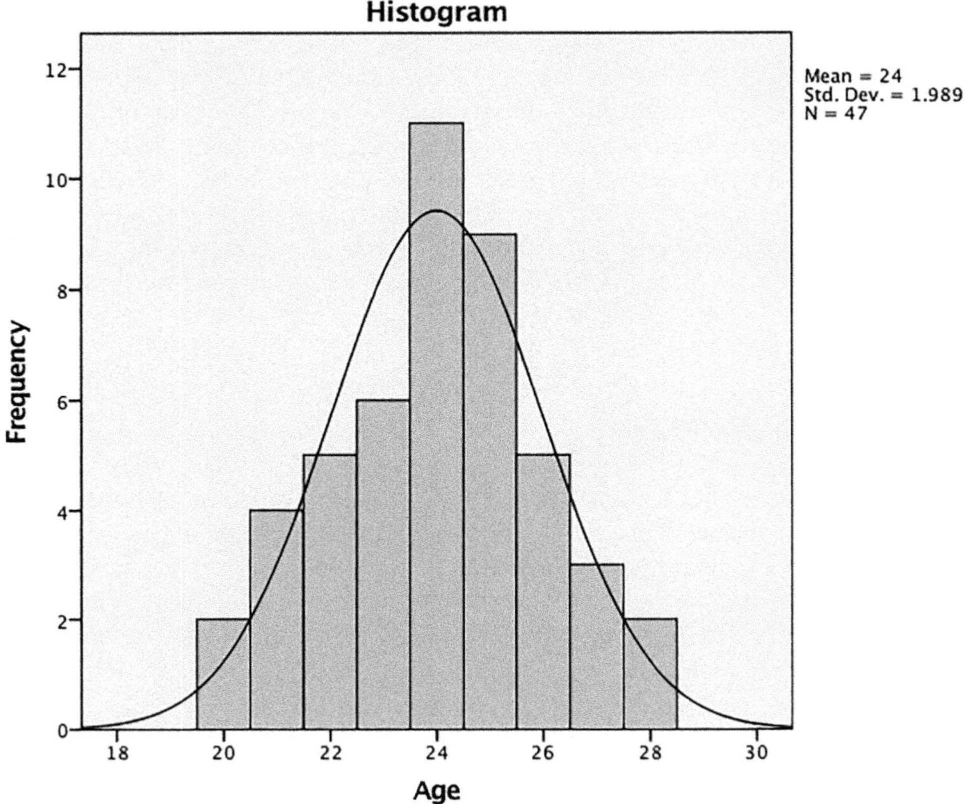

However, with the addition of the three outlying ages, the mean, median and mode are no longer identical.

Statistics

Age		
N	Valid	47
	Missing	0
Mean		26.51
Median		24.00
Mode		25

Now, notice the effect on the shape of the distribution. It is quite apparent that the curve is no longer normal.

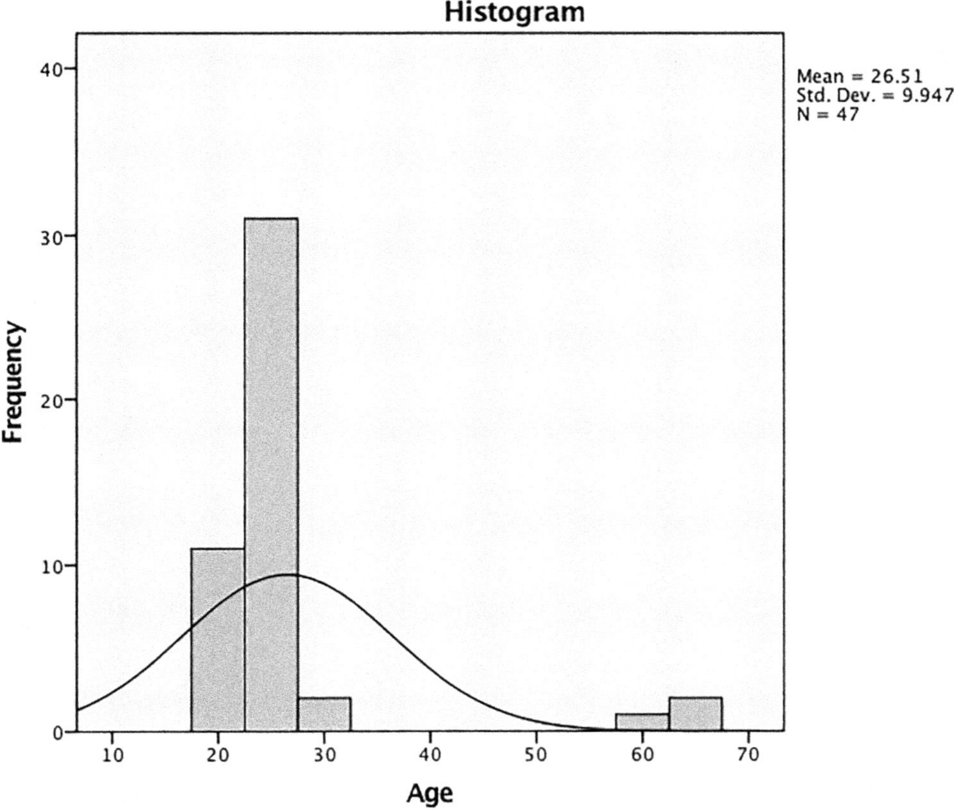

In Chapter 12 we talked about sampling and the difference between a population and a sample. Now as we start to talk about calculating values and using them to describe groups and to analyze differences, it is again important to review the distinction between samples and populations and how we calculate them a little differently. We defined a sample as a subset of the population and just above we provided the math formula for a sample mean. When we discuss the mean of a population we use different notation and in the statistical chapters you will see how it is used.

The formula for a population mean is where ***N* is the number in the population**.

$$\mu = \frac{\Sigma x}{N}$$

Terms to remember as we progress to other chapters:

STATISTIC **Term use for a measurement related to a sample**

PARAMETER **Term used for a measurement related to a population. May be the actual population value or one calculated based upon a sample from that population.**

Experiments are done to answer questions. They are situations created by scientists, created in very special ways, to allow the scientist to make judgments about the nature of things. Procedures, techniques and ideas have evolved and are still evolving which determine the ways in which experiments are carried out. An elaborate system is used and referred to as the scientific method. One part of the scientific method is the application of statistical inference to the outcome of an experiment—to the data collected during that experiment. Statistical inference is a way to make decisions consistently based upon the results in the face of uncertainty.

Scientists, do not to say, "I am certain such and such is true"; rather they say, "If I had to make a bet, I would bet on the fact that such and such is true". And "I would bet with these odds". The odds part is the most important; it tells you that scientists use statistics to calculate odds about their statements. No certainty is involved. Judgments are made, guesses if you like, decisions even, based upon sophisticated mathematics and, hopefully, knowledgeable and careful experimentation. But, in reality they are only guesses (based upon a reasonable and logical examination of the results) but can be questioned at any time and indeed this is the wonder and fascination of science and experimentation—the endless quest for better explanations. Guesses uncertainty is not a defect; it is scientific thought. Science works and it works simply because it always is trying to ensure there is opportunity to be proven wrong.

Statistical inference is the same as asking, "How do I calculate the odds of my being right?" Well you get odds on a certain kind of statement. You ask, "What are the odds that my experimental results occurred by chance alone?" If the odds were very low, you bet the experiment gave a reliable answer to your question "Is it true?" What are the odds that it is false? If the odds are small, it is false and bet it is true.

Experiments are designed to calculate the odds that nothing was going on. Researchers always run part of the experiment (testing an intervention) in such a way that nothing is going on. If one group of individuals receives a certain intervention (treatment) then another group will not receive the intervention (treatment). To decide about the effects of a certain drug, one group is given the drug and another group is given everything BUT the drug. When you look at the results, you compare one group with the other and if there is any difference, you ask yourself, "What are the odds that this difference occurred by chance?" In effect you are asking, "What are the odds that the drug had no effect?"

To understand how odds can be calculated, we must examine the behavior of systems that generate numbers, especially systems that generate numbers by chance alone—how numbers are generated at random.

If we take the six different numbers on the six faces of a single die (half of a pair of dice), we can get a series of random numbers by merely tossing the die over and over again and recording the number that faces up each time. The chance of any particular number coming up on a single role is 1/6. Plotting the distribution, we get on the x-axis, the numbers from 1 to 6 (the numbers occurring on the face of the die) and on the Y-axis, the probability of each particular number occurring.

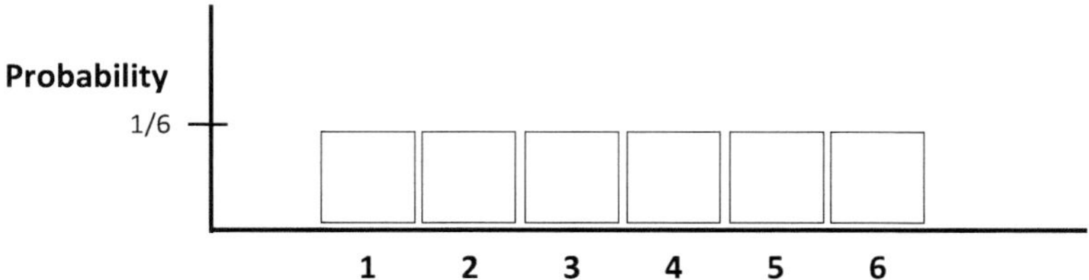

Rather Uninteresting!!! . . . Agreed!! But we are approaching a great discovery that is true of almost anything we measure (if measured on an interval or ratio scale). . . . The height of people or . . . the number of babies born on Tuesdays . . . the intelligence of people.

Suppose I toss a PAIR of dice. Now I ask, What is the distribution of the sum of two numbers appearing on the FACES of the dice? Well, how many ways could the dice fall? The first could fall in any of six ways, and for each of those, the second could also fall six ways. There are then, thirty-six (36) ways the PAIR could fall. However, some ways yield the same sum. For example, the first is a three (3) on the first die and the second is a three (3) on the second die yielding a sum of six (6), OR the first could be a two (2) and the second a four (4), also yielding a sum of six (6). The distribution for two dies thrown (pair of dice) is shown below:

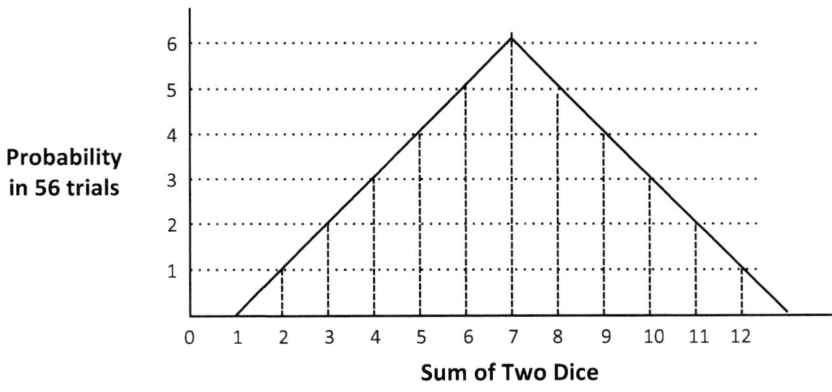

And the distribution for three dice thrown:

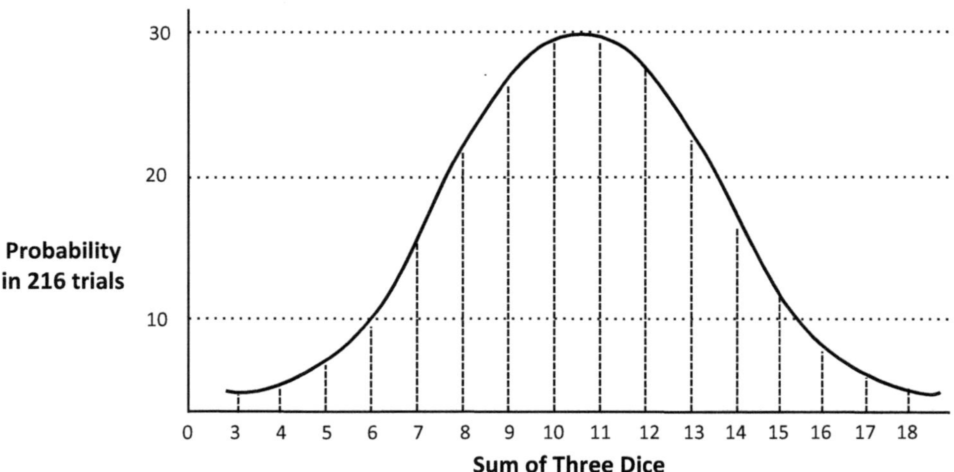

And finally, if I throw an enormous number of dice, an infinite amount, the shape of the curve would be as shown:

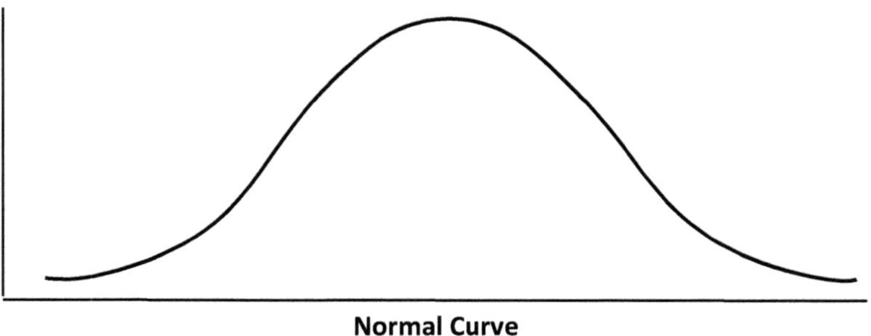

This graceful drawing is a normal distribution, or the normal curve. It depicts the probabilities of events which are the results of many things happening at random, just as the faces of the die occurred at random. Now we see how numbers behave at random; they are normally distributed, as are the heights of people, giraffes, monkeys, mice, etc. The curve below shows the distribution of IQ scores.

Only two numbers are needed to completely describe any normal curve, THE MEAN and a number that describes the amount of spread around the mean or the "variability". The second number is called the STANDARD DEVIATION. In the case of IQ, the standard deviation is fifteen (15). If the deviation for IQ was one (1) instead of 15, then

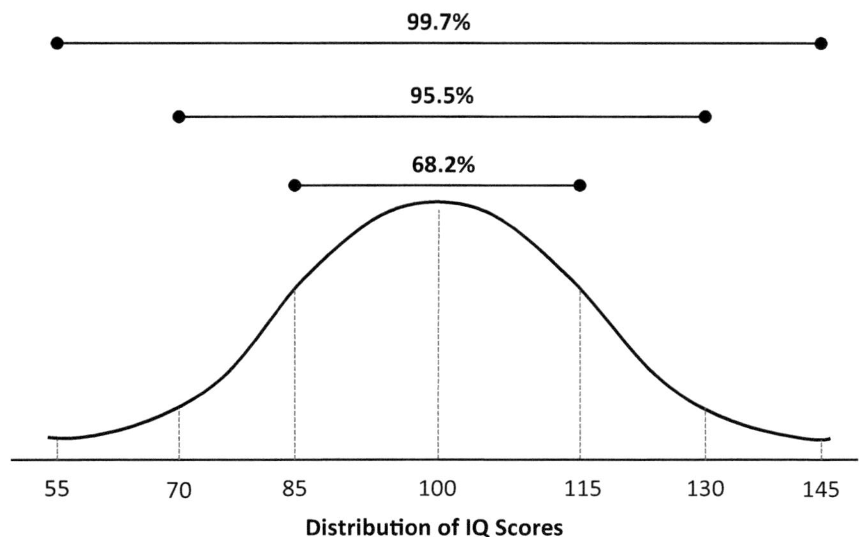

68% of the people would have IQs between 99 and 101. That is, people's IQ would vary less or deviate less from the mean.

A few more steps and we will have the whole picture. Let's look at two groups from an experiment. We have numbers for both groups and calculate the overall mean using the numbers from both groups. We use this overall mean as an estimate of the underlying mean of the distribution (estimate the mean of the population). We perform another set of operations to estimate the variability of the underlying distribution (the variability of the population). To do this we subtract the mean from each score, square the result (we square it to get rid of the + and −), divide by the number of scores and then take the square root of the result (to get back to our original scale of measurement). This number is the standard deviation. Now we ask, "What are the odds that these two groups came from the distribution with this mean and variance?" That's easy . . . because we know the individual group means and can look at the curve. For instance, suppose the overall mean is 100 and the standard deviation is 15, like the curve for IQ. Suppose also that the experimental group had a mean of 125 and the control group a mean of 75. We can ask, "What are the odds that we would get a difference of 50 in the mean between the experimental and control group IF both groups came from a distribution with a mean of 100 and a standard deviation of 15?" Easy for budding social work researchers, because the distribution of differences of two normally distributed variables is also normally distributed and has the same standard deviation. If we draw the curve of the distribution of differences it looks like this.

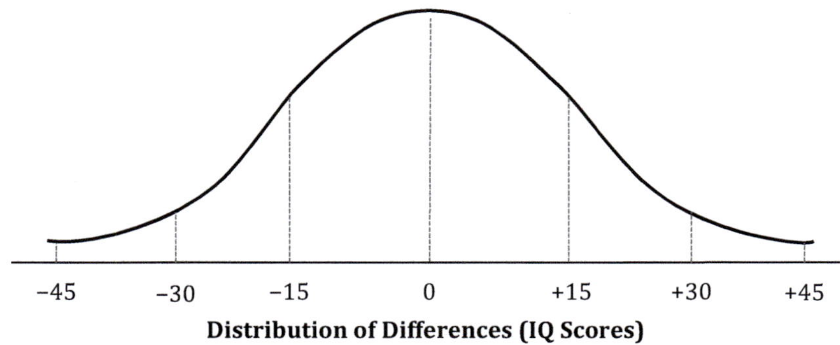

"What are the odds?" Since the difference in means of 50 or more is greater than three (3) standard deviations from the mean, we would expect a number that great to occur only 3 times out of 1000. The odds are 3 to 997. Very low. We assert, it's improbable that these two groups came from the same underlying distribution, AND it seems reasonable to assert that the experimental treatment had a real effect. OR to put it with true scientific caution. . . . It doesn't seem reasonable to assume that the experimental treatment had no effect. WHEW!!!!!

MEASURES OF VARIATION IN DISTRIBUTIONS—LOOKING AT THE WIDTH OF A DISTRIBUTION

Range

Range is probably the most familiar measurement you know associated with the width of a distribution. For years you have always been concerned about the "range of scores on an exam" and you already know that the range is the measure of the dispersion or width of a distribution that is equal to the highest values minus the lowest value. If the possible highest income reported by clients in your agency was $37,140 and the lowest was $3,670, the range of income of clients coming to your agency is between $3,670 to $37,140. ***The range requires ordering of the values is not appropriate for nominal level data but certainly appropriate for ordinal, interval and ratio level data.*** The range is not affected by weights of values, it does not make any difference if you have only one person making $3,670 and ten people making $376,140; the range is not affected. It is still the highest value minus the lowest value. The range does not provide a lot of information about the distribution of values since it only has two points, the highest and lowest, and does not say anything about all of the values across the distribution.

Deviation and Variance

As we saw in the previous section, determining the center of a distribution is very important to our description of the variable and values on the variable we are using to answer our questions. In addition, we need a way to measure width that has a relationship to the center of the distribution. We will first have to define what we are talking about. What is a **deviation**?

The terms used in research for differences in scores (values) are deviation and variance. **That is, a person or group differs from the norm (average, percentage, etc.) by some amount and this amount is called deviation.** ***The squared amount of this difference (deviation) is called variance.*** More precise mathematical definitions will be given later. At this point it is enough to conceptualize differences in terms of amount of deviation.

For example, there is a hypothetical Marital Satisfaction Scale (MAS) which has a total score of 100 with 100 being the highest satisfaction and 0 the lowest. Your score is 59 and the average score is 50. **Your deviation is 9.** In order to obtain your deviation, we first had to calculate some norm (mean) and then obtain how much you differ from the mean. The deviation could be conceptualized as follows:

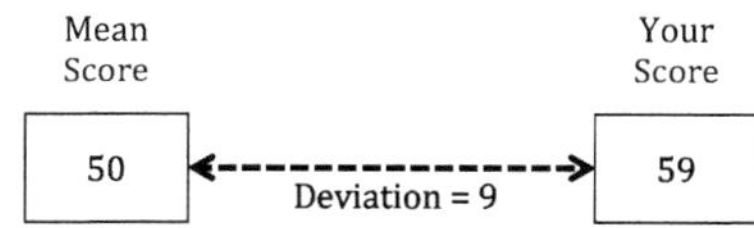

In the above example a simple average was the starting point (norm) from which to calculate the deviation or amount of difference. There are a lot of ways to determine a norm or base from which to discover differences (deviation). A social work researcher might use a ratio (percent) as a base from which to determine the amount of deviation. For example, in a large metropolitan area in 1980 there were 23 out of 230 elected officials who were women or 10% of the elected officials were women. We could use this as a norm or base to compare the number of elected women officials in 1990. Assume that in 1990 there were 46 elected women officials out of the same 230 positions. Thus in 1990, 20% of the officials were women. In this example, there is a deviation of +10%.

A social worker may want to find out if "physically challenged individuals spend more time seeking employment than non-physically challenged individuals". The measure would be total time spent per individual hunting for a job. Individuals would be categorized as challenged and non-challenged. Each group's average time spent (challenged and non-challenged) and the difference (deviation) between the groups would be evaluated to see if there was a significant difference. If the non-challenged group spent on average 75 hours seeking work and the challenged group spent on average 140 hours seeking work, then there is an average difference of 65 hours more spent job hunting by the challenged group.

Another question posed by a social worker might be, "Are Females in our clinic more often diagnosed depressed than Males?" One way to begin to answer this question would be to randomly select case records from your mental health facility until you have 100 Males and 100 Females. Then you could review the charts to see who had been diagnosed as depressed. The results of this preliminary investigation revealed the following *information*:

		GENDER	
		Males	**Females**
DIAGNOSIS	**Depressed**	20	60
	Not Depressed	80	20

This example allows us to begin to identify a difference between Males and Females in our mental health facility with respect to the diagnosis of depression. Later we will look at ways to statistically analyze this difference. Indeed, we will identify the relative amount of difference between these groups, but now we have only an example of descriptive results identifying differences.

One aim of research is to determine sources of variation. How do we begin to look at sources of variation? We note that 60% of the Females are diagnosed as depressed compared to only 20% of the Males. We begin to ask the question: Why would Females have a 40% higher rate of depression than Males? How can we begin to break down the sources of the higher rate of depression? We have a difference of 40% and we want to ask the question what variables could have contributed to this 40% difference?

What is variance? In statistical analysis, it is the squared deviation of a (value) score from the mean of (values) scores. Another way of saying this is it is the squared deviation from the mean or distance from the mean of the scores in a distribution. Let's review how to calculate the mean. Add all of the scores (values) and divide by the number of scores. Sure, that is simple stuff—now let's move on to deviation and variance and how we can determine these values. We want to calculate and use the amount of difference that values (scores) are from the mean. Remember there is a little problem in trying to determine these deviations. By definition the mean is the point on the distribution where all values (scores) above the mean are equal to all values (scores) below the mean, so if we do any calculations where we try to add, subtract or multiply or find the "average" deviation, it cannot be done using the actual numbers.

The way to resolve this problem is to square the amount of deviation from the mean for every value (score). This results in all numbers being positive and we can now perform calculations easily concerning the distribution as well as in statistical analysis presented in Chapters 15–21. By leaving the values squared it saves us from having to perform many difficult calculations (squaring and un-squaring), thus saving time. To put them back into the same metric that we have for the mean we simply have to un-square the results from the calculations.

One method of building social work knowledge is to discover differences, differences between groups or differences over time for individuals following an intervention. We might want to determine what the difference is between single mothers on welfare and single mothers not on welfare after the initiation of a new program to provide them assistance.

Remember that in order to use the deviation with respect to the mean we will have to un-square the value. If we un-square the value and divide by the number of values (n) we will obtain the standard (average) deviation for the values about the mean. We will show you this with an example in a few pages. Let's talk about how we can conceive of variance and differences from the average score. How do we begin to look at sources of variation? We note from practice that 60% of Females score high on a depression scale compared to only 20% of the Males who come to our clinic. Well we have already detected a source of variation in the amount of depression—gender. If you have some knowledge and have read about depression you might speculate that there are other sources of that variance, for example,

(1) Bio-chemical levels (first source of variance or V_1)
(2) Differences in seeking help (second source of variance or V_2)
(3) Depression test bias (third source of variance or V_3)
(4) Error (undetected sources of variance or Error).

We can conceptualize this mathematically as follows:

Total Variance $$V_{total} = V_1 + V_2 + V_3 + \text{Error}$$

The researcher would proceed to investigate what variables might account for the variance in scores and try to quantify how much each of the identified variables contributed to the total variance. (The identified sources of variance are the result of good knowledge of the situation and NOT statistical analysis.)

The total variance, the variance of all scores from the mean—the **sum of squares**—is the sum of all of the score deviations from the mean that have been squared. This is a critical moment in your understanding of variance and one that underpins many of the parts of the analysis chapters. ***The sum of squares (the total of all of the squared deviations from the mean) is the foundation for much of the statistical analysis of differences that are measured on an interval or ratio level.***

Let's look at an example. We will use the same data set to explain variance, use it again in Chapter 16 to perform a one-way analysis of variance (ANOVA) and once again in Chapter 18 to perform a two-way ANOVA. Using a single data set to explain the concept of variance and then using it in successive types of analysis will solidify your understanding of both the concept and subsequent data analyses. You will be able to see the conceptualization of variance and understand it both mathematically and graphically and finally to apply and analyze data to determine if there are differences between groups in terms of their exam scores.

We have a group of scores (values) from individuals on a social work licensure exam. The first thing to always do is look at the distribution of those scores. We can use SPSS to examine the distribution of the exam scores by calculating descriptive statistics and producing a frequency table and histogram.

SPSS Commands

Open the data set ***Ch14 Variance.***
Follow the steps below:

(1) Click ***Analyze.***
(2) Scroll down and select ***Descriptive Statistics.***
(3) Select ***Frequencies . . .***
(4) Move the variable ***Exam*** to the ***Variable(s)*** box.
(5) Ensure the box next to ***Display frequency tables*** is selected.
(6) Click the **Statistics . . .** button.
(7) In this example, we will request that SPSS calculate the ***Mean***, ***Median***, ***Mode***, ***Std. deviation***, ***Variance***, ***Range***, ***Minimum***, ***Maximum***, ***Skewness*** and ***Kurtosis***.

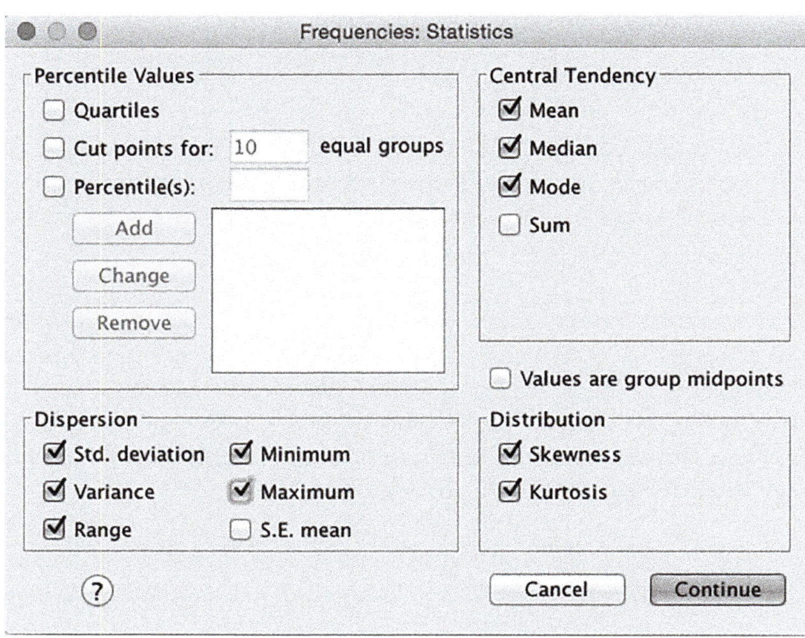

(8) Click ***Continue***.
(9) Click the ***Charts. . .*** button.
(10) Select ***Histograms*** and check the box next to ***Show normal curve on histogram***.

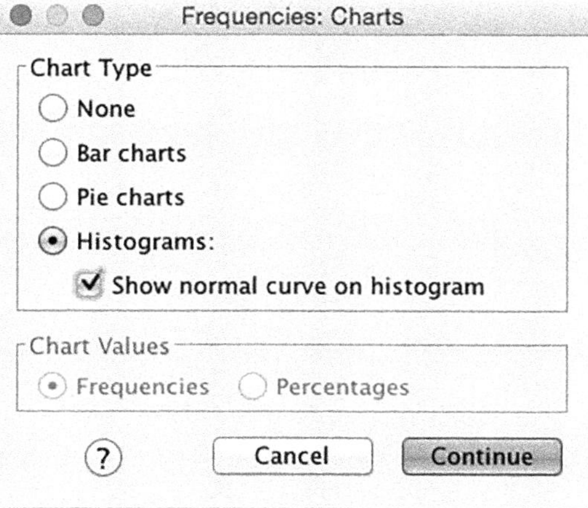

(11) Click ***Continue***.
(12) Click ***OK***.

SPSS will display the following outputs:

Statistics

Exam Score		
N	Valid	60
	Missing	0
Mean		16.50
Median		17.00
Mode		13[a]
Std. Deviation		6.385
Variance		40.763
Skewness		−.255
Std. Error of Skewness		.309
Kurtosis		−.485
Std. Error of Kurtosis		.608
Range		27
Minimum		2
Maximum		29

a. Multiple modes exist. The smallest value is shown.

Exam Score

		Frequency	Percent	Valid Percent	Cumulative Percent
Valid	2	1	1.7	1.7	1.7
	3	1	1.7	1.7	3.3
	4	1	1.7	1.7	5.0
	6	2	3.3	3.3	8.3
	8	2	3.3	3.3	11.7
	9	3	5.0	5.0	16.7
	11	3	5.0	5.0	21.7
	12	1	1.7	1.7	23.3
	13	5	8.3	8.3	31.7
	14	5	8.3	8.3	40.0
	15	1	1.7	1.7	41.7
	16	4	6.7	6.7	48.3
	17	4	6.7	6.7	55.0
	18	3	5.0	5.0	60.0
	19	4	6.7	6.7	66.7
	20	2	3.3	3.3	70.0
	21	3	5.0	5.0	75.0
	22	3	5.0	5.0	80.0
	23	3	5.0	5.0	85.0
	24	3	5.0	5.0	90.0
	25	2	3.3	3.3	93.3
	26	1	1.7	1.7	95.0
	27	2	3.3	3.3	98.3
	29	1	1.7	1.7	100.0
	Total	60	100.0	100.0	

With a range of 27, there may be too many scores to get a clear sense of the distribution by looking at the frequency table. Examining the histogram provides a visual representation of the distribution of exam scores:

Remember the way the mean (average) is calculated. You take all of the scores, add them together and then divide by the number of scores. If we look at this process in a little different way, we can start with the mean and then look at each score's position in the distribution in relation to the mean. For example, consider the diagram below.

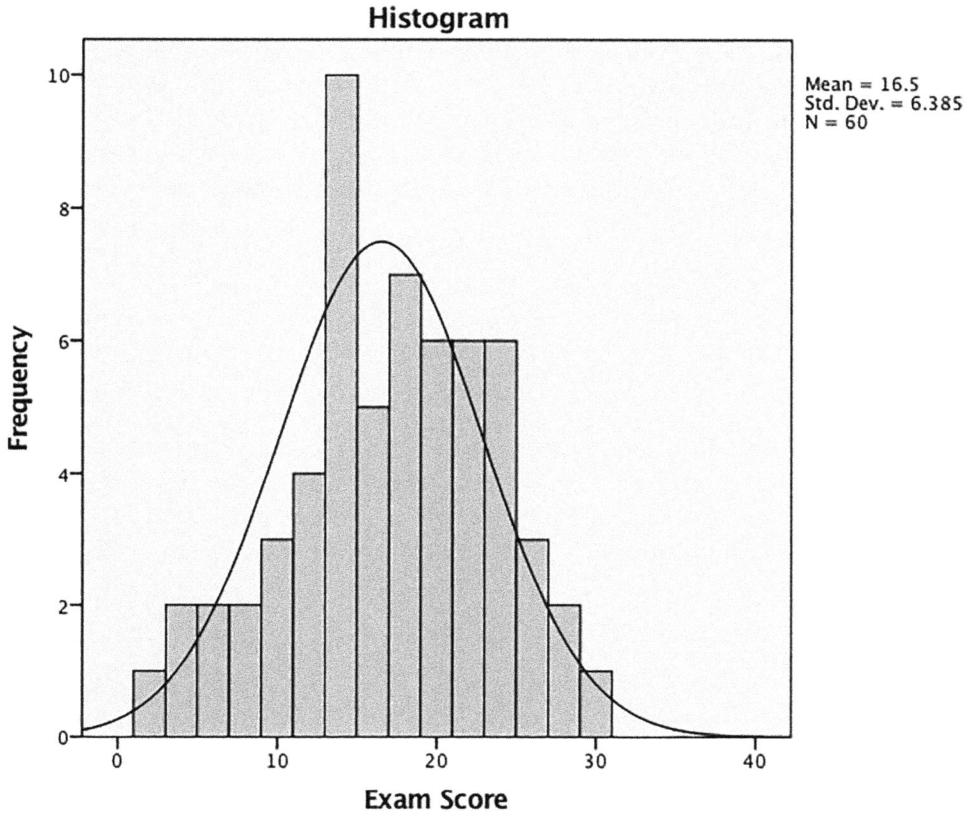

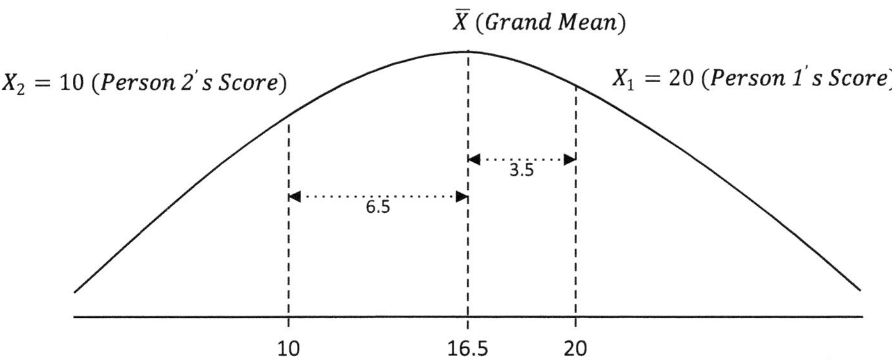

Look at Person 1 with an exam score of 20. The distance (deviation) of this person's score is 3.5 above the mean. Now look at Person 2. Their score is 10 and the distance (deviation) is 6.5 below the mean. We can look at all of the scores' deviations in terms of their distance from the mean. If we add all of those scores together with the + and − signs then of course they would equal 0. We want to be able to use the deviation score in many calculations; therefore, we will square each of those scores. If we want to get the total deviations from the mean, we could calculate all of them one by one by taking each score and subtracting the mean and squaring it. For example, we could take the score of Person 1, subtract the mean and square it with the result: $20 - 16.5 = 3.5$ then $3.5^2 = 12.25$. We can do the same for the second person: $10 - 16.5 = -6.6$ then $-6.5^2 = 42.25$.

This would look like this mathematically:

$$\Sigma(X_1 - \bar{X})^2 + (X_2 - \bar{X})^2 + (X_3 - \bar{X})^2 + \ldots$$

As you can see this is a long process and results in many fractions based upon calculations prior to squaring. These fractions then ultimately can lead to rounding errors depending on the number of decimal places used. A much better and simpler way to calculate the variance is to aggregate and then subtract using the following formula:

$$\Sigma X^2 - \frac{(\Sigma X)^2}{N}$$

Look at the exam data in the table below that has been arrayed by exam score and then each score has been squared.

SCORE	SCORE SQUARED	SCORE (Continued)	SCORE SQUARED (Continued)	SCORE (Continued)	SCORE SQUARED (Continued)
2	4	14	196	21	441
3	9	14	196	21	441
4	16	14	196	21	441
6	36	15	225	22	484
6	36	16	256	22	484
8	64	16	256	22	484
8	64	16	256	23	529
9	81	16	256	23	529
9	81	17	289	23	529
9	81	17	289	24	576

SCORE	SCORE SQUARED	SCORE (Continued)	SCORE SQUARED (Continued)	SCORE (Continued)	SCORE SQUARED (Continued)
11	121	17	289	24	576
11	121	17	289	24	576
11	121	18	324	25	625
12	144	18	324	25	625
13	169	18	324	26	676
13	169	19	361	27	729
13	169	19	361	27	729
13	169	19	361	29	841
13	169	19	361		
14	196	20	400	**990**	**18740**
14	196	20	400	ΣX	ΣX^2

We will use the easy formula to obtain the values needed. We are going to calculate all of these values by hand so that you can see conceptually what and how we determine the variance so that in the future you can see how statistical tests are used to determine if there are differences between groups.

$$\Sigma X^2 - \frac{(\Sigma X)^2}{N}$$

We add up all of the squared values as shown in Sum of X^2 which will give us a total of 18,740. Next, we have to sum up all of the X values which is 990 and we have to square that which will be 980,100. Then we divide that number 980,199 by *n* (60) which will give the sum of X quantity squared, divided by *n* which is 16,335. Then if we subtract that value from the first value 18,749 − 16,335 = 2,405 we will arrive at TOTAL Sum of Squares for this data—**the total variance**.

$$\begin{aligned}\text{Total Sum of Squares} &= 18740 - \frac{(990)^2}{60} \\ &= 18{,}740 - \frac{980{,}100}{60} \\ &= 18{,}740 - 16{,}355 \\ &= \mathbf{2{,}405}\end{aligned}$$

Let's revisit the descriptive statistics table we produced for these data using SPSS previously:

Statistics

Exam Score		
N	Valid	60
	Missing	0
Mean		16.50
Median		17.00
Mode		13[a]
Std. Deviation		6.385
Variance		40.763
Skewness		–.255
Std. Error of Skewness		.309
Kurtosis		–.485
Std. Error of Kurtosis		.608
Range		27
Minimum		2
Maximum		29

a. Multiple modes exist. The smallest value is shown.

The value of 40.7 is the variance of the data shown in the SPSS table. If we take our calculated Sum of Squares 2,405 and divide it by $n - 1$ ($n - 1$ and not n because we are estimating a parameter and which will be discussed in the degrees of freedom section later in this chapter) we obtain the same 40.7 number. Then if we take the square root of that value ($\sqrt{40.7}$) we will arrive at the value of 6.38 and it is the same value SPSS determined for standard deviation.

One objective of this exercise was to show you how you can derive the same results as SPSS from your own math calculations. Another objective was to help you to conceptualize variance and standard deviation using "real numbers" from a study and finally to show you that we can use the sums of squares to make calculations and not have to always rotate back and forth between square roots.

WHEW!!!!!!

Recall that one of **the important aspects of statistical analysis is to see if we can reduce error by identifying variables that can account for variance in the score**

that is identifying variables that account for differences. This process becomes a vital key to social work research.

Look at the distribution below:

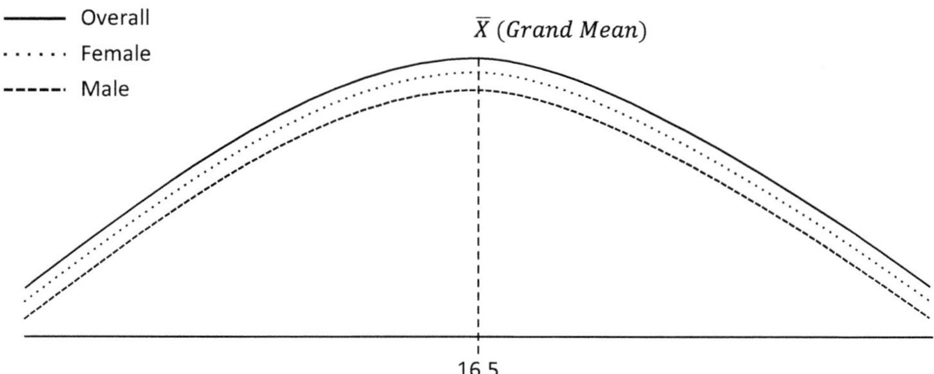

Grand Mean (GM) is the overall mean of all scores in the distribution before any variables have been identified. As you can see there is no difference in the Male and Female distribution of scores and their means with respect to each other and with respect to the overall distribution and the overall grand mean. When this occurs (no differences that are seen in the distribution and means) based upon a variable (gender in this case), then the variable does not account for any variance in the exam score and there is no difference between the subgroups (Males and Females). Another way of saying this is (you will see this later in the chapters on prediction) is that if we know the gender of a person, it would not help us at all to predict your score.

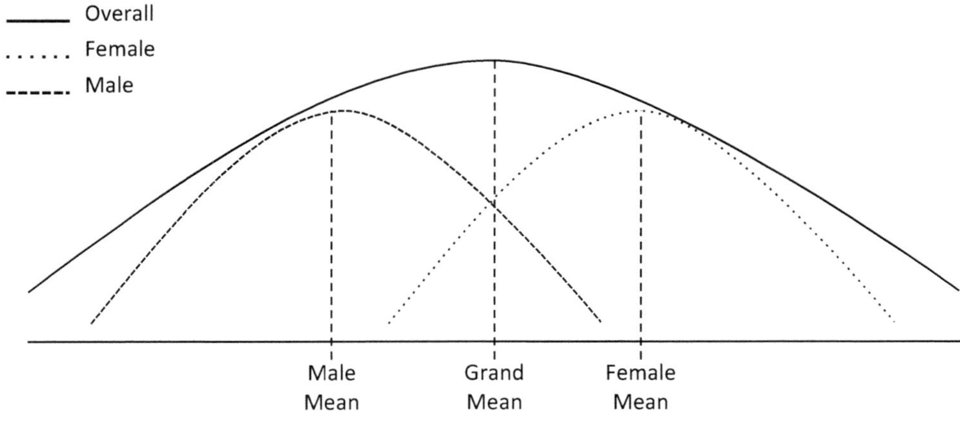

Now inspect the diagram above where the Male and Female scores are very different. There is a difference in the average Male score and the average Female score. If we look at the mean of the Females and the variation from that mean for all Female scores and if we look at the mean of the Male scores and the variation for all Male scores from the Male mean the amount of error of on the exam for all the scores is reduced if we use the mean of the Male subset and the mean of the Female subset as the start point for calculation of the deviation. What you are seeing is that some of the variation in exam score is accounted for by gender and thus error has also been reduced.

Thus, using the means of scores by gender as the start point, the exam score (using the variable gender) reduces the error and the variable gender has an effect and accounts for some of the variance in overall exam scores.

$$\mathbf{V_{total} = V_1\left(Gender\right) + Error}$$

A major reduction in error only occurs where there is a large enough difference between the groups on that variable. As we will see in later in the analysis chapters when there is a statistical significant difference between groups on the variable (in this case gender) then the variable accounts for differences on the exam score and reduces the overall error. ***Is there a significant difference on the dependent variable (exam score) between the groups (independent variable—gender) that would account for variance in the exam scores thereby reducing error?***

Ok, what about another variable and its effect on the exam score? Does the university attended have an effect on the exam score? Let's look at the diagram below.

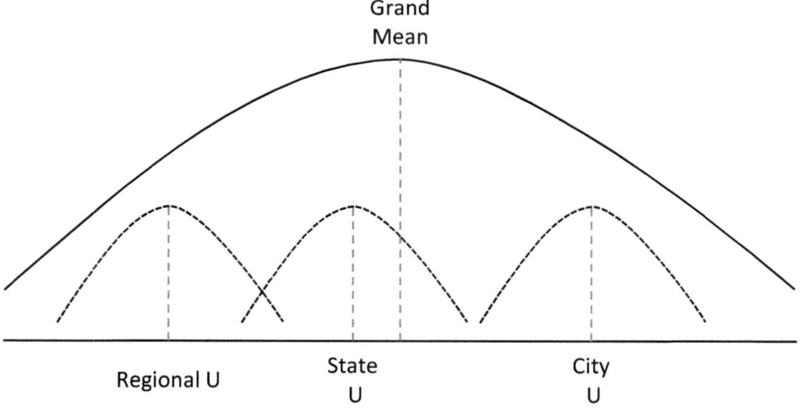

In the above example the equation would be:

$$\mathbf{V_{total} = V_1\left(University\ Attended\right) + Error}$$

There are three groups and in the diagram above each is different from the others. The way the diagram is presented it would appear that university attended would separate out individuals on their exam score and reduce error.

We might also have a situation as shown below where the university might make a difference in exam scores but where the difference is only between one group with respect to the other two groups.

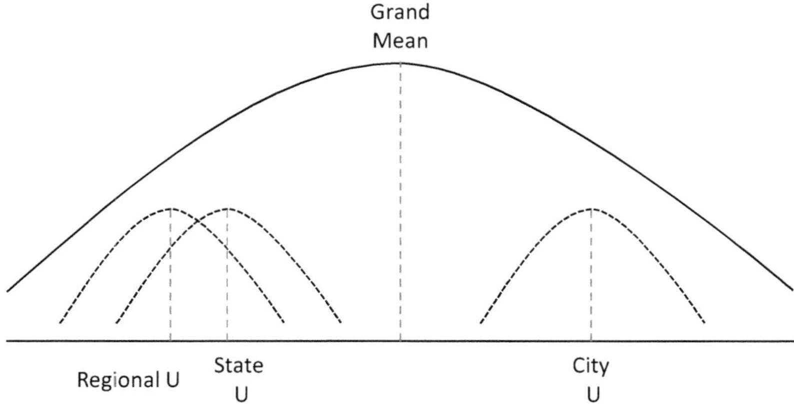

In this example, individuals who attended the City University have higher exam scores than individuals who attended State University and Regional University. In this distribution of exam scores, we are able to separate out those who attended City University (with higher exam scores) from those who attended State University and Regional University, both of whom have lower and about equal exam scores. We cannot, however, separate out State University graduates from Regional University graduates. Still we would be able to identify the City graduates from the other universities and reduce error.

Let's return to the situation where there are three different universities attended and all have very different means. What if both university attended and gender both were important variables in determining a person's exam score and that they acted together to account for the variance in the person's exam score? This situation is depicted in the diagram below with six groups. In this example, the difference between the groups could be significant and it would greatly reduce the error of a person's score from the mean. Also, it could lead to more accurately predicting the person's score.

The equation would be like the one below:

$$\begin{aligned} \mathbf{V_{total}} = {} & \mathbf{V_1}\,(\textbf{Gender}) + \\ & \mathbf{V_2}\,(\textbf{University Attended}) + \\ & \mathbf{V_3}\,(\textbf{Interaction of Gender and University} \\ & \textbf{Attended}) + \textbf{Error} \end{aligned}$$

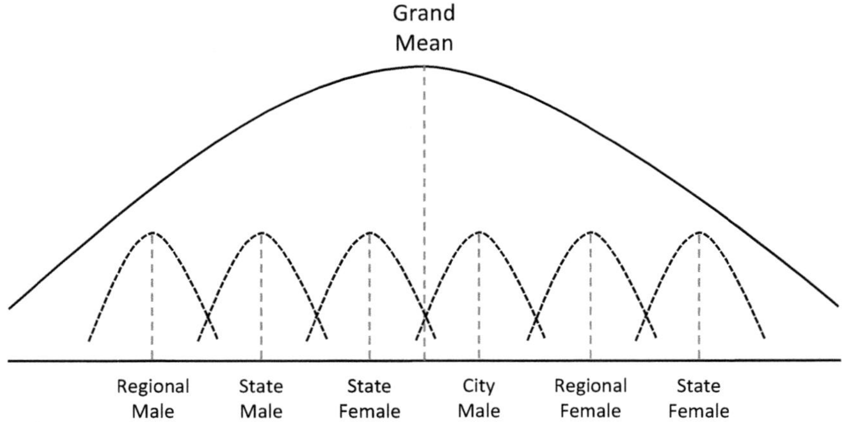

We are showing you what these look like and how to conceptualize them, and in Chapter 16 you will perform a statistical test to see if the Females and Males have significantly different exam scores—that is, are Male and Female scores significantly different and does gender reduce error? We will also investigate if university attended is an important variable in determining exam scores and finally in **Chapter 18 we will see if university attended and gender separately and interacting account for the variance in exam scores and reduce error**.

A graphic method to look at curves is to look at where the curve starts to make a change in direction. Think about waves in the ocean and when the wave starts to change from up to down. You can see in a graph that there can be many points in a curve—for example where there is a monitor on a patient in a hospital—where the line goes up and then starts to go down in some regular pattern. We can also look at a normal curve in the same way; that is, if we start on the left of the curve, we can see that it starts to go up and there is a point where it seems to become flat then starts to curve the other way. This pattern happens two times in a normal curve, once on the left side and once on the right side, and because it is a normal curve and equal on both sides, this change in direction will occur at exactly the same place on each side of the curve.

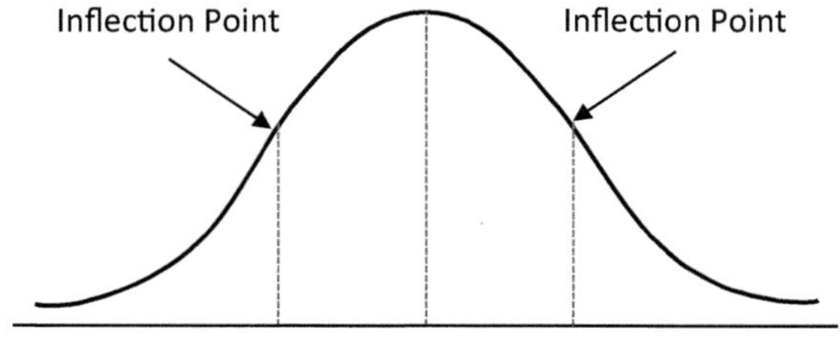

Here is the most important and critical point about normal curves—**the distance from the mean to where this change occurs on the curve is the standard deviation. It does not matter if the normal curve is narrow or wide; that change in the curve is always the standard deviation of the distribution. By simply looking at a normal curve you will also see that two standard deviations occur where you start to see a flattening out of the curve with relationship to the horizontal axis and at three standard deviations the curve is running almost parallel to the horizontal line.**

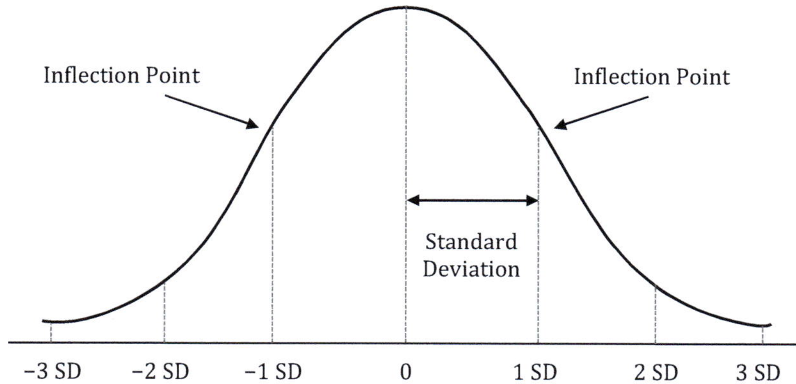

AREAS UNDER THE CURVE—THE FREQUENCY OF THINGS IN VARIOUS PORTIONS OF THE DISTRIBUTION

Social workers often want to know the percent of something with respect to a distribution. As shown earlier we discussed percent in terms of frequency but now it becomes important to discuss how we have standardized percentages of things under defined areas of the normal curve and how we use them to determine differences and similarities of groups. What are we saying? We are saying that when we have interval and ratio level data that is normally distributed, we can analyze differences between groups to see if there is a significant difference between them or not. For example, if Females have an average income of $33,000 and Males have an average income of $41,000 is there a significant difference between the income of Males and Females?

Normal distributions are the foundation of interval and ratio level data analysis. Remember that a normal curve is ***asymptotic*** which means that the **edges of the curve never touch the horizontal axis indicating that there is never 100% occurrence of any probability**—there is always a chance albeit an infinitesimal small one as the curve extends out to infinity that the occurrence of an event may happen. For example, almost 100%—99.999999%—of all incomes fall between $500 and $500,000,000 in a community but there is still a very slight change that someone has an income below $500 or $500,000,000. ***We always talk about probability and not certainty with regard to statistical calculations.***

Now that we know that many things are distributed normally or almost normally, the fact that the percentage of scores distributed to the left and right of the mean is always the same and is universal for normal curves. We have shown how to calculate the standard deviation; now let's look at regions under the curve. The region in the curve that is bounded by +1 SD above the mean and −1 SD below the mean contains 34.13% of the values above the mean and 34.13% of the values below the mean as shown in the figure below. As other texts refer to +1 SD = or −1 SD as 34% we will use the same convention. What happens to the percent at +2 SD or −2 SD? Approximately 14% of it is added to the right and left of the mean and when added to the 34% already to the right and left there is now a total of 48% of the values to the right of the mean and 48% of the values to the left of the mean. Finally, as shown in the figure below at ± 3 SD basically 50% of the values are above the mean and 50% of the values are below the mean. Of course, there is never 100% because the curve never touches the line in either direction.

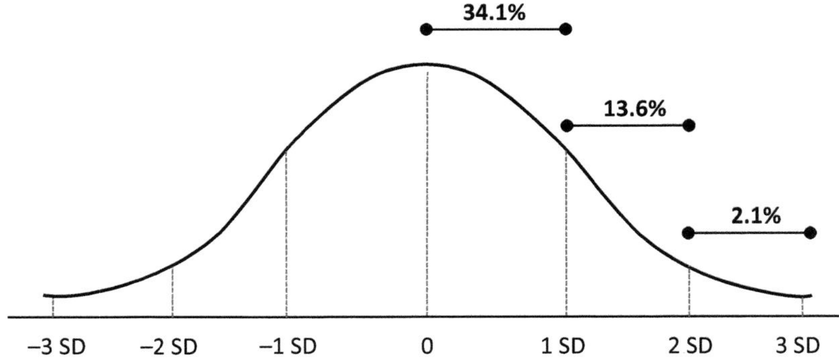

One of the problems in using raw data is we have to always refer to the mean and the SD of each and every distribution which leads to some problems in comparing, understanding and seeing differences due to score/scale differences. One way to overcome this problem is to set the mean at 0 and then refer to values with respect to the deviation from the mean of zero. This is called a **standard score or Z score**. For example, if the mean income in the community was $30,000 we could set the mean at zero that is $30,000. And if the SD was $5,000 then 1 SD + or − would be $25,000 and $35,000. If a particular individual had an income of $37,000 what percent of the community had incomes below this individual and what had incomes above this individual?

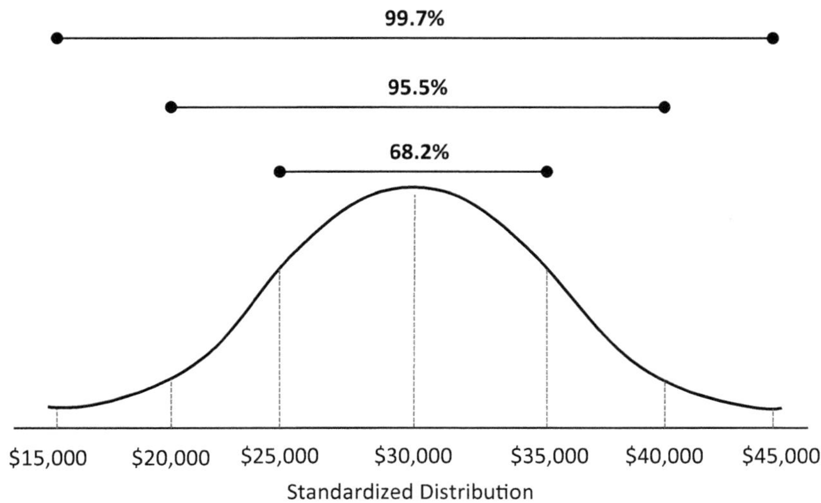

We have a formula that we can calculate this exactly:

$$Z = \frac{X - \mu}{\sigma}$$

For the person in our community the Z score would be:

> \$37,000 – \$30,000 / \$5,000 = \$7,000 / \$5,000 = 1.4
>
> Z = 1.4 or . . . approximately 92% of the population have incomes below and approximately 8% incomes above. In terms of percentiles we would say that this person's income is in the 92nd percentile.

Using this method (shown above) results in a ***standardized variable.*** What is a standardized variable? It is a normally distributed variable that has a mean of **μ and a standard deviation of σ**. We have done just that above. We utilized the mean of the community and the standard deviation of the community to determine the position of a single person's income relative to all other incomes in the community and the percent above and below that income. Other examples many of you are familiar with are the Graduate Record Exam and IQ where you can determine quite easily given their charts of the population values where your value (score) is in relationship to all the others in the population.

Now to return to the concept of variance for groups. As you have seen there is the variance of a population and also you can have variance of groups within that population. We introduced the question about the incomes of Females and Males to indicate differences in groups within the population. We said that Females have an average income of \$33,000 and Males \$41,000. Let's say that when we look at the whole population of Males and Females working the average income for the population was \$38,000; that is closer to the Male average than the Female average because more Males are presently working in this community. This is represented in the diagram below showing the overall population mean and distribution as well as the means and distributions of the Male and Female subgroups.

An important point will be made here about means and variances that is crucial to all of the analysis chapters. Look at the two groups—Females and Males—and look at the means and variance distributions. See the figure below:

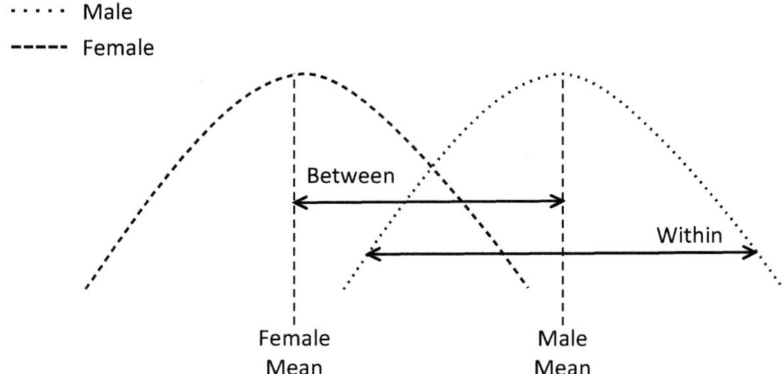

You can see that the variances of the two groups overlap some but there are differences in where they start and end, and there is variance within each of the Male and Female distributions. In effect, you see that the variance within is the variance within the Female distribution around its mean and the variance in the Male distribution is the variance around the Male mean. You can also see there is a difference (distance) between the means or a variance between the two means. You can see in the figure then we have labeled two variances—variance within (within the group) and variance between the groups (differences or variance between the means of Males and Females).

Another way to describe total variance in addition to the one we showed earlier is:

$$V_{\textbf{total}} = V_{\textbf{between}} + V_{\textbf{within}}$$

Later in the chapters on determining if there are significant differences between groups you will see that one of the ways to calculate it is the ratio of:

$$\frac{V\ between}{V\ within}$$

The greater the difference between groups and the less difference there is within groups the ratio will become larger, indicating the amount of difference between those in each group. This will become a key component as you start to analyze data.

In most experiments, odds of 19 to 1 or better are usually acceptable. This corresponds to a probability of 1/20 or .05. This figure is called the significance level, and an experimenter will report that their results were significant at the .05 level, or beyond. This means the experimenter's calculations indicate that the results could have occurred by chance less than 1 time in 20.

IT'S ALL ABOUT REJECTION

Ok. Let's look at it one more time from a different angle. The researcher has two groups: an experimental group, which receives some intervention to determine if this treatment has an effect, and a second group, a control group, which does not get the intervention. Measurements are made on both groups. The numbers from the measurements allow the experimenter to calculate the odds on whether or not the two groups are different. We have a tentative idea that the two groups will differ (or why do the study). We call this tentative idea the experimental hypothesis and symbolize it as H_e. The statistical statement we are getting odds on is the exact opposite of H_e; it states that the two groups do not differ. It is called the "Null Hypothesis", and is symbolized H_o. One and only one of these hypotheses can be true. We have to make a decision as to which one it is. A simple 2 × 2 table describes the situation.

		TRUTH	
		H_0 = True *No Effect*	**H_0 = False** *Effect*
RESEARCHER'S DECISION	**Accept H_0** *No Effect*	**CORRECT REJECTS** ($1 - \alpha$)	**MISS** *Type II Error* (β)
	Reject H_0 *Effect*	**FALSE ALARM** *Type I Error* (α, sig. level)	**HIT** ($1 - \beta$, power)

We see that four possibilities exist. If H_e is true and the experimenter decides that it is true we call it a HIT (note that true is defined as truth in the state of nature). The probability that the experimenter makes a HIT (**correctly rejecting the null**) is called the POWER of the experiment. POWER **is the probability of rejecting the null (no difference exists) and saying that a difference exists when in fact (in truth of nature) it exists and is symbolized as $1 - \beta$.** It is the power to detect real differences. We'll see in a moment what factors affect the power of an experiment.

The researcher may **decide to accept H_0 when in fact H_e is true, there is a difference**. This would be a MISS, **a failure to detect a real difference.** A MISS is also called a **TYPE II ERROR. The probability of a MISS is β.**

When **H_0 is true**, the experimenter has **two possible outcome decisions**, a **CORRECT REJECT 1 − α (accept H_0, there is no difference) when in truth there is no difference and a FALSE ALARM, α, also called a TYPE I ERROR.**

The researcher has only two choices:

(1) Accept the null
(2) Reject the null.

However, these two choices are paired with two possible states of truth (in nature) leaving the possibility of four different outcomes as shown above and in the curves shown below. If the researcher selects one of the two possible choices available, there are two possible outcomes to match that choice which have a probability of 1.

Since the researcher has calculated the odds that H_0 is true, and will decide against this only if these odds are 10 to 1 or better, the experimenter is setting the **FALSE ALARM (α)** rate at a minimum of 1 out of 20, or a probability of **.05**. This automatically sets **the CORRECT REJECT (1 − α)** rate at minimum of **.95**. The researcher can choose any significance level they want based upon what is being studied—.10 or even .01.

You may ask "Why choose .05?" To see that, notice in the curves the Significance Level affects not only the FALSE ALARM rate, but also the HIT rate or POWER. The distributions are plotted for both H_0 and H_e against the curves (realizing of course that only one can be TRUE at any one time).

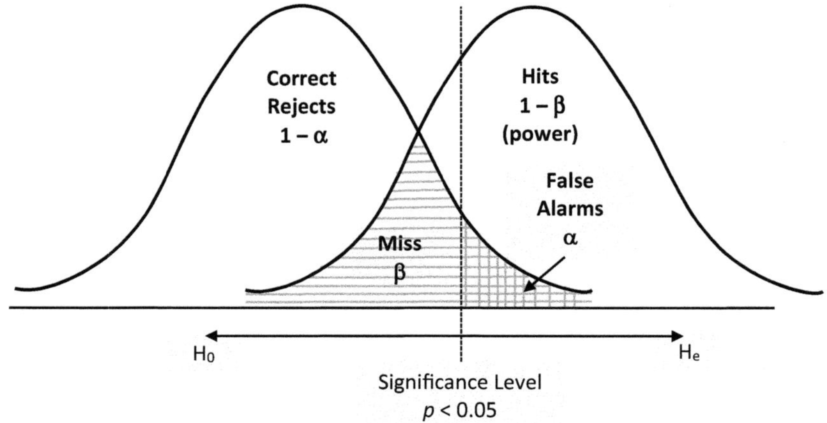

POWER AND FACTORS THAT DETERMINE THE AMOUNT OF POWER

Power is a term used to describe the ability of a statistical analysis (test) to reject the null hypothesis. Power is not a constant and varies in each application of a statistical test to the research data. We have just discussed the relationship of making a decision based upon data and what may in fact be truth in nature (researcher's decision and truth matrix). Throughout this book we have stressed that all research is based upon probabilities and not certainties, that we place bets on what is the state of nature and we place those bets based upon the confidence we have in our research and the differences we find. We are now going to define and look at how well those certain factors affecting research give enough power to confidently, with a degree of acceptable probability, reject the null hypothesis. Remember if we reject the null we are by definition accepting the experimental hypothesis (the hypothesis of difference).

The estimate of power is the probability found in the bottom right hand cell (researcher's decision and truth matrix) and of course refers to the ability to reject the null when the null is not true. This may seem reversed but it is the power to detect an effect when there is an effect—***not accepting the null*** when the null is not true.

There are four factors that affect power: (1) sample size, (2) decreasing variance, (3) effect size and (4) significance level. The first two are related to the sample, the third is the strength of the intervention and the fourth is related to the bet you want to make. We will discuss these in turn. Remember that **all of these factors interact to determine power—the decision to reject the null**. For example, you will see how a very large sample size can increase power in detecting differences when there is a small effect or that with a very big effect it can be seen with a small sample size.

The key to all research decisions concerning existence of differences is related to POWER. ***In effect what are the values of β and $1-\beta$ in any given research.***

In the examples below we will assume a population with a given mean and standard deviation. Then we will examine how changes in each of the factors can affect the researcher's decision about rejecting the null.

Sample Size

Recall that you are estimating the population mean μ from your sample. ***When you select only a very small number from a very large population, you are very likely to have the mean of the sample very different from the mean of the population.*** Let's say that you sampled the income of 40 people from a small community of 20,000 individuals. The probability of getting 40 individuals with an average income that is lower or higher than the whole population is fairly high, so your estimate of the income of the population would fall between a wide range of values. If you increase your sample of the population more and more and more, the variation of the sample mean from the population mean decreases and decreases. ***Finally, if you sample the whole population then the sample mean is the population mean!*** In any research study where an intervention is introduced, you compare the mean of the intervention group to the mean of the non-intervention group. The non-intervention group mean is use to represent the population mean because it is assumed to remain unchanged since it did not receive an intervention. If the size of the non-intervention group is small (small n) it can be a poor representative of the population due to the potential for large variation of the sample from the population. This must be taken into account when comparing the intervention group's mean to the non-intervention group mean when conducting a statistical analysis. The variation of the sample mean from the "real mean−μ" of the population has to be taken into account if you are going to test the effect of an intervention.

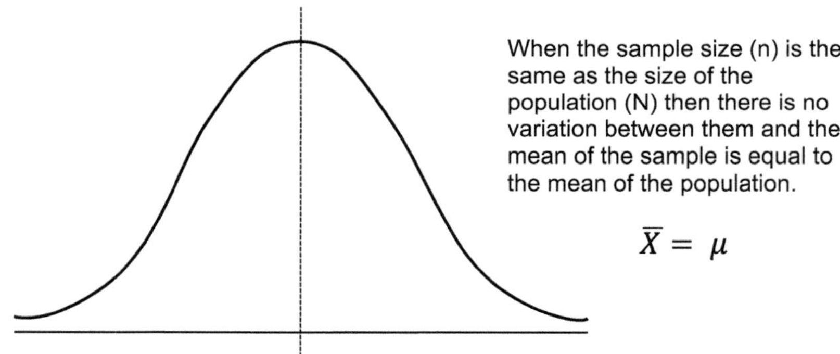

When the sample size (n) is the same as the size of the population (N) then there is no variation between them and the mean of the sample is equal to the mean of the population.
$\bar{X} = \mu$

With a small sample size, you can get a "screwy" estimate of the population mean!

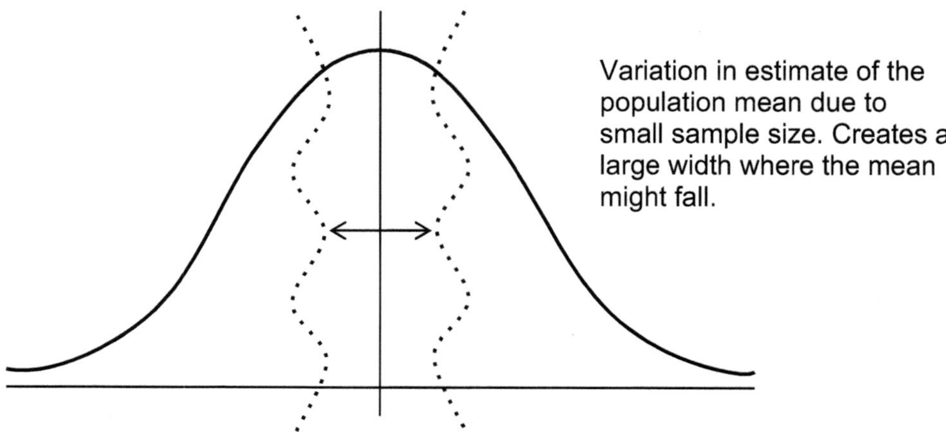

Variation in estimate of the population mean due to small sample size. Creates a large width where the mean might fall.

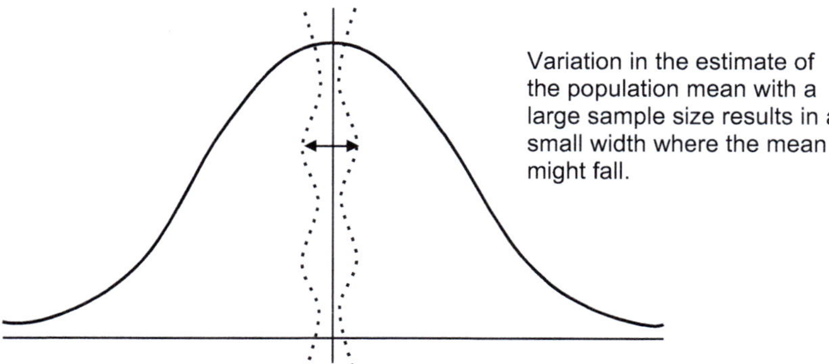

Variation in the estimate of the population mean with a large sample size results in a small width where the mean might fall.

Decrease Variance

The next way the researcher can improve power is to reduce variance within the group. Let's again look at the mean of income for the population. As we know the income of people varies with certain characteristics. If you include everyone in your sample, there is a lot of variation that is affected by certain characteristics, for example, education, race and gender. If you reduced the population to individuals with a certain educational level, a certain gender and a certain race, the amount of variation with respect to the mean income of that population will be reduced. In essence, the population is now more homogenous, less diverse and with less variation in mean income. As shown below, selecting a less diverse population from which to sample will reduce the potential variation and "bandwidth" in the population mean and therefore the estimation of the population mean from the sample mean.

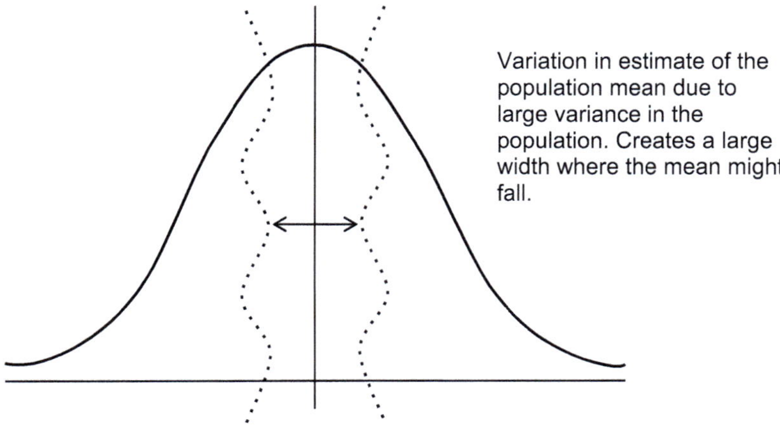

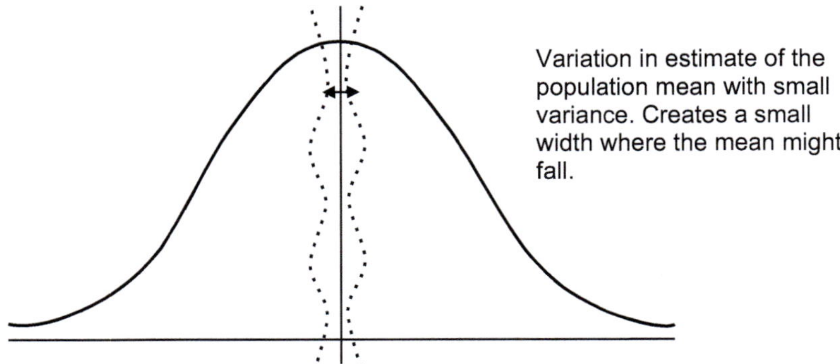
Variation in estimate of the population mean with small variance. Creates a small width where the mean might fall.

The more variance (error in estimating the population mean) the greater the effect size needed to detect significant differences between the non-intervention group and the intervention group. You can either control that variance by leaving out variables (as shown in this example) or control it by inclusion either as an IV or a covariate and seeing the effects of that variable. The important point is that reducing variance in the estimate of the population mean increases power to detect differences.

Increasing the Intervention (Effect Size) Pushes the Intervention Group Further Away

Effect size is the difference created by the intervention between the population mean (null) as estimated by the sample and the mean of the intervention group. You might think of effect size as the amount of bang in your intervention, the amount of antibiotic in a pill, the strength of a program to change a person's attitude or a host of other interventions that we undertake. When introducing an intervention, make it strong (powerful) because a small one is not easily detected—you want to make sure that the difference is pronounced.

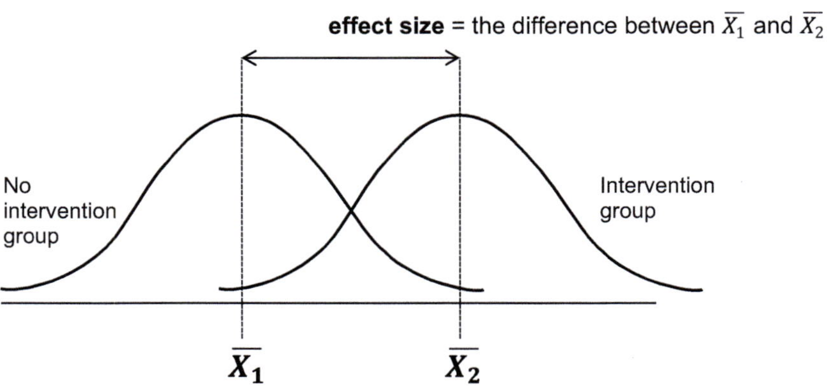
effect size = the difference between $\overline{X_1}$ and $\overline{X_2}$
No intervention group
Intervention group
$\overline{X_1}$
$\overline{X_2}$

Increasing the Significance Level Increases Power

Let's look at an example concerning child abuse. One group contains individuals not abusing a child and the other group those abusing a child. As shown earlier the distributions of groups usually overlap. Some of those who are not abusers appear to look like abusers and those who are abusers appear as non-abusers. We can increase the probability of making a Type I Error (calling it child abuse when it is not child abuse) by changing the significance level. Making the significant level less strict—for example moving it from .05 to .10 increases the power of the statistical test. In effect, you detect more differences but you also make more errors of saying there is a difference when there was no difference (getting more abusers but at the same time getting more non-abusers).

Changing the significance level is very different for a researcher than increasing sample size or reducing variance which are design issues in terms of data gathering. Changing the significance level is about what you are willing to accept in making decisions. The decision rule for setting the significance level can vary from situation to situation. You might be willing in a life or death situation to accept calling it one way or another. At what point are you willing to call it child abuse when there is no child abuse or the opposite, and what about the consequences to the child or to the parent? These are difficult decisions facing researchers in everyday studies. Some are more critical to life than others.

The SL (Significance Level) determines the small shaded area under the H_o curve when the SL is .05; that shaded area under the H_o curve is 1/20 of the total area under the H_o curve.

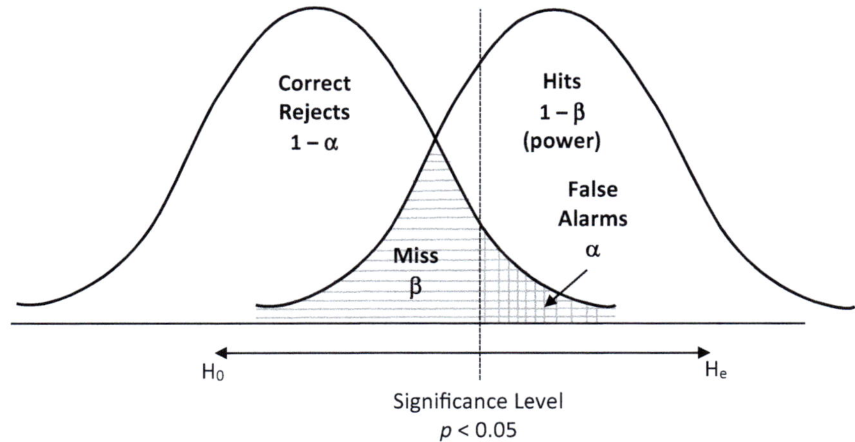

This SL also determines the HIT rate, since the researcher rejects H_e if the difference found is below the SL, when H_e is true in fact. If the researcher changes the SL to .001, moving the cut line to the right, the FALSE ALARM rate goes to .001, but the HIT rate is also reduced. Thus, the SL is one of the important factors affecting the POWER of the experiment. A SL of .05 seems a reasonable compromise for most researchers.

Finally, an example. In the American legal system, a person is presumed innocent, H_o, until proven guilty, H_e. The SL is the "shadow of doubt" which being stringent means the POWER is low to protect the innocent. A standard complaint against the police is that they are increasing the FALSE ALARM rate by getting phony confessions, while the police answer that they must get confessions to maintain a reasonable HIT rate.

DEGREES OF FREEDOM

Degrees of freedom become very important in determining probability when we perform statistical tests. You have already been introduced to probability and how numbers are generated. There are also constraints on what numbers can actually be generated given that you already have some numbers. Let's look at some examples. First, we will start with two dice. If I told you that you already have a total of 7 with a die roll and that one die is a 5, the only way you can get 7 is that the other die is a 2. However, if I told you that the number was a 7 and the other was a 3 then the only way to get a 7 is for the other number to be a 4.

When a number, some of the numbers, totals or averages in a set of numbers are already known, the other numbers may be restricted or constrained to only certain values they can assume; this is called ***degrees of freedom—the ability of numbers in a set of numbers to be able to assume any value and not be constrained to a particular value***. Look at the numbers that are in the tables below—you will see many like this in the statistical analysis chapters.

	Democrats	Republicans	TOTALS
Females		2	12
Males			13
TOTALS	11	14	25

In the table above with a total of 25 people, if I know there are 12 Females and 13 Males and that there are 14 Republicans and 11 Democrats and I identified that 2 Females are Republicans—can you solve how many are Female Democrats, Male Republicans and Male Democrats? In the set of numbers above with the totals identified, there is only one number that is free to move and once that number is identified the other three numbers are restricted and cannot move. In a set of numbers in a table (2 by 2 table) where the marginal totals are known there is ***1 degree of freedom—only one number can move—the rest are not free to move.***

A similar table but with a little more freedom!

	Females	Males	TOTAL
Republicans	2		10
Democrats			10
Independents			10
TOTAL	20	10	30

In this table with six cells and not four cells, and the marginal totals known, are the other cell values restricted? Do you know exactly what the other values are? Is there still freedom for any of the other cells to move and take on a value? Yes, there is. Now look at the next table.

	Females	Males	TOTAL
Republicans	2	8	10
Democrats			10
Independents			10
TOTAL	20	10	30

Still the numbers in the other cells are not restricted. You do not know what the values are for the remaining cells.

Look at the table below.

	Females	Males	TOTAL
Republicans	2	8	10
Democrats			10
Independents		2	10
TOTAL	20	10	30

With three cell values identified, all of the other cells become restricted—you will know the value of the numbers in all of the other remaining cells—10 Male Democrats, 10 Female Democrats and 8 Female Independents! In this case you have ***3 degrees of freedom***—3 can move before there are restrictions on the other numbers in the other cells. The formula for tables like these to determine the degrees of freedom is (R − 1)(C − 1) where R = number of rows and C = number of columns.

What about a distribution of interval numbers—how free they are to move if we already know the average of those numbers? Below is a short list of possible numbers—a total of 7 numbers. **We know the average of those numbers is 4.** The first six numbers have been free to move and their values are shown. Can you figure out the value of X in this set of numbers 4, 2, 5, 5, 4, 3, X? The value of X must be 5 in order to make all seven of the numbers average to 4. Whenever you have an array of numbers with the average of those numbers the degrees of freedom will always be **N − 1**.

Finally, we can look at a situation where we might have three averages and an overall average of those three averages. The degrees of freedom are again easy to determine. The same formula applies for degrees of freedom as for a set of numbers—it is **N − 1**. You have three numbers; two can move but the third is restricted.

Average 1 + Average 2 + Average 3 = TOTAL AVERAGE

If you know the total average, the first average can move freely, the second can move freely BUT the last average must add the right amount to average 1 and average 2 to make them all come together to match the total average.

Discussion Articles

Discuss how the authors dealt with probabilities, statistical significance. Power and effect size in light of the limitations they faced in the design.

Faul, A. C., Yankeelov, P., Rowan, N. L., Gillette, P., Nicholas, L. D., Borders, K. W., Beck, S., . . . Wiegand, M. (2007). Impact of geriatric assessment and self-management support on community dwelling older adults with chronic illness. *Journal of Gerontological Social Work*, *52*, 230–249. doi:10.1080/01634370802609288

Discuss the authors' concern with using parametric testing with non-normal data and their reasoning for not transforming and using nonparametric tests.

Treister, R., Nielsen, C. S., Stubhaug, A., Farrar, J. T., Pud, D., Sawilowsky, S., & Oaklander, A. N. (2015). Experimental comparison of parametric versus nonparametric analyses of data from the cold pressor test. *Journal of Pain*, *16*(6), 537–548. doi.org/10.1016/j.jpain.2015.03.001

Exercises for Chapter 13 arefound in eResources.

Chapter 14

DATA ENTRY AND CLEANING—MAKING SURE THAT THE ANSWERS I OBTAIN ARE COMPLETE AND WITHOUT ERROR

In Chapter 12 we discussed different techniques for gathering data. These data are collected through interviews, questionnaires, scales or other formats—so that they can help us to answer research questions. To answer these questions, we must first analyze the data. We must convert the raw data we have collected into useful information that can help us test a hypothesis, make a decision and reach a conclusion. The following chapters of this textbook will focus on specific techniques or methods that can be used to analyze different types of data. This chapter will focus on the important tasks that have to be done in order to prepare raw data for analysis. These tasks typically include coding, entering, inspecting and cleaning our collected data.

CODING DATA

Virtually all quantitative data analysis now involves the use of computer software such as IBM's SPSS statistical package. Raw data gathered by the researcher during the data collection phase must be formatted in certain ways in order to be readable by a computer program. Sometimes raw data can be directly entered into the electronic data set. If a survey question asked respondents to provide their current age rounded to the nearest half year (for example 36), the ratio level responses could be directly entered as they appear on the measurement instrument. Suppose, however, that the survey question asked respondents to identify their political affiliation as Republican, Democrat, Independent, or other. The responses to this item cannot be directly transferred to the electronic data set, are not as readily transferable. ***Coding*** is the term to describe the process the researcher uses to convert raw data into a standardized format for computer analysis.

For example, a basic *coding scheme* for the example survey question above might be:

1 = Republican
2 = Democrat
3 = Independent
4 = Other

Thus, whenever there is the response "Republican" to the question, a "1" is entered into the electronic data set for that person's response. Similarly, should the response be "Democrat", a "2" would be entered, and so forth. Note that this is a nominal level (or, categorical) variable and the numerical values for the coding scheme do not matter. The researcher could have just as easily adopted the following coding scheme:

4 = Republican
3 = Democrat
2 = Independent
1 = Other

Often, surveys and questionnaire items are designed to align with a predetermined coding scheme. You can probably think of many such examples:

Gender:

1 = Female
2 = Male

Race/Ethnicity:

1 = White
2 = Hispanic or Latino
3 = Black or African American
4 = Native American or American Indian

5 = Asian
6 = Pacific Islander
7 = Other

For closed-ended questions such as these, the researcher has selected or knows the coding scheme before administering the instrument to respondents. Data collection methods that allow for open-ended responses can be more challenging to code. In these cases, the researcher must examine responses before finalizing a coding scheme. For example, suppose you administered a survey to recent BSW graduates asking, "What is the most important personal characteristic for a social worker?" Because respondents were free to answer this question in any way they chose, a coding scheme cannot be developed until the responses have been reviewed. The following table depicts the raw data that you might have obtained:

Response	Frequency
"empathy"	22
"patience"	14
"openness"	9
"compassion"	9
"caring"	4
"flexible"	4
"dependable"	3
"trustworthy"	2
"knowledgeable"	1
"has expertise"	1
"adaptable"	1
"motivated"	1
"perceptive"	1
"organized"	1
"good listener"	1
"paycheck"	1

Now at first glance, we might decide to give each of these 16 responses a different code. However, there are a few problems with this approach. First, some of the responses are quite similar to one another (e.g., "empathy" and "compassion"). Second, a categorical variable with 16 unique levels may be more than we want to try to use in the analysis and not fit our research design and methodology. Finally, one of the responses (i.e., "paycheck") suggests that the respondent may have misunderstood the question and is one that we would not use in the analysis. We might address these problems by developing the following coding scheme:

1 = empathy, compassion or caring
2 = patience
3 = openness
4 = dependable or trustworthy
5 = flexible or adaptable
6 = other

While this scheme is certainly not the only possible approach given our raw data, it demonstrates how a researcher may condense diverse responses to an open-ended item into a more manageable number of categories. Note that the categories in this coding scheme have two very important characteristics: (1) they are ***mutually exclusive*** and (2) they are ***exhaustive. That is to say, every participant response must be able to be coded using one and only one code.*** (See Chapter 9.)

A researcher's data set may contain a large number of variables, and each variable can have its own coding scheme. ***Codebooks are used to organize and document the different coding schemes among all the variables included in a study. The initial codebook should be developed prior to data entry.***

ENTERING DATA

Data entry refers to the **process of entering the coded data** into a digital data set that can be read and analyzed by statistical software or other computer programs. While this process may not seem as exciting as data collection or data analysis, it is a vital step in the research process and one that requires ***careful attention***. Excessive errors in data entry make data inspection and cleaning tasks (discussed below) more complex and those that go undetected may impact the results of the analysis.

To briefly review, data sets consist of ***cells***, each of which contains a value. Cells are organized into ***rows*** **and** ***columns***. **Each row represents one case—the unit being studied.** ***In social work research, cases are often individuals but they could also be organizations, neighborhoods, schools, etc.*** In the picture below, the blue box represents one case. Each column represents one variable. The red box represents the variable *Age*. ***The cell where the row and column intersect contains the value for this case on this variable.*** So, we can see that the research subject with an ID number of 1004 is 20 years old.

	ID	Age	Race	Sex
1	1000	22	1	1
2	1001	23	1	1
3	1002	19	1	1
4	1003	22	2	1
5	1004	20	1	1
6	1005	22	2	2
7	1006	21	1	1
8	1007	23	2	1
9	1008	20	3	2
10	1009	19	1	1

In addition to this standard data set format, SPSS offers another "view" that may be useful during the data entry process. By clicking on the ***Variable View*** button at the bottom of the data set window, SPSS organizes the data in a variable-focused manner that allows the researcher to name and describe the variables included in the data set.

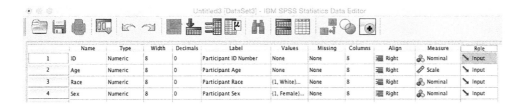

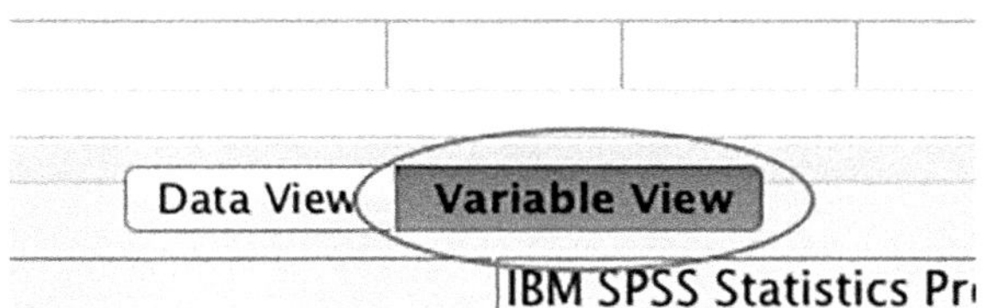

Untitled3 [DataSet3] - IBM SPSS Statistics Data Editor

	Name	Type	Width	Decimals	Label	Values	Missing	Columns	Align	Measure	Role
1	ID	Numeric	8	0	Participant ID Number	None	None	8	Right	Nominal	Input
2	Age	Numeric	8	0	Participant Age	None	None	8	Right	Scale	Input
3	Race	Numeric	8	0	Participant Race	{1, White}...	None	8	Right	Nominal	Input
4	Sex	Numeric	8	0	Participant Sex	{1, Female}...	None	8	Right	Nominal	Input

In the ***Variable View*** screen, ***each variable is a unique row while each column represents a different attribute for the variables in the data set***:

Name	Variables are named in this column. Each variable must have a unique name.
Type	This specifies the type of data entered for each variable. The default setting is numeric but also includes options such as currency, date or string.
Width	Specifies the column width for the display of variables.
Decimals	Specifies the number of decimal places displayed in cell values.
Label	Allows for the entry of a descriptive variable label. This is particularly helpful when variable names are unclear or non-descriptive.
Values	Allows for the assignment of descriptive value labels for each possible value of a variable. This allows for the entry of the codebook into the SPSS program. An example of this option is provided below.
Missing	Specifies particular values as missing. For example, 99 might be defined as a code for missing data.
Columns	Specifies the column width.
Align	Specifies how data will be aligned in the data set display.
Measure	Defines a variable as Nominal, Ordinal or Scale. SPSS treats interval and ratio level variables as Scale measurements.
Role	Specifies the role of a variable.

The following image shows how the ***Value Labels*** function can be used to assign descriptive labels to specific variable values. Because these descriptive labels are printed in the analysis output, interpretation does not require constant reference to an external codebook.

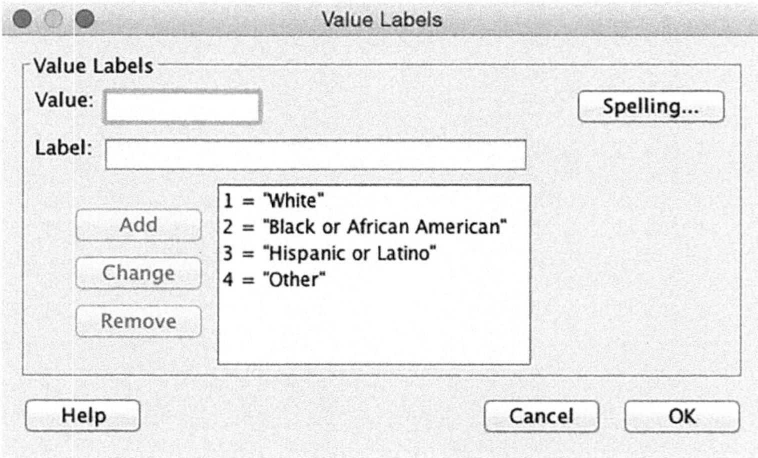

By naming and defining the variables at the outset of the data entry process, you can reduce the likelihood of confusing one variable for another or entering data in an incorrect format.

INSPECTING AND CLEANING DATA

It is hard to overemphasize the importance of thoroughly inspecting and cleaning your data before conducting any analysis. Data entry errors or other problems that are not identified and addressed in the data cleaning stage may skew results and lead to faulty conclusions. ***Plan on devoting plenty of time*** to thoroughly reviewing your data once it has been entered into the computer software. Frequently, the cleaning and inspection process takes much longer than the final analysis itself.

While the exact inspection and cleaning process may differ slightly depending on the nature of the collected data and the methods used to analyze it, almost all quantitative data cleaning approaches will need to examine three basic areas: (1) errors in data entry, (2) missing data and (3) characteristics of the data.

ERRORS IN DATA ENTRY

The best way to check for errors in data entry is to compare the electronic data set directly to the raw data. While this approach is recommended whenever possible, it becomes increasingly difficult as the number of cases and variables increase. As data sets become too complex for direct comparison, other strategies may be used in order to identify potential data entry problems.

The first step should include a careful examination of frequency tables and descriptive statistics (see Chapter 13). As you review the descriptive statistic output tables, consider such questions as:

- Do all values for a given variable fall within the expected range?
- Upon initial review, do means and standard deviations appear plausible?
- Are there any univariate outliers that might suggest a problem?

Let's look at an example of a very simple SPSS data set to illustrate how these situations might happen in research situations. Imagine that you are studying perceived happiness among residents of a retirement community. You have entered your raw data into an electronic data set consisting of four variables: (1) resident's age, (2) self-rated happiness (rated from 1 to 5), (3) number of activities the resident participated in over the last month, (4) number of unique visitors over the last month. There is a total of 14 cases. (In reality, a data set of this size would be easy to compare directly against the raw data but we will proceed as though it were too large to do so.)

Open the data set ***Ch14 DataInspection***

(1) Click ***Analyze***.
(2) Select ***Descriptive Statistics***.
(3) Select ***Frequencies***.
(4) Move all four variables into the ***Variable(s)*** box.
(5) Click on the ***Statistics . . .*** button.
(6) For this example, we will request ***Mean***, ***Median***, and ***Mode*** from the ***Central Tendency*** box and ***Std. deviation***, ***Range***, ***Minimum*** and ***Maximum*** from the ***Dispersion*** box.

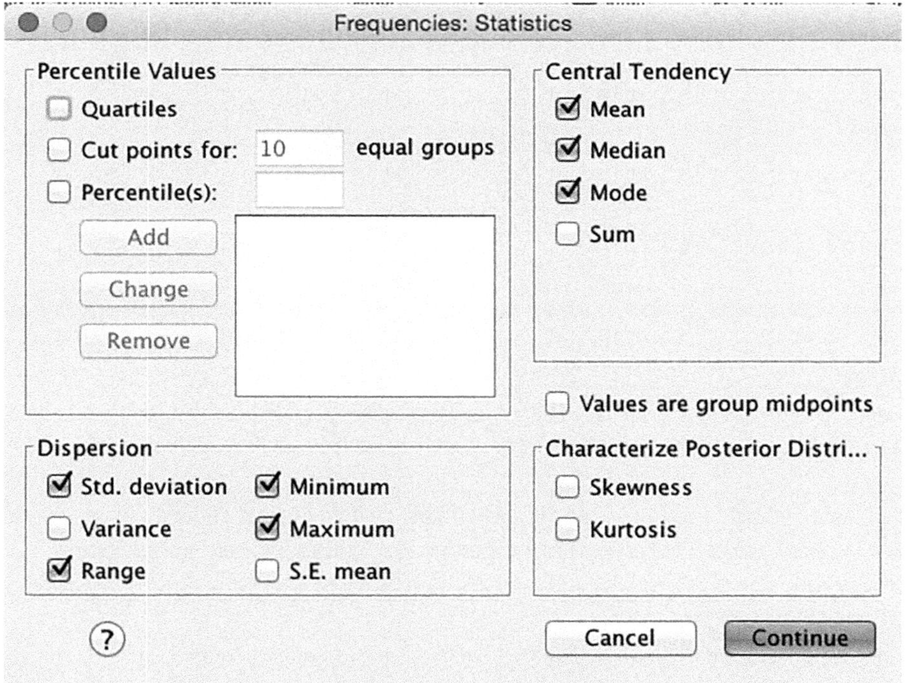

(7) Click ***Continue***.
(8) Click ***OK***.

We will first look at the descriptive statistics for the variable ***Age***:

Statistics

Resident's Age		
N	Valid	14
	Missing	0
Mean		78.07
Median		77.50
Mode		77
Std. Deviation		6.082
Range		21
Minimum		67
Maximum		88

We can see that the ages of residents in our sample range from 67 to 88 with a mean age of 78.07 and a standard deviation of 6.082. Since we are looking at residents of a retirement community the age range of 67–88 is plausible and does not raise any concerns regarding data entry.

We will next examine the ***Self-Rated Happiness*** variable. As this is an ***ordinal level measure, the frequency table may be more helpful to review than descriptive statistics table***:

Self-Rated Happiness

		Frequency	Percent	Valid Percent	Cumulative Percent
Valid	0	1	7.1	7.1	7.1
	Very unhappy	2	14.3	14.3	21.4
	Unhappy	3	21.4	21.4	42.9
	Neither happy nor unhappy	3	21.4	21.4	64.3
	Happy	4	28.6	28.6	92.9
	Very happy	1	7.1	7.1	100.0
	Total	14	100.0	100.0	

Upon careful review, we note a problem here. ***One case has a value of 0 entered for this variable. However, zero falls outside of the possible ranges for this variable as***

the ratings only range from 1 (very unhappy) to 5 (very happy). This is a clear sign that there has been a data entry error and we will need to compare the electronic data set against the raw data. Perhaps this was a missing value that was inadvertently input as a zero value. We need to correct this mistake and put in the proper code value.

Next, we will look at the ***Activities*** variable:

Statistics

Number of activities last month		
N	Valid	14
	Missing	0
Mean		6.71
Median		4.00
Mode		4
Std. Deviation		13.958
Range		55
Minimum		0
Maximum		55

Depending on the number of activities offered each month in this facility, the mean number of activities (6.71) may not appear suspect. However, note the relatively large standard deviation (13.958). This, coupled with a range of 55, is "strange" and we need to take an additional look at the data. The frequency table might help clarify if there is a problem:

Number of Activities Last Month

		Frequency	Percent	Valid Percent	Cumulative Percent
Valid	0	1	7.1	7.1	7.1
	1	1	7.1	7.1	14.3
	2	2	14.3	14.3	28.6
	3	2	14.3	14.3	42.9
	4	7	50.0	50.0	92.9
	55	1	7.1	7.1	100.0
	Total	14	100.0	100.0	

In the table, you can see that all residents participated in 0 to 4 activities last month with the exception of one person, who appears to have participated in 55. This is clearly an error and we will need to refer back to our raw data to determine the correct value. It is likely that this was meant to be entered as a 5 but was accidentally double-keyed.

Finally, we will examine the ***Visitors*** variable:

Statistics

Number of Visitors Last Month		
N	Valid	14
	Missing	0
Mean		2.57
Median		2.00
Mode		2[a]
Std. Deviation		2.138
Range		9
Minimum		0
Maximum		9

Number of Visitors Last Month

		Frequency	Percent	Valid Percent	Cumulative Percent
Valid	0	1	7.1	7.1	7.1
	1	3	21.4	21.4	28.6
	2	4	28.6	28.6	57.1
	3	4	28.6	28.6	85.7
	4	1	7.1	7.1	92.9
	9	1	7.1	7.1	100.0
	Total	14	100.0	100.0	

Once again there is an outlier. One case had 9 visitors last month—well above the mean of 2.57 visitors and 5 greater than the next highest value. However, unlike the previous example, this is not necessarily a data entry error. Despite being well above the average, it is entirely plausible that a resident might have had 9 visitors in the span of one month. Nevertheless, it would be prudent to refer back to the raw data just to confirm that this outlying value was entered correctly.

MISSING DATA

During the data inspection and cleaning process, the researcher must also consider the problem of missing data. ***Missing data occur when one or more cases have no recorded value for a given variable.***

There are a number of reasons that we may have missing values in our raw data. In the social sciences, perhaps the most common reason for missing data is nonresponse—when the person did not provide an answer to an item on a survey or questionnaire. This may be because the question was considered to be too private to answer or because the respondent is concerned that the answer would be socially undesirable. For example, some participants may hesitate to provide information related to yearly income or sexual history. Poorly designed survey items may be another cause of missing information. If a question is worded in such a way that the subject has difficulty in understanding the question, then they are more likely to skip over it. Researchers conducting longitudinal research often encounter missing data due to attrition. As the study progresses, some participants may die, move away or lose contact with the researcher thus resulting in a substantial amount of missing data in follow-up measures. Missing data may also result due to errors on the part of the researcher. For example, a portion of a measurement instrument may not have been given to a participant during data collection.

The first question that must be considered regarding missing data is whether it is *missing at random* or *missing not at random*. (Methodologists actually distinguish between *missing completely at random* and *missing at random* but this is beyond the scope of our introductory discussion here.)

Data are said to be missing at random if there is no relationship between the probability of missing data for a particular variable and the value of the variable itself or other variables.

Conversely, data that are missing not at random do indicate a relationship between the missing values and the unobserved values of the variable.

These concepts may be made a bit clearer if we think of some examples of how missing data may occur. Imagine a researcher has printed 200 questionnaires for research participants to complete and return. During data entry, the researcher finds that there was a printing error and the last page of about 5% of the questionnaires was left blank thus omitting the final question. Since there was no particular order in which the questionnaires were distributed to participants, it is likely that these missing values would be missing at random (we would still want to investigate) since the variables themselves were not related to the likelihood of missing.

Now imagine another situation in which a researcher has asked a question about the frequency of recreational drug use. It is observed that this question has a lower response rate than other items on the questionnaire. Perhaps people who frequently use recreational drugs were less likely to answer the question than those who never or seldom do so. Or, the researcher may notice that missing values on this question were more probable for people who reported an older age. Perhaps younger people were more willing to disclose information about drug use than older individuals. In either of these cases, the data would be missing not at random since there were systematic differences between those who answered and those who did not answer.

If data are missing not at random, the researcher must seek to account for the mechanism by which they are missing—it cannot be ignored. These techniques typically involve complex mathematical modeling procedures in order to establish parameter estimates for the missing values. By contrast, when data are missing at random, the missing data mechanism is considered *ignorable* and the researcher's options are more straightforward.

The most conventional responses for ***data that are missing at random include deletion and*** **imputation. Deletion entails the exclusion of missing data** from the analysis. **In *listwise deletion* (also known as *casewise deletion*) an entire case (all of the person's answers) is removed from the analysis if it has missing values for any of the variables in the analysis.** It is important to recognize that listwise deletion **may substantially reduce the sample size.**

Pairwise deletion attempts to remedy the problem that listwise deletion may cause, ***by excluding cases only for analyses involving the particular variables for which data are missing and including them in all other analyses***.

Imputation describes a series of techniques that are used to replace missing values with an estimate (or informed guess) before conducting the analysis. There are many different approaches to imputation ranging from relatively simple to highly complex. The most basic imputation method is *mean imputation*. Mean imputation involves the substitution of missing values with the mean of the observed variables for a given variable. Consider the following data set regarding income for households within a particular neighborhood:

HOUSEHOLD ID#	ANNUAL INCOME
1001	$27,000
1002	$32,500
1003	$21,500
1004	$33,000
1005	$24,000
1006	$23,000
1007	***Missing***
1008	$25,500
1009	$27,000

As you can see, we have no information regarding household 1007's annual income. However, given the small sample size, the researcher may be hesitant to exclude this household from the analysis. By calculating the mean of the other values for this variable and replacing the missing value with this value, the researcher can retain this case in other analyses involving income. Thus, the data set with the newly imputed value would look like:

HOUSEHOLD ID#	ANNUAL INCOME
1001	27,000
1002	32,500
1003	21,500
1004	33,000
1005	24,000
1006	23,000
1007	***26,688***
1008	25,500
1009	27,000

An advantage of this approach is that the sample size has not been reduced. However, mean imputation reduces the variability of the data leading to problems such as underestimates of the standard deviation. Mean imputation may also change the relationship among two or more variables (which is often a focus of the research) and thus must be used with caution.

Regression imputation is another basic imputation method. This method substitutes missing data on one variable with a predicted value based on other variables. Like mean imputation, regression imputation can also lead to statistical problems that may bias results. You will learn more about regression in Chapter 21.

The techniques discussed above are only the most basic and conventional approaches for handling missing data; statistical software packages often include methods for more advanced imputation techniques. There is no consensus regarding the most appropriate or effective approaches for dealing with missing data. How to approach missing data is one of the many challenging questions a researcher must grapple with when conducting a study.

CHARACTERISTICS OF THE DATA

Having inspected potential data entry errors and addressed the problem of missing data, it is time to look more closely at the characteristics of our data. This will often include the identification of univariate or multivariate outliers and an assessment of normality. Other characteristics may be explored based on the type of analysis we anticipate conducting. For example, if we plan on conducting an Analysis of Variance (ANOVA), we may investigate multicollinearity in our data or test for homogeneity of variance (see Chapters 16 and 18).

Regardless of the type of analysis to be conducted, we will almost always be interested in identifying outliers. Recall that ***outliers are extreme values***. A shown in Chapter 13, outliers may have a big effect on the analysis resulting in faulty interpretation. Once we have determined that an outlier is not due to a problem with data entry (as discussed above), we must decide whether to: (1) retain the outlier, (2) modify the outlier or (3) delete the outlier.

If the outlier is retained in the analysis, we must remember the extreme impact it may have on the results and the interpretation of the findings. Often, outlying cases may be of great interest to the researcher for additional exploration. For example, individuals who score exceptionally high or low on a psychometric scale may offer valuable insight into the phenomenon being measured by the instrument.

At times, we may want to keep the outlying case but reduce its effect on our analysis. *Value alteration* is the process of changing an outlying value to make it less extreme. One value alteration method entails changing the extreme value to a value one unit greater than the next highest value on that particular variable. For example, imagine we are conducting a study about self-harming behaviors among traumatized adolescent Females. We have asked the participants to report the number of times that they have engaged in deliberate self-harming behavior in the past seven days. We note that one participant (#7) reported more than three times as many self-harming episodes as any other participant. We do not want to exclude this case from our analysis but also recognize the substantial degree to which this outlier may skew our findings. As such, we opt to alter the score from 27 to 8 (one unit higher than the next most extreme value).

Participant	Self-Harming Episodes	
	Original Values	Altered Values
1	4	4
2	4	4
3	5	5
4	7	7
5	2	2
6	3	3
7	*27*	*8*
8	6	6
9	4	4
10	1	1

Sometimes, an outlier may indicate that the ***case (respondent) is not a member of the population we intended to sample (for example we are sampling social workers and a teacher was given the questionnaire)***. In such instances, deletion of the case will not impact our ability to state that the findings from the sample reflect accurately the population. Likewise, we may opt to delete an entire variable with problematic outliers if it is not central to our analysis or is highly correlated with other variables.

Regardless of how we manage outliers, it is **important to thoroughly document our approach**. ***In reporting the findings, you must describe the precise method(s) you used to deal with the outliers and offer an informed and clear rationale for those decisions.***

Recall that ***normal distributions*** are bell-shaped, unimodal and symmetrical with a mean, median and mode that are approximately equal. As demonstrated in Chapter 13, normality can be assessed graphically (e.g., histogram) or statistically (e.g., skewness and kurtosis). Normality is an assumption of parametric analyses and thus we will typically want to investigate the nature of our data's distribution during the data cleaning process.

In some cases of non-normality, a research may decide to *transform* the raw data. Transformation describes a series of mathematical processes that may be undertaken to change the shape of a variable's distribution. For example, if a variable is positively skewed, a square root transformation may result in a more normal distribution. While mathematically sound, the process of transformation can greatly complicate the interpretation of results and we will not go into that detail in this book.

Section 2

FINDING DIFFERENCES

Chapter 15

FINDING DIFFERENCES
Sample to Population Tests (One Sample Tests)

PART A: NONPARAMETRIC

Nominal Level Data

Chi-Square Goodness of Fit Test (SPSS Example)

See Chart—Sample to Population and Nominal Measurement

The Chi-Square Goodness of Fit test is used to test (1) if the sample is a good representation of the population—if the sample basically matches the population on a given variable or (2) if a hypothesized difference exists between the sample and the population. In the first case you hope the outcome will be that the sample is not different from the population and in the second case that the sample is different from the population. The test is calculated exactly the same in either case. The test compares the observed values (the data you collect) to the values you would expect to get from the population you took the sample from.

These questions are often posed and answered before any other analysis of data. This is done to ensure that the sample you have drawn is "truly" representative of the population.

Let's look at an example. Assume that you are working for a neighborhood center (Broadway Avenue Center) and have developed a very successful program that you would like to replicate in other centers in your section of the city. You recognize that the racial mix of a center might have an impact on the success of the program. You are concerned that the other centers in the city may have a different racial mix than your center. You want to find out if the racial mix in your center is basically the same as the other centers in the city. The monthly average per month for the other centers in the city is: Caucasians = 80%, African Americans = 15% and Other = 5%. You have collected data for the past six months and found that you have the following monthly average: Caucasians = 45%, African Americans = 47% and Other = 8%. You want to compare your center to all the other centers in your part of the city to see if they have the same racial mix of clients as your center. You can see that your center is a part of all the centers in the city; therefore, you are comparing your sample (center) to the population (all centers). You would like your center to have the same mix as all of the other centers in your city, then you think that the program would have a better chance of success if replicated in the other centers.

CHI-SQUARE GOODNESS OF FIT TEST—CONCEPTUAL FRAME

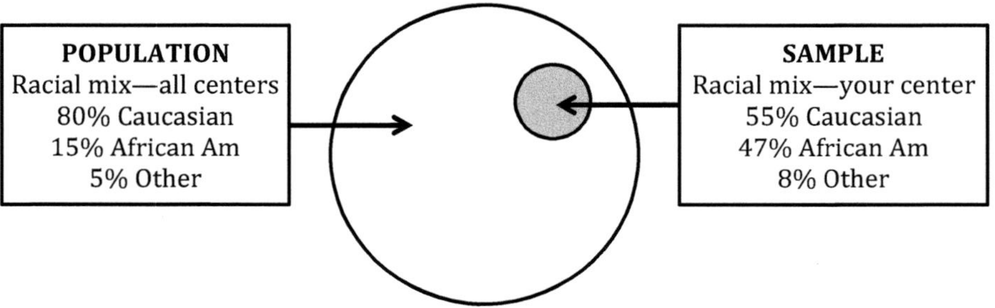

Study Question: Is there a difference between the racial composition of participants in the Broadway Avenue Center and the racial composition of other centers in the city?

This is a difference, cross-sectional design.

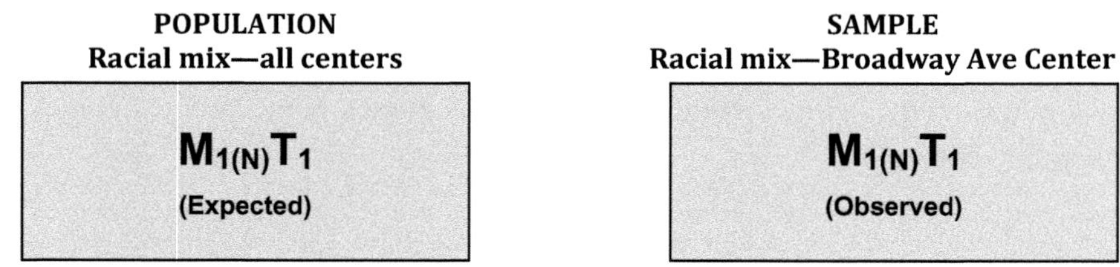

Hypotheses:

Difference: There is a difference between the racial composition of participants in the Broadway Avenue Center and other neighborhood centers in the city.

Null: There is no difference between the racial composition of participants in the Broadway Avenue Center and other neighborhood centers in the city. ***You hope to support the Null!***

Expected (E): The percentage of the races in the Broadway Avenue Center will be the same as the other neighborhood centers in the city.

Predicted (P): The percentage of the races in the Broadway Avenue Center will be the same as the other neighborhood centers in the city.

Observed (O): The actual racial percentage in the Broadway Avenue Center and the racial percentage in the other neighborhood centers in the city.

Level of Measurement: Nominal

Type of Design: Difference, cross-sectional

Number of Groups: 1 Group (sample)

Assumptions: (a) No more than 20% of the expected frequencies less than 5,
(b) No single expected frequency is less than 1

VARIABLE BOX—ONE GROUP (SAMPLE)

		SOURCE	
		Sample (A1)	***Population*** (A2)
RACE	***Caucasian*** (B1)	A1 B1	A2 B1
	African American (B2)	A1 B2	A2 B2
	Other (B3)	A1 B3	A2 B3

SPSS Commands

Open the data set ***Ch15 ChiSquare GoF 1***.
Follow the steps below:

(1) Click ***Analyze***.
(2) Scroll down and select ***Nonparametric Tests***.
(3) Select ***Legacy Dialogs***; Select ***Chi-square . . .***

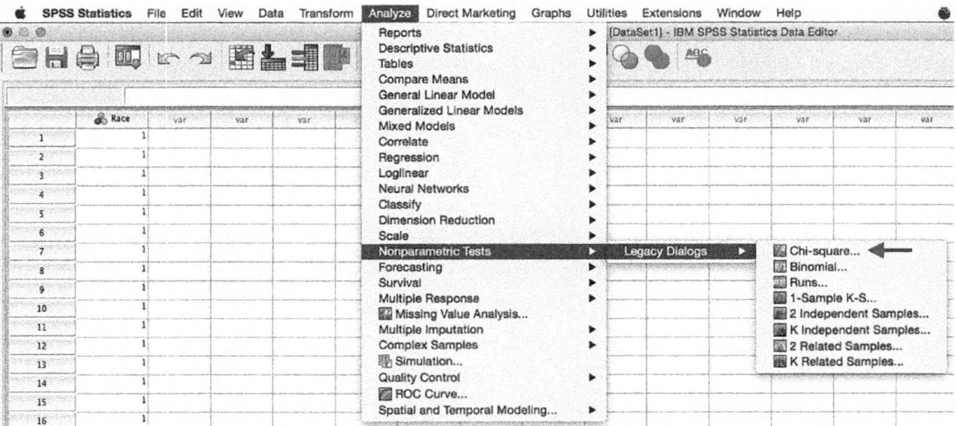

(4) Move the ***Race*** variable into the ***Test Variable List*** *box*.
(5) In the ***Expected Values*** box, enter .80 in the ***Value*** field (population value for Caucasian); click the ***Add*** button.
(6) Then enter .15 for African Americans (population value) and click the ***Add*** button.
(7) Then enter .05 for Other (population value) and click the ***Add*** button.

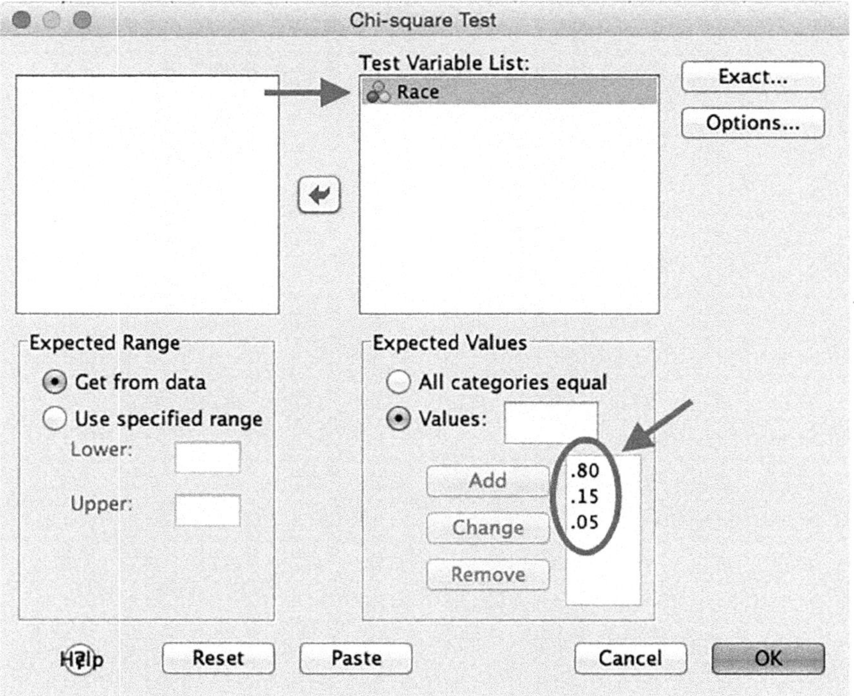

(8) Click ***OK*** to run.

Now look at the results. What do you see?

Race

	Observed N	Expected N	Residual
Caucasian	45	80.0	–35.0
African American	47	15.0	32.0
Other	8	5.0	3.0
Total	100		

Test Statistics

	Race
Chi-Square	85.379[a]
Df	2
Asymp. Sig.	.000

a. 0 cells (0.0%) have expected frequencies less than 5. The minimum expected cell frequency is 5.0.

What do you see in the results? **First, note that all of the assumptions of the test have been met (at least 5 expected in each cell and none with only 1).** Next look at the output (Race) box. The data from the neighborhood center is shown in the ***observed*** cells (Caucasian = 45, African American = 47, Other = 8). Next to them are the ***expected values*** you entered from the data of all the other centers (population) (Caucasian = .8, African American = .15 and Other = .5). The residuals shown on the right indicate the amount of difference between what was expected and what was observed if the racial composition of those attending your Center were the same as all the other centers. In the Test Statistics Box are the statistical results of the test. ***The first number shown (Chi-Square) is the value on the Chi-Square distribution that indicates the probability of the amount of difference between the data from your center and data from all the other centers occurring.*** It is a very large number so there appears to be a very big difference between your center and the other centers (population). The **df** refers to the degrees of freedom discussed in Chapter 14. Finally, you see the significance value—the probability of obtaining this amount of difference in the racial mix between those attending your center and the racial mix of those attending all the other centers in the city occurring by chance alone is .000 or less than 1 in 1,000. **When you obtain results of .000 on the computer print out, the convention is to report it as .001.**

Results might be written as follows:

A study was conducted at the Broadway Avenue Neighborhood Center over a period of 6 months to determine if the racial composition of the attendees was the same as the racial composition of all the other centers in the city.

Racial Composition of Broadway Avenue Neighborhood Center

Race	Observed	Expected
Caucasian	**45**	**80**
African American	**47**	**15**
Other	**8**	**5**
$X^2_{(2)} = 83.379; p < 0.001$		

The racial composition of the other community centers was Caucasian 80%, African American 15% and Other 5%. The racial composition of the Broadway Avenue Center was Caucasian 45%, African American 47% and Other 8%. There is a significant difference ($X^2_{(2)} = 83.379$, $p = .001$) between the racial composition at the Broadway Avenue Center and the other centers in the city with a much greater percent of African Americans attending the Broadway Avenue Center than Caucasians.

Practical Implications: There is a large difference between your center and the others in the city with respect to racial differences in those attending. Before replicating your programs in other centers, you might want to have a small pilot implementation at one other center that has a different racial ratio than yours to see how the program is accepted and attended before a city wide "roll out". You might want ask the participants in your program what they thought about it and see if there are differences in attitude according to race. Are there some other centers within the city that are similar to yours in racial participation? If so, then these might be good places to initiate replication first.

Let's turn to another example that looks at the proportion of Females elected in your county compared to the state. You noticed the proportion of elected Females in your county (Jefferson) was different from the state and you wanted to find out if this was a "big" difference. ***(Use of the test to support a hypothesis of a difference between a sample and a population.)*** You obtained the list of elected officials in your state in order to determine the proportion of Females. You formulated the following question, "Is there a difference in the proportion of Females elected in Jefferson County compared to the rest of the state?" From the question, you then developed the following hypothesis, "There is a difference between the proportion of Female elected officials in my county compared to the rest of the state". In this example, you were comparing one sample (Jefferson County) to the state (population). We will use the same test to answer the question but we have a different question and hypothesis we want to either support or reject.

CHI-SQUARE GOODNESS OF FIT TEST—CONCEPTUAL FRAME

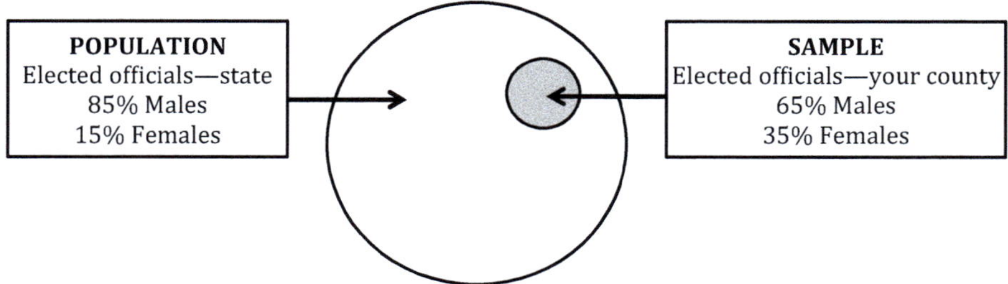

Study Question: Is there a difference between the proportion of Females elected in the county and the proportion elected in the state?

This is a difference, cross-sectional design.

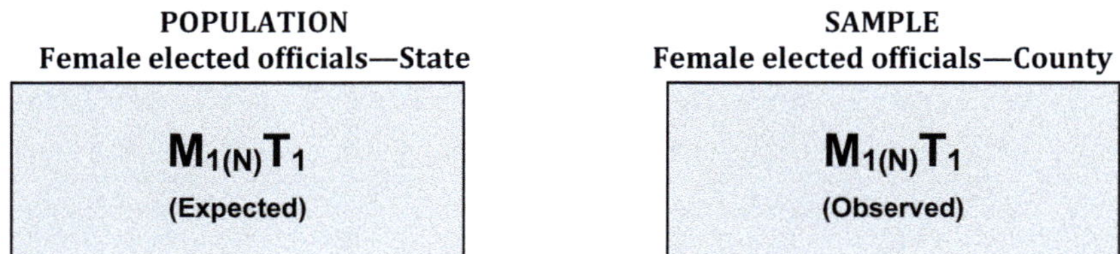

Hypotheses:

Difference: There is a difference between the proportions of Females elected in the county and the proportion elected in the state? ***You hope to support the Difference Hypothesis!***

Null: There is not a difference between the proportions of elected women in the county from the proportion elected in the state.

Expected (E): There will be no difference between the proportion of elected women in the county and the proportion of women elected in the state.

Predicted (P): There will be a difference between the proportion of elected women in the county and the proportion of elected women in the state.

Observed (O): The actual proportion of elected women in the county and the proportion of elected women in the state.

Level of Measurement: Nominal

Type of Design: Difference, cross-sectional

Number of Groups: 1 Group (sample)

Assumptions: (a) No more than 20% of the expected frequencies less than 5, (b) No single expected frequency less than 1

VARIABLE BOX—ONE GROUP (SAMPLE)

SOURCE—ELECTED OFFICIALS

		Sample (County) (A1)	***Population (State)*** (A2)
GENDER	***Females*** (B1)	A1 B1	A2 B1
	Males (B2)	A1 B2	A2 B2

SPSS Commands

Open the data set ***Ch15 ChiSquare GoF 2***.
Follow the steps below.

(1) Click ***Analyze.***

(2) Scroll down and select ***Nonparametric Tests.***

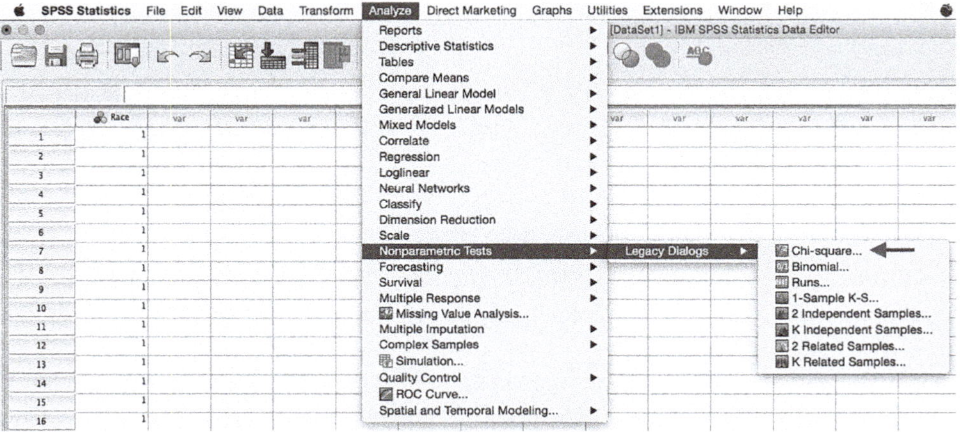

(3) Select ***Legacy Dialogs***; Select ***Chi-square . . .***

(4) Move the ***Gender*** variable into the ***Test Variable List*** box.
(5) In the ***Expected Values*** box, enter .85 in the ***Value*** field (population value for Males); click the ***Add*** button.
(6) Then enter .15 for (population value for Females) and click the ***Add*** button.

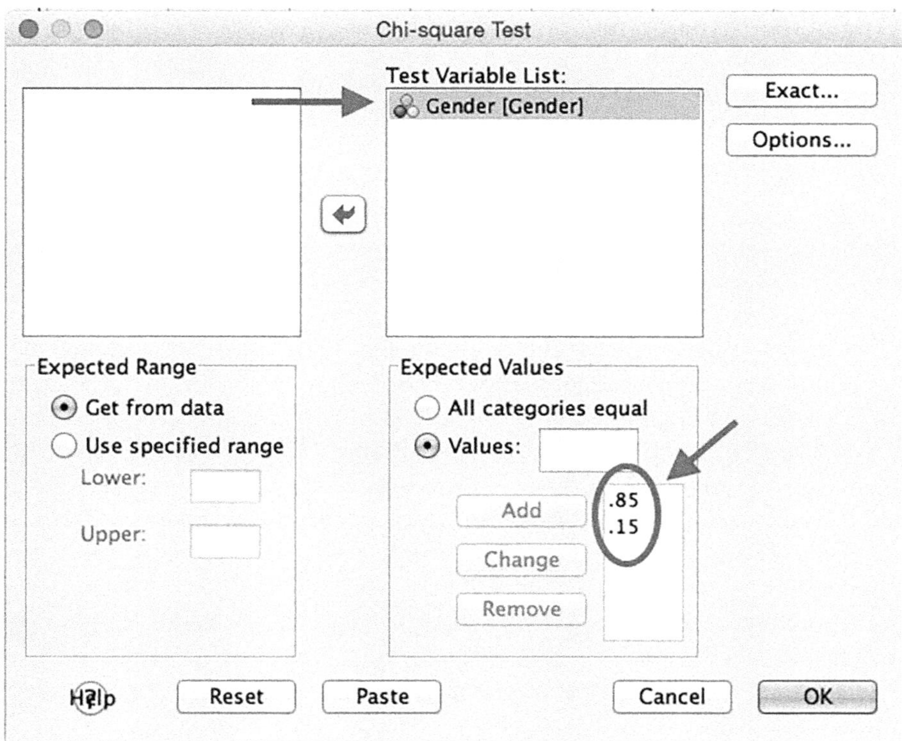

(7) Click ***OK*** to run.

*****You must always enter the variables in the order they are in the data or the results will be incorrect. In this example start with Males then Females.***

Gender

	Observed N	Expected N	Residual
Male	65	85.0	–20.0
Female	35	15.0	20.0
Total	100		

Test Statistics

	Gender
Chi-Square	31.373[a]
Df	1
Asymp. Sig.	.000

a. 0 cells (0.0%) have expected frequencies less than 5. The minimum expected cell frequency is 15.0.

Look at the table and Observed and Expected frequencies. The observed is the proportion in your county (sample) and the expected is the proportion for the total state (population). The residuals are the differences between what is expected and the observed and are typically referred to as the error of difference. The other table provides the value of the Chi-Square statistic and the level of significance and provides the data to answer the question "Is there a significant difference between the sample proportion and the population proportion?" The Chi-Square value shows where the value is on the Chi-Square distribution and the df (degrees of freedom) indicated how much freedom of movement the data points have (Chapter 13). The significance value reflects the amount of difference there is between what the expected amount would be (the proportion from the rest of the state) and observed amount (Jefferson County) and the probability you would observe this much difference by chance alone if there was no "real" difference. You can see that there is a 1 in 1000 probability that you would get this much difference simply by chance. **The note (a.) below the Test Statistic Box indicates that all of the assumptions of the test have been met (no cells having expected values of less than 5 and no single expected frequency less than 1).**

Results might be written as follows:

A Chi-Square Goodness of Fit test was run to test if there was a difference between the proportion of Female elected officials in Jefferson County and the proportion elected in the state.

Proportion of Female Elected Officials in Jefferson County

Race	Observed	Expected
Males	**65**	**85**
Females	**35**	**15**
$X^2_{(1)} = 31.373; p < 0.001$		

The results indicate that the percent (.35) of Female elected officials in Jefferson County was significantly higher than the percent (.15) of Female elected officials in the state ($X^2_{(1)} = 31.37; p = .01$).

Practical Implications: Given women's positions on various social issues, what might the reception be in Jefferson County compared to the state? You may want to find out if there is a difference in response to social issues in the county vs. the state? What might be the reasons for more elected women in the county compared to the state? Is there something different in the voter composition in the county vs. the state? Is there a difference between elected women in the county and the state on their positions and support for policies?

Chi-Square Goodness of Fit Test (Microsoft Excel Example)

See Chart—Sample to Population and Nominal Measurement

A Chi-Square Goodness of Fit test can also be run using Microsoft Excel. To do so, we will need to use the Chi-Square formula. This formula will be discussed in greater detail in subsequent chapters. In this section we will complete the Broadway Avenue Center example using only Microsoft Excel.

(1) Open Excel workbook ***Chapter15*. Click on worksheet *ChiSquare*.**

(2) Using our given data, we will first create a table depicting our observed and expected percentages for each racial group:

	A	B	C	D	E
2		**Goodness of Fit**			
3					
4		Race	Caucasian	African-American	Other
5		Observed %	45	47	8
6		Expected %	80	15	5

(3) Next, we will add a row using the following formula:

$$\frac{(observed - expected)^2}{expected}$$

For instance, for the Caucasian group, we will calculate:

$$\frac{(45-80)^2}{80} = \frac{-35^2}{80} = 15.3125$$

Having completed this step for each group, we will sum each of these values to determine a total value:

This total value—85.38 in this case—is our Chi-Square test statistic.

	A	B	C	D	E	F
4		Race	Caucasian	African-American	Other	
5		Observed %	45	47	8	
6		Expected %	80	15	5	Total:
7		(O - E)^2 / E	15.31	68.27	1.80	85.38
8						

(4) Having obtained the Chi-Square value ($\chi^2 = 85.38$), our final step entails determining the statistical significance of this value. To do this, we would refer to a table of Chi-Square critical values (www.nist.gov). We find that this Chi-Square value is significant at $p < 0.001$.

Ordinal Level Data

Kolmogorov-Smirnov (KS) 1 Sample Test (Normalcy)

In the previous section about nominal/categorical level variables, the question posed was "Is the sample representative of the population?" Now we want to answer the question "Is the data normally distributed?" **The KS 1 Sample test is usually conducted at the very start of a study to determine if the sample distribution you have obtained is normally distributed (Chapter 14). To perform most parametric statistical tests, you must have a normal distribution. This test is very useful when you plan to use parametric analysis later in your study as it can provide you with the answer to the question "Is the distribution normal?"—one of the major assumptions in any parametric test.**

The Chi-Square Goodness of Fit is appropriate for categorical data to determine if the sample is representative of the population while the KS 1 Sample is appropriate for ordinal, interval or ratio data to determine normality and thus representative of a normal population.

There is not a research design box or a variable box for the KS test because the test is not one that is used to test a difference/association, or the outcome of an intervention or to predict one variable from another. Rather, the test is to determine if the data you have has a particular form—the form of a normal distribution.

Let's use an example to demonstrate how this test determines if the sample is normal.

You are planning to conduct a study to determine if a treatment you are going to use with 25 couples in marital therapy will reduce marital conflict. In order to have a good design to test the intervention, you need to find out the amount of marital conflict for each couple (establish a baseline or average of conflict in the marriage) prior to the treatment to be able to compare it to the amount of conflict after treatment. The basic plan is to have each couple rate on a scale of 1–10 the amount of marital conflict in their marriage over a one-month period prior to treatment and then one month following the treatment. A measurement will be made prior to intervention and then post intervention. This type of study will be discussed in Chapter 16.

In order to make the pre-post comparison you have to determine if the couple's amount of marital conflict is normally distributed prior to the treatment to be able to use appropriate parametric tests of difference comparing pre- and post intervention. A KS 1 Sample test can be conducted to see if the distribution of marital conflict ratings prior to the intervention was normal.

Study Question: **Is the level of marital conflict in the sample of 25 couples normally distributed?**

Hypotheses:

Difference: The distribution of marital conflict in the sample of 25 couples is different from a normal distribution.
Null: The level of marital conflict in the sample of 25 couples is normally distributed. ***You want to support the null since you need the distribution to be normal so the sample can be used in future parametric statistical tests.***
Level of Measurement: Ordinal (**can be ratio or interval**)
Type of Design: No actual design; it is a test to determine if the sample is normally distributed
Number of Groups: 1 Group (sample)
Assumptions: Continuous data that is ordinal, interval or ratio.

SPSS Commands

Open the data set ***Ch15 One Sample K-S***.
Follow the steps below:

(1) Select *Analyze*.
(2) Select **Nonparametric Tests**.

(3) Select ***Legacy Dialogs***.

(4) Select ***1-Sample K-S . . .***

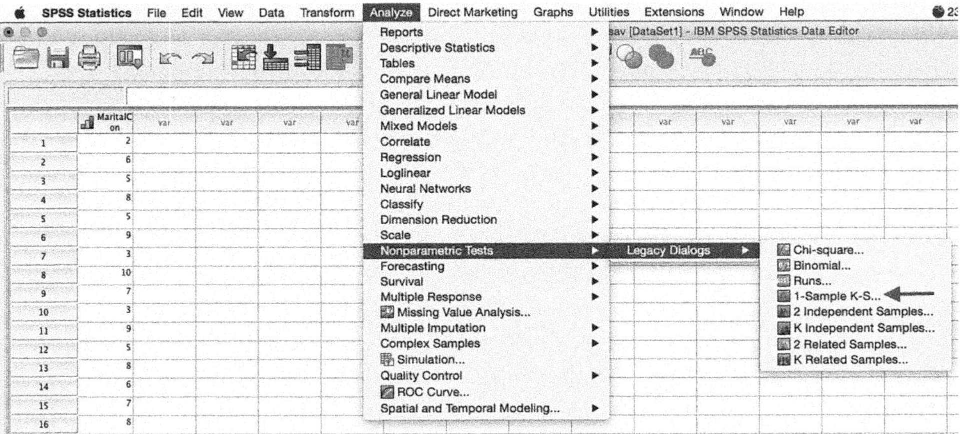

(5) Move variable ***MaritalCon*** over into the ***Test Variable List*** box.

(6) Under ***Test Distribution*** make sure that ***Normal*** is checked.

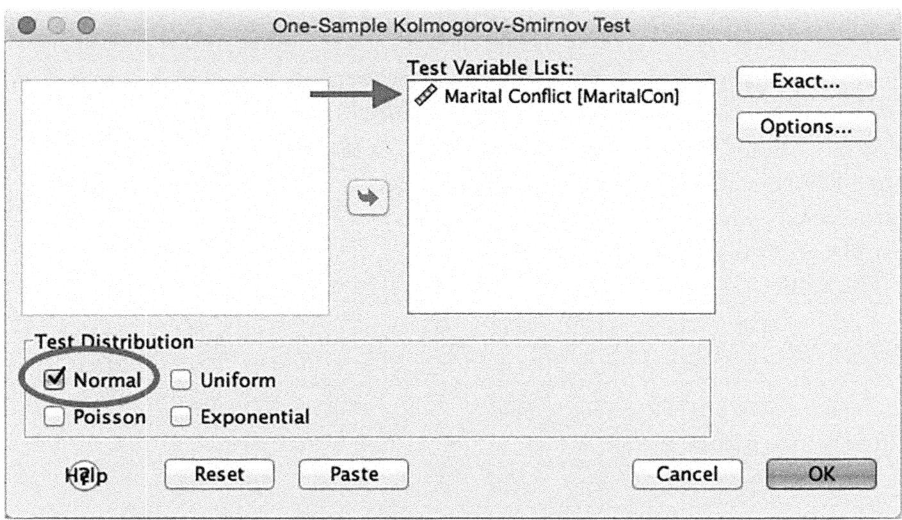

(7) Click ***OK***.

One-Sample Kolmogorov-Smirnov Test

		Marital Conflict
N		25
Normal Parameters[a, b]	Mean	5.88
	Std. Deviation	2.489
Most Extreme Differences	Absolute	.122
	Positive	.081
	Negative	–.122
Test Statistic		.122
Asymp. Sig. (2-tailed)		.200[c, d]

a. Test distribution is Normal.
b. Calculated from data.
c. Lilliefors Significance Correction.
d. This is a lower-bound of the true significance.

Note: ***Below the result box you see (a) the distribution is normal. This does NOT mean that you have a Normal Distribution!*** **It is indicating that you selected the normal distribution to test your data against!**

The **mean of the distribution is 5.88** indicating that the average amount of conflict was almost 6 for the 25 couples. **The standard deviation was 2.49. The KS Z is not significant (Asymp. 2-tailed = .200). This is the result you would like to have because it indicates that the distribution of the sample is not significantly different from normal and you will be able to use this data in future statistical analyses.** In this test, you actually DO NOT WANT THERE TO BE A SIGNIFICANT DIFFERENCE.

ONCE AGAIN: At the bottom of the chart you can see a note labeled (a) Test distribution is normal. This is NOT TELLING YOU THAT THE DISTRIBUTION IS NORMAL! What it is telling you is that you COMPARED your distribution to the normal distribution. You selected the Normal Distribution in your drop down box as your comparison distribution. You determine if the distribution is different from a normal distribution by looking at the significance levels.

PART B: PARAMETRIC

Interval/Ratio Level Data

One-Sample t-Test

See Chart—Sample to Population and Interval or Ratio Level Measurement

There are three different types of t-tests: (1) comparing a group (sample) mean to a population mean, (2) comparing two group (sample) means and (3) paired (replicated) group (sample) comparing the mean of the same group at one point in time to its mean at another point in time. The last two tests are not covered in this chapter but will be covered in later chapters. The first test, comparing a group (sample) mean to a population mean, is the most basic parametric test.

In order to compare a sample to a population, there must be a minimum of 10 and most preferably 20 in the group (sample) because you need enough values/scores (N in the sample size) to be able to obtain "an accurate" calculation of the mean. As you already know, if the group (sample) is small then you will not be able to get a good estimate of the mean and the variance of the group (sample), and it will not be representative of the population.

$$t = \frac{\bar{X} - \mu}{s / \sqrt{n}}$$

In the formula above, $\bar{X}$ = the sample mean, μ is the population mean, s = the standard deviation and n = the sample size. Using this formula t can be calculated.

As an example, consider that you are working as a social worker in child welfare seeing cases in a particular neighborhood of the city. You are interested to find out if the average income in this neighborhood is the same as the average of the city. Then you would collect a sample in the neighborhood and obtain the mean income for the neighborhood and compare it to the already collected and published average income for the city. This example provides a situation where you are determining if your neighborhood is different from the rest of the city. Now we will consider use of this test in a different research scenario where it is very important in the initial stages of a broader study to determine that the sample is not different from the population. Assume that you want to compare access to health care in your city to another city. From all that you have read you know that income is critical to an individual's access to health care. If you want your sample to really be representative of your city with respect to access to health care, it is important to determine if the average income of the group (sample) you selected was not statistically different from the city's average income.

If you had only wealthy people in the sample from your city, then the average would be significantly higher than the "real average" and they would be better able to afford health care and thus greater access. On the other hand, if you happen to only get individuals in the sample from your city that had lower incomes the average income would not reflect the "real average" income and they would not be as able to afford health care and thus have less access.

Now let's look at another example that will be used to calculate a t-test to the population. Assume that you are the social worker in charge of foster care and adoption in Metrocity and have been collecting data for the past year on how long it took to complete adoption. The average time to adoption for the state is 50 weeks. You want to find out if there is a difference between the average time to complete adoption in Metrocity and the average for the state.

ONE SAMPLE *t* TEST—CONCEPTUAL FRAME

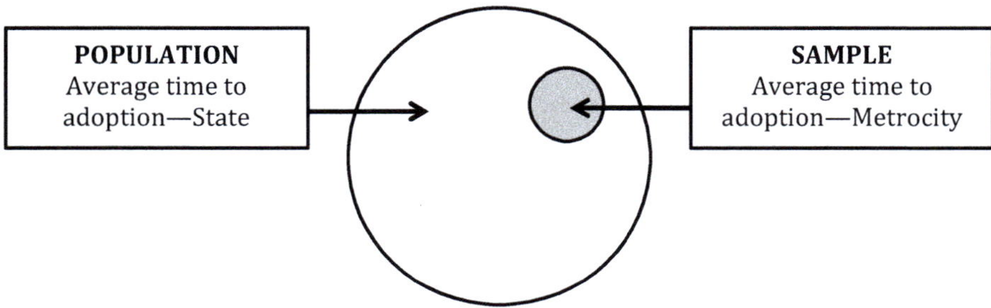

Study Question: **Is there a difference between the average length of time to adoption in Metrocity and the average length of time to adoption in the state?**

This is difference, cross-sectional design.

Hypotheses:

Difference: There is a difference between the average length of time to adoption in Metrocity compared to the state.

Null: There is no difference between the average length of time to adoption in Metrocity compared to the state.

Expected (E): There will be no difference between the average length of time to adoption in Metrocity and the state.

Observed (O): There will be a difference between the average length of time to adoption in Metrocity and the state.

Predicted (P): The actual average length of time for adoption in Metrocity and the state.

Level of Measurement: IV Nominal, DV Ratio

Type of Design: Difference, cross-sectional
Number of Groups: 1 Group (sample)
Assumptions: (a) Normal Distribution, (b) Independent Measures, (c) N no less than 10.

VARIABLE BOX—ONE GROUP (SAMPLE)
SOURCE—CITY AND STATE

	Sample (Metrocity) (A1)	***Population (State)*** (A2)
Weeks to Adoption	Mean	Mean

SPSS Commands

Open the data set ***Ch15 One Sample t.***
Follow the steps below:

(1) Click ***Analyze.***
(2) Select ***Compare Means.***
(3) Select ***One-Sample t-test***

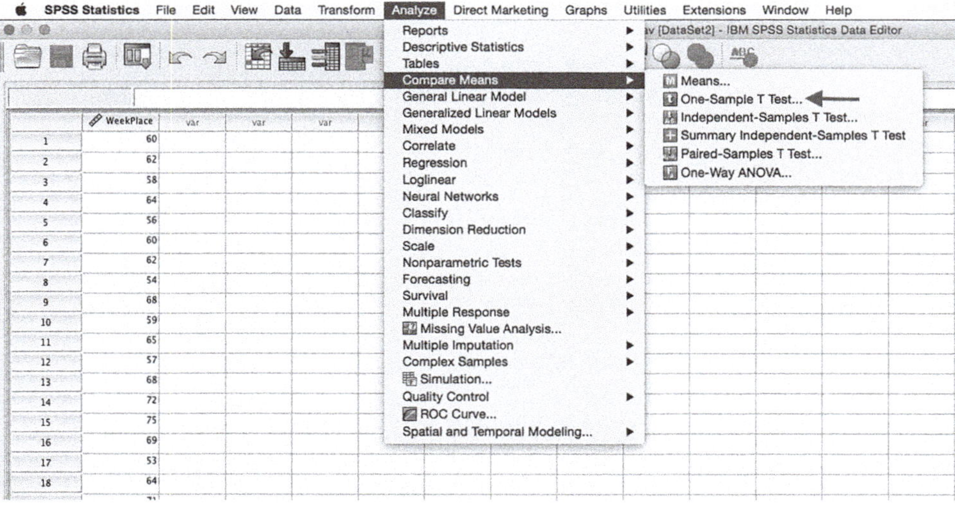

(4) Move the variable ***Weeks to placement [WeekPlace]*** into the ***Test Variable(s)*** box.
(5) Enter 50 (the population mean) in the ***Test Value*** box.

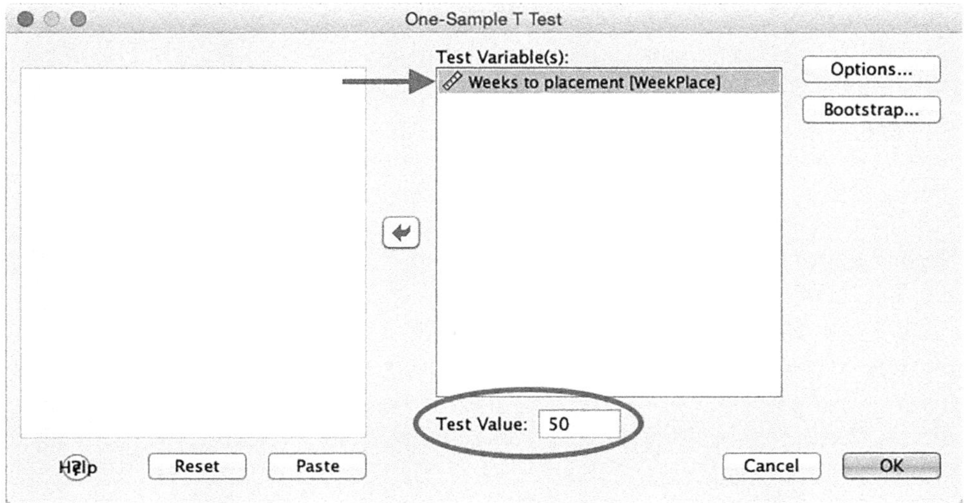

(6) Click ***OK***.

Let's review the output:

One-Sample Statistics

	N	Mean	Std. Deviation	Std. Error Mean
Weeks to placement [WeekPlace]	25	61.04	6.730	1.346

One-Sample Test

	Test Value = 50					
	t	Df	Sig. (2-tailed)	Mean Difference	95% Confidence Interval of the Difference	
					Lower	Upper
Weeks to placement [WeekPlace]	8.202	24	.000	11.040	8.26	13.82

The mean ($\bar{X}$) for Metrocity (sample) is 61.04 weeks, with a standard deviation of 6.73 weeks and is higher than the mean (μ) for the state of 50 weeks. The One-Sample Test box shows the value of t to be 8.20, with 24 degrees of freedom, and the significance is 0.001 (remember the convention that .000 is written as .001). The conclusion is that the time it takes to adopt children in Metrocity is significantly longer than the time it takes to adopt children in the rest of the state.

Results might be written as follows:

A study was conducted to compare the length of time to adopt in Metrocity compared to the state. The results of a one-sample t-test showed it took significantly longer to adopt children in Metrocity than in the state (Metrocity Mean = 61.04, SD = 6.72), (State Mean = 50 weeks). This result was significant, ($t_{(24)} = 8.20$; $p = .001$).

Practical Implications: Why do you think there was a difference? What factors might contribute to a longer time in Metrocity than the state? Are there fewer workers? Is there a difference in the children available for adoption? What is the ratio of adoptive parents to children? Are there some restrictions in Metrocity that are not in place elsewhere in the state? Is there a difference concerning within-family adoptions? Is there a difference in the training of the social workers? Is there greater turnover in Metrocity than in the state that may be related to inability of workers to quickly place children?

And others?

One Sample t-Test (Microsoft Excel Example)

See Chart—Sample to Population and Interval or Ratio Level Measurement

A one-sample *t*-test can also be run using Microsoft Excel. In this section we will conduct a one-sample *t*-test for the weeks to adoption example using Microsoft Excel.

(1) Open Excel workbook ***Chapter15***. Click on worksheet ***t-test***

For each of the 25 cases in our study we have been given the length of time (in weeks) to adoption. We are interested in whether there is a significant difference between the average length of time to adoption for our group (sample).

Metrocity and the average length of time to adopt for the state (population)—50 weeks.

(2) Before solving for the t value, we will need to calculate the mean, standard deviation, and standard error. In the following table, we have calculated each of these values for our data set. In the rightmost column, you will find the Microsoft Excel formula that can be used to complete these calculations.

		Formula:
sample size:	**25**	COUNT(B2:B26)
sample mean:	**61.04**	AVERAGE(B2:B26)
standard deviation:	**6.730**	STDEV.S(B2:B26)
standard error:	**1.346**	E6/SQRT(E4)

(3) We want to compare our sample mean with the population mean. In this example we know that the population mean is 50 weeks to adoption. We will also need to determine our degrees of freedom using the formula $df = (n - 1)$.

population mean:	**50**	
degrees of freedom:	**24**	n - 1

(4) We are now ready to solve for the t value using the formula:

$$t = \frac{\bar{X} - \mu}{s / \sqrt{n}}$$

(5) As you can see, we have already calculated the denominator ($s / \sqrt{n}$) when we determined the standard error. Likewise, we have already identified our sample mean and population mean. Thus we can easily obtain the t statistic using a basic Excel formula:

t statistic:	**8.202**	(E5-E9)/E7

(6) Finally, we will need to determine the p value for our t statistic. We could look at a table of critical values for the t distribution. Alternatively, we can instruct Microsoft Excel to calculate this value using the formula T.DIST.2T (2T indicates that our inquiry is 2-tailed).

p value:	**2.02252E-08**	T.DIST.2T(E12,E10)

Discussion Article

Critique the authors' use of the one-sample *t*-test. Critically reflect on the reasons for using this specific test as part of their study.

Frazier, T. W., & Edmonds, C. L. (2002). Curriculum predictors of performance on the major field test in psychology II. *Journal of Instructional Psychology*, *29*(1), 29–33. doi:10.1080/01634370802609288

Exercises for Chapter 15 are found in eResources.

Chapter 16

FINDING DIFFERENCES

Two Independent Groups (Samples) Tests

PART A: NONPARAMETRIC TESTS

Nominal Level Data

Chi-Square test for 2 × 2 tables

See Chart—Two Independent Groups and Nominal Measurement

This specific test analyzes the amount of difference between two nominal level variables. One of the variables often can be divided into two groups of people—Democrats and Republicans, on welfare and not on welfare, Females and Males, etc. Although some might conceptualize the relationship between the two variables as one being an independent variable and the other a dependent variable, it is better to look at the relationship in terms of time in that one happened before the other, for example gender before political party affiliation. It is even more preferable to view it simply as a relationship between the two variables irrespective of a temporal relationship. Even if there is a temporal relationship as in gender and party affiliation we could have just as easily started looking at political affiliation (Democrats and Republicans) and then determined the relationship/difference in the percentage of Males and Females in each party. The same relationship and percentage would exist starting with either variable.

Both variables in this example have ***only two options or levels (Female and Male—Democrat and Republican) and both are nominal*** and this test investigates the ratio of the distribution of categories for only two variables. **The type of design this test is used for is a difference/association design.** We are looking at group differences that can be examined as a snapshot in time (**cross-sectional**). Variables frequently used in social work where this test is appropriate are gender, race, ethnicity, source of payment, type of service received and below or above poverty level. ***BOTH of the variables*** in a **2 × 2 Chi-Square** can have ***only two levels (groups)—(thus 2 × 2)***. For example, you may have a variable with two levels (groups), e.g. working vs. not working; however, if you are interested in more than two levels (groups), e.g. working full time, working part-time and not working, the Chi-Square 2 × 2 is not the most appropriate test. **When you have more than two levels (groups) in either of the variables the correct test to use is Chi-Square for r × k that is discussed in Chapter 18.**

Conceptualization

We will begin by developing a conceptual framework to understand what happens when we analyze data using Chi-Square. Assume we want to find out what type of clients are using services offered by a welfare organization. It may be important for strategic planning purposes to know if there is a difference in utilization of services between White and African American clients with respect to gender. Since this is a very large agency serving a great number of clients, you randomly select from their database 100 White clients and 100 African American clients and record their gender.

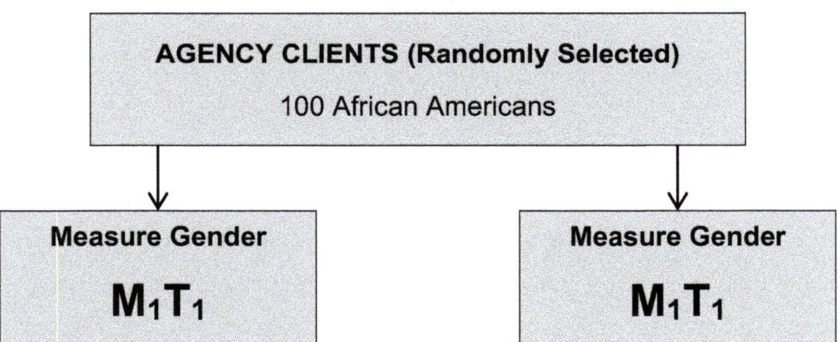

To help you to conceptualize and understand the test, let's look at some different ratios of gender and race. Clearly, these are hypothetical sets of data and not likely to be ones you would find in reality. However, they do provide a good way to demonstrate the statistical analysis methods involved in Chi-Square. What we are interested in are the **crosstabs (cross-tabulations)** in the 2 × 2 matrix. The crossed arrows indicate the crosstabs which show the ratios that are so important in the analysis. In the first example, out of the 100 White clients randomly selected there were 50 men and 50 women and out of the 100 African American clients there were 50 men and 50 women. If you knew these proportions and someone selected a different large group of clients from the same client database and told you their race, would you bet on what gender the person was? **If you knew the client was Female for example, what would you bet was their race?** ***Do you see any difference between White and African American clients with respect to gender?*** You have an equal chance (50%) of being correct and a (50%)

chance being incorrect irrespective if you know their gender or their race. The ratios are equal and indeed, there is no difference between the ratios of gender and race.

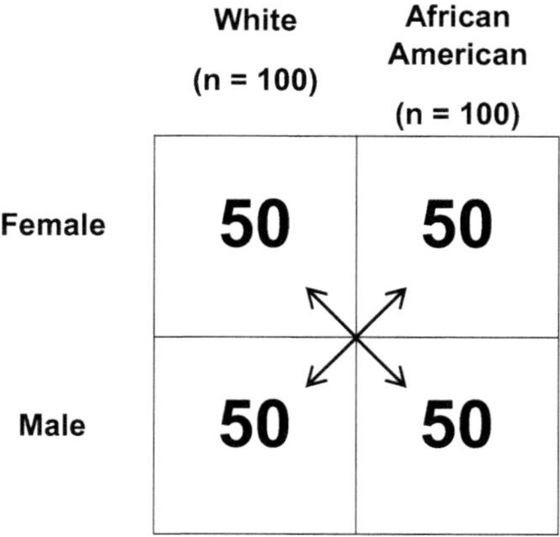

Now let's look at the next example. You again selected 100 White clients and 100 minority clients. You found that out of the 100 White clients there were 75 Females and only 25 Males. Of the 100 African American clients, there were 25 Females and 75 Males. If you look at the crosstabs (arrows) in this example, you will find a very different ratio from the first example.

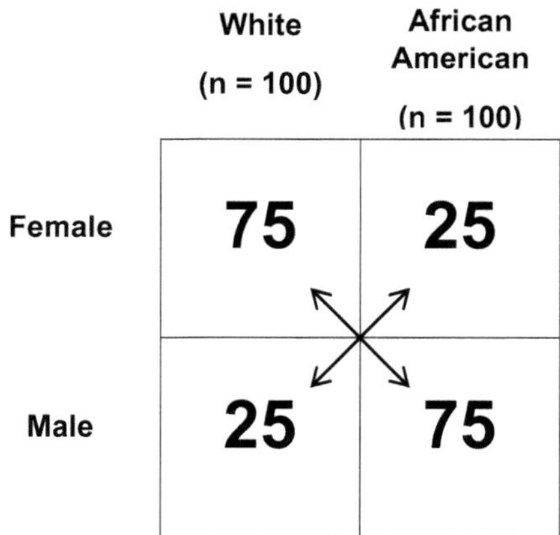

Using the ratios above, if a large group of clients was randomly selected from the same client database and you were told their gender, you would be much more confident in your bet on the client's race because there are some rather big differences in the ratios of the two genders. Thus, you would bet that a Female client was White and you would be correct 75% of the time and make a mistake only 25% of the time. If you were told the person was a Male, you would bet that the person was African American and you would be correct 75% of the time and wrong only 25%.

Finally, if the ratios in the agency were as shown below you would have found huge differences between the ratios of gender and race. Based upon these ratios, if the person was a Female you would bet the person was White and if the person was African American you would bet the person was a Male and you would make a wrong classification of gender only 1 out of 100 times.

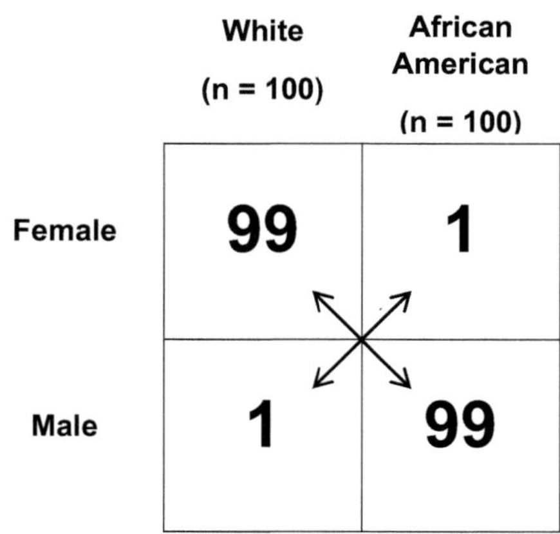

Now let's conceptualize a study and take you through the methods involved in answering a question with a Chi-Square 2 × 2 analysis. Suppose you have an interest in looking at gender and the percentage of Males and Females applying for welfare assistance at two different agencies.

Study Question: Is there a difference between the number of Males and Females that apply for welfare assistance at the Assist Agency and Help Agency?

This is a difference, cross-sectional design.

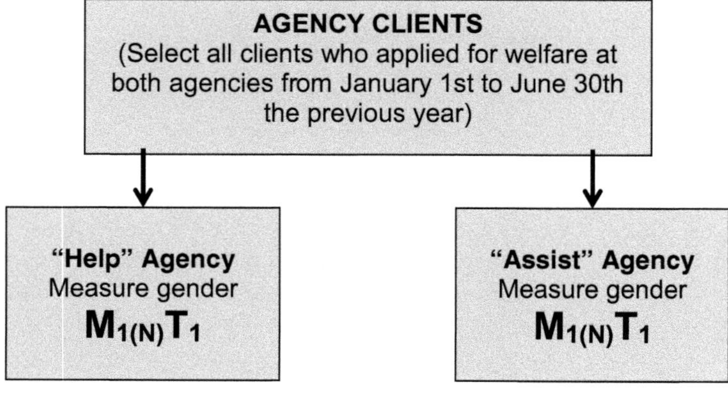

To refresh the notation for designs:

$M1_{(N)}$ = Measurement of the first nominal variable
T1 = First time the variable is measured
Thus, $M1_{(N)}T1$ = First time the first nominal variable is measured

Hypotheses:

Difference: There is a difference between the number of Females and Males applying for welfare assistance at ASSIST and HELP.

Null: There is no difference between the number of Females and Males applying for welfare assistance at ASSIST and HELP.

The way the difference hypothesis is stated, we are not making any prediction about which one of the agencies will have more Males or Females applying for welfare. As you recall from Chapter 10, this is a 2-tailed hypothesis, where there is not a predicted direction.

You selected all of the clients from both agencies who applied for welfare assistance between January 1 and June 30 of the previous year and you then coded their gender. This study can be shown using the variable box as a simple 2 × 2 box with Agency (with two groups/levels—Help and Assist) and Gender (with two groups/levels—Female and Male). From the examples and discussion of variable boxes in Chapter 9, the variable levels (groups) are placed outside the box (cells) and the measurement the number of people is recorded within cells of the box.

There are **only two levels of each nominal variable**, Agency (Assist and Help) and Gender (Female and Male), meeting the first requirement for using the test. The second is **independence of all measurements** and it was met as the selection of each person was independent of the selection of all others in the sample. **Thus, the *design requirements* of the test are met**.

The next step is to determine what we expect the ratio will be, what we predict the ratio will be and lastly what we observe the ratio is between the gender of the applicant and the agency they applied to. As you will recall from earlier chapters, **what we expect refers to what we expect the ratio will be in the case of the no difference (null) hypothesis. What we predict is the ratio stated in the difference hypothesis.** Finally, **what is observed is the actual data (numbers in the cells) that was gathered**. We can define these as follows for this example:

Expected (E): The number of Males and Females applying for assistance at ASSIST and HELP will be equal.

Predicted (P): Either ASSIST or HELP will have more Females than the other agency. (*Note: No direction is predicted only difference—2-tailed test*)

Observed (O): The actual distribution (data gathered) of Females applying for help at ASSIST and HELP.
Level of Measurement: IV Nominal (gender), DV Nominal (agency)
Type of Design: Difference, cross-sectional
Number of Groups: 2 Groups (samples)

The Chi-Square test has important ***assumptions that must be met*** or **the results of the test can be invalid.**

Assumptions: (a) No more than 20% of the expected frequencies less than 5, (b) No single expected frequency less than 1.

VARIABLE BOX—2 × 2 CHI-SQUARE

		AGENCY (A)	
		"ASSIST" Agency (A1)	***"HELP" Agency*** (A2)
GENDER (B)	***Males*** (B1)	A1 B1	A2 B1
	Females (B2)	A1 B2	A2 B2

> Let's start by arranging the data in a frequency table where the columns represent the two agencies (groups) and each row represents a category of the characteristic you are interested in. The columns are labeled C_1 (representing ASSIST) and C_2 (representing HELP). The rows are labeled R_1 (representing Males) and R_2 (representing Females).

MATH EXAMPLE—2 × 2 CHI-SQUARE

	"ASSIST" Agency C_1	**"HELP" Agency** C_2	**Total**
Males R_1	18 (R_1C_1)	10 (R_1C_2)	28 (R_1)
Females R_2	7 (R_2C_1)	24 (R_2C_2)	31 (R_2)
Total	25 (C_1)	34 (C_2)	**Grand Total 59**

The **observed** numbers (gathered data) are in the cells of the table. Cell R_1C_1 has the **observed** number of Males (18) applying for welfare assistance from ASSIST. Cell R_1C_2 has the **observed** number of Males (10) applying for welfare assistance from HELP. Cell R_2C1 has the **observed** number of Females (7) applying for welfare assistance from ASSIST and cell R_2C_2 has the **observed** number of Females (24) applying for welfare from HELP.

First determine what is the value we can ***expect*** for each cell, if the null hypothesis was indeed "true". The null hypothesis states there is no difference between the agencies with respect to gender. The proportion of Females who apply for welfare assistance at ASSIST would be the same as the proportion of Females applying for welfare assistance at ASSIST. And of course, then the proportion of Males who apply for welfare assistance at HELP is the same as the proportion of Males applying for welfare at HELP. **We can the calculate the EXPECTED frequency for each cell by multiplying the corresponding Row Total by the corresponding Column Total and then dividing it by the Grand Total.**

The calculation of the **expected (E)** value for all four cells is below.

The first cell is the R_1C_1 cell. Following the above formula method to obtain the **expected (E)**:

Total of Row 1 is 28. Total of Column 1 is 25 and the grand total is 59.

E for R_1C_1 is $28 \times 25 \div 59 =$ **11.86**
E for R_1C_2 is $28 \times 34 \div 59 =$ **16.14**
E for R_2C_1 is $31 \times 25 \div 59 =$ **13.14**
E for R_2C_2 is $31 \times 34 \div 59 =$ **17.86**

We can add these expected values to our table. ***Now we need to investigate if the assumptions of the test are met.*** Based on the values of the expected frequencies, ***we can conclude that the assumptions are met, because none of the cells have expected frequencies less than 5, and there is no observed cell frequency less than 1.***

The next is to evaluate the **difference between** the **observed (O)** and **expected (E)** frequencies. If the observed frequencies are similar to the expected frequencies, the difference between observed and expected will be small and it is more likely that after the statistical analysis we will not be able to reject the null hypothesis. However, if the differences between the observed frequencies and the expected frequencies are big, then it will be more likely that the agencies will differ with respect to gender and we will reject the null and accept the difference hypothesis.

OBSERVED AND EXPECTED VALUES—2 × 2 CHI-SQUARE

	"ASSIST" Agency C_1	"HELP" Agency C_2	Total
Males R_1	18 (*11.86*)	10 (*16.14*)	28 (R_1)
Females R_2	7 (*13.14*)	24 (*17.86*)	31 (R_2)
Total	25 (C_1)	34 (C_2)	**Grand Total 59**

The data in the table seems to indicate that the number of Male clients requesting welfare at ASSIST (Cell R_1C_1) is greater than what we would expect if there was no difference between Males and Females between the agencies. We also see that the number of Female clients requesting welfare assistance at HELP (Cell R_2C_2) to be more than what we can expect if there was no difference between Males and Females. Therefore, just by looking at the observed (O) data and comparing the observed numbers to the expected (E) values, we might begin to think that Males have a preference to apply at ASSIST and Females have a preference to apply at HELP.

Let's test it!

The **formula below will apply to ALL Chi-Square tests**, whether for a simple 2 × 2 Chi-Square (as in this example) or for the Chi-Square R × K (see Chapter 18).

$$\chi^2 = \Sigma \frac{(O-E)^2}{E}$$

O is the observed number in a cell and E is the expected number in a cell and Σ tells you to sum after calculating each value. We have already calculated the expected number in each cell. So, we can continue by calculating for each cell: $\frac{(O-E)^2}{E}$

Cell R_1C_1 is: $(18 - 11.86)^2 \div 11.86 = (6.14)^2 \div 11.86 = 37.70 \div 11.86 =$ **3.18**
Cell R_1C_2 is: $(10 - 16.14)^2 \div 16.14 = (6.14)^2 \div 16.14 = 37.70 \div 16.14 =$ **2.34**
Cell R_2C_2 is: $(7 - 13.14)^2 \div 13.14 = (6.14)^2 \div 13.14 = 37.70 \div 13.14 =$ **2.87**
Cell R_2C_2 is: $(24 - 17.86)^2 \div 17.86 = (6.14)^2 \div 17.86 = 37.70 \div 17.86 =$ **2.11**

Finally we sum (**Σ**) all the cell values: 3.18 + 2.34 + 2.87 + 2.11 = **10.50**

To determine degrees of freedom for the Chi-Square test, the formula is:

(R − 1)(C − 1) R = the number of rows and C = the number of columns

Thus, (2 − 1)(2 − 1) = 1 (df) degree of freedom

You can look up the significance of $\mathbf{X^2_{(1)} = 10.50}$ in any table of Chi-Square critical values such as the one found at www.itl.nist.gov.

Now that you understand the conceptualization, have calculated the value for Chi-Square and understand the statistical comparison to determine if there is a difference, we will conduct the statistical test using SPSS and Excel.

SPSS Commands

Open data set ***Ch16 Chi-Square 2x2***.
Follow the steps below.

(1) Go to ***Analyze***.
(2) Scroll down and select ***Descriptive Statistics***.
(3) Select ***Crosstabs . . .***

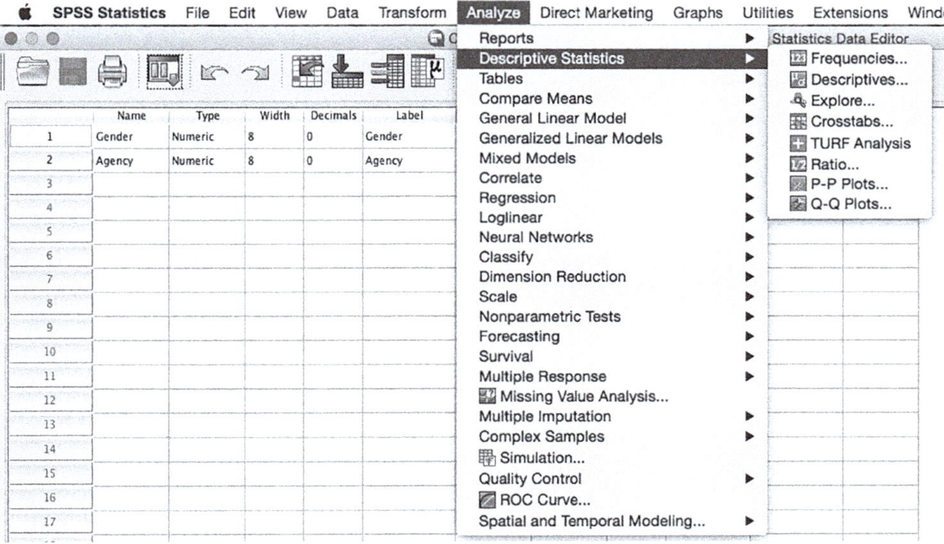

(4) Move the variable ***Gender*** into the ***Row(s)*** box; move the variable ***Agency*** into the ***Column(s)*** box.

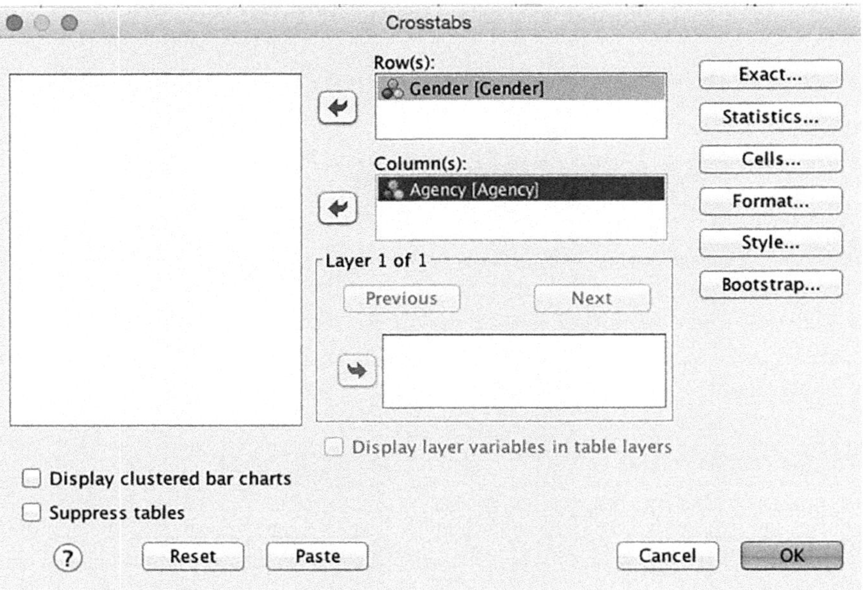

(5) Click the ***Statistics . . .*** button; check the box to select ***Chi-square***.

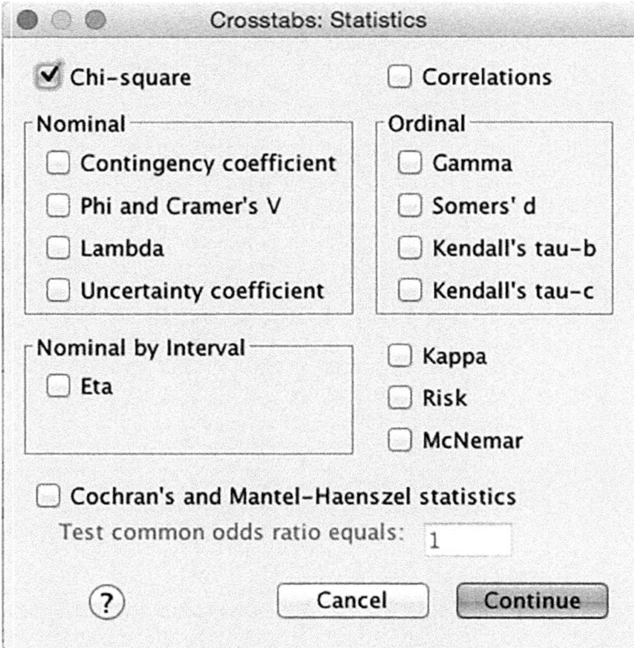

(6) Click ***Continue***.
(7) Click the **Cells . . .** button.

(8) Under ***Counts***, check the boxes by ***Observed*** and ***Expected***; under ***Percentages***, check the boxes by ***Row***, ***Column*** and ***Total***.

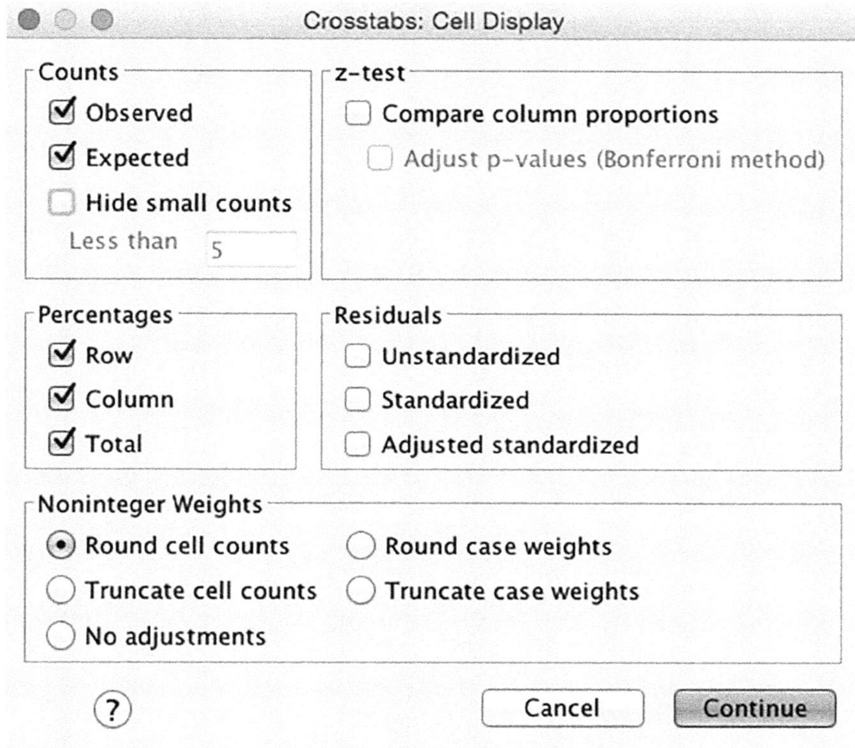

(9) Click ***Continue***.
(10) Click ***OK*** to run the analysis.

Gender * Agency Crosstabulation

			Agency		Total
			Help Agency	Assist Agency	
Gender	Male	Count	18	10	28
		Expected Count	11.9	16.1	28.0
		% within Gender	64.3%	35.7%	100.0%
		% within Agency	72.0%	29.4%	47.5%
		% of Total	30.5%	16.9%	47.5%

(*Continued*)

			Agency		Total
			Help Agency	Assist Agency	
	Female	Count	7	24	31
		Expected Count	13.1	17.9	31.0
		% within Gender	22.6%	77.4%	100.0%
		% within Agency	28.0%	70.6%	52.5%
		% of Total	11.9%	40.7%	52.5%
Total		Count	25	34	59
		Expected Count	25.0	34.0	59.0
		% within Gender	42.4%	57.6%	100.0%
		% within Agency	100.0%	100.0%	100.0%
		% of Total	42.4%	57.6%	100.0%

Chi-Square Tests

	Value	Df	Asymptotic Significance (2-sided)	Exact Sig. (2-sided)	Exact Sig. (1-sided)
Pearson Chi-Square	10.479[a]	1	.001		
Continuity Correction[b]	8.841	1	.003		
Likelihood Ratio	10.797	1	.001		
Fisher's Exact Test				.002	.001
Linear-by-Linear Association	10.302	1	.001		
N of Valid Cases	59				

a. 0 cells (0.0%) have expected count less than 5. The minimum expected count is 11.86.
b. Computed only for a 2 × 2 table.

In this example, we are interested in the distribution of gender; therefore, we examine the row where gender is displayed. First look at the **observed (O)** values (labeled 'Count' in the table) and the proportions—18 out of 28 Males go to the ASSIST agency (64%), and 24 out of 31 Females go to the HELP agency (77%). Basically, the proportions of the Males and Females are rather large and reversed by agency (see the crosstabs examples shown in the first part of the chapter). **A rule of thumb is if the proportional difference in percent is greater than 1.5 you are likely to have a significant difference.**

Start reading the crosstab from the upper row cell with the highest percentage value. In our example, we will say: **At least two-thirds of all Males (64%) apply for welfare**

at ASSIST while only 23% of all Females apply to ASSIST. Of the Females, 77% apply at HELP while only 36% of the Males apply to ASSIST.

Results might be written as follows:

At least 2/3 of all Males (64%) apply to ASSIST for welfare, while only 23% of the Females apply there. More than three quarters (77%) of all Females apply to HELP, while only 36% of Males apply there. This difference is significant ($X^2_{(1)} = 10.48, p = .001$).

Practical Implications: There seems to be a big difference between the Males and Females and their agency preference for welfare assistance. The study did not provide any reasons for why there is this difference. This may lead to you to another study where you may try to find answers about why this difference exists. Some potential questions might be:

Does one agency or the other have more Male or Female staff and is that related to the number of Females and Males attending the agency? Is there a difference in gender-related services provided by each agency? Are the hours of operation of the agencies more conducive to one gender or the other? Do the agencies differ in provision of transportation or assistance to the agency? Is there a difference in agencies with respect to providing assistance with child care?

Fischer Exact Test for 2 × 2 tables

See Chart—Two Independent Groups and Nominal Measurement

Research Design

The Fischer Exact test is a special application of the Chi-Square 2 × 2 that can be used in situations where you have two independent groups, and two nominal variables with two levels, and ***cannot meet the assumptions*** due to a **small sample size** or the requirement of **expected cell values of no less than 5** and **no single value of less than 1**. **When any of these assumptions cannot be met, use the Fisher Exact test** instead of the Chi-Square for 2 × 2.

Conceptualization

The conceptual framework is the same as the Chi-Square 2 × 2 test, but now we will be **calculating the exact probability of observing a specific set of frequencies in a 2 × 2 table**. Thus, we are calculating the probability of getting only these four specific numbers in these four specific cells.

The following study will show you how to apply the Fischer Exact test. Suppose you noticed in your caseload at the mental health agency that more men are using meth than Females. You wonder if the same will be true for the caseload of your co-worker, or are you the only one with a caseload of more Male meth users? Your question is as follows:

Study Question: Is the proportion of Male to Female meth users in my caseload different from that of my co-worker?

This is a difference/association, cross-sectional, independent measures design.

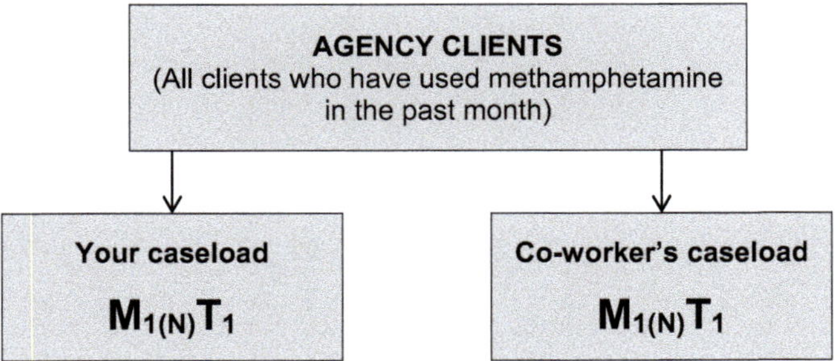

Hypotheses:

Difference: The proportion of Male to Female meth users in my caseload will be greater than the proportion of Male and Female meth users in my co-worker's caseload.

Null: The proportion of Male to Female meth users in the two caseloads will be the same.

Expected (E): The number of Males and Females using meth in the two caseloads will be equal.

Predicted (P): My caseload of meth users will have proportionally ***more Males*** than Females than the caseload of my co-worker.

Observed (O): The actual proportion of Males to Female meth users in the two caseloads.

Level of Measurement: IV Nominal (worker), DV Nominal (meth use)

Type of Design: Difference, cross-sectional

Number of Groups: 2 Groups (samples)

Assumptions: (a) No more than 20% of the expected frequencies less than 5, (b) No single observed frequency less than 1.

THEREFORE WE ARE USING FISHERS EXACT TEST.

As you can see from how the difference hypothesis is defined, **this time we are making a specific prediction about which caseload will have more Male meth users**

than Female meth users. This time, ***we have created a 1-tailed hypothesis, where we are predicting a direction of the difference***.

To conduct this study, you use the client database and determine the total of Male and Female meth clients for the past month in your caseload and you ask your co-worker to do the same. You then place this data into a simple 2 × 2 table with the variable worker divided into two separate workers (you and your co-worker) and the other variable gender divided into two groups (Female and Male). ***Conceptually the test is the same as the 2 × 2 Chi-Square test.***

VARIABLE BOX—2 × 2 FISHER'S EXACT TEST

		WORKER'S CASELOAD (A)	
		Worker 1 (A1)	***Worker 2*** (A2)
GENDER (B)	***Males*** (B1)	A1 B1	A2 B1
	Females (B2)	A1 B2	A2 B2

For the **Fisher's Exact** you have the same basic design and measurement as in a **Chi-Square 2 × 2 test except you have a small sample or one that does not meet the assumptions of the Chi-Square test**. In this study, the sample from your total caseload of meth users is 11 for the month and the caseload of meth users for your co-worker totals only 10.

Let's start by arranging the data in a frequency table where the columns represent the two workers' caseloads, and the rows represent gender.

MATH EXAMPLE—2 × 2 CHI-SQUARE WITH SMALL NUMBERS

	Worker 1 C_1	**Worker 2** C_2	**Total**
Males R_1	8	6	14
Females R_2	2	5	7
Total	10	11	**Grand Total** **21**

First investigate the assumptions to determine if a Chi-Square 2 × 2 test can be used. To investigate those assumptions, the expected (E) frequencies for each of our four cells need to be calculated.

The first cell is R_1C_1. Following the method to obtain the expected (E):

Total of Row 1 is 14. Total of Column 1 is 10 and the grand total is 21.

E for R_1C_1 is $14 \times 10 \div 21 =$ **6.66**

E for R_1C_2 is $14 \times 11 \div 21 =$ **7.33**

E for R_2C_1 is $10 \times 7 \div 21 =$ **3.33**

E for R_2C_2 is $11 \times 7 \div 21 =$ **3.66**

There are two expected frequencies (50%) that fall below 5. In a Chi-Square, there cannot be more than 20%. Therefore, the assumptions of the Chi-Square 2 × 2 test are not met and the Fischer Exact test must be used. Since there has already been a conceptualization of the Fisher's test how to determine if the assumptions of the Chi-Square are met, and the hand calculation of the Fisher Exact test is very laborious, we will proceed directly to SPSS to analyze the data.

SPSS Commands

Open the data set ***Ch16 FisherExact 2x2***.
Follow the steps below.

(1) Go to ***Analyze***.
(2) Scroll down and select ***Descriptive Statistics***.
(3) Select ***Crosstabs . . .***
(4) Move the variable ***Gender*** into the ***Row(s)*** box; move the variable ***Worker*** into the ***Column(s)*** box.
(5) Click the ***Statistics . . .*** button; check the box to select ***Chi-square***.
(6) Click ***Continue***.
(7) Click the ***Cells . . .*** button
(8) Under ***Counts***, check the boxes by ***Observed*** and ***Expected***; under ***Percentages***, check the boxes by ***Row***, ***Column*** and ***Total***.
(9) Click ***Continue***.
(10) Click ***OK*** to run the analysis.

Gender * Worker Crosstabulation

			Worker		Total
			Worker 1	Worker 2	
Gender	Male	Count	8	6	14
		Expected Count	6.7	7.3	14.0
		% within Gender	57.1%	42.9%	100.0%
		% within Worker	80.0%	54.5%	66.7%
		% of Total	38.1%	28.6%	66.7%
	Female	Count	2	5	7
		Expected Count	3.3	3.7	7.0
		% within Gender	28.6%	71.4%	100.0%
		% within Worker	20.0%	45.5%	33.3%
		% of Total	9.5%	23.8%	33.3%
Total		Count	10	11	21
		Expected Count	10.0	11.0	21.0
		% within Gender	47.6%	52.4%	100.0%
		% within Worker	100.0%	100.0%	100.0%
		% of Total	47.6%	52.4%	100.0%

Chi-Square Tests

	Value	Df	Asymptotic Significance (2-sided)	Exact Sig. (2-sided)	Exact Sig. (1-sided)
Pearson Chi-Square	1.527[a]	1	.217		
Continuity Correction[b]	.597	1	.440		
Likelihood Ratio	1.567	1	.211		
Fisher's Exact Test				.361	.221
Linear-by-Linear Association	1.455	1	.228		
N of Valid Cases	21				

a. 2 cells (50.0%) have expected count less than 5. The minimum expected count is 3.33.
b. Computed only for a 2×2 table.

Use the same approach to reporting results that we used with the Chi-Square 2×2. Results might be written as follows.

The percent of meth users in the caseload of Worker 1 is 80% Male while the percent of meth users in the caseload of Worker 2 is 55% Male. This difference was not significant, (Fisher's Exact, $p = .2$).

Practical Implications: Since there was not a significant difference between the caseloads in terms of gender it would appear that the assignment of meth clients based upon gender is relatively equally distributed between the workers although one worker does have more Males. It might be important to monitor assignments in the future. There are more Males than Females (although not significant) being seen, so a question might be, "Is there a need to focus treatment modalities that might be more effective for Males?" What are those treatment modalities? Is the staff trained appropriately? One question not addressed is, "What is the proportion of meth users to non-meth users in the agency caseload?"

Ordinal Level Data

Median Test (Ordinal or Interval or Ratio level converted to Ordinal)

See Chart—Two Independent Groups and Ordinal Measurement

Research Design

The Median test is another test that investigates differences between two independent groups, but this time the investigation **focuses on the difference between the two groups using a measure of central tendency, namely the median (the middle value that separates the upper half of the data from the lower half of the data). The reason for inclusion of interval or ratio level data with the Median test is if the assumptions of the distribution of the DV required for a t-test or ANOVA (for example, normal distribution, similar sample size) are not met then you can convert the data to ordinal level (SPSS will convert the data automatically) and use the Median test to compare the central tendency of the two groups**.

If you wanted to compare the income of two neighborhoods of the city, however, in one neighborhood there were a few people with very high incomes that would skew the average income much too high, then average income is really not a good representation of the incomes of that group. In this case you could utilize the income values but convert them to being above or below the median using the median to characterize the center of incomes for both neighborhoods.

This test can be used for ordinal level data and is appropriate when the assumptions for tests using interval or ratio level data cannot be met. The test determines if there is a **difference in the median income between the groups.** ***The median test does not require that the two groups be of similar size. Because the test utilizes the median and not the average, outliers or a non-normal distribution do not influence the test.*** When you use the Median test, you can still see if there is a difference in the middle of the groups—that is the median value.

We might want to find out if there is a difference in the income of clients using services offered by two welfare organizations. It may be important for strategic planning purposes to know if one agency has clients with higher income than the other. From the client database, you randomly select 100 clients from each welfare organization. Some individuals in one organization had very high incomes that were not representative of the incomes of clients in that organization and their incomes would make the average income extremely high and skewed as well, creating a very large variance and standard deviation. You still wanted to determine if one group was different from the other with respect to a measure of central tendency, so you decided to use the median as a way to see if one group had a higher median income than the other. The median was chosen as the measure of central tendency because it is not skewed by the very high incomes in one group.

The variable box below splits the dependent variable of interest (income) into two nominal groups—those above the median and those at or below the median:

VARIABLE BOX—MEDIAN TEST

		AGENCY (A)	
		Agency 1 (A1)	***Agency 2*** (A2)
INCOME (B)	***Income greater than combined median*** (B1)	A1 B1 (Cell a)	A2 B1 (Cell b)
	Income less than combined median (B2)	A1 B2 (Cell c)	A2 B2 (Cell d)

If both agencies have clients whose median income are the same, we can expect that half of the client sample from each agency will fall in income brackets above the median and half will fall in income brackets below the median. If this is the case, then Cells A and C will have about the same percent of clients as B and D. If this expectation is not seen in our data, we may conclude that the clients being served in one agency have a different median income than clients being served in the other agency.

Conceptualization

Now to conceptualize a study using different variables to demonstrate the methods involved in answering a question using the median test. Suppose you are employed by the Human Services Department of your state and work in one specific county. You have noticed that there seem to be two groups of women in the welfare system—those who receive welfare assistance for a while but then are able to function without any assistance, and those who cycle on and off receiving welfare assistance. You wonder if the difference between these two groups of women may be related to the number of jobs they have held prior to receiving welfare assistance.

You decided to do a small study and only look at one month of data from your agency. Based upon your practice experience you know you need to allow some time for the women to stay off welfare or to have the opportunity to cycle through the system. Thus, you selected four years ago as the appropriate time frame and of those 12 months of data you randomly selected one month to collect data on the clients—April. Data was gathered on all 25 women who received welfare assistance for the first time during the month of April and recorded the number of jobs each woman had prior to receiving assistance. You then reviewed the records of all 25 women to see if after receiving assistance and termination from the program they remained off the program or cycled back into the program during the next four years. The range of number of jobs held by the 25 women was from 1 to 10 jobs, thus the median test is appropriate since the data does not have a large range; it is small and the data was not normally distributed.

The number of independent samples (two) and level of measurement (ordinal) adhere to the requirements of the test. The one-shot snapshot part of the design may sound confusing, since you went back four years to select the sample of women (cyclers and non-cyclers). **Remember—this is a criterion for inclusion as a group and not a measurement of the DV. A longitudinal design is one where you select a DV, MEASURE IT and then at some point in the future MEASURE that DV again and compare it to the previous MEASUREMENT.** YOU ARE NOT MEASURING THE DV TWO TIMES, ONLY ONE TIME IN THE PRESENT. YOU ARE SELECTING THE TWO DIFFERENT GROUPS BASED UPON THEIR WELFARE ACTIVITY FROM FOUR YEARS AGO TO THE PRESENT. **Remember the key is that you only measured THE JOBS (DV) one time; thus it is snapshot.** You had to go back to a point where they were on welfare to select them and then allow time for them TO DEVELOP INTO ONE OF THE TWO GROUPS.

The sample size for both groups is not the same, but because similar sample size is not a requirement for this test, you can use the median test. Even if the sample size of both groups was larger and the range of jobs held was bigger (from 1 to 30), making your data more ratio level, you would still use this test if you had skewed data that was not normally distributed.

Study Question: Is there a difference in the number of jobs held by women prior to receiving welfare assistance for the first time who receive welfare assistance for a while but then are able to function without any further assistance in the future (group 1—No Cyclers), and the number of jobs held by women who receive welfare assistance for the first time but who then cycle on and off welfare assistance (group 2—Cyclers)?

This is a difference, cross-sectional design.

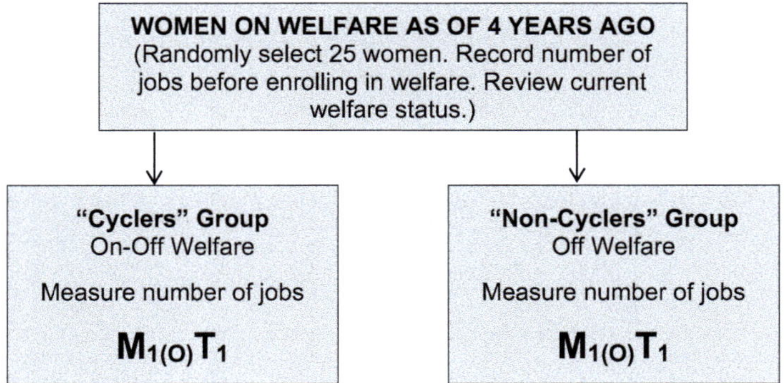

Hypotheses:

Difference: There is a difference between the No Cyclers and the Cyclers in the number of jobs held prior to the first time they received welfare assistance.

Null: There is no difference between the No Cyclers and the Cyclers in the number of jobs held prior to the first time they received welfare assistance.

Expected (E): The number of jobs held before receiving welfare assistance for the first time will be the same for the group of women who only receive welfare assistance once and the group of women who go on and off welfare assistance.

Predicted (P): The number of jobs held before receiving welfare assistance for the first time will be different for the two groups of women. (*Note: In this case our prediction has no direction—2-tailed test.*)

Observed (O): The actual number of jobs held by the two groups of women.

Level of Measurement: IV Nominal (welfare status), DV Ordinal (number of jobs—not normal in this example)

Type of Design: Difference, cross-sectional

Number of Groups: 2 Groups (samples)

Assumptions: (a) Ordinal level measurement, independent groups, no more than 20% of expected frequencies less than 5, (b) No single expected frequency less than 1. **If more than 20% and less than 1 use Fishers Exact test.**

VARIABLE BOX—MEDIAN TEST

		WELFARE STATUS (A)	
		"Non-cyclers" (A1)	*"Cyclers"* (A2)
Jobs (B)	***Number of jobs greater than combined median*** (B1)	**A** (A1 B1) (Cell a)	**B** (A2 B1) (Cell b)
	Number of jobs less than combined median (B2)	**C** (A1 B2) (Cell c)	**D** (A2 B2) (Cell d)

The data:

GROUP 1 (Non-Cyclers)	GROUP 2 (Cyclers)
1	1
3	7
1	3
1	10
3	2
8	7
1	8
3	3
6	8
2	7
2	
3	
2	
3	
2	

We have to calculate the grand median and array the combined data for both groups in descending magnitude from the highest to the lowest. The grand median is 3 jobs (see table below). At this time, we are not concerned about what group the middle value belongs to. There are 7 clients who have jobs at the median, with two belonging to the group who cycled on and off welfare assistance, and 5 belonging to the group who received welfare assistance only once.

##	Group	Number of jobs
1	Cycler	10
2	Non-Cycler	8
3	Cycler	8
4	Cycler	8
5	Cycler	7
6	Cycler	7
7	Cycler	7
8	Non-Cycler	6
9	Non-Cycler	3
10	Non-Cycler	3
11	Non-Cycler	3
12	Non-Cycler	3
13	Non-Cycler	**3**
14	Cycler	3
15	Cycler	3
16	Non-Cycler	2
17	Non-Cycler	2
18	Non-Cycler	2
19	Non-Cycler	2
20	Cycler	2
21	Non-Cycler	1
22	Non-Cycler	1
23	Non-Cycler	1
24	Non-Cycler	1
25	Cycler	1

Next, prepare a 2 × 2 table with the number of clients who held more jobs than the median of 3 and the number of clients who held 3 or fewer jobs. ***In this table, we have labeled the cells values inside the variable box as a, b, c, d, because the standard formula to calculate the only 2 × 2 χ^2 value uses this notation.***

	No Cyclers (Only receive welfare assistance once)	Cyclers (On and off welfare assistance)	Marginal Totals
Clients with number of jobs above combined median	2 (a)	6 (b)	8 **(a + b)**
Clients with number of jobs at or below combined median	13 (c)	4 (d)	17 **(c + d)**
Marginal Totals	15 **(a + c)**	10 **(b + d)**	25 **(a + b + c + d) = *n***

The following formula is used to calculate the median test:

$$\chi^2 = \frac{n\left(|ad - bc| - \frac{n}{2}\right)^2}{(a+b)(c+d)(a+c)(b+d)}$$

When we substitute the values from the above table we get the following:

$$\chi^2 = \frac{25\left(|8 - 78| - \frac{25}{2}\right)^2}{(8)(17)(15)(10)}$$

$$\chi^2 = \frac{25(|70| - 12.5)^2}{(8)(17)(15)(10)}$$

$$\chi^2 = \frac{25(57.5)^2}{(8)(17)(15)(10)}$$

$$\chi^2 = \frac{25(3{,}306.25)}{20{,}400}$$

$$\chi^2 = \frac{82{,}656.25}{20{,}400}$$

$$\chi^2 = 4.05$$

Degrees of freedom: (r − 1) (c − 1) = (2 − 1) (2 − 1) = 1

$$\mathbf{X^2_{(1)} = 4.05}$$

The significance can be determined by reviewing any table of Chi-Square critical values such as the one located at www.itl.nist.gov.

SPSS Commands

Open the data set ***Ch16 Median Test***.
Follow the steps below.

(1) Go to ***Analyze***.
(2) Scroll down and select ***Nonparametric Tests*** and then ***Legacy Dialogs***.
(3) Select ***K Independent Samples. . .***
(4) Under ***Test Type***, de-select the box next to ***Kruskal-Wallis H*** (the default selection) and check the box next to ***Median***.
(5) Move the variable number of ***Jobs*** to the ***Test Variable List*** box.
(6) Move the variable ***Welfare*** to the ***Grouping Variable*** box.

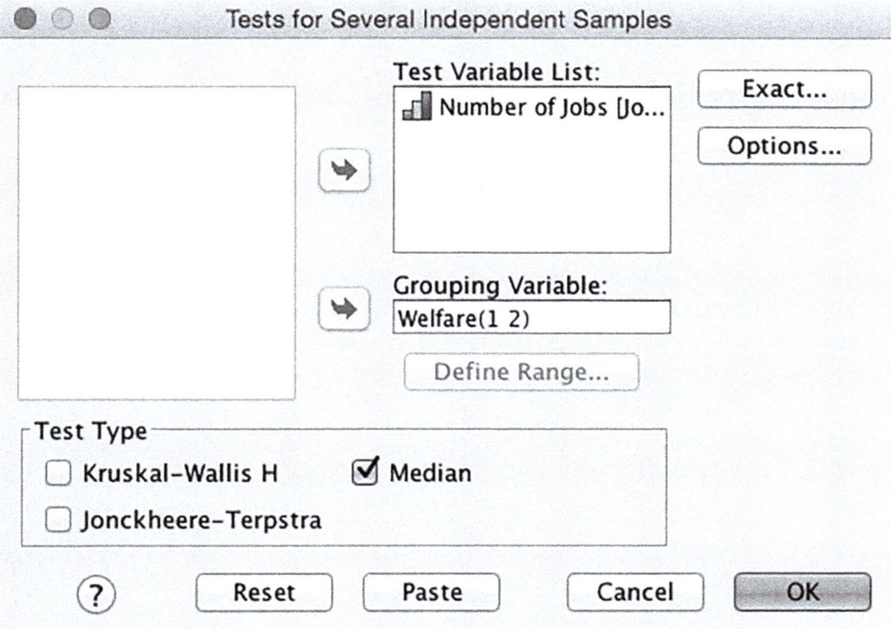

(7) Click ***Define Range . . .***
(8) Enter the minimum and maximum range for the grouping variable. In this example, the minimum is 1 ("cyclers") and the maximum is 2 ("non-cyclers").
(9) Click ***Continue***.
(10) Click ***OK*** to run the analysis.

Frequencies

		Welfare Status	
		"Cycler"	"Non-Cycler"
Number of Jobs	> Median	2	6
	≤ Median	13	4

Test Statistics[a]

	Number of Jobs
N	25
Median	3.00
Exact Sig.	.028

a. Grouping Variable: Welfare Status.

Results might be written as follows:

For the 15 women who received welfare assistance only once during the past 3 years (No Cyclers), only 2 out of 15 held more than the median amount of 3 jobs before receiving welfare. The other 13 women held less than the median number of jobs. For the 10 women who cycled on an off welfare since receiving it for the first time, 6 held more than the median amount of 3 jobs and 4 held the median of 3 jobs or less before entering welfare. This difference is significant (Median test $p = .028$).

Practical Implications: For the women cycling on and off welfare having more jobs, could this have been related to other factors? Are women more susceptible to being "dismissed" from work than men? What about lack of training, education and job skills, resulting in lower paying jobs that are often more susceptible to lay-offs? What about number of children and its impact on moving in and out of the labor market? What about single mothers compared to those with partners who may be able to supplement income and reduce cycling?

Wilcoxon-Mann-Whitney U Test

See Chart—Two Independent Groups and Ordinal Measurement

The Wilcoxon-Mann-Whitney U test is designed to test for differences between two groups, and like the median test the **dependent variable must at least be at least**

measured at the ordinal level. However, **the Wilcoxon-Mann-Whitney U is more powerful than the median test because it uses more of the information in the data** than the median test. The Wilcoxon-Mann-Whitney U compares every measurement with respect to the combined median of both groups and uses **each individual measurement by its rank value compared to all other individual measurement ranks in the calculations**. This **improves precision in testing the hypothesis**.

This test is a very powerful and an **excellent alternative to the Independent sample t-test or one-way ANOVA with two groups when the assumptions for these tests cannot be met**, or when you have ordinal level of measurement. ***The test is however sensitive to group sample size and requires that the two groups be relatively similar in size.***

The trade-off between the Median test and the Wilcoxon-Mann-Whitney U is that the Wilcoxon is more precise and powerful than the Median BUT the Mann-Whitney U REQUIRES ABOUT EQUAL SAMPLE SIZES.

Conceptualization

The process is different from the median test because it uses ranks. Initially, the values of the DVs **for the combined groups are ranked in order of increasing size**. The lowest rank of 1 is assigned to the lowest value in the combined groups, up to the highest rank that is assigned to the highest value in the combined groups. During the ranking, it is important to also keep a list of the group each score belongs to. After all the values are ranked, the rankings of each group are separately summed. After the sum of the ranks has been calculated for each group, the average rank for each is calculated. If the average rank in the two groups is about equal, it is very likely that the two client groups are not much different. If the sum and average ranks in the two groups are very different, it is more likely that the two groups may be significantly different.

Suppose you are a social worker at a community mental health clinic and you want to find out if Male and Female clients at intake rate their perceived mental health differently. From your experience working in the clinic you think that Females rate their mental health more negatively than Males. At intake, everyone rates their mental health on a scale from 1 to 5, with 1 = poor and 5 = excellent.

Study Question: Is there a difference between Male and Female clients on their self-rated mental health at intake?

This is a difference, cross-sectional design.

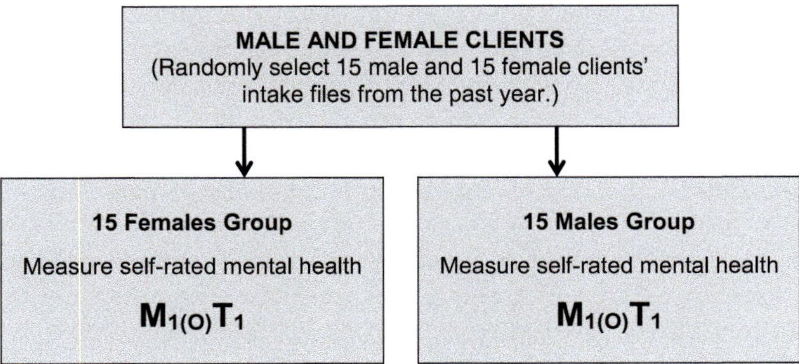

Hypotheses:

Difference: There is a difference between Male and Female clients on their self-rated mental health at intake, with Females rating their mental health more negatively than Males (1-tail directional).

Null: There is no difference between Male and Female clients on their self-rated mental health at intake.

Expected (E): The average rank for Males and Females on their self-rated mental health scores will be the same.

Predicted (P): The average rank for Females will be less than the average rank for Males on their self-rated mental health scores, indicating worse self-rated mental health for Females. *(We predict Females will have worse mental health ratings—a 1-tailed test.)*

Observed (O): The actual rankings for Males and Females on their self-rated mental health scores.

Level of Measurement: IV Nominal (gender), DV Ordinal (self-rated health)

Type of Design: Difference, cross-sectional

Number of Groups: 2 Groups (samples)

Assumptions: Ordinal level of measurement

VARIABLE BOX—WILCOXON-MANN-WHITNEY U

GENDER (A)

Females (A1)	***Males*** (A2)
Mean Rank	**Mean Rank**

A random sample of 15 Males and 15 Females who came to the agency in the past year for services was drawn. The answer of each of 30 clients on the self-rated mental health question was recorded and then all the answers from low (poor mental health) to high (very good mental health), were ranked making sure that each of the tied scores was given the average of the ranks they would have had if no ties had occurred. For example, if five scores were tied for the lowest position, to arrive at the rank for each score you gave the scores the ranks of 1, 2, 3, 4 and 5 because these were the lowest 5 ranks. Then to get the rank for each of these 5 individuals those rankings were added and divided by the number of ranks. Thus, 1 + 2 + 3 + 4 + 5 = 15 and then divide by 5 = 3. So, each individual was given a 3. The next score was assigned the rank of 6, because rank 1, 2, 3, 4 and 5 have already been assigned. If two scores were tied for the lowest position, each score would be assigned the rank of 1.5 (1 + 2)/2 and the next score assigned the rank of 3. It is important that to list which scores and ranks belonged to Male clients and which scores and ranks belonged to Female clients.

Actual Ratings of Mental Health at Intake

Male Ratings	Female Ratings
4	1
5	1
4	1
1	2
2	2
4	2
5	3
3	3
2	3
3	4
1	5
3	2
5	3
4	1
3	3

Order of Scores	Gender	Mental Health Rating	Rank	Formula for ties
1	Male	1	3.5	
2	Male	1	3.5	
3	Female	1	3.5	
4	Female	1	3.5	(1 + 2 + 3 + 4 + 5 + 6)/6 = 3.5
5	Female	1	3.5	
6	Female	1	3.5	
7	Male	2	9.5	
8	Male	2	9.5	
9	Female	2	9.5	
10	Female	2	9.5	(7 + 8 + 9 + 10 + 11 + 12)/6 = 9.5
11	Female	2	9.5	
12	Female	2	9.5	
13	Male	3	17	
14	Male	3	17	
15	Male	3	17	
16	Male	3	17	
17	Female	3	17	(13 + 14 + 15 + 16 + 17 + 18 + 19 + 20 + 21)/9 = 17
18	Female	3	17	
19	Female	3	17	
20	Female	3	17	
21	Female	3	17	
22	Male	4	24	
23	Male	4	24	
24	Male	4	24	(22 + 23 + 24 + 25 + 26)/5 = 24
25	Male	4	24	
26	Female	4	24	
27	Male	5	28.5	
28	Male	5	28.5	(27 + 28 + 29 + 30)/4 = 28.5
29	Male	5	28.5	
30	Female	5	28.5	

Calculate scores to ranks:

Calculate both the sum and mean ranks for Males and Females.

Males sum of ranks

3.5 + 3.5 + 9.5 + 9.5 + 17 + 17 + 17 + 17 + 24 + 24 + 24 + 24 + 28.5 + 28.5 + 28.5 = ***275.5***

MEAN RANK 275.5 ÷ 15 = *18.37*

Females sum of ranks

3.5 + 3.5 + 3.5 + 3.5 + 9.5 + 9.5 + 9.5 + 9.5 + 17 + 17 + 17 + 17 + 17 + 24 + 28.5 = ***189.5***

MEAN RANK 189.5 ÷ 15 = *12.63*

Now to calculate if the mean ranks for the two groups differ significantly. For this example, we will test if the mean rank of Males 18.37 differs significantly from the mean rank of Females 12.63.

The Wilcoxon-Mann-Whitney U formula is:

$$U_1 = R_1 - \frac{n_1(n_1+1)}{2}$$

Where n_1 = sample size for Group 1
R_1 = sum of the ranks in Group 1

Note: Either of the groups can be treated as sample 1. For this purpose, we will treat the Females as group 1 since we have equal group sizes. **However, if you are *using* a *table* to determine if the value is significant, you must calculate the U value on the group with the least individuals (smallest *n*).**

$$U_1 = 189.5 - \frac{15(16)}{2}$$

$$U_1 = 189.5 - 120$$

$$U_1 = 69.5$$

The smallest U value is used to consult the critical values table of U such as the one located at **www.itl.nist.gov**. In this case it will be the U value for Females, because the sum or ranks are the smallest for Females and the sample size is the same. The critical value for U with a sample size of 15 for both groups is 64.

SPSS Commands

Open the data set ***Ch16 Wilcoxon-Mann-Whitney U***.
Follow the steps below.

(1) Go to ***Analyze***.
(2) Scroll down and select ***Nonparametric Tests*** and then ***Legacy Dialogs***.
(3) Select ***2 Independent Samples . . .***
(4) Ensure that the box next to ***Mann-Whitney U*** is checked under the ***Test Type*** field.
(5) Move ***Mental Health*** into the ***Test Variable*** list.
(6) Move ***Gender*** into the ***Grouping Variable*** box.

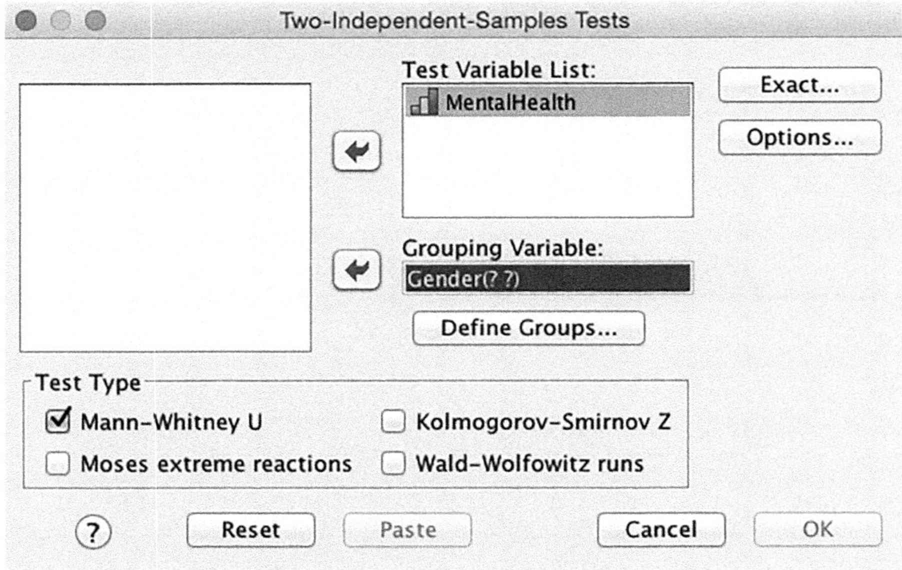

(7) Click ***Define Groups . . .***
(8) Under ***Define Groups***, add the code for Group 1 (Males) and the code for Group 2 (Females) based on how these groups were coded in the database (1 for Males, 2 for Females).
(9) Click ***Continue***.
(10) Click ***OK*** to run the analysis.

Ranks

	Gender	N	Mean Rank	Sum of Ranks
Mental Health	Males	15	18.37	275.50
	Females	15	12.63	189.50
	Total	30		

Test Statistics[a]

	Mental Health
Mann-Whitney U	69.500
Wilcoxon W	189.500
Z	−1.829
Asymp. Sig. (2-tailed)	.067
Exact Sig. [2*(1-tailed Sig.)]	.074[b]

a. Grouping Variable: Gender.
b. Not corrected for ties.

A 2-tailed test resulted in a p value of .067 which is not below the .05 threshold. ***Remember that you had a directional hypothesis—1-tailed. Therefore, you divide the significant level by 2 and to obtain the significance level for a 1-tailed (directional) test with the significance level now p = .034.***

Results might be written as follows:

A Wilcoxon-Mann-Whitney U test was performed to determine if Females rate their mental health worse than Males at intake at a community health clinic. The mean rank for Females was 12.63 and for Males was 18.37, indicating that Females rated their mental health worse than Males. These results are significant ($U = 69.5$; $p = 0.03$).

Note: Because this is a 1-tailed test, the 2-tailed p value provided in the SPSS output has to be divided by 2 to determine the p value for the 1-tailed test.

Practical Implications: If Females have a higher level of depression, then the agency might want to consider focusing on that problem earlier with Females. Concerns about and screening for suicide might be appropriate. What are the reasons it is more prevalent in Females? What social or personal factors might exist that are potential "causes" for depression in Females? Is there some sort of test bias that results in Females scoring worse? Are Males equally depressed but unwilling to admit it? Depression is a symptom of other problems so determining those should be a priority at intake. What are some factors you might want to investigate?

PART B: PARAMETRIC

Interval/Ratio Level Data

Independent Samples t-Test

See Chart—Two Independent Groups and Interval or Ratio Level Measurement

The ***t-test is the most basic of the parametric tests*** for investigating differences between two groups (IV) specifically on a variable/characteristic (DV) that is measured at an interval or ratio level. Examples of interval/ratio data frequently used in social work are income, age and total scores on attitude/opinion surveys. One of the assumptions of the t-test is that both groups must have a normal distribution. However, the t-test is robust and if you have **large and relatively equal size groups**, you do not always have to meet the normality assumption. **A more important assumption is that the standard deviations (homogeneity of variance) of both populations must be relatively equal.** Violation of the assumption of homogeneity of variance also can be accepted but ***much larger equal size groups are needed***. With unequal and smaller group sizes, if the assumption of homogeneity of variance is not met, there are likely to be serious effects on the results. **When group sizes are equal and normally distributed, 10 per group can provide a valid analysis; however, we prefer group sizes of at least 20.**

Conceptualization

We will start the conceptualization of parametric tests comparing means with a historical example from farming. We will follow this brief conceptual model with an example using licensure as the DV with Gender and University Attended as IVs that you were introduced to in Chapter 14. The farm example provides a very easy way to conceptualize means, variances, main effects and interactions.

The first question one might ask would be which type of seeds produces the most bushels of corn per acre?

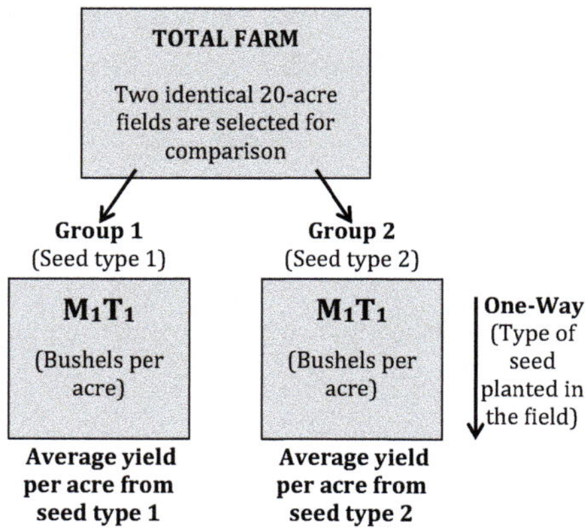

Another question might be which fertilizer produces the most corn per acre. A good farmer knows that some corn seeds have the best production with a certain fertilizer and others work best with another fertilizer. Thus, the following design might be appropriate:

VARIABLE BOX—TWO-WAY ANOVA

Two independent variables: (1) type of seed and (2) type of fertilizer
Two levels for each IV: 2 different types of seed and 2 different types of fertilizer

	Seed Type (A1)	**Seed Type (A2)**	
Fertilizer (B1)	A1B1	A2B1	**Row 1:** Effect of fertilizer B1
Fertilizer (B2)	A1B2	A2B2	**Row 2:** Effect of fertilizer B2
	Column 1: Effect of seed type A1	**Column 2:** Effect of seed type A2	

Clearly you can see identify the variables that produce the best results in the amount of corn you produce in a field. Let's say that the field had 40 acres and that it was divided evenly between the right half and the left half into 20 acres each and then you planted one half with seed type 1 and the other with seed type 2. Then you could measure how many bushels were produced per acre in the 20 acres of seed type 1 and how many bushels were produced per acre in the 20 acres of seed type 2. You could then total the bushels in each of those 20 acres, calculate the average per acre for each type of seed. You could also combine all the acres (40 total) and calculate the average per acre for the total farm. Now let's look at the second diagram. Here there are the same two types of seed but now we are using two different types of fertilizer. You can measure the amount of corn by the type of seed (the difference between the average amount of corn produced by each type of seed looking at the diagram from the top to the bottom)—that is the average of the seed type over or across (not counting the effect) of the fertilizer. In the diagram, you can see that seed type 1 had half of the acres fertilized with fertilizer A and half with fertilizer B and the same occurred with seed type 2. Since each seed type had the same type of fertilizer used on the same number of acres then the fertilizer type was balanced out in both cases and any effect on the amount of corn produced can be attributed to the seed type alone and not to an effect of the fertilizer.

Now if you look across (left to right) the diagram you will see the effect of the fertilizer. The average bushel per acre in the top row would be the average amount of corn produced using Fertilizer A. The average bushel per acre in the bottom row would be the average bushel per acre produced using Fertilizer B. Since both of the fertilizers had the same amount of seed type 1 and seed type 2 the average per acre in the rows is based upon the effect of the fertilizer and the effect of the seed type is balanced out and would have no effect since it is equal for both fertilizers.

Now to another very interesting aspect of a two-way analysis (or ultimately any multiple way analysis—more independent variables): the possibility to look at the interaction of the two independent variables. Remember the last question—does one type of seed work best with one type of fertilizer? If you compare the 4 cells you can obtain an answer to this question. In the top left corner, there are 10 acres where Seed 1 is paired with fertilizer A, in the top right corner 10 acres where Fertilizer A is paired with Seed 2, in the bottom left 10 acres where Fertilizer B is paired with Seed 1, and in the bottom right 10 acres where Fertilizer B is paired with Seed 2. With these pairings now we can look at all of the potential effects that impact the number of bushels of corn produced per acre. We can look at the effect (main effect) of the type of seed by comparing the variance in the average bushels per acre in the columns. We can look at the effect (main effect) of the type of fertilizer by comparing the variance in the average bushels per acre in the row. We can look at the interaction effect of variables—type of seed with type of fertilizer that appears in variance in the average of bushels per acre in the cells.

Let's return to the type of question that leads to the different types of analysis of variance (ANOVA). **A question that can be answered by the following tests—t-test or an independent sample (group) or a one-way Analysis of Variance (ANOVA)**—might be: Is there a difference between Females and Males on their licensure exam scores? In this example, there is **only 1 independent variable (Gender) with two levels**—Females and Males and 1 dependent variable licensure exam score. This question could be answered by using either a t-test or a one-way ANOVA. **(A t-test is the same as a one-way ANOVA that has only two levels of the independent variable.)**

Using the example from Chapter 14 again we want to **look at performance on the licensure exam score, however, using a different independent variable—university**. Is there a difference in licensure exam scores between those who attended a city university, a regional university or a state university? **You have the same dependent variable—licensure exam scores—but now the independent variable has three levels (groups—type of university).** ***With more than two levels of the independent variable (multiple groups) an ANOVA is required*** **and will be discussed in Chapter 18.**

Remember from Chapter 14 how to determine variance and standard deviation and

$$V_{total} = V_{between\ the\ groups} + V_{within\ the\ groups}$$

In order to compare differences between the groups to the difference within the groups the way to do that is to look at the ratio of between to within or:

$$\frac{V_{between}}{V_{within}}$$

Now we will perform a statistical test using the t-test and one-way ANOVA to determine if there is difference between Males and Females on their licensure exam score. The research design is shown below.

Study Question: Is there a difference on licensure exam scores between Females and Males?

This is a difference, cross-sectional design.

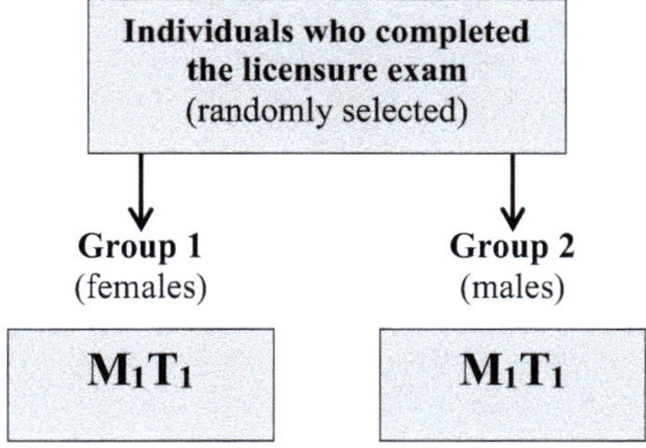

Hypotheses:

Difference: There is a difference on licensure exam scores between Females and Males.
Null: There is no difference between licensure exam scores of Females and Males.
Expected (E): The mean exam score of Females will be the same as the mean exam score of Males.
Predicted (P): The mean exam score of Females will be different than Males.
Observed (O): The actual mean exam score of Females and Males.
Level of Measurement: IV Nominal (gender), DV Interval (exam score)
Type of Design: Difference, cross-sectional
Number of Groups: 2 Groups (Samples)
Assumptions: (a) normal distribution, minimum of 10 per cell preferably 20 (b) independent measures

VARIABLE BOX— t-TEST

Females (A1)	***Males*** (A2)
Mean Exam Score $\bar{X}_1$	**Mean Exam Score** $\bar{X}_2$

Open the data set ***Ch16 t-Test ANOVA ANCOVA***. This is the same data that we used to calculate the basic variance values in Chapter 14. We will now use the data set to conduct both a t-test and an ANOVA.

First, examine the frequency tables of licensure exam scores for each gender.

SPSS Commands

Follow the steps below to produce these tables:

(1) Open the data set ***Ch16 t-Test ANOVA ANCOVA***. This is the same data that we used to calculate the basic variance values in Chapter 14. We will now use the data set to conduct both a t-test and an ANOVA.
(2) Click Analyze
(3) Scroll down and select ***Descriptive Statistics***.
(4) Select ***Frequencies . . .***
(5) Move the variables ***FemaleExam*** and ***MaleExam*** to the ***Variable(s)*** box.
(6) Ensure the box next to ***Display frequency tables*** is checked.
(7) Click ***OK*** to produce the frequency tables.

First, examine the frequency tables of licensure exam scores for each gender.

Review each of the two output tables, each of which presents the licensure exam scores for one gender.

FemaleExam

		Frequency	Percent	Valid Percent	Cumulative Percent
Valid	6	1	1.1	3.3	3.3
	8	2	2.3	6.7	10.0
	9	2	2.3	6.7	16.7
	13	1	1.1	3.3	20.0
	14	2	2.3	6.7	26.7
	15	1	1.1	3.3	30.0

	Frequency	Percent	Valid Percent	Cumulative Percent
16	2	2.3	6.7	36.7
17	2	2.3	6.7	43.3
18	2	2.3	6.7	50.0
19	3	3.4	10.0	60.0
20	1	1.1	3.3	63.3
22	1	1.1	3.3	66.7
23	2	2.3	6.7	73.3
24	2	2.3	6.7	80.0
25	2	2.3	6.7	86.7
26	1	1.1	3.3	90.0
27	2	2.3	6.7	96.7
29	1	1.1	3.3	100.0
Total	30	34.1	100.0	

MaleExam

		Frequency	Percent	Valid Percent	Cumulative Percent
Valid	2	1	1.1	3.3	3.3
	3	1	1.1	3.3	6.7
	4	1	1.1	3.3	10.0
	6	1	1.1	3.3	13.3
	9	1	1.1	3.3	16.7
	11	3	3.4	10.0	26.7
	12	1	1.1	3.3	30.0
	13	4	4.5	13.3	43.3
	14	3	3.4	10.0	53.3
	16	2	2.3	6.7	60.0
	17	2	2.3	6.7	66.7
	18	1	1.1	3.3	70.0
	19	1	1.1	3.3	73.3
	20	1	1.1	3.3	76.7
	21	3	3.4	10.0	86.7
	22	2	2.3	6.7	93.3
	23	1	1.1	3.3	96.7
	24	1	1.1	3.3	100.0
	Total	30	34.1	100.0	

We have constructed the table below to show you how the calculations proceed using the scores, the squared scores and the sum of square scores. This table is not generated by SPSS and is added to be an aid in your learning.

ALL SCORES	ALL SCORES SQUARED	FEMALE SCORE	FEMALE SCORE SQUARED	MALE SCORE	MALE SCORE SQUARED
2	4	6	36	2	4
3	9	8	64	3	9
4	16	8	64	4	16
6	36	9	81	6	36
6	36	9	81	9	81
8	64	13	169	11	121
8	64	14	196	11	121
9	81	14	196	11	121
9	81	15	225	12	144
9	81	16	256	13	169
11	121	16	256	13	169
11	121	17	289	13	169
11	121	17	289	13	169
12	144	18	324	14	196
13	169	18	324	14	196
13	169	19	361	14	196
13	169	19	361	16	256
13	169	19	361	16	256
13	169	20	400	17	289
14	196	22	484	17	289
14	196	23	529	18	324
14	196	23	529	19	361
14	196	24	576	20	400
14	196	24	576	21	441
15	225	25	625	21	441
16	256	25	625	21	441
16	256	26	676	22	484
16	256	27	729	22	484
16	256	27	729	23	529
17	289	29	841	24	576

ALL SCORES	ALL SCORES SQUARED	FEMALE SCORE	FEMALE SCORE SQUARED	MALE SCORE	MALE SCORE SQUARED
17	289				
17	289				
17	289				
18	324				
18	324				
18	324				
19	361				
19	361				
19	361				
19	361				
20	400				
20	400				
21	441				
21	441				
21	441				
22	484				
22	484				
22	484				
23	529				
23	529				
23	529				
24	576				
24	576				
24	576				
25	625				
25	625				
26	676				
27	729				
27	729				
29	841				
990	**18740**	**550**	**11,252**	**440**	**440**
ΣX	ΣX^2	ΣX_1	ΣX_1^2	ΣX_2	ΣX_2^2

Review the table above with the Sum of the Xs (**Σ*X***) and Sum of the Xs squared (**Σ*X*²**).

We will use this table and calculations in the formula for a 2-independent sample t-test so that you can conceptualize the process and to demonstrate the results obtained in SPSS. Remember that we will use the two groups to estimate the overall population mean and variance because we do not have the total population. While this looks incredibly difficult to understand, we will break it down and it will become much clearer for you.

$$t = \frac{\bar{X}_1 - \bar{X}_2}{\sqrt{\left(\frac{\left(\Sigma X_1^2 - \frac{(\Sigma X_1)^2}{N_1}\right) + \left(\Sigma X_2^2 - \frac{(\Sigma X_2)^2}{N_2}\right)}{N_1 + N_2 - 2}\right)\left(\frac{1}{N_1} + \frac{1}{N_2}\right)}}$$

$\bar{X}_1$ = Mean of Group 1
$\bar{X}_2$ = Mean of Group 2
N_1 = Number in Group 1
N_2 = Number in Group 2
ΣX_1^2 = Square each value in Group 1 then add them together
ΣX_2^2 = Square each value in Group 2 then add them together
$(\Sigma X_1)^2$ = Add all values in Group 1 then square that number
$(\Sigma X_1)^2$ = Add all values in Group 2 then square that number
$\left(\frac{1}{N_1} + \frac{1}{N_2}\right)$ = Correction for sample size
$\bar{X}_1$ = Mean for FEMALES = 18.333
$\bar{X}_2$ = Mean for MALES = 14.667
N_1 = Number of FEMALES = 30
N_2 = Number of MALES = 30
ΣX_1^2 = Square each value of the FEMALES then add together
= 11252
ΣX_2^2 = Square each value of the MALES then add together
= 7488
$(\Sigma X_1)^2$ = Add all FEMALE scores then square that number
= $(550)^2$ = 302,500
$(\Sigma X_2)^2$ = Add all MALE scores then square that number
= $(440)^2$ = 193,60

$$t = \frac{\bar{X}_1 - \bar{X}_2}{\sqrt{\left(\frac{\left(\sum X_1^2 - \frac{(\sum X_1)^2}{N_1}\right) + \left(\sum X_2^2 - \frac{(\sum X_2)^2}{N_2}\right)}{N_1 + N_2 - 2}\right)\left(\frac{1}{N_1} + \frac{1}{N_2}\right)}}$$

$$t = \frac{18.333 - 14.667}{\sqrt{\left(\frac{\left(11,252 - \frac{302,500}{30}\right) + (7,488 - \frac{193,600}{30}}{30 + 30 - 2}\right)\left(\frac{1}{30} + \frac{1}{30}\right)}}$$

$$t = \frac{3.666}{\sqrt{\left(\frac{(11,252 - 10,083.33) + (7,488 - 6453.33)}{58}\right)(.0333 + .0333)}}$$

$$t = \frac{3.666}{\sqrt{\left(\frac{(1,168.67) + (1,034.67)}{58}\right)(.0666)}}$$

$$t = \frac{3.666}{\sqrt{\left(\frac{2203.34}{58}\right)(.0666)}}$$

$$t = \frac{3.666}{\sqrt{(37.988)(.0.666)}}$$

$$t = \frac{3.666}{\sqrt{(2.5338}}$$

$$t = \frac{3.666}{1.5918}$$

$t = 2.3037$; $df = 58$; $p = .025$
($\text{df} = n - 2 = 60 - 2 = 58$) 2 is subtracted from the *n* because you have 2 groups

The *p* value for the calculated *t* score can be found by looking at a critical value table for the *t* distribution such as the one found www.itl.nist.gov.

SPSS Commands

Open the data set ***Ch16 t-Test ANOVA ANCOVA***.
Follow the steps below.

(1) Click ***Analyze***.
(2) Scroll down and select ***Compare Means***.
(3) Select ***Independent-Samples t-test . . .***
(4) Move the variable ***Exam*** into the ***Test Variable(s)*** box; move the variable ***Gender*** into the ***Grouping Variable*** box.

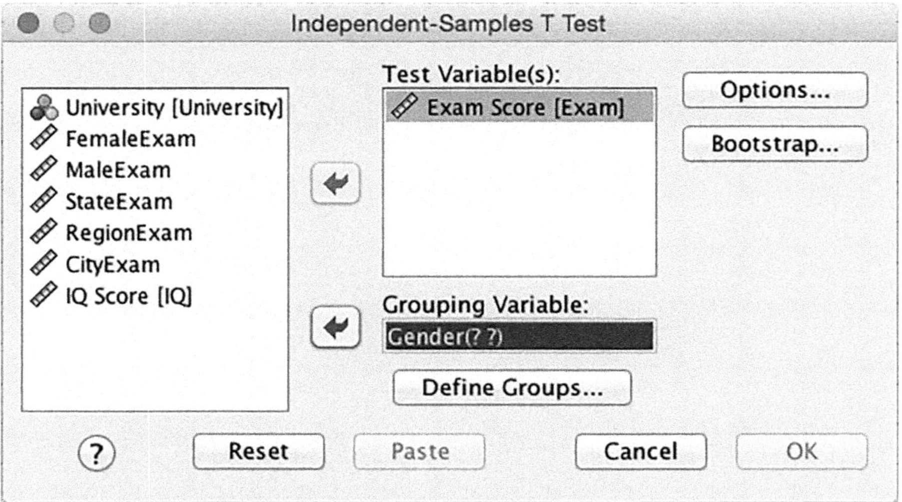

(5) Click on the button to ***Define Groups . . .***
(6) Type 1 (the value signifying Female) in the box beside ***Group 1***; type 2 (the value signifying Male) in the box beside ***Group 2***. Click ***Continue***.

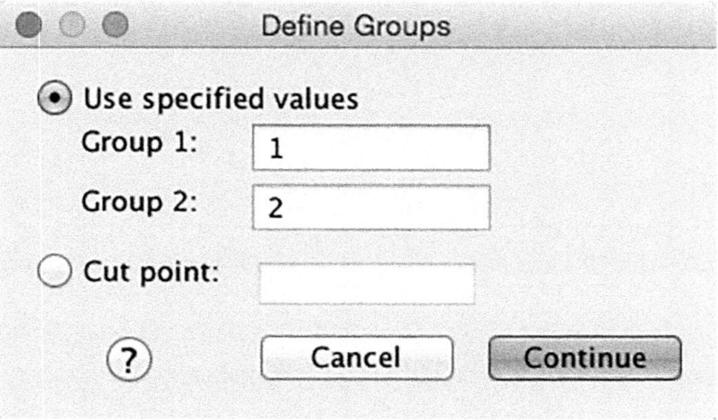

(7) Click ***OK*** to run the analysis.

Group Statistics

Exam Score	Gender	N	Mean	Std. Deviation	Std. Error Mean
	Female	30	18.33	6.348	1.159
	Male	30	14.67	5.973	1.091

Independent Samples Test

		Levene's Test for Equality of Variances		T-Test for Equality of Means						
		F	Sig.	T	Df	Sig. (2-tailed)	Mean Difference	Std. Error Difference	95% Confidence Interval of the Difference	
									Lower	Upper
Exam Score	Equal variances assumed	.151	.699	2.304	58	.025	3.667	1.591	.481	6.852
	Equal variances not assumed			2.304	57.786	.025	3.667	1.591	.481	6.852

In the descriptive statistics table, you can see the mean for the Males is 14.67 (SD = 5.973) and the mean for Females is 18.33 (SD = 6.348). Females had a higher licensure exam score than Males.

The first thing to check in the Independent Samples Test is the Levene's Test for Equality of Variances. ***The Levene's test is NON-SIGNIFICANT. This indicates that there is NOT A SIGNIFICANT DIFFERENCE IN THE VARIANCES OF THE TWO GROUPS; they are homogenous and you can read the Exam line where equal variances are assumed.***

If they are not equal then read the line Equal variances not assumed. In this example, you **read the line table marked equal variances assumed.**

The next step will be to calculate the effect size (see Chapter 12) using Cohen's D because the standard SPSS output does not provide an effect size for the t-test. First, we have to calculate the *Pooled SD (standard deviation)*. In the formula below, n = the number in the indicated group, and s = the standard deviation of the indicated group.

$$Pooled\ SD = \sqrt{\frac{(n_1 - 1)s_1^2 + (n_2 - 1)s_2^2}{(n_1 - 1) + (n_2 - 1)}}$$

$$Pooled\ SD = \sqrt{\frac{(29)6.348^2 + (29)5.973^2}{58}}$$

$$Pooled\ SD = \sqrt{\frac{1168.613 + 1034.625}{58}}$$

$$Pooled\ SD = \sqrt{\frac{2203.238}{58}}$$

$$Pooled\ SD = \sqrt{37.986}$$

$$Pooled\ SD = 6.1633$$

$$Cohen's\ d = \frac{\bar{X}_1 - \bar{X}_2}{Pooled\ SD}$$

$$Cohen's\ d = \frac{18.333 - 14.667}{6.1633}$$

$$Cohen's\ d = \frac{3.666}{6.1633}$$

$$\boldsymbol{Cohen's\ d} = .5948$$

The interpretation of the Cohen d statistic is:

Cohen's d effect size interpretations.

Cohen's *d* value	Interpretation
0–.19	Negligible or no effect size
.20–.49	Small effect size
.50–.79	Medium effect size
.80+	Large effect size

In the current example, we can observe a medium effect size.

The results could be written as follows:

An independent sample t-test was performed to determine if there was a difference between Females and Males on the licensure exam. The mean for Females was 18.333 and for Males 14.667, indicating that Females had higher licensure exam scores than Males. These results are significant ($t_{(58)} = 2.3037, p = .025$) with a medium effect size (Cohen's *d* = .5948).

Practical Implications: Why are the Females performing better? Are they all from the same university with the same training? Is there a difference in areas of social work interest between Males and Females that is tested on the exam? If there is a difference in interest is there a bias to an interest in the exam questions? Do the Females in the sample have a higher critical thinking score than Males and therefore do better on the exam? You may have many more questions.

The same data set will be used to calculate a one-way ANOVA with two groups. Remember the result of an ANOVA is the same as the t-test when there are only two groups. The calculations will not be exactly the same because we will be using the sums of squares between and not the mean scores of the Females and Males and we will use the sum of squares within for variance and not the standard deviation.

We will again present all of the parts to the study to demonstrate that the one-way ANOVA is designed the same and providing answers that are the same as the t-test. The ANOVA uses different calculation formulas so that you can progress beyond comparing only one IV and two groups in the same analysis with one DV (the limit of the t-test) to multiple IVs and multiple groups in ANOVAS.

Study Question: Is there a difference on licensure exam scores between Females and Males?

This is a difference, cross-sectional design.

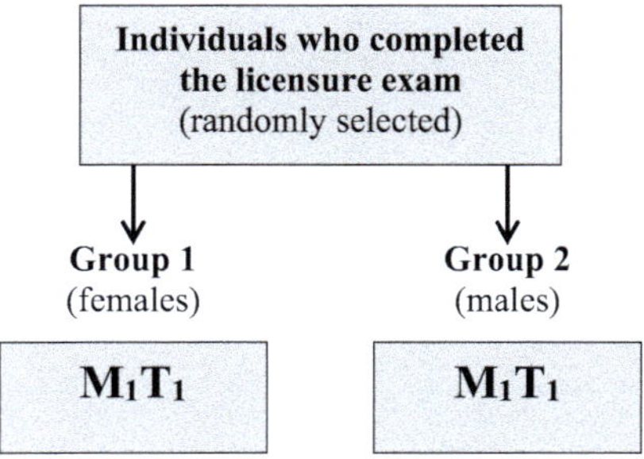

Hypotheses:

Difference: There is a difference on licensure exam scores between Females and Males.
Null: There is no difference on licensure exam scores between Females and Males.
Expected (E): The mean exam score of Females will be the same as the mean exam score of Males.
Predicted (P): The mean exam score of Females will be different than Males.
Observed (O): The actual mean exam score of Females and Males.

Level of Measurement: IV Nominal (gender), DV Interval (exam score)
Type of Design: Difference, cross-sectional
Number of Groups: 2 Groups (samples)
Assumptions: (a) Normal distribution, (b) Minimum of 10 per cell preferably 20 (c) Independent measures.

VARIABLE BOX—ONE-WAY ANOVA

Females (A1)	***Males*** (A2)
Exam Scores $\bar{X}_1$	**Exam Scores** $\bar{X}_2$

The ANOVA calculations are:

ANOVA CALCULATIONS

X_1 = Female Scores

X_2 = Males Scores

$$\Sigma X_1 = 550$$

$$\Sigma X_2 = 440$$

$$\Sigma X = 550 + 440 = 990$$

$$\Sigma X_1^2 = 11,252$$

$$\Sigma X_2^2 = 7,488$$

$$\Sigma X^2 = 11,252 + 7,488 = 18,740$$

$$\frac{(\Sigma X)^2}{N} = \frac{(990)^2}{60} = \frac{980100}{60} = 16,335$$

SS = Sum of Squares

$$SS_{Total} = \Sigma X^2 - \frac{(\Sigma X)^2}{N} = 18,740 - 16,355 = 2405$$

$$SS_{Between} = \frac{(\Sigma X_1)^2}{N_1} + \frac{(\Sigma X_2)^2}{N_2} - \frac{(\Sigma X)^2}{N} = \frac{(550)^2}{30} + \frac{(440)^2}{30} - \frac{(990)^2}{60}$$
$$= 1{,}008.33 + 6{,}453.33 - 16{,}335 = 16{,}536.60 - 16{,}335 = 201.66$$

$$SS_{Within} = SS_{Total} - SS_{Between} = 2405 - 201.66 = 2203.34$$

$$MS = Mean\ Square$$

$$MS_{Between} = \frac{SS_{Between}}{\#\ of\ Groups - 1} = \frac{201.66}{2-1} = 201.66$$

$$MS_{Within} = \frac{SS_{Within}}{N - \#\ of\ Groups} = \frac{2203.34}{60-2} = 37.989$$

$$F_{(1,158)} = \frac{MS_{Between}}{MS_{Within}} = \frac{201.66}{37.989} = 5.308;\ p = .025$$

Before running the data in SPSS, we will calculate partial eta squared using values from the ANOVA that are equivalent to Cohen's d in the t-test. The formula is:

$$Partial\ eta\ square = \frac{SS\ between}{SS\ between + SS\ error}$$
$$Partial\ eta\ square = \frac{201.66}{201.66 + 2203}$$
$$Partial\ eta\ square = \frac{201.66}{2404.66}$$
$$Partial\ eta\ square = 0.0839$$

General Partial Eta Squared Effect Size Interpretations

Partial Eta Squared	Interpretation
0–.009	Negligible or no effect size
.010–.058	Small effect size
.059–0.137	Medium effect size
.138+	Large effect size

The Partial Eta Squared Cutoff Points Are Very Important and Will Be Used Frequently in the Analysis Chapters

We can conclude that there was a ***medium effect size*** **(the same conclusion we arrived at for this data using the *t* statistic). The values for the size of the effect should be the equivalent since the one-way ANOVA for two independent groups is the same as the t-test for two independent groups.**

SPSS Commands

Open the data set ***Ch16 t-Test ANOVA ANCOVA***.
Follow the steps below.

(1) Click ***Analyze***.
(2) Scroll down and select ***General Linear Model***.
(3) Select ***Univariate . . .***
(4) Move the variable ***Exam*** to the ***Dependent Variable*** box; move the variable ***Gender*** to the ***Fixed Factor(s)*** box.

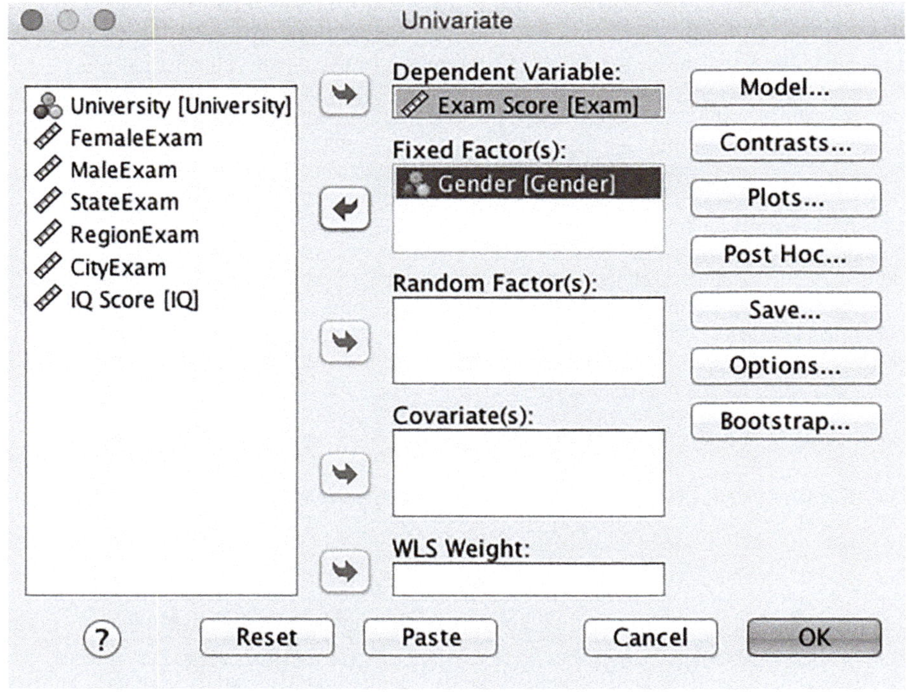

(5) Click ***Options . . .***
(6) Select ***Descriptive statistics***, ***Estimates of effect size***, ***Observed power*** and ***Homogeneity tests***.

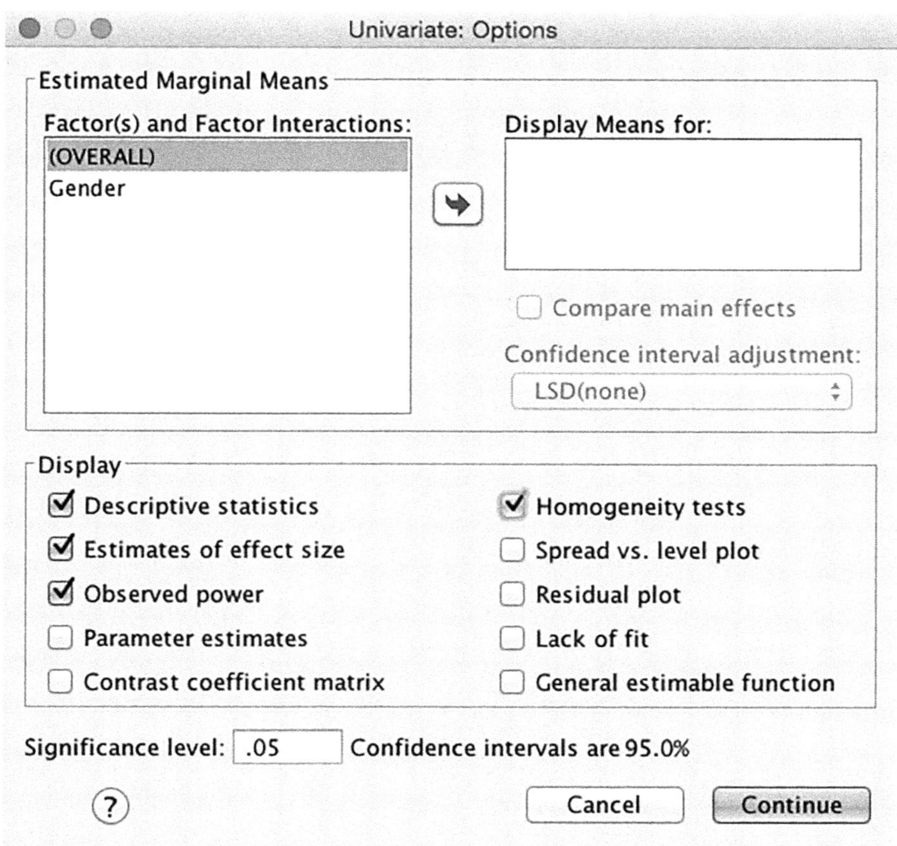

(7) Click ***OK*** to run the analysis.

Between-Subjects Factors

		Value Label	N
Gender	1	Female	30
	2	Male	30

Descriptive Statistics

Dependent Variable: Exam Score

Gender	Mean	Std. Deviation	N
Female	18.33	6.348	30
Male	14.67	5.973	30
Total	16.50	6.385	60

Levene's Test of Equality of Error Variances[a]

Dependent Variable: Exam Score

F	df1	df2	Sig.
.151	1	58	.699

Tests the null hypothesis that the error variance of the dependent variable is equal across groups.
a. Design: Intercept + Gender.

Tests of Between-Subjects Effects

Dependent Variable: Exam Score

Source	Type III Sum of Squares	Df	Mean Square	*F*	Sig.	Partial Eta Squared	Noncent. Parameter	Observed Power[b]
Corrected Model	201.667[a]	1	201.667	5.309	.025	.084	5.309	.620
Intercept	16335.000	1	16335.000	429.998	.000	.881	429.998	1.000
Gender	201.667	1	201.667	5.309	.025	.084	5.309	.620
Error	2203.333	58	37.989					
Total	18740.000	60						
Corrected Total	2405.000	59						

a. R Squared = .084 (Adjusted R Squared = .068).
b. Computed using alpha = .05.

The descriptive statistics table shows that Females have a higher average exam score than Males, suggesting that there may be a significant difference in the scores. **It is also clear that the assumption of equal variances in the two groups has been met because the Levene's test is not significant.** The next table shows the test of between-subjects effect (Gender) and includes the F statistic, significance of the statistic, the partial eta square indicating effect size and the power to detect differences. The F statistic is significant, the effect size is medium and there was sufficient power to perform the analysis. (See Chapter 14.)

The results might be written as follows:

A one-way between ANOVA was used to test if there were differences between Females and Males on the licensure exam score. The mean for Females was 18.333 and for Males 14.667, indicating that Females performed better on the licensure exam than Males. These results are significant ($F_{1,58}$ = 5.308, p = .025) with a medium effect size (partial eta squared = .084) and observed power of 62%.

Practical Implications: *These are the same as reported previously using the t-test.*

One-Way Between Analysis of Co-Variance (ANCOVA)

See Chart—Two Independent Groups and Interval or Ratio Level Measurement

Research Design

The one-way between analysis of co-variance (ANCOVA) is an extension of the one-way between ANOVA, but now will include ***another interval/ratio level variable that is used to take out (extract) variance that may affect differences in the DV***. Using a covariate (CV) in the analysis controls for the effect of that specific variable on the dependent variable. A researcher may want to exclude the effect of this variable because it can distort (create error) when you are trying to determine the effect of a specific IV on a specific DV. In an ***ANCOVA testing the difference between groups is done after the values of the dependent variable have been adjusted for differences related to the covariate (CV)***.

The assumptions required for the ANCOVA are the same as an ANOVA; however, there are three additional assumptions to be met (1) there must be a relationship between the dependent variable (DV) and the covariate (CV) and this relationship must be linear, (2) the regression line between the covariate and the dependent variable for both of the groups must be parallel and (3) the covariate must not be related to the independent group variable (IV).

Remember That the Dependent Variable (DV) and the Covariate (CV) Must Both Be Interval or Ratio Level Variables

Like an ANOVA, an ANCOVA may be used in all of the design types from exploratory to experimental. *An ANCOVA is frequently used to control for differences prior to the introduction of an intervention in the dependent variable. When you use the covariate this way, the initial amount of the dependent variable becomes the covariate and is used to equalize any pre-existing differences between those receiving the intervention and those not receiving the intervention. By using the initial level of the DV as a covariate, individual differences contributed by the covariate are removed as "undesirable variance" or "noise" in determining the actual effect of the intervention on the DV.*

When using the CV to determine and then subtract out the initial differences, it must be independent from the intervention/treatment and ***CV values must be gathered before the introduction of the intervention***. Of course, remember from the design section that random assignment to the intervention/treatment/experimental and to the no intervention/treatment/non-experimental/control group is an important prerequisite for an experimental design where an ANCOVA might be used. An ANCOVA should never be used as a substitute for assignment of individuals to treatment and no treatment groups.

If you are concerned about ***the effect of a variable on the DV there are three ways to control for its effect***:

(1) **The first is to make that variable an IV and test the impact on the DV; however, the variable has to be a nominal variable.** If the variable is naturally an interval/ratio level variable you have two other options
(2) **Control for the effect prior to any measurement of the DV.** For example, in the 400-yard race on a 1/4-mile track, the runner on the outside of the track (outside lane) will have to run further than the runner on the inside of the track (inside lane) to get to the common finish line. Of course, the purpose of the race is to determine the fastest runner by measuring the time to a common finish line. But everyone knows that if there are different distances to be run in the different lanes, the runners' time cannot be evaluated fairly because some are running shorter and some longer distances thus affecting their time. There is error in measuring the running time due to distance. The difference in distance is resolved by having the runner on the inside lane start the furthest back and as he or she moves to the outside lane each runner starts a prescribed distance further up the track to ensure that each runner runs exactly 400 yards to a single finish line for all runners. This procedure controls for the difference in distance prior to the race and is one way to control for the effect of the distance variable on running time. If you already know or suspect that a variable will affect the measurement of the DV, then you can select ways to "level the playing field" so that the measurement of the DV is not affected by that variable (CV). Sometimes you simply take out the variable before the study. Many examples occur in social work: only study women, only include one grade

level of children, only include individuals with depression in evaluating an intervention, only study a certain income level, etc. Limiting the effect of the variable by excluding group differences on that variable by selecting only one value on that variable takes the effect of that variable on the DV out of the equation. This is a method for controlling the effects of a variable that would produce a discrepancy (error) in the measurement of the DV that you have the opportunity to get rid of. Another often-used method is to ensure that all have the same level of the covariate. A very typical example is to provide training to everyone prior to the initiation of a study. For example, training all social workers on a particular intervention technique in working with individuals and testing to make sure that all have the same level of skill prior to start of a study. Here we see the "leveling of the playing field" by introducing the covariate and making sure everyone is the same

(3) **Control for the effects of the variable on the DV statistically by using an ANCOVA** if (a) it is very difficult to control the variable prior to the study, (b) it is very expensive or (c) it would make the study extremely lengthy by collecting information on the variable.

Remember from Chapter 9:

$$V_{T\ (DV)} = V_{1(IV)} + V_{2\ (IV)} + V_{3(IV)} + \text{Error}$$

The total variance of the DV is equal to the variance of variable 1 plus the variance of variable 2 plus the variance of variable 3 plus error. In this example the variables V1, V2, V3 have been identified and measured but any variance that is not measured by the variables V1, V2 or V3 would remain as error.

For a simple example, we will look at a situation where we are concerned with only one co-variable. In this example, the person's level of depression as measured on a standard depression scale (VT—total variance in the DV) is composed of the variance contributed by the IV (V1 variable of treatment/no treatment) plus error. If you are investigating the differences in depression of two groups, one that has treatment and one that does not, then a factor that can influence the amount of depression after treatment is the amount of depression prior to treatment. To control for the amount of depression prior to treatment you can measure the amount of depression for everyone prior to the intervention (pre-intervention) and then you take away the amount of depression each person has prior to treatment by subtracting it from the amount of depression following intervention (post-treatment). As you can see the playing field has been leveled based upon amount of depression prior to intervention. This is a classic way to utilize a covariate—to reduce error. You identify the source of the error, measure it and take it out of the measurement of differences—you reduce error!

Sometimes when you adjust (level) the means (averages) of the group by using the covariate, it will reduce the effect of the IV on the DV because the covariate may also be correlated with the IV thus removing some of the IV affect. In using designs where you are trying to determine the effect of an IV on the DV and also using a covariate, you need to be ***concerned and aware of (1) the possibility that the covariate may reduce the effect of the IV on the DV*** and ***(2) the covariate may produce more effect on the DV than the IV***. In this case you may have uncovered a variable that is acting as a moderator or mediator that should be studied.

When the covariate shares some variance with the variance accounted for, there is a reduction in the amount of accounted-for variance. When this happens, the covariate does not reduce error because the CV was not independent from the IV as required by the assumptions for using ANCOVA. When the covariate and the IV are not independent, you may get some effects on the results that you did not expect: (a) an outcome that was significant may become non-significant, (b) an outcome that was significant is still significant but not as significant as before and (c) an outcome that was non-significant before is significant now because the covariate was covering it up.

If you are going to use the level of the DV prior to intervention as the covariate then you must measure that level prior to intervention. Thus, the covariate *(the pre-measure of the DV) is measured at T_1 followed by an intervention and then the measurement of the DV at T_2*. These measurements are always on the same person. If you are not using the covariate to level the initial level for all participants in all groups prior to intervention, then you can measure the covariate at the same time as the DV both at T_1.

Conceptualization

The example used to explain the t-test and ANOVA will be used again for the ANCOVA.

In this example, it is not a measure of the DV prior to an intervention; it is measured at the same time as the DV.

We have basically the same question as before but with an addition. "Do Males and Females differ on their licensure exam, controlling for IQ?" The ANCOVA combines an ANOVA with a regression analysis (Chapter 21). We will not go into the regression analysis here but simply say it provides an estimate of the relationship between the covariate (IQ) and the DV (licensure exam score) and it will be discussed in Chapter 21. First, there is an estimate of the relationship between IQ and exam score and following that part of the analysis the influence of the individual's IQ is adjusted to remove the effects of it on the DV. Then the analysis of the effects of the IV (Gender) on the exam score (ANOVA portion) is performed on the adjusted exam scores (exam values with the effect of the IQ removed).

When you calculate differences using an ANCOVA, one degree of freedom is lost for each CV included in the analysis. This means that although power (see Chapter 14) is gained due to a decrease in error, it could be offset by the loss in degrees of freedom. If a good correlation exists between the CV and DV, the test will be more sensitive and able to detect differences (error reduction) that will offset the loss of a degree of freedom. ***Therefore, we suggest that a correlation of .25 be used as a minimum for inclusion as a covariate. Another important consideration is "Does the covariate have too high a correlation with the DV?" If the correlation is above .7, the covariate the same thing as the DV and may in fact be redundant and should not be used as a covariate.***

We will discuss correlation in greater depth in a later chapter. We can use SPSS to produce a basic correlation matrix to examine the degree of correlation between the DV (exam score) and the CV (IQ):

Correlations

		Exam Score	IQ Score
Exam Score	Pearson Correlation	1	**.248**
	Sig. (2-tailed)		.056
	N	60	60
IQ Score	Pearson Correlation	.248	1
	Sig. (2-tailed)	.056	
	N	60	60

As you can see, the DV and covariate in this example have a correlation of 0.248—the minimal suggested degree of correlation.

How the covariate reduces error. In an ANCOVA every group mean is adjusted based upon the covariate. For example, if one gender had an above-average mean on the CV (IQ) compared to the other gender, then their group mean score on the DV (exam score) will be lowered. In contrast, if one gender had a below-average mean on the CV (IQ) the mean score on their DV (exam score) will be raised. The amount of adjustment in the group mean score on the DV depends on how far above or below the average that group score is on the CV (IQ). **By adjusting the mean of exam scores the ANCOVA analysis provides the best estimate of how Males and Females would have performed in terms of the licensure exam if they had all possessed equivalent IQs.** In this way, there is a level playing field for the two groups with respect to IQ (its effect is taken out of the exam score) and the error variance (within variance) is reduced. Conceptually it is the same as making sure the distance run on the track is the same for all athletes so that the time to the finish line was not affected by the different distances run based upon the lane assignment of the runner.

As you recall from our conceptual framework for an ANOVA, averaged squared deviations from the means—variances—are partitioned into variance associated with different levels of the IV (between-group variance) and variance associated with differences in scores within groups (within-group or error variance).

The table for the ANCOVA is similar to the one for ANOVA, the only difference is that the values for the sum of squares and degrees of freedom have been adjusted for the effects of the covariate. The between-groups degrees of freedom are still the number of groups−1, the total degrees of freedom are still N − 1, but the within-groups degrees of freedom are now N−number of groups−1. **The statistic for the ANCOVA now becomes the ratio of the adjusted between-groups mean squares to the adjusted within-groups mean square.**

We will not do the math calculations for the ANCOVA since you have already completed a calculation for the ANOVA and the calculations for the ANCOVA follow the same procedures and then take out the variance contributed by the covariate.

We will use the same example as the one we used to illustrate the one-way between ANOVA where we investigated if there is a difference in Male and Female scores on the licensure exam. We will control for IQ using the Weschler Adult Intelligence Scale (WAIS). The scores on the IQ test range from 0 to 200 with a national average of 100 and an SD of 15. The study question is similar to the one-way ANOVA with the addition of the covariate.

Study Question: Is there a difference between Males and Females on their licensure exam score after controlling for IQ?

This is a difference, cross-sectional design.

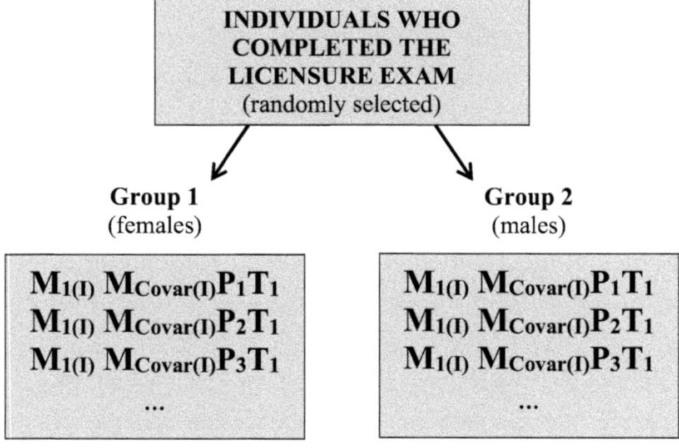

Look at the design above and you will note that we have to measure the interval level DV exam score (M_1) and the interval level CV the IQ (M_{covar}) for each person at a particular point in time (T_1) and we have to have each measurement for the DV and the CV linked together for each person (P_1).

Hypotheses:

Difference: There is a difference between Males and Females on their licensure exam scores after controlling for IQ as measured by the Weschler Adult Intelligence Scale (WAIS).

Null: There is no difference between Males and Females on their licensure exam score after controlling for IQ as measured by the WAIS.

Expected (E): The adjusted mean licensure exam score of Males will be the same as the adjusted mean licensure exam score of Females, after controlling for IQ.

Predicted (P): The adjusted mean licensure exam score of Males will be different from the adjusted mean licensure exam score of Females, after controlling for IQ.

Observed (O): The actual adjusted mean licensure exam score for Females and Males, after controlling for IQ.

Level of Measurement: IV Nominal (gender), DV Interval (exam score), CV Interval (IQ)

Type of Design: Difference, cross-sectional

Number of Groups: 2 Groups (samples)

Assumptions: (a) Normal distribution, minimum of 10 per cell preferably 20 (b) Independent measures, (c) Linear relationship between DV and covariate, (d) Regression line between the covariate and the dependent variable for both of the groups must be parallel, (e) The covariate must not be related to the IV.

VARIABLE BOX—ONE-WAY ANCOVA

Females (A1)	***Males*** (A2)
Exam Scores *X – covariate*	**Exam Scores** *X – covariate*

SPSS Commands

Open the data set ***Ch16 t-Test ANOVA ANCOVA***.
Follow the steps below.

(1) Click ***Analyze***.
(2) Scroll down and select ***General Linear Model***.

(3) Select ***Univariate*** . . .

(4) Move the variable ***Exam*** to the ***Dependent Variable*** box; move the variable ***Gender*** to the ***Fixed Factor(s)*** box; Move the variable ***IQ*** to the ***Covariate(s)*** box.

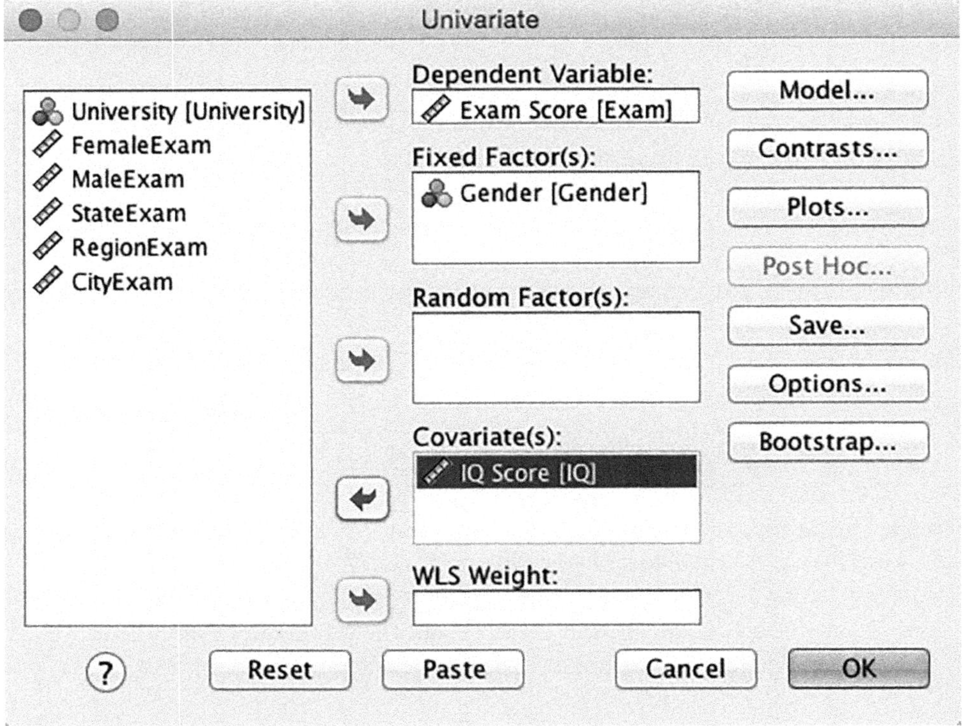

(5) Click ***Options*** . . .

(6) Select ***Descriptive statistics***, ***Estimates of effect size***, ***Observed power*** and ***Homogeneity tests***.

(7) Under the ***Estimated Marginal Means*** menu, move ***Gender*** from the ***Factor(s) and Factor Interactions*** box to the ***Display Means for*** box.

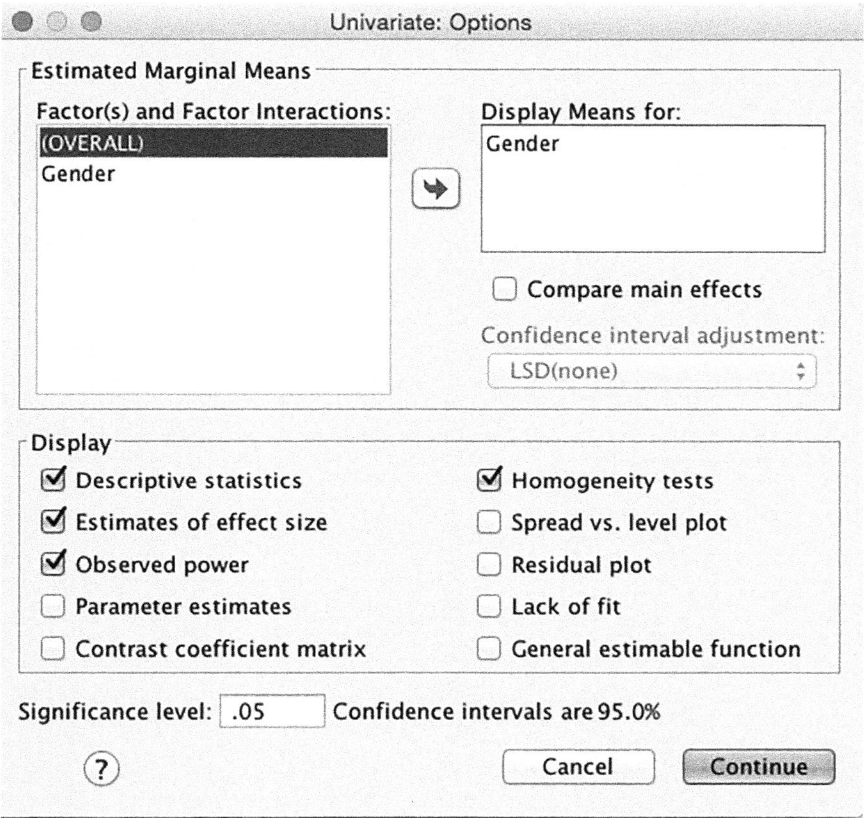

(8) Click ***Continue***.
(9) Click ***OK*** to run the analysis.

Between-Subjects Factors

		Value Label	N
Gender	1	Female	30
	2	Male	30

Descriptive Statistics

Dependent Variable: Exam Score

Gender	Mean	Std. Deviation	N
Female	18.33	6.348	30
Male	14.67	5.973	30
Total	16.50	6.385	60

Levene's Test of Equality of Error Variances[a]

Dependent Variable: Exam Score

F	df1	df2	Sig.
1.052	1	58	.309

Tests the null hypothesis that the error variance of the dependent variable is equal across groups.

a. Design: Intercept + IQ + Gender.

Tests of Between-Subjects Effects

Dependent Variable: Exam Score

Source	Type III Sum of Squares	df	Mean Square	*F*	Sig.	Partial Eta Squared	Noncent. Parameter	Observed Power[b]
Corrected Model	327.875[a]	2	163.937	4.499	.015	.136	8.997	.747
Intercept	69.510	1	69.510	1.907	.173	.032	1.907	.274
IQ	126.208	1	126.208	3.463	.068	.057	3.463	.448
Gender	180.288	1	180.288	4.947	.030	.080	4.947	.590
Error	2077.125	57	36.441					
Total	18740.000	60						
Corrected Total	2405.000	59						

a. R Squared = .136 (Adjusted R Squared = .106).

b. Computed using alpha = .05.

Gender

Dependent Variable: Exam Score

Gender	Mean	Std. Error	95% Confidence Interval	
			Lower-Bound	Upper-Bound
Female	18.237[a]	1.103	16.028	20.447
Male	14.763[a]	1.103	12.553	16.972

a. Covariates appearing in the model are evaluated at the following values: IQ Score = 99.95.

The difference between Males and Females is still significant. The adjusted mean (estimated marginal mean) for Males changed from 14.667 to 14.763 and for Females from 18.333 to 18.227 after controlling for IQ with a mean of 99.9. The overall mean did not change from 16.50. Gender differences are still significant for licensure exam scores but the significance is not as great (.025 to .030) indicating that there was a very slight change in score based upon IQ. Both power and effect size remain small.

The results could be written as follows:

A one-way between ANCOVA was performed to test if Females and Males differ on their licensure exam scores. IQ was controlled for in the analysis with an average IQ of 99.95. IQ was not significant ($p = .068$). The estimated marginal mean for Females was 18.227 (SE = 1.103) and for Males was 14.763 (SE = 1.103), indicating that Females had better licensure exam scores than Males. These results are significant ($F_{157} = 4.907$; $p = .03$) with a medium effect (partial eta squared = .08) and 59% power.

Practical Implications: The implications are the same as reported for the t-test on this same data EXCEPT now you can say that IQ does not have a significant effect on licensure score. Gender, while significant and having a medium effect, only accounts for only approximately 8% of the difference in the scores, indicating the need to search for other variables that have a greater effect.

Articles for Discussion

Critique the author's use of the Fisher Exact and the Wilcoxon-Mann-Whitney U test in this study. Reflect on the reasons for using these specific tests as part of the study.

Banks, A., & Faul, A. (2007). Reduction of face-to-face contact hours in foundation research courses: Impact on student's knowledge gained and course satisfaction. *Social Work Education, 26*(8), 780–793. doi:10.1080/02615470601140500

Discuss the author's use of the KS test and the independent t-test in their study. Why is it important in their research? Also discuss the amount of control in the study design.

Raheb, G., Kahleghi, E., Moghanibashi-Mansourieh, A., Farhoudian, A., & Teymouri, R. (2016). Effectiveness of social work intervention with a systematic approach to general health in opioid addicts in addiction treatment centers. *Psychological Research on Behavior Management*, *9*, 309–315. Retrieved from www.ncbi.nlm.nih.gov/pmc/articles/PMC5118021

Discuss the findings about which tests are more frequently used and how they are reported. Do you believe that the tests used are strong enough, correctly reported in the literature? What do you think should be done in social work research concerning designs and analytical methods?

Ham, A. D., Huggins-Hoyt, K. Y., & Pettus, J. (2016). Assessing statistical change indices in selected social work intervention research studies. *Research on Social Work Practice*, *26*(1), 44–52. doi:10.1177/1049731515581496

Exercises for Chapter 16 are found in eResources.

Chapter 17

FINDING DIFFERENCES

Two Related or Matched Groups (Samples) Tests

PART A: NONPARAMETRIC

Nominal Level Data

McNemar Change Test

See Chart—Two Matched or Related Groups and Nominal Measurement

The McNemar test is used to determine if a change took place after an intervention when the variable is nominally measured. The test does not measure the amount of change that took place, only that it did take place. It is a very basic explanatory design with no control group and sometimes used in program evaluation.

Conceptual Framework

We will begin by developing a conceptual framework to understand how the data is analyzed. This test can be visualized and analyzed using a 2 × 2 table. Let's assume that the pretest has two possibilities (X = for and Y = against) and the posttest has the same two possibilities (X = for and Y = against).

	Posttest: X For	Posttest: Y Against	Row total
Pretest: X For	A	B	A + B
Pretest: Y Against	C	D	C + D
Column total	A + C	B + D	N

Discordant pairs (pairs that are not matching) are found in Cells B and C (where there was a change from before to after). Mathematically the null hypothesis is $p_B = p_C$ and $p_B \neq p_C$ is the difference hypothesis.

The formula for calculating the exact probability for the McNemar test is:

$$\chi^2 = \frac{(b-c)^2}{b+c}$$

Assume a program is introduced into nursing home to get residents to become more involved in social activities with others. The outcome is for the elderly to change their leisure activity from watching TV alone to playing games with other people. At the beginning of the intervention, they had to choose if they would rather watch TV alone or if they would prefer playing games with other people. The intervention focused on the importance of socialization with others as contributing to happiness and better health and promoted game playing as a way to achieve these goals.

Study Question: Does the intervention program result in more socialization through game playing?

This is an explanatory pre-post, repeated measures design with no control group.

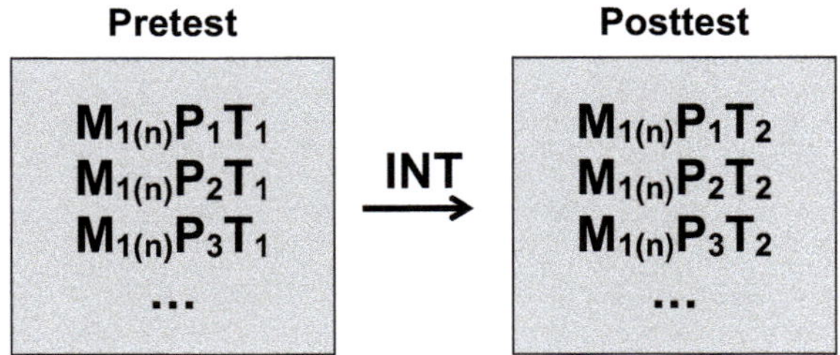

Hypotheses:

Difference: The intervention will create a change in the leisure activity from watching TV alone to game playing activity.

Null hypothesis: The intervention will not create a change in the preferred leisure time activity.

Expected (E): No difference.

Predicted (P): Leisure activity will change from watching TV alone to playing games with others.

Observed (O): The actual distribution of choices for leisure activity.

Level of Measurement: Nominal

Type of Design: Explanatory, repeated measures no control

Number of Groups: 2 Groups (samples)

Assumptions: None

VARIABLE BOX—McNEMAR TEST

	Posttest: Watch TV	Posttest: Play Games	Row Total
Pretest: Watch TV	A	B	A + B
Pretest: Play Games	C	D	C + D
Column Total	A + C	B + D	*N*

Ideally, you want your intervention to show that residents changed their preferred leisure time activity from watching TV alone to playing games with others (B). We would not like the residents to change their preferred leisure time activity from playing games with others to watching TV (C). If the intervention has no effect, the probability of B will be the same as the probability of C. Also the probability of A will be the same as the probability of D. If the intervention actually has an effect, these probabilities will be significantly different from one another.

The results after the intervention were:

	Posttest: Watch TV	Posttest: Play Games	Row Total
Pretest: Watch TV	5	15	20
Pretest: Play Games	3	6	9
Column Total	8	21	*29*

Using the formula to find the value for the McNemar test:

$$\chi^2 = \frac{(b-c)^2}{b+c}$$

$$\chi^2 = \frac{(15-3)^2}{15+3}$$

$$\chi^2 = \frac{(12)^2}{18}$$

$$\chi^2 = \frac{144}{18}$$

$$\chi^2 = 8$$

The critical value of X^2 with 1 degree of freedom is 6.54 (this can be found in any table of Chi-Square critical values such as the one found at www.itl.nist.gov). Since the calculated value of Chi-Square = 8, the change was significant at $p < .01$.

Let's look at a different example that involves social workers in Child Protective Services (CPS). The training section of CPS wanted to institute new training that provided the workers with Solution-Focused Intervention. They were interested in determining if the workers changed their preferred method of intervention after training. They were not interested in the amount of change in the preferred method only if they changed their preferred method of intervention. There were 20 workers involved in the training and before the training they were asked to write down if they preferred cognitive or solution-focused interventions. Out of the 20 workers, 17 preferred cognitive intervention and 3 preferred solution-focused intervention.

Training was provided and after the training, 4 workers who had preferred cognitive still preferred cognitive methods, but 13 of those who preferred cognitive methods changed their preference to solution-focused methods. Of the 3 who had preferred solution-focused methods, 2 remained preferring solution-focused methods and 1 had changed to preferring cognitive methods.

Study Question: Does training in Solution-Focused Intervention create a change in the preferred method to solution focused by CPS workers?

This is an explanatory pre-post, repeated measures design with no control group.

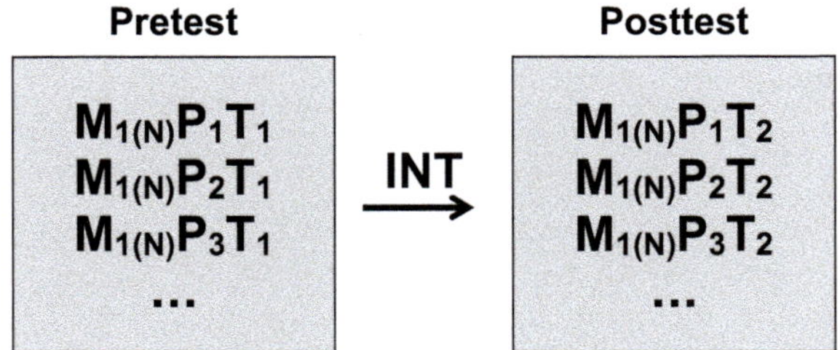

Hypotheses:

Explanatory: Solution-Focused Training will create a change in the method used by CPS workers to more solution focused (directional hypothesis, 1 tailed).

Null: Solution-Focused Training will not create a change in the method used by CPS workers.

Expected (E): Workers' preferred method would remain the same before and after the training.

Predicted (P): Workers will change to solution focused as their preferred method after the training.

Observed (O): The amount of workers who changed their preferred to solution focused after training.
Level of Measurement: IV Nominal (Training), DV Nominal (Method)
Type of Design: Explanatory, repeated measures, no control
Number of Groups: 2 Groups (samples)
Assumptions: Matching

VARIABLE BOX—McNEMAR TEST

	Cognitive—After	Solution Focused—After	Row Total
Cognitive—Before	Stays the same (A)	Changes from COG to SF (B)	A + B
Solution Focused—Before	Changes from SF to COG (C)	Stays the same (D)	C + D
Column Total	A + C	B + D	N

SPSS Commands

Open the data set ***Ch17 McNemar***.
Follow the steps below.

(1) Click ***Analyze***.
(2) Scroll down and select ***Nonparametric Tests***.
(3) Select ***Legacy Dialogs***; select ***2 Related Samples . . .***

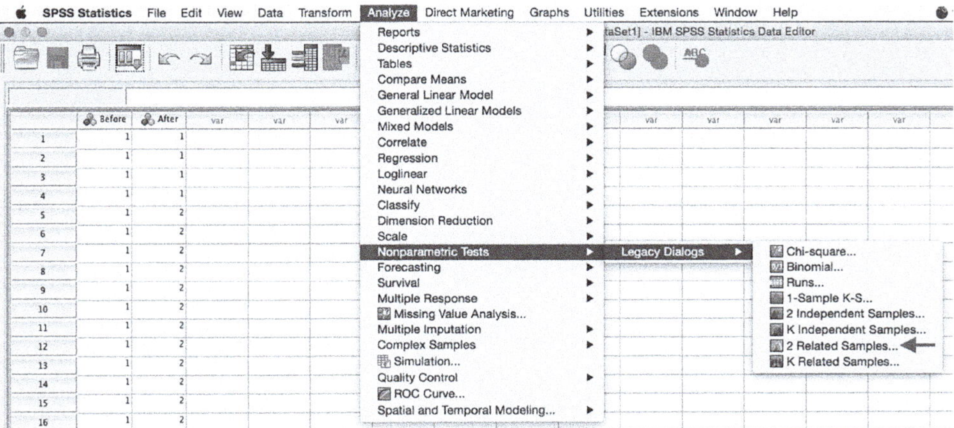

(4) Move the ***Before*** and ***After*** variables into the ***Test Pairs*** list.
(5) Select ***McNemar*** in the ***Test Type*** box.
(6) Click ***OK*** to run.

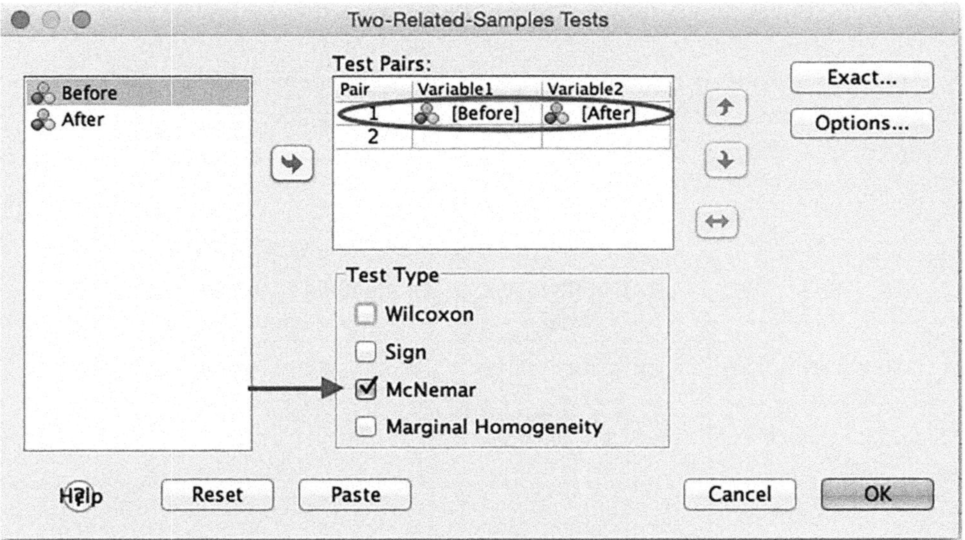

Look at the output:

Before and After

Before	After	
	Cognitive	Solution Focused
Cognitive	4	13
Solution Focused	1	2

Test Statistics[a]

	Before and After
N	20
Exact Sig. (2-tailed)	.002[b]

a. McNemar test.
b. Binomial distribution used.

The output provides the before and after results. There was a significant difference between preferred method before and preferred method after. You can conclude that the training made a difference in moving the workers from cognitive to solution-focused methods.

Results might be written as follows:

A pre-post design with no control was used to determine if CPS workers changed from cognitive as their preferred method of practice to solution focused after training in solution-focused methods. There was a significant change between pre- and post-measures on the preferred method of practice. Of the 20 workers who participated in the training, 17 preferred cognitive intervention and 3 preferred solution-focused intervention before the start of training. After the training, 4 workers who had preferred cognitive at the start of the job still preferred cognitive methods. Thirteen (13) of those who preferred cognitive methods had changed to preferring solution-focused methods. Of the 3 who preferred solution-focused methods, 2 still preferred solution-focused methods but 1 changed the preference to cognitive methods. The change from cognitive to solution-focused methods after training was significant (McNemar test $p = .001$ one talied).

Practical Implications: The training resulted in a change for workers who preferred cognitive to solution focused and thereby helped the agency to have a more consistent approach/method to resolving client problems. Transfer from one social worker to another could be more easily accomplished (if needed) due to the client receiving the same method of intervention. Training was effective and might be utilized with all new employees as the method of preference prior to assignment of cases. The agency and researcher should be aware that 4 persons who preferred cognitive at the start of the training still preferred that method. An interview or follow-up with these individuals might help to determine reasons for not changing. In addition, it would be important to talk to the person who switched from solution focused to cognitive to find out why this person changed after the introduction of more solution-focused training.

Ordinal Level Data

Wilcoxon Signed Rank Test

See Chart—Two Matched or Related Groups (Samples) and Ordinal Measurement

The Wilcoxon Signed Rank test measures before and after change like the McNemar; however, the ***magnitude of the change can be determined since the measurement is ordinal***.

Let's look at a study where a video is shown to a group of people to see how the video impacts their perception of social work. Participants rate their perception of social work before and after a video that depicts social work very positively. The study's goal is to find out if this video will change the perception of social work to a more positive one. **The Wilcoxon Signed Rank test requires at least ordinal level data and is appropriate when you have interval or ratio data that is not normally distributed.**

Recall that the McNemar test is also a before and after test using NOMINAL DATA and based upon the Chi-Square distribution. With ranks (ordinal data) the Wilcoxon Signed Rank test provides more precision and ability to discriminate if there are differences.

Individual measurements prior to intervention act like a "control group" or a reflection of the population. The measurement of each individual difference between the prior and post-intervention reflects the effect or difference of the intervention. This method is sometimes referred to as the individual being their "own control". For example, a group of 25 freshman students are shown a video that is very positive about social work. Before the video is shown, they are asked to rate the importance of social work on a 5-point scale, ranging from not important at all to very important. After the video is shown, they are asked to rate the importance of social work again. The goal of this explanatory study is to find out if the student's perceptions of social work will change as a result of this video.

Study Question: Does a positive video about social work change freshmen students' perception of social work?

This is an explanatory pre-post, repeated measures design with no control group.

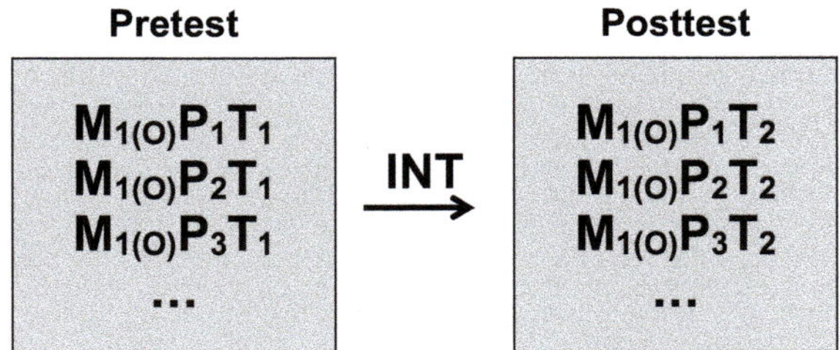

Hypotheses:

Explanatory: A positive video about social work will improve freshmen students' perception of social work.

Null: A positive video about social work will not change freshmen students' perception of social work.

Expected (E): Freshmen students' perception about social work will be the same before and after the video.

Predicted (P): Freshmen students' perception of social work will be more positive after watching the video.

Observed (O): The change that takes place in perception of social work after watching the video.

Level of Measurement: IV Nominal (Video), DV Ordinal (Perception of Social Work)

Type of Design: Explanatory, repeated measures, no control

Number of Groups: 2 Groups (samples) related
Assumptions: (a) Ordinal DV (b) Underlying distribution is continuous.

VARIABLE BOX—Wilcoxon Signed Ranks
TIME

	T_1 PRE RANK	Intervention VIDEO	T_2 POST RANK
P_1			
P_2			
P_3			
P_4			
P_5			
$P_{\dots}$			

The following table shows the results:

Social Work Perceptions

Student #	Before (X_i)	After (Y_i)	$Y_i - X_i$ (Z_i)	Sign of Z_i	$\|Z_i\|$	Rank of $\|Z_i\|$	Negative Ranks	Positive Ranks
1	1	1	0		0			
2	1	2	+1	+	1	5		5
3	1	2	+1	+	1	5		5
4	1	2	+1	+	1	5		5
5	2	4	+2	+	2	13.5		13.5
6	2	4	+2	+	2	13.5		13.5
7	2	4	+2	+	2	13.5		13.5
8	2	2	0		0			
9	2	4	+2	+	2	13.5		13.5
10	2	4	+2	+	2	13.5		13.5
11	3	5	+2	+	2	13.5		13.5
12	3	5	+2	+	2	13.5		13.5
13	3	3	0		0			
14	3	5	+2	+	2	13.5		13.5
15	3	3	0		0			

(Continued)

Student #	Before (X_i)	After (Y_i)	Y_i–X_i (Z_i)	Sign of Z_i	$\lvert Z_i \rvert$	Rank of $\lvert Z_i \rvert$	Negative Ranks	Positive Ranks
16	3	2	–1	–	1	5	5	
17	4	3	–1	–	1	5	5	
18	4	5	+1	+	1	5		5
19	4	5	+1	+	1	5		5
20	4	5	+1	+	1	5		5
21	4	5	+1	+	1	5		5
22	5	5	0		0			
23	5	5	0		0			
24	5	5	0		0			
25	5	5	0		0			
						Rank Totals:	10	143

The first step is to exclude any of the observations where $Z_i = 0$; *in this case, the adjusted sample size is 17*. We have excluded in the analysis 8 values where there was no change in perceptions before and after the video. The next two columns show the value and absolute value of $Y_i – X_i$ (Z_i and $|Z_i|$). The last two columns shows the rank with a mean rank assigned to tied scores. Tie ranks are calculated by adding the ranks together and dividing by the number of ties. The value 1 occurs 9 times. The ranks corresponding to these values are 1, 2, 3, 4, 5, 6, 7, 8 and 9 with a sum of 45 and when divided by 9 = 5 which is the value given each of these 9 ranks. The next value is 2 of which there were 8 instances. The ranks corresponding to these values are 10, 11, 12, 13, 14, 15, 16, 17 and when summed = 108. Dividing this by 8 = 13.5 which is the rank given to each of these 8 scores. The positive and negative ranks are then summed. As depicted in the table, $\boldsymbol{W_+ = 143}$ while $\boldsymbol{W_- = 10}$.

S is then calculated as the smaller of these two rank sums: $\boldsymbol{S = \min(W_+, W_-)}$

The critical value is then obtained for the adjusted sample size (17 in this example). *S* is compared against the critical value, and the H_0 is rejected if *S* is less than or is equal to the critical value. For a 1-tailed significance of 0.05, the critical value is 41 (as can be determined by referring to a table of critical values such as those available at www.nist.gov); therefore, the *S* value is smaller than the critical value and the H_0 is rejected.

SPSS Commands

Open the data set ***Ch17 Wilcoxon***.
Follow the steps:

(1) Click ***Analyze***.
(2) Scroll down and select ***Nonparametric Tests***.
(3) Select ***Legacy Dialogs***; select ***2 Related Samples . . .***

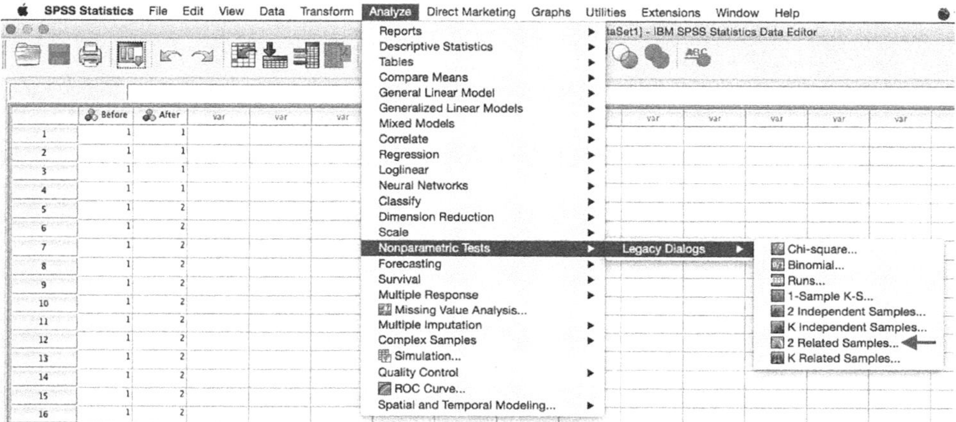

(4) Move the ***SW_Before*** and ***SW_After*** variables into the ***Test Pairs*** list.
(5) Select ***Wilcoxon*** in the ***Test Type*** box.
(6) Click ***OK*** to run.

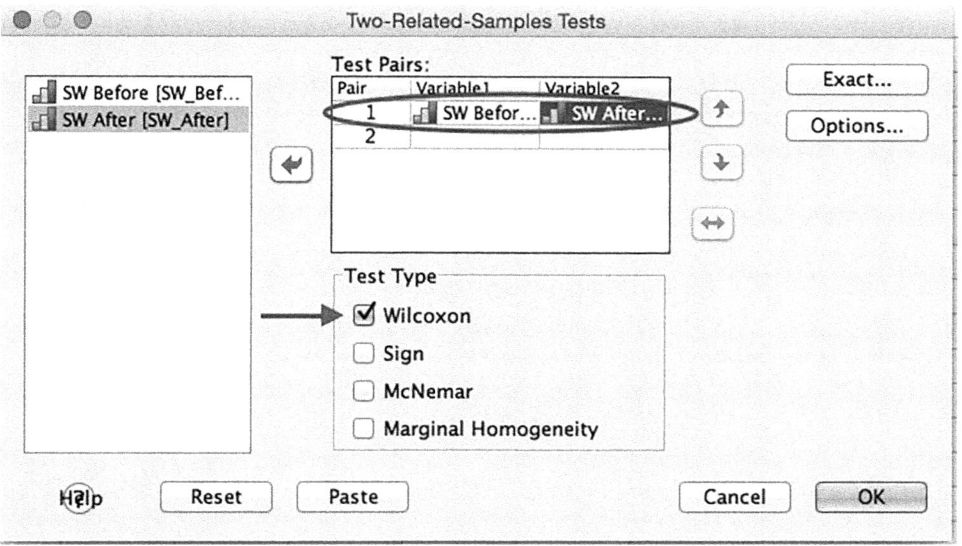

Review the SPSS output tables:

Ranks

		N	Mean Rank	Sum of Ranks
SW After—SW Before	Negative Ranks	2[a]	5.00	10.00
	Positive Ranks	15[b]	9.53	143.00
	Ties	8[c]		
	Total	25		

a. SW After < SW Before.
b. SW After > SW Before.
c. SW After = SW Before.

Test Statistics[a]

	SW After—SW Before
Z	–3.242[b]
Asymp. Sig. (2-tailed)	.001

a. Wilcoxon Signed Ranks test.
b. Based on negative ranks.

Results might be written as follows:

A pre-post explanatory design with no control was used to determine if the perception of social work by students changes after watching a video portraying social work positively. There was a significant positive change from the pre- to post-measurement of the perception of social work. Fifteen of the 25 students who watched the video became more positive in their perception of social work after the video. Eight did not change their perception and two became more negative in their perception. The positive change in perception was significant (Wilcoxon Z = −3.242; *p* = .0005 one tailed).

Practical Implications: The video used was very effective in changing the perception of freshmen students toward social work to a more positive one. It is important to interview those who did not change and those who reacted negatively to the video to determine how it might be improved. Who were the students—their majors—would it hold for certain majors and not others? This study was conducted with freshman students and does not generalize to the greater population. A study needs to be conducted to find out if the same results would be obtained in the community.

PART B: PARAMETRIC

Interval or Ratio Level Data

Paired-Samples t-test

See Chart—Two Related or Matched Groups and Interval or Ratio Measurement

As previously discussed in Chapter 15, comparing a group (sample) mean to a population and in Chapter 16, comparing two group (sample) means, the t-test is the most basic of the parametric tests. Now we will discuss the third type of t-test, namely the paired sample t-test (replicated).

The paired sample t-test is used to analyze the same type of data as a repeated measure Analysis of Variance (ANOVA) and the same results will be obtained from both tests. **This test is appropriate for an explanatory before and after design with no control group and is used in program evaluation where frequently only one group is tested before an intervention (pretest) and tested after the intervention (posttest) using interval or ratio data.** The average pre-intervention score of the group is compared to the average post-intervention score of that same group.

We will demonstrate the use of the paired t-test by analyzing the results of an intervention for teenage girls with low self-esteem. The focus of the social worker led group is to improve self-esteem and prior to the start of the group meetings each girl completed a pretest on self-esteem. All girls participated in the group for 10 weeks to improve their self-esteem. Following the 10 weeks of group self-image improvement meetings, the girls completed the same self-esteem test. Self-esteem was measured on a Self-Esteem Scale with a total score that could range between 4 and 16, with higher scores indicating poor self-esteem. For example, I feel that I cannot do anything right. 1 = Never 5 = Always.

Study Question: Do the self-esteem group sessions improve self-esteem in the teenage girls?

This is an explanatory repeated measures pre-post non control design.

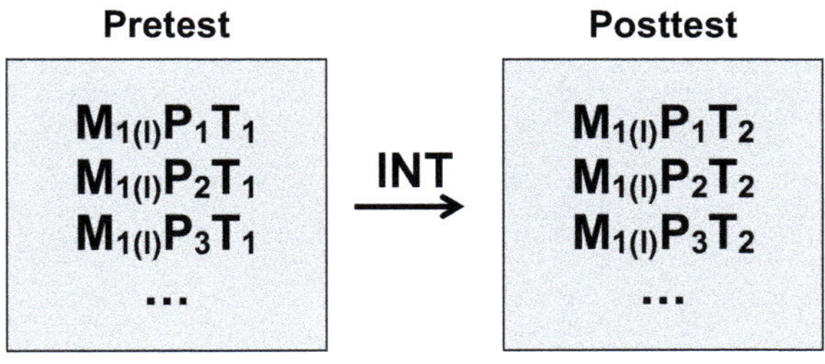

Hypotheses:

Explanatory: Group meetings will improve the teenage girl's self-esteem **(1-tailed)**.

Null: Group meetings will not improve the teenage girl's self-esteem.

Expected (E): The girls will have the same level of self-esteem before and after the group meetings.

Predicted (P): The girls will have increased self-esteem after 10 weeks of group meetings.

Observed (P): The change in self-esteem of the teenage girls following 10 weeks of group meetings.

Level of Measurement: IV Nominal (meetings), DV Interval (self-esteem score)

Type of Design: Explanatory, related, no control

Number of Groups: 2 Groups (samples) related

Assumptions: (a) Matched (b) Similar distributions (c) N of 10+.

VARIABLE BOX—PAIRED GROUP (SAMPLE) t-TEST

TIME

	T_1 PRE SCORE	Intervention GROUP MEETINGS	T_2 POST SCORE
P_1			
P_2			
P_3			
P_4			
P_5			
$P_{...}$			

CONCEPTUAL FRAMEWORK

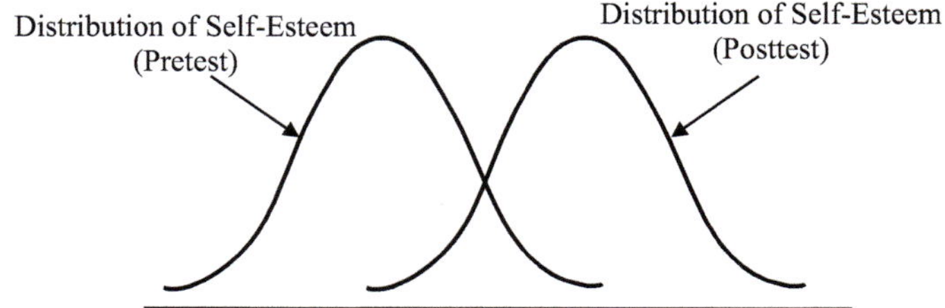

Esteem (Pre)	Esteem (Post)	Difference
7	6	–1
7	9	2
4	7	3
8	10	2
6	4	–2
3	7	4
9	8	–1
5	9	4
6	6	0
8	10	2
7	6	–1
7	9	2
4	7	3
8	10	2
6	4	–2
3	7	4
9	8	–1
5	9	4
6	6	0
8	10	2
7	6	–1
7	9	2
4	7	3
8	10	2
6	4	–2
3	7	4
9	8	–1
5	9	4
6	6	0
8	10	2

A very simple difference score formula can be used to calculate the paired sample t-test:

$$t = \frac{\bar{X}_{dif}}{s_{dif/\sqrt{N}}}$$

Where $\bar{X}_{dif}$ = the mean of the difference scores
S_{dif} = the standard deviation of these scores
N = number of pairs

$$t = \frac{1.3}{2.09 / \sqrt{30}}$$

$$t = \frac{1.3}{2.09 / 5.47}$$

$$t = \frac{1.3}{.38}$$

$$t = 3.42$$

With the degrees of freedom being one less than the total number of pairs (30 − 1 = 29), you can look at any t distribution table (such as the one found at www.nist.gov) and see that the critical value (p = 0.05) is 2.04. Because our obtained value exceeds this amount, we can conclude that there is a significant difference between pre- and posttest scores on self-esteem.

Now lets do the same using SPSS.

SPSS Commands

Open the data set ***Ch17 Paired t-test.***
Follow the steps below:

(1) Click ***Analyze.***
(2) Scroll down and select ***Compare Means.***
(3) Select ***Paired-Samples t-test . . .***

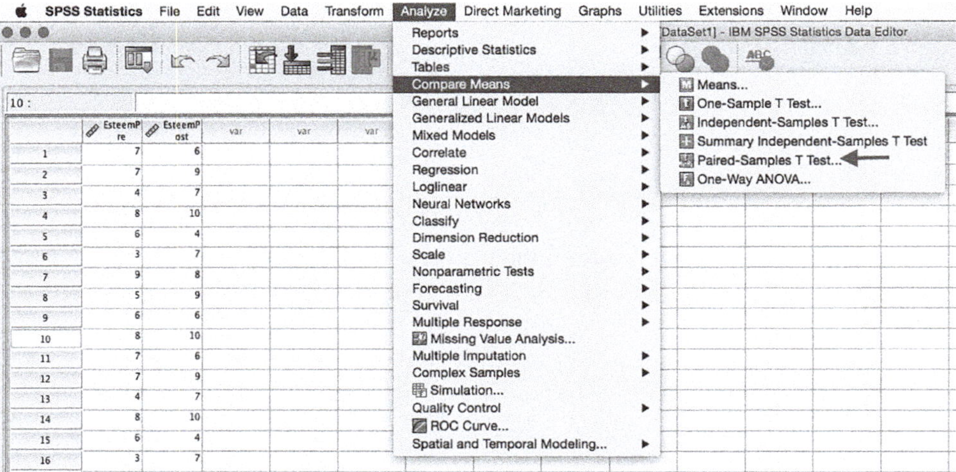

(4) Move the ***EsteemPre*** and ***EsteemPost*** variables to the ***Paired Variables*** list.
(5) Click ***OK*** to run.

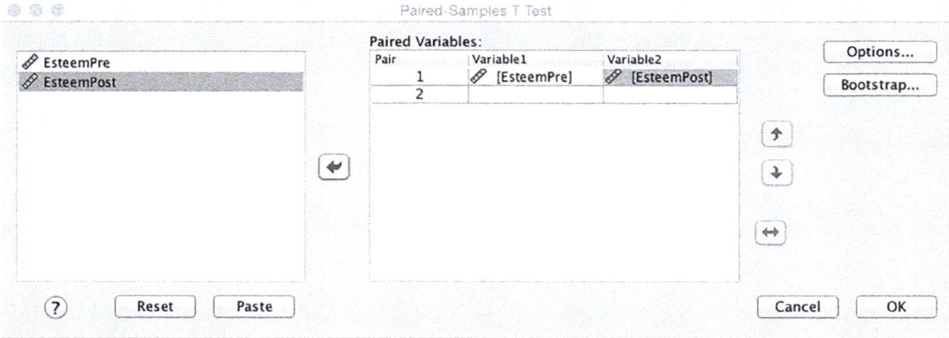

Look at the results;

Paired-Samples Statistics

		Mean	N	Std. Deviation	Std. Error Mean
Pair 1	EsteemPre	6.30	30	1.822	.333
	EsteemPost	7.60	30	1.886	.344

Paired-Samples Correlations

		N	Correlation	Sig.
Pair 1	EsteemPre and EsteemPost	30	.367	.046

Paired-Samples Test

		Paired Differences							
		Mean	Std. Deviation	Std. Error Mean	95% Confidence Interval of the Difference				
					Lower	Upper	T	Df	Sig. (2-tailed)
Pair 1	EsteemPre— EsteemPost	−1.300	2.087	.381	−2.079	−.521	−3.412	29	.002

The results might be written as follows.

A pre-post with no control design was used to determine if the self-esteem of teen-age girls improved after 10 weeks of group meetings focused on improving self-esteem. Self-esteem was measured on a scale with a total score that ranged from 4 to 16, with higher scores indicating better self-esteem. At the start of the meetings, the mean self-esteem score was 6.3 (SD = 1.822). After ten weeks of group meetings to improve self-esteem, the mean self-esteem score was 7.60 (SD = 1.886). The increase in mean score between pre- and posttest was 1.2. A paired sample t-test indicated that this increase was significant ($t_{(29)} = 3.412, p = .001$ one tailed).

Client Self-Esteem Following 10 Weeks of Group Meetings

	Pretest	Posttest
Esteem Score	$M = 6.3$ ($SD = 1.82$)	$M = 7.6$ ($SD = 1.88$)
$t_{(29)} = 3.41; p = .002$		

Practical Implications: There was a change in the self-esteem of the participants in the group sessions but since there was no control group or any comparison the question might arise would girls who did not attend the group also improve their self-esteem during this same 10-week period? Replication of this study with a control group would be a positive next step. There was only a relatively small change (although significant) in the self-esteem score. Although significant, does this relative small change make a difference in their everyday life? Finally, are there other variables that might occur during those 10 weeks that might account for the positive change in self-esteem other than the weekly sessions, for example getting more positive comments at school?

Repeated Measures ANOVA

See Chart—Two Related or Matched Groups and Interval or Ratio Measurement

In Chapter 16 you were introduced to ANOVAS. In this chapter, another type of ANOVA is introduced, the repeated measures ANOVA, where you are looking at differences WITHIN groups. Different names are used such as repeated, paired or replicated indicating that the ***same people are assessed two times*** and the ***mean of the first measurement is compared to the mean of the second measurement***. You can see that the variance measured is within the group and measured on two different occasions, T_1 and T_2.

In a repeated measure ANOVA, the dependent variable is always an interval or ratio level variable and has to be normally distributed to meet assumptions. Also, for the most basic repeated measure ANOVA there are only two measurement occasions. This type of basic repeated measure ANOVA is exactly the same as the paired sample t-test. Three or more measurement occasions will be discussed later.

Let's look at a simple one-way repeated measures ANOVA with two groups (samples). Since it is the same as the paired sample t-test (but will give you more information for the results), let's use the same example we used when we looked at the paired sample t-test, namely where you are interested to see if a 10-week group anxiety reduction treatment will reduce anxiety levels in clients. Our study question, hypotheses, expected, predicted and observed values, level of measurement, type of design, number of samples, assumptions and conceptual framework all remain the same; the only difference is we are conducting a one-way within ANOVA to test for differences.

Study Question: Do the self-esteem group sessions improve self-esteem in the teenage girls?

This is an explanatory repeated measures pre-post no control design.

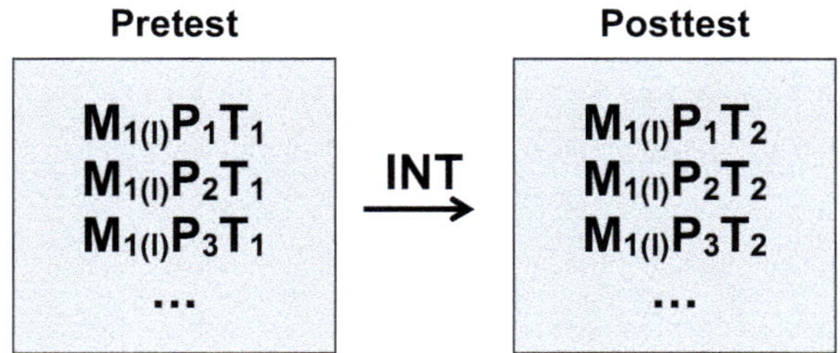

Hypotheses:

Explanatory: Group meetings will improve self-esteem of the teenage girls.
Null: Group meetings will not improve self-esteem of the teenage girls.
Expected (E): The girls will have the same level of self-esteem before and after the group meetings.
Predicted (P): The girls will have increased self-esteem after 10 weeks of group meetings.
Observed (O): The change in self-esteem of the teenage girls following 10 weeks of group meetings.
Level of Measurement: IV Nominal (meetings), DV Interval (self-esteem score)
Type of Design: Explanatory, repeated measures no control
Number of Groups: 2 Groups (samples) related
Assumptions: (a) Matched pairs with similar distributions, (b) N of 10+.

VARIABLE BOX—REPEATED MEASURES ANOVA

TIME

	T_1 PRE SCORE	Intervention GROUP MEETINGS	T_2 POST SCORE
P_1			
P_2			
P_3			
P_4			
P_5			
$P_{...}$			

SPSS Commands

Open the data set ***Ch17 One-Way Repeat Measures ANOVA ANCOVA***. Follow the steps below:

(1) Click ***Analyze***.

(2) Scroll down and select ***General Linear Model***.

(3) Select ***Repeated Measures . . .***

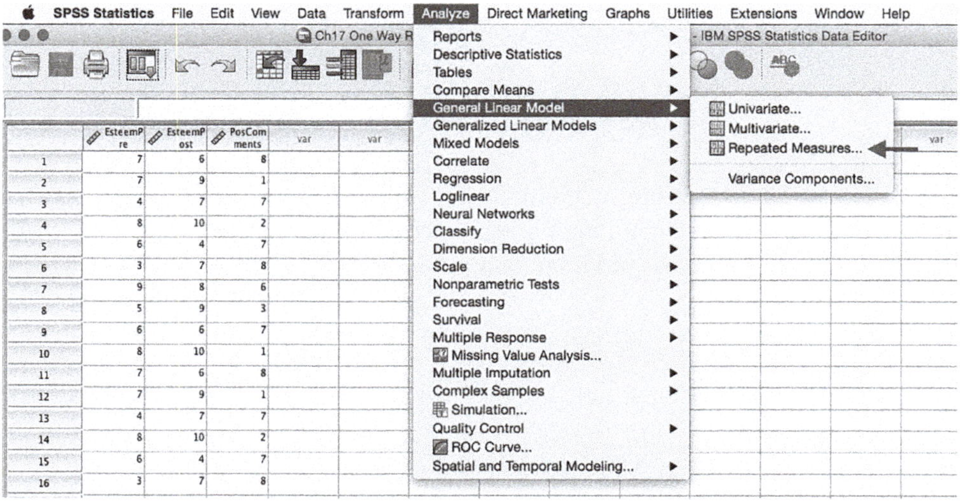

(4) Name the ***Within-Subject Factor "TIME"***; choose *2* for ***Number of Levels***.
(5) Click ***Add***.

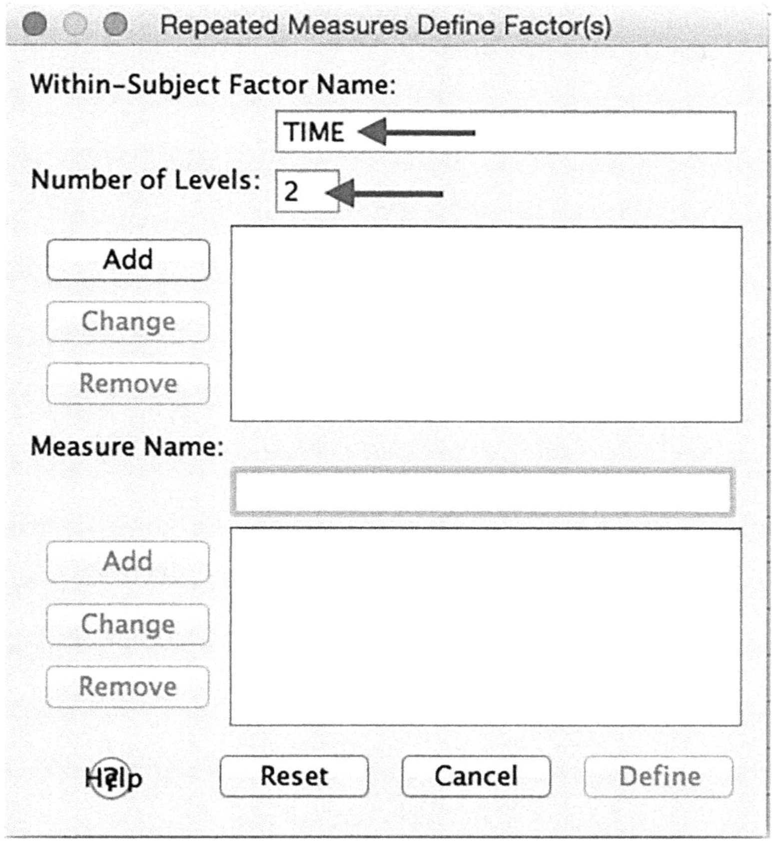

(6) Under ***Measure Name*** type ***"ESTEEM" (this name MUST be DIFFERENT from any variable name in your database)***.
(7) Click ***Add***.
(8) Click ***Define***.

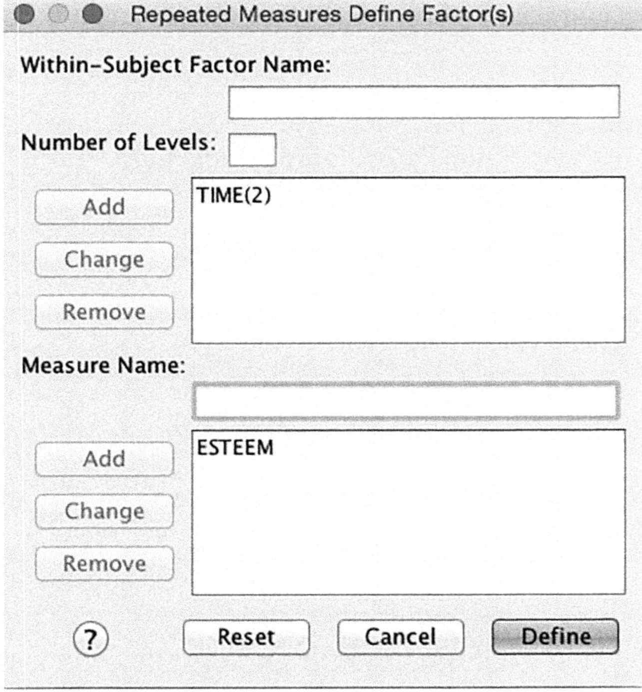

(9) Move ***EsteemPre*** to 1 and ***EsteemPost*** to 2 in the ***Within-Subjects Variables*** box.
(10) Click on ***Options . . .***

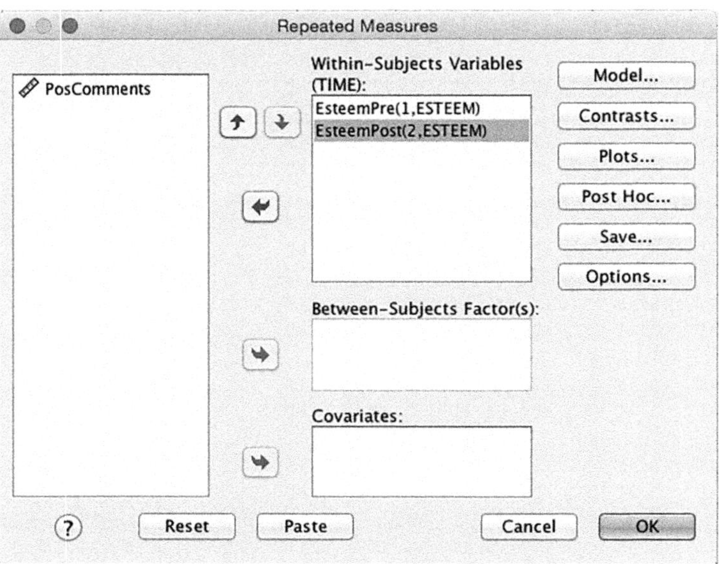

(11) Select ***Descriptive statistics***, ***Estimates of effect size*** and ***Observed power***.
(12) Click ***Continue***.

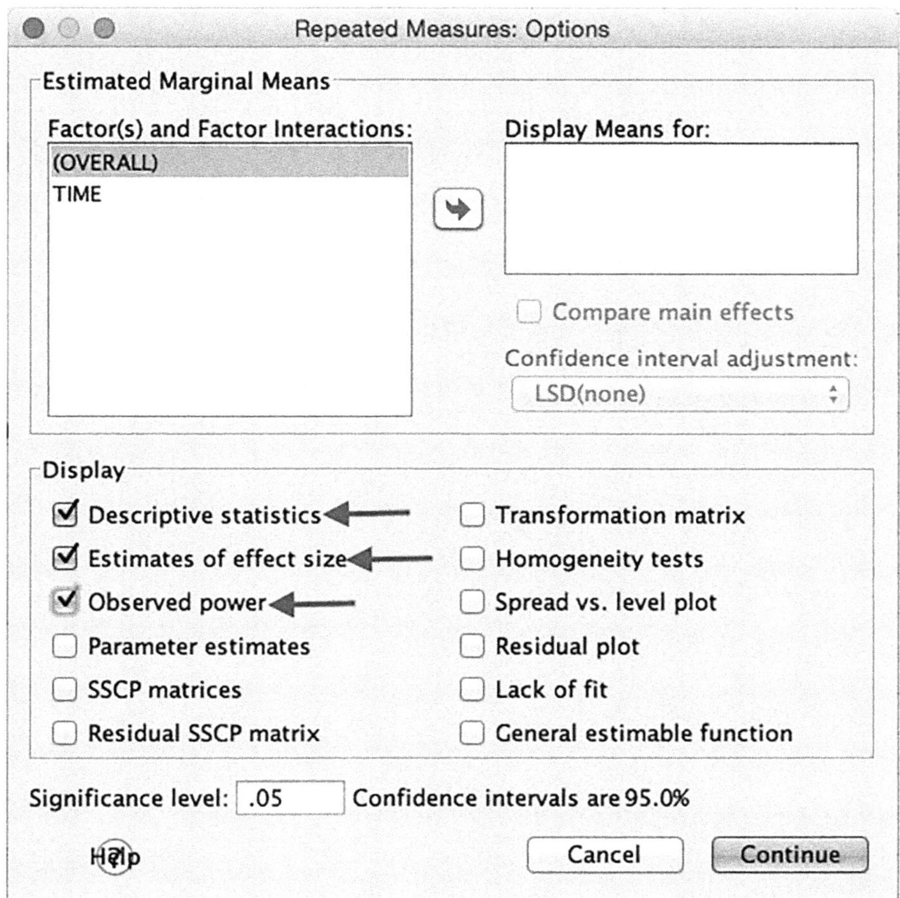

(13) Click ***OK*** to run.

Let's review the output:

Within-Subjects Factors

Measure: ESTEEM	
TIME	Dependent Variable
1	EsteemPre
2	EsteemPost

Descriptive Statistics

	Mean	Std. Deviation	N
EsteemPre	6.30	1.822	30
EsteemPost	7.60	1.886	30

Multivariate Tests[a]

Effect		Value	*F*	Hypothesis df	Error df	Sig.	Partial Eta Squared	Noncent. Parameter	Observed Power[c]
TIME	Pillai's Trace	.286	11.641[b]	1.000	29.000	.002	.286	11.641	.909
	Wilks' Lambda	.714	11.641[b]	1.000	29.000	.002	.286	11.641	.909
	Hotelling's Trace	.401	11.641[b]	1.000	29.000	.002	.286	11.641	.909
	Roy's Largest Root	.401	11.641[b]	1.000	29.000	.002	.286	11.641	.909

a. Design: Intercept; within-subjects design: TIME.
b. Exact statistic.
c. Computed using alpha = .05.

Mauchly's Test of Sphericity[a]

Measure: ESTEEM

Within-Subjects Effect	Mauchly's W	Approx. Chi-Square	Df	Sig.	Epsilon[b]		
					Greenhouse-Geisser	Huynh-Feldt	Lower-bound
TIME	1.000	.000	0	.	1.000	1.000	1.000

Tests the null hypothesis that the error covariance matrix of the orthonormalized transformed dependent variables is proportional to an identity matrix.
a. Design: Intercept; within-subjects design: TIME.
b. May be used to adjust the degrees of freedom for the averaged tests of significance. Corrected tests are displayed in the Tests of Within-Subjects Effects table.

Tests of Within-Subjects Effects

Measure: ESTEEM

Source		Type III Sum of Squares	Df	Mean Square	*F*	Sig.	Partial Eta Squared	Noncent. Parameter	Observed Power[a]
TIME	Sphericity Assumed	25.350	1	25.350	11.641	.002	.286	11.641	.909
	Greenhouse-Geisser	25.350	1.000	25.350	11.641	.002	.286	11.641	.909
	Huynh-Feldt	25.350	1.000	25.350	11.641	.002	.286	11.641	.909
	Lower-bound	25.350	1.000	25.350	11.641	.002	.286	11.641	.909
Error(TIME)	Sphericity Assumed	63.150	29	2.178					
	Greenhouse-Geisser	63.150	29.000	2.178					
	Huynh-Feldt	63.150	29.000	2.178					
	Lower-bound	63.150	29.000	2.178					

a. Computed using alpha = .05.

Tests of Within-Subjects Contrasts

Measure: ESTEEM

Source	TIME	Type III Sum of Squares	df	Mean Square	*F*	Sig.	Partial Eta Squared	Noncent. Parameter	Observed Power[a]
TIME	Linear	25.350	1	25.350	11.641	.002	.286	11.641	.909
Error(TIME)	Linear	63.150	29	2.178					

a. Computed using alpha = .05.

Tests of Between-Subjects Effects

Measure: ESTEEM

Transformed Variable: Average

Source	Type III Sum of Squares	df	Mean Square	*F*	Sig.	Partial Eta Squared	Noncent. Parameter	Observed Power[a]
Intercept	2898.150	1	2898.150	616.402	.000	.955	616.402	1.000
Error	136.350	29	4.702					

a. Computed using alpha = .05.

Client Self-Esteem Following 10 Weeks of Group Meetings

	Pretest	Posttest
Esteem Score $F_{(1,29)} = 11.64; p = .002$	$M = 6.3$ ($SD = 1.82$)	$M = 7.6$ ($SD = 1.88$)

In this specific analysis, you should ignore the multivariate tests table, because we are performing a univariate analysis. The first table you inspect is the ***Mauchly's Test of Sphericity***. This analysis is testing if the dependent variable variance-covariance matrices are equal or homogeneous (refer to as homogeneity of variance) for repeated subjects design (looking at the same assumption as the Levene test for independent groups). The null hypothesis is that the variances are equal. ***If this test is not significant, read results in the Sphericity Assumed row—if significant read the corrected Greenhouse-Geisser row.***

In reading the Sphericity Assumed row you see that the F test is significant, accounting for 28.6% of the variance, with a large effect size. The observed power is 90%.

The results might be written as follows:

A pre-post design with no control was used to determine if the self-esteem of teenage girls improved after 10 weeks of group meetings focused on improving self-esteem. Self-esteem was measured on a scale with a total score that ranged from 4 and 16, with higher scores indicating better self-esteem. At the start of the meetings, the mean self-esteem score was 6.3 (*SD* = 1.822). After ten weeks of group meetings to improve self-esteem, the mean self-esteem score was 7.60 (*SD* = 1.886). The increase in mean score between pre- and posttest was 1.3. A one-way repeated measures ANOVA found the difference in self-esteem scores pre to post was significant (*F*(1,29) = 11.641, *p* = .001 one tailed).

Practical Implications: Since a One-Way ANOVA for two repeated groups is the same as a paired t-test the practical implication would be the same as shown for the paired t-test earlier in this chapter.

Repeated Measures ANCOVA

See Chart—Two Related or Matched Groups and Interval or Ratio Measurement

As discussed in the previous chapters on ANOVA, it is sometimes important to include a covariate to exclude the affects of a particular variable on the DV so that you can better see the affect of the IV on the DV.

Let's go back to the example of self-esteem improvement. There may be other variables that would improve self-esteem as well as the 10 weeks of group sessions.

One that might be important in improving self-esteem would be the amount of positive comments the teenagers receive in school. The greater the number of positive comments the more it may improve self-esteem. You decide that you will include the number of positive self-comments as a covariate in the study.

Study Question: Does the self-esteem improvement group improve self-esteem in the teenage girls, controlling for positive comments?

This is an explanatory repeated measures pre-post no control design with a covariate.

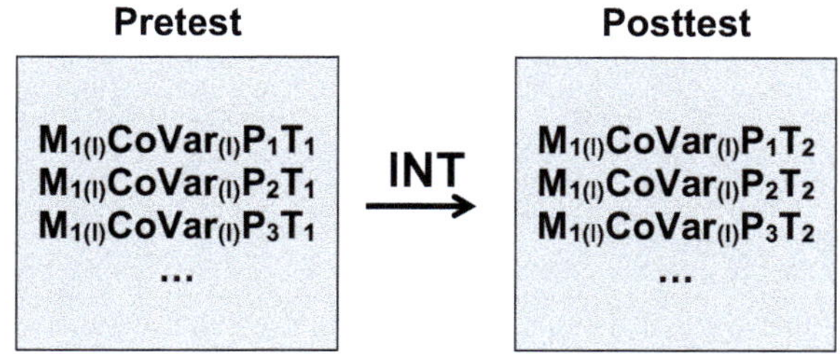

Hypotheses:

Explanatory: Group meetings will improve self-esteem of the teenage girls, controlling for positive school comments.
Null: Group meetings will not improve self-esteem of the teenage girls, controlling for positive school comments.
Expected (E): The girls will have the same level of self-esteem before and after the group meetings, controlling for positive school comments.
Predicted (P): The girls will have increased self-esteem after 10 weeks of group meetings, controlling for positive school comments.
Observed (O): The change in self-esteem of the teenage girls following 10 weeks of group meetings, controlling for positive school comments.
Level of Measurement: IV Nominal (meetings), DV Interval (self-esteem score), Covariate Ratio (school comments)
Type of Design: Explanatory, repeated measures, no control
Number of Groups: 2 Groups (samples) related
Assumptions: (a) Matched pairs, (b) Similar distributions, (c) N of 10+

VARIABLE BOX—REPEATED MEASURES ANCOVA

TIME

	T_1 PRE SCORE	Intervention GROUP MEETINGS	T_2 POST SCORE
P_1	Covariate extracted		Covariate extracted
P_2	Covariate extracted		Covariate extracted
P_3	Covariate extracted		Covariate extracted
P_4	Covariate extracted		Covariate extracted
P_5	Covariate extracted		Covariate extracted
$P_{...}$	Covariate extracted		Covariate extracted

Design

Conceptual Framework

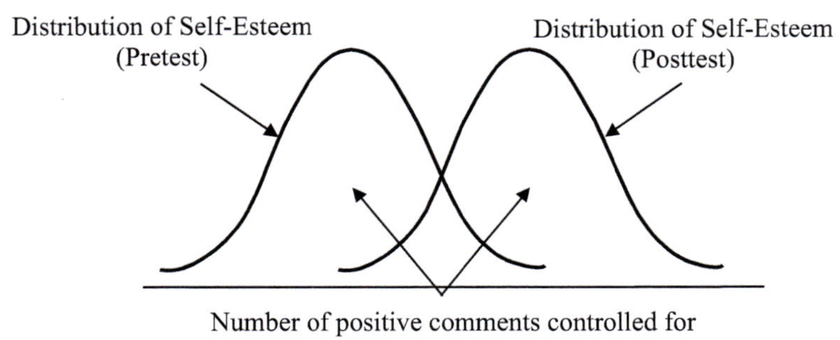

SPSS Commands

Open the data set ***Ch17 One-Way Repeat Measures ANOVA ANCOVA***. Follow the steps below:

(1) Click ***Analyze***.
(2) Scroll down and select ***General Linear Model***.
(3) Select ***Repeated Measures . . .***

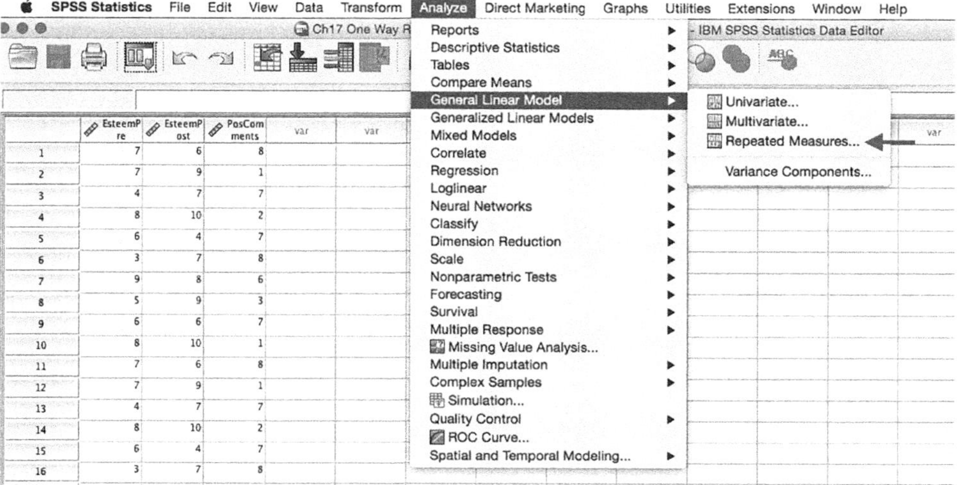

(4) Name the ***Within-Subject Factor "TIME"***; choose ***2*** for ***Number of Levels***.
(5) Click ***Add***.

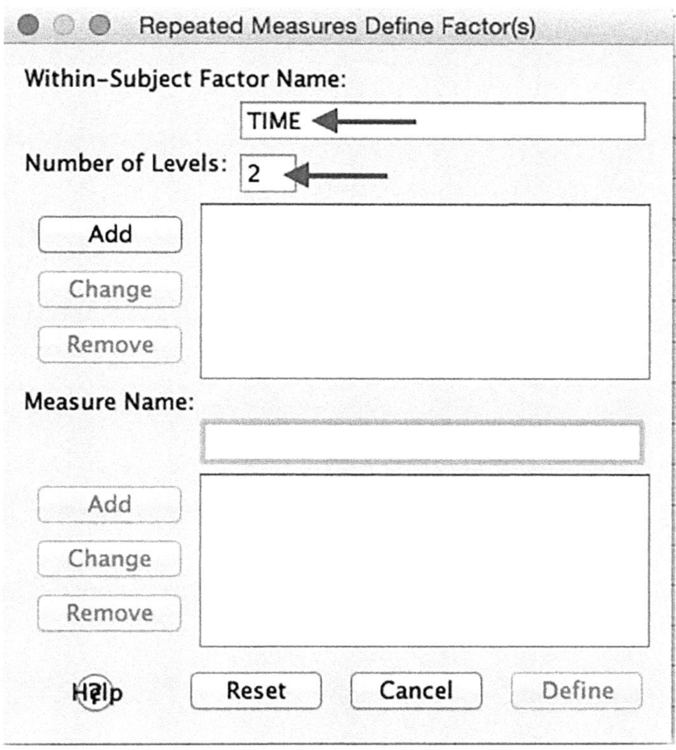

(6) Under ***Measure Name*** type "esteem" (this name should be different from any variable name in your database).
(7) Click ***Add.***
(8) Click ***Define.***

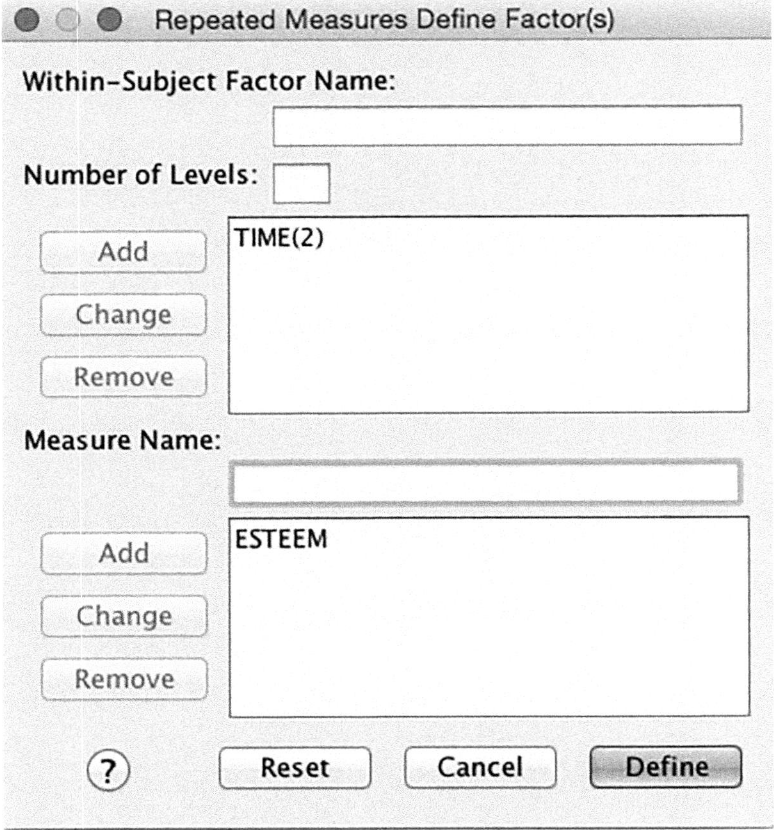

(9) Move ***EsteemPre*** to 1 and ***EsteemPost*** to 2 in the ***Within-Subjects Variables*** box.
(10) Move ***PosComments*** to ***Covariates*** box.

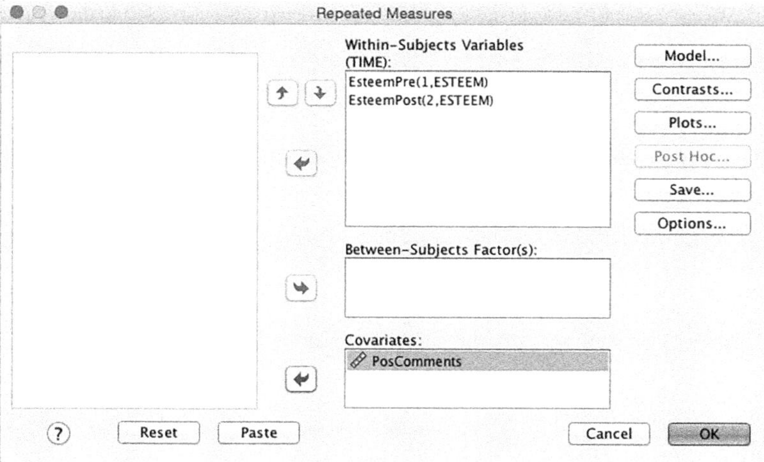

(11) Click on ***Options . . .***
(12) Select ***Descriptive statistics***, ***Estimates of effect size*** and ***Observed power***.
(13) Click ***Continue***.

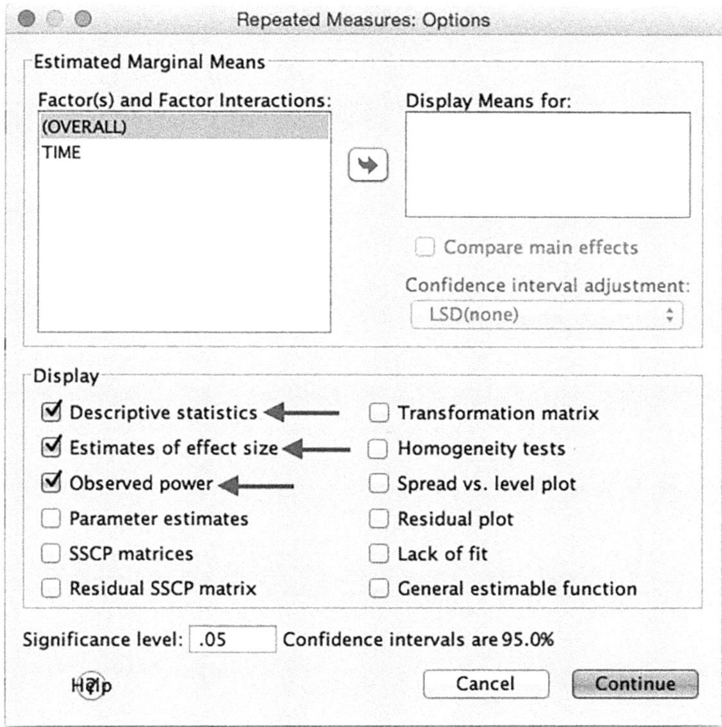

(14) Click on ***EM Means . . .***
(15) Move (overall) and time to the ***Display Means for*** box.

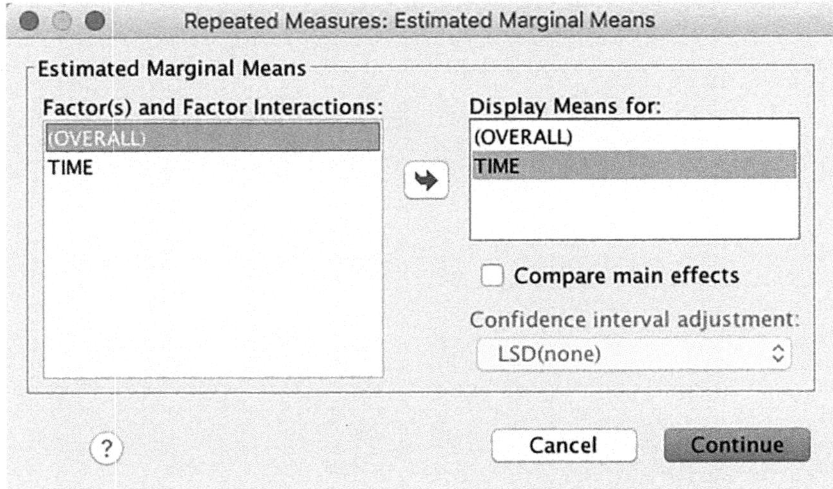

(16) Click ***OK*** to run.

Let's look at the output:

Within-Subjects Factors

Measure: ESTEEM

TIME	Dependent Variable
1	EsteemPre
2	EsteemPost

Descriptive Statistics

	Mean	Std. Deviation	N
EsteemPre	6.30	1.822	30
EsteemPost	7.60	1.886	30

Multivariate Tests[a]

Effect		Value	*F*	Hypothesis df	Error df	Sig.	Partial Eta Squared	Noncent. Parameter	Observed Power[c]
TIME	Pillai's Trace	.302	12.125[b]	1.000	28.000	.002	.302	12.125	.919
	Wilks' Lambda	.698	12.125[b]	1.000	28.000	.002	.302	12.125	.919
	Hotelling's Trace	.433	12.125[b]	1.000	28.000	.002	.302	12.125	.919
	Roy's Largest Root	.433	12.125[b]	1.000	28.000	.002	.302	12.125	.919
TIME * PosComments	Pillai's Trace	.125	4.001[b]	1.000	28.000	.055	.125	4.001	.489
	Wilks' Lambda	.875	4.001[b]	1.000	28.000	.055	.125	4.001	.489
	Hotelling's Trace	.143	4.001[b]	1.000	28.000	.055	.125	4.001	.489
	Roy's Largest Root	.143	4.001[b]	1.000	28.000	.055	.125	4.001	.489

a. Design: Intercept + PosComments; within-subjects design: TIME.
b. Exact statistic.
c. Computed using alpha = .05.

Mauchly's Test of Sphericity[a]

Measure: ESTEEM

Within-Subjects Effect	Mauchly's W	Approx. Chi-Square	df	Sig.	Epsilon[b]		
					Greenhouse-Geisser	Huynh-Feldt	Lower-bound
TIME	1.000	.000	0	.	1.000	1.000	1.000

Tests the null hypothesis that the error covariance matrix of the orthonormalized transformed dependent variables is proportional to an identity matrix.
a. Design: Intercept + PosComments; within-subjects design: TIME.
b. May be used to adjust the degrees of freedom for the averaged tests of significance. Corrected tests are displayed in the Tests of Within-Subjects Effects table.

Tests of Within-Subjects Effects

Measure: ESTEEM

Source		Type III Sum of Squares	Df	Mean Square	*F*	Sig.	Partial Eta Squared	Noncent. Parameter	Observed Power[a]
TIME	Sphericity Assumed	23.927	1	23.927	12.125	.002	.302	12.125	.919
	Greenhouse-Geisser	23.927	1.000	23.927	12.125	.002	.302	12.125	.919
	Huynh-Feldt	23.927	1.000	23.927	12.125	.002	.302	12.125	.919
	Lower-bound	23.927	1.000	23.927	12.125	.002	.302	12.125	.919
TIME * PosComments	Sphericity Assumed	7.895	1	7.895	4.001	.055	.125	4.001	.489
	Greenhouse-Geisser	7.895	1.000	7.895	4.001	.055	.125	4.001	.489
	Huynh-Feldt	7.895	1.000	7.895	4.001	.055	.125	4.001	.489
	Lower-bound	7.895	1.000	7.895	4.001	.055	.125	4.001	.489
Error(TIME)	Sphericity Assumed	55.255	28	1.973					
	Greenhouse-Geisser	55.255	28.000	1.973					
	Huynh-Feldt	55.255	28.000	1.973					
	Lower-bound	55.255	28.000	1.973					

a. Computed using alpha = .05.

Tests of Within-Subjects Contrasts

Measure: ESTEEM

Source	TIME	Type III Sum of Squares	df	Mean Square	*F*	Sig.	Partial Eta Squared	Noncent. Parameter	Observed Power[a]
TIME	Linear	23.927	1	23.927	12.125	.002	.302	12.125	.919
TIME * PosComments	Linear	7.895	1	7.895	4.001	.055	.125	4.001	.489
Error(TIME)	Linear	55.255	28	1.973					

a. Computed using alpha = .05.

Tests of Between-Subjects Effects

Measure: ESTEEM

Transformed Variable: Average

Source	Type III Sum of Squares	Df	Mean Square	*F*	Sig.	Partial Eta Squared	Noncent. Parameter	Observed Power[a]
Intercept	1163.690	1	1163.690	646.798	.000	.959	646.798	1.000
PosComments	85.974	1	85.974	47.786	.000	.631	47.786	1.000
Error	50.376	28	1.799					

a. Computed using alpha = .05.

1. Grand Mean

Measure: esteem			
Mean	Std. Error	95% Confidence Interval	
		Lower-Bound	Upper-Bound
6.950[a]	.173	6.595	7.305

a.Covariates appearing in the model are evaluated at the following values: PosComments = 5.00.

2. Time

Measure: esteem				
Time	Mean	Std. Error	95% Confidence Interval	
			Lower-Bound	Upper-Bound
1	6.300[a]	.300	5.686	6.914
2	7.600[a]	.190	7.212	7.988

a. Covariates appearing in the model are evaluated at the following values: PosComments = 5.00.

Mauchly's test is not significant so you can proceed in interpreting the rest of the result, reading the Sphericity Assumed row. The F test for TIME is significant (when the positive comments have been removed from affecting the self-esteem score) accounting for .30% of the variance. The interaction term of TIME by Positive Comments was not significant indicating that positive comments were not significant with respect to the change in self-esteem. Remember when there is ***a Covariate you cannot report the value of the mean (from descriptives)*** which is the mean before the exclusion of the positive comments—***you report the Standard Estimate of the Mean!*** If you look at the standard error of the means pre and post you will notice that the value of the mean did not change but the standard error is much lower. This indicates that taking out the effect of positive comments as a covariate on self-esteem reduced the error of the estimate of the mean, making us much more confident about the actual measurement of self-esteem.

The results might be written as follows.

A pre-post design with a covariate and no control was used to determine if the self-esteem of teenage girls improved after 10 weeks of group meetings, controlling for positive comments in the classroom. Self-esteem was measured on a scale with a total score that ranged from 4 to 16, with higher scores indicating better self-esteem. At the start of the meetings, the mean self-esteem score was

6.3 (SE = .333). After ten weeks of group meetings to improve self-esteem, the mean self-esteem score was 7.60 (SE = .334). The increase in mean score between pre- and posttest was 1.3. A one-way repeated measures ANOVA found the difference in self-esteem scores pre to post was significant after controlling for positive comments in the classroom ($F_{(1,28)}$ = 11.641, p = .001 one tailed), with a large effect size .302 and 92% power. The time-positive comments interaction was significant ($F_{(1,28)}$ = 4.001, p = .027), with a medium effect size and 49% power.

Client Self-Esteem Following 10 Weeks of Group Meetings With Covariate

	Pretest	Posttest
Esteem Score	M = 6.3 (SD = 1.82)	M = 7.6 (SD = 1.88)
$F_{(1,28)} = 12.13;\ p = .002$		

Practical Implications: This study, by including the covariate of positive school comments as a covariate answered the question if the affect of positive school comments made a difference in the self-esteem score. Positive comments did improve self-esteem but did not quite reach significance. Maybe if there was a greater increase in positive comments in school, there would be an even greater increase in self-esteem. However, there still remains the concern if the small change in scores is important to their daily life as well as the need to determine the generalizability of the findings.

Discussion Article

Critique the reason to use matched samples in this study. How did the authors apply the design and how did they analyze it? How might you use this in a study you design?

Koh, E., & Tests, M. F. Propensity score matching of children in kinship and non-kinship care: Do permanency outcomes differ? *Social Work Research*, *32*(2), 105–116. Retrieved from https://academic.oup.com/swr/article/32/2/105/162075

Exercises for Chapter 17 are found in eResources.

Chapter 18

FINDING DIFFERENCES

Multiple (k) Independent Groups (Samples) Tests

PART A: NONPARAMETRIC

Nominal Level Data

Chi-Square Test r × k

See Chart—Multiple (k) Independent Groups and Nominal Measurement

As noted previously in Chapter 16, Chi-Square can be utilized when there are more than two groups (levels) of either one of the variables (more than two rows and/or more than two columns). In an r × k Chi-Square, rows are labeled r and columns labeled k. The Chi-Square test for r × k tables is easily understood as simply progressing to additional nominal group (level) categories from the basic 2 × 2 Chi-Square. The following equation is used to test if there are differences in the ratios of the nominal categories in an r × k Chi-Square.

$$X^2 = \sum_{i=1}^{r}\sum_{j=1}^{k}\frac{\left(n_{ij} - E_{ij}\right)^2}{E_{ij}}$$

You apply the same formula and calculations you used for the Chi-Square 2 × 2 but now you have to calculate for all the cells in the rows and columns. The formula that was used in Chapter 16 to calculate the 2 × 2 Chi-Square, $\frac{(O-E)^2}{E}$, you actually use again for **every cell in the r (row) × k (column) matrix**. Sum (Σ) all of those calculations. This will become very clear when you see the numerical example. The degrees of freedom for an r × k Chi-Square is calculated by: $df = (r - 1)(k - 1)$ with r = the number of rows and k = the number of columns.

Assume that you have been working in a community project and noticed there seems to be a relationship between the level of an individual's education and their income. You want to find out if there is a difference in a person's income with respect to their education. You know from the literature that there is an income gap between Males and Females which might distort the distribution of incomes and in order to control for this difference, you only collected data on Females for this particular study. You selected a sample of 160 Females randomly from the community service project and had a short interview with each person. Based upon their education they were categorized into three groups (levels), high school or below, some college education and college graduate or above. Income was also categorized into three groups (levels), high income $60,000 and above, middle income between $35,000 and $59,999 and low income below $35,000.

Study Question: Do people with different educational levels differ in their income levels?

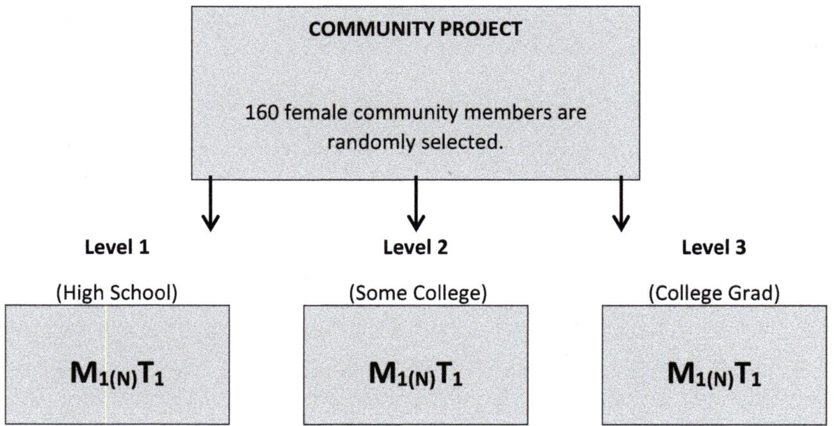

Hypotheses:

Difference: Females with different educational levels will have different income levels.

Null: Females with different educational levels will not have different income levels.

Expected (E): Females with different educational levels will proportionally be equal in the different income levels.

Predicted (P): Females with different educational levels will proportionally be unequal in the different income levels.

Observed (O): The actual distribution of educational and income levels.

Level of Measurement: IV Nominal (education) DV Nominal (income)
Type of Design: Difference, cross-sectional, independent measures
Number of Groups: 3 Groups (samples)
Assumptions: (a) No more than 20% of the expected frequencies less than 5, (b) No expected frequency less than 1.

VARIABLE BOX—CHI-SQUARE 3 × 3

		EDUCATION (A)		
		High School or Less (A1)	***Some College*** (A2)	***College Graduate +*** (A3)
INCOME (B)	***Low Income*** (B1)	A1 B1	A2 B1	A3 B1
	Middle Income (B2)	A1 B2	A2 B2	A3 B2
	High Income (B3)	A1 B3	A2 B3	A3 B3

Calculate the expected for each cell as you did in Chapter 16 for 2 × 2 Chi-Square. Those values are shown in the table below.

	High School or Less		Some College		College graduate+		Total
	Observed	Expected	Observed	Expected	Observed	Expected	
Low Income	10	*18.8*	10	*12.5*	30	*18.8*	50
Middle Income	10	*15*	10	*10*	20	*15*	40
High Income	40	*26.3*	20	*17.5*	10	*26.3*	70
Total	60		40		60		160

We can now compute X^2 using the formula:

$$X^2 = \sum_{i=1}^{r}\sum_{j=1}^{k}\frac{\left(n_{ij} - E_{ij}\right)^2}{E_{ij}}$$

REMEMBER THIS FORMULA SIMPLY TELLS YOU TO SUM UP ALL OF THE

$$\frac{(O-E)^2}{E}$$

FOR EVERY CELL IN THE VARIABLE BOX, THE MATH CALCULATION IS BELOW.

$$X^2 = \frac{(10-18.8)^2}{18.8} + \frac{(10-15)^2}{15} + \frac{(40-26.3)^2}{26.3} + \frac{(10-12.5)^2}{12.5} + \frac{(10-10)^2}{10} + \frac{(20-17.5)^2}{17.5} + \frac{(30-18.8)^2}{18.8} + \frac{(20-15)^2}{15} + \frac{(10-26.3)^2}{26.3}$$

$$\mathbf{X^2 = 32.29}$$

Degrees of freedom (r − 1)(k − 1) = (3 − 1)(3 − 1) = (2)(2) = **4**

You can look up the significance of $X^2_{(4)}$ **= 32.39** in any table of Chi-Square critical values such as the one found at www.itl.nist.gov.

SPSS Commands

Open the data set ***Ch18 ChiSquare RxK***.
Follow the steps below:

(1) Click ***Analyze***.
(2) Scroll down and select ***Descriptive Statistics***.
(3) Select ***Crosstabs . . .***
(4) Move ***Income*** into the ***Row(s)*** box; move ***Education*** into the ***Column(s)*** box.

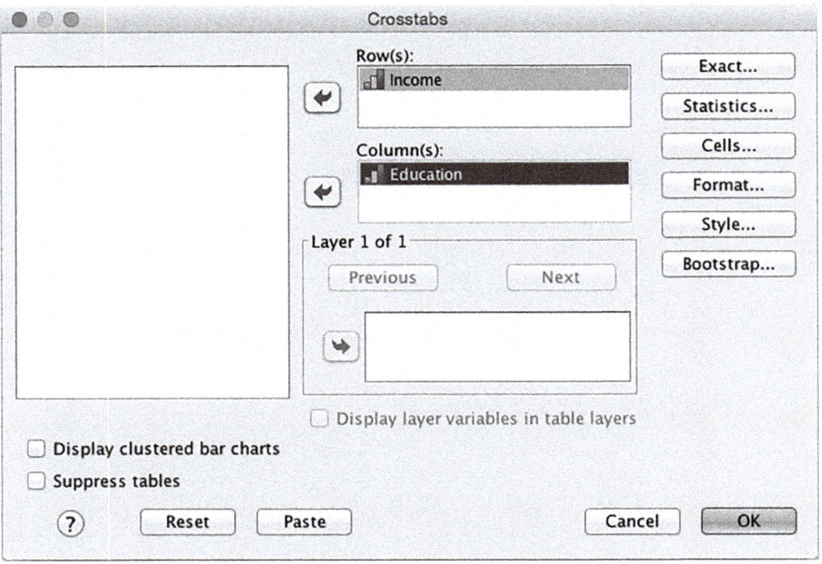

(5) Click the ***Statistics . . .*** button.
(6) Check the box next to ***Chi-square***; click ***Continue***.

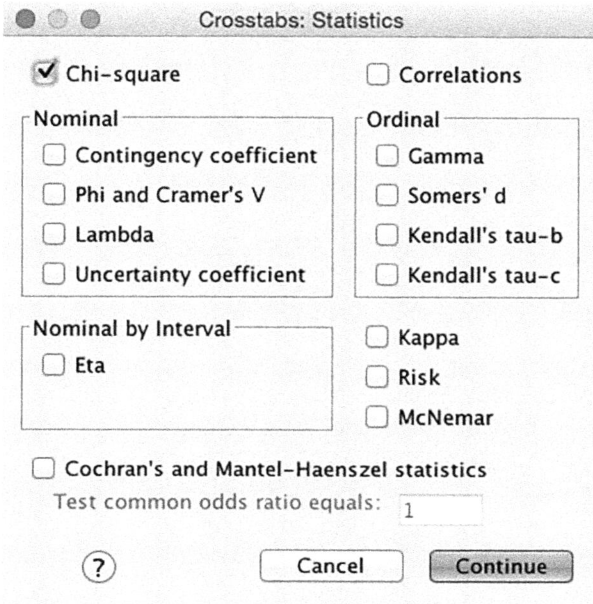

(7) Click the ***Cells . . .*** button.
(8) In the ***Counts*** box select ***Observed*** and ***Expected***; in the ***Percentages*** box select ***Row***, ***Column*** and ***Total***.

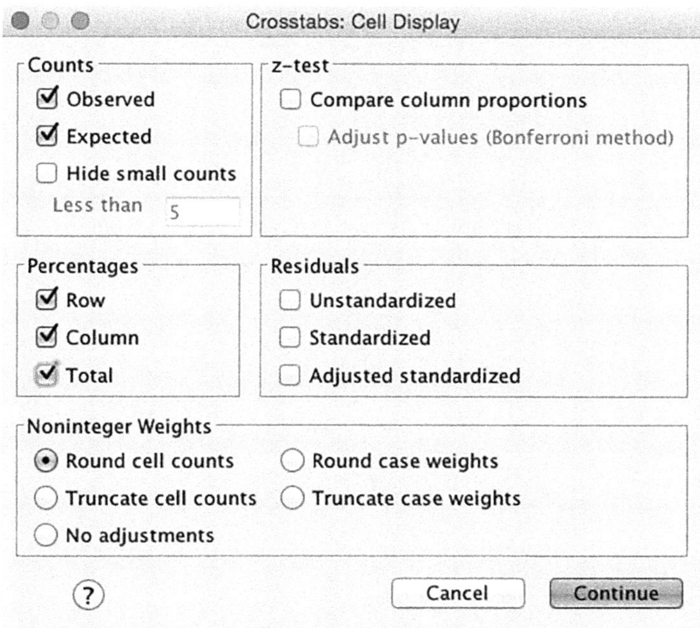

(9) Click ***Continue***.
(10) Click ***OK*** to run the analysis.

Income * Education Crosstabulation

			Education			Total
			High School or Less	Some College	College Grad+	
Income	Low Income	Count	40	20	10	70
		Expected Count	26.3	17.5	26.3	70.0
		% within Income	57.1%	28.6%	14.3%	100.0%
		% within Education	66.7%	50.0%	16.7%	43.8%
		% of Total	25.0%	12.5%	6.3%	43.8%
	Middle Income	Count	10	10	20	40
		Expected Count	15.0	10.0	15.0	40.0
		% within Income	25.0%	25.0%	50.0%	100.0%
		% within Education	16.7%	25.0%	33.3%	25.0%
		% of Total	6.3%	6.3%	12.5%	25.0%
	High Income	Count	10	10	30	50
		Expected Count	18.8	12.5	18.8	50.0
		% within Income	20.0%	20.0%	60.0%	100.0%
		% within Education	16.7%	25.0%	50.0%	31.3%
		% of Total	6.3%	6.3%	18.8%	31.3%
Total		Count	60	40	60	160
		Expected Count	60.0	40.0	60.0	160.0
		% within Income	37.5%	25.0%	37.5%	100.0%
		% within Education	100.0%	100.0%	100.0%	100.0%
		% of Total	37.5%	25.0%	37.5%	100.0%

Chi-Square Tests

	Value	Df	Asymptotic Significance (2-sided)
Pearson Chi-Square	32.286[a]	4	.000
Likelihood Ratio	34.300	4	.000
Linear-by-Linear Association	28.191	1	.000
N of Valid Cases	160		

a. 0 cells (0.0%) have expected count less than 5. The minimum expected count is 10.00.

Results might be written as follows:

Of the Females with low income, 57% were high school graduates or below while only 14% were college graduates or above. Females with middle incomes were distributed evenly between high school graduates or below (25%) and some college (25%) with most of this income group being college graduates or above (50%). Finally, the high-income group consisted of 60% college graduates or above, 20% with some college and 20% who had a high school education or below. These differences were significant: ($X^2_{(4)} = 32.29, p = .001$).

Practical Implications: What else would you want to know after you found these differences? What is the difference between Female incomes and Male incomes? What other differences might be related to difference in incomes—number of children—marital status—types of jobs available in the community? Maybe you want to find out if there are some specific differences in jobs with respect to income that may not be related to formal education, for example high-level tech jobs with high pay. Is child care supplied by the employer? Is child care available in the community and at what cost?

Ordinal Level Data

Extension of the Median Test

See Chart—Multiple (k) Independent Groups and Ordinal Measurement

The extension of the median test is the same as the median test discussed in Chapter 16 but now there are **more than two groups (k groups)**. The same assumptions apply to the extension (k group) of the median test as the two group median test. **The extension of the median test can be used when you have ordinal data or interval or ratio level data when (1) the groups (samples) are not similar in size or (2) the data is non-normal.** It is important to know what your data looks like be in order to **make sure you actually do have an ordinal DV**. If you have **many scores that are tied and clustered around the median, you may need to change to a nominal level test (Chi-Square)**, because the data may not actually be distributed ordinally.

We will continue the process of using previous examples as the foundation for more advanced tests. In Chapter 16 you conducted a study about women on welfare who cycled on and off and those who went off welfare and stayed off. In that example, you only had two groups but now you want to re-conceptualize the situation a little differently. You have been thinking that maybe there is a difference between three groups of women (1) those who are on welfare and go off and remain off, (2) those who are continually cycling on and off welfare and (3) those who are always on welfare. **You**

wanted to continue the research about number of jobs but now with three different groups of women.

Study Question: Is there a difference in the number of jobs held between women who get off welfare, those who cycle in and out of welfare, and those who never get off welfare.

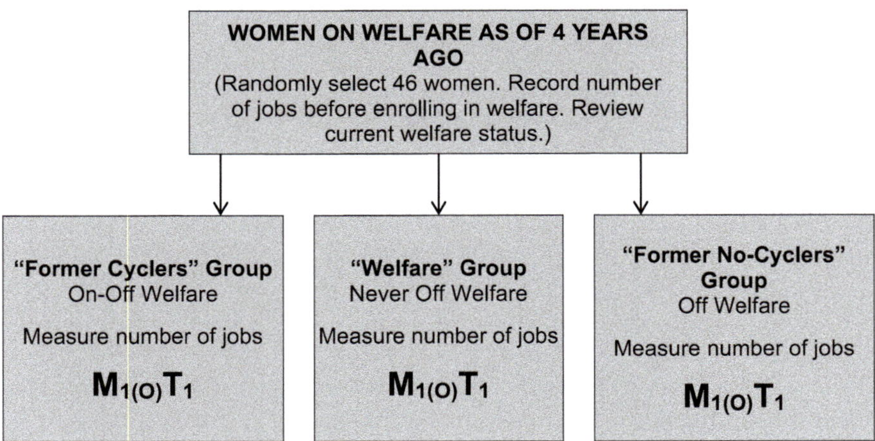

Hypotheses:

Difference: There is a difference in the number of jobs held between women who get off welfare, those who cycle in and out of welfare and those who never get off welfare.

Null: There is no difference in the number of jobs held between women who get off welfare, those who cycle in and out of welfare and those who never get off welfare.

Expected (E): The distribution of jobs held between women who get off welfare, those who cycle in and out of welfare and those who never get off welfare will be the same.

Predicted (P): The distribution of jobs held between women who get off welfare, those who cycle in and out welfare, and those who never get off welfare will be different.

Observed (O): The actual distribution of jobs between women who get off welfare, those who cycle in and out of welfare, and those who never get off welfare.

Level of Measurement: IV Ordinal (welfare), DV Ordinal (Jobs)

Type of Design: Difference, cross-sectional, independent measures

Number of Groups: 3 Groups (samples)

Assumptions: (a) Ordinal level of data, **(b)** Sample size does not have to be the same

VARIABLE BOX—MEDIAN TEST

Variable Box—Extension of the Median Test

		WELFARE STATUS (A)		
		"On and Off Welfare" (A1)	***"Never Off Welfare"*** (A2)	***"Off Welfare"*** (A3)
Jobs (B)	***Number of jobs greater than combined median*** (B1)	A1 B1	A2 B1	A3 B1
	Number of jobs less than combined median (B2)	A1 B2	A2 B2	A3 B2

Off Welfare	On and Off Welfare	Never Off Welfare
2	7	5
1	6	0
3	5	0
2	8	1
1	8	2
3	10	0
2	9	2
2	7	9
3	6	8
4	5	10
8	4	8
3	1	9
2	7	7
1	4	0
1		0
		1
		2

Like the calculations for the 2 group median test we have to first calculate the grand mean by combining all the scores from the three groups and arranging them in descending order (arrange them from the highest to the lowest). The grand median is 3 jobs.

##	Group	Number of jobs	Ranking
1	on and off welfare	10	1.5
2	never off welfare	10	1.5
3	on and off welfare	9	4
4	never off welfare	9	4
5	never off welfare	9	4
6	off welfare	8	8
7	on and off welfare	8	8
8	on and off welfare	8	8
9	never off welfare	8	8
10	never off welfare	8	8
11	on and off welfare	7	12.5
12	on and off welfare	7	12.5
13	on and off welfare	7	12.5
14	never off welfare	7	12.5
15	on and off welfare	6	15.5
16	on and off welfare	6	15.5
17	on and off welfare	5	18
18	on and off welfare	5	18
19	never off welfare	5	18
20	off welfare	4	21
21	on and off welfare	4	21
22	on and off welfare	4	21
23	**off welfare**	**3**	**24.5**
24	**off welfare**	**3**	**24.5**
25	off welfare	3	24.5
26	off welfare	3	24.5
27	off welfare	2	30.5
28	off welfare	2	30.5
29	off welfare	2	30.5
30	off welfare	2	30.5
31	off welfare	2	30.5
32	never off welfare	2	30.5
33	never off welfare	2	30.5
34	never off welfare	2	30.5
35	off welfare	1	38

##	Group	Number of jobs	Ranking
36	off welfare	1	38
37	off welfare	1	38
38	off welfare	1	38
39	on and off welfare	1	38
40	never off welfare	1	38
41	never off welfare	1	38
42	never off welfare	0	44
43	never off welfare	0	44
44	never off welfare	0	44
45	never off welfare	0	44
46	never off welfare	0	44

Fill in the variable box constructed earlier. In the cells place the actual values (observations) and the expected values. Place into the appropriate cells the number of actual values (observations) that are above and below the grand median in for each of the three welfare status groups. When a value is the same as the median, you might wonder which cell does it go into—above or below. **The preferred method is to only put those values that are definitely above the grand mean as above, and then all other values are placed in the category as being below the mean, including those that are equal to the grand mean.**

		WELFARE STATUS (A)			
		On and Off Welfare	***Off Welfare***	***Never Off Welfare***	***Marginal Total***
Jobs (B)	***Number of jobs greater than combined median*** (B1)	13 (O) *6.7 (E)*	2 (O) *7.17 (E)*	7 (O) *8.13 (E)*	22
	Number of jobs less than combined median (B2)	1 (O) *7.3 (E)*	13 (O) *7.83 (E)*	10 (O) *8.87 (E)*	24
	Marginal Total	14	15	17	$n = 46$

The expected values are shown in italics. The same formula is used to calculate the extension of the median test as we have done before with the r x k Chi-Square.

$$X^2 = \sum_{i=1}^{r}\sum_{j=1}^{k}\frac{\left(n_{ij} - E_{ij}\right)^2}{E_{ij}}$$

For calculation purposes for **each cell you perform**

$$\frac{(O-E)^2}{E}$$

Then sum (Σ) them all together.

The calculation would be as follows:

$$X^2 = \frac{(13-6.7)^2}{6.7} + \frac{(2-7.17)^2}{7.17} + \frac{(7-8.13)^2}{8.13} + \frac{(1-7.3)^2}{7.3} + \frac{(13-7.83)^2}{7.83} + \frac{(10-8.87)^2}{8.87}$$

$$\mathbf{X^2 = 18.83}$$

Degrees of freedom are (r – 1)(k – 1) = (2 – 1)(3 – 1) = (1)(2) = 2.

You can look up the significance of $X^2_{(2)}$ = **18.83** in any table of Chi-Square critical values such as the one found at www.itl.nist.gov. In this case, we find that it is statistically significant at the $p < 0.001$ level.

SPSS Commands

Open the data set ***Ch18 MedianExtension***.
Follow the steps below:

(1) Go to ***Analyze***.
(2) Scroll down and select ***Nonparametric Tests***; select ***Legacy Dialogs***.
(3) Select ***K Independent Samples . . .***
(4) Under ***Test Type***, check the box by ***Median*** and ensure that no other tests are selected.
(5) Move ***Number of Jobs*** into the ***Test Variable List***.
(6) Move ***Welfare*** into the ***Grouping Variable*** box.

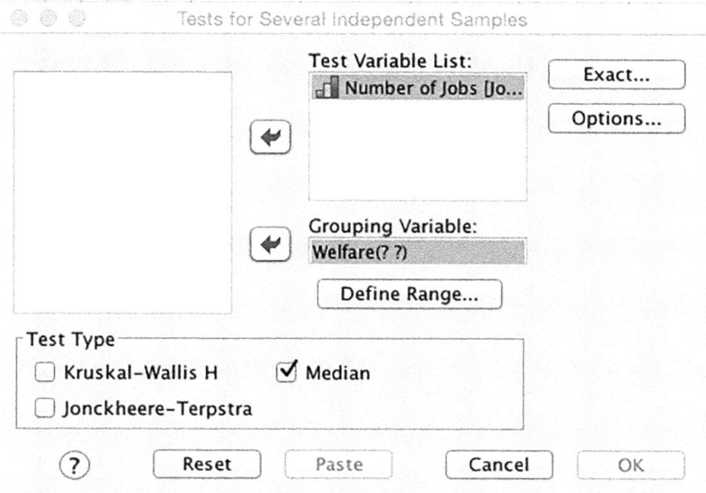

(7) Click the ***Define Range . . .*** button.
(8) Under ***Range for Grouping Variables*** enter ***1*** into the ***Minimum*** box and ***3*** into the ***Maximum*** box (as our welfare status variable has three levels).

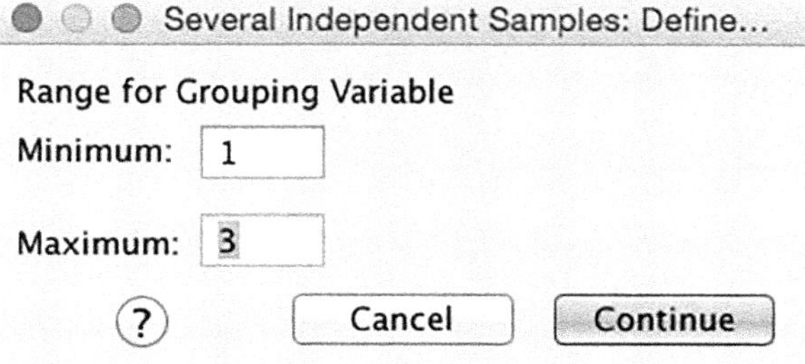

(9) Click ***Continue***.
(10) Click ***OK*** to run the analysis.

Let's look at the output:

Frequencies

		Welfare Status		
		Off welfare	On and off welfare	Never off welfare
Number of Jobs	> Median	2	13	7
	≤ Median	13	1	10

Test Statistics[a]

	Number of Jobs
N	46
Median	3.00
Chi-Square	18.830[b]
Df	2
Asymp. Sig.	.000

a. Grouping Variable: Welfare Status.
b. 0 cells (0.0%) have expected frequencies less than 5. The minimum expected cell frequency is 6.7.

Results might be written as follows.

For women off welfare 13 out of 15 were below the median of 3 jobs. Women who were never off welfare were relatively equally distributed with 7 above the median of 3 and 10 below the median of 3. The group of women who cycle on and off welfare had the greatest number, 11 women, above the mean with only 1 below the mean. There is a significant difference between the number of jobs held by their welfare status (Median test $X^2_{(2)} = 18.83, p < .001$).

Practical Implications: Women who get off welfare have much fewer number of jobs than the other groups. Does this mean that they stay in a job longer? If so why? Does this mean that they have better qualifications for employment and thus better and more stable jobs? Is there something about their other characteristics that is different from the other two groups? As noted earlier what other factors—number of children, others in a supportive role and other ones you can think of—may affect the number of jobs? Are the cyclers the least qualified, have the most children and basically have the opposite characteristics of those who stay off welfare? What are the characteristics of those who never get off and what places them in the middle of number of jobs compared to those women who get off and those who cycle?

Kruskal-Wallis One-Way Analysis of Ranks Test

See Chart—Multiple (k) Independent Groups and Ordinal Measurement

The Kruskal-Wallis One-Way Analysis of Ranks is very often used and appropriate when you have multiple independent samples. In Chapter 16 you were introduced to the Wilcoxon-Mann-Whitney U test that is used when you have two independent groups (samples) with a nominal IV and ordinal DV that tests differences in mean ranks. **The Kruskal-Wallis also tests mean ranks difference but now there can be more than two groups.** This test becomes **the best choice when a one-way ANOVA with more than two groups (levels) of an IV cannot be used because (1) the N is too small or (2) the data does not meet the assumptions of the ANOVA**. The ***Kruskal-Wallis tests differences in the mean ranks of k groups.***

Conceptualization

You think there might be a difference in the amount of human trafficking related to different types of cities and there is a difference in the amount of trafficking between border, port, central large and central small cities. Border cities are defined as any city that has an entry point between the US and Mexico or Canada. Port cities are defined as a US city that is a major shipping port with an international entry. A central large city is defined as a city over 1 million in population and is not a border or port city, and a central small city is defined as a city with a population between 500,000 and 1 million that is not a border or port city. This type of study lends itself to the Kruskal-Wallis test because the data from these cities is non-normal (you could not use an ANOVA to test the differences) and there is an ordinal DV (human-trafficking rate).

Study Question: Is there is a difference in human-trafficking rates between border, port, central big and central small cities?

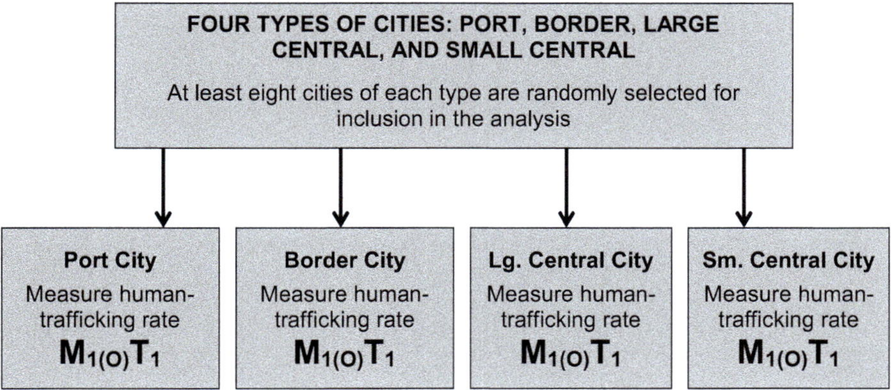

Hypotheses:

Difference: There is a difference in human-trafficking rates between border, port, central large and central small cities.

Null: There is no difference in human-trafficking rates between border, port, central large and central small cities.

Expected (E): The human-trafficking rates will be the same for different types of cities.

Predicted (P): The human-trafficking rates will be different for different types of cities.
Observed (O): The actual human-trafficking rates for different types of cities.
Level of Measurement: IV Nominal (City), Ordinal DV (human trafficking)
Type of Design: Difference, Cross-Sectional
Number of Groups: 4 Groups (samples)
Assumptions: (a) Ordinal level of measurement (b) Non-normal ratio DV changed to ordinal, (c) Relatively equal group sizes.

VARIABLE BOX—KRUSKAL-WALLIS

CITY TYPE

Port City	***Border City***	***Large Central City***	***Small Central City***
Mean Rank	Mean Rank	Mean Rank	Mean Rank

The scores (values) on the variable are converted to ranks, ignoring group membership, similar to the median test.

Type of City	Trafficking Rate	Rank
Port	1.07	1
Large City	1.20	2.5
Large City	1.20	2.5
Port	1.24	4
Port	1.31	5
Small City	1.32	6
Large City	1.40	7
Port	1.46	8
Port	1.49	9
Small City	1.52	10
Small City	1.60	11
Large City	1.70	12
Port	1.79	13
Small City	1.82	14
Small City	1.93	15.5
Large City	1.93	15.5
Border	1.95	17.5

Type of City	Trafficking Rate	Rank
Port	1.95	17.5
Small City	2.04	19
Border	2.08	20.5
Small City	2.08	20.5
Port	2.27	22
Large City	2.29	23
Small City	2.35	24
Large City	2.58	25
Large City	2.60	26
Border	2.90	27
Border	2.95	28.5
Border	2.95	28.5
Port	2.99	30
Border	3.00	31
Border	3.09	32
Border	3.10	33
Port	3.11	34
Border	3.12	35
Border	3.20	36
Border	3.40	37
Border	3.50	38
Border	3.94	39

Do the four mean ranks differ from each other: border city (mean rank = 31), port city (mean rank = 14.35), vs. large central city (mean rank = 14.19) and small central city (mean rank = 15.00)? The formula to calculate the Kruskal-Wallis test is:

$$KW = \frac{12}{N(N+1)} \sum_{j=1}^{k} \overline{n_j(\bar{R}_j - \bar{R})^2}$$

k = number of groups (samples)
n_j = number of values (scores) in each of the separate groups
N = total number of values (scores) in the total sample (the sum of all nj)
$\bar{R}_j$ = the mean of the ranks in each of the separate groups (samples)
$\bar{R}$ = the mean of the ranks total (all groups combined—total sample)

The calculation follows:

$$KW = \frac{12}{N(N+1)} \sum_{j=1}^{k} \overline{n_j(\bar{R}_j - \bar{R})^2}$$

$$KW = \frac{12}{39(40)}\left[13(31-20)^2 + 10(14.35-20)^2 + 8(14.19-20)^2 + 8(15-20)^2\right]$$

$$KW = \frac{12}{1560}\left[13(11)^2 + 10(5.62)^2 + 8(5.81)^2 + 8(5)^2\right]$$

$$KW = 0.007\left[13(121) + 10(31.92) + 18(33.76) + 8(25)\right]$$

$$KW = 0.007[1573 + 319.22 + 270.08 + 200]$$

$$KW = 0.007[2362.30]$$

$$KW = 18.18$$

You can look up the significance of **KW = 18.18** in any table of critical values such as the one found at www.itl.nist.gov. In this case, we find that it is statistically significant at the $p < 0.001$ level.

SPSS Commands

Open the data set ***Ch18 KruskalWallis***.
Follow the steps below:

(If you have the raw scores the computer will rank those scores automatically for you.)

(1) Go to ***Analyze***.
(2) Scroll down and select ***Nonparametric Tests***; select ***Legacy Dialogs***.
(3) Select ***K Independent Samples . . .***
(4) Under ***Test Type***, check the box by ***Kruskal Wallis H*** and ensure that no other tests are selected.
(5) Move ***Traffic*** into the ***Test Variable List***.
(6) Move ***CityType*** into the ***Grouping Variable*** box.

(7) Click the ***Define Range...*** button.
(8) Under ***Range for Grouping Variables*** enter ***1*** into the ***Minimum*** box and ***4*** into the ***Maximum*** box (as our city type variable has four levels).

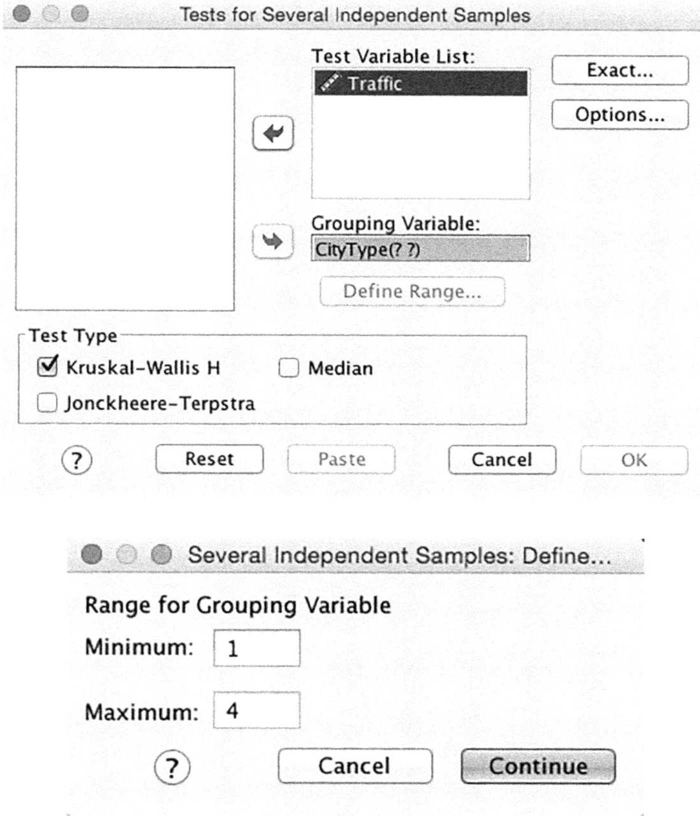

(9) Click ***Continue***.
(10) Click ***OK*** to run the analysis.

Ranks

	City Type	N	Mean Rank
Traffic	Border	13	30.96
	Port	10	14.40
	Central Big	8	14.19
	Central Small	8	15.00
	Total	39	

Test Statistics[a,b]

	Traffic
Chi-Square	18.053
Df	3
Asymp. Sig.	.000

a. Kruskal-Wallis Test.
b. Grouping Variable: City Type.

Due to the precision of the computer and rounding difference when hand-calculated, there is a slight difference to the value you will obtain using SPSS.

Hand calculation = 18.18 *SPSS = 18.05*

However, both are significant at the p <.001 level.

The results might be written as follows.

A Kruskal-Wallis test was performed to test for differences in human-trafficking rates between border, port, central large and central small cities. The mean rank for border cities was 30.96, for central small cities 15.00, for port cities 14.40 and for central large cities 14.19. The results were significant ($X^2_{(3)} = 18.053, p = .001$).

Practical Implications: Why are border cities higher in trafficking than port cities? Are there stricter and more concentrated enforcement efforts at ports? Are there more opportunities for trafficking in border cities; if so, what are they? Why do smaller cities have a higher trafficking rate than port or big central cities? What factors (variables) might contribute to this higher rate? Is there a difference in the type of human trafficking in these different cities?

PART B: PARAMETRIC

Interval/Ratio Level Data

One-Way Between - Subjects ANOVA

See Chart—Multiple (k) Independent Groups and Interval or Ratio Measurement

The one-way between ANOVA test for multiple (k) independent groups (samples) is the same as the one-way between ANOVA test for two independent samples we discussed in Chapter 16, except this time we have more than two groups (levels) of the independent nominal level variable.

In a one-way between-group ANOVA, we examine the difference in effects by testing the difference in group means. The variance provided by an effect (variable) is identified and tested with respect to the error variance. Remember **V total = V between + V error. And the ratio of those variances become the F test to see if there is a significant difference between the groups.**

Let's look at an example of a simple one-way between ANOVA for k independent groups. The example from Chapter 13 and 16 looking at the variables gender, university attended and licensure exam score will be used for multiple independent groups (samples) ANOVA.

CONCEPTUAL FRAMEWORK: ONE-WAY ANOVA

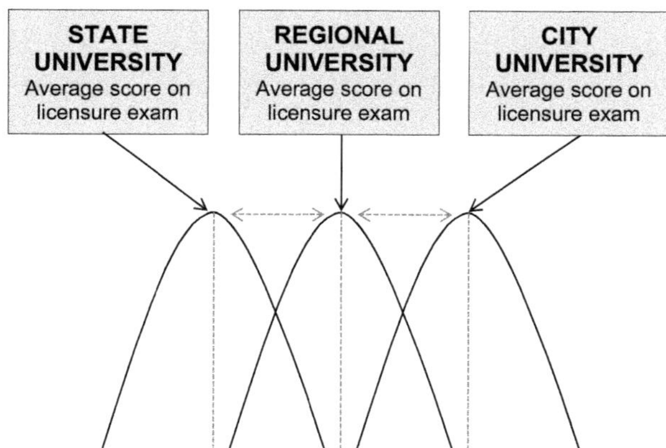

Study Question: Is there a difference in performance on the licensure exam between graduates of State University, Regional University or City University?

This is a difference, cross-sectional independent measures design.

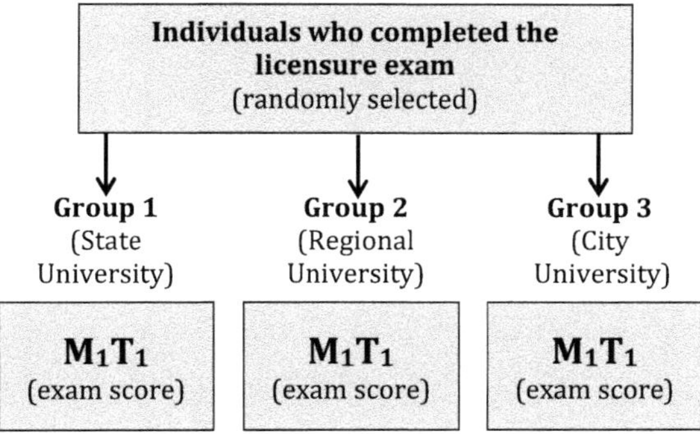

Hypotheses:

Difference: There is a difference in performance on the licensure exam between State U, Regional U and City U graduates.

Null: There is no difference in performance on the licensure exam between State U, Regional U and City U graduates.

Expected (E): There will be no difference in performance on the licensure exam between State U, Regional U and City U graduates.

Predicted (P): There will be a difference in performance on the licensure exam between State U, Regional U and City U graduates.

Observed (O): Actual scores on the licensure exam for State U, Regional U and City U graduates.

Level of Measurement: IV Nominal (University), DV Interval (scores on licensure exam)

Type of Design: Difference, cross-sectional, independent measures

Number of Groups: 3 Groups (samples)

Assumptions: (a) Normal Distribution, (b) Close to equal size in groups

VARIABLE BOX—Multiple (k) Group ANOVA

State U Grad. (A1)	***Regional U Grad.*** (A2)	***City U Grad.*** (A3)
Mean Exam Score $\bar{X}_1$	**Mean Exam Score** $\bar{X}_2$	**Mean Exam Score** $\bar{X}_3$

State University Exam Score	State University Exam Score Squared	Regional University Exam Score	Regional University Exam Score Squared	City University Exam Score	City University Exam Score Squared
2	4	6	36	9	81
3	9	8	64	11	121
4	16	8	64	11	121
6	36	9	81	14	196
12	144	9	81	14	196
13	169	11	121	14	196
13	169	13	169	17	289
13	169	13	169	18	324
14	196	14	196	19	361
16	256	15	225	19	361

State University Exam Score	State University Exam Score Squared	Regional University Exam Score	Regional University Exam Score Squared	City University Exam Score	City University Exam Score Squared
16	256	16	256	19	361
17	289	16	256	20	400
18	324	17	289	21	441
19	361	17	289	21	441
22	484	18	324	22	484
23	529	20	400	23	529
24	576	21	441	25	625
24	576	22	484	27	729
25	625	23	529	27	729
26	676	24	576	29	841
310	**5864**	**300**	**5050**	**380**	**7826**
ΣX_1	ΣX_1^2	ΣX_2	ΣX_2^2	ΣX_3	ΣX_3^2

We will calculate the ANOVA using the same method we did when there were only two groups (levels). We will now calculate the ANOVA with 3 groups.

ANOVA Calculations

$\mathbf{X}_1$ = State University graduate's exam scores
$\mathbf{X}_2$ = Regional University graduate's exam scores
$\mathbf{X}_3$ = City University graduate exam's scores

$$\Sigma X_1 = 310$$

$$\Sigma X_2 = 300$$

$$\Sigma X_3 = 380$$

$$\Sigma X = 310 + 300 + 380 = 990$$

$$\Sigma X_1^2 = 5{,}864$$

$$\Sigma X_2^2 = 5{,}050$$

$$\Sigma X_3^2 = 7{,}826$$

$$\Sigma X^2 = 5{,}864 + 5{,}050 + 7{,}826 = 18{,}740$$

$$\frac{(\Sigma X)^2}{N} = \frac{(990)^2}{60} = \frac{980100}{60} = 16{,}335$$

$$SS = Sum\ of\ Squares$$

$$SS_{Total} = \Sigma X^2 - \frac{(\Sigma X)^2}{N} = 18{,}740 - 16{,}355 = 2405$$

$$SS_{Between} =$$

$$\frac{(\Sigma X_1)^2}{N_1} + \frac{(\Sigma X_2)^2}{N_2} + \frac{(\Sigma X_3)^2}{N_3} - \frac{(\Sigma X)^2}{N} = \frac{(310)^2}{20} + \frac{(300)^2}{20} + \frac{(380)^2}{20} - \frac{(990)^2}{60}$$

$$= 4{,}805 + 4{,}500 + 7{,}220 - 16{,}335 = 16{,}525 - 16{,}335 = 190.0$$

$$SS_{Within} = SS_{Total} - SS_{Between} = 2405 - 190.0 = 2215.0$$

$$MS = Mean\ Square$$

$$MS_{Between} = \frac{SS_{Between}}{\#\ of\ Groups - 1} = \frac{190.0}{3 - 1} = 95.0$$

$$MS_{Within} = \frac{SS_{Within}}{N - \#\ of\ Groups} = \frac{2215.0}{60 - 3} = 38.86$$

$$F_{(2,57)} = \frac{MS_{Between}}{MS_{Within}} = \frac{100.83}{38.655} = 2.445; p = .096$$

The effect size (partial eta squared) can be calculated as follows:

$$Partial\ eta\ square = \frac{SS\ between}{SS\ between + SS\ error}$$

$$Partial\ eta\ square = \frac{190}{190 + 2215}$$

$$Partial\ eta\ square = \frac{190}{2405}$$

$$Partial\ eta\ square = 0.079$$

The partial eta squared statistic shows how much variance is accounted for by university attended and is evaluated using the following cut-off points:

Partial Eta Squared Effect Size Interpretations

Partial Eta Squared	Interpretation
0–.009	Negligible or no effect size
.010–.058	Small effect size
.059–0.137	Medium effect size
.138+	Large effect size

Based upon the value of the Partial Eta Square calculated above the University Attended had a Medium Effect Size.

SPSS Commands

Open the data set ***Ch18 ANOVA ANCOVA***.

Follow the steps below:

(1) Click ***Analyze***.
(2) Scroll down and select ***General Linear Model***.
(3) Select ***Univariate . . .***
(4) Move the variable ***Exam Score [Exam]*** to the ***Dependent Variable*** box; move the variable ***University*** to the ***Fixed Factor(s)*** box.

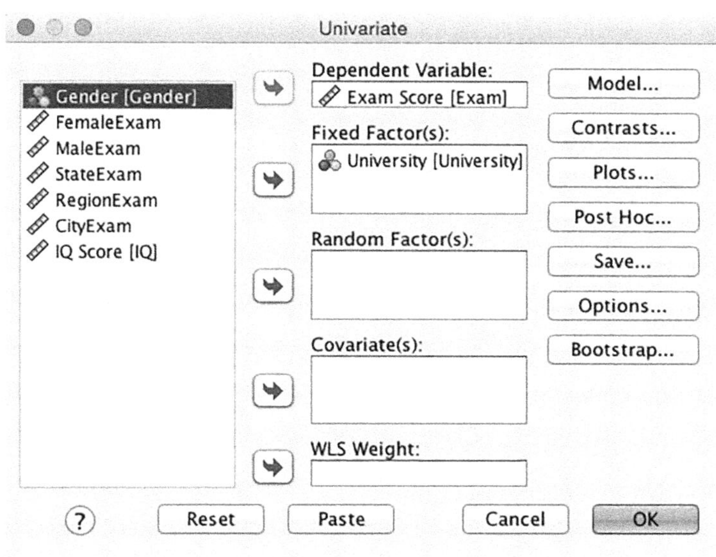

(5) Click ***Options. . .***
(6) Select ***Descriptive statistics***, ***Estimates of effect size***, ***Observed power*** and ***Homogeneity tests***.
(7) Click Continue
(8) Click ***Post Hoc . . .***
(9) Move ***University*** to the ***Post Hoc Test for*** box; in the ***Equal Variances Assumed*** box, select ***Bonferroni***; in the ***Equal Variances Not Assumed*** box, select ***Tamhane's T2***.

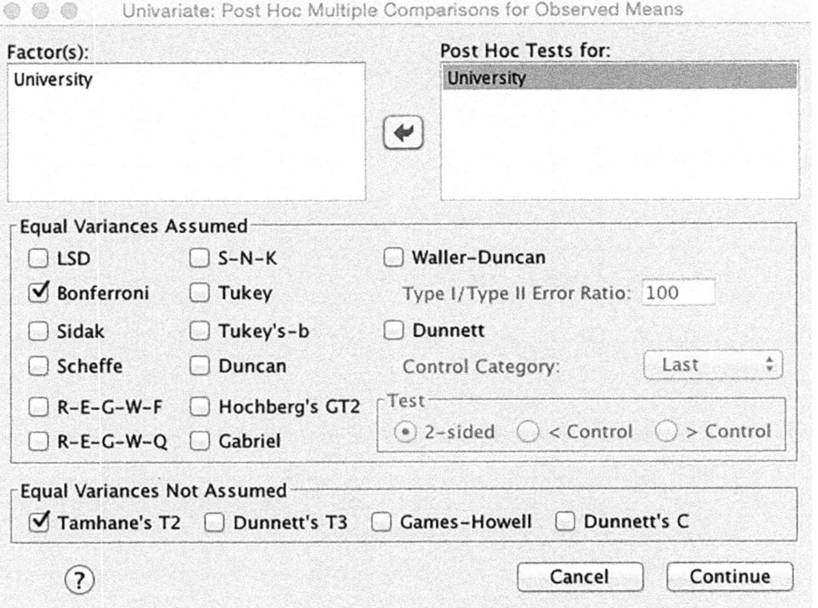

(10) Click ***Continue***.
(11) Click ***OK*** to run the analysis.

Post Hoc is conducted to determine (1) if there is a significant difference between the groups (means are significantly different) and (2) where the differences are—which groups differ significantly. POST HOC CAN ONLY BE USED FOR FIXED FACTORS AND CANNOT BE USED FOR REPEATED MEASURES DESIGNS!

Bonferroni is the most common method used to test for differences. It is based upon the t-test and adjusts for multiple comparisons. Tukey is the next most common used and is based upon the standardized range. It is most powerful when you have large N. For smaller Ns Bonferroni is preferred. If you have 1 to 4 groups use Bonferroni; if you have more than 4 groups use Tukey. To do a Post Hoc all you need to do is to click on Post Hoc and insert the variable you want to investigate. **If you do not have homogeneity**

of variances, use the Tamhane's T2 test to investigate post hoc differences, not Bonferroni or Tukey. We "clicked" both to save time and space in the example.

Between-Subjects Factors

		Value Label	N
University	1	State U	20
	2	Regional U	20
	3	City U	20

Descriptive Statistics

Dependent Variable: Exam Score

University	Mean	Std. Deviation	N
State U	15.50	7.466	20
Regional U	15.00	5.380	20
City U	19.00	5.648	20
Total	16.50	6.385	60

Levene's Test of Equality of Error Variances[a]

Dependent Variable: Exam Score

F	df1	df2	Sig.
1.246	2	57	.295

Tests the null hypothesis that the error variance of the dependent variable is equal across groups.
a. Design: Intercept + University.

Tests of Between-Subjects Effects

Dependent Variable: Exam Score

Source	Type III Sum of Squares	df	Mean Square	*F*	Sig.	Partial Eta Squared	Noncent. Parameter	Observed Power[b]
Corrected Model	190.000[a]	2	95.000	2.445	.096	.079	4.889	.473

(*Continued*)

Tests of Between-Subjects Effects

Dependent Variable: Exam Score

Source	Type III Sum of Squares	df	Mean Square	*F*	Sig.	Partial Eta Squared	Noncent. Parameter	Observed Power[b]
Intercept	16335.000	1	16335.000	420.359	.000	.881	420.359	1.000
University	190.000	2	95.000	2.445	.096	.079	4.889	.473
Error	2215.000	57	38.860					
Total	18740.000	60						
Corrected Total	2405.000	59						

a. R Squared = .079 (Adjusted R Squared = .047).
b. Computed using alpha = .05.

Multiple Comparisons

Dependent Variable: Exam Score

	(I) University	(J) University	Mean Difference (I-J)	Std. Error	Sig.	95% Confidence Interval	
						Lower-Bound	Upper-Bound
Bonferroni	State U	Regional U	.50	1.971	1.000	–4.36	5.36
		City U	–3.50	1.971	.243	–8.36	1.36
	Regional U	State U	–.50	1.971	1.000	–5.36	4.36
		City U	–4.00	1.971	.141	–8.86	.86
	City U	State U	3.50	1.971	.243	–1.36	8.36
		Regional U	4.00	1.971	.141	–.86	8.86
Tamhane	State U	Regional U	.50	2.058	.993	–4.66	5.66
		City U	–3.50	2.093	.279	–8.75	1.75
	Regional U	State U	–.50	2.058	.993	–5.66	4.66
		City U	–4.00	1.744	.080	–8.36	.36
	City U	State U	3.50	2.093	.279	–1.75	8.75
		Regional U	4.00	1.744	.080	–.36	8.36

Based on observed means.
The error term is Mean Square(Error) = 38.860.

The results might be written as follows:

A one-way between ANOVA was performed to determine if there was a difference in performance on the licensure exam between graduates of State U, Regional U and

City U. The mean score on the licensure exam for State U graduates was 15.5, for Regional U 15.0 and for City U 19.0. Although there was a trend toward difference, it did not reach significance ($F_{(2,57)}$ = 2.445 p = .096), with a medium effect size (partial eta squared = .079) and 47% power.

We instructed you to conduct the both Post Hoc tests because this saves time by not having to run the SPSS program again if the result is significant. *If there is not a significant F in the overall test, you do not perform the Post Hoc* test to determine *where the significant difference occurs*. Thus, there is no report of the Post Hoc tests in the write up of the results.

Practical Implications: Although there was not a significant difference between the universities there was a trend toward difference with State U and Region U having similar averages and City U being about 4 points higher. Is there a difference in the preparation of City U students for the exam compared to the other universities? Are the students attending City U different from the other universities (age, ethnicity, selection of social work practice, practicum sites and many more) and could any of these account for the difference in exam scores?

ONE-WAY Between—Subjects ANOVA with Post Hoc

See Chart—Multiple (k) Independent Groups and Interval or Ratio Measurement

Study Question: **Is there a difference in hours dedicated to exercise among senior adults receiving telephone coaching, video coaching and in-person coaching?**

This is a difference/association cross-sectional independent measures design.

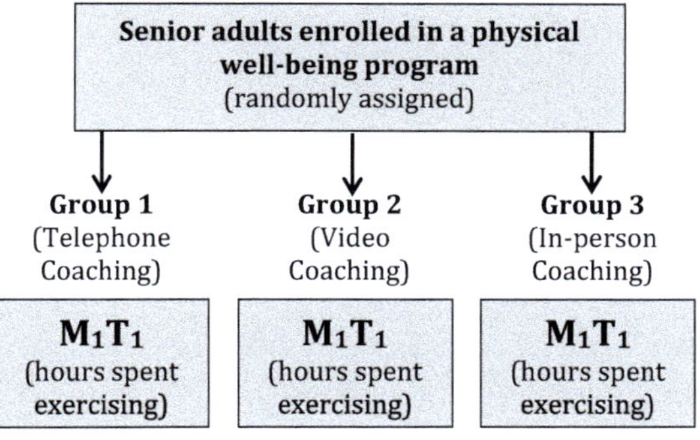

Hypotheses:

Difference: There is a difference in hours dedicated to exercise among senior adults receiving telephone coaching, video coaching and in-person coaching.

Null: There is no difference in hours dedicated to exercise among senior adults receiving telephone coaching, video coaching and in-person coaching.

Expected (E): No difference in hours dedicated to exercise among senior adults receiving telephone coaching, video coaching and in-person coaching.

Predicted (P): A difference in hours dedicated to exercise among senior adults receiving telephone coaching, video coaching and in-person coaching.

Observed (O): Total hours spent exercising during the month-long physical well-being program.

Level of Measurement: IV Nominal (type of coaching), DV Ratio (total hours spent in exercise)

Type of Design: Difference, cross-sectional, independent measures

Number of Groups: 3 Groups (samples)

Assumptions: (a) Normal distribution, (b) Close to equal size in groups

VARIABLE BOX—ANOVA

Telephone Coaching (A1)	***Video Coaching*** (A2)	***In-Person Coaching*** (A3)
Mean Total Hours $\overline{X}_1$	**Mean Total Hours** $\overline{X}_2$	**Mean Total Hours** $\overline{X}_3$

SPSS Commands

Open the data set ***Ch18 ANOVA Post Hoc***.
Complete the following steps:

(1) Click ***Analyze***.
(2) Scroll down and select ***General Linear Model***.
(3) Select ***Univariate. . .***
(4) Move the variable ***Hours Exercised Per Week*** to the ***Dependent Variable*** box; move the variable ***Coaching Method*** to the ***Fixed Factor(s)*** box.
(5) Click ***Options. . .***
(6) Select ***Descriptive statistics***, ***Estimates of effect size***, ***Observed power*** and ***Homogeneity tests***.
(7) Click ***Continue***.

(8) Click ***Post Hoc . . .***

(9) Move ***Coach*** to the ***Post Hoc Test for*** box; in the ***Equal Variances Assumed*** box, select ***Bonferroni***; in the ***Equal Variances Not Assumed*** box, select ***Tamhane's T2***.

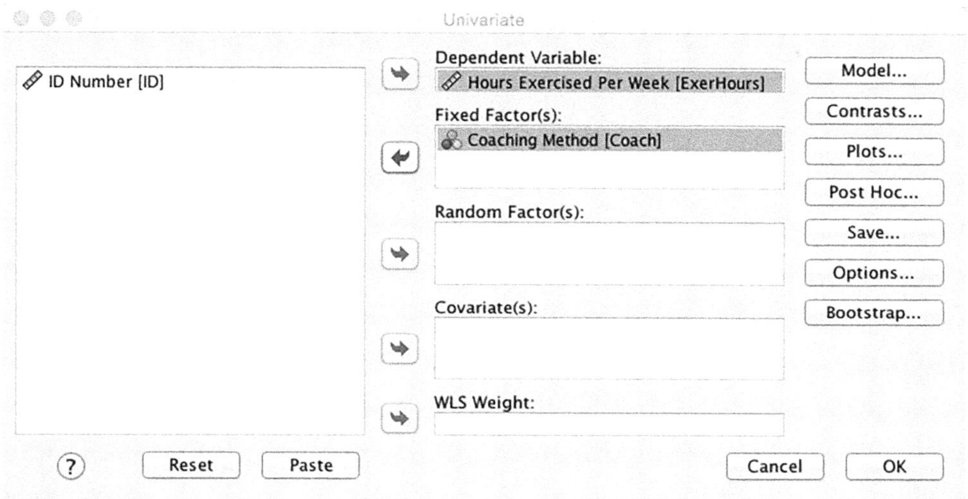

Univariate: Post Hoc Multiple Comparisons for Observed Means

Factor(s):
Coach

Post Hoc Tests for:
Coach

Equal Variances Assumed
LSD
Bonferroni
Sidak
Scheffe
R-E-G-W-F
R-E-G-W-Q
S-N-K
Tukey
Tukey's-b
Duncan
Hochberg's GT2
Gabriel
Waller-Duncan
Type I/Type II Error Ratio: 100
Dunnett
Control Category: Last
Test
2-sided
< Control
> Control

Equal Variances Not Assumed
Tamhane's T2
Dunnett's T3
Games-Howell
Dunnett's C

Cancel
Continue

(10) Click ***Continue***.
(11) Click ***OK*** to run the analysis.

Let's review the output tables:

Between-Subjects Factors

		Value Label	N
Coaching Method	1	Telephone Coaching	40
	2	Video Coaching	40
	3	Personal Coaching	40

Descriptive Statistics

Dependent Variable: Hours Exercised

Coaching Method	Mean	Std. Deviation	N
Telephone Coaching	4.69	2.283	40
Video Coaching	5.08	1.890	40
Personal Coaching	7.44	2.362	40
Total	5.73	2.489	120

Levene's Test of Equality of Error Variances[a]

Dependent Variable: Hours Exercised

F	df1	df2	Sig.
2.135	2	117	.123

Tests the null hypothesis that the error variance of the dependent variable is equal across groups.
a. Design: Intercept + Coach.

Tests of Between-Subjects Effects

Dependent Variable: Hours Exercised

Source	Type III Sum of Squares	df	Mean Square	*F*	Sig.	Partial Eta Squared	Noncent. Parameter	Observed Power[b]
Corrected Model	177.254[a]	2	88.627	18.510	.000	.240	37.019	1.000
Intercept	3944.533	1	3944.533	823.813	.000	.876	823.813	1.000

Tests of Between-Subjects Effects

Dependent Variable: Hours Exercised

Source	Type III Sum of Squares	df	Mean Square	*F*	Sig.	Partial Eta Squared	Noncent. Parameter	Observed Power[b]
Coach	177.254	2	88.627	18.510	.000	.240	37.019	1.000
Error	560.213	117	4.788					
Total	4682.000	120						
Corrected Total	737.467	119						

a. R Squared = .240 (Adjusted R Squared = .227).
b. Computed using alpha = .05.

Coaching Method

Multiple Comparisons

Dependent Variable: Hours Exercised

	(I) Coaching Method	(J) Coaching Method	Mean Difference (I-J)	Std. Error	Sig.	95% Confidence Interval	
						Lower-Bound	Upper-Bound
Bonferroni	Telephone Coaching	Video Coaching	−.39	.489	1.000	−1.58	.80
		Personal Coaching	−2.75*	.489	.000	−3.94	−1.56
	Video Coaching	Telephone Coaching	.39	.489	1.000	−.80	1.58
		Personal Coaching	−2.36*	.489	.000	−3.55	−1.17
	Personal Coaching	Telephone Coaching	2.75*	.489	.000	1.56	3.94
		Video Coaching	2.36*	.489	.000	1.17	3.55
Tamhane	Telephone Coaching	Video Coaching	−.39	.469	.796	−1.53	.76
		Personal Coaching	−2.75*	.519	.000	−4.02	−1.48
	Video Coaching	Telephone Coaching	.39	.469	.796	−.76	1.53
		Personal Coaching	−2.36*	.478	.000	−3.53	−1.19
	Personal Coaching	Telephone Coaching	2.75*	.519	.000	1.48	4.02
		Video Coaching	2.36*	.478	.000	1.19	3.53

Based on observed means.
The error term is Mean Square(Error) = 4.788.
*. The mean difference is significant at the .05 level.

The results might be written as follows:

A one-way between ANOVA was performed to determine if there was a difference in hours dedicated to exercise among senior adults receiving telephone coaching, video coaching and in-person coaching. The mean score for hours dedicated to exercise for telephone coaching was 4.69, for video caching 5.08 and for personal coaching 7.44, indicating that personal coaching resulted in the most hours dedicated to exercise. This result was significant ($F(2,117) = 18.51$, $p = .001$) with a large effect size (partial eta squared = .24) and 100% power. A Bonferroni post hoc comparison was conducted to determine where the differences between the group existed and it was found that all of the three methods were significantly different from each other at $p = .001$.

One-Way Between-Subjects ANCOVA

See Chart—Multiple (k) Independent Variables and Interval or Ratio Measurement

CONCEPTUAL FRAMEWORK: ONE-WAY ANCOVA

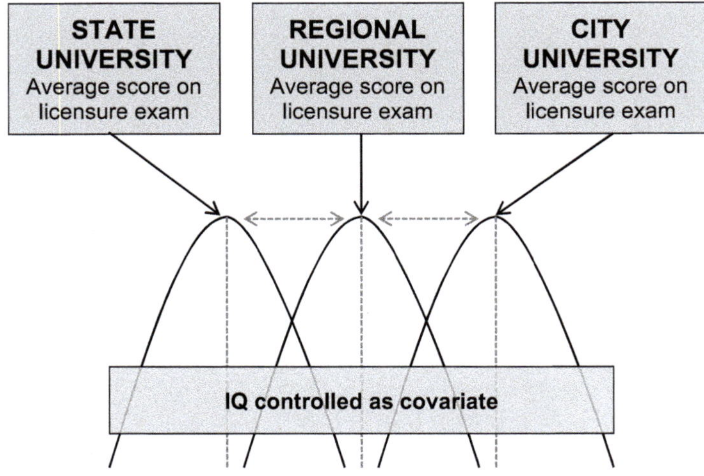

Study Question: **Is there a difference in performance on the licensure exam between State U, Regional U and City university graduates, controlling for IQ?**

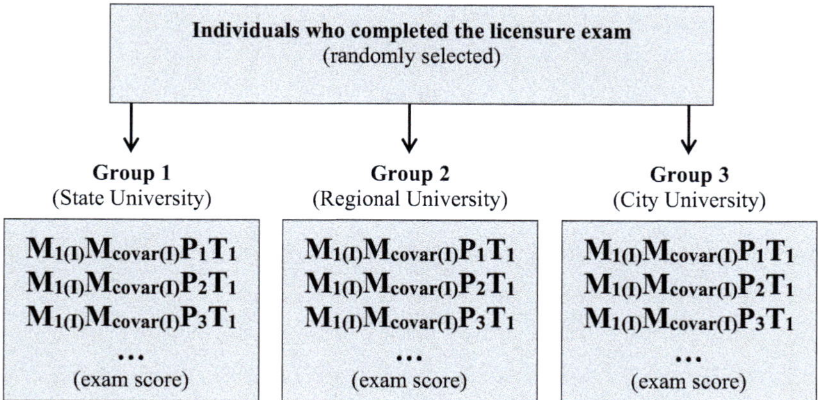

Hypotheses:

Difference: There is a difference in performance on the licensure exam between graduates of State U, Regional U and City U, controlling for IQ.

Null: There is no difference in performance on the licensure exam between graduates of State U, Regional U and City, controlling for IQ.

Expected (E): There will be no difference in performance on the licensure exam between State U, Regional U and City U graduates, controlling for IQ.

Predicted (P): There will be a difference in performance on the licensure exam between State U, Regional U and City graduates, controlling for IQ.

Observed (O): Actual scores on the licensure exam for State U, Regional U and City U graduates, controlling IQ.

Level of Measurement: IV Nominal (university), DV Interval (scores on licensure exam), Covariate Interval (IQ)

Type of Design: Difference, cross-sectional, independent measures

Number of Groups: 3 Groups (samples)

Assumptions: (a) Normal distribution, (b) Homogeneity of variance, (c) Relationship of DV and Covar

VARIABLE BOX—ANCOVA

State U Grad. (A1)	***Regional U Grad.*** (A2)	***City U Grad.*** (A3)
Exam Scores X_1–covariate	**Exam Scores** X_2–covariate	**Exam Scores** X_3–covariate

SPSS Commands

Open the data set ***Ch18 ANOVA ANCOVA***.
Follow the steps below:

(1) Click ***Analyze***.
(2) Scroll down and select ***General Linear Model***.
(3) Select ***Univariate . . .***
(4) Move the variable ***Exam Score [Exam]*** to the ***Dependent Variable*** box; move the variable ***University*** to the ***Fixed Factor(s)*** box.
(5) Move the covariate ***IQ*** to the ***Covariate(s)*** box.

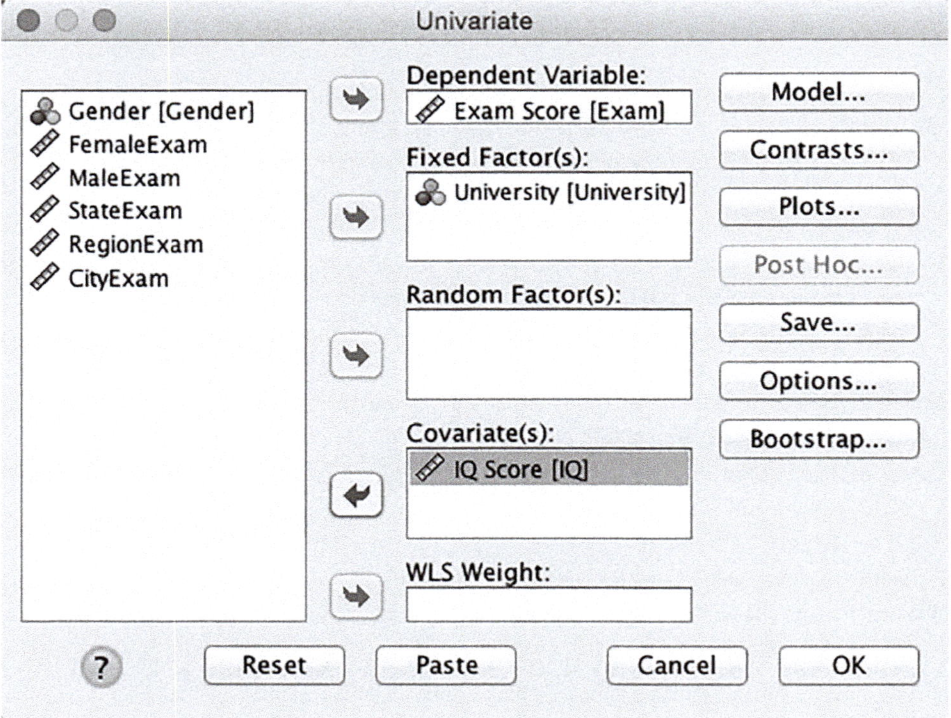

(6) Click ***Options . . .***
(7) Select ***Descriptive statistics***, ***Estimates of effect size***, ***Observed power*** and ***Homogeneity tests***.
(8) Click ***Continue***.
(9) Select ***EM Means***.
(10) Move ***Overall and University to Display Means***.
(11) Click ***Continue***.
(12) Click ***OK*** to run the analysis.

Between-Subjects Factors

		Value Label	N
University	1	State U	20
	2	Regional U	20
	3	City U	20

Descriptive Statistics

Dependent Variable: Exam Score

University	Mean	Std. Deviation	N
State U	15.50	7.466	20
Regional U	15.00	5.380	20
City U	19.00	5.648	20
Total	16.50	6.385	60

Levene's Test of Equality of Error Variances[a]

Dependent Variable: Exam Score

F	df1	df2	Sig.
.424	2	57	.656

Tests the null hypothesis that the error variance of the dependent variable is equal across groups.
a. Design: Intercept + IQ + University.

Tests of Between-Subjects Effects

Dependent Variable: Exam Score

Source	Type III Sum of Squares	df	Mean Square	*F*	Sig.	Partial Eta Squared	Noncent. Parameter	Observed Power[b]
Corrected Model	287.719[a]	3	95.906	2.537	.066	.120	7.610	.596
Intercept	49.980	1	49.980	1.322	.255	.023	1.322	.204
IQ	97.719	1	97.719	2.585	.114	.044	2.585	.352
University	140.132	2	70.066	1.853	.166	.062	3.706	.370
Error	2117.281	56	37.809					
Total	18740.000	60						
Corrected Total	2405.000	59						

a. R Squared = .120 (Adjusted R Squared = .072).
b. Computed using alpha = .05.

University

Dependent Variable: Exam Score				
University	Mean	Std. Error	95% Confidence Interval	
			Lower-Bound	Upper-Bound
State U	15.906[a]	1.398	13.106	18.706
Regional U	14.971[a]	1.375	12.216	17.726
City U	18.623[a]	1.395	15.829	21.417

a. Covariates appearing in the model are evaluated at the following values: IQ Score = 99.95.

When you take out the effect of IQ on the scores, the difference between universities is even less. The scores on the licensure exam change from 15.5 to 15.906 for State U graduates; 15.0 to 14.971 for Regional U graduates and from 19.0 to 18.623 for City U graduates after controlling for IQ.

Results might be written as follows.

A one-way between ANCOVA was used to test for differences in performance on the licensure exam between graduates of State U, Regional U and City U. IQ was controlled in the analysis using the WAIS as the covariate. The effect of IQ was not significant ($F_{(1, 56)} = .155$ $p = .114$). The estimated mean score (controlling for IQ) on the licensure exam for State U graduates was 15.906, Regional U graduates 14.971 and City U graduates 18.623. This difference was not significant ($F_{(2,56)} = 1.853$ $p = .166$) with a medium effect size (partial eta squared = .062) and 35% power.

Practical Implications: After you controlled for IQ you found out that the university had less effect on exam but there was still some relationship. The questions and thoughts proposed concerning the ANOVA conducted with with universities where IQ was not included as a covariate will still be important to investigate in the future.

Two-Way Between ANOVA

See Chart—Multiple (k) Independent Groups and Interval or Ratio Measurement

The two-way between ANOVA is used when you have ***two variables (two IVs)*** with ***two or more groups/levels*** and they are independent. The assumptions and requirements for ANOVAS still apply.

We have already tested gender and university separately to see if they have an effect on licensure exam performance. Now we will find out if both variables interacting (combined together) have an effect on the exam. In this example, there are two variables (2 IVs), Gender with two groups (levels), Female and Male, and University graduated with three groups (levels), State, Regional and City. The dependent variable is still the licensure exam score. There is a complete crossing of all groups/levels of variables as you can see in the variable box. A very important rule of thumb is there must be 10 values (scores) in each of the cells in the variable box matrix. Thus, as you add additional variables or additional groups (levels) to a variable more cells are created and the sample size increases very quickly and dramatically.

Study Question: Is there a difference in exam scores based on gender and university attended?

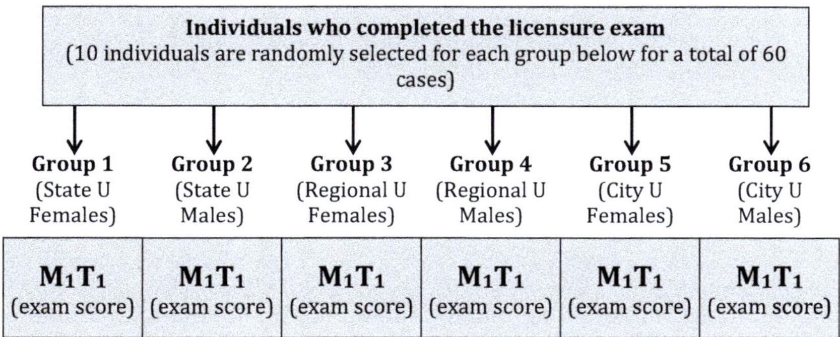

Hypotheses:

Difference: There is a difference in exam scores based on gender and university attended.

Null: There is no difference in exam scores based gender and university attended.

Expected (E): There will be no difference in exam scores based on gender and university attended.

Predicted (P): There will be a difference in exam scores based on gender and university attended.

Observed (O): Actual exam scores for each group based gender and university attended.

Level of Measurement: IV Nominal (gender), IV Nominal (university attended), DV Interval (exam score)

Type of Design: Difference, cross-sectional, independent measures

Number of Groups: 6 Groups (samples)

Assumptions: (a) Normal distribution, (b) Close to equal group sizes, (c) At least 10 per cell.

VARIABLE BOX—TWO-WAY ANOVA

Two independent variables: (1) university attended and (2) gender Multiple levels for each IV: 3 university types and 2 genders

		GENDER		
		Female (A1)	**Male (A2)**	
UNIVERSITY TYPE	**State University (B1)**	A1B1	A2B1	**Row 1:** Effect of State U
	Regional University (B2)	A1B2	A2B2	**Row 2:** Effect of Regional U
	City University (B2)	A1B3	A2B3	**Row 2:** Effect of City U
		Column 1: Effect of being Female	**Column 2:** Effect of being Male	

STATE UNIVERSITY				REGIONAL UNIVERSITY				CITY UNIVERSITY			
FEMALE		MALE		FEMALE		MALE		FEMALE		MALE	
X_1	X_1^2	X_2	X_2^2	X_3	X_3^2	X_4	X_4^2	X_5	X_5^2	X_6	X_6^2
13	169	2	4	6	36	11	121	14	196	9	81
16	256	3	9	8	64	13	169	17	289	11	121
18	324	4	16	8	64	13	169	19	361	11	121
19	361	6	36	9	81	16	324	19	361	14	196
22	484	12	144	9	81	17	289	20	400	14	196
23	529	13	169	14	196	20	400	23	529	18	324
24	576	13	169	15	225	21	441	25	625	19	361
24	576	14	196	16	256	22	484	27	729	21	441
25	625	16	256	17	289	23	529	27	729	21	441
26	676	17	289	18	324	24	576	29	841	22	484
210	**4576**	**100**	**1288**	**120**	**1616**	**180**	**3434**	**220**	**5060**	**160**	**2766**
ΣX_1	ΣX_1^2	ΣX_2	ΣX_2^2	ΣX_3	ΣX_3^2	ΣX_4	ΣX_4^2	ΣX_5	ΣX_5^2	ΣX_6	ΣX_6^2

ANOVA Calculations

X_1 = State University Female grad exam scores
X_2 = State University Male grad exam scores

X_3 = Regional University Female grad exam scores
X_4 = Regional University Male grad exam scores
X_5 = City University Female grad exam scores
X_6 = City University Male grad exam scores

$$\mathbf{\Sigma X_1 = 210}$$

$$\mathbf{\Sigma X_2 = 100}$$

$$\mathbf{\Sigma X_3 = 120}$$

$$\mathbf{\Sigma X_4 = 180}$$

$$\mathbf{\Sigma X_5 = 220}$$

$$\mathbf{\Sigma X_6 = 160}$$

$$\mathbf{\Sigma X = 200 + 100 + 120 + 180 + 220 + 160 = 990}$$

$$\mathbf{\Sigma X_1^2 = 4{,}576}$$

$$\mathbf{\Sigma X_2^2 = 1{,}288}$$

$$\mathbf{\Sigma X_3^2 = 1{,}616}$$

$$\mathbf{\Sigma X_4^2 = 3{,}434}$$

$$\mathbf{\Sigma X_5^2 = 5{,}060}$$

$$\mathbf{\Sigma X_6^2 = 2{,}766}$$

$$\mathbf{\Sigma X^2 = 4{,}576 + 1{,}288 + 1{,}616 + 3{,}434 + 5{,}060 + 2{,}766 = 18{,}740}$$

$$\mathbf{\frac{(\Sigma X)^2}{N} = \frac{(990)^2}{60} = \frac{980100}{60} = 16{,}335}$$

$$SS = Sum\ of\ Squares$$

$$SS_{Total} = \Sigma X^2 - \frac{(\Sigma X)^2}{N} = 18,740 - 16,355 = 2405$$

$$SS_{Between} =$$

$$\frac{(\Sigma X_1)^2}{N_1} + \frac{(\Sigma X_2)^2}{N_2} + \frac{(\Sigma X_3)^2}{N_3} + \frac{(\Sigma X_4)^2}{N_4} + \frac{(\Sigma X_5)^2}{N_5} + \frac{(\Sigma X_6)^2}{N_6} - \frac{(\Sigma X)^2}{N}$$

$$= \frac{(210)^2}{10} + \frac{(100)^2}{10} + \frac{(120)^2}{10} + \frac{(180)^2}{10} + \frac{(220)^2}{10} + \frac{(160)^2}{10} - \frac{(990)^2}{60}$$

$$= 4,410 + 1,000 + 1,440 + 3,240 + 4,840 + 2,560 - 16,335$$

$$= 17,490 - 16,335 = 1,135$$

$$SS_{Within} = SS_{Total} - SS_{Between} = 2405 - 190.0 = 2215.0$$

SPSS Commands

Open the data set ***Ch18 ANOVA ANCOVA***.
Follow the steps below:

(1) Click ***Analyze***.
(2) Scroll down and select ***General Linear Model***.
(3) Select ***Univariate . . .***
(4) Move the variable ***Exam*** to the ***Dependent Variable*** box; move the variables ***University*** and ***Gender*** to the ***Fixed Factor(s)*** box.
(5) Click ***Options. . .***
(6) Select ***Descriptive statistics***, ***Estimates of effect size***, ***Observed power*** and ***Homogeneity tests***.
(7) Click ***Continue***.
(8) Click ***Post Hoc . . .***
(9) Move ***University*** to the ***Post Hoc Test for*** box (Post Hoc testing is unnecessary for ***Gender*** as it only has two levels); in the ***Equal Variances Assumed*** box, select ***Bonferroni***. (Note that the Tamhane's T2 is not available when you run a two-way between-subjects ANOVA.)
(10) Click ***Plots. . .***
(11) Move ***University*** to the ***Horizontal Axis*** box; move ***Gender*** to the ***Separate Lines*** box.
(12) Click ***Add***.

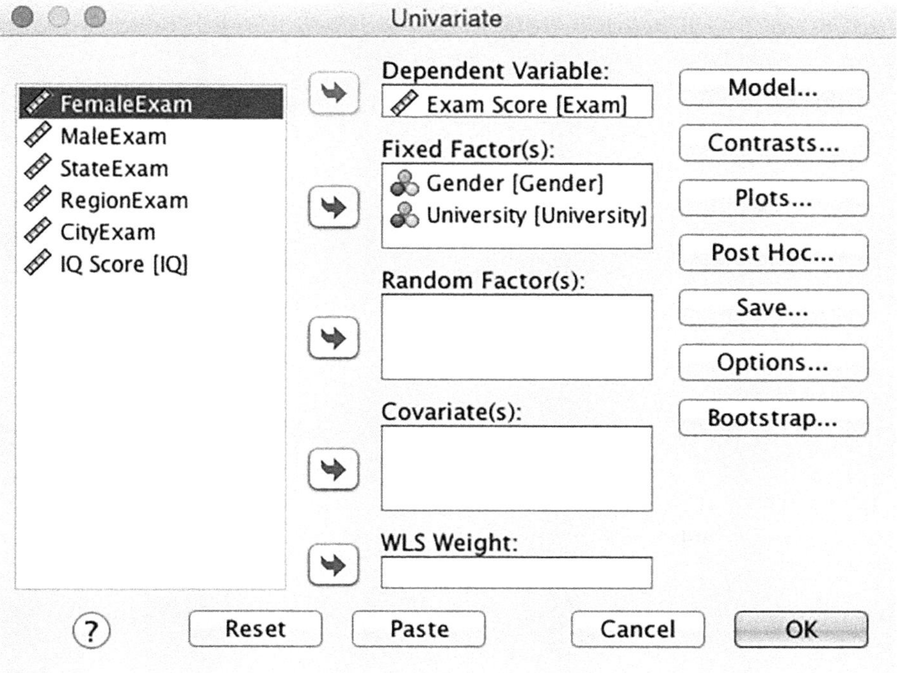

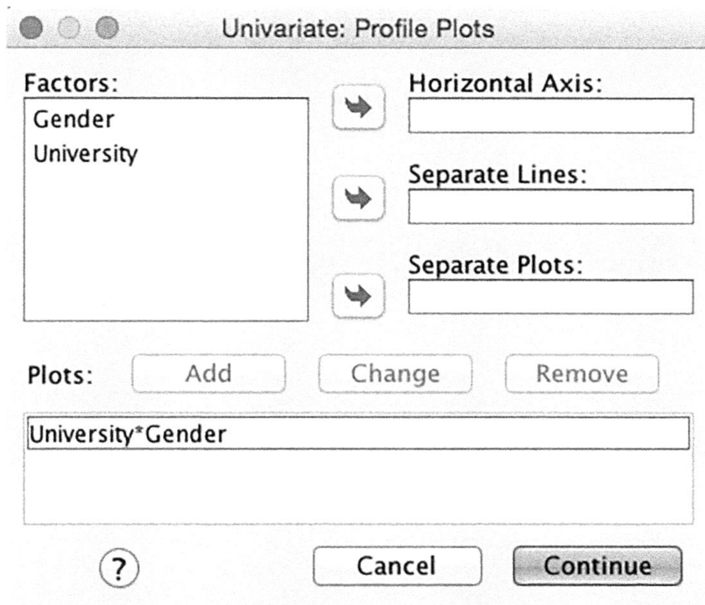

(13) Click ***Continue***.
(14) Click ***OK*** to run the analysis.

Between-Subjects Factors

		Value Label	N
Gender	1	Female	30
	2	Male	30
University	1	State U	20
	2	Regional U	20
	3	City U	20

Descriptive Statistics

Dependent Variable: Exam Score

Gender	University	Mean	Std. Deviation	N
Female	State U	21.00	4.295	10
	Regional U	12.00	4.422	10
	City U	22.00	4.944	10
	Total	18.33	6.348	30
Male	State U	10.00	5.657	10
	Regional U	18.00	4.643	10
	City U	16.00	4.784	10
	Total	14.67	5.973	30
Total	State U	15.50	7.466	20
	Regional U	15.00	5.380	20
	City U	19.00	5.648	20
	Total	16.50	6.385	60

Levene's Test of Equality of Error Variances[a]

Dependent Variable: Exam Score

F	df1	df2	Sig.
.587	5	54	.710

Tests the null hypothesis that the error variance of the dependent variable is equal across groups.
a. Design: Intercept + Gender + University + Gender * University.

Tests of Between-Subjects Effects

Dependent Variable: Exam Score

Source	Type III Sum of Squares	df	Mean Square	*F*	Sig.	Partial Eta Squared	Noncent. Parameter	Observed Power[b]
Corrected Model	1155.000[a]	5	231.000	9.979	.000	.480	49.896	1.000
Intercept	16335.000	1	16335.000	705.672	.000	.929	705.672	1.000
Gender	201.667	1	201.667	8.712	.005	.139	8.712	.826
University	190.000	2	95.000	4.104	.022	.132	8.208	.704
Gender * University	763.333	2	381.667	16.488	.000	.379	32.976	.999
Error	1250.000	54	23.148					
Total	18740.000	60						
Corrected Total	2405.000	59						

a. R Squared = .480 (Adjusted R Squared = .432).
b. Computed using alpha = .05.

Multiple Comparisons

Dependent Variable: Exam Score

Bonferroni

(I) University	(J) University	Mean Difference (I-J)	Std. Error	Sig.	95% Confidence Interval	
					Lower-Bound	Upper-Bound
State U	Regional U	.50	1.521	1.000	–3.26	4.26
	City U	–3.50	1.521	.076	–7.26	.26
Regional U	State U	–.50	1.521	1.000	–4.26	3.26
	City U	–4.00*	1.521	.033	–7.76	–.24
City U	State U	3.50	1.521	.076	–.26	7.26
	Regional U	4.00*	1.521	.033	.24	7.76

First examine the Descriptive Statistics table. A two-way ANOVA allows you to see if gender and university interact to produce an effect on exam scores and indeed it does. For example, Females at City U have their highest scores and the lowest at Regional U while the Males have their highest scores at Regional U and lowest at State U. This interaction is confirmed by looking at the Test of Between-Subjects Effect Table with the interaction of gender and university being the most significant of all effects at p =.001.

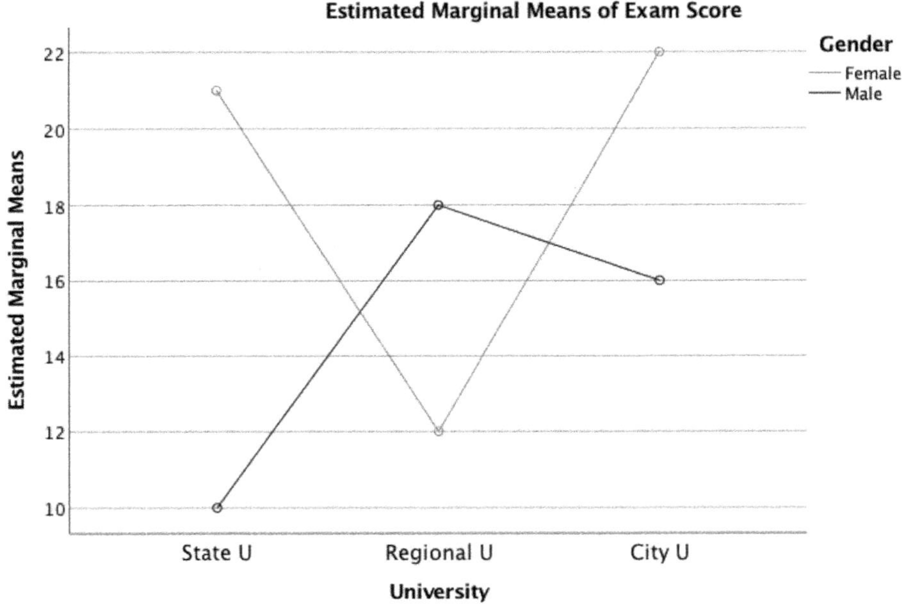

The main effect of gender $p = .005$ and university $p = .022$ is also supported. Post hoc multiple comparisons show that the difference in the effect of university on exam score occurs between the City and Regional University. Finally, the plot of estimated marginal mean provides graphic evidence of the interaction effect between gender and university on exam score. Females at both State U and City U perform well on the exam but Females at Regional U do not perform as well. Males perform best when they graduated from Regional U and were above the Females from that university. However, Males at State U and City U perform below Males from Regional U and worse than Females at those schools.

A post hoc requires a minimum of 3 groups. If you obtain an overall significance in the ANOVA when you have more than 3 groups/levels then you should perform post hoc analysis to determine where the significant differences are occurring.

Results might be written as follows:

The licensure scores of social workers were analyzed using a two-way between-subjects ANOVA with 3 groups/levels of university (State, Regional, City) and 2 groups/levels of gender (Female, Male). All effects were found to be statistically significant. The main effect of gender showed that Females (*M* = 18.333, *SD* = 6.348) achieved significantly higher scores on the licensure exam than did

Males (*M* = 14.667; *SD* = 5.973), ($F_{(1,54)}$ = 8.71, *p* = .005; partial eta squared = 0.14) indicating a large effect with 83% power. The main effect of university was significant ($F_{(2,54)}$ = 4.10, *p* = .02, partial eta squared = 0.132) indicating a medium effect with 70% power. This difference in universities was assessed using the Bonferroni multiple comparison test with the only significant difference occurring between City U (Mean = 19.0, *SD* = 5.65) and Regional U (Mean = 15.0, *SD* = 5.38) *p* = .033. The difference between City U and State U (Mean 15.5, *SD* = 7.47) trended toward significance *p* = .076. There was no difference between State U and Regional U. The interaction effect between gender and university was significant, ($F_{(2,54)}$ = 16.49, *p* = .001, partial eta squared = 0.38) indicating a strong effect with 99% power.

Practical Implications: Since City U is the university with the best exam scores it would be important to see how their curriculum fits with the questions on the exam. The other two universities might need to change their curriculum to improve their graduates score on the exam. Since Females perform better at City U and there is an interaction with gender and university, not only is there a curriculum difference that is related to the performance, but maybe Females are more likely to take a particular curriculum at these different universities. If you look at the plot where there is a gender inversion at Regional U (Males are much higher than Females), it indicates an area to investigate to determine why this particular university is different from the other two universities.

Two-Way Between-Subjects ANCOVA

See Chart—Multiple (k) Independent Groups and Interval or Ratio Measurement

Study Question: Is there a difference in exam scores based on university attended and gender, controlling for IQ?

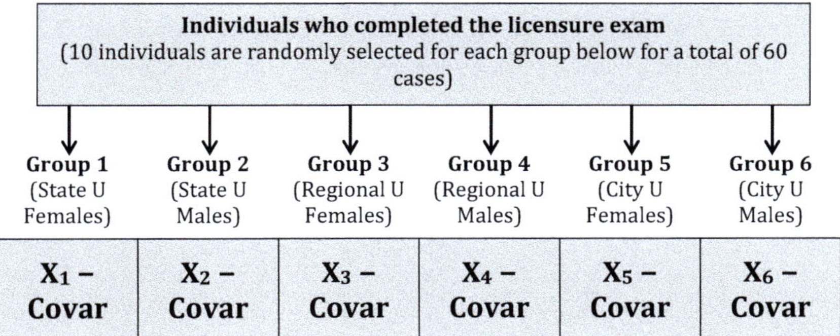

Hypotheses:

Difference: There is a difference in performance on the licensure exam based on university attended and gender, controlling for IQ.
Null: There is no difference in performance on the licensure exam based on university attended and gender, controlling for IQ.
Expected (E): No difference in performance on the licensure exam based on university attended and gender, controlling for IQ.
Predicted (P): Difference in performance on the licensure exam based on university attended and gender, controlling for IQ.
Observed (O): Actual performance scores on the licensure exam for each group based on university attended and gender, controlling for IQ.
Level of Measurement: IV Nominal (gender), IV Nominal (university attended), DV Interval (exam score), CV Interval (IQ)
Type of Design: Difference/association, cross-sectional, independent measures
Number of Groups: 6 Groups (samples)
Assumptions: (a) Normal distribution, (b) Close to equal group sizes; (c) At least 10 per cell, (d) Correlation between DV and Co Var, (e) Homogeneity of variance.

VARIABLE BOX—TWO-WAY ANOVA

Two independent variables: (1) university attended and (2) gender Multiple levels for each IV: 3 university types and 2 genders

Covariate of IQ removed from DV scores for all individuals

		GENDER		
		Female (A1)	**Male (A2)**	
	State University (B1)	A1B1	A2B1	**Row 1:** Effect of State U
UNIVERSITY TYPE	**Regional University (B2)**	A1B2	A2B2	**Row 2:** Effect of Regional U
	City University (B2)	A1B3	A2B3	**Row 2:** Effect of City U
		Column 1: Effect of being Female	**Column 2:** Effect of being Male	

SPSS Commands

Open the data set ***Ch18 ANOVA ANCOVA***.
Follow the steps below:

(1) Click ***Analyze***.
(2) Scroll down and select ***General Linear Model***.
(3) Select ***Univariate. . .***
(4) Move the variable ***Exam Score*** to the ***Dependent Variable*** box; move the variables ***University*** and ***Gender*** to the ***Fixed Factor(s)*** box; move the covariate ***IQ*** to the ***Covariate(s)*** box.

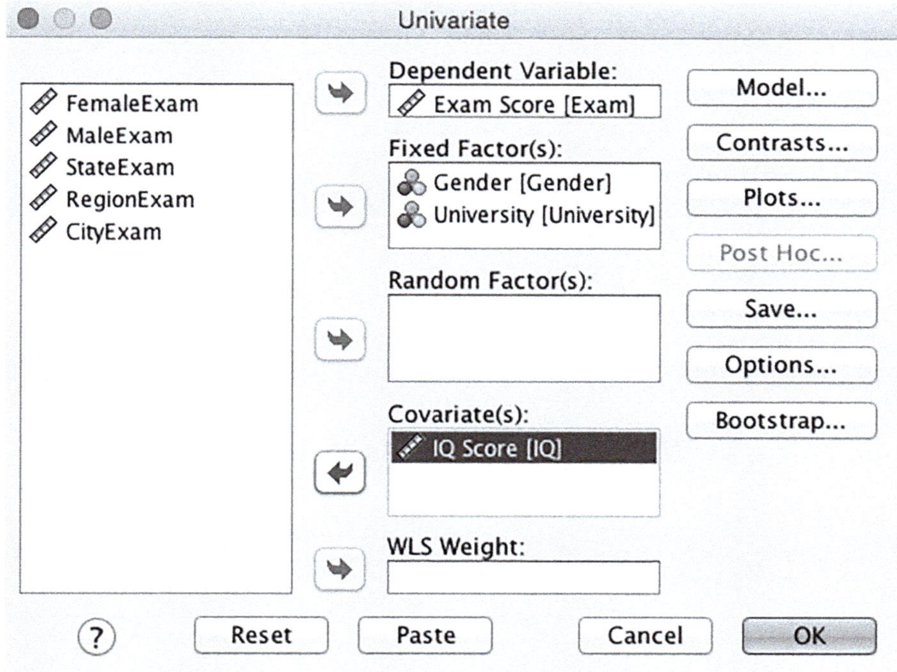

(5) Click ***Options . . .***
(6) Select ***Descriptive statistics***, ***Estimates of effect size***, ***Observed power*** and ***Homogeneity tests***.
(7) Move ***Gender***, ***University*** and ***Gender*University*** to the ***EM Means*** box.

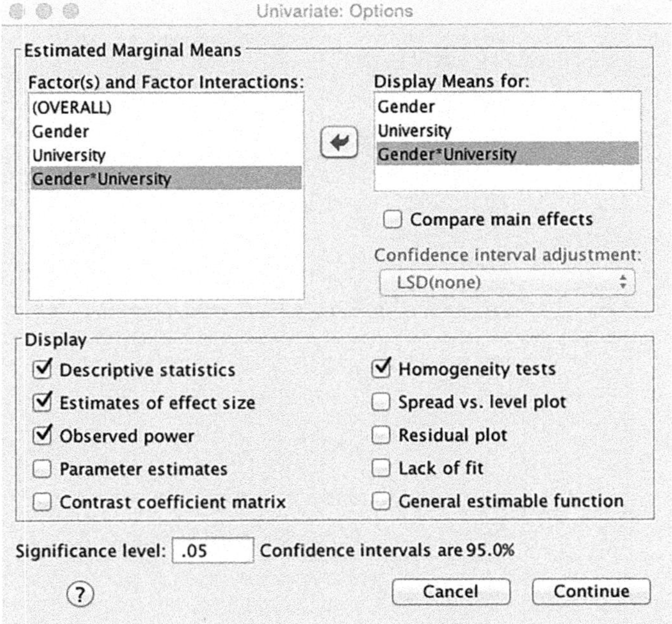

(8) Click ***Continue***.
(9) Click ***Plots . . .***
(10) Move ***University*** to the ***Horizontal Axis*** box; move ***Gender*** to the ***Separate Lines*** box.
(11) Click ***Add***.

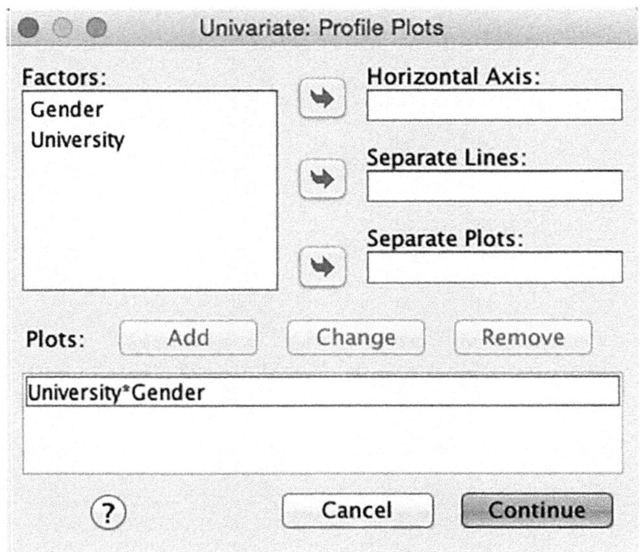

(12) Click ***Continue***.
(13) Click ***OK*** to run the analysis.

Between-Subjects Factors

		Value Label	N
Gender	1	Female	30
	2	Male	30
University	1	State U	20
	2	Regional U	20
	3	City U	20

Descriptive Statistics

Dependent Variable: Exam Score

Gender	University	Mean	Std. Deviation	N
Female	State U	21.00	4.295	10
	Regional U	12.00	4.422	10
	City U	22.00	4.944	10
	Total	18.33	6.348	30
Male	State U	10.00	5.657	10
	Regional U	18.00	4.643	10
	City U	16.00	4.784	10
	Total	14.67	5.973	30
Total	State U	15.50	7.466	20
	Regional U	15.00	5.380	20
	City U	19.00	5.648	20
	Total	16.50	6.385	60

Levene's Test of Equality of Error Variances[a]

Dependent Variable: Exam Score

F	df1	df2	Sig.
.782	5	54	.567

Tests the null hypothesis that the error variance of the dependent variable is equal across groups.
a. Design: Intercept + IQ + Gender + University + Gender * University.

Tests of Between-Subjects Effects

Dependent Variable: Exam Score

Source	Type III Sum of Squares	df	Mean Square	*F*	Sig.	Partial Eta Squared	Noncent. Parameter	Observed Power[b]
Corrected Model	1185.413[a]	6	197.569	8.586	.000	.493	51.515	1.000
Intercept	7.619	1	7.619	.331	.567	.006	.331	.087
IQ	30.413	1	30.413	1.322	.255	.024	1.322	.204
Gender	189.984	1	189.984	8.256	.006	.135	8.256	.805
University	157.133	2	78.566	3.414	.040	.114	6.829	.617
Gender * University	713.857	2	356.929	15.511	.000	.369	31.022	.999
Error	1219.587	53	23.011					
Total	18740.000	60						
Corrected Total	2405.000	59						

a. R Squared = .493 (Adjusted R Squared = .435).
b. Computed using alpha = .05.

1. Gender

Dependent Variable: Exam Score

Gender	Mean	Std. Error	95% Confidence Interval	
			Lower-Bound	Upper-Bound
Female	18.284[a]	.877	16.525	20.043
Male	14.716[a]	.877	12.957	16.475

a. Covariates appearing in the model are evaluated at the following values: IQ Score = 99.95.

2. University

Dependent Variable: Exam Score

University	Mean	Std. Error	95% Confidence Interval	
			Lower-Bound	Upper-Bound
State U	15.731[a]	1.091	13.542	17.920
Regional U	14.983[a]	1.073	12.832	17.135
City U	18.785[a]	1.089	16.601	20.969

a. Covariates appearing in the model are evaluated at the following values: IQ Score = 99.95.

3. Gender * University

Dependent Variable: Exam Score

Gender	University	Mean	Std. Error	95% Confidence Interval	
				Lower-Bound	Upper-Bound
Female	State U	20.983[a]	1.517	17.941	24.026
	Regional U	12.017[a]	1.517	8.974	15.059
	City U	21.851[a]	1.522	18.798	24.905
Male	State U	10.479[a]	1.573	7.324	13.635
	Regional U	17.950[a]	1.518	14.907	20.994
	City U	15.719[a]	1.537	12.637	18.801

* Covariates appearing in the model are evaluated at the following values: IQ Score = 99.95.

Graph of the Interaction of Gender and University Attended on Exam Score with IQ Removed as a Co-variate

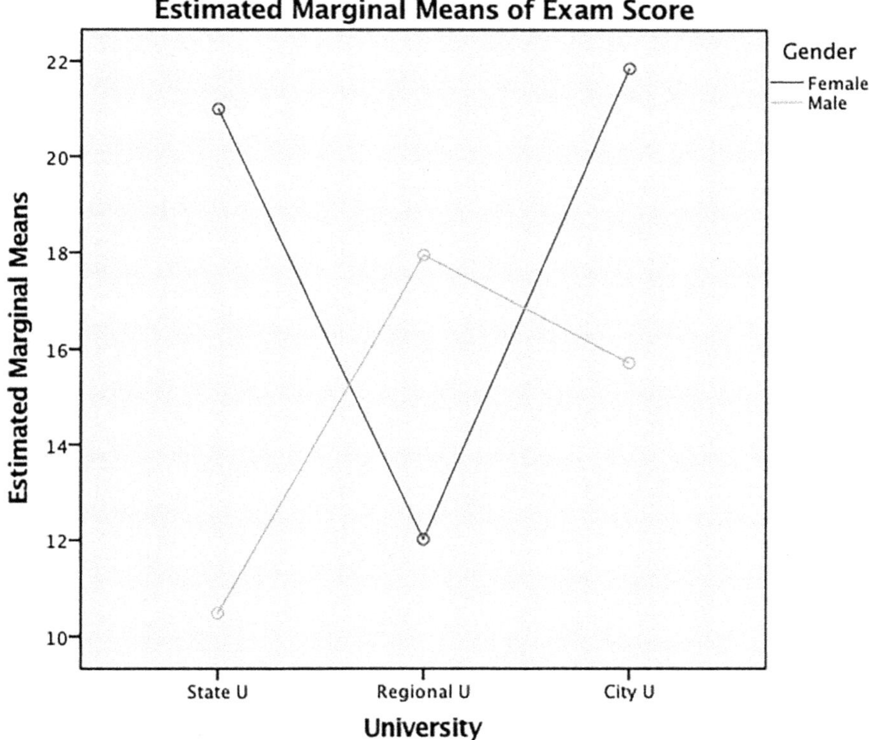

Results might be written as follows.

The licensure exam scores of were analyzed using a two-way between-subjects ANCOVA with two variables, University (State, Regional, City), Gender (Female, Male) and IQ (measured by the WAIS) as a covariate. IQ was not significant $F_{(1,53)} = 1.32, p = .255$; partial eta squared = .024 with a small effect and 20% power.

The main effect of gender showed that Females ($M = 18.28$, $SE = .877$) had significantly higher scores on the licensure exam than did Males ($M = 14.716$, $SE = .877$); ($F_{(1,53)} = 8.256, p = .006$, partial eta squared = .135) with a medium effect and 80% power. The main effect of university, State U ($M = 15.73$, $SE = 1.09$), Regional U ($M = 14.983$, $SE = 1.073$), City U ($M = 18.785$, $SE = 1.089$) was significant ($F_{(2,53)} = 3.14$, $p = .04$, partial eta squared = .114) with a medium effect and 62% power.

The interaction effect between gender and university, Females State U ($M = 20.89$, $SE = 1.52$), Females Regional U ($M = 12.02$, $SE = 1.52$), Females City U ($M = 21.85$, $SE = 1.52$), Males State U ($M = 10.48$, $SE = 1.57$), Males Regional U ($M = 17.95$, $SE = 1.52$), Males City U ($M = 15.72$, $SE = 1.54$) was significant ($F_{(2,53)} = 15.51$, $p = .001$, partial eta squared = .37) with a large effect and 99% power.

Practical Implications: Since there were no major changes controlling for IQ, the same implications for the two-way ANOVA without IQ as a CoVar still apply.

Discussion Article

Critique the use of the Kruskal-Wallis test as well as the ANOVAS AND ANCOVAS in this study. Reflect on why the reasons they were used. How might you use them if you created a study?

Lam, L. C., Tam, C. W., Lui, V. W., Chan, W. C., Chan, S. S., Chiu, H. F., . . . Chan, W. M. (2009). Modality of physical exercise and cognitive function in Hong Kong older Chinese community. *International Journal of Geriatric Psychiatry*, *24*, 48–53. Retrieved from https://onlinelibrary.wiley.com/doi/abs/10.1002/gps.2072

Exercises for Chapter 18 are found in eResources.

Chapter 19

FINDING DIFFERENCES

Multiple (k) Related/Repeated Groups (Samples)

PART A: NONPARAMETRIC

Nominal Level Data

Cochran Q Test

See Chart—Multiple (k) Related or Matched Groups and Nominal Measurement

The ***Cochran Q is used to analyze data with more than two related samples that are nominally measured*** whereas the **McNemar is used to analyze data with only two related samples**. In the Cochran Q, there can be more than two possible conditions of the independent variable. It may be used for both difference studies as well as explanatory studies, and we will provide you with a design for each type.

For a difference design assume that you are an entering social work student who is taking four basic social work courses: SW 401 (Practice), SW 402 (Policy), SW 403 (Diversity) and SW 404 (Research). The question is, "Are all the classes in the first semester (Practice, Policy, Diversity, Research) of equal difficulty?" Since you are only concerned with difficult or easy, you develop a nominal level dependent variable with two levels: Difficult and Easy. In this study, the classes would be considered matched across each student because each student rates every class.

Study Question: Do first year social work students perceive the 4 basic social work classes (practice, policy, diversity research) as having the same degree of difficulty.

This is a difference multiple repeated measures design with no control group.

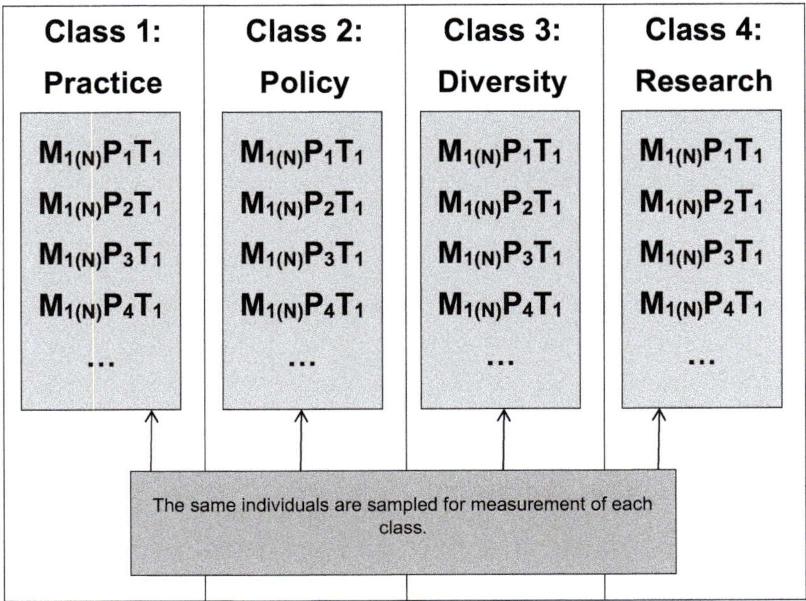

Hypotheses:

Difference: There will be a difference in the difficulty ratings of the basic social work classes.

Null: There will be no difference in the difficulty ratings of the basic social work classes.

Expected (E): There will be no difference in the difficulty ratings of the basic social work classes.

Predicted (P): There will be a difference in the difficulty ratings of the basic social work classes.

Observed (O): The actual distribution of difficulty for classes.

Level of Measurement: DV Nominal (type of class)

Type of Design: Difference, repeated measures, no control

Number of Groups: 4 Groups (samples)

Assumptions: (a) Same person rates all categories

VARIABLE BOX—COCHRAN Q TEST

		Class			
		Practice	***Policy***	***Diversity***	***Research***
Student	***Student 1***	Rating: *Difficult* or *Easy*	Rating: *Difficult* or *Easy*	Rating: *Difficult* or *Easy*	Rating: *Difficult* or *Easy*
	Student 2	Rating: *Difficult* or *Easy*	Rating: *Difficult* or *Easy*	Rating: *Difficult* or *Easy*	Rating: *Difficult* or *Easy*
	Student 3	Rating: *Difficult* or *Easy*	Rating: *Difficult* or *Easy*	Rating: *Difficult* or *Easy*	Rating: *Difficult* or *Easy*
	Student...	Rating: *Difficult* or *Easy*	Rating: *Difficult* or *Easy*	Rating: *Difficult* or *Easy*	Rating: *Difficult* or *Easy*

Suppose you collected the following data:

STUDENT	PRACTICE	POLICY	DIVERSITY	RESEARCH	ROW TOTAL	ROW TOTAL ^{2}
1	0	1	0	1	**2**	**4**
2	0	1	0	1	**2**	**4**
3	0	1	1	1	**3**	**9**
4	0	1	1	1	**3**	**9**
5	0	1	0	1	**2**	**4**
6	0	0	0	1	**1**	**1**
7	0	0	0	1	**1**	**1**
8	0	1	0	0	**1**	**1**
9	0	1	1	1	**3**	**9**
10	0	1	1	1	**3**	**9**
11	0	0	0	1	**1**	**1**
12	1	1	0	0	**2**	**4**
13	0	0	0	0	**0**	**0**
14	0	0	0	0	**0**	**0**
15	1	1	0	1	**3**	**9**
16	1	1	0	1	**3**	**9**
17	0	1	1	1	**3**	**9**
18	0	1	1	1	**3**	**9**
19	0	0	0	1	**1**	**1**
20	0	0	0	1	**1**	**1**
21	0	1	0	1	**2**	**4**

(*Continued*)

STUDENT	PRACTICE	POLICY	DIVERSITY	RESEARCH	ROW TOTAL	ROW TOTAL ²
22	1	1	0	1	**3**	**9**
23	0	1	0	1	**2**	**4**
24	0	1	1	1	**3**	**9**
25	0	1	1	1	**3**	**9**
COLUMN TOTAL	**4**	**18**	**8**	**21**	**51**	**133**

Using the data above, we can calculate Cochran Q using the following formula:

$$Q = \frac{(k-1)\left[k\sum_{j=1}^{k} G_j^2 - \left(\sum^{kj=1} G_j\right)^2\right]}{k\sum_{i=1}^{N} L_i - \sum_{i=1}^{N} L_i^2}$$

$$Q = \frac{(4-1)\left[4\left(4^2+18^2+8^2+21^2\right)-51^2\right]}{4(51)-133}$$

$$Q = \frac{(3)\left[4(16+324+64+441)-2601\right]}{71}$$

$$Q = \frac{(3)\left[4(845)-2601\right]}{71}$$

$$Q = \frac{(3)[3380-2601]}{71}$$

$$Q = \frac{(3)[779]}{71}$$

$$Q = \frac{2337}{71} = 32.92$$

We can compare these results to those we obtain using SPSS.

SPSS Commands

Open the data set ***Ch19 CochranQ1***.
Follow the steps below:

(1) Click ***Analyze***.
(2) Scroll down and select ***Nonparametric Tests***.
(3) Select ***Legacy Dialogs***.
(4) Select ***K Related Samples . . .***

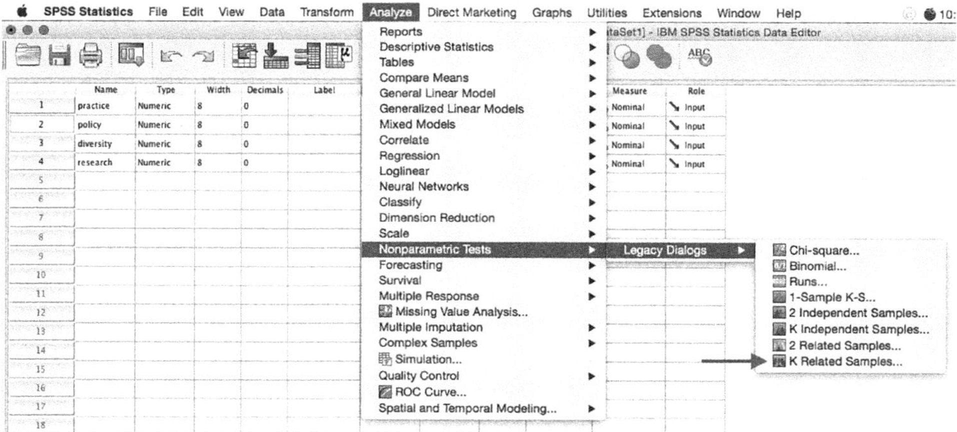

(5) Move each of the four variables ***(practice***, ***policy***, ***research*** and ***diversity***) into the ***Test Variables*** box.
(6) Under ***Test Type***, select ***Cochran's Q*** and un-check the other boxes.
(7) Click ***OK*** to run the analysis.

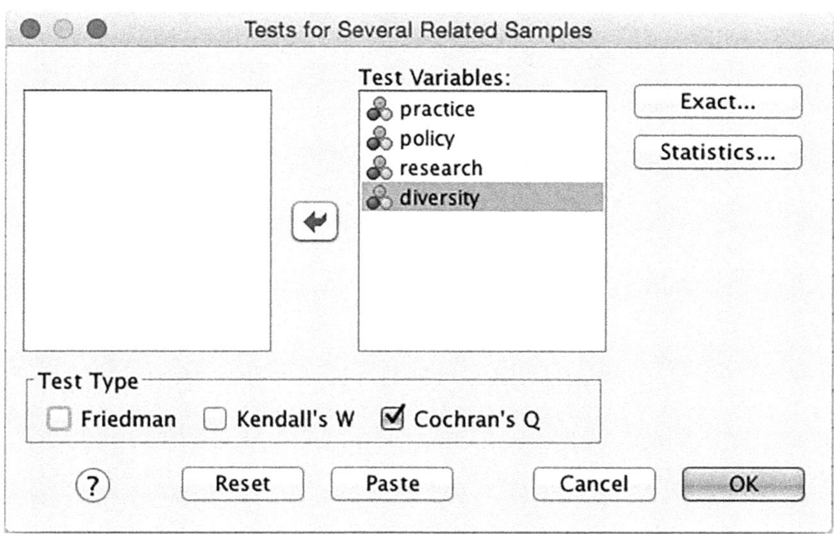

Please note that the data in the SPSS set was coded 1 and 2 not 0 and 1 as it is in the data we calculated by hand. This is to reduce the chances that 0 might be confused with missing data.

Look at the output tables:

Frequencies

	Value	
	1	2
Practice	21	4
Policy	7	18
Research	4	21
Diversity	17	8

Test Statistics

N	25
Cochran's Q	32.915[a]
Df	3
Asymp. Sig.	.000

a. 1 is treated as a success.

Note that the SPSS results are virtually identical to those we calculated by hand above.

Look at the SPSS frequency distribution table where 1 = easy and 2 = difficult. What is your preliminary conclusion about easy and difficult courses from looking at this table? Which courses are rated easy and which difficult? Finally, look at the actual test statistics and decide if the differences between the courses in difficulty was statistically significant.

Results might be written as follows:

First-year social work students were asked to rate 4 social work courses, practice, policy, diversity and research. Out of 25 students practice was seen as easy by 21, and diversity by 17 whereas only 7 said policy was easy and only 4 indicated that research was easy. The results of a Cochran Q found that the perception of difficulty of between these classes was statistically significant (Cochran's $Q_{(3)}$ = 32.915, p = .001).

Practical Implications: Practice is always a favorite class of social work students as it is perceived as providing the skills needed to be an effective professional. Diversity follows practice closely in low difficulty, possibly because of the values and concern for social justice that is part of its material and fits with application in practice. Policy and research may be seen as less closely related to the practice of social work, especially research. Researchers need to continue investigating reasons listed by students that underlie their easy and difficult ratings. A comparison of the application of materials in the four different courses may reveal that there is not a solid connection made between coursework and importance to practice application in policy and research. Methods to teach policy and research may be different from the way practice and diversity is taught in that there may be less interactive learning and role play sessions that may be related to the perception of easy and difficult.

Now let's create a different design. This design measures a change in outcome. There are three methods used to change a person's perception of social work (1) a video depicting the positive work in many areas by social workers, (2) a talk delivered by a professional social worker and (3) a testimonial presentation by a woman and her family about how much the social worker helped them to recover from a multitude of problems (former client). All three methods will be given to incoming freshmen who have indicated that they are interested in the "helping professions". Since we want to see the impact of each method on each person, we know that the order of presentation of the methods will affect their perception. That is, if the social worker presentation is followed by the video and then the former client for every person in the study, there is an effect of order that will influence the results.

Therefore, we counterbalance the methods so that when we look at all of the individuals, the effect of order is removed. Counterbalancing would look as follows with order shown by the numbers in the cells.

Order of Exposure to the Three Presentation Formats

	Video	Social Worker	Former Client
Person 1	1st	2nd	3rd
Person 2	3rd	1st	2nd
Person 3	2nd	3rd	1st
Person 4	1st	2nd	3rd
Person 5	3rd	1st	2nd
Person 6	2nd	3rd	1st
. . .	. . .	. . .	. . .

As you can see, the order of presentation is removed in that the video is 1st for 1/3 of the sample, 2nd for 1/3 of the sample and 3rd for 1/3 of the sample, and the same is true for the other two methods. Thus, when we aggregate the findings across students, we will be able to analyze the scores as not being influenced by the order of presentation.

Study Question: Do the three methods of presenting social work (video, social worker, former client) have the same effect on incoming freshman who are interested in the helping professions?

This is an explanatory multiple repeated measures design with no control group.

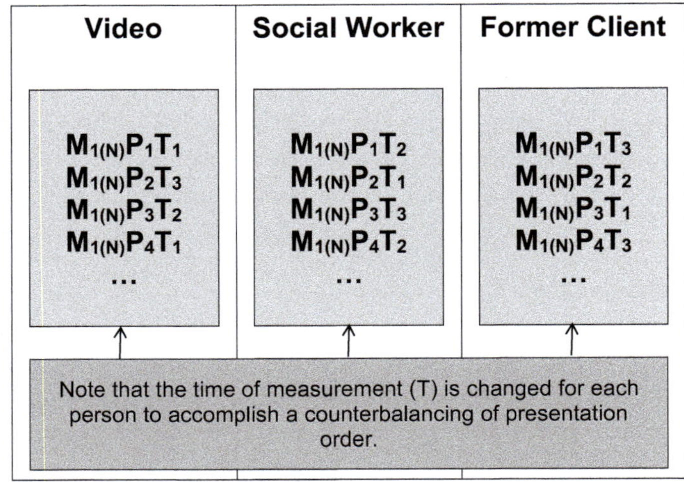

Hypotheses:

Explanatory: The different presentation methods will result in a different amount of change (outcome) in perception of social work.
Null: There will be no difference in the amount of change (outcome) between the different presentation methods.
Expected (E): The outcome for each method will be similar.
Predicted (P): The outcome for method will be different.
Observed (O): The actual outcome for each method.
Level of Measurement: IV Nominal (Method), DV Nominal (outcome)
Type of Design: Explanatory multiple repeated measures design with no control group
Number of Groups: 3 Groups (samples)—Methods
Assumptions: (a) Matched, (b) 10 per group

VARIABLE BOX—COCHRAN *Q* TEST

Presentation Method

		Video	***Social Worker***	***Former Client***
	Student 1	Rating: *Positive* or *No Change*	Rating: *Positive* or *No Change*	Rating: *Positive* or *No Change*
Student	***Student 2***	Rating: *Positive* or *No Change*	Rating: *Positive* or *No Change*	Rating: *Positive* or *No Change*
	Student 3	Rating: *Positive* or *No Change*	Rating: *Positive* or *No Change*	Rating: *Positive* or *No Change*
	Student . . .	Rating: *Positive* or *No Change*	Rating: *Positive* or *No Change*	Rating: *Positive* or *No Change*

SPSS Commands

Open the data set ***Ch19 CochranQ2***
Follow the steps below:

(1) Click ***Analyze***.
(2) Scroll down and select ***Nonparametric Tests***.
(3) Select ***Legacy Dialogs***.
(4) Select ***K Related Samples . . .***

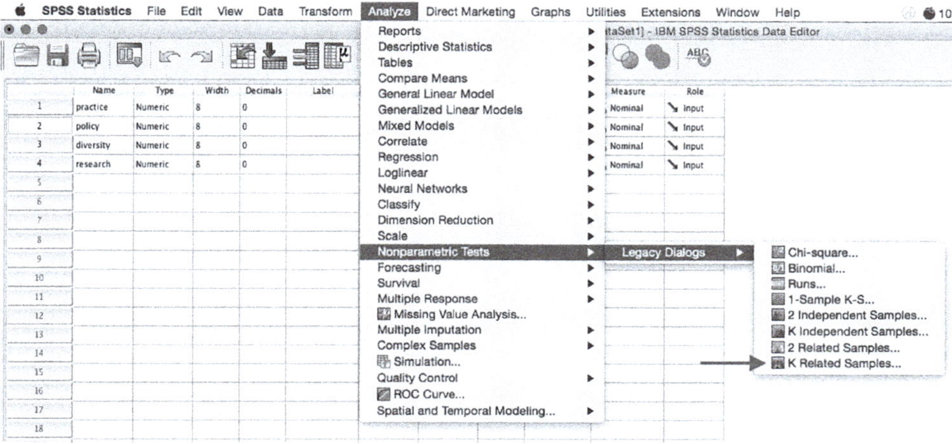

(5) Move each of the three variables (***Video***, ***SWorker*** and ***FmrClient***) into the ***Test Variables*** box.
(6) Under ***Test Type***, select ***Cochran's Q*** and un-check the other boxes.
(7) Click ***OK*** to run the analysis.

Now, let's look at the output tables for this analysis. Remember that a 1 indicates a positive change in the student's perception of social work while a 2 indicates that there was not a positive change.

Frequencies

	Value	
	1	2
Video	13	12
SWorker	4	21
FmrClient	13	12

Test Statistics

N	25
Cochran's Q	8.526[a]
Df	2
Asymp. Sig.	.014

a. 1 is treated as a success.

What is your preliminary conclusion looking at this table? Which of the methods seem to be effective and which do not seem to be very effective? Which seems to be the most effective? Finally, look at the test statistics and decide if the difference in outcome is statistically significant.

Results might be written as follows:

A Cochran Q test was run to determine if there is a difference (outcome) between presentation methods (Video, Social Worker, Recipient) influencing students who are interested in a helping profession career toward a more positive view of social work. Both video and a talk by a recipient produced a positive outcome to study social work for 13 out of 25 students whereas a talk by a social worker only produced a positive outcome for 4 students. The difference between the methods was significant (Cochran's $Q_{(2)} = 8.526, p = .014$).

Practical Implications: The findings need to be replicated and have a much larger sample but it seems that both the video and a talk by a mother and family have much more success in moving students who are interested in the helping professions to be more positive to entering social work. A talk from a social worker is not nearly as effective. Those who are recruiting potential social workers (after replication of these methods with other groups and across other institutions) might investigate which of these two methods, video or recipient, works better with particular groups or in particular conditions. In appealing to the general public (not those interested in a helping profession), performing the same study would see if these methods might be successful in creating a more positive view of social work in the general public.

Ordinal Level Data

Friedman Test

See Chart—Multiple (k) Related or Matched Groups and Ordinal Measurement

The Friedman Test is an Analysis of Variance by ranks. There are two types of designs that are suitable for the Friedman test. The first is a design already found in the example used for the Cochran Q where the method was repeated for every person. Remember the prospective social work major was exposed to all three of the methods of influencing their decision to become a social worker. This design is such that the group of individuals is studied under the many (k) different conditions. The second design is where you create matching sets of individuals and then randomly assign individuals within each set to one of the conditions. We will show you both designs that are appropriate for the Friedman test.

The first type is a design where the ***same group of individuals*** is studied in different conditions. For example, you have been working with a group of teenage children at your youth service center and you are concerned about the way they are assessed in the school. You think that maybe the assessment methods are not equivalent and that students will perform differently on the different methods of evaluation. You are working with the school system and teachers to make sure that there is comparability of assessment methods. The study includes three different types of assessments collected on the same individual: (1) end-of-week quiz, (2) the week's homework and (3) in-class project for the week. Students were in the fall semester of their sophomore year of high school. Scores for all three assessments could range from 0 to 10. ***The data was not normal and did not meet the criteria for a parametric test thus the Friedman (ordinal data nonparametric) is very appropriate to use.***

Study Question: Do students perform differently on the different assessment strategies used to test them during a one-week period in a sophomore English class?

This is a difference multiple repeated measures design with no control group.

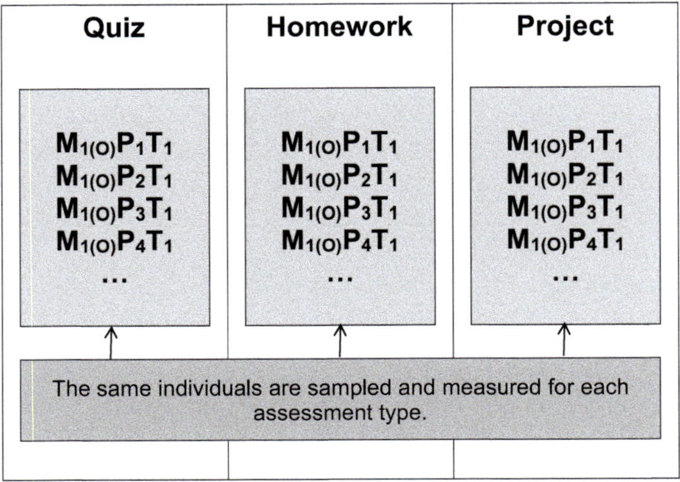

Hypotheses:

Difference: Students will perform differently on the different assessment methods used.

Null: Students will not perform differently on the different assessment methods used.

Expected (E): The performance of the students will be the same on all assessment methods.

Predicted (P): The performance of the students will be different on the three assessment methods.

Observed (O): The actual performance of the students on the different assessment methods.

Level of Measurement: IV Nominal (Assessment Method), DV Ordinal (performance)

Type of Design: Difference, repeated measures, no control

Number of Groups: 3 Groups (samples)

Assumptions: (a) Same person completes all assessments

VARIABLE BOX—FRIEDMAN TEST

		Assessment Method		
		Quiz	***Homework***	***Project***
Student	***Student 1***	Assessment Score (Ordinal)	Assessment Score (Ordinal)	Assessment Score (Ordinal)
	Student 2	Assessment Score (Ordinal)	Assessment Score (Ordinal)	Assessment Score (Ordinal)
	Student 3	Assessment Score (Ordinal)	Assessment Score (Ordinal)	Assessment Score (Ordinal)
	Student . . .	Assessment Score (Ordinal)	Assessment Score (Ordinal)	Assessment Score (Ordinal)

Now, let's look at the data:

Student	Scores			Ranks		
	Quiz	Homework	Project	Quiz	Homework	Project
1	8.6	9.1	6.7	2	3	1
2	8.8	8.9	7.4	2	3	1
3	6.7	7.3	5.7	2	3	1
4	8.3	9.1	9.3	1	2	3
5	8.2	8.5	8	2	3	1
6	8.3	7.8	9.2	2	1	3
7	5.5	7.1	6.5	1	3	2
8	8.7	9.3	7.2	2	3	1
9	8.8	8.3	8.1	3	2	1
10	9.3	9.6	8.4	2	3	1
11	8.6	7.5	6.5	3	2	1
12	8.7	9.4	10	1	2	3
13	8.8	9.7	9.3	1	3	2
14	8.2	7.8	7.5	3	2	1
15	8.8	8.3	9.4	2	1	3
16	7.4	7.9	9.8	1	2	3
17	6.9	8.2	7.6	1	3	2
18	9.4	8.7	9.5	2	1	3
19	7.5	7.2	8.4	2	1	3
20	7.4	7.6	6.8	2	3	1
21	8.5	7.8	9.3	2	1	3
22	8.7	8.7	8.2	2.5	2.5	1
23	8.2	9.2	7.6	2	3	1
24	9.4	9.6	9	2	3	1
25	6.8	7.3	8.2	1	2	3
R_j				46.5	57.5	46

We can use the formula to calculate the F_r value:

$$F_r = \left[\frac{12}{Nk(k+1)}\sum_{j=1}^{k} R_j^2\right] - 3N(k+1)$$

$$F_r = \left[\frac{12}{(25)(3)(4)}\left(46.5^2 + 57.5^2 + 46^2\right)\right] - (3)(25)(4)$$

$$F_r = 3.4$$

SPSS Commands

Open the data set ***Ch19 Friedman1***.
Follow the steps below:

(1) Click ***Analyze***.
(2) Scroll down and select ***Nonparametric Tests***.
(3) Select ***Legacy Dialogs***.
(4) Select ***K Related Samples . . .***

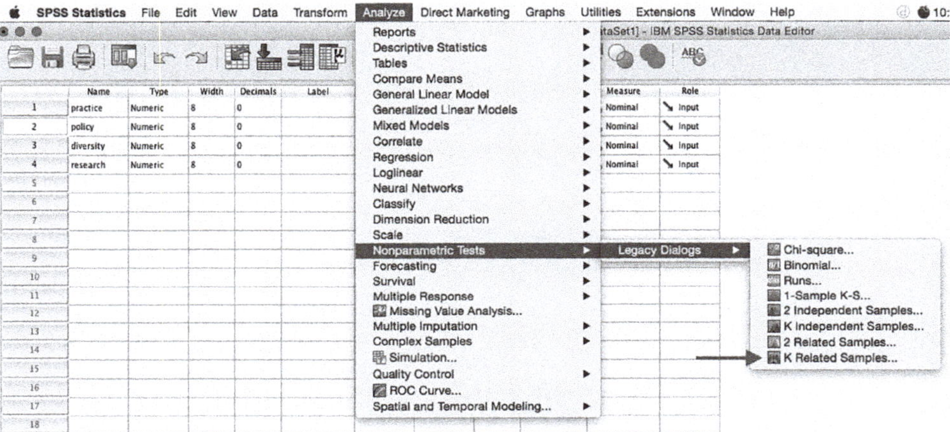

(5) Move each of the three variables (***Quiz***, ***HW*** and ***Project***) into the ***Test Variables*** box.
(6) Under ***Test Type***, select ***Friedman*** and de-select any other boxes.
(7) Click ***OK*** to run the analysis.

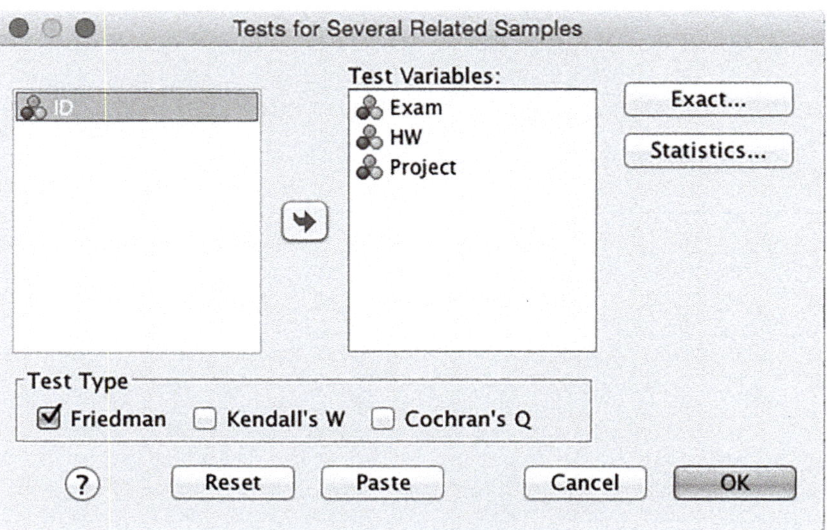

Examine the output tables:

Ranks

	Mean Rank
Quiz	1.86
HW	2.30
Project	1.84

Test Statistics[a]

N	25
Chi-Square	3.414
Df	2
Asymp. Sig.	.181

a. Friedman Test

Look the ranks table of the Friedman test. What is your preliminary conclusion by just looking at this table? Which of the three assessment strategies resulted in the best performance by students? Now look at the test statistics and decide if the difference in performance is statistically significant.

Results might be written as follows:

A Friedman test was run to determine if there was a difference in score using different assessment strategies in a sophomore English class. Students performed slightly better on homework assignments (mean rank = 2.30), than the quiz (mean rank = 1.86) or the project (mean rank = 1.84). However, the differences between assessment strategies were not significant (Friedman $X^2_{(2)} = 3.414, p = .181$).

Practical implications: There appears to be no group differences between the types of assessment. However, this assessment did not include assessments for a complete semester or a year. If assessments were evaluated over a longer period, differences may emerge. Another aspect to be studied is the individual differences in children and their particular ability to perform under different assessment strategies. It could be that a particular assessment strategy works well with one type of student and another strategy with another type of student. It is extremely important for social workers to recognize that assessment strategies we use or others use can significantly affect the assessment itself. From your experience, you might be able to help develop another study that would start to identify which assessment works best with which type of child. For example, is gender, race or language capability related to difference in performance on a particular assessment strategy?

The second type of design that can be analyzed using the Friedman test is where **respondents are matched and then placed into a set**. Once individuals have been matched and placed into a set, **each individual from that set is randomly assigned to a different intervention**. For example, there are 25 sets of single mothers on welfare consisting of 3 mothers per set. Each one of these sets (consisting of 3 mothers) are matched on age, length of time on welfare, level of education and number of children. Thus, one set might consist of 3 mothers who are 29 years old have been on welfare for 7 months, with 15 years of education and 2 children. Another set might consist of mothers with a different age, different amount of time on welfare and a different number of children. After matching women on these variables and developing 25 sets (a total of 75 women) you might want to see which type of training would result in the best ability to budget money. The agency would then implement the best method. Management of the budget was rated on a scale of 1–5 with 5 the best budget management and 1 being the worst budget management.

Study Question: Does the type budget training provided to women on welfare differ in their ability to manage a budget?

This is an explanatory multiple repeated measures design with no control group.

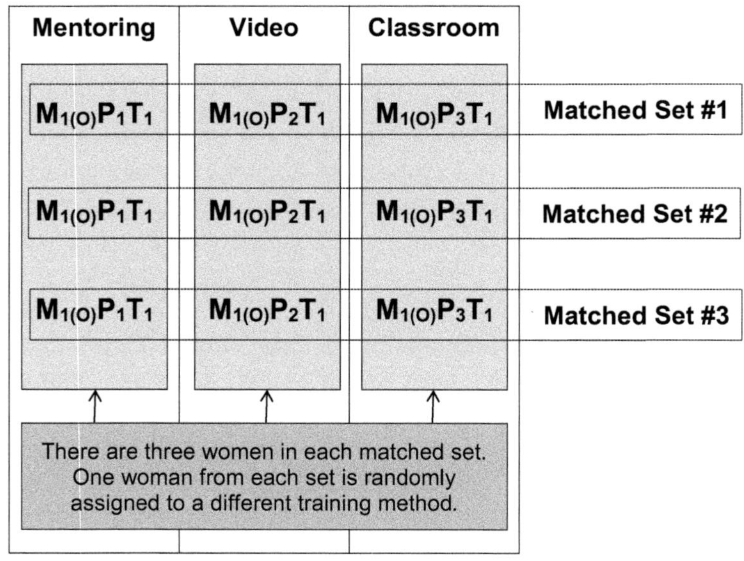

Hypotheses:

Difference: The type of training makes a difference in the ability to manage a budget for women on welfare.

Null: The type of training does not make a difference in the ability to manage a budget for women on welfare.

Expected (E): The type of training provided to women on welfare does not make a difference in their ability to manage a budget.

Predicted (P): The type of training provided to women on welfare makes a difference in their ability to manage a budget.

Observed (O): The actual ranking of the ability to manage a budget.

Level of Measurement: IV Nominal (Type of Training), DV Ordinal (rank of ability to manage budget)

Type of Design: Explanatory, repeated measures, no control

Number of Samples: Twenty-five matched sets of 3, randomly assigned to type of training

Assumptions: (a) Matched respondents

VARIABLE BOX—FRIEDMAN TEST

Type of Budget Training

	Mentoring (A)	***Video (B)***	***Classroom (C)***
Matched Set 1	Person 1: *Rating (ordinal)*	Person 2: *Rating (ordinal)*	Person 3: *Rating (ordinal)*
Matched Set 2	Person 1: *Rating (ordinal)*	Person 2: *Rating (ordinal)*	Person 3: *Rating (ordinal)*
Matched Set 3	Person 1: *Rating (ordinal)*	Person 2: *Rating (ordinal)*	Person 3: *Rating (ordinal)*
Matched Set . . .	Person 1: *Rating (ordinal)*	Person 2: *Rating (ordinal)*	Person 3: *Rating (ordinal)*

SPSS Commands

Open the data set ***Ch19 Friedman2***.
Follow the steps below:

(1) Click ***Analyze***.
(2) Scroll down and select ***Nonparametric Tests***.
(3) Select ***Legacy Dialogs***.
(4) Select ***K Related Samples . . .***

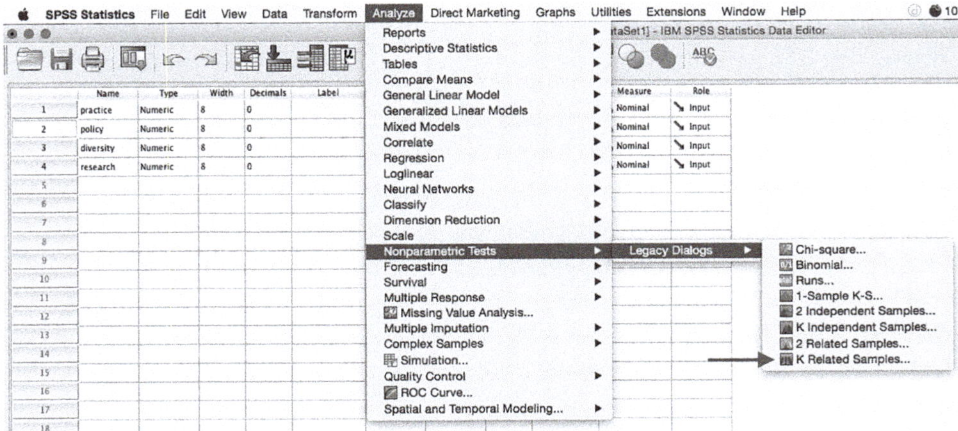

(5) Move each of the three variables ***(classroom*****,** ***videos*** and ***mentoring)*** into the ***Test Variables*** box.
(6) Under ***Test Type***, select ***Friedman*** and de-select any other boxes.
(7) Click ***OK*** to run the analysis.

Examine the output tables:

Friedman Test

Mean Rank	
Classroom	2.36
Videos	2.18
Mentoring	1.46

Test Statistics[a]

N	25
Chi-Square	14.921
Df	2
Asymp. Sig.	.001

a. Friedman Test

Look carefully at the Ranks Table. What is your conclusion? Which of the three types of training resulted in the highest mean rank for budget management? Now look at the Test Statistics and decide if the difference in outcome is significant.

Results might be written as follows:

A Friedman test was run to determine if the type of training (mentoring, video or classroom) provided to women on welfare makes a difference in their ability to manage a budget. It is clear that women on welfare are much better at managing a budget when they have been trained using mentoring training (mean rank = 1.46) compared to videos (mean rank = 2.18) and classroom (2.36). This difference between type of training was significant (Friedman test $X^2_{(2)} = 14.921$, $p = .001$).

Practical Implications: While mentoring is clearly the best method, we can see that both classroom and video produce above average outcomes for budget management. Thus, all methods are successful. Mentoring may be the most expensive method in terms of social worker or trainer time, and if cost is a factor, then the other two methods are certainly acceptable. Another possibility would be to combine either classroom or videos with mentoring, which would reduce individual face-to-face time while adding to the potential of the classroom and mentoring methods. A study to determine if different combinations would be equally effective as mentoring alone might be warranted in terms of cost. If cost could be reduced, then that money and time might be available for other programs and individuals. Finally, this study was carried out with only women; it is important to also conduct this same study with men to see which method is best for that population.

PART B: PARAMETRIC

Interval/Ratio Level Data

One-Way Within-Subjects ANOVA

See Chart—Multiple (k) Related or Matched Groups and Interval or Ratio Measurement

Chapter 17 introduced the repeated measures ANOVA. In this chapter, there are two types of designs where repeated measures are used with more than two groups. The one-way within subject's ANOVA looks at the same individuals across three or more levels of a single independent variable with a measurement for each person under each level of the independent variable. In other words, you have data on the same person on more than one condition of the IV (WITHIN SUBJECT).

The study involved 10 people who were receiving welfare. The IV was readiness to work with 3 different (levels) methods used to determine readiness: (1) video of simulated job interview, (2) case file and (3) current resume. A panel of 5 expert judges (senior workers in the State Job Training Program) rated each client's readiness to work using all three methods. The variable readiness to work and the three (levels) methods are: Video, Case or Resume, and the DV is the Rating by the panel.

The 5 judges rated each client on a scale from 1 to 30 on each method.

The ratings were then averaged for each client for each method for client to obtain a score for each method for each client. Since there could be an effect of order (time), the order of method was counterbalanced across clients.

Study Question: Is there a difference between the method of determining a client's readiness to work?

This is a difference multiple repeated measures design.

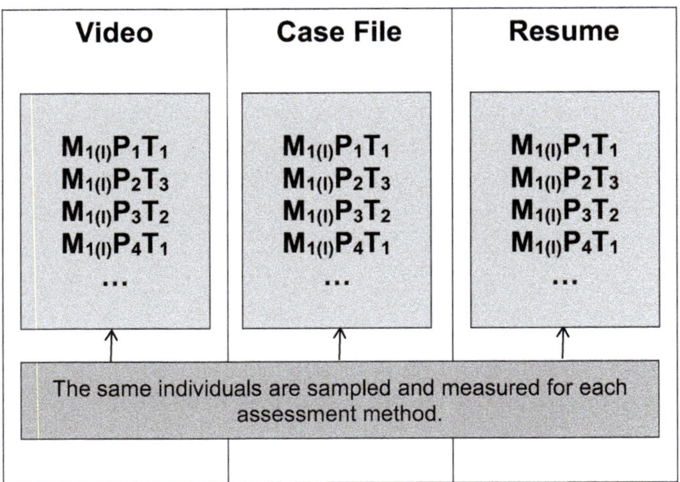

Hypotheses:

Difference: The method used to determine readiness for work will result in a different score for the client.

Null: The method used to determine readiness for work will not result in a different score for the client.

Expected (E): Clients will receive similar scores on all three methods to determine readiness for work.

Predicted (P): Clients will receive different scores on the three methods used to determine readiness for work.
Observed (O): The actual scores received on all methods for readiness to work.
Level of Measurement: IV Nominal (method), DV Interval (ratings on readiness to work)
Type of Design: Difference, repeated measures design, no control
Number of Groups: 3 Groups (method)
Assumptions: (a) Normal distribution, (b) Homogeneity of variance (c) At least 10 per group.

VARIABLE BOX—ONE-WAY WITHIN-SUBJECTS ANOVA

Method Used to Determine "Readiness to Work"

	Video (A)	***Case File (B)***	***Resume (C)***
Trainee 1	Composite score of five expert judges	Composite score of five expert judges	Composite score of five expert judges
Trainee 2	Composite score of five expert judges	Composite score of five expert judges	Composite score of five expert judges
Trainee 3	Composite score of five expert judges	Composite score of five expert judges	Composite score of five expert judges
Trainee . . .	Composite score of five expert judges	Composite score of five expert judges	Composite score of five expert judges

No attempt is made to perform the mathematical calculations because they are rather long and the basis has been previously developed in Chapter 17. The analysis will be carried out only in SPSS.

SPSS Commands

Open the data set ***Ch19 One Way Within ANOVA ANCOVA.***
Follow the steps below:

(1) Click ***Analyze.***
(2) Scroll down and select ***General Linear Model.***
(3) Select ***Repeated Measures . . .***

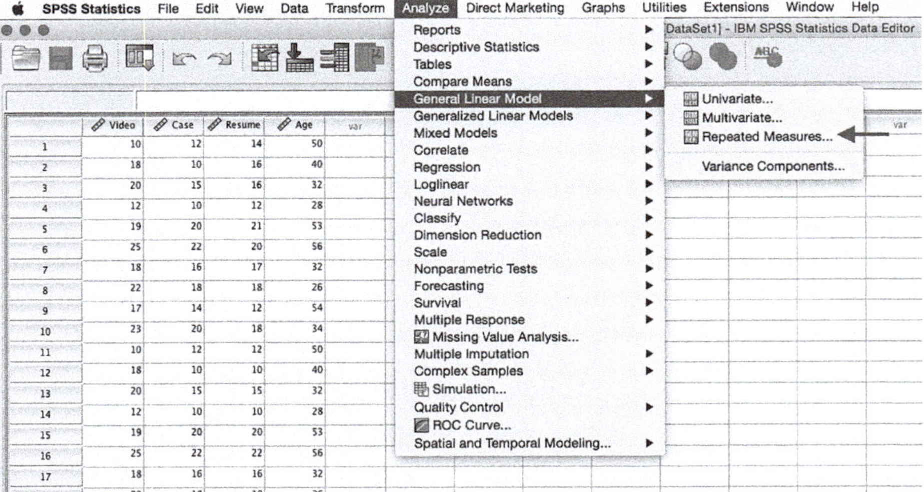

(4) In the ***Within-Subject Factor Name*** box type method (this represents our IV—the method used to determine readiness for work); in the ***Number of Levels*** box type ***3***.
(5) Click ***Add***.

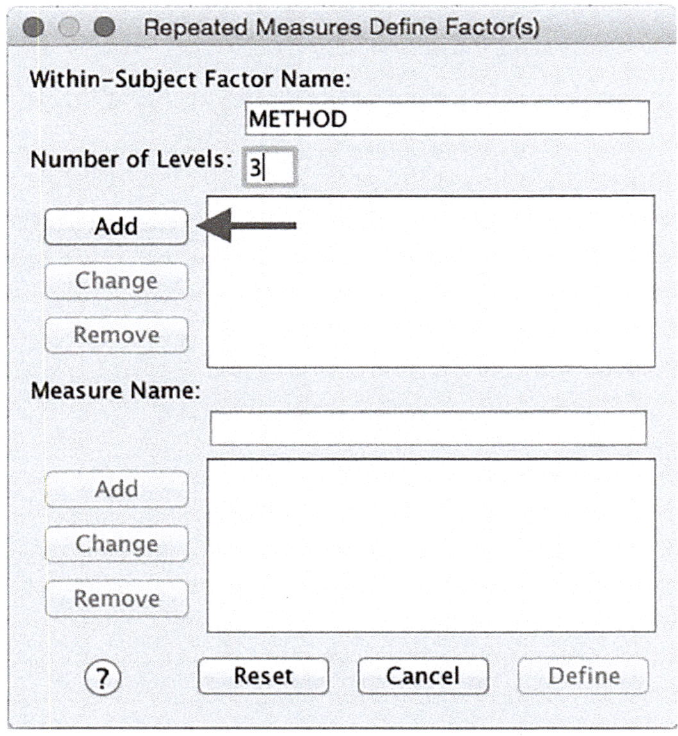

(6) In the ***Measure Name*** box type *READINESS* (it is important that this is a different label than any of the variable names in the data set).
(7) Click ***Add***.

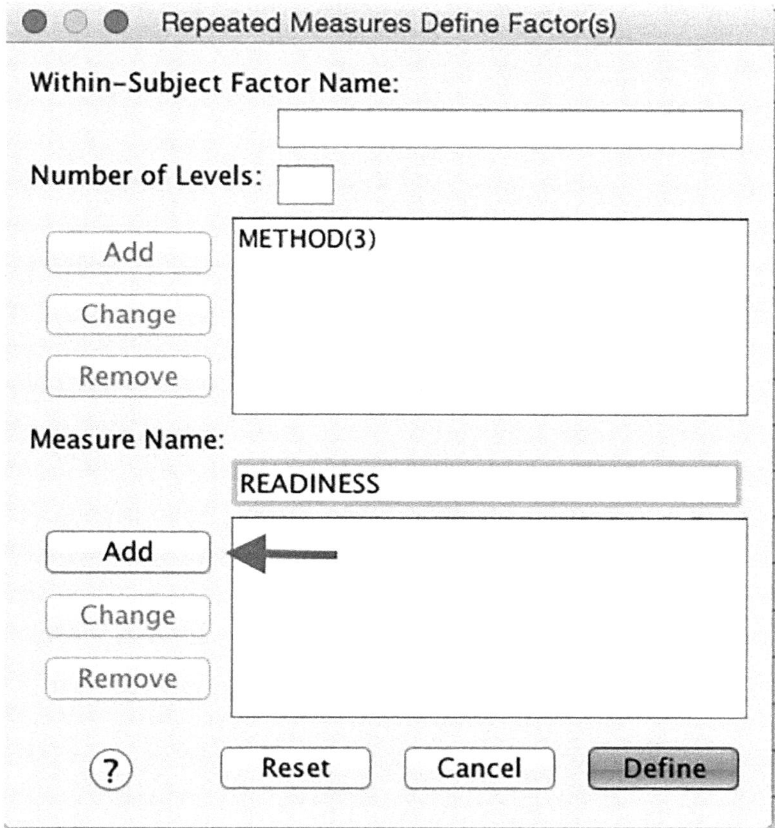

(8) Click ***Define***.
(9) Define the Within-Subject Factor (METHOD) by moving the variables ***Video***, ***Case*** and ***Resume*** into the ***Within-Subject Variables*** box. ***Video*** should be used to define the first level (***1,*** *READINESS*), ***Case*** should be used to define the second level (***2,*** *READINESS*), and ***Resume*** should be used to define the third level (***3,*** *READINESS*).
(10) Click ***Options***.
(11) Select ***Descriptive statistics***, ***Estimates of effect size*** and ***Observed power***.
(12) Click ***Continue***.
(13) Click ***OK*** to run the analysis

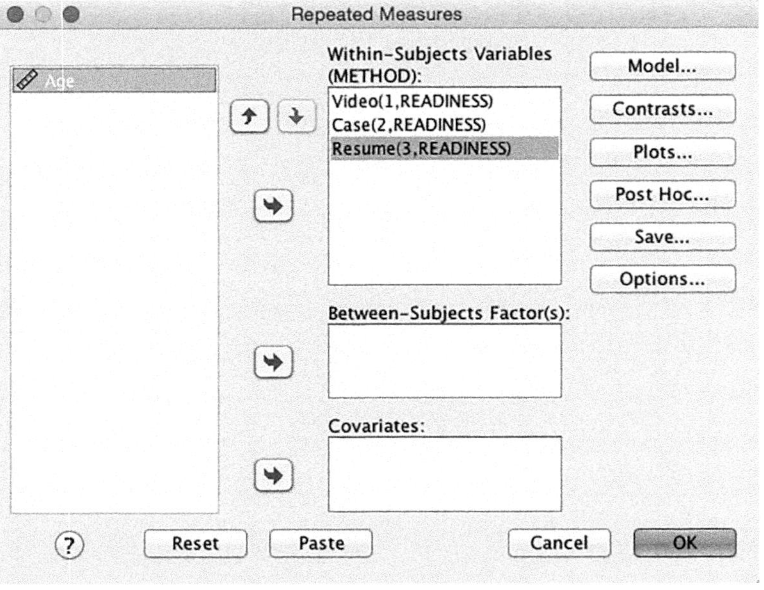
Repeated Measures
Age
Within-Subjects Variables (METHOD):
Video(1,READINESS)
Case(2,READINESS)
Resume(3,READINESS)
Model...
Contrasts...
Plots...
Post Hoc...
Save...
Options...
Between-Subjects Factor(s):
Covariates:
Reset
Paste
Cancel
OK

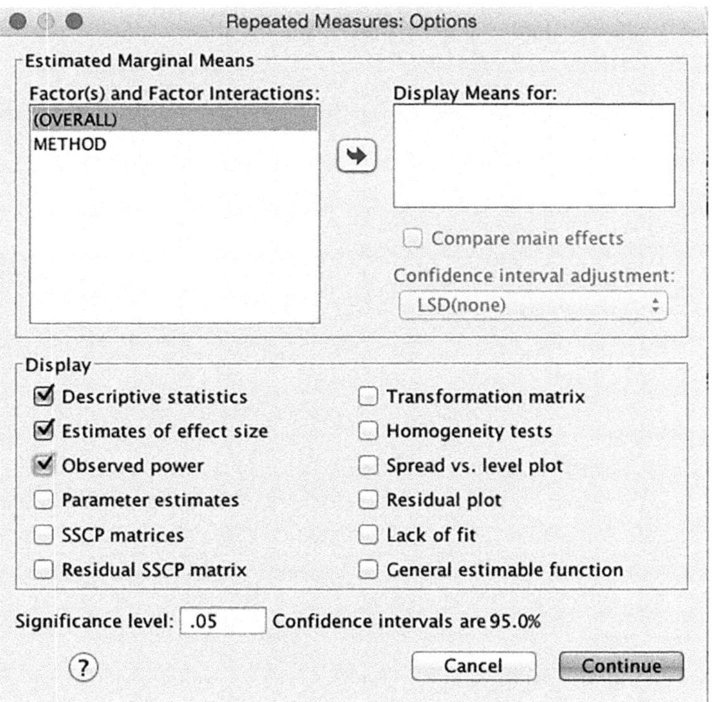
Repeated Measures: Options
Estimated Marginal Means
Factor(s) and Factor Interactions:
(OVERALL)
METHOD
Display Means for:
Compare main effects
Confidence interval adjustment:
LSD(none)
Display
Descriptive statistics
Estimates of effect size
Observed power
Parameter estimates
SSCP matrices
Residual SSCP matrix
Transformation matrix
Homogeneity tests
Spread vs. level plot
Residual plot
Lack of fit
General estimable function
Significance level: .05 Confidence intervals are 95.0%
Cancel
Continue

Let's review the output:

Within-Subjects Factors

Measure: READINESS	
METHOD	Dependent Variable
1	Video
2	Case
3	Resume

Descriptive Statistics

	Mean	Std. Deviation	N
Video	18.40	4.524	20
Case	15.70	4.156	20
Resume	16.05	3.634	20

Multivariate Tests[a]

Effect		Value	F	Hypothesis df	Error df	Sig.	Partial Eta Squared	Noncent. Parameter	Observed Power[c]
METHOD	Pillai's Trace	.503	9.103[b]	2.000	18.000	.002	.503	18.206	.948
	Wilks' Lambda	.497	9.103[b]	2.000	18.000	.002	.503	18.206	.948
	Hotelling's Trace	1.011	9.103[b]	2.000	18.000	.002	.503	18.206	.948
	Roy's Largest Root	1.011	9.103[b]	2.000	18.000	.002	.503	18.206	.948

a. Design: Intercept; within-subjects design: method.
b. Exact statistic.
c. Computed using alpha = .05.

Mauchly's Test of Sphericity[a]

Measure: READINESS

Within-Subjects	Mauchly's W	Approx. Chi-Square	df	Sig.	Epsilon[b]		
					Greenhouse-Geisser	Huynh-Feldt	Lower-bound
METHOD	.699	6.438	2	.040	.769	.823	.500

Tests the null hypothesis that the error covariance matrix of the orthonormalized transformed dependent variables is proportional to an identity matrix.

a. Design: Intercept; within-subjects design: method.

b. May be used to adjust the degrees of freedom for the averaged tests of significance. Corrected tests are displayed in the Tests of Within-Subjects Effects Table.

Tests of Within-Subjects Effects

Measure: READINESS

Source		Type III Sum of Squares	Df	Mean Square	F	Sig.	Partial Eta Squared	Noncent. Parameter	Observed Power[a]
METHOD	Sphericity Assumed	86.233	2	43.117	13.382	.000	.413	26.764	.996
	Greenhouse-Geisser	86.233	1.538	56.081	13.382	.000	.413	20.577	.985
	Huynh-Feldt	86.233	1.647	52.371	13.382	.000	.413	22.035	.989
	Lower-bound	86.233	1.000	86.233	13.382	.002	.413	13.382	.934
Error METHOD	Sphericity Assumed	122.433	38	3.222					
	Greenhouse-Geisser	122.433	29.216	4.191					
	Huynh-Feldt	122.433	31.285	3.913					
	Lower-bound	122.433	19.000	6.444					

a. Computed using alpha = .05.

Tests of Within-Subjects Contrasts

Measure: READINESS

Source	METHOD	Type III Sum of Squares	df	Mean Square	F	Sig.	Partial Eta Squared	Noncent. Parameter	Observed Power[a]
METHOD	Linear	55.225	1	55.225	12.600	.002	.399	12.600	.920
	Quadratic	31.008	1	31.008	15.046	.001	.442	15.046	.957
Error (METHOD)	Linear	83.275	19	4.383					
	Quadratic	39.158	19	2.061					

a. Computed using alpha = .05.

Tests of Between-Subjects Effects

Measure: READINESS

Transformed Variable: Average

Source	Type III Sum of Squares	df	Mean Square	F	Sig.	Partial Eta Squared	Noncent. Parameter	Observed Power[a]
Intercept	16766.817	1	16766.817	376.775	.000	.952	376.775	1.000
Error	845.517	19	44.501					

a. Computed using alpha = .05.

Ignore the multivariate tests table. It is applicable when there are two dependent variables, which is not the case in this example and will not be covered in this book. First look at the **Mauchly's test of sphericity**. This test is used to determine if the dependent variable variance-covariance matrices are equal or **homogeneous (refer to as homogeneity of variance)** for a **within subject design**. In order to continue the analysis, the assumption of equal variances has to be met. (You remember this **assumption of equal variances for the independent measures ANOVA was tested by Levene's test.**) **The null hypothesis is that the variances are equal.** If this **test is not significant, you can proceed with interpreting the rest of the results, reading the Sphericity Assumed row**. **If the test is significant, you need to read the corrected Greenhouse-Geisser row.**

Since Mauchly's test is significant (.04), we must read the results from the Greenhouse-Geiser row. The F test is significant (.001) and has a large effect size accounting for about 41% of the variance with 98% power.

The results might be written as follows:

A one way within-subject design was conducted to test if the different methods used to determine a client's readiness to work affect the readiness score. Three different methods were used to evaluate readiness to work: (1) a video, (2) their resume and (3) their case file. Scores for each method could range between 1 and 30, with a higher rating indicating greater readiness to work. Each method was scored by 5 expert work readiness judges with the methods counterbalanced across clients and judges. The scores for all 5 judges for each client for each method were aggregated. A one way within-subject ANOVA was used to analyze the data. The mean score for video was 18.4 ($SD = 4.65$), case record 15.7 ($SD = 4.27$) and resume 16.4 ($SD = 3.06$). The methods were found to be significantly different ($F_{(2,18)} = 13.38$, $p = .001$), with a large effect size (partial eta square = .413) and 98% power.

Practical Implications: When developing programs to assist individuals to prepare to re-enter the workforce, videos are the best method of preparation. Having tested the three different methods, it would be important to see how this method generalizes to other types of training and situations. It is important for social workers to recognize that the approach we adopt with clients can be extremely important in the success they have. Helping agencies to develop their capability to use the appropriate training method might require training for agency personnel (which would also be evaluated in a research study). Lessons learned in this study about how to develop and implement the use of video to become ready for work and to demonstrate that readiness are important for transfer of the method.

One-Way Within-Subjects ANCOVA

See Chart—Multiple (k) Related or Matched Groups and Interval or Ratio Measurement

As discussed in previous chapters, the introduction of a covariate allows the researcher to control for a particular variable that is expected to have an effect on the dependent variable. The researcher can extract that effect (which if not extracted would remain as an error) when testing the effects of the IV on the DV.

We are still interested to see if the methods used to determine a client's readiness to work differ from one another; however, this time, you want to control for the age of the clients as a potential factor that could influence the difference found in the methods. For example, being older might result in a more impressive resume, or it could result in a more negative evaluation of a video where the age of the client is clearly visible.

Study Question: Does the method of determining a client's readiness to work affect the score of readiness to work, controlling for age?

This is a difference multiple repeated measures design.

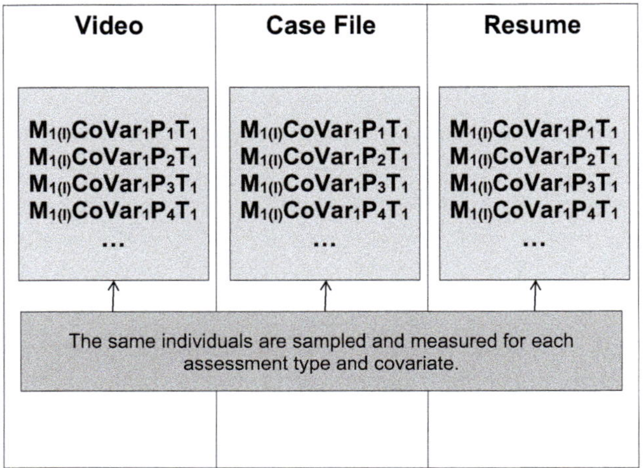

Hypotheses:

Difference: The method used to determine readiness for work will result in a different score for the client, controlling for age.

Null: The method used to determine readiness for work will not result in a different score for the client, controlling for age.

Expected (E): Clients will receive similar scores on all three methods to determine readiness for work, controlling for age.

Predicted (P): Clients will receive different scores on the three methods used to determine readiness for work, controlling for age.

Observed (O): The actual scores received on all methods for readiness to work, controlling for age.

Level of Measurement: IV Nominal (Method) DV Interval (Score on readiness to work) CV Interval (Age)

Type of Design: Difference, repeated measures, no control

Number of Groups: 3 Groups (Method)

Assumptions: (a) Normal distributions, (b) Homogeneity of variance (c) At least 10 per group.

VARIABLE BOX—ONE WAY WITHIN-SUBJECTS ANCOVA

Method Used to Determine "Readiness to Work"

	Video (A)	***Case File (B)***	***Resume (C)***
Trainee 1	Composite score of five expert judges *(Age extracted)*	Composite score of five expert judges *(Age extracted)*	Composite score of five expert judges *(Age extracted)*
Trainee 2	Composite score of five expert judges *(Age extracted)*	Composite score of five expert judges *(Age extracted)*	Composite score of five expert judges *(Age extracted)*
Trainee 3	Composite score of five expert judges *(Age extracted)*	Composite score of five expert judges *(Age extracted)*	Composite score of five expert judges *(Age extracted)*
Trainee . . .	Composite score of five expert judges *(Age extracted)*	Composite score of five expert judges *(Age extracted)*	Composite score of five expert judges *(Age extracted)*

SPSS Commands

Open the data set ***Ch19 One Way Within ANOVA ANCOVA***
Follow the steps below:

(1) Click ***Analyze***.
(2) Scroll down and select ***General Linear Model***.

(3) Select ***Repeated Measures . . .***

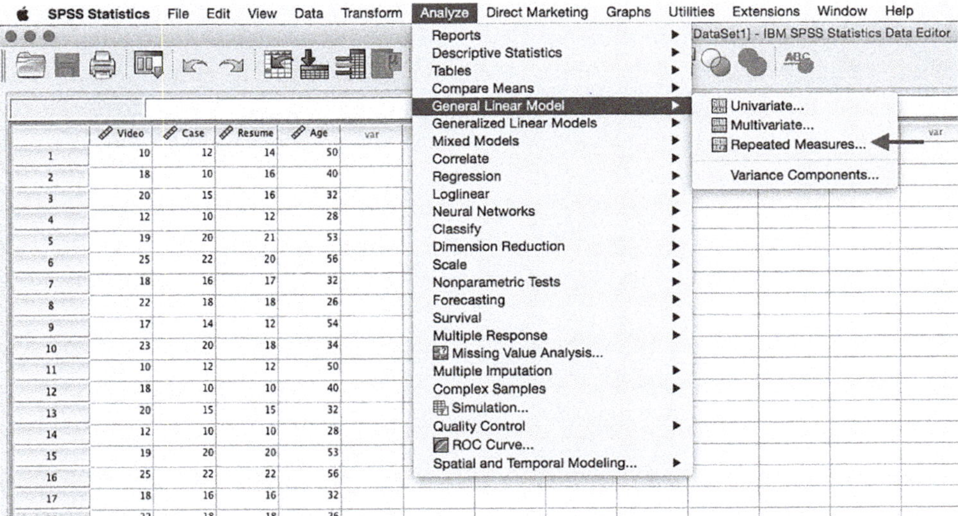

(4) In the ***Within-Subject Factor Name*** box type method (this represents our IV—the method used to determine readiness for work); in the ***Number of Levels*** box type ***3***.

(5) Click Add.

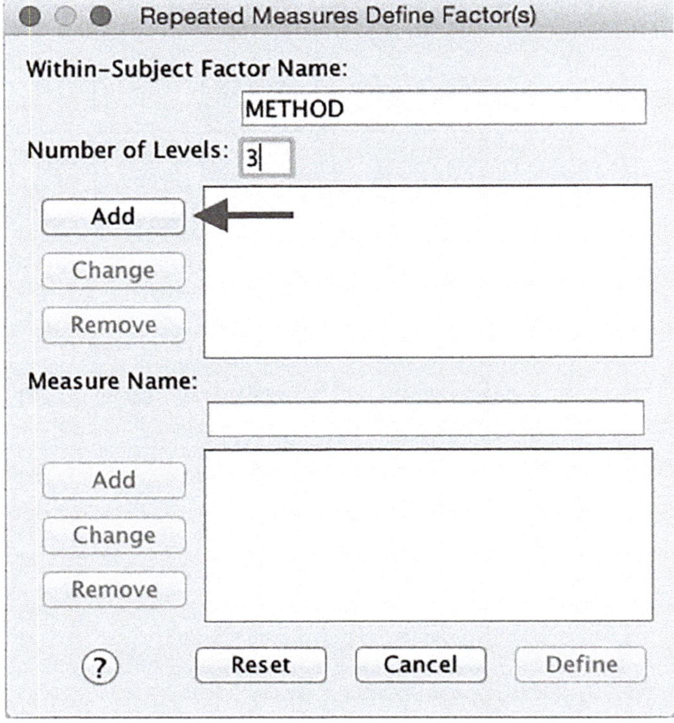

(6) In the ***Measure Name*** box type readiness (it is important that this is a different label than any of the variable names in the data set).
(7) Click ***Add***.

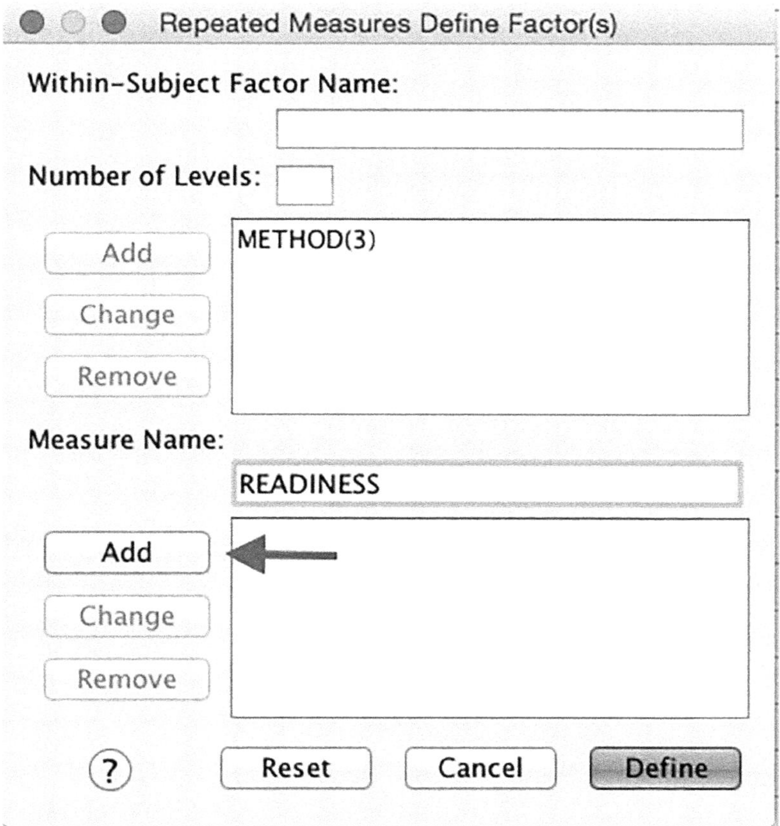

(8) Click ***Define***.
(9) Define the ***Within-Subject Factor Variables (METHOD)*** box by moving the variables ***Video***, ***Case*** and ***Resume*** into the ***Within-Subject Variables*** box. ***Video*** should be used to define the first level (***1, READINESS***), ***Case*** should be used to define the second level (***2, READINESS***), and ***Resume*** should be used to define the third level (***3, READINESS***).
(10) Move the variable ***Age*** to the ***Covariates*** box.
(11) Click ***Options***.
(12) Select ***Descriptive statistics***, ***Estimates of effect size*** and ***Observed power***.
(13) Under ***EM Means*** move method to the ***Display Means for*** box.
(14) Click ***Continue***.
(15) Click ***OK*** to run the analysis.

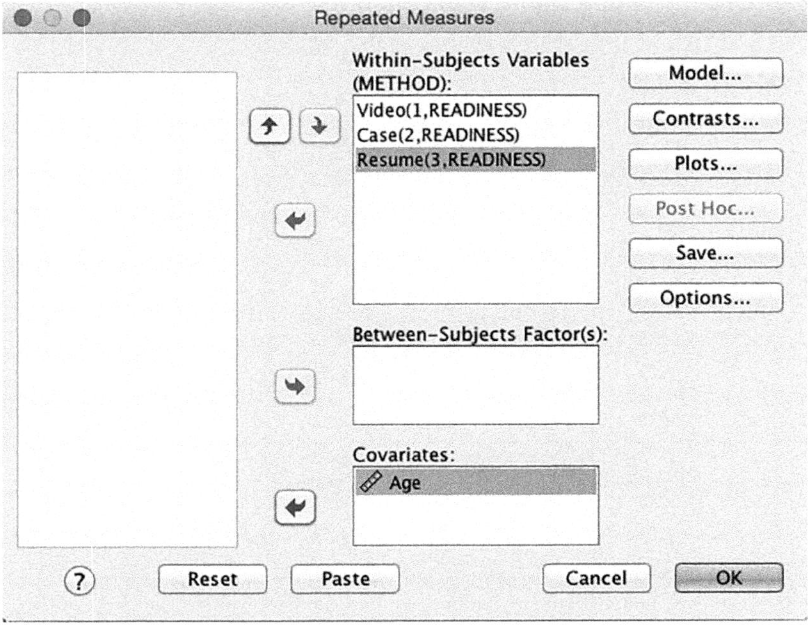

Repeated Measures

Within-Subjects Variables (METHOD):
Video(1,READINESS)
Case(2,READINESS)
Resume(3,READINESS)

Between-Subjects Factor(s):

Covariates:
Age

Model... Contrasts... Plots... Post Hoc... Save... Options...

Reset Paste Cancel OK

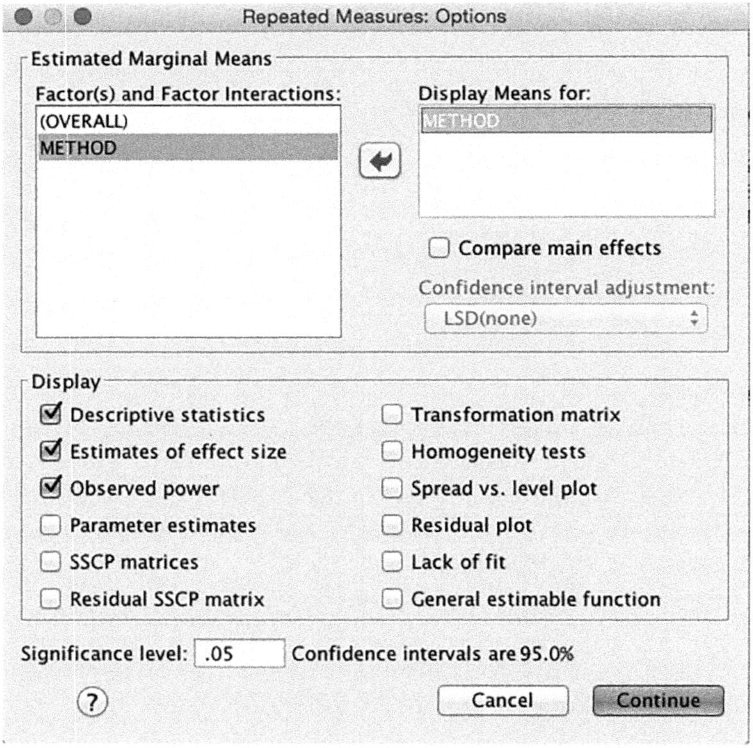

Repeated Measures: Options

Estimated Marginal Means

Factor(s) and Factor Interactions:
(OVERALL)
METHOD

Display Means for:
METHOD

Compare main effects

Confidence interval adjustment:
LSD(none)

Display

- [x] Descriptive statistics
- [x] Estimates of effect size
- [x] Observed power
- [ ] Parameter estimates
- [ ] SSCP matrices
- [ ] Residual SSCP matrix
- [ ] Transformation matrix
- [ ] Homogeneity tests
- [ ] Spread vs. level plot
- [ ] Residual plot
- [ ] Lack of fit
- [ ] General estimable function

Significance level: .05 Confidence intervals are 95.0%

Cancel Continue

Let's review the output tables:

Within-Subjects Factors

Measure: READINESS	
METHOD	Dependent Variable
1	Video
2	Case
3	Resume

Descriptive Statistics

	Mean	Std. Deviation	N
Video	18.40	4.524	20
Case	15.70	4.156	20
Resume	16.05	3.634	20

Multivariate Tests[a]

Effect		Value	F	Hypothesis df	Error df	Sig.	Partial Eta Squared	Noncent. Parameter	Observed Power[c]
METHOD	Pillai's Trace	.317	3.952[b]	2.000	17.000	.039	.317	7.903	.628
	Wilks' Lambda	.683	3.952[b]	2.000	17.000	.039	.317	7.903	.628
	Hotelling's Trace	.465	3.952[b]	2.000	17.000	.039	.317	7.903	.628
	Roy's Largest Root	.465	3.952[b]	2.000	17.000	.039	.317	7.903	.628
METHOD * Age	Pillai's Trace	.146	1.457[b]	2.000	17.000	.261	.146	2.915	.268
	Wilks' Lambda	.854	1.457[b]	2.000	17.000	.261	.146	2.915	.268
	Hotelling's Trace	.171	1.457[b]	2.000	17.000	.261	.146	2.915	.268
	Roy's Largest Root	.171	1.457[b]	2.000	17.000	.261	.146	2.915	.268

a. Design: Intercept + Age; within-subjects design: method.

b. Exact statistic.

c. Computed using alpha = .05.

Mauchly's Test of Sphericity[a]

Measure: READINESS							
Within-Subjects Effect	Mauchly's W	Approx. Chi-Square	Df	Sig.	Epsilon[b]		
					Greenhouse-Geisser	Huynh-Feldt	Lower-bound
METHOD	.717	5.653	2	.059	.779	.887	.500

Tests the null hypothesis that the error covariance matrix of the orthonormalized transformed dependent variables is proportional to an identity matrix.

a. Design: Intercept + Age; within-subjects design: method.

b. May be used to adjust the degrees of freedom for the averaged tests of significance. Corrected tests are displayed in the Tests of Within-Subjects Effects table.

Tests of Within-Subjects Effects

Measure: READINESS

Source		Type III Sum of Squares	Df	Mean Square	F	Sig.	Partial Eta Squared	Noncent. Parameter	Observed Power[a]
METHOD	Sphericity Assumed	31.267	2	15.634	5.038	.012	.219	10.076	.783
	Greenhouse-Geisser	31.267	1.559	20.056	5.038	.020	.219	7.854	.703
	Huynh-Feldt	31.267	1.775	17.617	5.038	.015	.219	8.942	.745
	Lower-bound	31.267	1.000	31.267	5.038	.038	.219	5.038	.565
METHOD * Age	Sphericity Assumed	10.725	2	5.363	1.728	.192	.088	3.456	.339
	Greenhouse-Geisser	10.725	1.559	6.880	1.728	.200	.088	2.694	.296
	Huynh-Feldt	10.725	1.775	6.043	1.728	.196	.088	3.067	.317
	Lower-bound	10.725	1.000	10.725	1.728	.205	.088	1.728	.238
Error (METHOD)	Sphericity Assumed	111.708	36	3.103					
	Greenhouse-Geisser	111.708	28.062	3.981					
	Huynh-Feldt	111.708	31.947	3.497					
	Lower-bound	111.708	18.000	6.206					

a. Computed using alpha = .05.

Tests of Within-Subjects Contrasts

Measure: READINESS

Source	METHOD	Type III Sum of Squares	df	Mean Square	F	Sig.	Partial Eta Squared	Noncent. Parameter	Observed Power[a]
METHOD	Linear	17.631	1	17.631	4.075	.059	.185	4.075	.480
	Quadratic	13.636	1	13.636	7.255	.015	.287	7.255	.722
METHOD * Age	Linear	5.400	1	5.400	1.248	.279	.065	1.248	.185
	Quadratic	5.325	1	5.325	2.833	.110	.136	2.833	.357
Error (METHOD)	Linear	77.875	18	4.326					
	Quadratic	33.833	18	1.880					

a. Computed using alpha = .05.

Tests of Between-Subjects Effects

Measure: READINESS

Transformed Variable: Average

Source	Type III Sum of Squares	df	Mean Square	F	Sig.	Partial Eta Squared	Noncent. Parameter	Observed Power[a]
Intercept	891.039	1	891.039	19.415	.000	.519	19.415	.986
Age	19.428	1	19.428	.423	.523	.023	.423	.095
Error	826.088	18	45.894					

a. Computed using alpha = .05.

METHOD

Measure: READINESS

METHOD	Mean	Std. Error	95% Confidence Interval	
			Lower-Bound	Upper-Bound
1	18.400[a]	1.039	16.217	20.583
2	15.700[a]	.926	13.755	17.645
3	16.050[a]	.817	14.333	17.767

a. Covariates appearing in the model are evaluated at the following values: Age = 40.50.

Remember you are including a covariate to report the estimated marginal means and not the mean. In this example because the extracted covariate only minimally affected method variables, the estimated and marginal means are the same. Mauchly's test was not significant (.059) so you can read the Sphericity Assumed row for the results.

Results might be written as follows.

A one way within-subject ANCOVA was conducted to test if the different methods used to determine a client's readiness to work affect the readiness score, controlling for age. Three different methods were used to evaluate readiness to work: (1) a video, (2) their resume and (3) their case file. Scores for each method could range between 1 and 30, with a higher rating indicating greater readiness to work. Each method was scored by 5 expert work readiness judges with the methods counterbalanced across clients and judges. The scores for all 5 judges for each client for each method were aggregated. The estimated marginal means were: video = 18.4 (*SE* = 1.039), case file = 15.7 (*SE* = .926) and resume = 16.1 (*SE* = .817). The methods were found to be significantly different when controlling for age ($F_{(2,36)} = 5.038$, $p = .012$, with a large effect size (partial eta squared = .219)

and 78% power. The covariate age was not significant ($F_{(2,36)}$ = 1.728, with a medium effect size (partial eta squared = .088) and 34% power.

Practical Implications: Since age was not a significant covariate and did not change the outcome of the methods, refer to the practical implications for this data with no covariate.

One-Way Within-Subjects ANOVA (Panel Design)

See Chart—Multiple (k) Related or Matched Groups and Interval or Ratio Measurement

Another type of repeated measures ANOVA design is one where ***the same person is measured at least three times or more***. This design as you will recall from Chapter 11 is a panel study. In other words, you have data on the same subject on one specific DV, and measurement is conducted at multiple points in time. In Chapter 17 we introduced you to a similar design with only a pre- and post-measurement (two time periods) whereas now there are multiple measurements over time.

The example used is one where children receive anger management training in a community social work program. The level of anger is measured before the start of the program, at the end of the program and again after 6 months. Anger was measured using an anger management scale where the score could range between 5 and 25.

Study Question: Does the anger management program reduce the anger of the children and maintain the reduction over a 6-month period?

This is an explanatory multiple repeated measures panel design with no control.

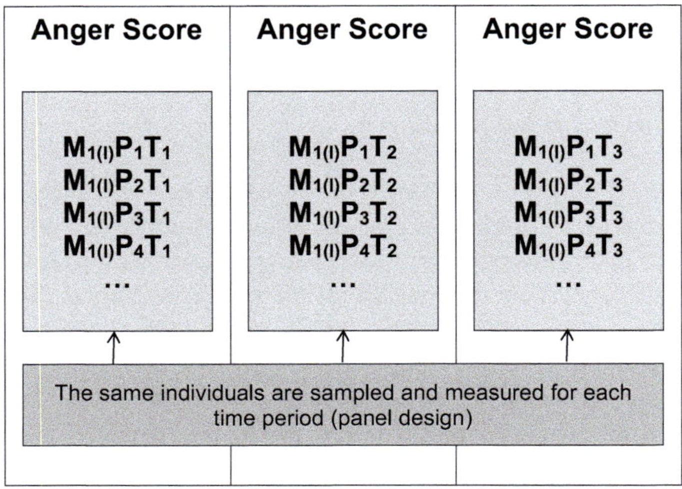

Hypotheses:

Explanatory: The anger management program will reduce the anger of the children and continue to maintain that reduction over time.
Null: The anger management program will not reduce the anger of the children over time.
Expected (E): Children will have the same anger scores at every measurement.
Predicted (P): Children will have reduced anger at each consecutive measurement.
Observed (O): The actual anger scores at each measurement.
Level of Measurement: IV Nominal (anger program), DV Interval (Anger Score)
Type of Design: Explanatory, repeated measures (panel), no control
Number of Groups: 3 Groups (different points in time)
Assumptions: (a) Normal distribution, (b) Homogeneity of variance (c) At least 10 per group

VARIABLE BOX—ONE-WAY PANEL ANOVA

	Time Measured		
	Time 1 (Pre)	***Time 2 (Post)***	***Time 3 (Follow-up)***
Child 1	Anger Score	Anger Score	Anger Score
Child 2	Anger Score	Anger Score	Anger Score
Child 3	Anger Score	Anger Score	Anger Score
Child …	Anger Score	Anger Score	Anger Score

SPSS Commands

Open the data set ***Ch19 Panel ANOVA ANCOVA***.
Follow the steps below:

(1) Click ***Analyze***.
(2) Scroll down and select ***General Linear Model***.
(3) Select ***Repeated Measures . . .***
(4) In the ***Within-Subject Factor Name*** box type time; in the ***Number of Levels*** box type ***3***.
(5) Click ***Add***.
(6) In the ***Measure Name*** box type anger (it is important that this is a different label than any of the variable names in the data set).
(7) Click ***Add***.
(8) Click ***Define***.
(9) Define the Within-Subject Factor by moving the variables ***anger1***, ***anger2*** and ***anger3*** in the appropriate order into the ***Within-Subject Variables*** box.

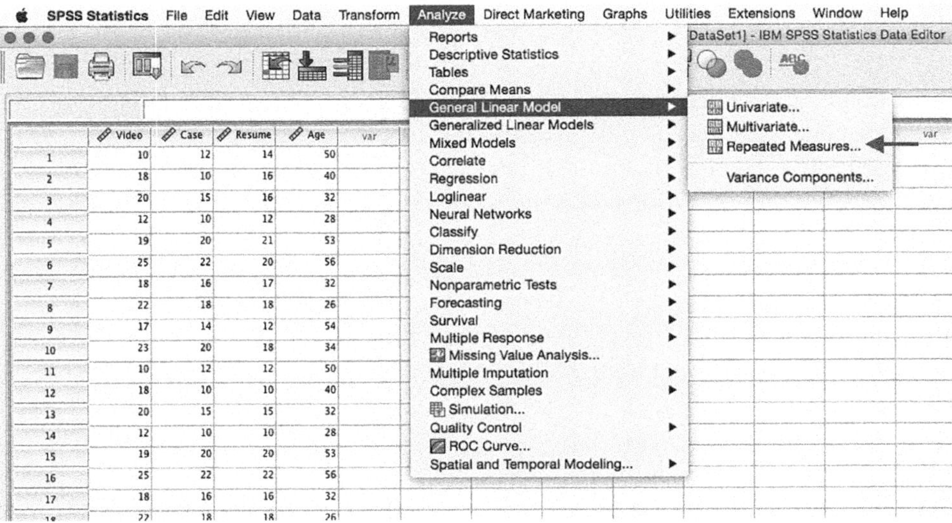

Repeated Measures Define Factor(s)

Within-Subject Factor Name: TIME

Number of Levels: 3

Add

Change

Remove

Measure Name:

Add

Change

Remove

? Reset Cancel Define

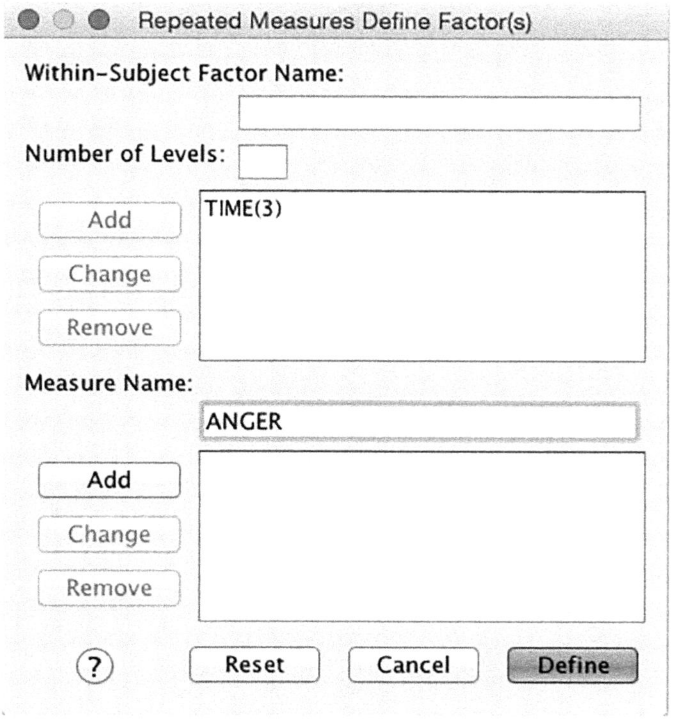
Repeated Measures Define Factor(s)
Within-Subject Factor Name:
Number of Levels:
Add
Change
Remove
TIME(3)
Measure Name:
ANGER
Add
Change
Remove
?
Reset
Cancel
Define

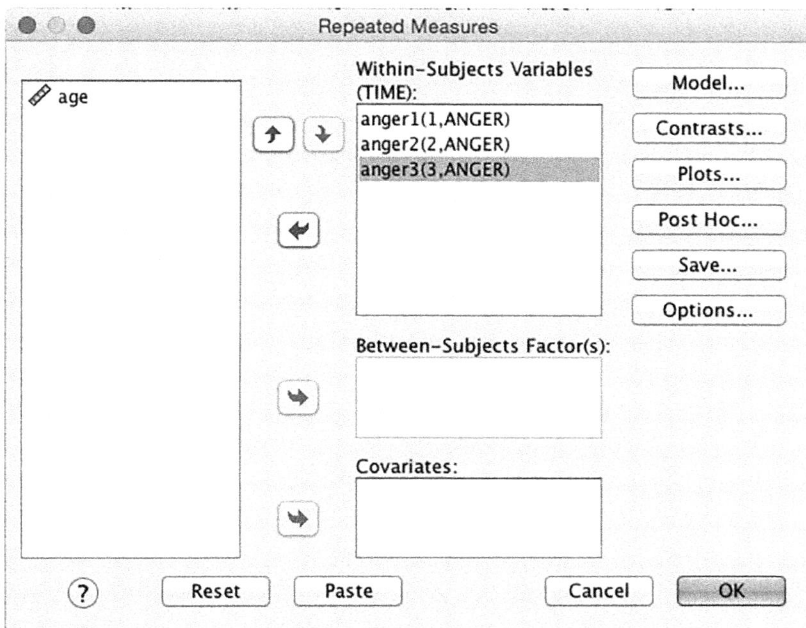
Repeated Measures
age
Within-Subjects Variables
(TIME):
anger1(1,ANGER)
anger2(2,ANGER)
anger3(3,ANGER)
Model...
Contrasts...
Plots...
Post Hoc...
Save...
Options...
Between-Subjects Factor(s):
Covariates:
?
Reset
Paste
Cancel
OK

(10) Click ***Options***.
(11) Select ***Descriptive statistics***, ***Estimates of effect size*** and ***Observed power***.

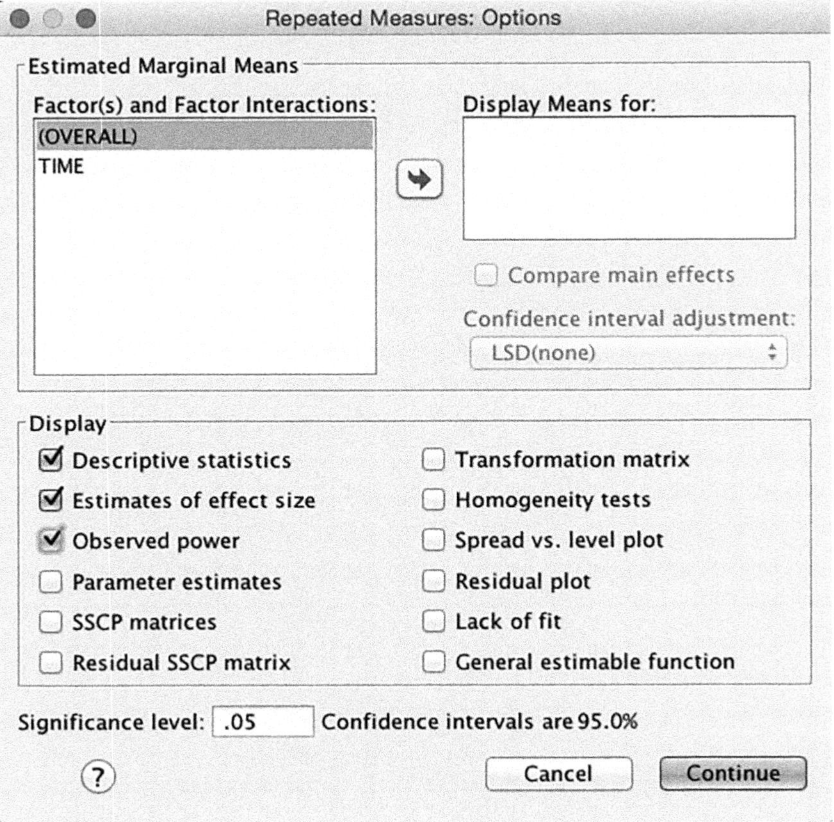

(12) Click ***Continue***.
(13) Click ***OK*** to run the analysis.

Within-Subjects Factors

Measure: ANGER	
TIME	Dependent Variable
1	anger1
2	anger2
3	anger3

Descriptive Statistics

	Mean	Std. Deviation	N
anger1	20.10	4.181	50
anger2	14.72	3.620	50
anger3	10.76	4.269	50

Multivariate Tests[a]

Effect		Value	F	Hypothesis df	Error df	Sig.	Partial Eta Squared	Noncent. Parameter	Observed Power[c]
TIME	Pillai's Trace	.755	74.011[b]	2.000	48.000	.000	.755	148.021	1.000
	Wilks' Lambda	.245	74.011[b]	2.000	48.000	.000	.755	148.021	1.000
	Hotelling's Trace	3.084	74.011[b]	2.000	48.000	.000	.755	148.021	1.000
	Roy's Largest Root	3.084	74.011[b]	2.000	48.000	.000	.755	148.021	1.000

a. Design: Intercept; within-subjects design: time.
b. Exact statistic.
c. Computed using alpha = .05.

Mauchly's Test of Sphericity[a]

Measure: ANGER

Within-Subjects Effect	Mauchly's W	Approx. Chi-Square	df	Sig.	Epsilon[b]		
					Greenhouse-Geisser	Huynh-Feldt	Lower-bound
TIME	.215	73.766	2	.000	.560	.564	.500

Tests the null hypothesis that the error covariance matrix of the orthonormalized transformed dependent variables is proportional to an identity matrix.
a. Design: Intercept; within-subjects design: time.
b. May be used to adjust the degrees of freedom for the averaged tests of significance.
Corrected tests are displayed in the Tests of Within-Subjects Effects Table.

Tests of Within-Subjects Effects

Measure: ANGER

Source		Type III Sum of Squares	Df	Mean Square	F	Sig.	Partial Eta Squared	Noncent. Parameter	Observed Power[a]
TIME	Sphericity Assumed	2197.693	2	1098.847	133.999	.000	.732	267.998	1.000
	Greenhouse-Geisser	2197.693	1.120	1961.363	133.999	.000	.732	150.145	1.000
	Huynh-Feldt	2197.693	1.128	1947.712	133.999	.000	.732	151.197	1.000
	Lower-bound	2197.693	1.000	2197.693	133.999	.000	.732	133.999	1.000
Error (TIME)	Sphericity Assumed	803.640	98	8.200					
	Greenhouse-Geisser	803.640	54.904	14.637					
	Huynh-Feldt	803.640	55.289	14.535					
	Lower-bound	803.640	49.000	16.401					

a. Computed using alpha = .05.

Tests of Within-Subjects Contrasts

Measure: ANGER

Source	TIME	Type III Sum of Squares	df	Mean Square	F	Sig.	Partial Eta Squared	Noncent. Parameter	Observed Power[a]
TIME	Linear	2180.890	1	2180.890	144.097	.000	.746	144.097	1.000
	Quadratic	16.803	1	16.803	13.274	.001	.213	13.274	.946
Error (TIME)	Linear	741.610	49	15.135					
	Quadratic	62.030	49	1.266					

a. Computed using alpha = .05.

Tests of Between-Subjects Effects

Measure: ANGER

Transformed Variable: Average

Source	Type III Sum of Squares	df	Mean Square	F	Sig.	Partial Eta Squared	Noncent. Parameter	Observed Power[a]
Intercept	34625.607	1	34625.607	1068.382	.000	.956	1068.382	1.000
Error	1588.060	49	32.409					

a. Computed using alpha = .05.

Again, we ignore the multivariate tests table. Look at the Mauchly's test of sphericity. This test is significant; thus, you need to read the Greenhouse-Geisser row where you find that the F test is significant and accounts for 73% of the variance, indicating a large effect size. The observed power is 100%.

The results might be written as follows:

A panel design with a one-way repeated ANOVA was used to determine if children's anger is reduced after being in an anger management program. Anger was measured on a scale with a total score that ranged between 5 and 25, with higher scores indicating more anger. At the beginning of the anger management program, the mean anger score of the children was 20.10 (*SD* = 4.18). At the end of the anger management program, the mean anger score of the children was 14.72 (*SD* = 3.62). After six months, the anger scores reduced further to a mean of 10.76 (*SD* = 4.27). The reduction in anger scores was significant ($F_{(1.1,54.9)}$ = 133.99; $p = .0005$ one tailed), with a large effect size (partial eta square = 0.73) and 100% power.

Practical Implications: The program seems to have a rather long-term effect in that the reduction in anger continued six months after the end of the sessions. It would be important to find out what was happening between the end of the program and the follow-up period that might be contributing to this continuing decrease in anger. Future research might be focused on these reduction factors. In addition, replications of this program need to be conducted with different groups in different locations to find out if this anger management intervention can generalize across diverse individuals and settings. Another aspect is the persons providing the program. An investigation if different providers using the same program will produce the same positive results is a good idea.

We will conduct the same study as above but introduce a covariate—Age—to control for the age of the children.

Study Question: **Does the anger management program reduce the anger of the children and maintain the reduction over a 6-month period, controlling for age?**

This is an explanatory multiple repeated measures panel design with no control.

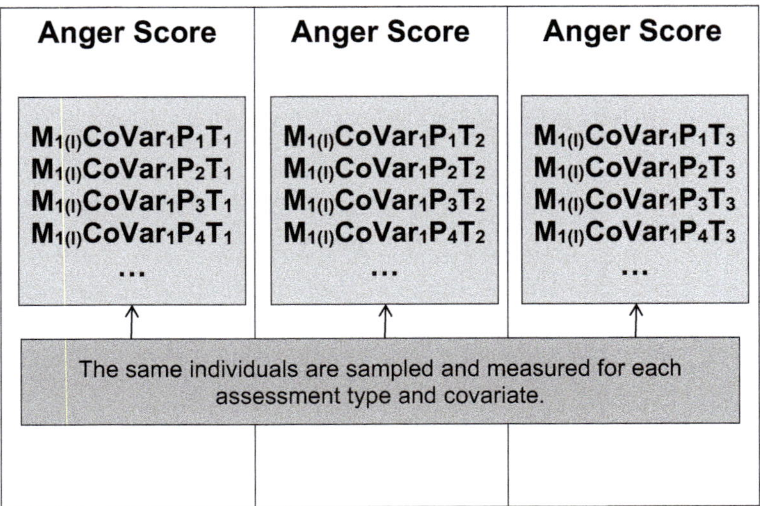

Hypotheses:

Explanatory: The anger management program will reduce the anger of the children, controlling for the age of the children.

Null: The anger management program will not reduce the anger of the children, controlling for the age of the children.

Expected (E): Children will have the same anger scores at every measurement occasion, controlling for the age of the children.

Predicted (P): Clients will have reduced anger at every consecutive measurement occasion, controlling for the age of the children.

Observed (O): The actual anger scores at each measurement occasion, after controlling for the age of the children.

Level of Measurement: IV Nominal, (anger program), DV Interval (anger score) CV Ratio (age)

Type of Design: Explanatory, repeated measures, no control

Number of Groups: 3 Groups (Different points in time)

Assumptions: (a) Normal distribution, (b) Homogeneity of variance, (c) At least 10 per group

SPSS Commands

Open the data set ***Ch19 One-Way Panel ANOVA ANCOVA***.
Follow the steps below:

(1) Click ***Analyze***.
(2) Scroll down and select ***General Linear Model***.
(3) Select ***Repeated Measures . . .***

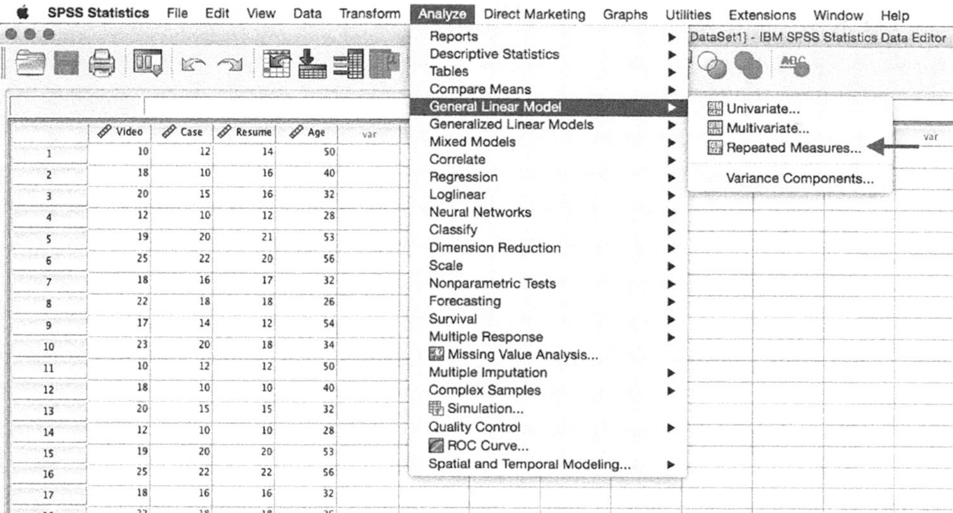

(4) In the ***Within-Subject Factor Name*** box type time; in the ***Number of Levels*** box type ***3***.

(5) Click ***Add***.

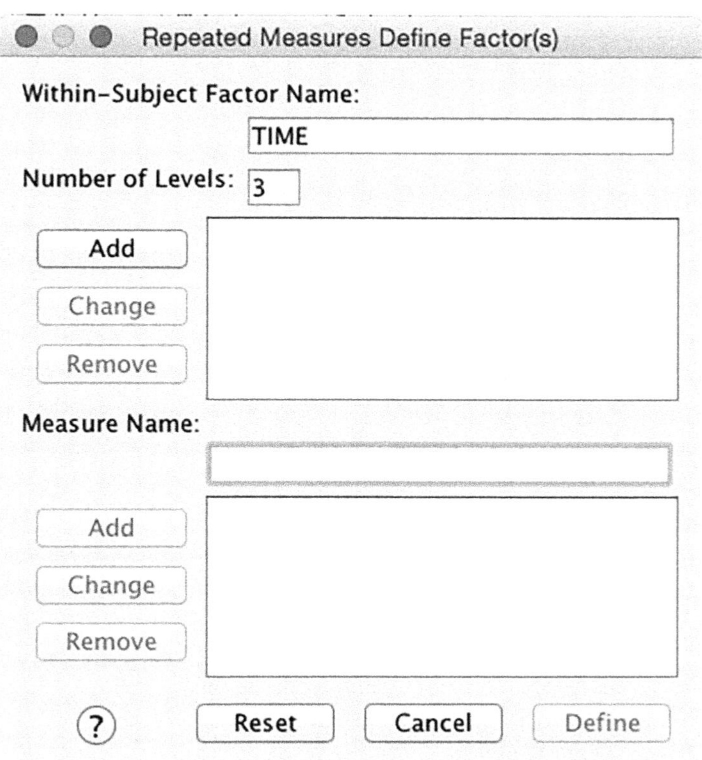

(6) In the ***Measure Name*** box type ***ANGER*** (it is important that this is a different label than any of the variable names in the data set).
(7) Click ***Add***.

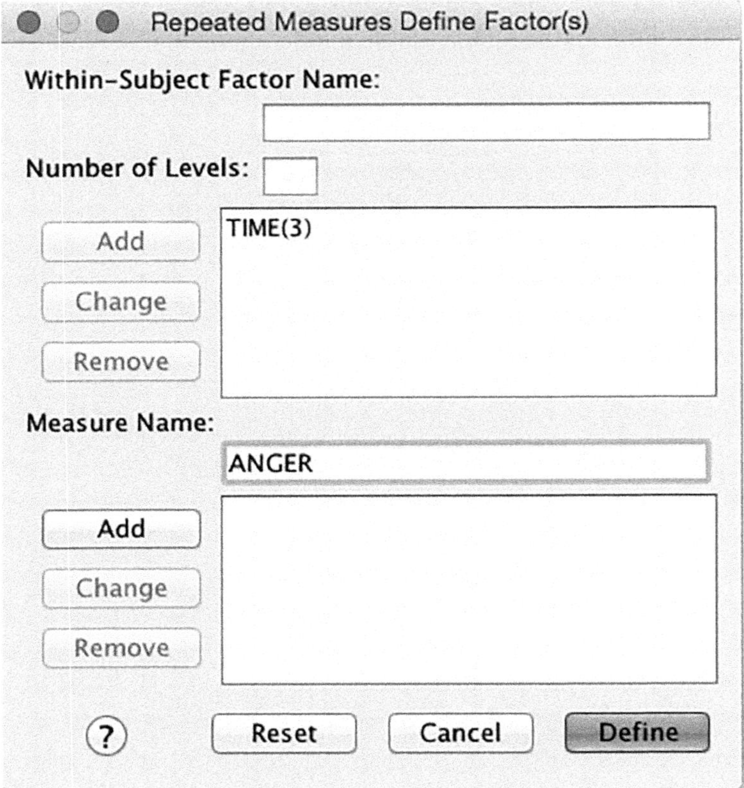

(8) Click ***Define***.
(9) Define the Within-Subject Factor by moving the variables ***anger1***, ***anger2*** and ***anger3*** in the appropriate order into the ***Within-Subject Variables*** box.
(10) Move the variable age into the ***Covariates*** box.
(11) Click ***Options . . .***
(12) Select ***Descriptive statistics***, ***Estimates of effect size*** and ***Observed power***.
(13) Under ***Estimated Marginal Means*** move time into the ***Display Means for*** box.
(14) Click ***Continue***.
(15) Click ***Plots . . .***
(16) Move the factor time to the ***Horizontal Axis*** line; click ***Add***.
(17) Click ***Continue***.
(18) Click ***OK*** to run the analysis.

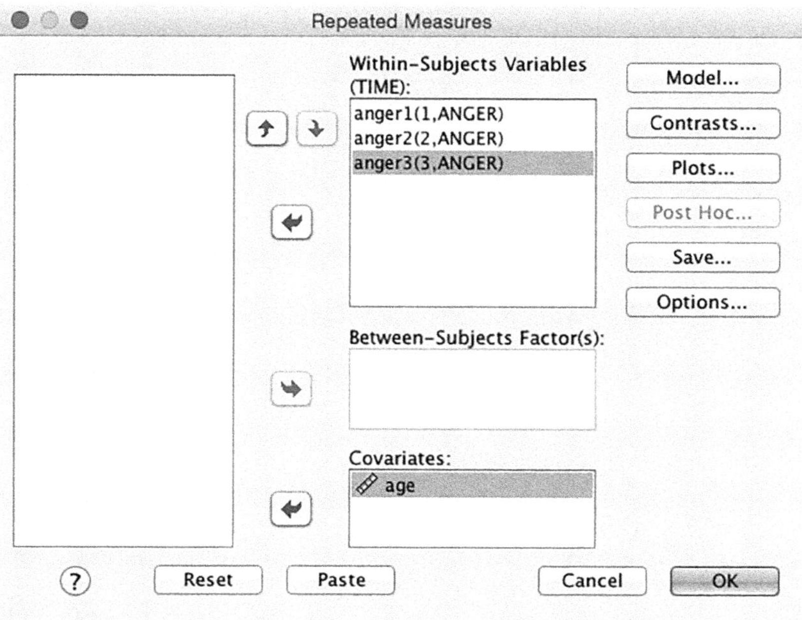

Repeated Measures: Options

Estimated Marginal Means

Factor(s) and Factor Interactions:

(OVERALL)

TIME

Display Means for:

TIME

Compare main effects

Confidence interval adjustment:

LSD(none)

Display

☑ Descriptive statistics
☑ Estimates of effect size
☑ Observed power
☐ Parameter estimates
☐ SSCP matrices
☐ Residual SSCP matrix
☐ Transformation matrix
☐ Homogeneity tests
☐ Spread vs. level plot
☐ Residual plot
☐ Lack of fit
☐ General estimable function

Significance level: .05 Confidence intervals are 95.0%

Cancel Continue

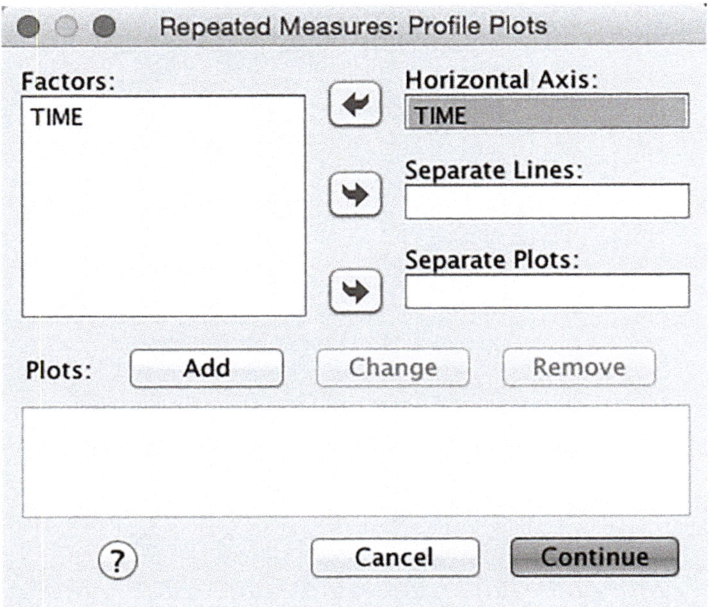

Let's review the output tables:

Within-Subjects Factors

Measure: ANGER

TIME	Dependent Variable
1	anger1
2	anger2
3	anger3

Descriptive Statistics

	Mean	Std. Deviation	N
anger1	20.10	4.181	50
anger2	14.72	3.620	50
anger3	10.76	4.269	50

Multivariate Tests[a]

Effect		Value	F	Hypothesis df	Error df	Sig.	Partial Eta Squared	Noncent. Parameter	Observed Power[c]
TIME	Pillai's Trace	.090	2.315[b]	2.000	47.000	.110	.090	4.630	.446
	Wilks' Lambda	.910	2.315[b]	2.000	47.000	.110	.090	4.630	.446
	Hotelling's Trace	.099	2.315[b]	2.000	47.000	.110	.090	4.630	.446
	Roy's Largest Root	.099	2.315[b]	2.000	47.000	.110	.090	4.630	.446
TIME * age	Pillai's Trace	.020	.479[b]	2.000	47.000	.622	.020	.958	.124
	Wilks' Lambda	.980	.479[b]	2.000	47.000	.622	.020	.958	.124
	Hotelling's Trace	.020	.479[b]	2.000	47.000	.622	.020	.958	.124
	Roy's Largest Root	.020	.479[b]	2.000	47.000	.622	.020	.958	.124

a. Design: Intercept + age; within-subjects design: time.
b. Exact statistic.
c. Computed using alpha = .05.

Mauchly's Test of Sphericity[a]

Measure: ANGER

Within-Subjects Effect	Mauchly's W	Approx. Chi-Square	df	Sig.	Epsilon[b]		
					Greenhouse-Geisser	Huynh-Feldt	Lower-bound
TIME	.214	72.454	2	.000	.560	.576	.500

Tests the null hypothesis that the error covariance matrix of the orthonormalized transformed dependent variables is proportional to an identity matrix.
a. Design: Intercept + age; within subjects design: time.
b. May be used to adjust the degrees of freedom for the averaged tests of significance.
Corrected tests are displayed in the Tests of Within-Subjects Effects table.

Tests of Within-Subjects Effects

Measure: ANGER

Source		Type III Sum of Squares	df	Mean Square	F	Sig.	Partial Eta Squared	Noncent. Parameter	Observed Power[a]
TIME	Sphericity Assumed	71.801	2	35.900	4.322	.016	.083	8.643	.739
	Greenhouse-Geisser	71.801	1.120	64.117	4.322	.038	.083	4.840	.562
	Huynh-Feldt	71.801	1.152	62.343	4.322	.037	.083	4.977	.569
	Lower-bound	71.801	1.000	71.801	4.322	.043	.083	4.322	.531

(*Continued*)

Tests of Within-Subjects Effects

Measure: ANGER

Source		Type III Sum of Squares	df	Mean Square	F	Sig.	Partial Eta Squared	Noncent. Parameter	Observed Power[a]
TIME * age	Sphericity Assumed	6.167	2	3.083	.371	.691	.008	.742	.108
	Greenhouse-Geisser	6.167	1.120	5.507	.371	.569	.008	.416	.094
	Huynh-Feldt	6.167	1.152	5.354	.371	.575	.008	.427	.095
	Lower-bound	6.167	1.000	6.167	.371	.545	.008	.371	.092
Error (TIME)	Sphericity Assumed	797.473	96	8.307					
	Greenhouse-Geisser	797.473	53.753	14.836					
	Huynh-Feldt	797.473	55.282	14.425					
	Lower-bound	797.473	48.000	16.614					

a. Computed using alpha = .05.

Tests of Within-Subjects Contrasts

Measure: ANGER

Source	TIME	Type III Sum of Squares	Df	Mean Square	F	Sig.	Partial Eta Squared	Noncent. Parameter	Observed Power[a]
TIME	Linear	69.128	1	69.128	4.504	.039	.086	4.504	.548
	Quadratic	2.673	1	2.673	2.110	.153	.042	2.110	.296
TIME * age	Linear	4.939	1	4.939	.322	.573	.007	.322	.086
	Quadratic	1.228	1	1.228	.969	.330	.020	.969	.162
Error (TIME)	Linear	736.671	48	15.347					
	Quadratic	60.802	48	1.267					

a. Computed using alpha = .05.

Tests of Between-Subjects Effects

Measure: ANGER

Transformed Variable: Average

Source	Type III Sum of Squares	df	Mean Square	F	Sig.	Partial Eta Squared	Noncent. Parameter	Observed Power[a]
Intercept	467.026	1	467.026	14.184	.000	.228	14.184	.958
Age	7.634	1	7.634	.232	.632	.005	.232	.076
Error	1580.426	48	32.926					

a. Computed using alpha = .05.

TIME

Measure: ANGER

TIME	Mean	Std. Error	95% Confidence Interval	
			Lower-Bound	Upper-Bound
1	20.100[a]	.597	18.899	21.301
2	14.720[a]	.515	13.685	15.755
3	10.760[a]	.608	9.539	11.981

a. Covariates appearing in the model are evaluated at the following values: age = 15.00.

Shown below is the plot of the mean number of anger outbursts at the 3 time periods controlling for age.

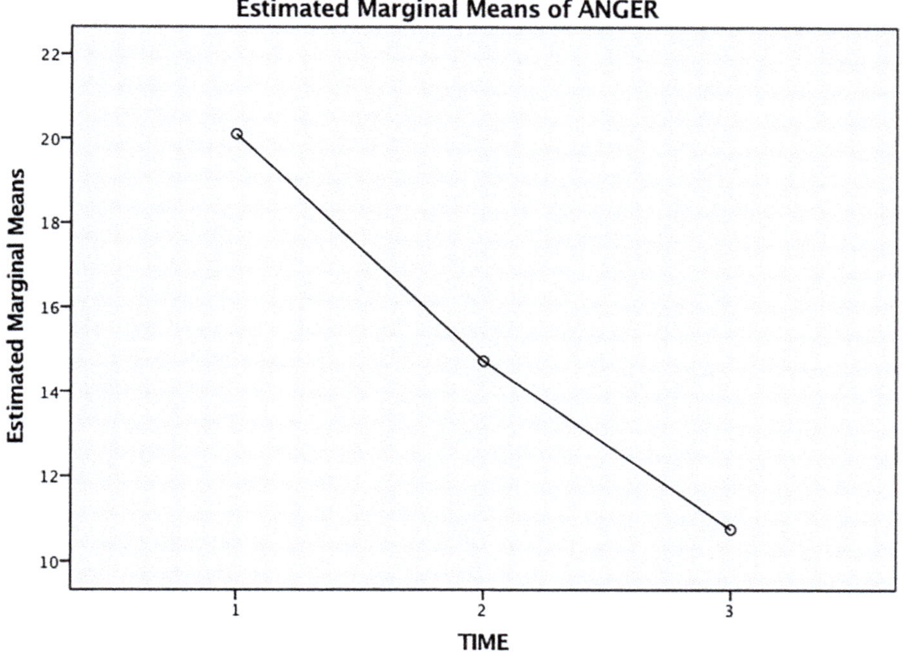

Do not use the multivariate tests table; the first table of importance is the Mauchly's test of sphericity. It is significant; therefore, read the corrected Greenhouse-Geisser row.

In the Greenhouse-Geisser row for Tests of Within Subjects Effects, you see that the F test for the effect of time is significant. The effect of time by age interaction is not significant.

Results might be written as follows:

A panel design with a one-way repeated ANCOVA was used to determine if children's anger is reduced after being in an anger management program, controlling for the age of the children. Anger was measured on a scale with a total score that ranged between 5 and 25, with higher scores indicating more anger. At the beginning of the anger management program, the mean anger score of the children was 20.10 (*SE* = 0.597). At the end of the anger management program, the mean anger score of the children was 14.72 (*SE* = 0.515). After six months, the anger scores reduced further to a mean of 10.76 (*SE* = 0.608). The main effect of anger reduction over time was significant ($F_{(1.12, 53.75)}$ = 4.332, *p* = .019 one tailed) with a medium effect (partial eta squared = .083) and .56% power. Age was not significant ($F_{(1.12, 53.75)}$ = .371, *p* = .569) with no effect (partial eta square = .008).

Since controlling for age did not change the results, the implications developed for the previous problem still apply.

Section 3

FINDING RELATIONSHIPS AND MAKING PREDICTIONS

Chapter 20

MEASURES OF ASSOCIATION/ CORRELATION

PART A: NONPARAMETRIC

Nominal Level Data

Phi Coefficient

See Chart—Measures of Association/Correlation and Nominal Measurement

Recall in Chapter 16 the Chi-Square test for two independent samples was discussed and the Chi-Square test for two independent variables compares the ratios of the distributions of categories for variables that only have two levels. The phi coefficient measures the amount of association between two categorical variables that have only two levels. Therefore, it is directly related to the Chi-Square 2 × 2 test for two independent variables. As with all measures of association, the value of the statistic can range between −1 and 1.

Let's return to the example in Chapter 16. The question was: "*Is there a difference between the number of Males and Females who apply for welfare at the Assist Agency and those who apply for welfare at the Help Agency?*"

The 2 × 2 table for this example looked like this:

		Agency	
		Help	Assist
Gender	Male	18 (a)	10 (b)
	Female	7 (c)	24 (d)

a, b, c and d in the table represent the frequencies of the observation. The phi coefficient (Φ) is determined by the following formula:

$$\Phi = \frac{ad - bc}{\surd\{(a+b)(c+d)(a+c)(b+d)\}}$$

The phi statistic is related to Chi-Square (χ^2) in the following way:

$$\Phi^2 = \frac{\chi^2}{N} \text{ or } \chi^2 = N\Phi^2$$

Previously we focused on looking at the difference between the number of Females and Males seeking welfare at the Assist Agency or at the Help Agency. This time we will also include in the analysis a measurement of the amount of relationship between gender and agency selected. The question and hypotheses will be changed slightly.

Study Question: "Is there a relationship between Agency selected for welfare assistance and Gender?"

This is an association, cross-sectional, independent measures design.

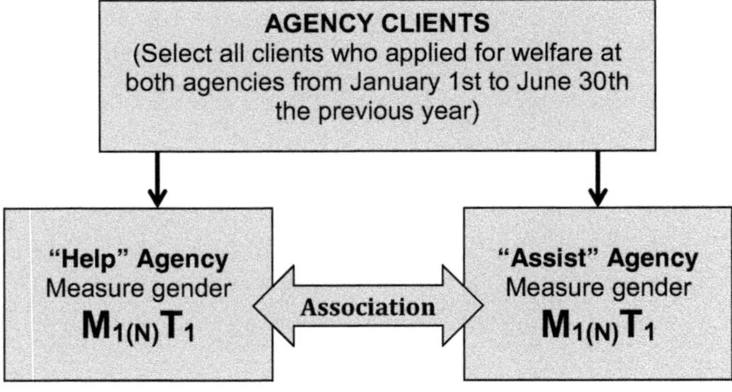

Hypotheses:

Association: There a relationship between Agency selected for welfare assistance and Gender.

Null: There is no relationship between Agency selected for welfare assistance and Gender.

Expected (E): There is no relationship betweenAagency selected for welfare assistance and Gender.

Predicted (P): There a relationship between Agency selected for welfare assistance and Gender.

Observed (O): The actual relationship between Agency selected for welfare assistance and Gender.

Level of Measurement: Nominal (Agency), Nominal (Gender)

Type of Design: Association, cross-sectional

Number of Groups: 2 Groups (samples)

Assumptions: (a) No more than 20% expected frequencies less than 5, (b) No expected frequency less than 1

VARIABLE BOX— Phi Coefficient

		AGENCY (A)	
		"Assist" Agency (A1)	***"Help" Agency*** (A2)
GENDER (B)	***Males*** (B1)	A1 B1	A2 B1
	Females (B2)	A1 B2	A2 B2

SPSS Commands:

Open the data set ***Ch20 Chi-Square 2×2***.
Follow the steps below:

(1) Go to ***Analyze***.
(2) Select ***Descriptive Statistics***.
(3) Go to ***Crosstabs . . .***
(4) Move ***Gender*** into the ***Row(s)*** box.
(5) Move ***Agency*** into the ***Column(s)*** box.

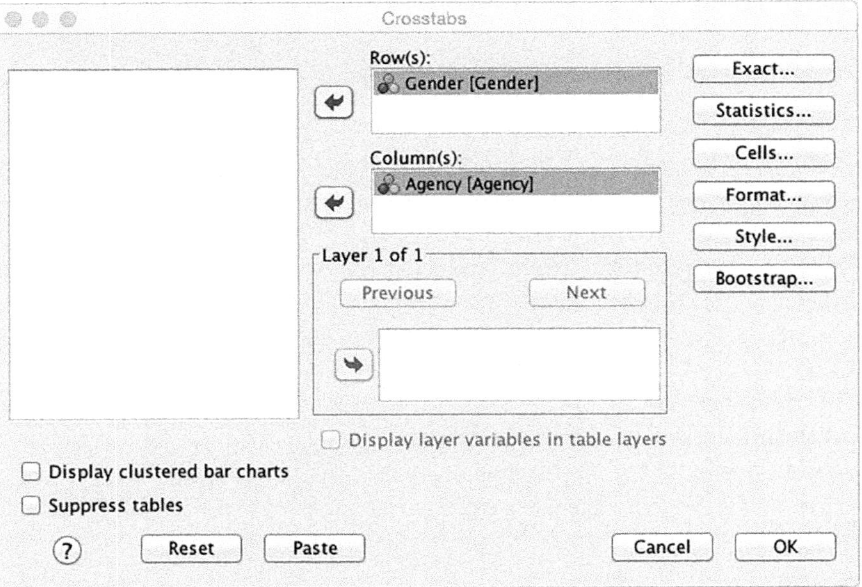

(6) Click on ***Statistics . . .***
(7) Select ***Chi-square*** and ***Phi and Cramer's V***.
(8) Click ***Continue***.

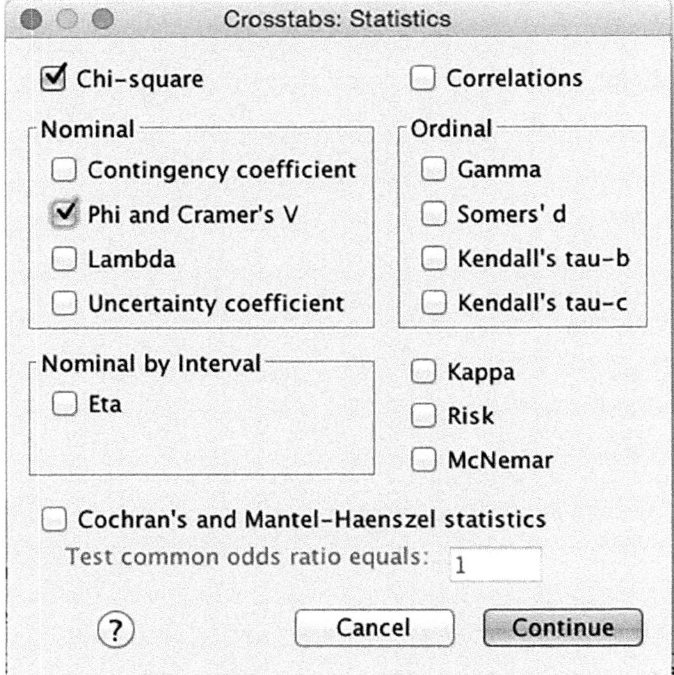

(9) Click on ***Cells . . .***
(10) Select ***Observed***, ***Expected***, ***Row***, ***Column*** and ***Total***.

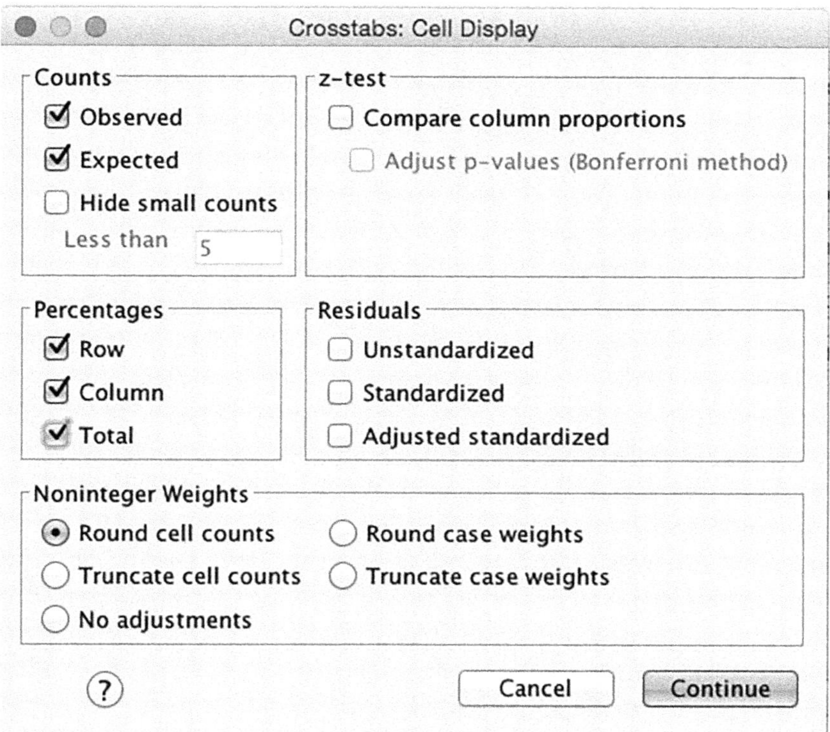

(11) Click ***Continue***.
(12) Click ***OK*** to run the analysis.

Let's look at the output:

Case Processing Summary

	Cases					
	Valid		Missing		Total	
	N	Percent	N	Percent	N	Percent
Gender * Agency	59	100.0%	0	0.0%	59	100.0%

Gender * Agency Crosstabulation

			Agency		Total
			Help Agency	Assist Agency	
Gender	Male	Count	18	10	28
		Expected Count	11.9	16.1	28.0
		% within Gender	64.3%	35.7%	100.0%
		% within Agency	72.0%	29.4%	47.5%
		% of Total	30.5%	16.9%	47.5%
	Female	Count	7	24	31
		Expected Count	13.1	17.9	31.0
		% within Gender	22.6%	77.4%	100.0%
		% within Agency	28.0%	70.6%	52.5%
		% of Total	11.9%	40.7%	52.5%
Total		Count	25	34	59
		Expected Count	25.0	34.0	59.0
		% within Gender	42.4%	57.6%	100.0%
		% within Agency	100.0%	100.0%	100.0%
		% of Total	42.4%	57.6%	100.0%

Chi-Square Tests

	Value	Df	Asymptotic Significance (2-sided)	Exact Sig. (2-sided)	Exact Sig. (1-sided)
Pearson Chi-Square	10.479[a]	1	.001		
Continuity Correction[b]	8.841	1	.003		
Likelihood Ratio	10.797	1	.001		
Fisher's Exact Test				.002	.001
Linear-by-Linear Association	10.302	1	.001		
N of Valid Cases	59				

a. 0 cells (0.0%) have expected count less than 5. The minimum expected count is 11.86.
b. Computed only for a 2 × 2 table.

Symmetric Measures

		Value	Approximate Significance
Nominal by Nominal	Phi	.421	.001
	Cramer's V	.421	.001
N of Valid Cases		59	

The same reporting method applied earlier to crosstab tables will be used to describe these results. However, now you have an additional statistic to report that is found in the Symmetric Measures output box—the phi statistic with a value of .421 and is significant at .001. Based on the Cohen d convention a correlation below 0.20 is small, between 0.20 and 0.50 is medium and above 0.5 is strong.

Recognize that finding an association between genders and agency selected is simply the obverse of finding an association between gender and agency.

The results as reported in Chapter 16 will now have the correlation added as follows:

At least 2/3 of all Males (64%) apply to ASSIST for welfare, while only 23% of the Females apply there. More than three quarters (77%) of all Females apply to HELP, while only 36% of Males apply there. This difference is significant, $X^2_{(1)} = 10.48, p = .001$. The phi coefficient ($\Phi = 0.42, p = .001$) indicates a medium relationship between gender and agency selected to apply for welfare.

Practical Implications: The same implications apply as those suggested in Chapter 16. Since there is a significant relationship between the agency selected and gender we should now start to identify what other variables might contribute to Females selecting Assist and Males selecting Help. Is there a difference in operating hours? Is there accommodation for children in one of the agencies? What is the gender composition of the staff at each agency? Do the agencies provide different services?

Cramer's V

See Chart—Measures of Association/Correlation and Nominal Measurement

In Chapter 18, Chi-Square r × k (where there are more than two levels on either or both of the two nominal variables) was discussed. The Cramer's V coefficient is the statistic that measures the amount of association between two categorical variables in a Chi-Square r × k design. You have seen how the phi statistic is related to Chi-Square 2 × 2 and Cramer's V has a similar relationship to the Chi-Square r × k as follows:

$$Cramer's\ V = \sqrt{\frac{X^2}{N(k-1)}}$$

where k = the smaller of the number of rows (r) or columns (c).

Although the Cramer's V statistic is interpreted much like the Pearson's r (rho) correlation discussed later in the parametric section of this chapter (where a value close to +1 or −1 indicates a strong relationship and a value close to 0 indicates a weak relationship) the interpretation of the value of Cramer's V cannot be interpreted as a linear relationship between 0 and 1. Interpretation of the Cramer's V should include additional evaluation based upon the proportions found in the Crosstabs Table. Adding levels to either of the variables can change the value of Cramer's V.

We will use the example from Chapter 18 where the question was "Do individuals with higher education levels have higher SES levels?" Data was collected on 160 individuals who live in the community and based upon their income they were categorized into 3 levels. High SES included individuals with income $60,000 and above, Middle SES with incomes between $35,000 and $59,999 and Low SES with incomes below $35,000. Amount of education was categorized into 3 levels—high school or below, some college education and college graduate or above.

The r × k table for the data was:

		Education		
		High School or Below	Some College	College Grad or Above
SES	Low SES	40	20	10
	Middle SES	10	10	20
	High SES	10	10	30

Previously the research focused on differences between education and SES. ***This time we are also interested in the association (relationship)*** between education and SES. Therefore, the question and hypotheses need to be expressed in terms of relationship.

Study Question: Is there a relationship between level of education and level of SES?

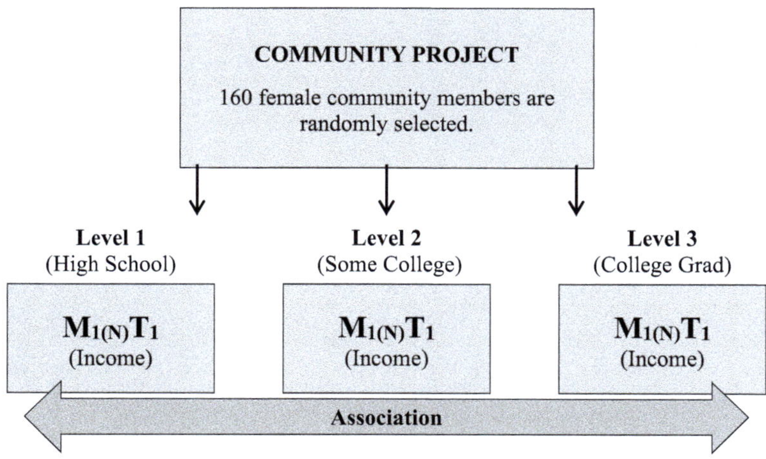

Hypotheses:

Relationship: There is a relationship between level of education and level of SES.
Null: There is no relationship between level of education and level of SES.
Expected (E): There is no relationship between level of education and level of SES.
Predicted (P): There is a relationship between level of education and level of SES.
Observed (O): The actual distribution of educational levels and SES levels.
Level of Measurement: Nominal (Educational levels), Nominal (SES levels)
Type of Design: Relationship, cross-sectional
Number of Groups: 2 Groups (samples)
Assumptions: (a) No more than 20% expected frequencies less than 5, (b) No expected frequency less than 1

VARIABLE BOX

EDUCATION (A)

		High School or Less (A1)	***Some College*** (A2)	***College Graduate +*** (A3)
INCOME (B)	***Low Income*** (B1)	A1 B1	A2 B1	A3 B1
	Middle Income (B2)	A1 B2	A2 B2	A3 B2
	High Income (B3)	A1 B3	A2 B3	A3 B3

SPSS Commands

Open the data set ***Ch20 chi square r × k***.
Follow the steps below:

(1) Go to ***Analyze***.
(2) Go to ***Descriptive Statistics***.
(3) Select ***Crosstabs . . .***
(4) Move ***SES*** into the ***Row(s)*** box, Move ***Education*** into ***Column(s)*** box.

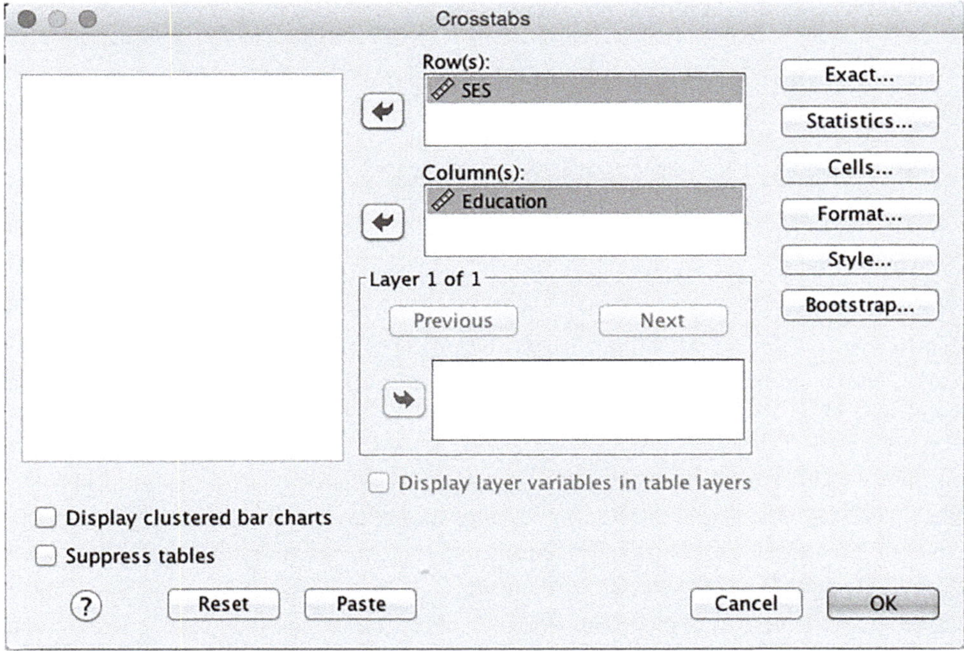

(5) Click on the ***Statistics . . .*** button.
(6) Select ***Chi-square*** and ***Phi and Cramer's V***.
(7) Click ***Continue***.
(8) Click on the ***Cells . . .*** button.
(9) Check the following: ***Observed***, ***Expected***, ***Row***, ***Column*** and ***Total***.
(10) Click ***Continue***.
(11) Click ***OK*** to run the analysis.

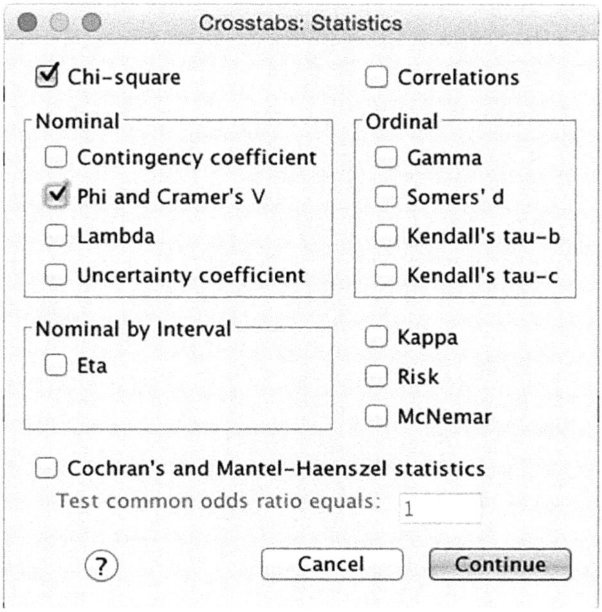

Crosstabs: Statistics

- [x] Chi-square
- [ ] Correlations

Nominal
- [ ] Contingency coefficient
- [x] Phi and Cramer's V
- [ ] Lambda
- [ ] Uncertainty coefficient

Ordinal
- [ ] Gamma
- [ ] Somers' d
- [ ] Kendall's tau-b
- [ ] Kendall's tau-c

Nominal by Interval
- [ ] Eta

- [ ] Kappa
- [ ] Risk
- [ ] McNemar

- [ ] Cochran's and Mantel-Haenszel statistics

Test common odds ratio equals: 1

? Cancel Continue

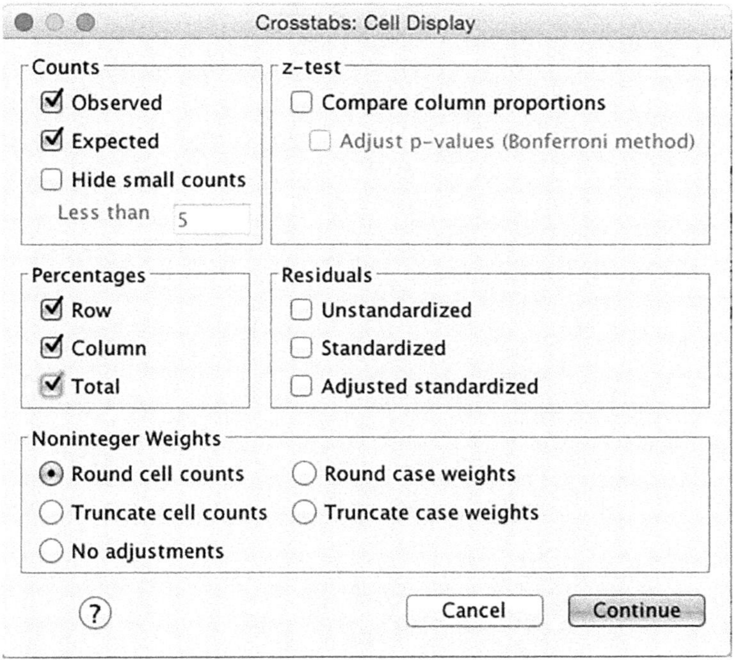

Crosstabs: Cell Display

Counts
- [x] Observed
- [x] Expected
- [ ] Hide small counts

Less than 5

z-test
- [ ] Compare column proportions
- [ ] Adjust p-values (Bonferroni method)

Percentages
- [x] Row
- [x] Column
- [x] Total

Residuals
- [ ] Unstandardized
- [ ] Standardized
- [ ] Adjusted standardized

Noninteger Weights
- (•) Round cell counts
- ( ) Round case weights
- ( ) Truncate cell counts
- ( ) Truncate case weights
- ( ) No adjustments

? Cancel Continue

Case Processing Summary

	Cases					
	Valid		Missing		Total	
	N	Percent	N	Percent	N	Percent
SES * Education	160	100.0%	0	0.0%	160	100.0%

SES * Education Crosstabulation

			Education			Total
			High School	Some College	College Graduate	
SES	Low SES	Count	40	20	10	70
		Expected Count	26.3	17.5	26.3	70.0
		% within SES	57.1%	28.6%	14.3%	100.0%
		% within Education	66.7%	50.0%	16.7%	43.8%
		% of Total	25.0%	12.5%	6.3%	43.8%
	Middle SES	Count	10	10	20	40
		Expected Count	15.0	10.0	15.0	40.0
		% within SES	25.0%	25.0%	50.0%	100.0%
		% within Education	16.7%	25.0%	33.3%	25.0%
		% of Total	6.3%	6.3%	12.5%	25.0%
	High SES	Count	10	10	30	50
		Expected Count	18.8	12.5	18.8	50.0
		% within SES	20.0%	20.0%	60.0%	100.0%
		% within Education	16.7%	25.0%	50.0%	31.3%
		% of Total	6.3%	6.3%	18.8%	31.3%
Total		Count	60	40	60	160
		Expected Count	60.0	40.0	60.0	160.0
		% within SES	37.5%	25.0%	37.5%	100.0%
		% within Education	100.0%	100.0%	100.0%	100.0%
		% of Total	37.5%	25.0%	37.5%	100.0%

Chi-Square Tests

	Value	Df	Asymptotic Significance (2-sided)
Pearson Chi-Square	32.286[a]	4	.000
Likelihood Ratio	34.300	4	.000
Linear-by-Linear Association	28.191	1	.000
N of Valid Cases	160		

a. 0 cells (0.0%) have expected count less than 5. The minimum expected count is 10.00.

Symmetric Measures

		Value	Approximate Significance
Nominal by Nominal	Phi	.449	.000
	Cramer's V	.318	.000
N of Valid Cases		160	

We will use the same format for reporting results. Similar to the phi coefficient, we have an additional statistic to include in the results—the Cramer's V. This statistic is found in the Symmetric Measures table just below Phi. The Cramer's V coefficient is 0.32 (rounded) and is significant and a moderate relationship.

The results might be written as follows:

More than half of people with Low SES (57%) have a high school diploma or lower and only 14% have graduated from college. Of those individuals with a Middle SES, 50% were college graduates while 25% had some college and 25% had high school or below. For those with a High SES, 60% were college graduates with 20% having some college. This difference is significant ($X^2_{(4)} = 32.29, p = 001$). The Cramer's V coefficient (.318) indicates a moderate relationship between education and SES.

Practical Implications: It would be important to focus educational efforts and measures to engage students from lower SES in learning activities. New methods for engaging learners from lower SES should be tested. Methods for training educators to work with lower SES students to continue education and become engaged in higher educational goals should be developed and tested.

Ordinal Level Data

Spearman Rank Order Coefficient

See Chart—Measures of Association/Correlation and Ordinal Measurement

The Spearman r (rho) is one of the oldest nonparametric tests, and used to determine if there is a linear relationship between two variables. **Both variables must be measured on *at least* an ordinal level.** The SPSS program will transform interval or ratio level data to ordinal level automatically for you. The Spearman r is similar to the Pearson r; however, **the Pearson r requires normally distributed interval or ratio level** data for calculation. The Spearman uses ordinal level data; therefore, if you have non-normal data, using the Spearman is a better alternative than using the Pearson and not meeting the assumptions. The Spearman r correlation ranges between −1 and 1. The Spearman r differs from the Pearson r correlation in that the raw numbers are converted to ranks before computations are done. When converting to ranks, the smallest value on X becomes a rank of 1, etc. Let's look at the following X–Y pairs and how they change when the values are converted to ranks. (Note that this is far too small a data set for analysis and is only used for demonstration purposes so that you can more easily understand the operations of the test.)

X actual number	Y actual number	X rank	Y rank
5	7	2	3
2	2	1	1
7	9	3	4
8	4	4	2

The first actual value of X is 5 and is converted into a 2 because 5 is the second lowest value of X. The next actual value of X is 2 and converted into a 1 since it is the lowest. The same procedure is used for the rest of the X values and also for all of the Y values. The formula used to calculate the Spearman Rank Order Coefficient is:

$$r = 1 - \frac{6\Sigma D^2}{n\left(n^2 - 1\right)}$$

n = number of pairs and D equals difference between ranks.

Suppose we are interested in determining if there is a relationship between the final exam scores of social work students in two classes: policy and practice. We only have a small sample and the exam does not have a large range; thus, you do not meet the assumptions of the Pearson r and should use the Spearman.

Question: What is the relationship between the final exam scores of social work students in their policy class and their practice class?

This is a relationship, cross-sectional repeated measures design.

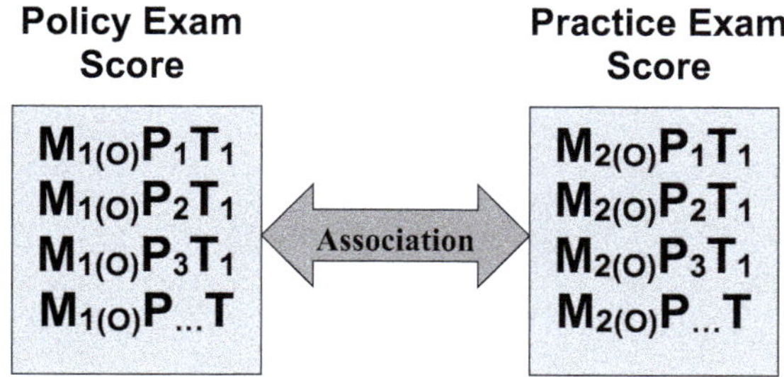

Hypotheses:

Relationship: There is a relationship between the final exam score in the policy class and the final exam score in the practice class.

Null: There is no relationship between the final exam score in the policy class and the final exam score in the practice class.

Expected (E): There will be no relationship between the final exam score in the policy class and the final exam score in the practice class.

Predicted (P): There will be a relationship between the final exam score in the policy class and the final exam score in the practice class.

Observed (O): The actual relationship between the final exam score in the policy class and the final exam score in the practice class.

Level of Measurement: Ordinal (exam score in policy class), Ordinal (exam score in practice class)

Type of Design: Association, cross-sectional

Number of Groups: 2 Groups (samples)

Assumptions: (a) Ordinal level data, (b) Interval/ratio data that does not meet the assumptions of normality

VARIABLE BOX

FINAL EXAM SCORE

	Policy Class	*Practice Class*
Student 1	Raw Score → Rank	Raw Score → Rank
Student 2	Raw Score → Rank	Raw Score → Rank
Student …	Raw Score → Rank	Raw Score → Rank

SPSS Commands

Open the data set ***Ch20 Spearman Rank Order***.
Follow the steps below:

(1) Go to ***Analyze***.
(2) Scroll down to ***Correlate***.
(3) Select ***Bivariate . . .***
(4) In the ***Correlation Coefficients*** box, ensure that only ***Spearman*** is selected.
(5) Move ***PolicyExam*** and ***PracticeExam*** into the ***Variables*** box.

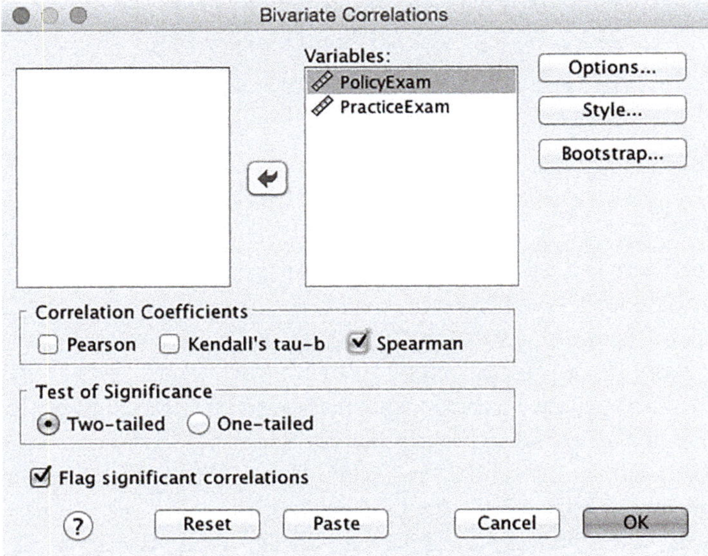

(6) Click ***OK*** to run the analysis.

Let's look at the output:

Correlations

			Policy Exam	Practice Exam
Spearman's rho	Policy Exam	Correlation Coefficient	1.000	.818**
		Sig. (2-tailed)	.	.001
		N	12	12
	Practice Exam	Correlation Coefficient	.818**	1.000
		Sig. (2-tailed)	.001	.
		N	12	12

**. Correlation is significant at the 0.01 level (2-tailed).

The ***strength of the correlation coefficients*** can be found in the table below:

COEFFICIENT VALUE	STRENGTH
0 to .01 or –.01	**VERY WEAK**
.01 to .03 or –.01 to –.03	**WEAK**
.03 to .05 or –.03 to –.05	**MODERATE**
.05 above or –.5 below	**STRONG**

The results show that the relationship between the policy exam score and the practice exam score is positive, strong and significant. The results might be written as follows:

A Spearman rank order coefficient was calculated to investigate the relationship between the final exam score in a policy class and the final exam score in a practice class for a sample of social work students. The results indicate there is a significant strong positive correlation between the policy exam score and the practice exam score (Spearman's rho = 0.82, p = .001).

Practical Implications: Social Work students are consistent in their examinations across important social work subjects. These findings indicate that students might be able to integrate what they have learned in policy into practice because of the strong correlation. This would need to be evaluated by testing to see if in their practice activities, classes, practicum and seminars they are utilizing knowledge of policy in their interactions with agencies and clients and critical application of learning materials for effective professional social workers.

Kendall tau b

See Chart—Measures of Association/Correlation and Ordinal Measurement

The assumptions of the Kendall tau b are similar to Spearman r. The distinction between them is the ***Kendall tau b takes into account the difference between pairs of scores that are higher on both variables (concordant) and reducing this difference by subtracting pairs where the score is higher on one variable but lower on the other (discordant)***. Kendall tau b is calculated using the following formula:

$$T = \frac{n_c - n_d}{\frac{1}{2}n(n-1)}$$

n_c is the number of concordant pairs, and n_d is the number of discordant pairs in the data set. ***Once again remember that a concordant pair is when a person who has a***

higher value on one variable also has a higher score on the other variable. A discordant pair is when there is a higher value on one variable and lower value on the other variable. ***n*** is the number of pairs. ***A tied pair is not regarded as concordant or discordant. If there are a large number of ties, the total number of pairs should be adjusted, or the Gamma statistic should be used (see the section on Gamma later in this chapter).*** **The *Kendall tau b* is the *appropriate statistical test when the number of rows and columns are basically equal* since the calculations are based upon concordant and discordant pairs.**

We will look more closely at concordant and discordant pairs utilizing another example comparing scores on the Troubled Childhood Scale and the Marital Problems Scale for 11 clients. It is important to note that in this example the values (scores) are interval level; however, it is a small n and they are not normally distributed, so the Kendall tau B rank order test is preferred to parametric tests. The raw scores are shown below.

Troubled Childhood Scale (X)		Marital Problems Scale (Y)	
X_1	27	Y_1	60
X_2	28	Y_2	70
X_3	30	Y_3	72
X_4	31	Y_4	62
X_5	32	Y_5	66
X_6	33	Y_6	80
X_7	35	Y_7	86
X_8	37	Y_8	95
X_9	38	Y_9	73
X_{10}	39	Y_{10}	75
X_{11}	40	Y_{11}	94

In a sample of n observations, we can have $n(n - 1) \div 2$ total pairs. So, in our sample where we have 11 observations, we can have $11(11 - 1) \div 2 = 55$, thus, there are ***55 possible pairs***. Let's look at the **1 and 2 pair** (X_1Y_1) and (X_2Y_2). If $X_2 - X_1$ and $Y_2 - Y_1$ have the same sign, it is a concordant pair. If we replace the values we find:

X_2 (28) $-X_1$ (27) and Y_2 (70) $-Y_1$ (60) is a **concordant pair**. They both go down. Let's look at the **8 and the 10 pair** $(X_8\ Y_8)$ and $(X_{10}\ Y_{10})$. If $X_{10} - X_8$ and $Y_{10} - Y_8$ have different signs, it is a discordant pair. If we replace the values we find: X_{10} (39) $-X_8$ (37) and Y_{10} (75) $-Y_8$ (95) is a **discordant pair. One is going up and the other is going down. A tie is a pair where both = 0.**

Having seen how the pairs are calculated we will now use SPSS to calculate Kendall Tau b because hand calculation is rather laborious.

Study Question: What is the relationship between the amount of trouble in childhood and marital problems?

This is a relationship, cross-sectional repeated measures design.

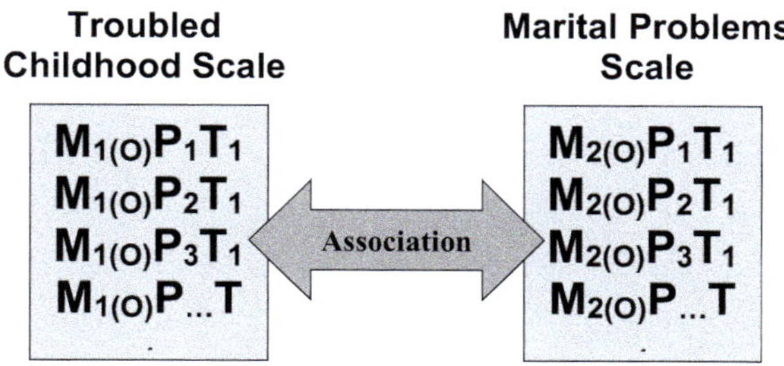

Hypotheses:

Relationship: There is a relationship between the amount of trouble in childhood and marital problems.

Null: There is no relationship between the amount of trouble in childhood and marital problems.

Expected (E): There will be no relationship between the amount of trouble in childhood and marital problems.

Predicted (P): There will be a relationship between the amount of trouble in childhood and marital problems.

Observed (O): The actual relationship between the amount of trouble in childhood and marital problems.

Level of Measurement: Ordinal (troubled childhood), Ordinal (marital problems)

Type of Design: Relationship, cross-sectional

Number of Groups: 2 Groups (samples)

Assumptions: Ordinal level data or interval ratio data that does not meet the assumptions of normality

SPSS Commands

Open the data set ***Ch20 Kendall Tau B***.
Follow the steps below:

(1) Click ***Analyze***.
(2) Scroll down to ***Correlate***.
(3) Select ***Bivariate . . .***

(4) In the ***Correlation Coefficients*** box, ensure that only ***Kendall's tau-b*** is selected.
(5) Move both variables (***TCScale*** and ***MPScale***) into the ***Variables*** box.

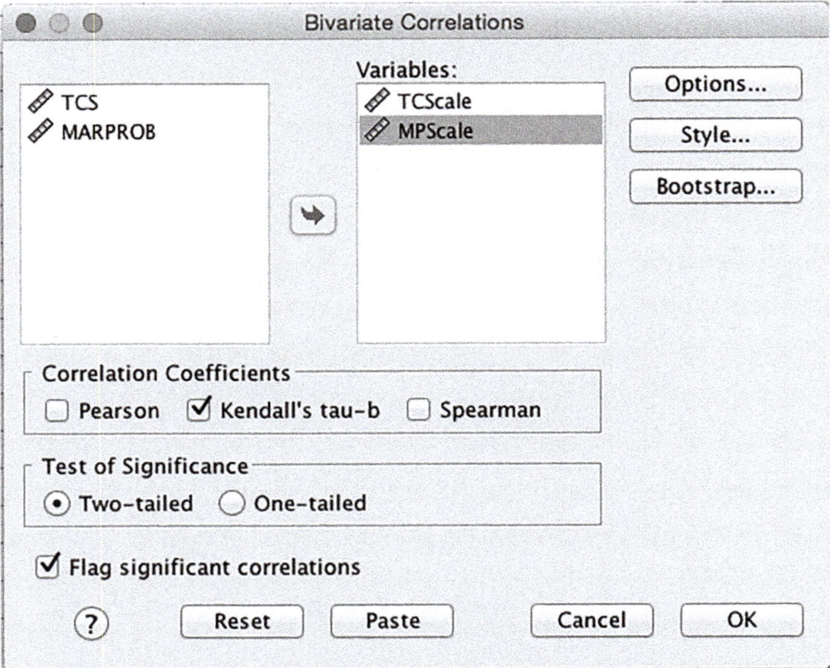

(6) Click ***OK*** to run the analysis.

Let's look at the output.

Correlations

			Troubled Childhood Scale	Marital Problems Scale
Kendall's tau_b	Troubled Childhood Scale	Correlation Coefficient	1.000	.600*
		Sig. (2-tailed)	.	.010
		N	11	11
	Marital Problems Scale	Correlation Coefficient	.600*	1.000
		Sig. (2-tailed)	.010	.
		N	11	11

*. Correlation is significant at the 0.05 level (2-tailed).

The relationship between the Troubled Childhood Scale score and the Marital Problem Scale score is positive, strong and significant. Remember because of the reduction of the discordant pairs **the Kendall tau b is more conservative than Spearman r in determining the amount of relationship**.

The results might be written as follows:

A Kendall tau b rank order correlation was calculated to investigate the relationship between the amount of trouble in childhood and the amount of marital problems as an adult. The results indicate that there is a strong significant positive correlation between amount of trouble in childhood and marital problems as an adult (Kendall tau b = 0.60, *p* = 0.01).

Practical Implications: While this is clearly not a causal study, one implication (the AS IF idea) might be to reduce the amount of problems in a child's younger years so it could potentially reduce marital problems. Intervention within families with young children to reduce the family problems could potentially prove a deterrent to adult marital problems. Seeing parents model effective ways to deal with marital problems may also provide the child with methods to use in their own future marriage. Potential studies related to this finding might be: (1) to query adults who are having marital problems about the problems in their childhood and to determine the frequency of those problems, (2) to investigate if there are some particular childhood problems specifically related to adult marital problems and (3) to determine if different types of childhoods/family constellations are related to present or absence as well as types of adult marital problems.

Kendall tau b Partial Rank Order Coefficient

See Chart—Measures of Association/Correlation and Ordinal Measurement

The Kendall tau b *partial* rank order correlation coefficient is based upon the Kendall tau b rank order correlation coefficient; however, with the *tau b partial you can determine the relationship between more than two variables. This test allows the researcher to control or mathematically* take out the variance contributed by one variable **(we will label it Z) to the variable dependent variable (Y) so that you can obtain a more accurate estimate of the specific variance accounted for in Y by X**. The example will clarify this process.

Let's go back to our example. Suppose you are interested in the amount of correlation between a person's **score on the Troubled Childhood Scale (TCS) (variable X)** and their **score on the Marital Problems Scale (MPS) (variable Y)**. You also know that the **years of marriage (variable Z) will have an effect on the Marital Problems Scale**. *You want to know* ***the association of the Troubled Childhood Scale score to the score on the Marital Problems Scale if you make the years of marriage constant. You want to take out the association (variance) that is related to years of marriage.*** (Much like extracting a covariate.)

Study Question: What is the relationship between the amount of trouble in childhood and marital problems, holding years of marriage constant?

This is a relationship, cross-sectional, repeated measures design.

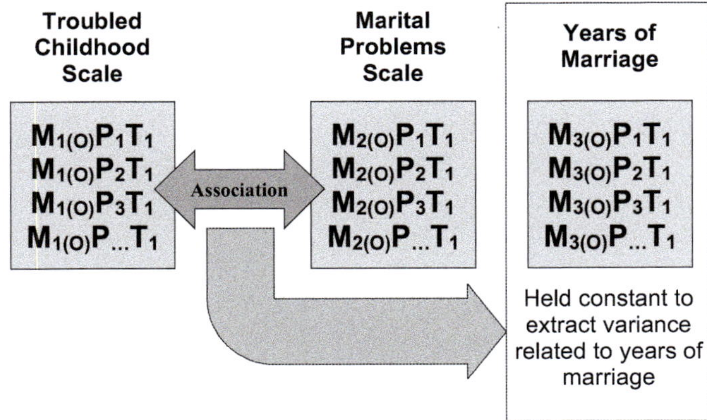

Hypothesis:

Relationship: There is a relationship between the amount of trouble in childhood and marital problems, holding years of marriage constant.

Null: There is no relationship between the amount of trouble in childhood and marital problems, holding years of marriage constant.

Expected (E): There will be no relationship between the amount of trouble in childhood and marital problems, after holding years of marriage constant.

Predicted (P): There will be a relationship between the amount of trouble in childhood and marital problems, after holding years of marriage constant.

Observed (O): The actual relationship between the amount of trouble in childhood and marital problems, after holding years of marriage constant.

Level of Measurement: Ordinal (TCS), Ordinal (MPS) Ordinal (years of marriage)

Type of Design: Relationship, cross-sectional

Number of Groups: 2 Groups (samples)
Assumptions: Ordinal level data or interval/ratio data that does not meet the assumptions of normality.

SPSS Commands

Open the data set ***Ch20 Kendall Tau B***.
Follow the steps below:

(1) Click ***Analyze***.
(2) Scroll down to ***Correlate***.
(3) Select ***Bivariate . . .***
(4) In the ***Correlation Coefficients*** box, ensure that only ***Kendall's tau-b*** is selected.
(5) Move all variables (***TCScale***, ***MPScale*** and ***YearsMar***) into the ***Variables*** box.

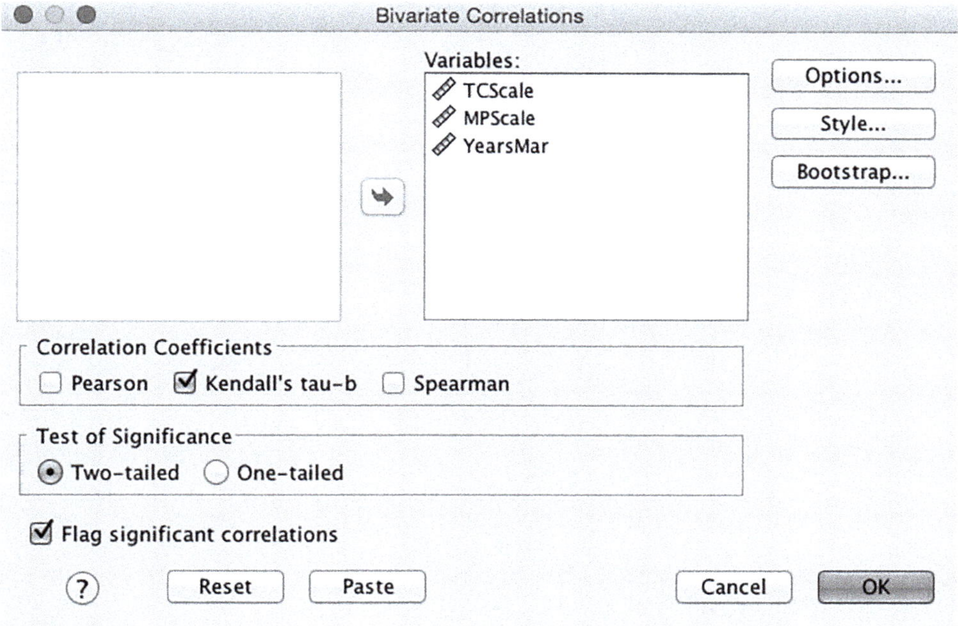

(6) Click ***OK*** to run the analysis.

You are interested in three relationships found in the output:

X **(Troubled Childhood Scale) ×** ***Y*** **(Marital Problems Scale)**
Y **(Marital Problems Scale) ×** ***Z*** **(Years of Marriage)**
X **(Troubled Childhood Scale) ×** ***Z*** **(Years of Marriage)**

Correlations

			TCScale	MPScale	YearsMar
Kendall's tau_b	TCScale	Correlation Coefficient	1.000	.663**	.294**
		Sig. (2-tailed)	.	.000	.003
		N	50	50	50
	MPScale	Correlation Coefficient	.663**	1.000	.175
		Sig. (2-tailed)	.000	.	.081
		N	50	50	50
	YearsMar	Correlation Coefficient	.294**	.175	1.000
		Sig. (2-tailed)	.003	.081	.
		N	50	50	50

**. Correlation is significant at the 0.01 level (2-tailed).

TCScale to MPScale (*X* to *Y*) = .633
MPScale to Years of Marriage (*Y* to *Z*) = .175
TCScale to Years of Marriage (*X* to *Z*) = .294

Now we need to do some calculations. SPSS does not have a program that calculates the Kendall Tau partial correlation. You have to use the following formula to calculate the relationship between Troubled Childhood Scale and the Marital Problems Scale scores, keeping Years of Marriage constant:

$$r_{xy*z} = \frac{r_{xy} - r_{xz}r_{yz}}{\sqrt{1 - r_{xz}^2}\sqrt{1 - r_{yz}^2}}$$

Inserting the values from the table into the formula we will get:

$$r_{xy*z} = \frac{.663 - .(.294)(.175)}{\sqrt{1 - .086}\sqrt{1 - .031}}$$

$$r_{xy*z} = \frac{.611}{\sqrt{.914}\sqrt{.969}}$$

$$r_{xy*z} = \frac{.611}{(.956)(.984)}$$

$$r_{xy*z} = \frac{.611}{.941}$$

$$\boldsymbol{r_{xy*z}} = .649$$

The results might be written as follows:

A Kendall tau b partial rank order correlation was calculated to investigate the relationship between a troubled childhood and marital problems, controlling for years of marriage. After controlling for years of marriage, results indicate there is a significant moderate positive correlation between scores on the Troubled Childhood Scale and scores on the Marital Problems Scale (partial Kendall tau b = .649, p = .001).

Practical Implications: It is important to replicate this study so that we can determine if the findings that the years of marriage is not a major contributor to marital problems. Should this be found in replications then we could conclude that it is not an important factor and would not guide practice whereas childhood troubles would. Other factors to have a look at might be age at marriage, length of time together before marriage and, as stated in the previous practical implications, the need to continue to investigate and be more specific with those childhood "troubles".

Gamma

See Chart—Measures of Association/Correlation and Ordinal Measurement

Gamma is another measure of correlation between two ordinal level variables and is also based on the difference between concordant pairs (C) and discordant pairs (D). Gamma is computed using the following formula:

$$Gamma = \frac{(C - D)}{(C + D)}$$

As you can see, the Gamma statistic is the difference between the number of concordant pairs and the number of discordant pairs, **divided by the total of all concordant and discordant pairs**. Therefore, as the ratio of concordant pairs to discordant pairs increases, the value of gamma increases indicating a stronger association. **Clearly, the Gamma statistic ignores all ties. Values can range between −1 and 1.** ***When the data contains many tied observations, the Gamma statistic is preferred over the Kendall Tau.*** *While ignoring ties is important where there are a great many ties, another problem can arise by* ***overestimating the strength of the relationship*** *because ties are not taken into account.* ***The researcher has to make the decision to use it when there are quite a few ties but not so many ties that leaving them out increases the strength of the relationship too much.*** Remember that ***both of the measures have to be ordinal***.

Let's look at an example from an agency that wanted to investigate the relationship between the level of income of a family and their need for health care. Both variables were ordinal and ordered—from low to high income and from low to high health care need.

Study Question: What is the relationship between the need for health care and the level of income?

This is a relationship, cross-sectional, repeated measures design.

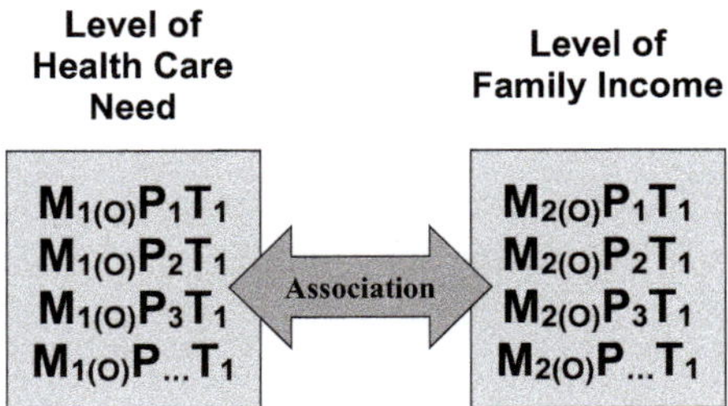

Hypotheses

Relationship: There is a relationship between the need for health care and the level of income.
Null: There is no relationship between the need for health care and the level of income.
Expected (E): There will be no relationship between the need for health care and the level of income.
Predicted (P): There will be a relationship between the need for health care and the level of income.
Observed (O): The actual relationship between the need for health care and the level of income.
Level of Measurement: Ordinal (need for health care), Ordinal (income level) both ordered
Type of Design: Relationship, cross-sectional, repeated measures

VARIABLE BOX—GAMMA

	Level of Health Care Need	*Level of Family Income*
Individual 1	1—"Not Much Need" to 5—"High Need"	1—"Above $40,000" to 5—"Below $9,999"
Individual 2	1—"Not Much Need" to 5—"High Need"	1—"Above $40,000" to 5—"Below $9,999"
Individual . . .	1—"Not Much Need" to 5—"High Need"	1—"Above $40,000" to 5—"Below $9,999"

Number of Groups: Two groups (samples)
Assumptions: (a) Ordinal level data (b) Ordering in both variables.

SPSS Commands

Open the data set ***Ch20 Gamma***.
Follow the steps below:

(1) Click ***Analyze***.
(2) Scroll down and select ***Descriptive Statistics***.
(3) Select ***Crosstabs . . .***
(4) Move the variable ***Need HealthNeed*** into the ***Row(s)*** box
(5) Move the variable ***Income*** into the ***Column(s)*** box.

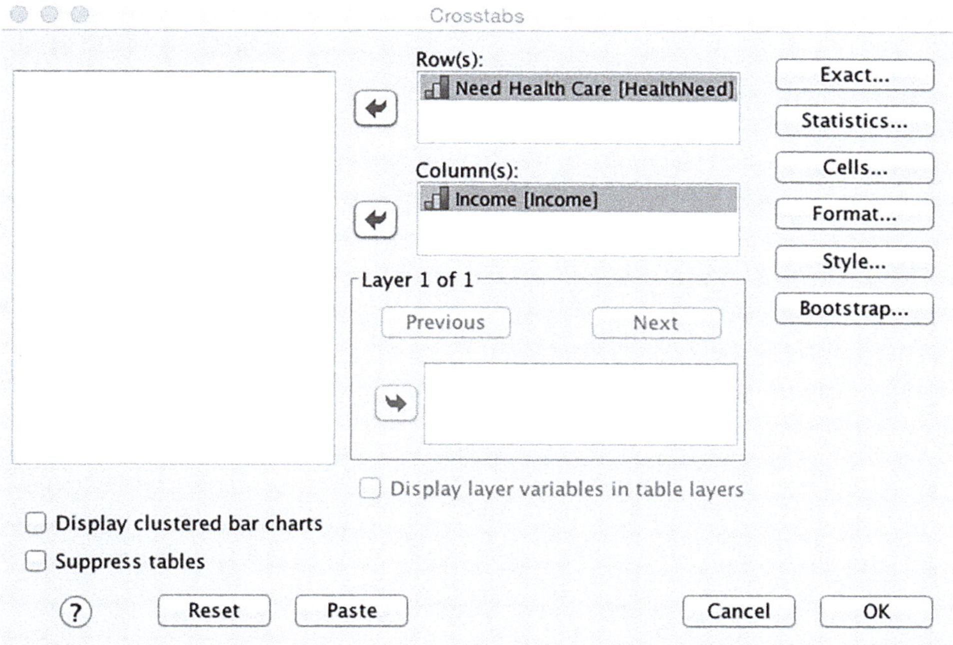

(6) Click the ***Statistics . . .*** button.
(7) Select ***Gamma*** in the ***Ordinal*** box; click ***Continue***.
(8) Click the **Cells . . .** button.
(9) Select ***Row***, ***Column*** and ***Total*** in the ***Percentages*** box; click ***Continue***.
(10) Click ***OK*** to run the analysis.

Need Health Care * Income Crosstabulation

			Income					Total
			Above $40,000	$30,000 to $39,999	$20,000 to $29,999	$10,000 to $19,999	Below $9,999	
Need Health Care	Not Much Need	Count	6	3	1	0	0	10
		% within Need Health Care	60.0%	30.0%	10.0%	0.0%	0.0%	100.0%
		% within Income	66.7%	30.0%	8.3%	0.0%	0.0%	20.0%
		% of Total	12.0%	6.0%	2.0%	0.0%	0.0%	20.0%
	Below Average Need	Count	2	6	2	0	0	10
		% within Need Health Care	20.0%	60.0%	20.0%	0.0%	0.0%	100.0%
		% within Income	22.2%	60.0%	16.7%	0.0%	0.0%	20.0%
		% of Total	4.0%	12.0%	4.0%	0.0%	0.0%	20.0%
	Average Need	Count	1	1	6	2	0	10
		% within Need Health Care	10.0%	10.0%	60.0%	20.0%	0.0%	100.0%
		% within Income	11.1%	10.0%	50.0%	22.2%	0.0%	20.0%
		% of Total	2.0%	2.0%	12.0%	4.0%	0.0%	20.0%
	Above Average Need	Count	0	0	2	5	3	10
		% within Need Health Care	0.0%	0.0%	20.0%	50.0%	30.0%	100.0%
		% within Income	0.0%	0.0%	16.7%	55.6%	30.0%	20.0%
		% of Total	0.0%	0.0%	4.0%	10.0%	6.0%	20.0%
	High Need	Count	0	0	1	2	7	10
		% within Need Health Care	0.0%	0.0%	10.0%	20.0%	70.0%	100.0%
		% within Income	0.0%	0.0%	8.3%	22.2%	70.0%	20.0%
		% of Total	0.0%	0.0%	2.0%	4.0%	14.0%	20.0%
Total		Count	9	10	12	9	10	50
		% within Need Health Care	18.0%	20.0%	24.0%	18.0%	20.0%	100.0%
		% within Income	100.0%	100.0%	100.0%	100.0%	100.0%	100.0%
		% of Total	18.0%	20.0%	24.0%	18.0%	20.0%	100.0%

Symmetric Measures

		Value	Asymptotic Standard Error[a]	Approximate T[b]	Approximate Significance
Ordinal by Ordinal	Gamma	.886	.044	15.462	.000
N of Valid Cases		50			

a. Not assuming the null hypothesis.
b. Using the asymptotic standard error assuming the null hypothesis.

The results could be written as follows:

A Gamma statistic was calculated to investigate the relationship between health care need and income. Those with incomes above $40,000, 60%, had no health care needs while 70% of those with incomes below $10,000 had high health care needs. Results indicate that there is a significant strong positive correlation between health care needs and amount of income (Gamma = .886, *p* = .001.

Practical Implications: This study needs to be replicated in many different areas with different cost of living to determine what the level of income might be in relationship to health care needs. What specific health care needs are met for those with high incomes and what ones are not met with those with low incomes? What is the relationship between health care needs and access to health care for these different incomes groups? What does this finding indicate for social work practice with different income groups and what should social workers be aware of when working with different income groups with respect to health care?

Kendall tau c—Correlation to a Criterion

See Chart—Measures of Association/Correlation and Ordinal Measurement

The Kendall tau correlation is a method to determine the correlation between a group of rankings and a criterion. A criterion ranking is a previously established external ranking that a researcher can use to compare the ranking obtained in their research to an established criterion. This following is a situation where this type of analysis would be applicable. You are training new social workers in an agency that provides services to families. The training is aimed at teaching social workers new to the agency to recognize the severity of the problems in families that come for services. The agency has made training videos of families that depict different levels of severity that have been ranked on the level of severity by experts. After the training in recognizing severity of problems in families, these videos are shown to the social work trainees and they are to rank the families in terms of severity of their problems. There are 5 videos that have been previously ranked by the experts and assigned a rank from 1 to 5. Thus, each video has been assigned a rank by the experts, for example video of

Family (A) is ranked as the most severe and receives a ranking of 1 while the video of Family (B) is rated as the least severe and receives a ranking of 5. The other 3 Families are also ranked so that each of the 5 Families has a numerical ranking between **1 and 5 with no ties**. Now you have the criterion rankings by expert family social workers and you want to see if the trainees rank the families in the same order as the experts. If the training has been successful, then the correlation between the rankings of the trainees and the experts will be high.

The formula for the Kendall tau c is shown below. It calculates a value representing the excess of concordant over discordant pairs, multiplied by a term representing an adjustment for size.

$$Tau\ C = (\mathrm{C} - \mathrm{D})\left[\frac{2\mathrm{m}}{\mathrm{n}^2(\mathrm{m}-1)}\right]$$

C = concordant pairs
D = discordant pairs
m = the number of rows or columns, **whichever is smaller**
n = the sample size

Let's continue using the example above. We are interested to see how positive the training was in assisting them to determine the severity of family problems. We will test the outcome of the training by comparing their ability to assess families compared to experts. If there is a high degree of agreement (correlation), then the training was a success. The trainees were asked to rate the 5 families on a 1–5 Likert scale with no ties allowed (could not rate any family the same as another family) on the rating of the amount of severity of family problems.

Study Question: What is the relationship between the rating of severity of family problems as depicted in the videos by social work trainees compared to the rating of experts?

This is a relationship, cross-sectional, correlation to a criterion design.

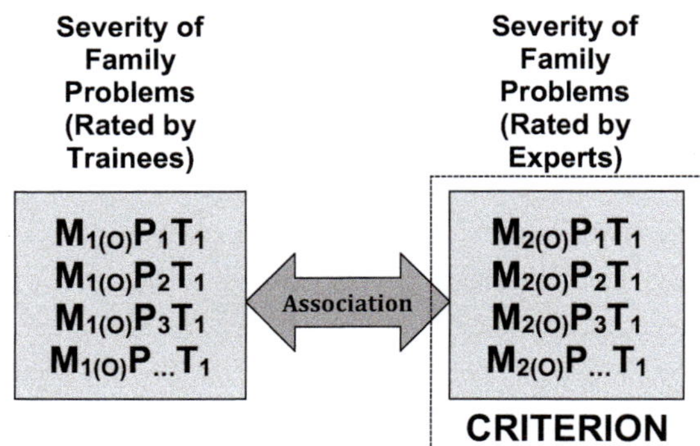

Hypothesis:

Relationship: There is a relationship between the rating of trainees and the rating of experts on the severity of family problems in the videos.
Null: There is no relationship between the ratings of trainees and the rating of experts on the severity of family problems in the videos.
Expected (E): There will be no relationship between the ratings of trainees and the ratings of experts on the severity of family problems in the videos.
Predicted (P): There will be a relationship between the ratings of trainees and the ratings of experts on the severity of family problems in the videos.
Observed (O): The actual relationship between the ratings of trainees and the ratings of experts on the severity of family problems in the videos.
Level of Measurement: Ordinal (trainees rating), Ordinal (criterion rating by experts)
Type of Design: Relationship, cross-sectional
Number of Groups: 2 Groups (samples)
Assumptions: (a) Ordinal level data (b) One of the two samples sample is the criterion

VARIABLE BOX—KENDALL TAU C

	Severity of Family Problems	*Severity of Family Problems*
Trainee 1	1–5 ranking as determined by student trainee	1–5 ranking as determined by expert (criterion)
Trainee 2	1–5 ranking as determined by student trainee	1–5 ranking as determined by expert (criterion)
Trainee . . .	1–5 ranking as determined by student trainee	1–5 ranking as determined by expert (criterion)

SPSS Commands

Open the data set ***Ch20 Kendall Tau C***.
Follow the steps below:

(1) Click ***Analyze***.
(2) Scroll down and select ***Descriptive Statistics***.
(3) Select ***Crosstabs . . .***
(4) Move the variable ***TrainRate*** into the ***Row(s)*** box.
(5) Move the variable ***ExpRate*** into the ***Column(s)*** box.
(6) Click the ***Statistics . . .*** button,
(7) Select ***Kendall's tau-c*** in the ***Ordinal*** box; click ***Continue***.
(8) Click ***OK*** to run the analysis.

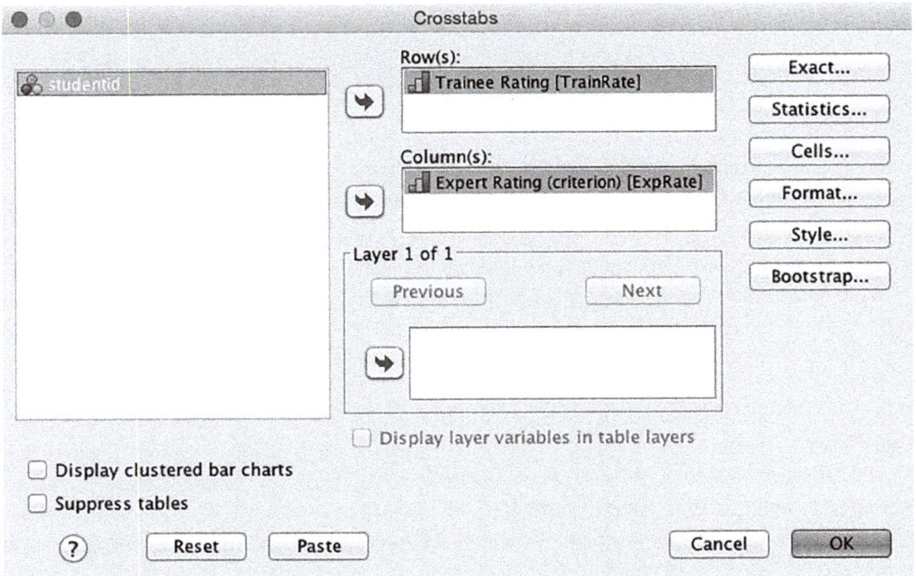

Look at the output:

Trainee Rating * Expert Rating (Criterion) Crosstabulation

Count

		Expert Rating (criterion)					Total
		Most Severe	Mod Severe	Average	Less Severe	No Problems	
Trainee Rating	Most Severe	3	1	0	1	0	5
	Mod Severe	2	1	1	1	0	5
	Average	0	0	3	1	1	5
	Less Severe	0	2	1	1	1	5
	No Problems	0	1	0	1	3	5
Total		5	5	5	5	5	25

Symmetric Measures

		Value	Asymptotic Standard Error[a]	Approximate T[b]	Approximate Significance
Ordinal by Ordinal	Kendall's tau-c	.476	.141	3.382	.001
N of Valid Cases		25			

a. Not assuming the null hypothesis.

b. Using the asymptotic standard error assuming the null hypothesis.

There is a relationship between the rankings of the trainees and the rankings of the experts (criterion). In the crosstabs table, at both ends of the ratings (most severe and no problems) there was greater agreement between the trainees and the experts (criterion) than in the middle of the scale. For the family that was rated most severe by the experts, 3 of the trainees rated it most severe and 2 as moderately severe with no ratings lower. For the family that was rated with no problems by the experts, 3 of the trainees rated the family as having no problems, 1 with less problems and 1 with average problems. Thus, the trainees were able to pick out the families with the most severe problems and those with the least severe problems.

The results might be written as follows:

A Kendall tau c correlation was calculated to investigate the relationship between the ranking of severity of family problems by expert social workers (criterion) and social workers who have just completed training to recognize family problems. The results indicate that there is a moderate and significant correlation between rankings by the trainees and the experts (Kendall tau c = .476, $p = .001$).

Practical Implications: Since the trainees most frequently matched the experts on the most and least severe ratings the prior education/training appears to be successful. However, there are problems with the trainees successfully identifying those families in the middle range. It would seem that future training needs to include more emphasis and time spent on identifying those families that are in the middle range.

Kendall W Coefficient of Concordance

See Chart—Measures of Association/Correlation and Ordinal Measurement

The type of design where the Kendall W is the appropriate test to use is a study where each individual provides a rating on a set of different variables. The purpose of the research would be to determine if there is consistency in the rankings of the variables across all individuals and if there is a difference in the mean ratings of the variables. Remember in this test the same person rates all variables, thus it is a related measures design. The Kendall's W ranges from 0 (no agreement) to 1 (compete agreement). In effect, it is a test of inter-rater reliability for data that is ordinal.

Let's look at an example. We have randomly sampled 22 people and asked each of them to rate on a scale from 1 to 8 what is an important condition (these conditions are pre-selected by the researcher) about a place to live. Each condition is different and related to what is important about a place to live. These ratings were forced in that a **person had to assign only one rank to each variable and could not use that rank again. Thus, on the 8 conditions (people, housing, recreation, taxes, arts, cost of living, climate, transportation) the person had to choose which was number 1**

(most favorable), number 2 and so on until they got to the least favorable, number 8, with no ties and no omissions.

In the example above, we have the condition (i) and the rater (*j*). We have a total of *n* conditions (in our example $n = 8$) and we have a total of m raters (in our example 22). Therefore, the total rank is:

$$R_i = \sum_{j=1}^{m} r_{ij}$$

The mean value of the total ranks is: $\bar{R} = \frac{1}{2} m(n+1)$

The sum of squared deviations, *S*, is: $S = \sum_{i=1}^{n} \left(R_i - \bar{R}\right)^2$

Kendall's W statistic is: $W = \frac{12S}{m^2\left(n^3 - n\right)}$

Study Question: What is the agreement among respondents concerning the importance of various conditions about a place to live?

This is a relationship, cross-sectional, repeated measures design.

Condition 1: People	Condition 2: Climate	Condition 3: Arts	Condition 4: Recreation	Condition 5: Housing	Condition ...: ...
$M_{1(O)}P_1T_1$	$M_{2(O)}P_1T_1$	$M_{3(O)}P_1T_1$	$M_{4(O)}P_1T_1$	$M_{5(O)}P_1T_1$	$M_{...(O)}P_1T_1$
$M_{1(O)}P_2T_1$	$M_{2(O)}P_2T_1$	$M_{3(O)}P_2T_1$	$M_{4(O)}P_2T_1$	$M_{5(O)}P_2T_1$	$M_{...(O)}P_2T_1$
$M_{1(O)}P_{...}T_1$	$M_{2(O)}P_{...}T_1$	$M_{3(O)}P_{...}T_1$	$M_{4(O)}P_{...}T_1$	$M_{5(O)}P_{...}T_1$	$M_{...(O)}P_{...}T_1$

Degree of agreement among all raters

Hypothesis:

Relationship: There is agreement among the raters concerning what condition is important about a place to live.

Null: There is no agreement among the raters concerning what condition is important about a place to live.

Expected (E): There will be no agreement among the raters concerning what condition is important about a place to live.

Predicted (P): There will be agreement among the raters concerning what condition is important about a place to live.

Observed (O): The actual agreement among the raters concerning what condition is important about a place to live.
Level of Measurement: Ordinal (ratings)
Type of Design: Relationship, cross-sectional, repeated individual

VARIABLE BOX—KENDALL W

	Condition 1	Condition 2	Condition 3	Condition 4	Condition 5	Condition 6	Condition 7	Condition 8
Rater 1	Ranking 1–8	Ranking 1–8	Ranking 1–8	Ranking 1–8	Ranking 1–8	Ranking 1–8	Ranking 1–8	Ranking 1–8
Rater 2	Ranking 1–8	Ranking 1–8	Ranking 1–8	Ranking 1–8	Ranking 1–8	Ranking 1–8	Ranking 1–8	Ranking 1–8
Rater. . .	Ranking 1–8	Ranking 1–8	Ranking 1–8	Ranking 1–8	Ranking 1–8	Ranking 1–8	Ranking 1–8	Ranking 1–8

Number of Samples: 8 Groups (samples)
Assumptions: (a) Ordinal level data, (b) Related samples, (c) Forced rankings.

SPSS COMMANDS

Open the data set ***Chapter 20 Kendall W***.
Follow the steps below:

(1) Go to ***Analyze***.
(2) Scroll to ***Nonparametric Tests***.
(3) Select ***Legacy Dialogs***.
(4) Select ***K Related Samples . . .***
(5) Move all of the variables with the exception of ***Rater*** into the ***Test Variables*** box.
(6) Under ***Test Type***, select ***Kendall's W*** only.

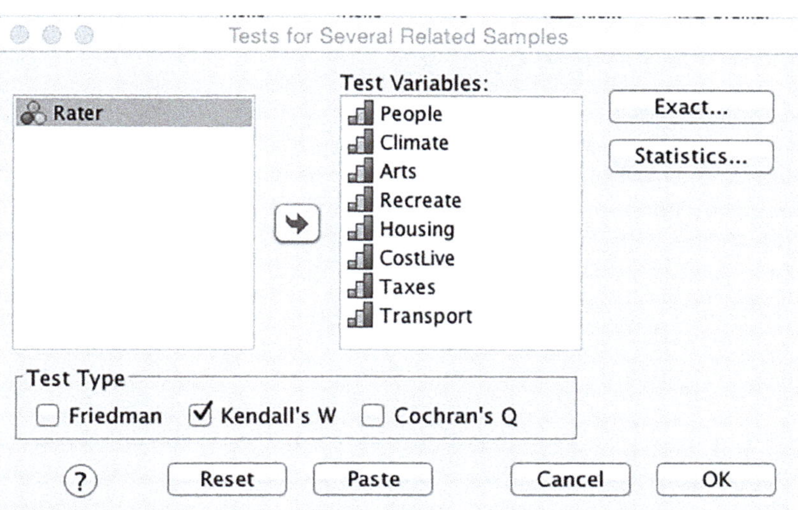

(7) Click ***OK*** to run the analysis.

Let's look at the output:

Ranks

	Mean Rank
People	1.58
Climate	6.53
Arts	4.27
Recreate	3.75
Housing	2.88
CostLive	5.27
Taxes	3.90
Transport	7.82

Test Statistics

N	30
Kendall's W[a]	.673
Chi-Square	141.230
df	7
Asymp. Sig.	.000

a. Kendall's Coefficient of Concordance

We see that "people" are the most important aspect about a place to live and "transportation" is the least important. Overall agreement among raters was 67% (rounded).

The results might be written as follows:

A Kendall's W (coefficient of concordance) was calculated to assess the agreement between raters concerning what is the most important condition about a place to live. From the results, it is clear that among all raters, people are evaluated as the most important (mean rank = 1.58), followed by housing (mean rank = 2.88). The least important condition about a place to live is transportation (mean rank = 7.82). The agreement between raters is 67% (Kendall's $W = 0.67$, $p = 0.001$), indicating a high level of agreement.

Practical Implications: It is important to be concerned with community planning. Therefore, the results of this study could become part of a message about what is important to the people in the community. This would be especially critical during interactions with leaders in the community who have ability to influence policy. From these results, it is clear that in terms of infrastructure housing is the most important issue facing your community and one that should gain major attention. With respect to continued research, additional studies can be conducted to determine what types of housing are important and in what areas of the city.

PART B: PARAMETRIC

Interval/Ratio Level Data

Pearson R

See Chart—Measures of Association/Correlation and Interval or Ratio Measurement

The Pearson correlation coefficient measures the relationship/association between two interval or ratio level variables. The correlation can range between −1 and +1. A positive correlation occurs when the values increase on one variable and also increase on the other variable. A negative value occurs when the values on one variable increase and the values on the other variable decrease. The Pearson r is calculated by using the covariance of the two variables as the numerator and the product of their standard deviations as the denominator using the following formula:

$$r = \frac{\sum_{i=1}^{n}(X_i - \bar{X})(Y_i - \bar{Y})}{\sqrt{\sum_{i=1}^{n}(X_i - \bar{X})^2}\sqrt{\sum_{i=1}^{n}(Y_i - \bar{Y})^2}}$$

To interpret the strength of the relationship, use the following table:

COEFFICIENT VALUE	STRENGTH
0 to .01 or −.01	**VERY WEAK**
.01 to .03 or −.01 to −.03	**WEAK**
.03 to .05 or −.03 to −.05	**MODERATE**
V	**STRONG**

We are interested in children in the welfare system. Specifically, we want to know if there is a relationship between the Global Assessment of Function (GAF) and the amount of trauma a child has experienced as measured by the Traumatic Events Screening Inventory (TESI).

Study Question: What is the relationship between the GAF scores of children in the child welfare system and their TESI?

This is a relationship, cross-sectional, repeated measures design.

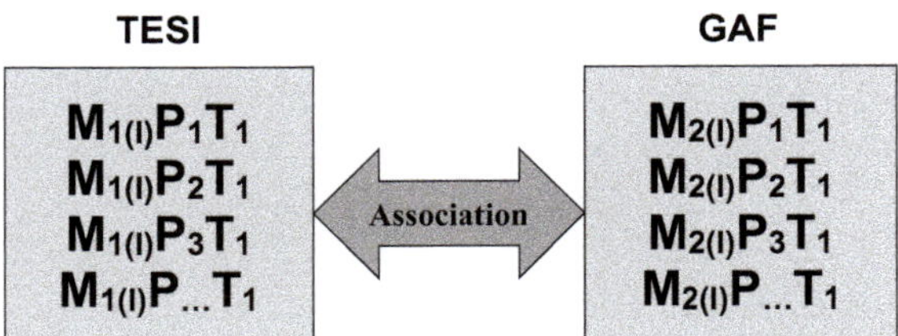

Hypotheses:

Relationship: There is a relationship between the GAF scores of children in the child welfare system and their TESI.

Null: There is no relationship between the GAF scores of children in the child welfare system and their TESI.

Expected (E): There will be no relationship between the GAF scores of children in the child welfare system and their TESI.

Predicted (P): There will be a relationship between the GAF scores of children in the child welfare system and their TESI.

Observed (O): The actual relationship between the GAF scores of children in the child welfare system and their TESI.

Level of Measurement: GAF Interval, TESI Interval

Type of Design: Relationship, cross-sectional

VARIABLE BOX—PEARSON R

	GAF	TESI
Child 1	GAF score	TESI score
Child 2	GAF score	TESI score
Child. . .	GAF score	TESI score

Number of Groups: 2 Groups (samples)

Assumptions: (a) Interval level data, (b) Normal distribution.

SPSS Commands

Open the data set ***Ch20 Pearson***.

Follow the steps below:

(1) Click ***Analyze***.

(2) Scroll down to ***Correlate***.

(3) Select ***Bivariate . . .***
(4) Move the variables ***GAF*** and ***TESI*** into the ***Variables*** box.
(5) Under ***Correlation Coefficients***, ensure that ***Pearson*** is checked.

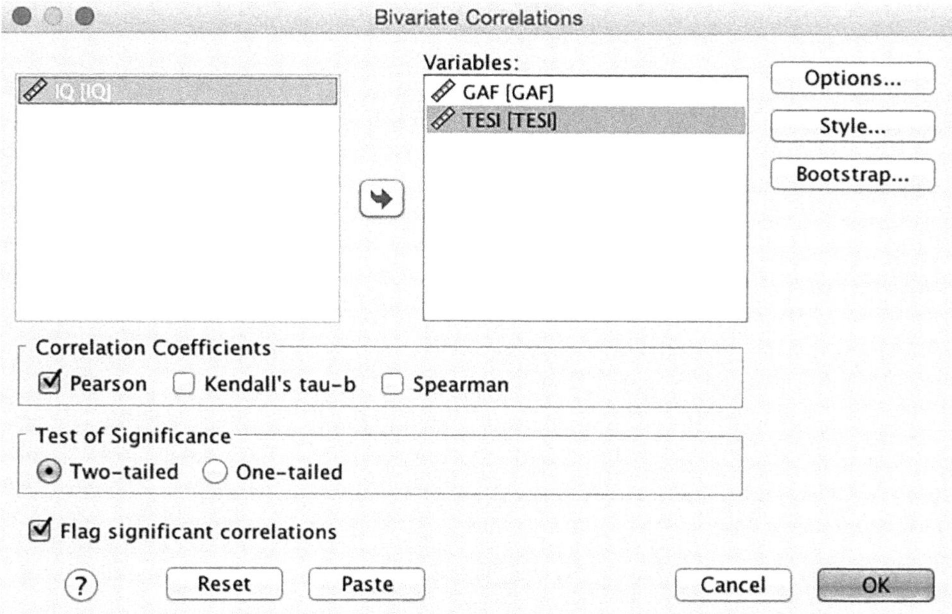

(6) Click ***OK*** to run the analysis.

Let's look at the results:

Correlations

		GAF	**TESI**
GAF	Pearson Correlation	1	−.604**
	Sig. (2-tailed)		.000
	N	500	500
TESI	Pearson Correlation	−.604**	1
	Sig. (2-tailed)	.000	
	N	500	500

**. Correlation is significant at the 0.01 level (2-tailed).

The results show that the relationship between GAF and TESI is negative, strong and significant. Thus, with a greater amount of trauma the child's level of functioning is lower and, conversely, the less trauma the higher the level of functioning.

The results might be written as follows:

A Pearson *r* coefficient was calculated to determine the relationship between the GAF scores of children in the child welfare system and their trauma as measured by the Traumatic Events Screening Inventory. The results indicate that there is a significant strong negative correlation between GAF and trauma ($r = -.604$, $p = .001$).

Practical Implications: It is very important for social workers to be aware of trauma in children in all areas of social work practice. These results clearly point to the very powerful negative effect of trauma on all aspects of a child's life. Determining if there is trauma in the child's history, the extent of this trauma and the reaction of the child to this trauma are very important in their development. Further research could be conducted to determine what types of trauma are more closely associated with certain areas of functioning. Also determining the effects of varying amounts of trauma and its impact on functioning are areas of import to social work.

Pearson Partial Correlation Coefficient

See Chart—Measures of Association/Correlation and Interval or Ratio Measurement

The Pearson partial r coefficient is similar to the Pearson r coefficient, but it allows for **more than two variables** to be tested as we have already seen for ordinal level data with the Kendall Tau B Partial. Therefore, the researcher is able to control or mathematically take out the amount of variance contributed by a covariate in order to ascertain more specifically the correlation or variance contributed by only one variable (the variable of the most interest). This time, however, in contrast to the Kendall Tau B Partial, the calculation can be done using SPSS.

Let's look at the previous example. We are still interested in how GAF scores are correlated with the TESI scores for children in the welfare system. We also know that IQ contributes to the score on the GAF. We want to control for the effect of IQ on the GAF so that we can determine more precisely the effect of trauma on the GAF.

Study Question: What is the relationship between the GAF scores of children in the child welfare system and their TESI after controlling for IQ?

This is a relationship, cross-sectional, repeated measures design.

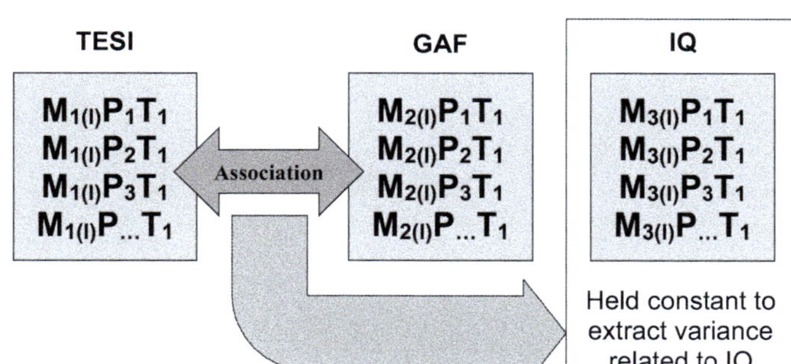

Hypotheses:

Relationship: There is a relationship between the GAF scores of children in the child welfare system and their TESI, controlling for IQ.

Null: There is no relationship between the GAF scores of children in the child welfare system and their TESI, controlling for IQ.

Expected (E): There will be no relationship between the GAF scores of children in the child welfare system and their TESI, controlling for IQ.

Predicted (E): There will be a relationship between the GAF scores of children in the child welfare system and their TESI, controlling for IQ.

Observed (O): The actual relationship between the GAF scores of children in the child welfare system and their TESI, controlling for IQ.

Level of Measurement: GAF Interval, TESI Interval IQ Interval

Type of Design: Relationship, cross-sectional

Number of Groups: 3 Groups (samples)

Assumptions: (a) Interval/ratio level data, (b) Normal distribution.

VARIABLE BOX—PEARSON PARTIAL CORRELATION

	GAF	TESI
Child 1	GAF score	TESI score
Child 2	GAF score	TESI score
Child. . .	GAF score	TESI score

SPSS Commands

Open the data set ***Ch20 Pearson***.
Follow the steps below:

(1) Click ***Analyze***.
(2) Scroll down to ***Correlate***.

(3) Select ***Partial...***
(4) Move the variables ***GAF*** and ***TESI*** into the ***Variables*** box.
(5) Move the variable ***IQ*** into the ***Controlling for*** box.

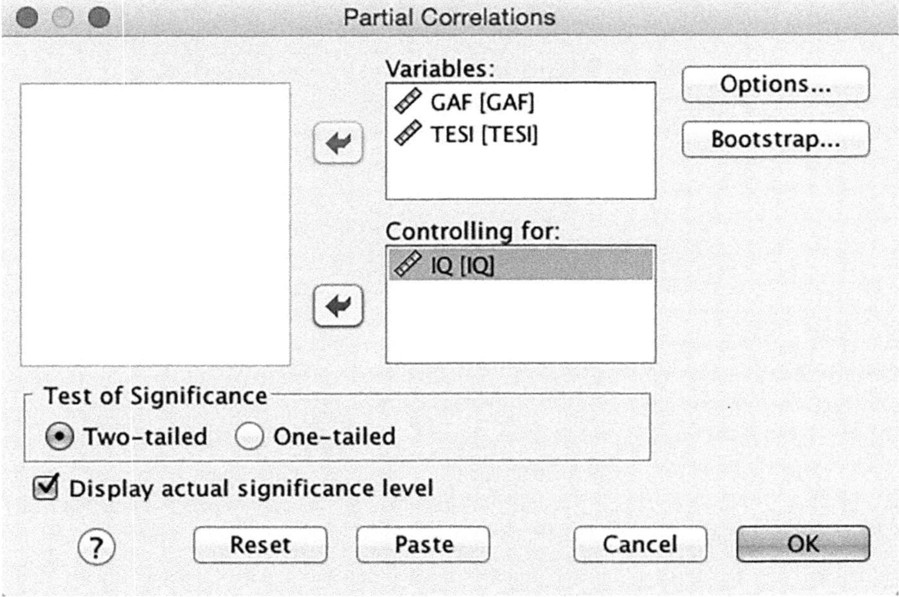

(6) Click ***OK*** to run the analysis.

Let's look at the output:

Correlations

Control Variables			GAF	TESI
IQ	GAF	Correlation	1.000	–.597
		Significance (2-tailed)	.	.000
		Df	0	497
	TESI	Correlation	–.597	1.000
		Significance (2-tailed)	.000	.
		Df	497	0

The results show that the relationship between GAF and TESI remains strong and negative, even after controlling for IQ.

The results might be written as follows.

A Pearson partial r coefficient was calculated to determine the relationship between the functioning of children in the child welfare system as measured by the GAF and the amount of trauma as Measured by the Traumatic Event Survey Inventory (TESI), controlling for IQ. The results indicate that there is a significant strong negative correlation between functioning and trauma, after controlling for IQ ($r_{(47)} = -0.597, p = .001$).

Practical Implications: Remember that in the previous example the correlation between trauma and the GAF as .604. Now after controlling for IQ, the correlation was basically not reduced at all (only reduced to .597) indicating that the relationship between trauma and the GAF is very strong. Trauma is highly related to functioning and IQ does not have any import on this relationship. For social workers, it means that irrespective of IQ in our clients, trauma plays a highly significant role in their functioning. Further research should be aimed at identifying variables and taking out their effect on functioning (reducing error) in order to determine each variable's effect on overall functioning. In practice, we as social workers should place more emphasis on the role of trauma and other potential factors on functioning and not use intelligence as a sole predictor of functioning. This result clearly points to the effect of the environment on the functioning of a child.

Articles for Discussion

Critique the author's use of the Spearman rho in the study. Discuss reason why it was used and if there was another way to design and conduct the study.

Ruscingo, G., Zipp, G., & Olsen, V. (2010). Admission variables and academic success in the first year of the professional phase in a doctor of physical therapy program. *Journal of AlliedHealth, 39*(3), 138–142. Retrieved from www.ncbi.nlm.nih.gov/pubmed/21174017

Exercises for Chapter 20 are found in eResources.

Chapter 21

FINDING RELATIONSHIPS—MAKING PREDICTIONS

PART A: NONPARAMETRIC

Lambda

See Chart—Prediction and Nominal Measurement

The Lambda statistic is an appropriate predictor statistic for nominal level variables. Specifically, it measures the percent of improvement when a ***predictor variable*** is used to estimate the value of a ***predicted variable*** compared to the estimate that would occur by chance. The key difference between Lambda and Cramer's V is there is an ***antecedent*** **(predictor)** and ***consequent*** **(predicted)** variable based upon a chronological relationship between the variables—***one variable comes before the other variable in time***. Lambda is an asymmetrical statistic in that one variable (A) comes before the other variable (B) and prediction only occurs in one direction A→B (asymmetrical) and not in both directions (symmetrical). The Lambda statistic will tell you ***how well you can predict B from A when you use the value of A to predict the value of B***. The value of Lambda can **range from 0 to 1**. In essence the statistic is a measure of the relative ***reduction in prediction error*** of one variable when you know the value of the other variable.

The following formula is used to calculate Lambda:

When the ***predicted variable*** is in the row:

$$\lambda a = \frac{\sum_{i} \max\left(O_{ij}\right) - \max\left(R_{i}\right)}{N - \max\left(R_{i}\right)}$$

When the ***predicted variable*** is in the column:

$$\lambda b = \frac{\sum_{j} \max\left(O_{ij}\right) - \max\left(C_{j}\right)}{N - \max\left(C_{j}\right)}$$

Let's explore a conceptual example. Remember Lambda is a statistic that shows the ***amount of error reduced*** in the ***predicted/consequent*** variable if you know the ***predictor/antecedent condition*** in an ***r* × *k table***. The table below has some hypothetical data showing the relationship between variable **A *predictor*/antecedent** and variable **B *predicted/consequent***.

	A1	A2	A3	Total
B1	***21***	7	6	34
B2	10	10	6	26
B3	6	***24***	9	***39***
B4	5	5	***17***	27
TOTAL	**42**	**46**	**38**	**126**

The table above looks like data that would be very appropriate for a Cramer's V test and it certainly is. As shown in Chapter 20, ***Cramer's V is a measure of association between two variables in an r by k table***. Therefore, the Cramer's V is the ***overall* calculation of the association** between variables but it does not provide any prediction value. The output of the Cramer's V for the data is provided below. You can see the amount of association between the variables.

Symmetric Measures

		Value	Approx. Sig.
Nominal by Nominal	Phi	.549	.000
	Cramer's V	**.388**	.000
N of Valid Cases		126	

The amount of association between the two variables (Cramer V) is .39 (rounded) indicating a high moderate correlation. This is only the **overall association** between A and B and **does not provide a prediction**. In some of the studies that have nominal variables, one variable may precede another variable. In these cases, you may want to determine how well you can predict the second variable (error reduction) using the first variable. This type of design is one where there is chronological order of the two nominal variables and the reduction in error of prediction can be calculated using Lambda.

Again we will provide a math solution followed by a conceptual frame and finally calculate Lambda using SPSS.

$$\textbf{Lambda} = \frac{\sum_{j=i}^{k} nmj - \max(Ri)}{N - Max(Ri)}$$

N = the total number on the sample

$\sum_{j=i}^{k} nmj$ = the sum of the highest frequency in Column 1 (**21**) + the highest frequency in Column 2 (**24**) + the highest frequency in Column 3 (**17**) for a total of **62**
Max (Ri) is the largest row total = **39**

Thus $\textbf{Lambda} = \frac{62-39}{126-39} = .26$

Now let's move to the conceptual model. Using the data in the table above, assume that you are trying to predict the value of B but did not have an **antecedent** predictor condition of A. Then you would have to choose between B1, B2, B3, B4 equally. That means with 4 rows your chance of making a correct selection is .25 (25%) and 25% of the total 126 would result in 31.5 correct guesses by chance alone. But what if you could use A as a predictor? Then from the choices of B conditions in the A1 Column you should pick B1 as the best guess for B to maximize the number of correct selections and not B2, 3 or 4. Knowing the value A1 then picking B1 you would be correct 21/42 or 50% of the time. Knowing the value of A2, then you should pick B3 and you would be correct 24/46 or 52% and if you know A3, then you should pick B4 and you would be correct 17/38 or 45%.

Let's look at another example. We want to see if we can improve the prediction of what type of social work job is selected by graduates of social work programs from 3 different universities—a state university, a regional university and a city university. The types of jobs were categorized into 4 areas: 1) child welfare, 2) mental health, 3) health and 4) school.

Study Question: If we know what university the social worker graduated from can we predict the type of job they select?

This is a prediction design.

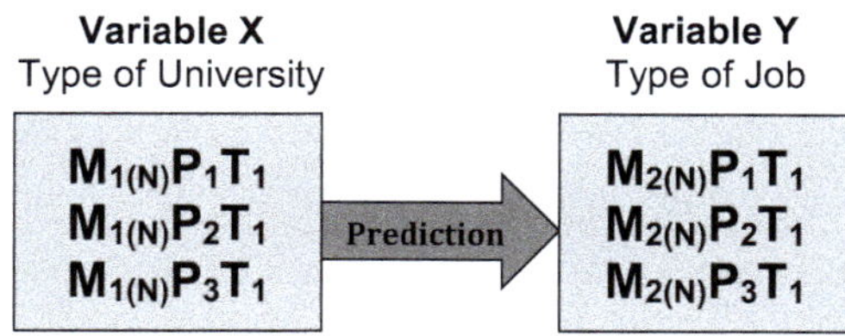

Hypotheses:

Prediction: The prediction of job type will improve if the university the social worker graduated from is known.

Null: The prediction of job type will not improve if the university the social worker graduated from is known.

Expected (E): No improvement in prediction.

Predicted (P): Improvement in prediction.

Observed (O): Actual improvement in predictability.

Level of Measurement: University (Nominal Predictor), Job Type (Nominal Predicted)

Type of Design: Prediction

Number of Groups: 3 Groups (samples)

Assumptions: (a) No more than 20% expected frequencies less than 5, (b) No single expected frequency less than 1 (c) One variable is the antecedent and the other variable is the consequent variable

VARIABLE BOX—LAMBDA

UNIVERSITY (A)

		Regional University (A1)	***State University*** (A2)	***City University*** (A3)
JOB TYPE (B)	***Child Welfare*** (B1)	A1 B1	A2 B1	A3 B1
	Mental Health (B2)	A1 B2	A2 B2	A3 B2
	Health (B3)	A1 B3	A2 B3	A3 B3
	School (B1)	A1 B4	A2 B4	A3 B4

SPSS Commands

Open the data set ***Ch21 Lambda***.
Follow the steps below.

(1) Click ***Analyze***.
(2) Scroll down and select ***Descriptive Statistics***.
(3) Select ***Crosstabs . . .***
(4) Move ***Job Type*** into the ***Row(s)*** box; move ***University*** into the ***Column(s)*** box.

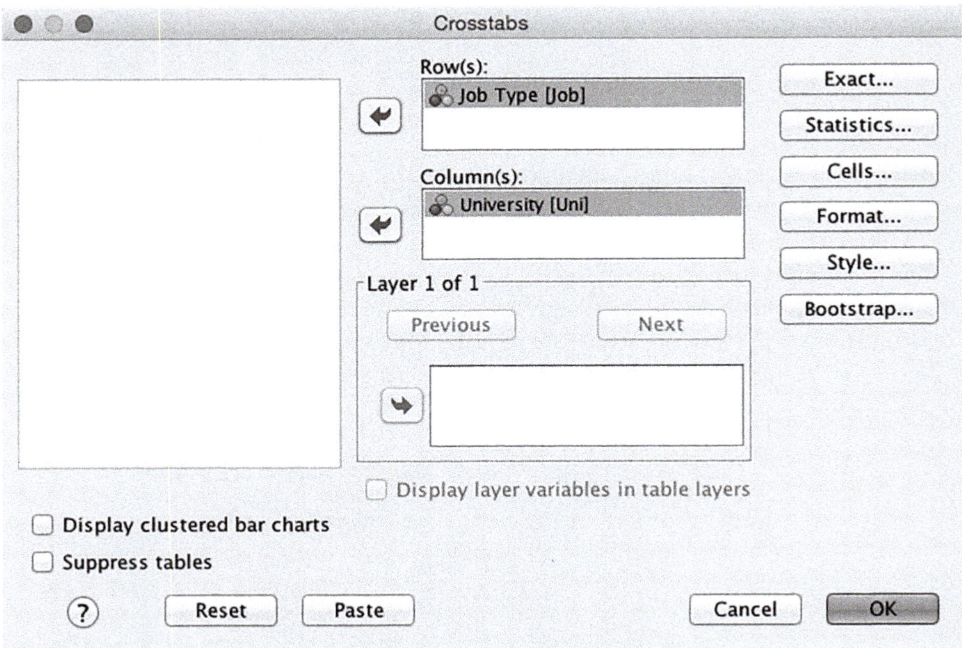

(5) Click the ***Statistics . . .*** button.
(6) Check the box next to ***Chi-square***.
(7) Under the ***Nominal*** heading, check the box next to ***Lambda***; click ***Continue***.
(8) Click the ***Cells . . .*** button.
(9) Under ***Counts***, select ***Observed*** and ***Expected***; under ***Percentages***, select ***Row***, ***Column*** and ***Total***.
(10) Click ***OK*** to run the analysis.

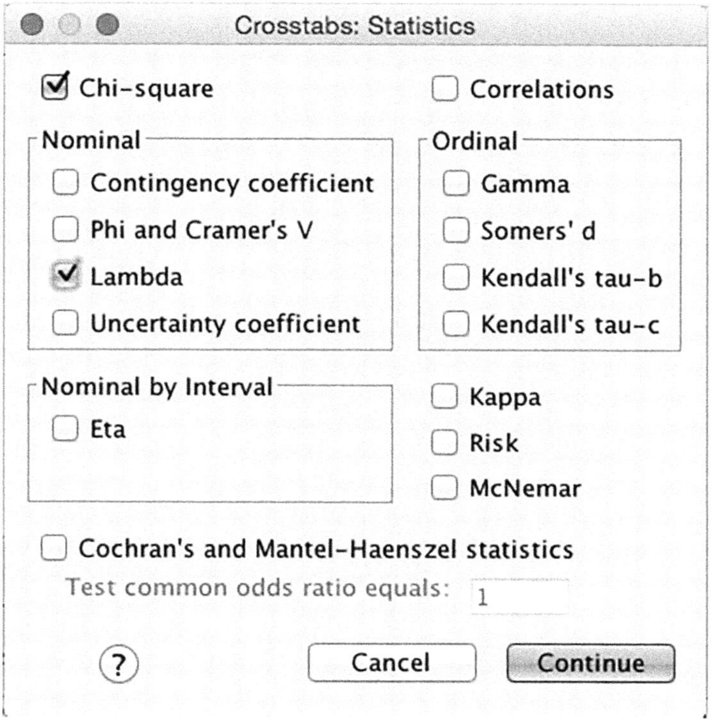

Crosstabs: Statistics

☑ Chi-square ☐ Correlations

Nominal
☐ Contingency coefficient
☐ Phi and Cramer's V
☑ Lambda
☐ Uncertainty coefficient

Ordinal
☐ Gamma
☐ Somers' d
☐ Kendall's tau-b
☐ Kendall's tau-c

Nominal by Interval
☐ Eta

☐ Kappa
☐ Risk
☐ McNemar

☐ Cochran's and Mantel-Haenszel statistics
Test common odds ratio equals: 1

? Cancel Continue

Job Type * University Crosstabulation

			University			Total
			Regional	State	City	
Job Type	Child Welfare	Count	21	7	6	34
		Expected Count	11.3	12.4	10.3	34.0
		% within Job Type	61.8%	20.6%	17.6%	100.0%
		% within University	50.0%	15.2%	15.8%	27.0%
		% of Total	16.7%	5.6%	4.8%	27.0%
	Mental Health	Count	10	10	6	26
		Expected Count	8.7	9.5	7.8	26.0
		% within Job Type	38.5%	38.5%	23.1%	100.0%
		% within University	23.8%	21.7%	15.8%	20.6%
		% of Total	7.9%	7.9%	4.8%	20.6%
	Health	Count	6	24	9	39
		Expected Count	13.0	14.2	11.8	39.0

(Continued)

Job Type * University Crosstabulation

			University			Total
			Regional	State	City	
		% within Job Type	15.4%	61.5%	23.1%	100.0%
		% within University	14.3%	52.2%	23.7%	31.0%
		% of Total	4.8%	19.0%	7.1%	31.0%
	School	Count	5	5	17	27
		Expected Count	9.0	9.9	8.1	27.0
		% within Job Type	18.5%	18.5%	63.0%	100.0%
		% within University	11.9%	10.9%	44.7%	21.4%
		% of Total	4.0%	4.0%	13.5%	21.4%
Total		Count	42	46	38	126
		Expected Count	42.0	46.0	38.0	126.0
		% within Job Type	33.3%	36.5%	30.2%	100.0%
		% within University	100.0%	100.0%	100.0%	100.0%
		% of Total	33.3%	36.5%	30.2%	100.0%

Chi-Square Tests

	Value	Df	Asymptotic Significance (2-sided)
Pearson Chi-Square	37.951[a]	6	.000
Likelihood Ratio	35.475	6	.000
Linear-by-Linear Association	19.641	1	.000
N of Valid Cases	126		

a. 0 cells (0.0%) have expected count less than 5. The minimum expected count is 7.84.

Directional Measures

			Value	Asymptotic Standard Error[a]	Approximate T[b]	Approximate Significance
Nominal by Nominal	Lambda	Symmetric	.293	.072	3.653	.000
		Job Type Dependent	.264	.072	3.292	.001
		University Dependent	.325	.086	3.234	.001
	Goodman and Kruskal tau	Job Type Dependent	.105	.036		.000[c]
		University Dependent	.151	.050		.000[c]

a. Not assuming the null hypothesis.
b. Using the asymptotic standard error assuming the null hypothesis.
c. Based on Chi-Square approximation.

The same method applied to reporting results from the cells in the cross tables in previous chapters will be used. There is additional output to read in the directional measures table. The value for **Lambda** when **job** is the **dependent predicted variable** is. **264** and significant at **.001**. If the prediction of job type had been based on chance alone, the chance of making the correct prediction would have been 25% (4 categories of job type—the outcome variable), resulting in 75% errors. The value of Lambda indicates there was a .26 (26%) reduction in error.

The results might be written as follows:

Half (50%) of the social workers who graduated from Regional U obtained child welfare jobs with another 24% working in mental health positions. Of those who attended State U 52% went into health jobs and another .22% into mental health jobs. Most City U social work graduates went into school social work positions (45%) with the next highest percent working in health care (24%). The Lambda coefficient indicates that knowing the type of university the student graduated from will reduce the error of prediction in the type of social work job where they are employed by 26% ($\lambda = 0.26, p = .001$).

Practical Implications: Recruiters from agencies providing services can more selectively focus their activities on those universities that are providing social workers who go into their area of service. It would be interesting to determine if there are differences in the curricula of these universities and if those differences are related to the ultimate jobs their graduates select. Is there a relationship between the particular jobs accepted and those available in close proximity geographically to the universities?

Somers' d

See Chart—Prediction and Ordinal Measurement

In the previous chapter, Gamma, a symmetrical test that measures the amount of association between the two variables, was introduced. It is not a prediction statistic whereas ***Somers' d* is the prediction statistic based upon Gamma.** ***Gamma should not be used in a design where there is an antecedent condition (IV) and consequent condition (DV) or when you designate an independent variable and a dependent variable. Somers' d should be used.*** In addition, Gamma is based upon using concordant and discordant pairs and eliminates ties from the calculation as does *Somers' d*. However, *Somers' d* differs from Gamma in that it includes ***ties from rows (Antecedent/IV) but does not include ties from the columns (Consequent/DV)***. The formula is:

$$d_{yx} = \frac{(C - D)}{(C + D + Y_0)}$$

Where C = concordant pairs
D = discordant pairs
Y_0 = pairs tied on Y
Scores can range between −1 and 1.

We want to investigate if there is an increase in income with an increase in years of staying sober. The a priori prediction is: the more years (increase) of sobriety the higher (increase) the income. Based upon practice experience as well as literature there is support for this ordered prediction. The study was based on data already collected from a small sample of individuals attending a program at the local substance abuse agency.

Study Question: Will income increase as years maintaining sobriety increases?

This is a prediction design.

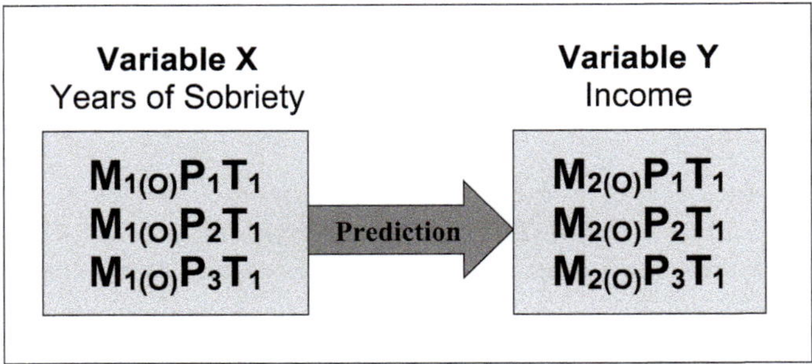

Hypotheses:

Prediction: Income will increase as years maintaining sobriety increases.
Null: Income will not increase as years maintaining sobriety increases.
Expected (E): Income will not increase as years maintaining sobriety increases.
Predicted (P): Income will increase as years maintaining sobriety increases.
Observed (O): The actual values for income and years of sobriety.
Level of Measurement: Predictor Ordinal (Years of sobriety), Predicted Ordinal (Income)
Type of Design: Prediction
Number of Groups: 3 Groups (samples)
Assumptions: (a) Ordinal level of measurement for Predictor variable/IV and ordinal level of measurement for Predicted variable/DV or non-normal ratio predicted variable (b) Relatively equal group sizes (c) Determine a priori the order of the results.

VARIABLE BOX—SOMERS' d

		Years of Sobriety (A)		
		One Year (A1)	***Two Years*** (A2)	***Three Years*** (A3)
JOB TYPE (B)	***Less than $20K*** (B1)	A1 B1	A2 B1	A3 B1
	$20K–$29K (B2)	A1 B2	A2 B2	A3 B2
	$30K–$39K (B3)	A1 B3	A2 B3	A3 B3
	More than $40K (B1)	A1 B4	A2 B4	A3 B4

SPSS Commands

Open the data set ***Ch21 SomersD1***
Follow the steps below:

(1) Click ***Analyze***.
(2) Scroll down and select ***Descriptive Statistics***.
(3) Select ***Crosstabs . . .***
(4) Move ***YearsSob*** into the ***Row(s)*** box; move ***Income*** into the ***Column(s)*** box.

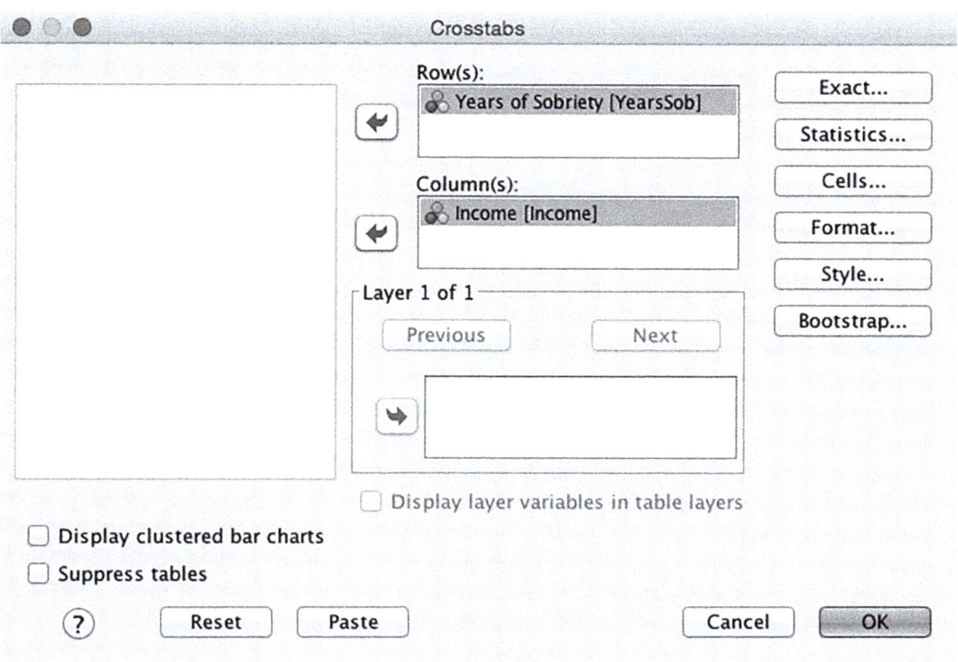

(5) Click the ***Statistics . . .*** button.
(6) Check the box next to ***Chi-square***.
(7) Under the ***Ordinal*** heading, check the box next to ***Somers' d***; click ***Continue***.

Crosstabs: Statistics

- [x] Chi-square
- [ ] Correlations

Nominal
- [ ] Contingency coefficient
- [ ] Phi and Cramer's V
- [ ] Lambda
- [ ] Uncertainty coefficient

Ordinal
- [ ] Gamma
- [x] Somers' d
- [ ] Kendall's tau-b
- [ ] Kendall's tau-c

Nominal by Interval
- [ ] Eta

- [ ] Kappa
- [ ] Risk
- [ ] McNemar

- [ ] Cochran's and Mantel-Haenszel statistics

Test common odds ratio equals: 1

? Cancel Continue

(8) Click the ***Cells . . .*** button.
(9) Under ***Counts***, select ***Observed*** and ***Expected***; under ***Percentages***, select ***Row***, ***Column*** and ***Total***.
(10) Click ***OK*** to run the analysis.

			Income				Total
			Below 20K	20–29K	30–39K	Over 40K	
Years of Sobriety	1 Year	Count	4	2	0	0	6
		Expected Count	1.7	1.7	1.0	1.7	6.0
		% within Years of Sobriety	66.7%	33.3%	0.0%	0.0%	100.0%
		% within Income	80.0%	40.0%	0.0%	0.0%	33.3%
		% of Total	22.2%	11.1%	0.0%	0.0%	33.3%
	2 Years	Count	1	3	1	1	6
		Expected Count	1.7	1.7	1.0	1.7	6.0
		% within Years of Sobriety	16.7%	50.0%	16.7%	16.7%	100.0%
		% within Income	20.0%	60.0%	33.3%	20.0%	33.3%
		% of Total	5.6%	16.7%	5.6%	5.6%	33.3%
	3 Years	Count	0	0	2	4	6
		Expected Count	1.7	1.7	1.0	1.7	6.0
		% within Years of Sobriety	0.0%	0.0%	33.3%	66.7%	100.0%
		% within Income	0.0%	0.0%	66.7%	80.0%	33.3%
		% of Total	0.0%	0.0%	11.1%	22.2%	33.3%
Total		Count	5	5	3	5	18
		Expected Count	5.0	5.0	3.0	5.0	18.0
		% within Years of Sobriety	27.8%	27.8%	16.7%	27.8%	100.0%
		% within Income	100.0%	100.0%	100.0%	100.0%	100.0%
		% of Total	27.8%	27.8%	16.7%	27.8%	100.0%

Chi-Square Tests

	Value	Df	Asymptotic Significance (2-sided)
Pearson Chi-Square	15.200[a]	6	.019
Likelihood Ratio	18.993	6	.004
Linear-by-Linear Association	11.359	1	.001
N of Valid Cases	18		

a. 12 cells (100.0%) have expected count less than 5. The minimum expected count is 1.00.

Directional Measures

			Value	Asymptotic Standard Error[a]	Approximate T[b]	Approximate Significance
Ordinal by Ordinal	*Somers' d*	Symmetric	.737	.085	8.758	.000
		Years of Sobriety Dependent	.700	.082	8.758	.000
		Income Dependent	.778	.089	8.758	.000

a. Not assuming the null hypothesis.
b. Using the asymptotic standard error assuming the null hypothesis.

The tables above clearly show that income increases as the number of years sober increases.

The results might be written as follows:

A *Somers' d* statistic was calculated to investigate if an increase in years sober would predict an increase in income. For those who have been sober only 1 year, 4 out of 6 had incomes below $20,000. For those sober 3 years or more 4 out of 6 had incomes above $40,000. The results indicate that years of sobriety is a strong positive indicator of amount of income (*Somers' d* = .737, *p* = .001).

Practical Implications: These findings would be useful in talking to prospective individuals for treatment to show that if you remain sober your livelihood would become better. It is also something you would use with those who might support a "staying sober" program in that if individuals remain sober they are less likely to need financial assistance in the future. Additionally, with more income they would pay more taxes and improve the financial base of the community and not take resources from it.

Let's look at one more example. You are interested in studying the relationship between the level of education and attitudes toward abortion. You have 5 levels of education on an ordinal scale: (1) Some High School, (2) High School Graduate, (3) Some College, (4) College Graduate, (5) Graduate Degree. You have 5 attitudes toward abortion that are also on an ordinal scale: (1) Very Negative, (2) Negative, (3) No Opinion, (4) Positive, (5) Very positive. The study has two ordinal variables, ***education (antecedent) as the predictor variable (IV)*** and ***attitude toward abortion (consequent) as the predicted (DV) variable.***

Study Question: Does more education predict a more favorable attitude toward abortion?

This is a prediction design.

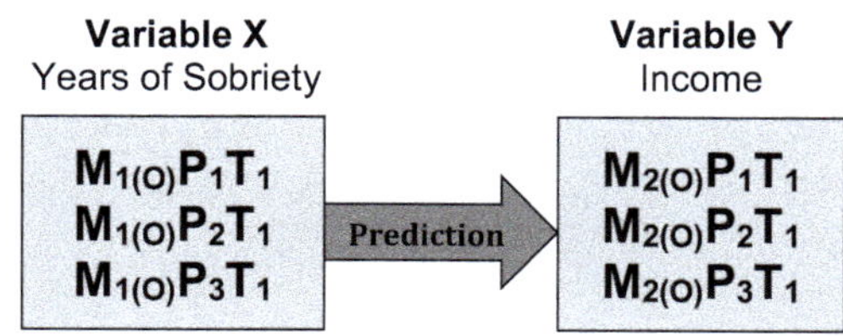

Hypotheses:

Prediction: More education will predict a more favorable attitude toward abortion.
Null: More education will not predict a more favorable attitude toward abortion.
Expected (E): Amount of education will not predict attitude toward abortion.
Predicted (P): More education will predict a more favorable attitude toward abortion.
Observed (O): The actual attitude toward abortion by educational level.
Level of Measurement: Predictor Ordinal (Educational level), Predicted Ordinal (attitude toward abortion)
Type of Design: Prediction
Number of Groups: 5 Groups (samples)
Assumptions: (a) Ordinal level of measurement for both Predictor/IV and Predicted/DV or *non-normal* interval level Predictor/IV and/or Predicted/DV, (b) Relatively equal group sizes, (c) Determine a priori the order of prediction.

SPSS Commands

Open the data set ***Ch21 SomersD2***.
Follow the steps below:

(1) Click ***Analyze***.
(2) Scroll down and select ***Descriptive Statistics***.
(3) Select ***Crosstabs . . .***
(4) Move ***Education*** into the ***Row(s)*** box; move ***Attitude*** into the ***Column(s)*** box.
(5) Click the ***Statistics . . .*** button.
(6) Check the box next to ***Chi-square***.
(7) Under the ***Ordinal*** heading, check the box next to ***Somers' d***; click ***Continue***.
(8) Click the ***Cells . . .*** button.
(9) Under ***Counts***, select ***Observed*** and ***Expected***; under ***Percentages***, select ***Row***, ***Column*** and ***Total***.
(10) Click ***OK*** to run the analysis.

Level of Education * Abortion Attitude Crosstabulation

			Abortion Attitude					Total
			Very Negative	Negative	No Opinion	Positive	Very Positive	
Level of Education	Some High School	Count	7	7	4	2	0	20
		% within Level of Education	35.0%	35.0%	20.0%	10.0%	0.0%	100.0%
		% within Abortion Attitude	87.5%	30.4%	16.0%	6.7%	0.0%	20.0%
		% of Total	7.0%	7.0%	4.0%	2.0%	0.0%	20.0%
	High School Graduate	Count	0	10	7	3	0	20
		% within Level of Education	0.0%	50.0%	35.0%	15.0%	0.0%	100.0%
		% within Abortion Attitude	0.0%	43.5%	28.0%	10.0%	0.0%	20.0%
		% of Total	0.0%	10.0%	7.0%	3.0%	0.0%	20.0%
	Some College	Count	0	2	10	7	1	20
		% within Level of Education	0.0%	10.0%	50.0%	35.0%	5.0%	100.0%
		% within Abortion Attitude	0.0%	8.7%	40.0%	23.3%	7.1%	20.0%
		% of Total	0.0%	2.0%	10.0%	7.0%	1.0%	20.0%
	College Graduate	Count	0	3	3	10	4	20
		% within Level of Education	0.0%	15.0%	15.0%	50.0%	20.0%	100.0%
		% within Abortion Attitude	0.0%	13.0%	12.0%	33.3%	28.6%	20.0%
		% of Total	0.0%	3.0%	3.0%	10.0%	4.0%	20.0%
	Graduate Degree	Count	1	1	1	8	9	20
		% within Level of Education	5.0%	5.0%	5.0%	40.0%	45.0%	100.0%
		% within Abortion Attitude	12.5%	4.3%	4.0%	26.7%	64.3%	20.0%
		% of Total	1.0%	1.0%	1.0%	8.0%	9.0%	20.0%
Total		Count	8	23	25	30	14	100
		% within Level of Education	8.0%	23.0%	25.0%	30.0%	14.0%	100.0%
		% within Abortion Attitude	100.0%	100.0%	100.0%	100.0%	100.0%	100.0%
		% of Total	8.0%	23.0%	25.0%	30.0%	14.0%	100.0%

Chi-Square Tests

	Value	Df	Asymptotic Significance (2-sided)
Pearson Chi-Square	74.351[a]	16	.000
Likelihood Ratio	72.923	16	.000
Linear-by-Linear Association	40.482	1	.000
N of Valid Cases	100		

a. 15 cells (60.0%) have expected count less than 5. The minimum expected count is 1.60.

Directional Measures

			Value	Asymptotic Standard Error[a]	Approximate T[b]	Approximate Significance
Ordinal by Ordinal	*Somers' d*	Symmetric	.562	.066	8.346	.000
		Level of Education Dependent	.573	.066	8.346	.000
		Abortion Attitude Dependent	.551	.066	8.346	.000

a. Not assuming the null hypothesis.
b. Using the asymptotic standard error assuming the null hypothesis.

Inspection of the table indicates that the predicted relationship is supported—the higher the level of education the more positive the attitude toward abortion. **In the directional measures table read the line where abortion attitudes are the dependent variable—.551 with a significance of .001.**

The result might be written as follows:

A *Somers' d* statistic was calculated to investigate if an increase in education would predict an increase in positive attitude toward abortion. For those who completed some high school 7/20 had a very negative attitude toward abortion and 7/20 had a negative attitude. For those with a graduate degree 9/20 had a very positive attitude toward abortion and 8/20 had a positive attitude. The results indicate level of education is a strong positive predictor of a positive attitude toward abortion (*Somers' d* = 0.55, *p* = .001).

Practical Implications: Supporting more education for the population would likely result in a more liberal attitude toward abortion. An area to investigate might be to determine if education related only to abortion and reproductive health result in a more positive attitude toward abortion than years of formal education or conversely, is it the general and more liberal attitude that often comes with advanced education needed to foster the more liberal attitude toward abortion? What other factors might be important in relationship to abortion attitude—religion, race, age?

PART B: PARAMETRIC

Interval/Ratio Level Data

Simple Linear Regression

See Chart—Prediction and Interval or Ratio Measurement

A **simple linear regression** is a statistical method to test a **hypothesized relationship between two interval or ratio level variables**. The hypothesized relationship is a statement of **how the Predicted (DV) variable changes/moves with respect to a change in the Predictor (IV)**. This type of analysis is used to answer the question "Does the predicted variable (DV) increase or decrease with respect to an increase or decrease in the predictor variable (IV) and/or what is the amount of this change?" Again, similar to all tests discussed in this chapter, there is a directional hypothesis; that is, there are antecedent (predictor/IV) and consequent (predicted/DV) conditions.

There are some very important assumptions that must be met to make sure the results of the test are valid.

(1) Variables must be ***interval or ratio. (Variables measured on an ordinal level should not be used). However, when many items that are measured on an ordinal scale are aggregated the total can be used as an interval level measurement. For example a scale with 20 items rated 1–5 measuring attitude toward refugees would have a range of scores from 20 to 100 and could be used as an interval scale.***
(2) The relationship between the **variables must be linear**.
(3) The **observations must be independent**.
(4) For **each value of the predictor (IV), the distribution must be normal**.

The following discussion related to regression will use a specific example of 5th grade students in a low-income inner city school. In your social work practice and in coursework you have noted that the success students have on the end of semester **Overall Performance Examination (predicted variable—DV) depends** to some extent on their **Attitude Toward School (predictor variable—IV)**. The question you have is "***How much will the overall performance examination (predicted—DV) increase as a result of a positive increase in Attitude Toward School (predictor—IV)***?"

The student's Attitude Toward School is measured by 7 questions. Each question has 5 possible alternatives on a Likert scale ranging from 1 (very negative attitude) to 5 (very positive attitude). Thus, aggregate scores have a range from 7 to 35. Let's first look conceptually at the relationship in terms of this example. A relationship consists of two sets of data and a set of pairs. The relationship can be in terms of a set of ordered pairs. The ordered pair in this example is: (Attitude and Performance). There are 50 students in the data set, therefore there are 50 ordered pairs.

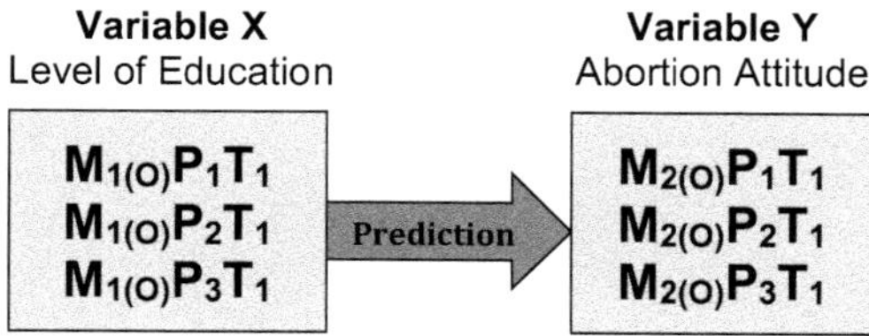

Let's look at two plots that both **depict a relationship**. Inspection of the first plot shows a group of dots that run on a diagonal from the bottom left to the upper right corner providing the first visual clue that a potential linear relationship exists.

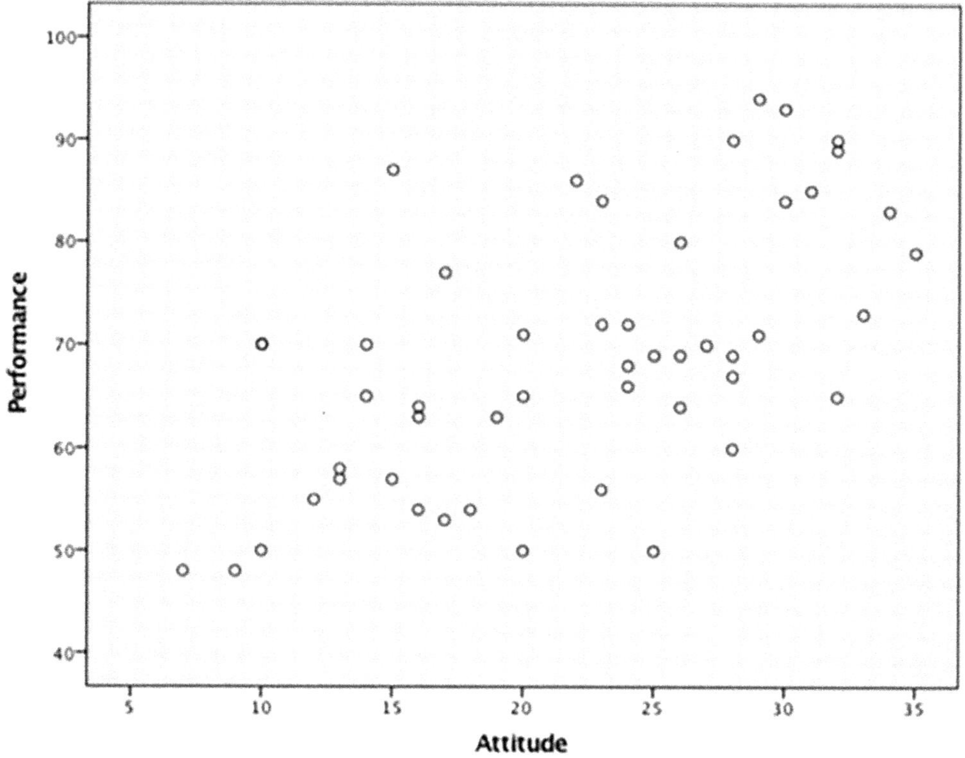

The second graph is an overlay of an ellipse on the previous graph with a line through the center of the ellipse providing a much stronger visual picture that a potential linear relationship exists.

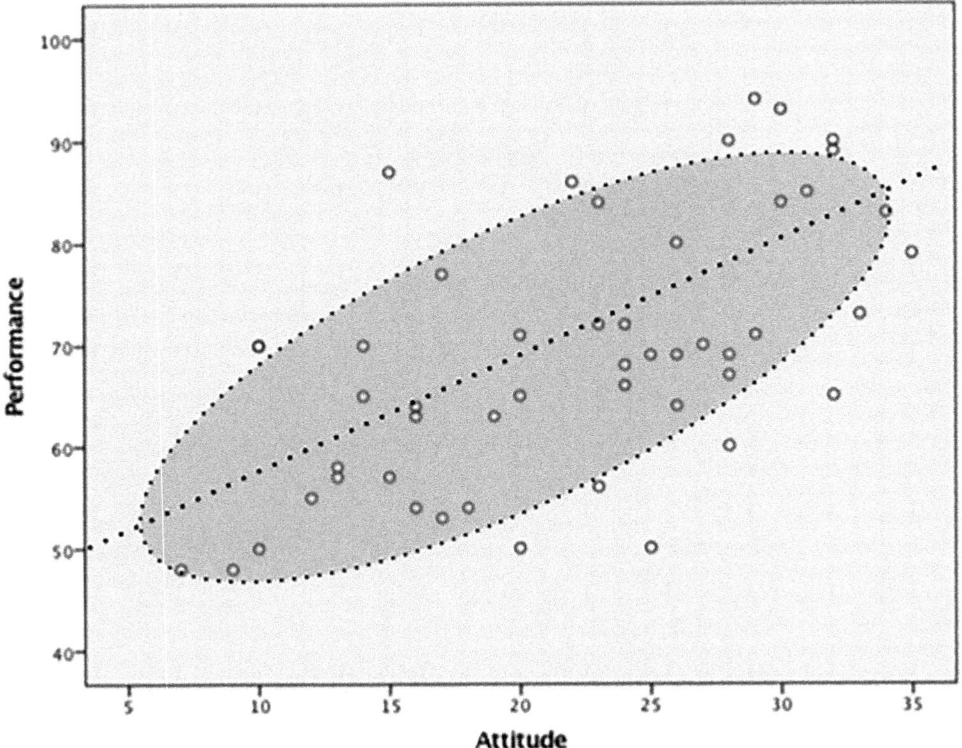

As an ***ellipse narrows it visually depicts that all the Y values for a particular value of X are coming closer together***. This would pull the ellipse tighter and tighter. If the values of Y are not close together for each value of X, then you would have a scatterplot where the dots would be all over the graph and it would take a circle to try to encompass them. One of the ways to "eyeball" data for regression analysis is to prepare scatterplots like these and see if there appears to be an ellipse or circle pattern. The tighter the ellipse, the greater the relationship; the closer to a full circle, the less relationship.

SPSS Commands

Open the data set ***Ch21 Regression***.
Follow the steps below:

(1) Click ***Graphs***.
(2) Scroll down and select ***Legacy Dialogs***.
(3) Select ***Scatter/Dot . . .***
(4) Select ***Simple Scatter***; click ***Define***.
(5) Select ***Define***.
(6) Move ***Performance*** to the Y-axis box; move ***Attitude*** to the X-axis box.
(7) Click ***OK*** to produce the graph.

Let's look at the output. This scatterplot will provide you with the same graph as the first one shown above with no ellipse. It appears to show a linear relationship and in general seems to have the possibility of putting an ellipse over the data and to see how narrow the ellipse would be and to draw a line for the diagonal orientation. A positive relationship would be when X increases, Y increases on the diagonal from bottom left to upper right. A negative relationship would be when X increases, Y decreases and the diagonal would start in the upper left and move to the lower right. Both can be strong relationships, the difference being in the direction of the relationship between X and Y—decreasing or increasing.

Now let's look at a set of data where there is not a relationship so that you can compare it to the one you have just seen.

SPSS Commands

Open the data set ***Ch21 Nonlinear***.
Follow the steps below:

(1) Click ***Graphs***.
(2) Scroll down and select ***Legacy Dialogs***.
(3) Select ***Scatter/Dot . . .***
(4) Select ***Simple Scatter***; click ***Define***.
(5) Select ***Define***.
(6) Move ***Performance*** to the Y-axis box; move ***Attitude*** to the X-axis box.
(7) Click ***OK*** to produce the graph.

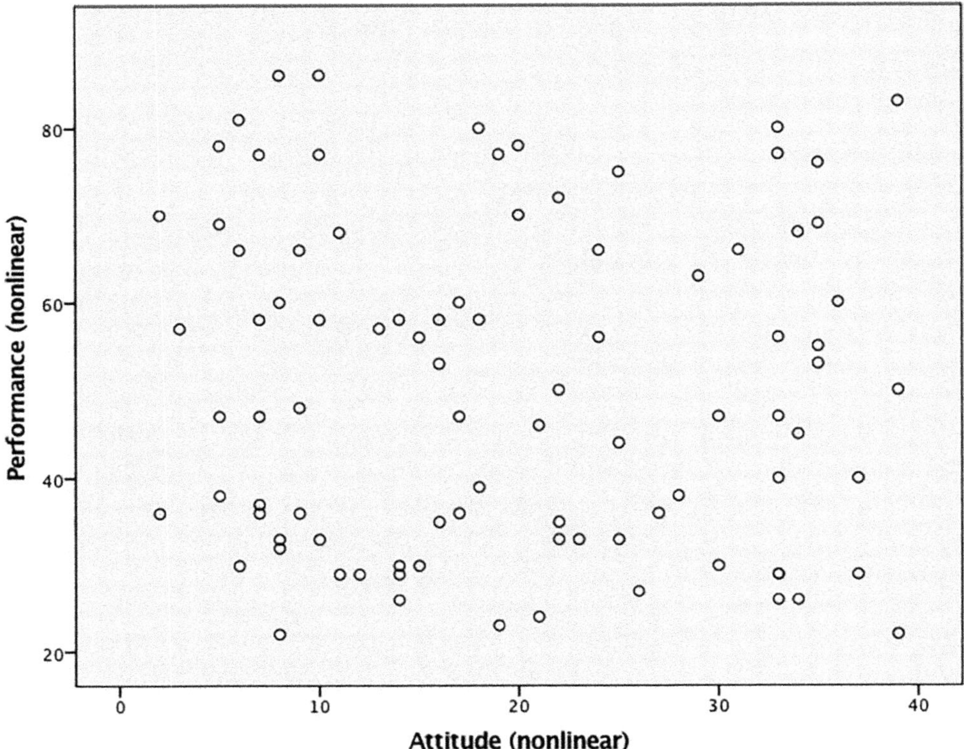

You can see that an ellipse would not adequately cover the XY pairs. If you look at the values of Y for each value of X you can see they are vertically dispersed over a great range indicating knowing X does not help to predict Y. **REMEMBER the closer together the Ys are at each value of X, the stronger the relationship and the better the prediction of Y.**

A graph of the some XY data followed by the equation for a linear relationship (a straight line) is shown below.

$$y_{pred}\,(\textit{exam performance}) = \alpha + \beta x\,(\textit{attitude toward school})$$

a and **β** are unknown
α = value of Y (Predicted/DV) when X (Predictor/IV) is 0
α is a **constant—*the intercept—where the regression line crosses the*** Y-axis
β = a ***constant that multiplies*** (X) the predictor/IV. β is a calculated value that will ***minimize the amount of error/distance from the line for ALL values of Y.*** **Thus, β is**

the value of the slope (angle) of the line. The slope of the line shows **how much the predicted Y (Predicted/DV) increases for each increase in the value of X (Predictor/IV)**. This slope can be either positive or negative.

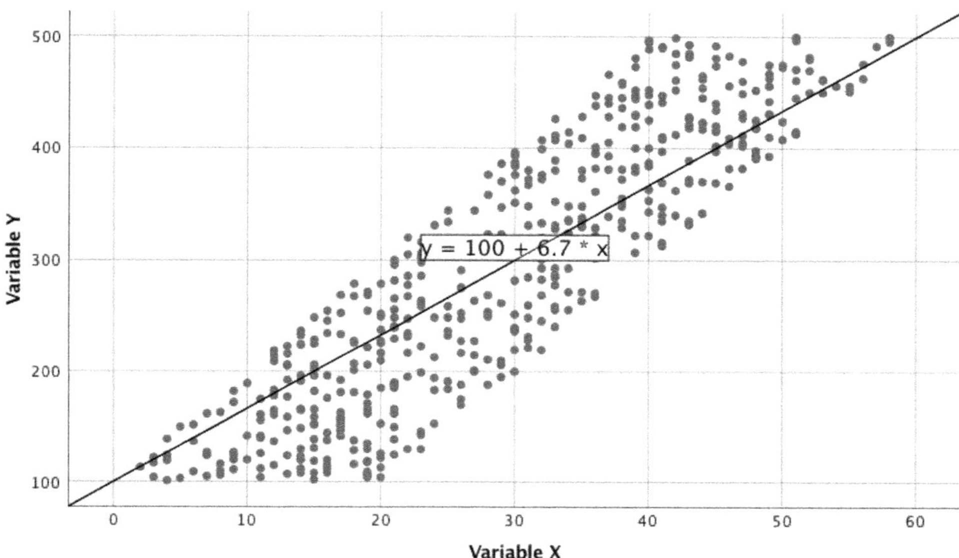

The ***standardized equation for a regression line is:***

$$y_{z\ pred}(perf) = \beta x_z(att)$$

Where
$\mathbf{y_{z\ pred}}$ = the Z score value that is being predicted (dependent variable)
$\mathbf{x_z}$ = the Z score value of the independent variable (predictor)
β = the coefficient of $\mathbf{x_z}$. You multiply $\mathbf{x_z}$ by **β (beta weight) to predict Y**.

The intercept is where the line intercepts Y when X is zero. But in the standardized regression equation it is not included because when the equation is standardized it becomes zero. **Remember from Chapter 14 that standardization sets starting values for different distributions at zero (0). When a regression is standardized, then we are able to both visually and mathematically compare differences because then the regressions are all on the same scale. In standardized regressions both axes (X and Y) are set at zero.** ***A standardized regression equation can be described as: If you change X by one SD, it will change Y by the standardized beta value multiplied by the SD of Y.***

$$y_{z\ pred}(perf) = \beta x_z(att)$$

So if X_z ***increases by 1,*** $Y_{z\ pred}$ ***will be the same as β. Therefore, the value of β will tell us the proportion of the standardized value Y that will be*** Y_{pred}:

$$y_{z\ pred}(perf) = \beta(1)$$

This equation will provide us with the ***best "guess" of the value of Y given the value of X***. Of course these estimates of Y do not suggest that attitude (X) and performance (Y) are related exactly like this or all values of Y will fall right on the prediction line. This estimate of Y is based on only using this one variable (attitude) to predict student performance differences. Of course we know that many other variables can contribute to the difference in Y. Remember the equation $\mathbf{V_T = V_1 + V_2 + \ldots + (error)}$ that many variables can and do combine to make up the total variance of a single variable. **Also you recall that there is always error present in the equation because there is no perfect prediction (Remember from Chapter 14—there is always the CHANCE!).** We understand that there will always be error in our prediction and ***in regression analysis the error is called the residual***. The residual is the amount of ***difference between all of the "real" data points (values of the observed Ys) and the regression line that is the predicted value of Y* for a specific value of X**. If you look at the graph below, the dark lines represent the residuals (errors) between the predicted value of Y from a specific value of X and the observed (actual value) of Y at that value of X.

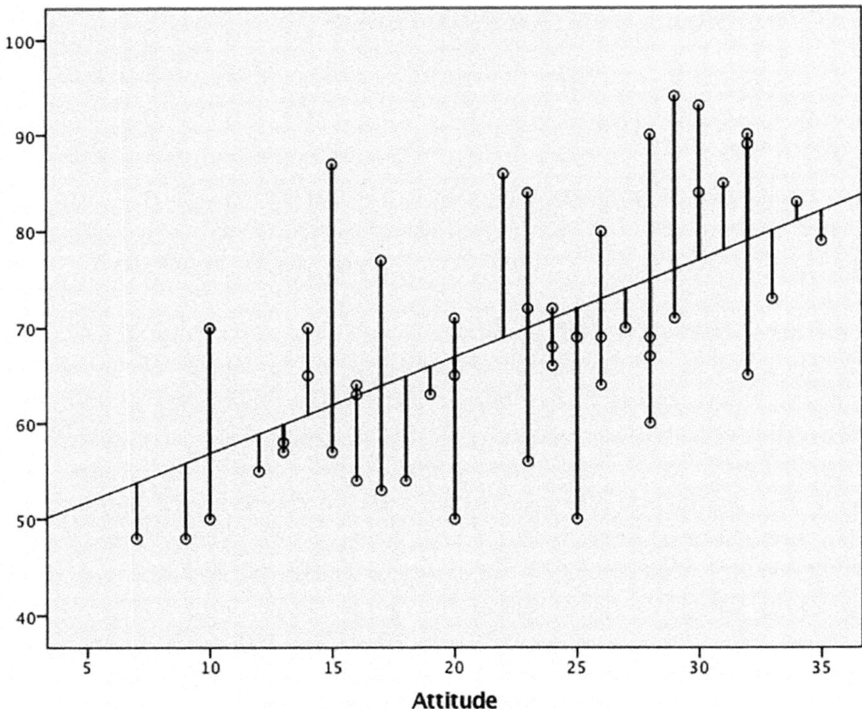

The total amount of residual would be all of the difference between all of the actual observed values of Y and the predicted values of Y for all values of X added together. The statistical analysis used in simple linear regression is to try to find from all of the potential straight lines the line that best summarizes the relationship between two variables—in this example X (Attitude) and Y (Performance). ***We call this line the REGRESSION LINE, the line that MINIMIZES the total amount of ERROR (residual).***

Let's analyze some data using SPSS to perform a linear regression.

Study Question: How much will the score on the Overall Performance Examination (Predicted/DV) increase as a result of an increase in positive Attitude Toward School (Predictor/IV)?

This is a prediction design.

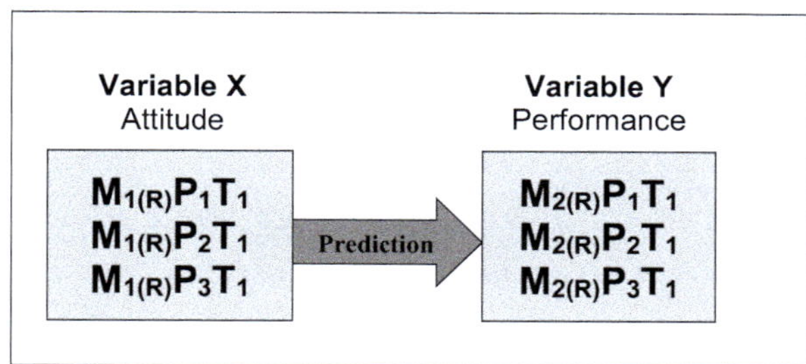

Hypotheses:

Prediction: The more positive the Attitude Toward School, the higher the score on the Overall Performance Examination.

Null: Attitude Toward School will not predict the score on the Overall Performance Examination.

Expected (E): There will be no predictive relationship between Attitude Toward School and score on the Overall Performance Examination.

Predicted (P): The more positive the Attitude Toward School, the higher the score on the Overall Performance Examination.

Observed (O): The ability of Attitude Toward School to predict score on the Overall Performance Examination.

Level of Measurement: Predictor Interval (Attitude), Predicted Interval (Performance Examination score)

Type of Design: Predictive

Number of Groups: 2 Samples same group

Assumptions: (a) Interval level data, (b) Normal distribution of Y (DV) at each value of X (IV), (c) Linear relationship between variables, (d) Normal distribution of X (IV) the Predictor

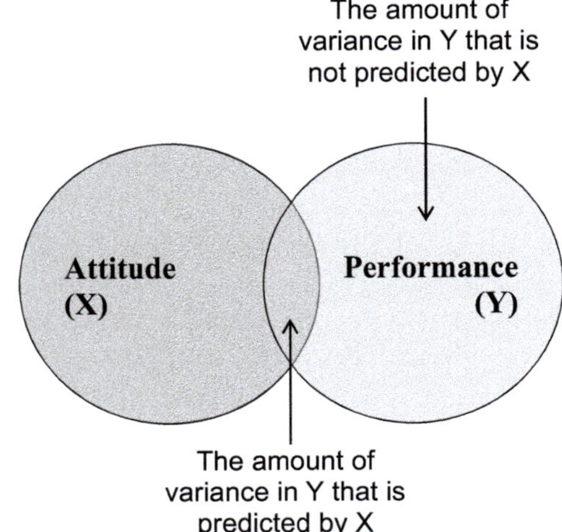

SPSS Commands

Open the data set ***Ch21 Regression***.
Follow the steps below:

(1) Click ***Analyze***.
(2) Scroll down and select ***Regression***.
(3) Select ***Linear . . .***
(4) Move ***Performance*** into the ***Dependent*** box.
(5) Move ***Attitude*** into the ***Independent(s)*** box.

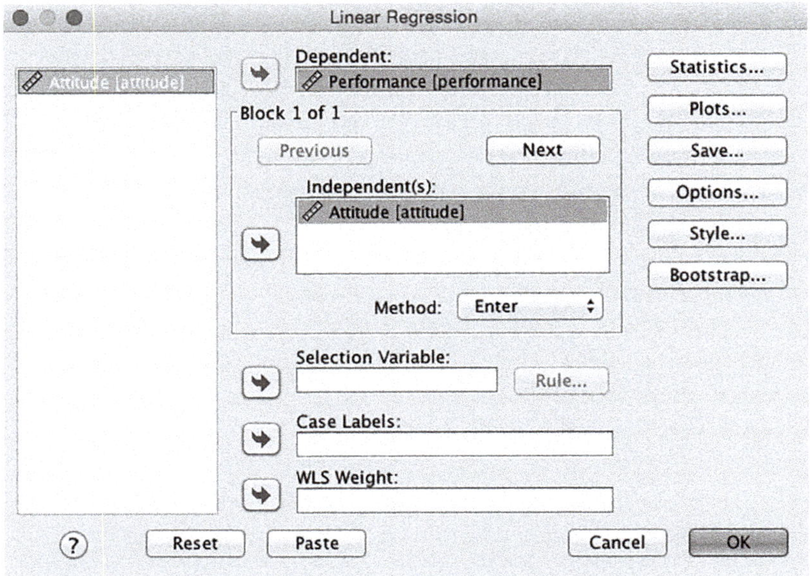

(6) Click the ***Statistics . . .*** button.
(7) Check the boxes next to ***Estimates***, ***Model fit*** and ***Descriptives***.

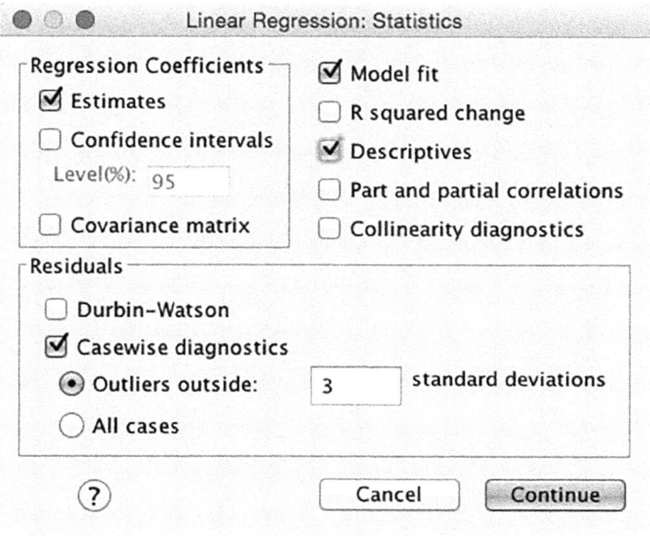

(8) Under ***Residuals***, check the box next to ***Casewise diagnostics*** and request ***Outliers outside 3 standard deviations***.
(9) Click ***Continue***.
(10) Click the ***Plots . . .*** button.
(11) Under the ***Standardized Residual Plots*** heading, request both the ***Histogram*** and the ***Normal probability plot***.
(12) Move ***ZRESID*** (standardized residuals) into the Y-axis and ***ZPRED*** (the standardized predicted value) into the X-axis.

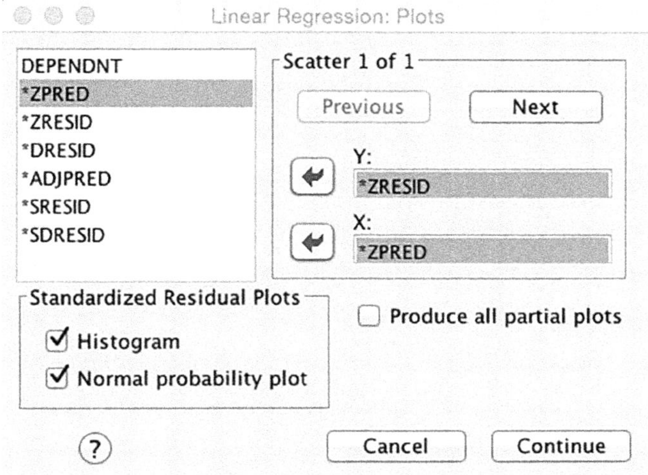

(13) Click ***Continue***.
(14) Click ***OK*** to run the analysis.

Let's look at the output:

Descriptive Statistics

	Mean	Std. Deviation	N
Performance	68.9400	12.80850	50
Attitude	21.9600	7.55918	50

Correlations

		Performance	Attitude
Pearson Correlation	Performance	1.000	.596
	Attitude	.596	1.000
Sig. (1-tailed)	Performance	.	.000
	Attitude	.000	.
N	Performance	50	50
	Attitude	50	50

Variables Entered/Removed[a]

Model	Variables Entered	Variables Removed	Method
1	Attitude[b]	.	Enter

a. Dependent Variable: Performance.
b. All requested variables entered.

Model Summary[b]

Model	R	R Square	Adjusted R Square	Std. Error of the Estimate
1	.596[a]	.356	.342	10.38898

a. Predictors: (Constant), Attitude.
b. Dependent Variable: Performance.

ANOVA[a]

Model		Sum of Squares	Df	Mean Square	F	Sig.
1	Regression	2858.140	1	2858.140	26.481	.000[b]
	Residual	5180.680	48	107.931		
	Total	8038.820	49			

a. Dependent Variable: Performance.
b. Predictors: (Constant), Attitude.

Coefficients[a]

Model		Unstandardized Coefficients		Standardized Coefficients	T	Sig.
		B	Std. Error	Beta		
1	(Constant)	46.753	4.555		10.264	.000
	Attitude	1.010	.196	.596	5.146	.000

a. Dependent Variable: Performance.

Residuals Statistics[a]

	Minimum	Maximum	Mean	Std. Deviation	N
Predicted Value	53.8253	82.1149	68.9400	7.63737	50
Residual	−22.01144	25.09199	.00000	10.28242	50
Std. Predicted Value	−1.979	1.725	.000	1.000	50
Std. Residual	−2.119	2.415	.000	.990	50

a. Dependent Variable: Performance.

Look at the descriptive statistics and correlations tables that contain means, standard deviations and correlations providing information for the initial assessment of the data. The mean for performance is 68.94, SD = 12.81, and for attitude 21.96, SD = 7.59. The correlation between performance and attitude is .596 indicating a potential linear relationship between the variables. The next table to review is the Model Summary

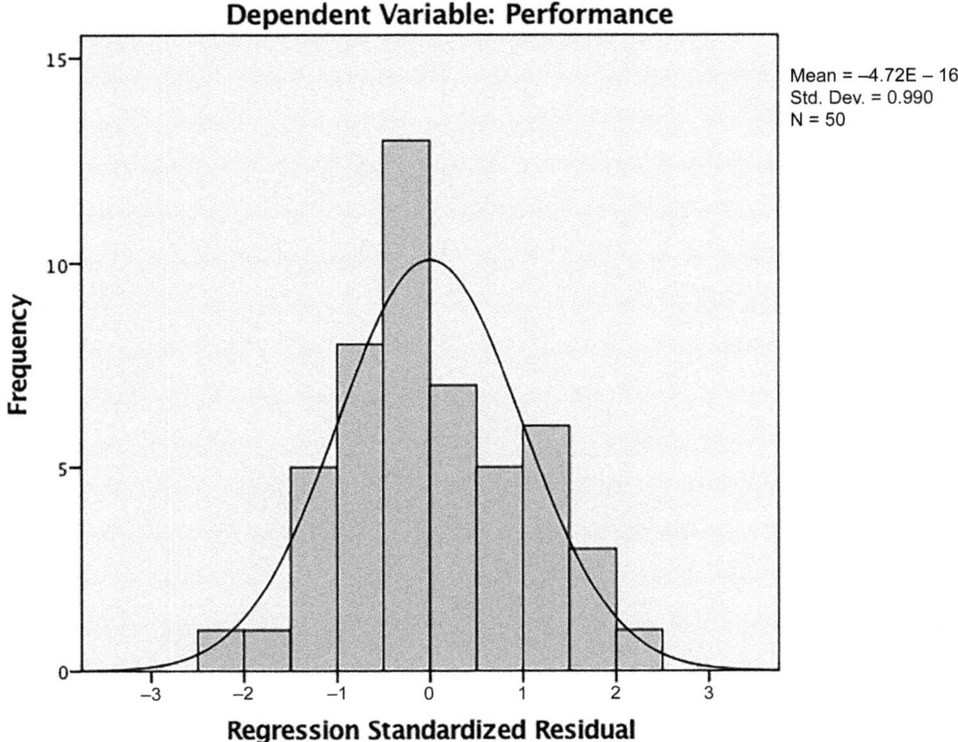

Table, that includes the R, the R Square, Adjusted R Square, and SE of the Estimate. ***The R^2 value is important because (as noted earlier) it shows the amount of variance in the Predicted variable/DV (Examination Performance) that can be attributed to the Predictor variable/IV (Attitude Toward School).***

The adjusted R^2 is an estimate of the amount of variance that could be attributed to attitude toward school that could be used to predict exam performance if this linear estimate was used with another (new and different) sample. Sample size and the number of variables (more than one predictor variable becomes a multiple regression model as shown in the next section) are used to correct for potential overestimates of the relationship in future applications of the model. ***When you write the results section, you should not use the R^2 value. Use the Adjusted R^2 value that indicates the likely amount of variance that could be attributed to the predictor variable(s) when they are used in future studies.*** The example has an **adjusted** ***R^2 of 0.342, indicating that 34% (rounded) of the variation in Performance could be attributed to Attitude Toward School and might then be used in future research and program planning.***

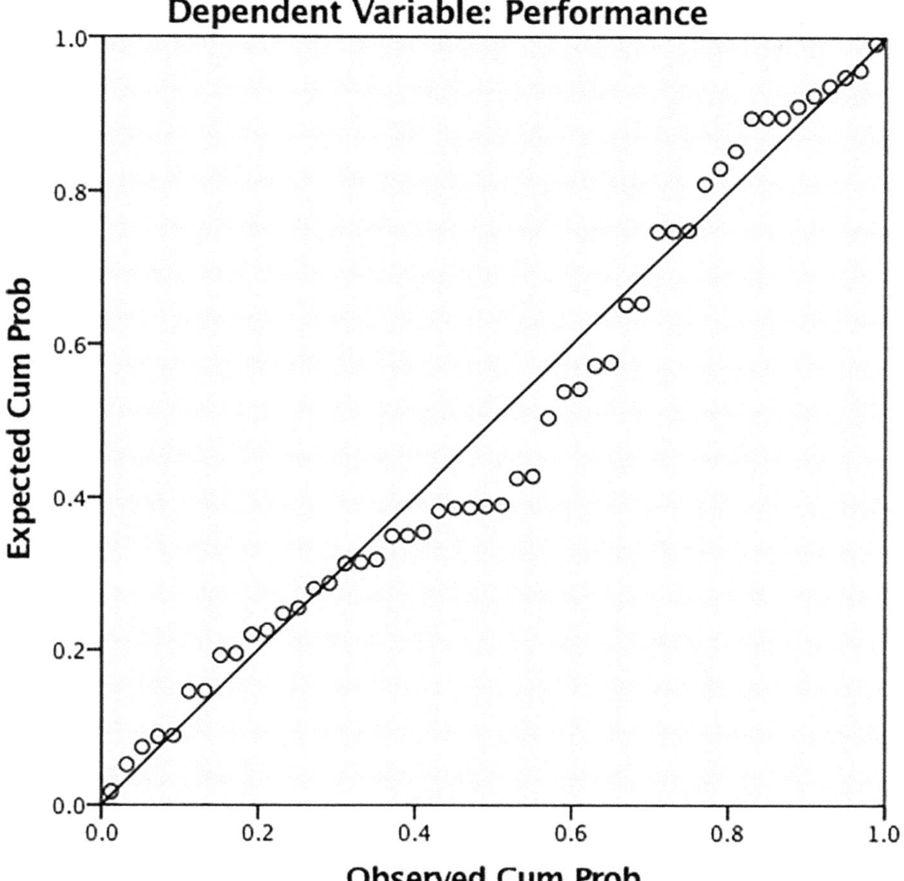

Look at the SE of the estimate and compare it to the mean of the Predicted DV that can be found in the residuals statistics table. Look at the SE of the estimate and compare it to the mean of the Predicted DV that can be found in the residuals statistics table. **The SE should be relatively small compared to the mean of the predicted value.** The mean of the predicted value is 68.94, and the SE of 10.39 (rounded) indicating it is sufficiently small to progress with the analysis. In simple linear regression (only one variable), the SE will be bigger than in multiple regression due to the inability of a single variable to account for a large amount of variance in the predicted variable. Once again we refer to the basic idea that usually it takes a number of variables (IVs) to produce a good predict a single DV. $V_T = V_1 + V_2 + V_3 + \text{error}$.

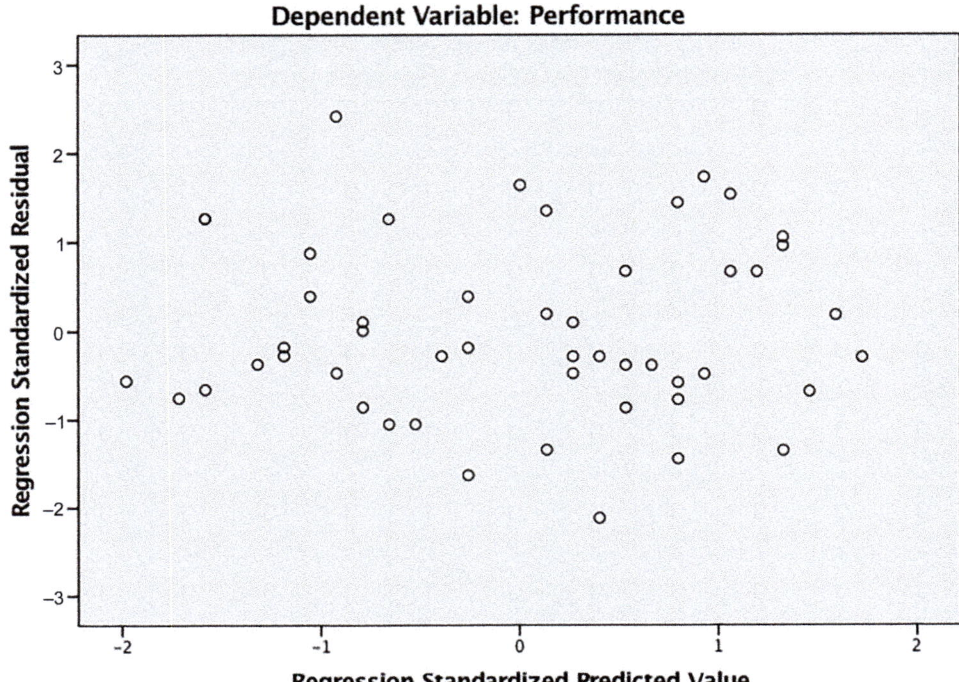

Review the ANOVA table. If the F statistic is significant as in the example ($F_{(1,48)} = 26.48$, $p = .001$) then the regression equation is statistically significant and we can continue to examine the results of the regression coefficients. The values in the coefficients table are very important because they provide the values we use in the regression equation. Recall the regression equation:

$$y_{pred}(perf) = \alpha + \beta x\ (att)$$

Based on the **unstandardized (B)** coefficients in the coefficients table and by placing the values into the equation we can conclude that

$$y_{pred}(perf) = 46.753 + (1.01)\ (att)$$

For example, if we have an attitude score of 7, the predicted performance score of that student will be 46.753 + (1.01) (7) = 53.823. For a student with an attitude score of 8, the predicted performance score of that student will be 46.753 + (1.01) (8) = 54.833. You can see that the two predicted Y values differ by 1.01 (the value of the X coefficient) when the corresponding X value differ by exactly 1.

Based on the ***standardized equation*** for a regression line we can conclude that:

$$y_{z\,pred}(perf) = .(596)\,(x_z)$$

In a **simple linear regression, the standardized beta weight for attitude is exactly the same as the value of Pearson r**. If we change X by one SD of X, then we will change Y by the standardized beta value times the SD of Y. **You can see that beta weight tells us how much change a 1 SD increase in attitude will produce in a standardized score for performance.** This can be demonstrated by using the values in the example. If we change X by one SD (7.55), then we will change Y by the standardized beta value (.596) times the SD of Y (10.28) = 6.126. **The *t* statistic tests of the specific regression coefficient (see Attitude in the coefficients table) is statistically significant, $p = .001$.** The conclusion is that Attitude Toward School significantly predicts the Performance score.

Next we will examine the charts. These charts help to assess assumptions of normality, linearity and homoscedasticity (see Chapter 14). Let's look more closely at these assumptions before interpreting the charts.

Linearity is an important assumption that must be met in basic linear regression analysis. If the **form of the relationship** between X and Y is **curvilinear**; for example a **U** or **S shape line** is a **serious violation of the assumption of linearity**. If you use a linear regression model when the data is nonlinear it will give you an incorrect analysis. Regression calculates a line that minimizes the residuals (error), which is the difference between the actual Y values and the predicted Y values for every X value. If the data are not basically linear, then each point on the regression line will be incorrectly calculated. Before performing a linear regression analysis, it is always a good procedure to create a scatterplot showing the relationship of the actual (observed values) of X and Y and to visually inspect the relationship. If the scatterplot seems to be linear (see ellipses in the first part of this chapter), then go ahead and run the linear regression analysis. After running the analysis, the normal probability plot will show how well the residuals lie along a straight line. This gives another visual indication of linearity. In the example the normal probability shown below indicates linearity. As you can see there are some values a little off the line but there is not a large U shape or a large S shape curve of the data points—it is rather straight.

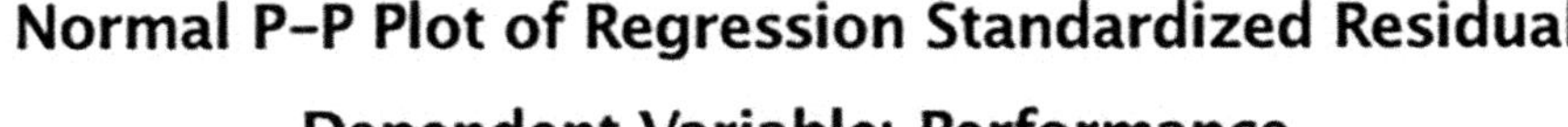

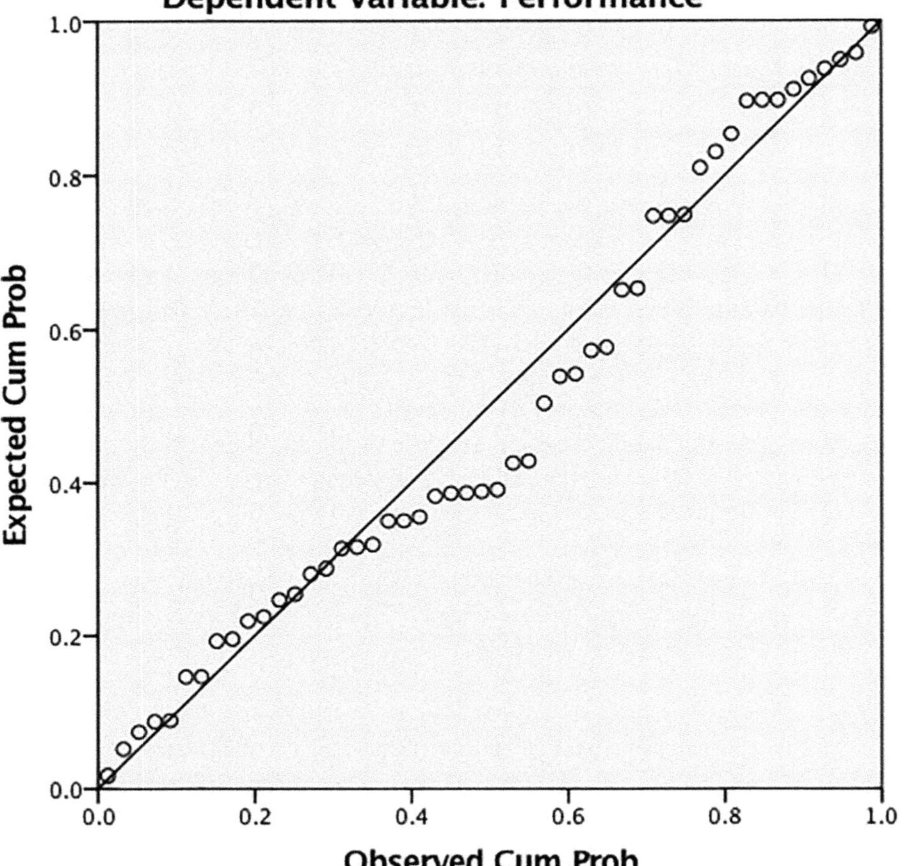

Normality is another important assumption that must be met. As we know, residuals refer to the differences between the observed scores and the predicted scores. If the analysis is perfect, the differences between the observed scores and the predicted scores will be zero (basically it never happens). One way to evaluate normality in the results of a regression line is to inspect the shape of the distribution of the residuals. The distribution needs to assume the shape of a normal curve to meet the assumption of normality. To see if this distribution of residuals is assuming the shape of a normal distribution, you can look at a histogram of residuals (depicting the distribution of errors). If the distribution is severely skewed, the data may be transformed with a square root or logarithmic transformation. In our example, the distribution of residuals shown below indicates normality.

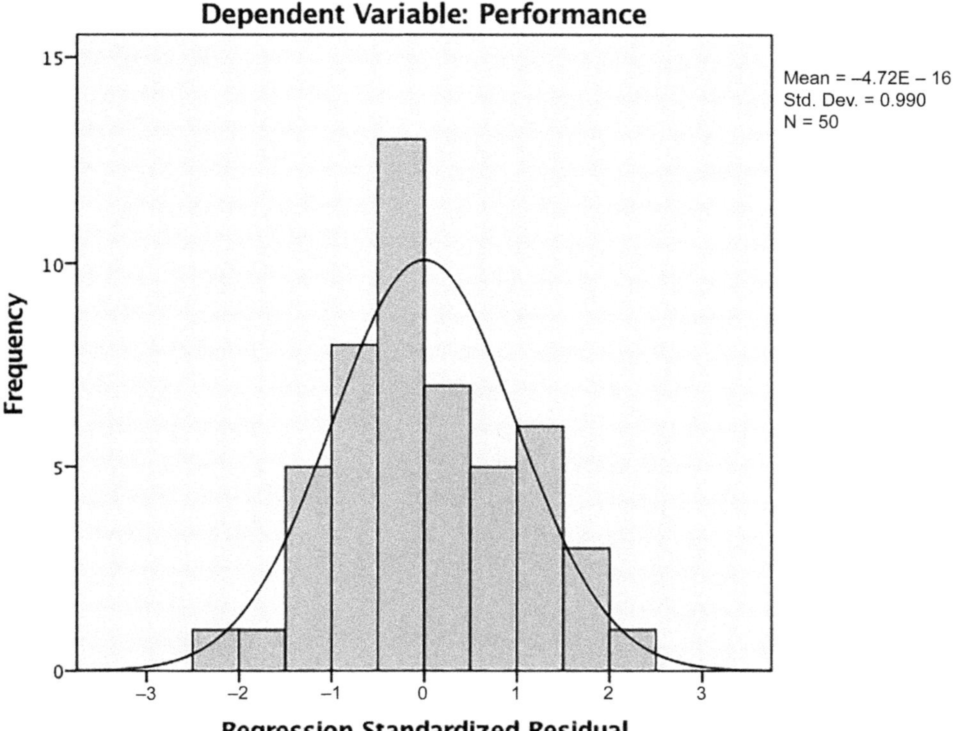

Homoscedasticity is another important assumption to be met. In a regression analysis ***you want homoscedasticity or equality of variances. As you have already learned, this same property is very important in statistics which is used to find differences. In the regression model the variance for each value of the predictor/IV variable and the variability of the predicted/DV variable is about the same.*** **In other words, the variance around the regression line (Y values/data points—distribution above and below the line) should be relatively equal for all values of X.** To meet the assumption of homoscedasticity, you want similar distributions of Y around the regression line for each value of X. The graph below shows distributions of Ys for each value of X with a curve of those values for each of the X values.

A scatterplot of the predicted standardized value against the standardized residual value helps to visualize homoscedasticity between predicted DV scores and errors of that prediction. When you **cannot visualize a rectangle around the standardized zero** then you need to be concerned about the non-normality of the residuals—-*hetero*scedasticity—the **variance of the residuals (errors) around the predicted value of Y is not the same for all values of X**. Homoscedasticity in a simple linear

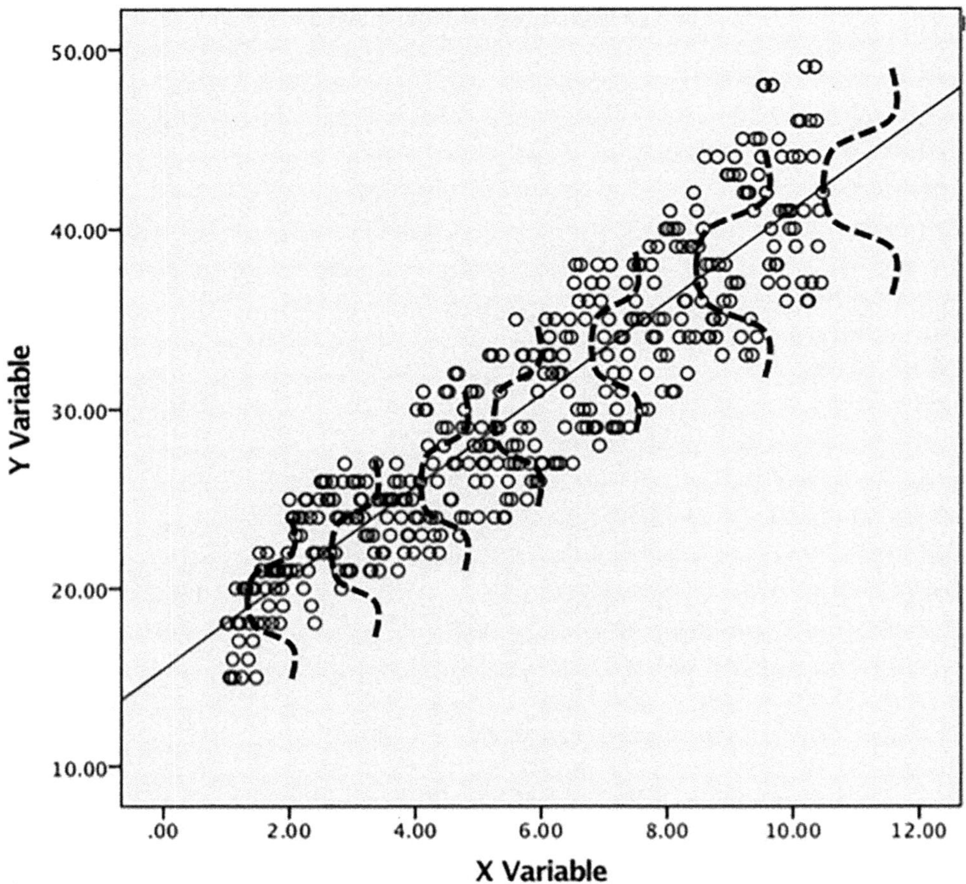

regression analysis is always difficult to visualize in this type of scatterplot, because **non-rectangular patterns can indicate the need for more variables to improve the prediction and not a strong violation of normality**. This is the scatterplot for the example:

There is not clear rectangularity, but this could be a result of not including additional variables along with attitude as predictors of performance. We will show you in the next section (multiple regression) how to do a regression analysis using multiple variables.

Results might be written as follows.

A simple linear regression analysis was performed to investigate if an increase in Attitude Toward School would predict an increase in Performance Evaluation

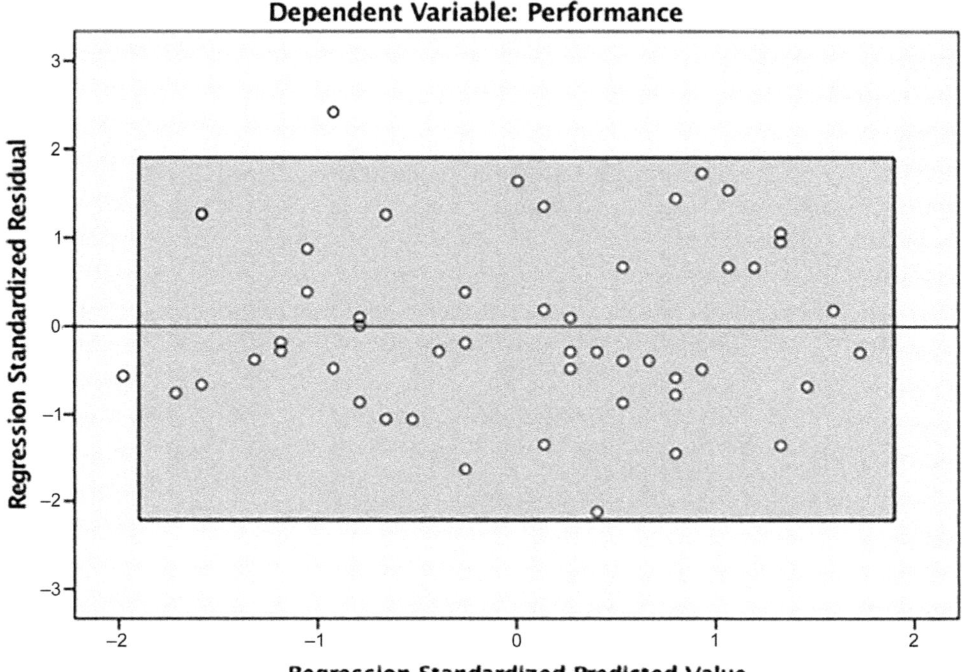

scores. The R^2 statistic was statistically significant ($F_{(1, 48)} = 26.48$, $p = .001$, R^2 adjusted = 0.342) indicating that 34% of the variance in performance could be attributed to the attitude of students toward statistics. An increase of one standard deviation in attitude (7.55 points, the *SD* of attitude) will result in an increase of 7.63 points in performance (.596 standardized beta weight * 12.8 the *SD* of performance = a 7.63 point increase).

Practical Implications: If we can improve the student's attitude toward the subject, then we would be able to improve their overall performance in the course. Therefore, we should set up programs that dispel myths and concerns about such courses long before individuals have to take the required course. Replication is also important to determine if this model will fit when using it to predict performance in another situation. This prediction was developed specifically for making the best estimate for this data and we do not know if in future situations it will be a good model for prediction. Additionally, we should try to determine other variables that could be included in predicting performance. If there are other variables that predict performance, they might be ones to focus on with interventions.

Multiple Regression

See Chart—Prediction Multiple Variables and Interval or Ratio Measurement

Multiple regression is similar to simple linear regression; however, in multiple regression there are two or more predictor/IV variables and only one predicted/DV variable. Multiple regression is used because by selecting a group of variables you are likely to increase the ability to predict the predicted variable (DV). Multiple regression can be used in two ways when there is **some amount of relationship between the predictor variables** and the **predicted variable:** (1) to find the ***best group of predictor variables*** or (2) to test the ***importance of individual predictors in explaining variance*** in the predicted variable.

Before we go into more detail about multiple regression, let's first review ***partial and semi-partial correlations*** as a background to multiple regression analysis. We briefly discussed partial Pearson r analysis in the previous chapter. In this chapter we will have a more technical discussion about partial and semi-partial correlations. Partial and semi-partial correlations help us to better understand the relationship between variables. Partialing is a term that means what it says, that is "***to take a part of something***". Utilizing the method of ***partialing out effects***, a researcher can control the effect of one or more variables in the relationship between two variables. The methodology allows the researcher ***to find out to what extent the relationship between the predicted/DV variable and predictor/IV . . . is influenced by or determined by another IV***. In some cases the relationship between a predictor/IV and a predicted/DV can be misunderstood if another predictor/IV has not been controlled.

Let's return to our example of the Overall Performance Examination and Attitude Toward School. The relationship between the Overall Performance Examination (predicted/DV) and the Attitude Toward School (predictor/IV) has already been investigated. However, you wonder if both the Overall Performance Examination and Attitude Toward School is influenced by the student's level of math ability. One way to control for math ability would be to only include students with the same math ability to be part of the study, but typically this is not practical and would pose problems in trying to generalize results to those with different math ability. Multiple regression analysis is a statistical method that can be used to control for or hold constant the influence of the math. Math ability of the students is determined by a standardized test of math ability. Scores on the math ability test can range between 0 and 20.

SPSS Commands

Open data set ***Ch21 MultiRegression***.
Follow the steps below:

(1) Click ***Analyze***.
(2) Scroll down and select ***Descriptive Statistics***.

(3) Select ***Descriptives . . .***
(4) Move ***Performance***, ***Attitudes*** and ***Math*** into the ***Variable(s)*** box.
(5) Click ***OK***.

Descriptive Statistics

	N	Minimum	Maximum	Mean	Std. Deviation
Attitude	50	7	35	21.96	7.559
Performance	50	48	94	68.94	12.808
Math	50	3	20	11.84	4.622
Valid N (listwise)	50				

Now, using the same data set, we will examine correlations:

(1) Click ***Analyze***.
(2) Scroll down and select ***Correlate***.
(3) Select ***Bivariate . . .***
(4) Move ***Attitude***, ***Performance*** and ***Math*** into the ***Variables*** box.
(5) Under ***Correlation Coefficients***, check the box next to ***Pearson***.
(6) Click ***OK***.

Correlations

		Attitude	Performance	Math
Attitude	Pearson Correlation	1	.596**	.521**
	Sig. (2-tailed)		.000	.000
	N	50	50	50
Performance	Pearson Correlation	.596**	1	.887**
	Sig. (2-tailed)	.000		.000
	N	50	50	50
Math	Pearson Correlation	.521**	.887**	1
	Sig. (2-tailed)	.000	.000	
	N	50	50	50

**. Correlation is significant at the 0.01 level (2-tailed).

The table shows that attitude and math ability both correlate with performance. If you have to choose only one predictor, it would make sense to choose math because it has the highest correlation (.88) and based upon this correlation is the strongest predictor of performance. Furthermore, you can see that it also controls part of the correlation between attitude and performance.

To make sure that math is a strong predictor, we will first run a simple linear regression between only math and performance.

Study Question: How much will the score on the Overall Performance Exam (Predicted/DV) increase with an increase in Math ability (Predictor/IV)?

This is a prediction design.

Hypotheses:

Prediction: An increase in Math ability will result in an increase in the score on the Overall Performance Exam.
Null: An increase in Math ability will not result in an increase in the score on the Overall Performance Exam.
Expected (E): There will be no relationship between Math ability and score on the Overall Performance Exam.
Predicted (P): An increase in Math ability will result in an increase in the Overall Performance Exam.
Observed (O): The actual relationship between Math ability and score on the Overall Performance Exam.
Level of Measurement: Predictor—Interval (Math ability score), Predicted—Interval (Overall Performance Exam score)
Type of Design: Prediction
Number of Groups: 2 Samples same group
Assumptions: (a) Interval level data, (b) Normal distributions, (c) Linear relationship between variables

Conceptual framework:

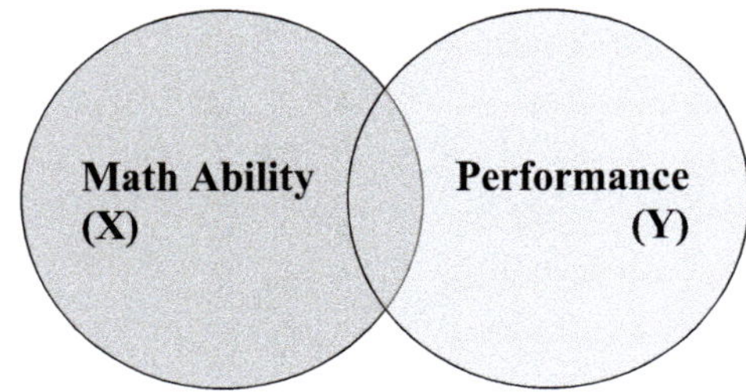

SPSS Commands

Open the data set ***Ch21 MultiRegression***.
Follow the steps below:

(1) Click *Analyze*.
(2) Scroll down and select ***Regression***.

(3) Select ***Linear . . .***
(4) Move ***Performance*** into the ***Dependent*** box.
(5) Move ***Attitude*** into the ***Independent(s)*** box.

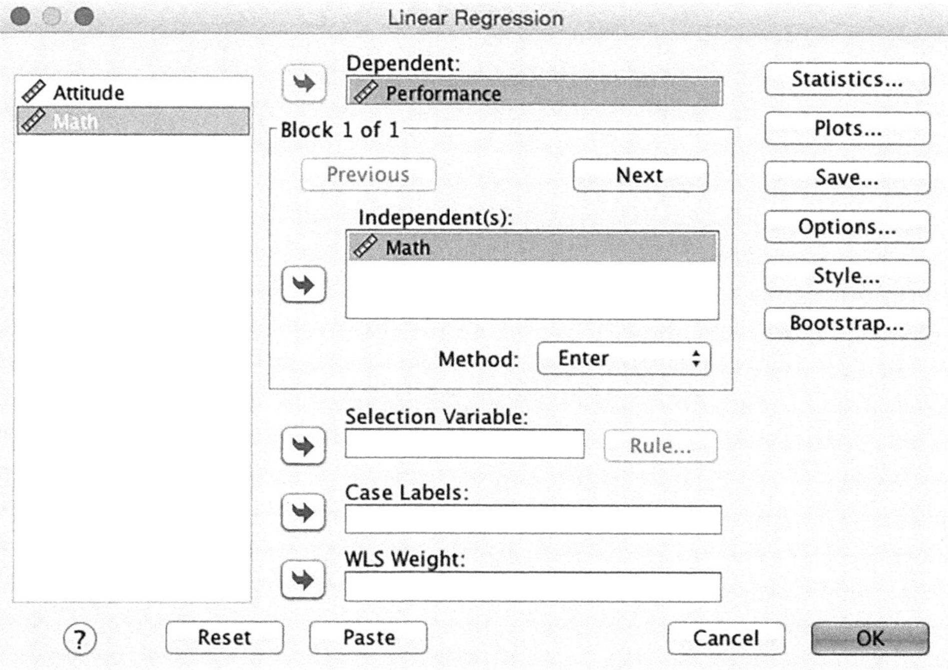

(6) Click the ***Statistics . . .*** button.
(7) Check the boxes next to ***Estimates***, ***Model fit*** and ***Descriptives***.
(8) Under ***Residuals***, check the box next to ***Casewise diagnostics*** and request ***Outliers outside 3 standard deviations***.
(9) Click ***Continue***.
(10) Click the ***Plots . . .*** button.
(11) Under the ***Standardized Residual Plots*** heading, request both the ***Histogram*** and the ***Normal probability plot***.
(12) Move ***ZRESID*** (standardized residuals) into the Y-axis and ***ZPRED*** (the standardized predicted value) into the X-axis.
(13) Click ***Continue***.
(14) Click ***OK*** to run the analysis.

Linear Regression: Statistics

Regression Coefficients
- [x] Estimates
- [ ] Confidence intervals
  Level(%): 95
- [ ] Covariance matrix

- [x] Model fit
- [ ] R squared change
- [x] Descriptives
- [ ] Part and partial correlations
- [ ] Collinearity diagnostics

Residuals
- [ ] Durbin-Watson
- [x] Casewise diagnostics
  - (•) Outliers outside: 3 standard deviations
  - ( ) All cases

? Cancel Continue

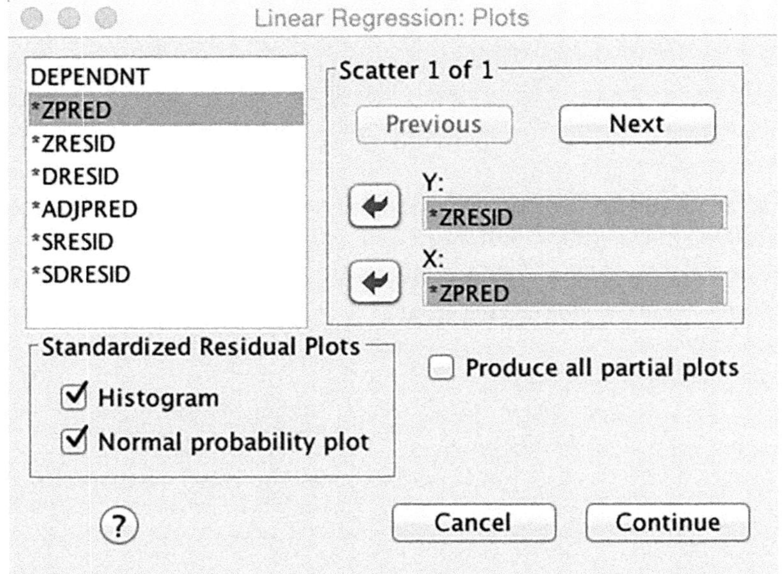

Let's look at the output:

Regression

Descriptive Statistics

	Mean	Std. Deviation	N
Performance	68.94	12.808	50
Math	11.84	4.622	50

Correlations

		Performance	Math
Pearson Correlation	Performance	1.000	.887
	Math	.887	1.000
Sig. (1-tailed)	Performance	.	.000
	Math	.000	.
N	Performance	50	50
	Math	50	50

Variables Entered/Removed[a]

Model	Variables Entered	Variables Removed	Method
1	Math[b]	.	Enter

a. Dependent Variable: Performance.
b. All requested variables entered.

Model Summary[b]

Model	R	R Square	Adjusted R Square	Std. Error of the Estimate
1	.887[a]	.787	.783	5.971

a. Predictors: (Constant), Math.
b. Dependent Variable: Performance.

ANOVA[a]

Model		Sum of Squares	Df	Mean Square	F	Sig.
1	Regression	6327.390	1	6327.390	177.462	.000[b]
	Residual	1711.430	48	35.655		
	Total	8038.820	49			

a. Dependent Variable: Performance.
b. Predictors: (Constant), Math.

Coefficients[a]

Model		Unstandardized Coefficients		Standardized Coefficients		
		B	Std. Error	Beta	t	Sig.
1	(Constant)	39.830	2.343		17.001	.000
	Math	2.459	.185	.887	13.322	.000

a. Dependent Variable: Performance.

Residuals Statistics[a]

	Minimum	Maximum	Mean	Std. Deviation	N
Predicted Value	47.21	89.00	68.94	11.364	50
Residual	−13.957	13.667	.000	5.910	50
Std. Predicted Value	−1.913	1.766	.000	1.000	50
Std. Residual	−2.337	2.289	.000	.990	50

a. Dependent Variable: Performance.

First look at the descriptive statistics and correlations table where you can see how the data is structured. There is a strong correlation between math ability and performance with $R^2 = 0.79$ and the adjusted $R^2 = 0.78$, indicating that 78% of the variation in performance could be attributed to math ability. The mean of the predicted value is 68.94 with the SE of the estimate being 5.97. Clearly math ability is a stronger predictor than attitude because the SE of the estimate is lower than with attitude. We can

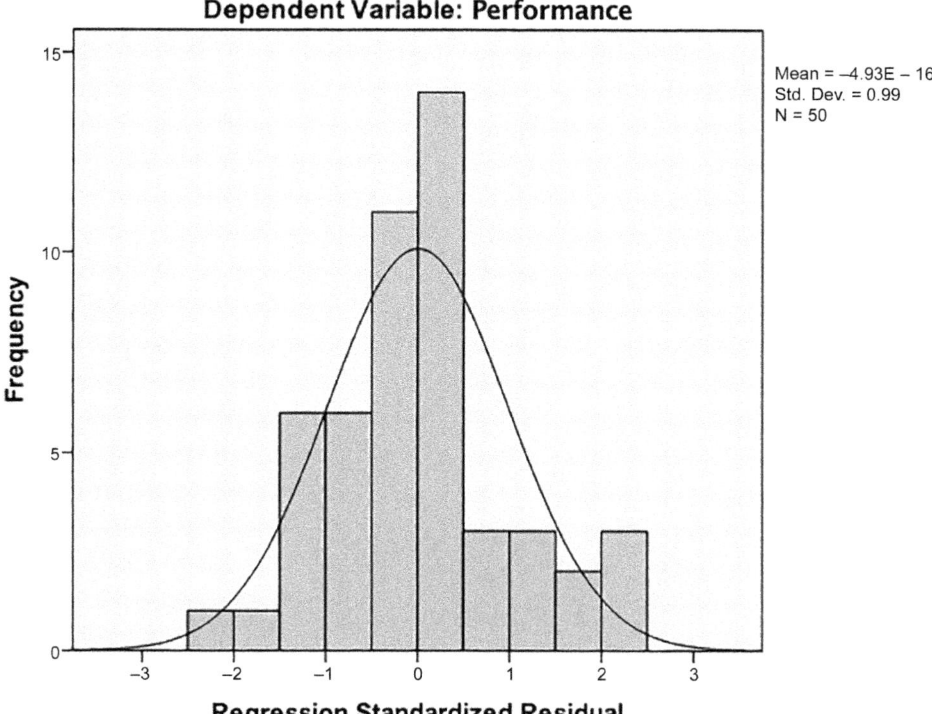

conclude that the SE is sufficiently small compared to the mean of the Y_{pred}. There is a significant F statistic so we can go ahead and examine the results of the regression coefficients. Based on the unstandardized coefficients in the coefficients table we can conclude that

$$y_{pred}(perf) = 39.83 + 2.46 * (math)$$

The t-test is also significant indication that math ability is a very strong predictor of the score on the Overall Performance Examination. The residuals have a normal distribution, with a relatively straight line indicating meeting the assumption of linearity. The last plot is again difficult to interpret because other predictors may be needed in the regression analysis to more completely predict performance. The plot does, however, suggest a better rectangular shape than the earlier attitude/performance regression analysis.

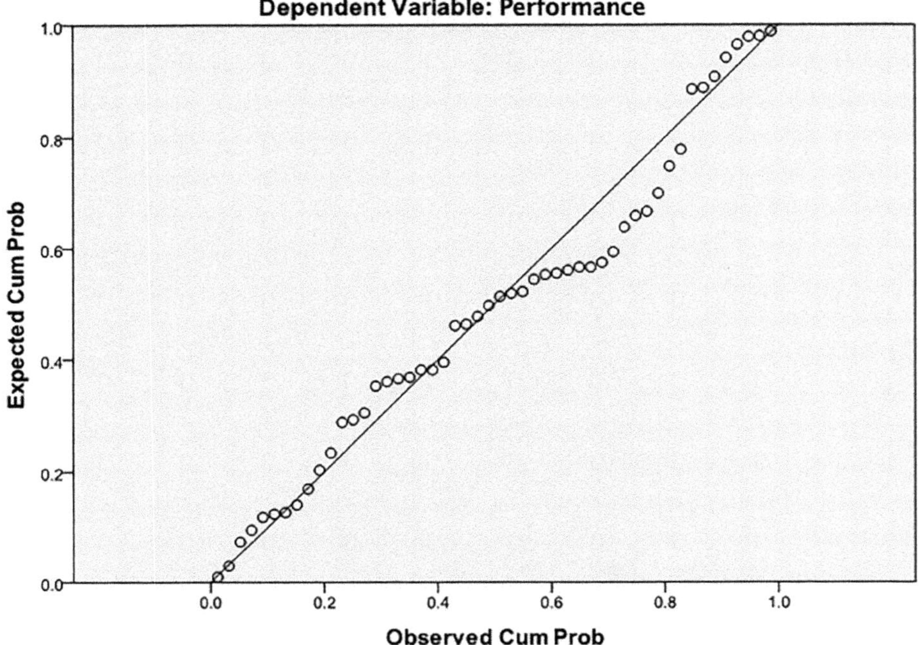
Normal P–P Plot of Regression Standardized Residual
Dependent Variable: Performance
Expected Cum Prob
Observed Cum Prob
0.0
0.2
0.4
0.6
0.8
1.0

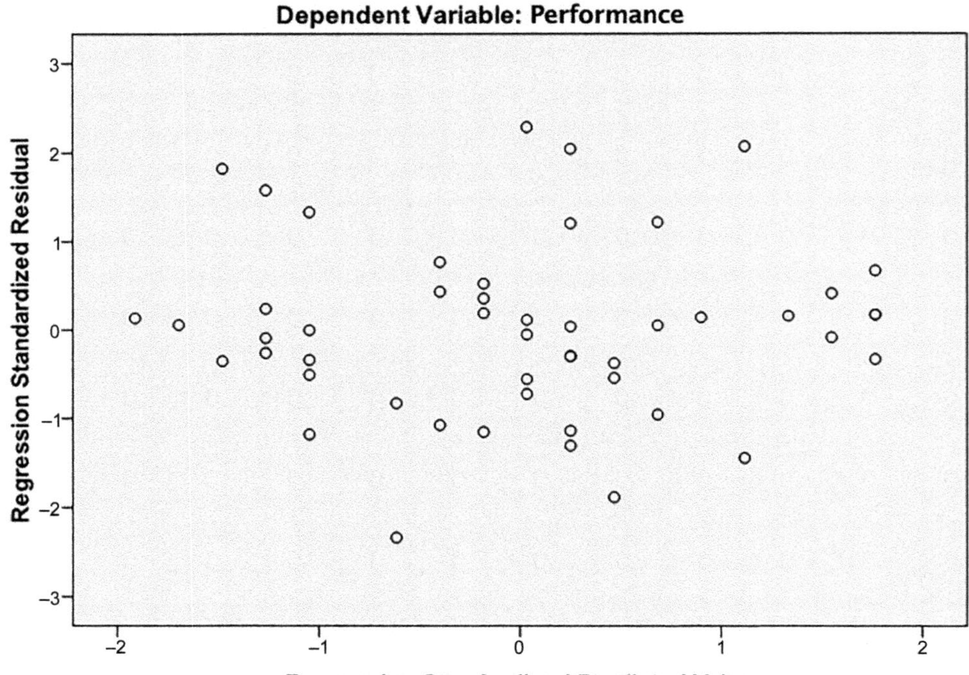
Dependent Variable: Performance
Regression Standardized Residual
Regression Standardized Predicted Value
3
2
1
0
−1
−2
−3

The results might be written as follows:

A simple linear regression analysis was performed to investigate if an increase in Math ability will result in an increase in the score on the Overall Performance Examination. The R^2 statistic was statistically significant ($F_{(1,48)} = 177.46, p = 0.001$, R^2 adjusted = 0.78), indicating that 78% of the variance in performance could be attributed to Math ability. An increase of one standard deviation in Math ability (4.62 points) will result in a 11.40 point increase (0.89 * 12.81) in performance.

Based on the results of the linear regression of math on performance and the previous one with attitude and performance, one can reach the conclusion that math is a stronger predictor than attitude of performance. Math can be viewed as contributing about 78% of the variance in performance and attitude about 34% of performance but these two variables do appear to overlap in their prediction. It therefore would make sense to combine these two variables in a multiple regression analysis to determine how much the prediction is improved if we use both variables.

Let's revisit the regression problem again. X is the predictor variable (IV) and Y is the predicted variable (DV). *Y′ is the prediction of variable Y based upon the regression line—the value of Y predicted at each value of* X. Y is the actual value of Y at each value of X and Y′ is the predicted value of Y at each value of X. Therefore, Y−Y′ is the error or residual variable (what is left over after the contribution of the predictor variables is removed).

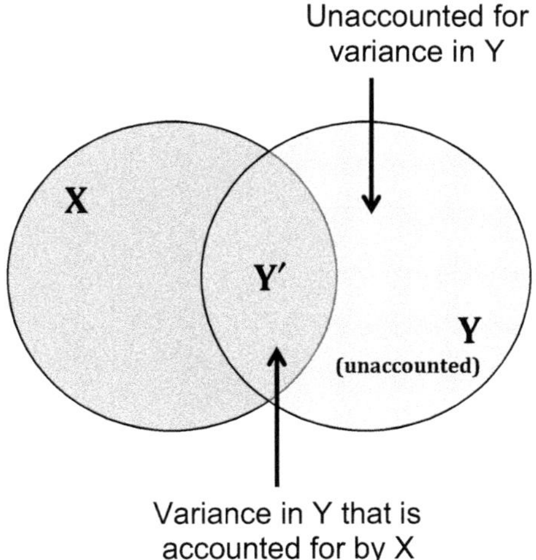

Now, let's go back to our example where we have three variables, attitudes, math ability and performance. Let's carefully look at the Venn diagram.

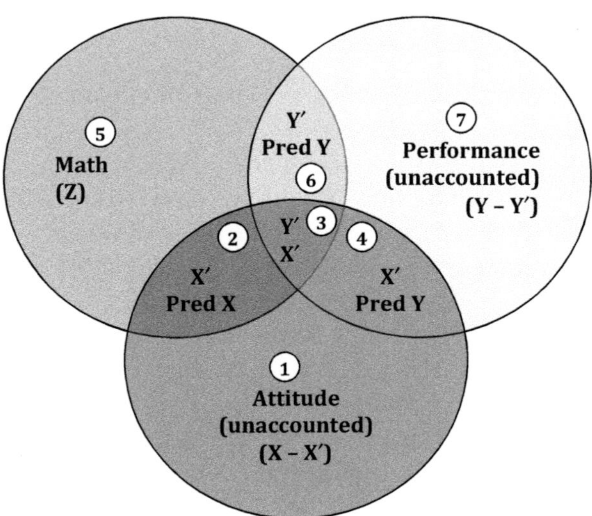

Note: In Parts 1, 5, 7 there is no overlap of the variables.

(1) Combining Parts 2 and 3 shows the overlap of Attitude and Math and indicates the amount of variance in Attitude accounted for by Math. The amount of variance in Attitude not accounted for by Math is shown in Parts 1 and 4.
(2) Combining Parts 6 and 3 shows the overlap of Math and Performance and indicates the amount of variance in Performance accounted for by Math. The amount of variance in Performance not accounted for by Math is shown in Parts 4 and 7.

There are six variables that are important in this example of multiple regression analysis.

(a) Attitude (Parts 1, 2, 3, 4)
(b) Amount of Variance in Attitude attributed to Math (Parts 2, 3)
(c) Amount of Variance in Attitude not attributed to Math (Parts 1, 4)
(d) Performance (Parts 3, 4, 6, 7)
(e) Amount of Variance in Performance attributed to Math (Parts 3, 6)
(f) Amount of Variance in Performance not attributed to Math (Parts 4, 7)

Look at the Venn diagram. If we correlate the amount of Variance not attributed to Math (Parts 4, 7) with the amount of Variance in Attitude not attributed to Math (Parts 1, 4), we get the amount of Variance in Performance attributed to attitude with no influence of Math (PART 4 ONLY).

First, we use math ability (2, 3, 5, 6) to predict attitude (1, 2, 3, 4), with the result of predicted attitude (2, 3) and non-predicted (error) attitude (1, 4). Then we use math ability (2, 3, 5, 6) to predict performance (3, 4, 6, 7), with the result of predicted performance (3, 6) and non-predicted (error) performance, (4, 7). Therefore, we have six variables of interest: attitude (1, 2, 3, 4), predicted attitude (2, 3) and non-predicted (error) attitude (1, 4), performance (3, 4, 6, 7), predicted performance (3, 6) and non-predicted (error) performance (4, 7). Then when we correlate non-predicted (error) performance (4, 7) with non-predicted (error) attitude (1, 4), we get the relationship between attitude and performance with the influence of math removed (4).

Let's go back to the example and do a partial correlation on performance, attitude and math, where we control for the influence of math. Here are the results:

Correlations

		Attitude	Performance
Attitude	Pearson Correlation	1	.596**
	Sig. (2-tailed)		.000
	N	50	50
Performance	Pearson Correlation	.596**	1
	Sig. (2-tailed)	.000	
	N	50	50

**. Correlation is significant at the 0.01 level (2-tailed).

Correlations

		Performance	Math
Performance	Pearson Correlation	1	.887**
	Sig. (2-tailed)		.000
	N	50	50
Math	Pearson Correlation	.887**	1
	Sig. (2-tailed)	.000	
	N	50	50

**. Correlation is significant at the 0.01 level (2-tailed).

Correlations

Control Variables			Attitude	Performance
Math	Attitude	Correlation	1.000	.341
		Significance (2-tailed)	.	.017
		Df	0	47
	Performance	Correlation	.341	1.000
		Significance (2-tailed)	.017	.
		Df	47	0

The correlation between attitude and performance was .596; however, controlling for math the correlation became only .341 indicating that math has a strong predictive value. Now look at semi-partial correlations. The order of correlations is as follows:

(0) Original correlation—zero order correlation (no factors held constant)
(1) Hold constant one factor—first order correlation
(2) Hold constant two factors—second order correlation, etc.

Back to the example. In multiple regression, we use multiple variables to predict the predicted variable. We already saw that both attitude about statistics and math ability correlate with course performance. Based on the results of the above linear regression and the previous one using attitude to predict course performance we can conclude that math ability is a more important predictor for performance than attitude, Math ability accounts for 88% of the variance in performance, whereas attitude towards statistics accounts for 59% of the variance in performance. **However, in our partial Pearson r analysis we did see that when the effect of math ability is removed, there is still some left-over variance in performance that is only accounted for by attitude. It makes sense to combine these two variables in one multiple regression analysis, to see how much our prediction will improve using both variables.**

The predictor variable (IV) must overlap to some extent with the predicted variable (DV). The more the predictor(s) overlap with the predicted variable, the better the prediction. The relationship among the predictors is important because if the correlation among them is very high (they overlap a lot), one of the predictors is redundant.

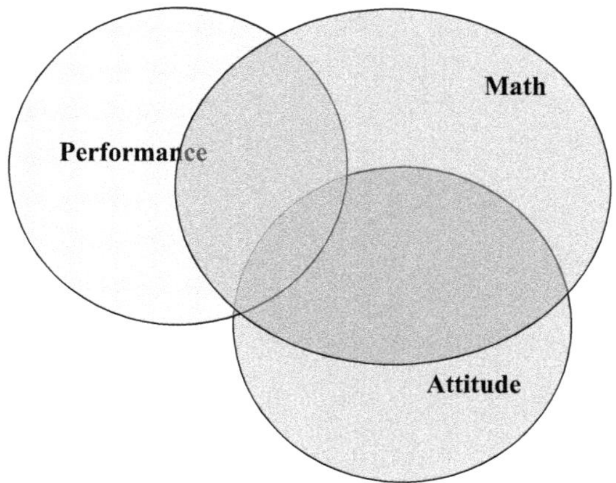

A redundant predictor is one that explains the same variance as the another predictor. In the Venn diagram above the predictors would have almost the same area of variance attributed to them in the predicted variable. You can see that the variance attributed to attitude in Performance is completely within the variance attributed to Math. Thus, Attitude does not add to the variance attributed to in Performance as Math is already doing it. Attitude in this example would become redundant (unnecessary to use) in a multiple regression analysis. Multiple regression requires selection of predictors that correlate well with the predicted variable (variance can be attributed to that predictor) but do not correlate too much with each other (overlap in the predicted variable) and thus the same variance in the predicted variable is attributed to both. **A thorough examination of the literature of the variables related to your question is invaluable in determining predictors to be included in the design.**

There are some very important criteria to be met. **Normality, linearity and homoscedasticity** have already been discussed with respect to simple linear regression in terms of how they can negatively affect the analysis. Other factors also become very important.

Sample size. As discussed in Chapter 12, power is greatly influenced by the size of the sample. You recall when conducting an ANOVA (Chapter 16), the recommendation was a minimum of 10 scores per cell. Thus, with an increase in the number of IVs or with additional levels in the IVs, the sample size will need to be increased significantly. In multiple regression, a similar situation occurs. With additional predictors, the sample needs to be increased in relationship to the number of predictors. As a rule of thumb, we recommend 15 participants per predictor to ensure enough power.

Multicollinearity. This is the term for the previously discussed "overlap problem" of predictors. When one or more predictor variables are very highly correlated, it can cause severe distortion in the regression analysis. With collinearity the effect of individual variables is difficult to determine. It is always important to control for multicollinearity by evaluating the bivariate and partial correlations between the predictors. There are many other ways to assess multicollinearity. A Pearson r correlation (in a bivariate analysis) of .80 or higher between two predictor variables indicates multicollinearity. Multicollinearity may exist when not many t values are significant and the R^2 is above .75. You can also look at the Variance Inflation Factor (VIF) and if it is greater than 4 you might have a situation of multicollinearity. We recommend when there is multicollinearity to delete one of the two highly correlated predictors or (less preferable) to combine those two predictors into a single composite variable.

Outliers. A large number of outliers in multiple regression analysis will create critical errors. As we have noted in previous chapters if the outliers are less than 10% of the total N and are not too extreme they can be retained in the data analysis. However, if they are extreme or greater than 10% you should not use them in the analysis. Another important type of outlier is a **multivariate outlier**. A multivariate outlier is a data point that is an outlier on many predictor variables. In this example, a multivariate outlier would be a pair of scores (math and attitude) where both math and attitude for the individual would be highly deviant from the rest of the data. We suggest that you run the regression analysis both ways, with and without outliers. If there is a difference in the results, get rid of the outliers if you are not deleting too many (stay below the 10% of the N rule of thumb). Typically, your prediction when you remove outliers improves.

Predictors

Do not automatically drop low predictors from the analysis. In initial studies of a phenomena predictor variables must start somewhere and you might not have high value predictors. That is, if you have an R^2 value that is not very high, do not **automatically exclude variables as they might be important** to the prediction. Refining your study to determine critical variables (as we have discussed in the reduction of error in many chapters) is a way to improve the prediction. Remember to keep predictor variables that have been found in previous research or have been developed from theory. Non-significant predictors may be left in the model because theory suggests they are important and until there are many replications indicating that they are not important predictors they should be left in the model. However, after a number of studies indicate that they are not good predictors, they should be left out and the theory modified to exclude these variables.

Another problem that can arise is to include predictor variables that should be left out (misspecification). A good way to determine if a predictor variable should be included and kept in a multiple regression analysis is to conduct **bivariate analyses with each of the predictor variables (IV) and the predicted variable (DV). If the bivariate relationship is not significant, almost all of the time it is not a good predictor variable.** Another way to make sure you do not include unnecessary variables is to look at the t value for the variable and if it is at .10 or less it is probably a good predictor; if it is greater than .10 it should be excluded.

If you have developed a multiple regression prediction using variables from theory/literature, non-significant predictors may be left in the model. We leave them in because theory suggests they are important and until there are many replications indicating that they are not important predictors, they should be in the model. However, after a number of studies indicate that they are not predictors then they should be left out and the theory modified to exclude these variables.

There are different ways in SPSS to build multiple regression models. The most **frequently used is to enter *all predictors into the equation at the same time (ENTER method)*.** This method is chosen if you have no reason to develop a specific order for entering the predictor variables. The **ENTER** method option is typically selected when the prediction **model is derived from theory** and all variables have basically the same importance in the prediction. It is used when **you want to find out the overall association of all of the predictors with the predicted variable and also to find out the importance of each individual predictor**.

STEP **methods create a regression model one variable at a time rather than all at the same time.** The reason for using the different step methods is **to build a model with only the "important" predictors** in it. With the **FORWARD method, bivariate correlation coefficients are computed for each predictor variable with the predicted variable**. After they are calculated, the predictor variable with the largest correlation is entered first, then the second largest correlation and so on with each succeeding lower correlation. Each predictor variable, once placed into the model, remains in the regression equation. This procedure continues until no more predictor variables contribute significantly to the prediction.

In the **BACKWARD** method, all predictor variables are placed into the regression analysis at the same time and multiple R^2 and partial correlation coefficients are computed. **Then the predictor variable that has the smallest partial correlation coefficient with the predicted variable is *removed* from the regression equation.** Then the predictor variable that has the second smallest partial correlation coefficient is removed. **This procedure stops when the variance in the predicted variable significantly drops (it has reached a predictor variable that is explaining a significant amount of variance).**

In the STEPWISE method, the forward and backward methods are combined. The **contribution of each predictor variable already entered into the analysis** (it has already been analyzed for attribution of variance to the predicted variable) is then **reassessed after each new predictor variable is entered into the equation**. Predictor variables that no longer contribute significantly to the variance in the predicted variable are removed. The model solution is complete when there are no more significant predictor variables. Concerns about using the stepwise methods of analysis are (1) they are more dependent upon the sample characteristics and may not be the best way to try to determine the relationship of the predictor and predicted variables when applied to the population and (2) they tend to be more oriented toward single predictors than the analysis of all of the variables simultaneously.

Let's now finally return to our example where we want to see how both Attitude Toward School and Math Ability predict Overall Exam Performance.

Study Question: Can the score on the Overall Performance Exam—Predicted variable (DV) be predicted by Math ability and Attitude Toward School—Predictor variables (IVs)?

This is a prediction design.

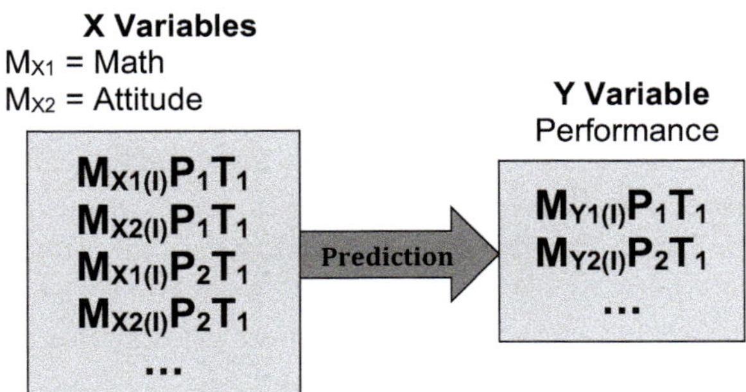

Hypotheses:

Prediction: Attitude Toward School and Math Ability will predict the score on the Overall Performance Exam.

Null: Attitude Toward School and Math Ability will not predict performance on the Overall Performance Examination.

Expected (E): There will be not be a predictive relationship between Attitude Toward School, Math Ability and score on the Overall Performance Examination.

Predicted (P): There will be a predictive relationship between Attitude Toward School, Math Ability and score on the Overall Performance Examination.

Observed (O): The actual relationship between Attitude Toward School, Math Ability and Overall Performance Examination.

Level of Measurement: IV Interval (Attitude toward School), IV Interval (Math Ability), DV Interval (Overall Performance Examination)

Type of Design: Predictive

Number of Groups: 3 Samples same group

Assumptions: (a) Interval level data, (b) Normal distributions, (c) Linear relationship between variables, (d) Homoscedasticity, (e) No multicollinearity.

Conceptual framework:

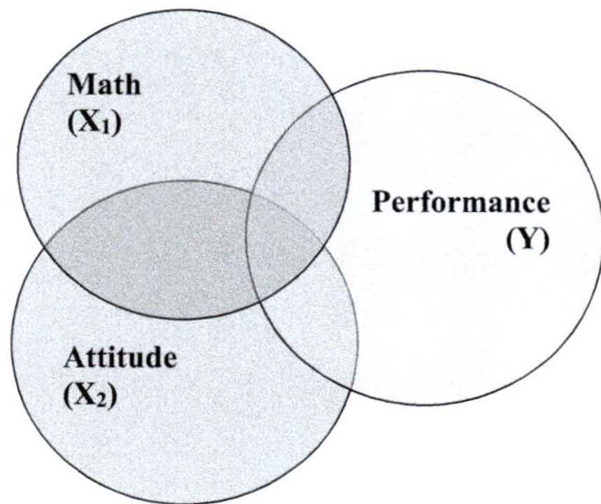

SPSS Commands

Open the data set ***Ch21 MultiRegression***.
Follow the steps below:

(1) Click ***Analyze***.
(2) Scroll down and select ***Regression***.
(3) Select ***Linear . . .***
(4) Move ***Performance*** into the ***Dependent*** box.
(5) Move ***Math*** and ***Attitude*** into the ***Independent(s)*** box.

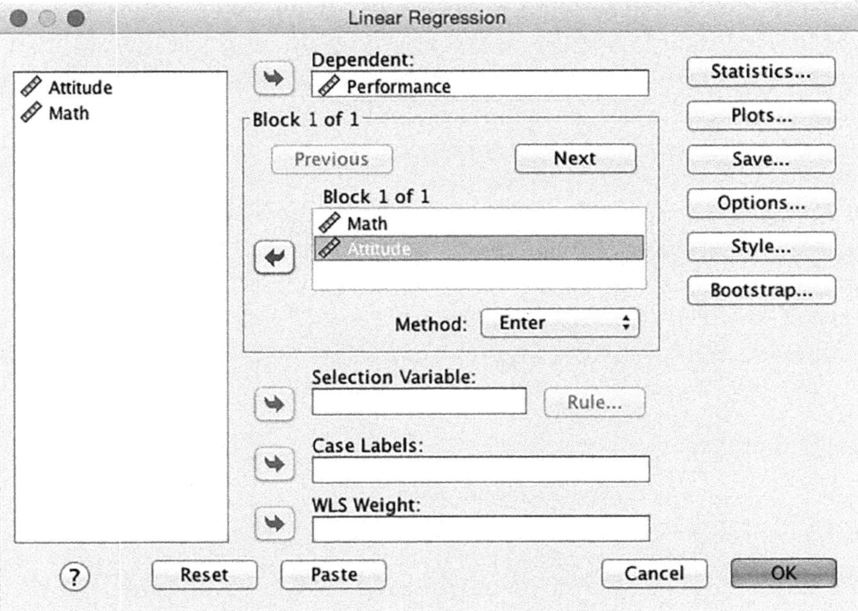

(6) Click the ***Statistics . . .*** button.

(7) Check the boxes next to ***Estimates***, ***Model fit***, ***Descriptives***, ***Part and partial correlations*** and ***Collinearity diagnostics***.

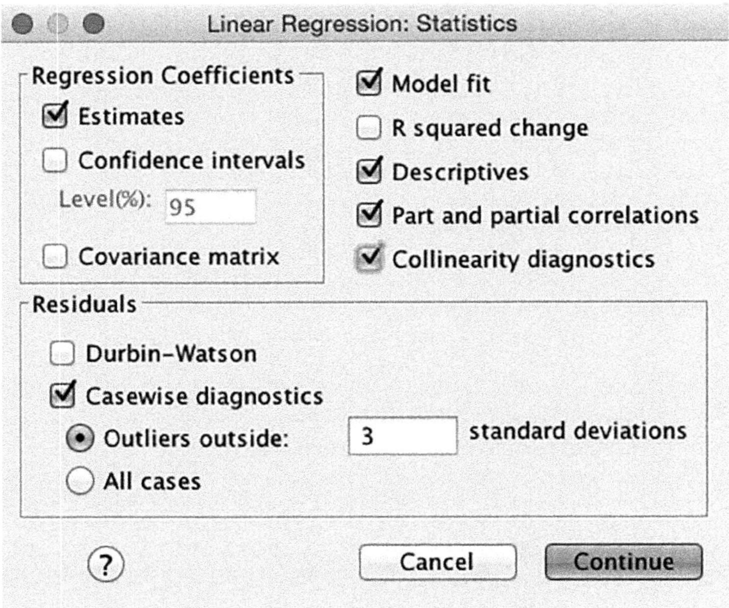

(8) Under ***Residuals***, check the box next to ***Casewise diagnostics*** and request ***Outliers outside 3 standard deviations***.
(9) Click ***Continue***
(10) Click the ***Plots . . .*** button.
(11) Under the ***Standardized Residual Plots*** heading, request both the ***Histogram*** and the ***Normal probability plot***.
(12) Move ***ZRESID*** (standardized residuals) into the Y-axis and ***ZPRED*** (the standardized predicted value) into the X-axis.

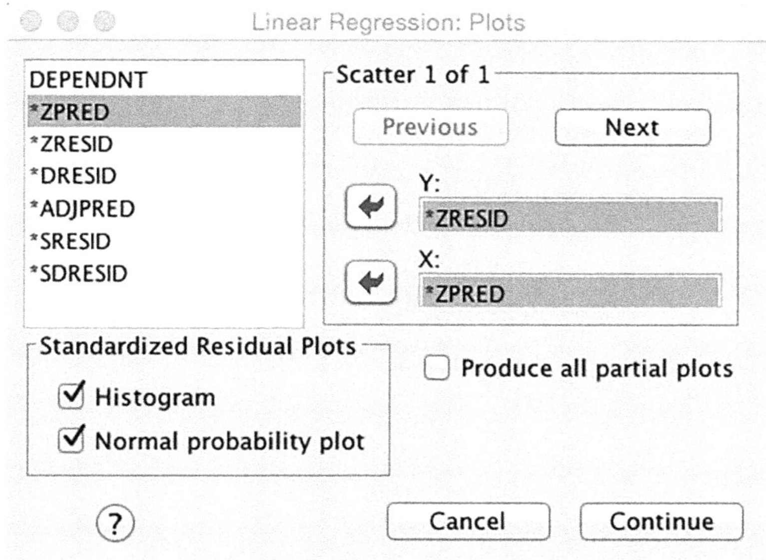

(13) Click ***Continue***.
(14) Click ***OK*** to run the analysis.

Look at the output:

Descriptive Statistics

	Mean	Std. Deviation	N
Performance	68.94	12.808	50
Math	11.84	4.622	50
Attitude	21.96	7.559	50

Correlations

		Performance	Math	Attitude
Pearson Correlation	Performance	1.000	.887	.596
	Math	.887	1.000	.521
	Attitude	.596	.521	1.000
Sig. (1-tailed)	Performance	.	.000	.000
	Math	.000	.	.000
	Attitude	.000	.000	.
N	Performance	50	50	50
	Math	50	50	50
	Attitude	50	50	50

Variables Entered/Removed[a]

Model	Variables Entered	Variables Removed	Method
1	Attitude, Math[b]	.	Enter

a. Dependent Variable: Performance.
b. All requested variables entered.

Model Summary[b]

Model	R	R Square	Adjusted R Square	Std. Error of the Estimate
1	.901[a]	.812	.804	5.673

a. Predictors: (Constant), Attitude, Math.
b. Dependent Variable: Performance.

ANOVA[a]

Model		Sum of Squares	Df	Mean Square	F	Sig.
1	Regression	6525.984	2	3262.992	101.373	.000[b]
	Residual	1512.836	47	32.188		
	Total	8038.820	49			

a. Dependent Variable: Performance.
b. Predictors: (Constant), Attitude, Math.

Coefficients[a]

Model		Unstandardized Coefficients		Standardized Coefficients			Correlations			Collinearity Statistics	
		B	Std. Error	Beta	t	Sig.	Zero-order	Partial	Part	Tolerance	VIF
1	(Constant)	36.125	2.679		13.483	.000					
	Math	2.193	.205	.791	10.675	.000	.887	.841	.675	.729	1.372
	Attitude	.312	.126	.184	2.484	.017	.596	.341	.157	.729	1.372

a. Dependent Variable: Performance.

Collinearity Diagnostics[a]

Model	Dimension	Eigenvalue	Condition Index	Variance Proportions		
				(Constant)	Math	Attitude
1	1	2.882	1.000	.01	.01	.01
	2	.067	6.538	.58	.78	.01
	3	.051	7.539	.41	.21	.98

a. Dependent Variable: Performance.

Residuals Statistics[a]

	Minimum	Maximum	Mean	Std. Deviation	N
Predicted Value	44.89	89.97	68.94	11.541	50
Residual	−10.700	12.192	.000	5.556	50
Std. Predicted Value	−2.084	1.822	.000	1.000	50
Std. Residual	−1.886	2.149	.000	.979	50

a. Dependent Variable: Performance.

Charts

Look at the descriptive statistics and correlations table to see the structure of the data. The same outcomes emerge as before in that there is a very strong correlation between math ability and performance, and a weaker correlation between attitude and performance, although still significant and strong. The model summary table shows that R^2 is 0.81 and the adjusted **R^2 is 0.80, indicating that 80% of the variance in the overall performance exam performance can be attributed to math ability *and* attitude toward school**. As shown in the descriptive table, the mean of the performance (predicted value) is 68.94 and the SE of the estimate is 5.67. The ANOVA table shows that

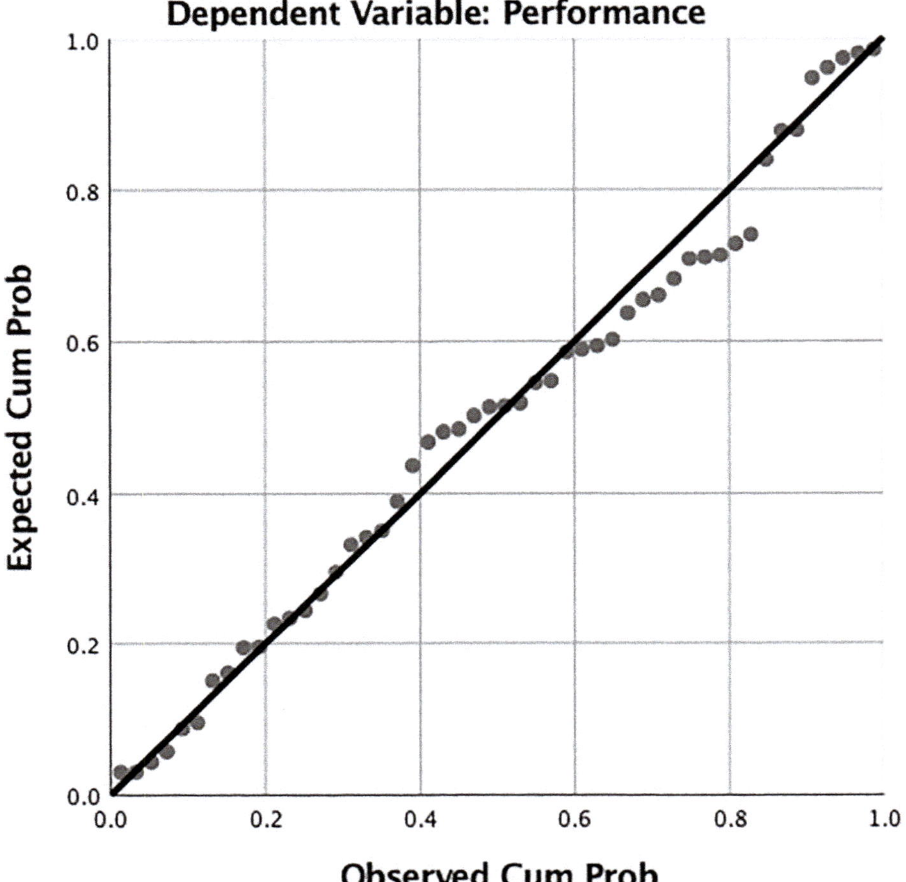

the F statistic is significant ($F_{(2,47)} = 101.37, p = .001$), indicating that we can proceed with the analysis. Based on the unstandardized coefficients in the coefficients table the following equation can be written:

$$y_{pred}(perf) = 36.15 + .312 * (att) \ + \ 2.193 * (math)$$

In the coefficient table the following can be found. The t-test is significance for math ability as a predictor (p = .001), and attitude toward school as a predictor (p = .017) are both significant confirming the other results. The VIF statistics indicate that there is not a problem of multicollinearity which is also confirmed with a bivariate correlation of .521 between attitude and math (found in the correlations table). The zero-order

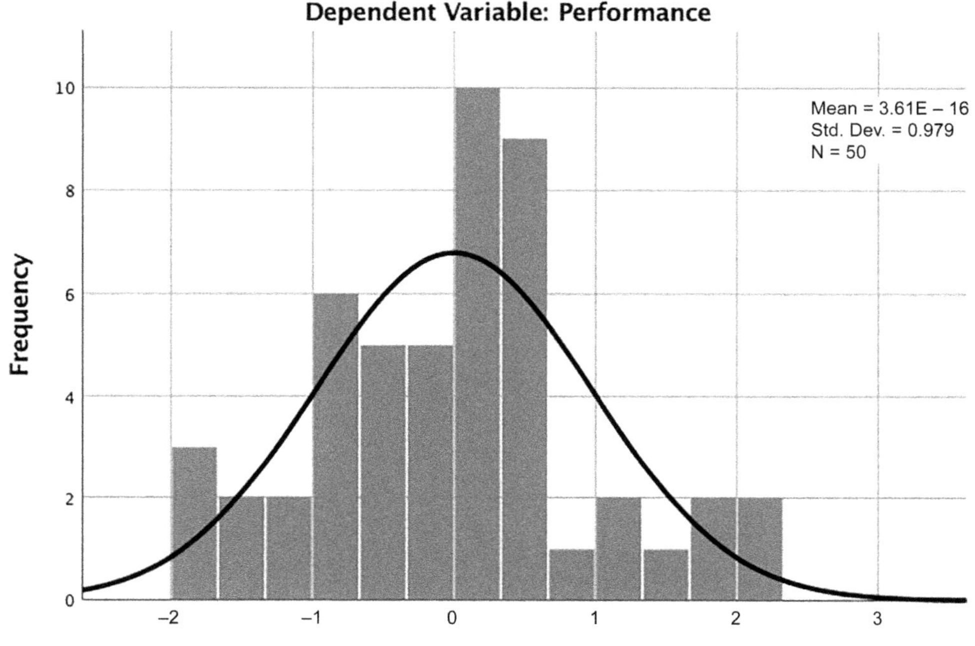
Dependent Variable: Performance
Mean = 3.61E – 16
Std. Dev. = 0.979
N = 50
Frequency
0
2
4
6
8
10
–2
–1
0
1
2
3
Regression Standardized Residual

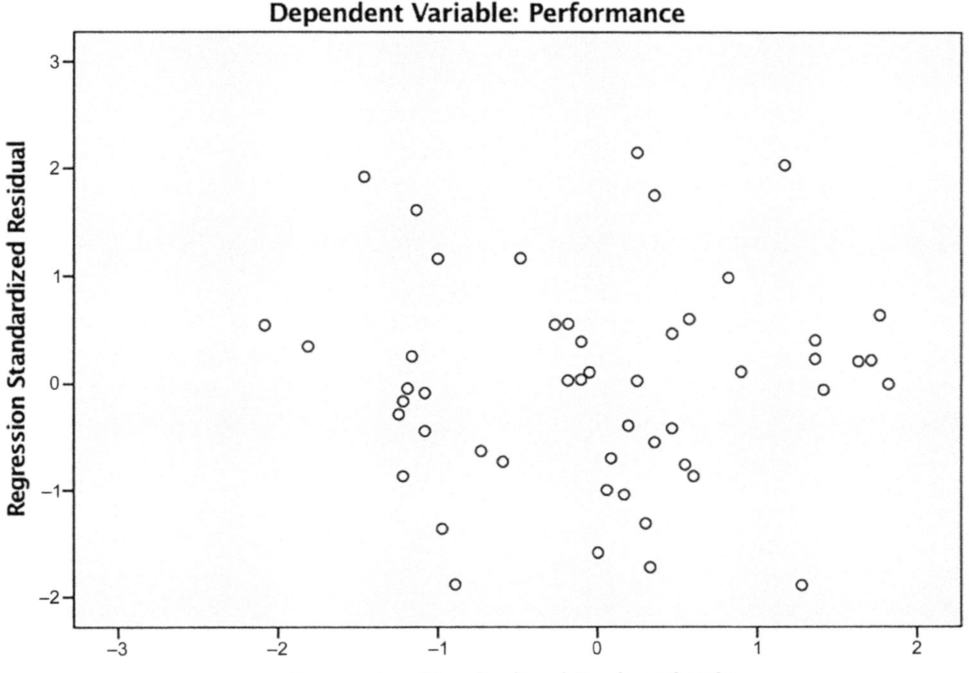
Dependent Variable: Performance
Regression Standardized Residual
3
2
1
0
–1
–2
–3
–2
–1
0
1
2
Regression Standardized Predicted Value

correlations are simply bivariate correlations between each of the predictors and the dependent variable. The partial correlation coefficients are the correlation between the IV and DV after all remaining IVs have been partialed out or controlled for. Based on the table we see that the partial correlation between math and performance, controlling for attitude is 0.841, and between attitude and performance, controlling for math, is 0.341. The partial correlation, when squared, shows the unique contribution of each predictor. If we square 0.157, we get 0.02, indicating that **attitude contributes 2% to the prediction**. If we square math ability, we see that the **unique contribution of math ability is 46%**. However, our R^2 value is 0.80, indicating that 80% of the variance can be attributed to both variables—that which is unique to each variable AND the amount attributed to both variables when they overlap. We have just determined that **the two predictors alone uniquely accounted for 48% of the variance. The difference between these two values is 32%. This represents the total amount of overlapping predictive value of the two predictors.**

Results might be written as follows:

A multiple regression analysis was performed to investigate if the variance in overall performance exam scores could be attributed to math ability and attitude toward school. It was hypothesized that a positive increase in math ability and attitude toward school would result in a positive increase in the overall performance exam score. The R^2 statistic was statistically significant ($F_{(2, 47)} = 101.373, p = .001$), R^2 adjusted = .804 indicating that 80% of the variance in the score on the overall performance exam can be attributed to the math ability and attitude toward school. Math ability contributed significantly to the prediction of performance in the (Standardized beta = .791, unique contribution based on part correlation = .44). Attitude Toward School contributed significantly to the prediction of performance (Standardized beta = .184, unique contribution based on part correlation = .02).

Practical Implications: Much of the conclusions from the simple linear regressions of attitude on performance and math on performance are still applicable. However, with the multiple regression model we have determined that while both are important to performance, math is much more important than attitude. Interestingly there is a great overlap between attitude and math, suggesting that there is another underlying factor (construct) that appears in both variables and should be the subject of future studies.

Articles for Discussion

What do the research findings say about the view of social workers toward their clients? Why do you think these results were found? Why was the regression analysis used? How would you implement these findings into practice changes?

Cohen, B. (1985). Applying the "Unmotivated" label to clients in social service agencies. *The Journal of Sociology and Social Welfare*, *12*(2), 274–286. Retrieved from http://scholarworks.wmich.edu/jssw/vol12/iss2/4

Why did the author use regression and a prediction model in this study? Discuss the results and their impact on social work. How can the results be used in practice?

Cohen-Mansfield, J., Dakheel-Ali, M., & Jensen, B. (2013). Predicting service use and intent to use services of older adult residents of two naturally occurring retirement communities. *Social Work Research*, *37*(4), 313–329. doi:10.1093/swr/svt026

Exercises for Chapter 21 are found in eResources.

GLOSSARY

1-Tailed Test: see Directional Hypothesis

2-Tailed Test: see Non-Directional Hypothesis

A phase: in a single subject design the period where there is no intervention occurring

A priori: before the event—a prediction before something happens—the probability of a future event calculated from previous knowledge

AB Design: a single subject design with a baseline phase (A phase) followed by a single intervention phase (B phase)

ABABAB Design: a single subject design where there is a series of interventions followed by a period of non-intervention to measure the effect of the intervention over time and to determine the long-term effects of the intervention—in social work practice it is often a situation of testing whether the client can "go it on their own" for a period of time and then come back to receive more intervention

ABCD Designs: a single subject design where there are multiple intervention targets but all are parts of a broader overall single target (one problem with multiple parts)

Alpha α: in a regression equation the intercept of the regression line with the Y-axis

ANCOVA: a parametric statistical test using interval or ratio level measurement to determine the amount of difference in the means of the dependent variable between independent groups with statistical control of a variable related to the dependent variable—allows for that variance to be subtracted from the values of the dependent variable—adjusting the means

ANCOVA—One-Way Between With Multiple (k) Groups and a Covariate: a parametric statistical test using interval or ratio level measurement to determine the amount of difference in the means of the dependent variable between more than two independent groups with statistical control of a variable related to the dependent variable—allows for that variance to be subtracted from the values of the dependent variable—adjusting the means (see chart in eResources)

ANCOVA—Repeated Measures: a parametric statistical test using interval or ratio measurement with matched/paired groups after adjusting the dependent variable based upon the variance attributed to the covariate to determine if there was a difference between the groups measured MORE THAN 1 time (T1, T2)—typically used in a pre-post design (see chart in eResources)

ANCOVA—Repeated Measures With k groups and a Covariate: a parametric statistical test using interval or ratio level measurement with k matched/paired groups after adjusting the dependent variable based upon the variance attributed to the covariate to determine if there was a difference between the k groups measured MORE THAN one time (T1, T2)—typically used in a pre-post design (see chart in eResources)

ANCOVA—Two-Way Between With Multiple (k) Groups and a Covariate: a parametric statistical test using interval or ratio level measurement to determine the amount of difference in the means of the dependent variable with MORE THAN ONE INDEPENDENT VARIABLE and BETWEEN more than two independent groups WITH statistical control of a variable related to the dependent variable that allows for that variance to be subtracted from the values of the dependent variable—adjusting the means (see chart in eResources)

Annotated Bibliography: method to catalogue your literature search includes: (1) specific: bibliographic information (author, title, etc.) (2) a summary of what was written, (3) a critical evaluation of what was written and (4) how the material can be utilized in your research or practice

ANOVA: a parametric statistical test using interval or ratio level measurement to determine the amount of difference in the means of the dependent variable between independent groups

ANOVA—One-Way Between With Multiple (k) Groups: a parametric statistical test using interval or ratio level measurement to determine the amount of difference in the means of the dependent variable between more than two independent groups (see chart in eResources)

ANOVA—One-Way Within With Multiple (k) Groups: a parametric statistical test using interval or ratio data with k matched/paired groups to determine if there was a difference between MORE THAN two groups measured MORE THAN 1 time (T1 and T2)—typically used in a pre-post design (see chart in eResources)

ANOVA—Repeated Measures: a parametric statistical test using interval or ratio data with matched/paired groups to determine if there was a difference between the groups measured MORE THAN one time (T1, T2)—typically used in a pre-post design (see chart in eResources)

ANOVA—Two-Way Between With Multiple (k) Groups: a parametric statistical test using ratio or interval measurement to determine the amount of difference in the means of the dependent variable with MORE THAN one INDEPENDENT VARIABLE and between MORE THAN two groups (see chart in eResources)

Axial Coding: in objectivist grounded theory (qualitative research), the second in the sequence of coding information that can be viewed as surrounded and having some influence on the open coding categories

B Design: in a single subject design where there is no baseline established prior to the introduction of the intervention

B Phase: in a single subject design the period when there is intervention occurring

Back Translation: translating from one language into another language using one translator, then translating a second time with a different translator into the original language to ensure the correctness of the translation

Backward Planning: in program evaluation developing the program starting with the goals/outcome (problem resolution) and working backward to determine the necessary resources to accomplish the resolution of the program and outcome achievement

Baseline: in a single subject design the measurement of the occurrence of the target (behavior/attitude/problem) of the intervention prior to initiation of any intervention

Beneficence Principle: a principle in research ethics that states a person upon whom research is being performed must be protected from both psychological and physical harm

Beta β: in a regression equation the slope of the regression line

Bi-modal Distribution: a frequency distribution that has two values that are the highest occurring value or very similar

Bracketing: in the phenomenological approach (qualitative research) the researcher brackets their experience by acknowledging their experience in the situation, presenting it and then as much as possible excluding it from the combined experienced description provided by the participant

Case Study: the study of a specific (delineated/circumscribed) occurrence at a specific time and specific place

Causality: a cause and effect relationship—if the effect always happens if the cause always happens—able to be experimentally shown

Central Tendency Measures: the values in a distribution that are used to indicate the center of the distribution (Mean, Median, Mode)

Chance: the probability of something happening at random

Chi-Square Goodness of Fit Test: a nonparametric statistical test using nominal measurement to determine if the sample is a good representation of the population (see chart in eResources)

Chi-Square r x k Multiple Independent Samples/Groups test: a statistical test using nominal level data to determine the amount of difference between two independent groups/samples with more than two levels in at least one of the groups/samples (see chart in eResources)

Chi-Square Two Independent Sample/Groups: a statistical test using nominal level data to determine the amount of difference in two independent samples/groups

Closed-Ended Question: a type of question where the possible answers are provided to the respondent and no alternative responses are allowed

Cluster Sampling: sampling method that is a multiple stage process wherein the researcher moves from larger "clusters" of units to smaller "clusters" to obtain the sample

Cochran Q Test: a nonparametric statistical test used to determine the amount of difference between more than two related (k) samples/groups using nominal level of measurement (see chart in eResources)

Coding: putting raw data into categorical groups (nominal and ordinal level data)—creating the variables in a data set

Cohen's d: a method to determine effect size for the t-test (comparison of two independent groups)

Cohort Design: a type of longitudinal design where the sample selected from the population to form a pool of participants does not change but the participants selected from the pool change over time—for example, the graduating class of 2000 is the same group over time but the participants selected can be different but all from the class of 2000

Concept: an abstract idea that has been created by putting numerous individual observations together

Conceptual Equivalent: measuring the same constructs in another culture/language

Confidence Interval: the range of values (scores) in which the researcher is willing to say the parameter will occur based upon statistics calculated from the sample

Confidentiality: when the participant can be identified by the researcher, but guaranteed his/her identity will not be made public

Confirmability: refers to the need for objectivity in the researcher in qualitative research and is strengthened by use of reflection

Constant: a value that does not change

Construct: a concept that has properties that can be measured and used in science to develop questions

Constructivist Grounded Theory: a less structured post-modern form of grounded theory

Content/Construct Validity: the ability of the measure to capture all of the aspects (content) of the variable being measured

Contingency Table-Crosstab Table: a table that shows the frequency of occurrence of two or more nominal or ordinal level variables

Continuous Variable: a variable that can assume any value in a set of values that are ordered (infinite number of values)

Control: during the research process when the researcher reduces the number and effect of variables other than the IV(s) that could affect the outcome

Control Group: the group(s) of individuals in an experimental design that do not receive the intervention and are used for comparison to those receiving the intervention

Convenience Sampling: a non-probability sampling method where all participants are selected because they are readily available—least representative but cost effective

Correlation: a statistic that shows the amount and direction of a relationship between two variables—typically a correlation coefficient ranges from −1 (where one variable increases while the other variable decreases) to +1 (where both variables increase)

Cost Benefit: the cost of the program compared to the total monetary value of all benefits accrued as a result of the program

Cramer V: a statistical measurement of the amount of relationship (association) between two categorical variables with more than two levels (k) (see chart in eResources)

Credibility: using well-established research methods, random sampling and having experts and/or participants check on the accuracy of the materials (Qualitative Research)—similar to internal validity in Quantitative Research

Criterion Validity: testing the measurement against other measures of the same construct

Criterion Validity—Concurrent: testing the measurement against other known measures of the same construct at the same time

Criterion Validity—Predictive: using the measurement to predict an eternal criterion that measures the same construct

Critical Incident Case Study: a type of case study that provides a thorough investigation into a specific instance of a phenomena

Cronbach's Alpha: the value found (correlation coefficient) by using all of the possible split half combinations in the scale to determine internal consistency

Cross-Sectional Design: a type of research design where the dependent variable is measured only at a single point in time (T1)

Cultural Competence: being as aware as possible of the beliefs, norms, customs and behavior of others and acting appropriately upon that knowledge

Cumulative Case Study: a type of case study that compiles and aggregates information from several previously conducted case studies of a single phenomenon occurring at different sites and different times

Cyclic Baseline: in a single subject design where the occurrence of the target (behavior/attitude/problem) occurs in a specific repetitive pattern prior to any intervention—low on weekend and high during the week

Decreasing Baseline: in a single subject design where the occurrence of the target (behavior/attitude/problem) is continually becoming less prior to any intervention

Deductive Reasoning: starts with generalizations and theory and tests the generalizations: and theory based upon specific situations

Degrees of Freedom: the number of ways that the data are free to move—the number of values (observations) of the variable after the number of data restrictions (parameters) are estimated

Dependability: research is dependable if the same results are found when the study is conducted in the same exact way over and over again (Qualitative Research—similar to reliability in Quantitative Research)

Dependent/Predicted Variable: a variable in which change can be accounted for or caused by an independent variable, occurs chronologically after another variable or is predicted by another variable

Descriptive/Exploratory Designs: a category of research design where the focus of the research is to determine frequency, amount and conditions relating to variables about which there is little information

Deviation From the Mean: how much a single score is different from the mean of the distribution

Deviation Score: the difference of an individual score from the mean of that distribution

Difference/Relationship Designs: a category of research designs that attempts to determine if differences or relationships exist and if so the amount of difference or relationship

Directional Hypothesis: a hypothesis that states the direction (greater, lesser) of the relationship between the IV and the DV—there is greater depression in older individuals than younger individuals

Discrete Variable: a variable that can assume only a certain number of values—typically a categorical variable

Distribution: the frequency pattern of scores/values, the total number of scores/observation on a variable in a data set

Effectiveness: in program evaluation the amount of change from the previous level (was the program effective in achieving the outcome)

Efficiency: in program evaluation the amount of change related to the amount of cost to produce the change (to achieve the outcome)

Error: the amount of unexplained variance in the DV (Experimental Designs) or the predicted variable (Prediction Designs) that cannot be accounted for by the IV or Predictor variable

Ethnocentrism: recognizing differences in culture but still evaluating results based upon the cultural background of the researcher

Ethnographic Approach: a method of qualitative research characterized by its focus on and examination of the shared culture of a group

Expected Value (E): the expected value of the dependent variable that there is no difference (Null Hypothesis)

Experimental Group: in an experimental design the group that receives the intervention

Experimental Pre-Post Design: a type of longitudinal design with two measurement periods (Time 1) pre-intervention and (Time 2) post-intervention that includes a minimum of two groups—experimental group and control group

Explanatory/Predictive Designs: a category of research designs where (1) an independent variable is manipulated by the researcher and the dependent variable is measured to determine the effect of the IV on the DV (2) where the researcher measures the predictor variable and determines how well it can predict the predicted variable

Exploratory Case Study: a type of case study conducted on a small scale to identify and refine questions and to form the basis for designing a more extensive study

External Validity: the ability of the results to generalize to the population—based upon the adequacy of the sample to represent the population as opposed to internal validity which is related to the process of the research itself

F Statistic: a statistic that is used to compare the difference in variance between two groups—used in ANOVA

Face Validity: when the statement appears to be measuring what it is supposed to be measuring simply on the basis of the words

False Alarm: a Type I Error

Fisher ExactTesttest—Two Independent Samples/Groups: a statistical test to determine the amount of difference between two independent samples/groups when the dependent variable is measured at the nominal level and when the assumptions of the Chi-Square Two Independent Samples/Groups test are NOT MET (see chart in eResources)

Focus Group: a variant of an interview and consists of a small number of participants who are asked to respond to a specified set of questions in a group setting so that they can interact with each other

Formative Evaluation: in program evaluation determining how well the program is developing toward "rolling out"—actual start

Frequency: the amount/number of observations in a category—most often referring to the number in a cell—found in a frequency table

Frequency Table: a table that shows the frequency/amount of things/observations in each category of the variable

Friedman Analysis of VarianceTest by Ranks: a nonparametric statistical test used to determine the amount of difference between more than two related (k) samples/groups using ordinal level data (see chart in eResources)

Gamma: a statistical test using ordinal level of measurement to determine if there is a linear relationship between two variables taking into account the difference between the pairs of scores (concordant—discordant) and dividing the result by the total of all pairs (ignores ties) (see chart in eResources)

Generalize: using the findings from the sample to infer it is the same for the population

Grounded Theory Approach: a method of qualitative research aimed at discovering/uncovering/revealing theory that is generated from the experiences of those who have lived it

Histogram: a graphic representation of the distribution of the values of a variable with the vertical axis representing the frequency of the scores and the horizontal axis representing the values on the variable—using a bar for the frequencies

History: the amount of change that can occur in the results due to the occurrence of a significant event—one of the threats to internal validity

Homoscedasticity: equality of variance—important in both Regression and ANOVA

Humanism: belief system that sees all people as having dignity, worth and capability of self-fulfillment

Hypothesis: a statement/declarative sentence about the relationship between two or more variables

Experimental Hypothesis: prediction (best guess) in a statement/declarative form that there is a relationship between two or more variables

Experimental Hypothesis: a prediction that there is no relationship between two or more variables and is the direct opposite of the experimental hypothesis

Ideology: a rigidly fixed belief system—unlikely to change

Illustrative Case Study: a type of case study in qualitative research aimed at a problem or issue (individual, family, group or organization) to more fully elucidate it and illuminate it—highly descriptive—to portray

Implementation Evaluation: in program evaluation assessing how well the initiation of the program is progressing AND how well the program is functioning after implementation (does not measure the outcome, only the functioning)

Increasing Baseline: Increasing Baseline in a single subject design when the occurrence of the target (behavior/attitude/problem) is ever increasing prior to any intervention

Independent/Predictor Variable: a variable that can be used to account for, cause or change a dependent variable; a variable that occurs chronologically before another variable; a variable that is a predictor of another variable

Inductive Reasoning: reasoning that starts with observations (specifics) and uses them to generalize and create theory

Informed Consent: researcher must provide the potential participant with the following information: what the research is about, what will happen to them in the study, if there is any risk or harm that might happen to them, any benefits to them or others because of the study and that they can drop out of the study at any time with no negative results—the participant has the information needed to make an informed decision prior to the research process

Instrumental Case Study: a type of case study that aims to understand the overarching problem and situation and not a specific individual or to understand a particular issue or situation related to a human service organization—to characterize the context

Instruments: the amount of change that can occur in the results due to change in the measurement instruments or the administration of those instruments—a threat to internal validity

Interaction: the effect of one independent variable (factor) on another independent variable (factor) as it affects the dependent variable—age and gender interact on the health of an individual

Internal Validity: the type of validity that is related to the process of the research (see Threats to Internal Validity) as opposed to External Validity which is related to the sampling of individuals into the research study

Inter-observer Reliability: the consistency of measurement across many observers/judges—the correlation coefficient is a measure of inter-observer reliability

Interval Measurement: a level measurement where the distance between each unit of measurement is equal (equal-interval scale) but there is no known zero (things CANNOT be compared using ratios)

Interview: a method of obtaining information by talking to respondents using a questionnaire or interview guide—can be conducted in three ways: (1) face to face, (2) telephone, (3) Internet

Intrinsic Case Study: a type of case study that aims to understand the unique and individual characteristics of a particular situation for a particular person

Jargon Trap: using words or phrases with participants or other researchers when the words or phrases have no meaning to them—the meaning is only understood within the profession

Justice Principle: the principle in research ethics that states (1) all participants in the study are treated equally and (2) benefits from the research will be equal to all

Kendall Tau B Partial Rank Order Coefficient: a statistical test using ordinal level measurement to determine if there is a linear relationship between two or more variables taking into account the difference between the pairs of scores (concordant—discordant) AND controlling—mathematically taking out the variance contributed by the third variable (see chart in eResources)

Kendall Tau B Rank Order Coefficient: a statistical test using ordinal level measurement to determine if there is a linear relationship between two variables taking into account the difference between the pairs of scores (concordant—discordant) (see chart in eResources)

Kendall Tau C: a statistical test using ordinal level measurement to determine the amount of relationship (association) between the ranking of one group compared to an external criterion (see chart in eResources)

Kendall W: a statistical test using ordinal level measurement to determine if there is consistency and a difference in the mean ratings of multiple variable across individuals (see chart in eResources)

Key Informants: individuals who by virtue of the position in the group/community or organization have specific and detailed information that is important to the research

Kolmogorov-Smirnov 1 Sample Test: a test to determine if the data in a single sample is normally distributed

Kruskal-Wallis Test (One-Way Analysis of Ranks): a nonparametric statistical test using ordinal level measurement to compare the ranks of more than two groups—often used when ranks are the data categories (Likert scales) or when the assumptions of the ANOVA cannot be met (see chart in eResources)

Lack of Cultural Awareness: assuming that participants will respond as the person developing the research responds and not incorporating cultural differences into the research process

Lambda: a nonparametric statistical method using nominal level measurement to determine the percent of improvement in prediction when a predictor variable is used to estimate the value of a predicted variable—how well you can predict B from A when you use the value of A to predict B (see chart in eResources)

Leptokurtic Distribution: a distribution of values that is very steep and with little or no tails

Levene's Test: a statistical test used to determine if the variances in the dependent variable for the independent samples/groups is the same—used in an ANOVA

Linear Relationship: a form of relationship between two variables that can basically be fitted to a straight line—most of the values/scores of the y variable are close to the slope of a straight line plotted on the x variable

Linguistic Equivalent: using the same words in another culture/language

Logic Model: in program evaluation a model that lists step by step the assumptions, materials, processes and objectives for the program from inception to outcome

Longitudinal Design: a type of research design where the dependent variable is measured at more than one point in time (T1, T2, T. . .)

Loss of Participants: the amount of change that can occur in the results due to participants not completing the study and not from the IV—a threat to internal validity

Mail Survey: a survey using a questionnaire that is conducted using the postal service

Marginals: the rows and column totals in a frequency table—crosstabs—Chi-Square tests

Maturation: the amount of change that can occur in the results due to the passage of time and not from the IV—one of the threats to internal validity

Mauchly's Test of Sphericity: a statistical test to determine the homogeneity of variance in the sample/groups in a repeated measures design

McNemar Change Test: a nonparametric statistical test using nominal level measurement to determine if there was a change after an intervention with two-matched or related groups (see chart in eResources)

Mean: the weighted center of the distribution—the average of all the values in a set of data—half of the weight of the values are to the right of the mean and half are to the left of the mean

Measurement Equivalent: if linguistic and conceptual equivalence have been accomplished, you can use the scale or statements to compare culturally different groups because the same thing is being measured with a common metric

Median: the value in the distribution that is midway between the highest and lowest values

Median Test: a statistical test that uses the median to determine the amount of difference between two independent samples/groups when the dependent variable is measured at the interval or ratio level and THE ASSUMPTIONS OF THE T-TEST OR ANOVA CANNOT BE MET (see chart in eResources)

Median Test—Extension: a nonparametric statistical test that is the same as the median test where more than two groups are compared (see chart in eResources)

Member Checking: in qualitative research when all of the collected material is given to the participants and they provide feedback on accuracy

Miss: a Type II Error

Mixed Method: a research design that includes a minimum of one qualitative and one quantitative research component in the design

Mode: the most frequently occurring value in the distribution or more than one value if they have high values compared to the rest of the distribution

Multicollinearity: in regression analysis when predictor variables are highly correlated—overlap of predictors creating a problem for analysis

Multiple Baseline Design: in a single subject design where there are multiple and different target problems that are related and a single intervention employed (multiple problems with single intervention)

Narrative Approach: a method of conducting qualitative research that uses the lived story (written or spoken account) as the basis of inquiry for an individual of what happened in chronological order

Needs Assessment: in program evaluation the first phase in the process to identify and elucidate the problem

Negatively Skewed Distribution: a skewed distribution that has the tail skewed to the left

Nominal Measurement: a level of measurement that places things into groups by name—where measurement is based upon inclusion into mutually exclusive and exhaustive categories

Non-Directional Hypothesis: a hypothesis that does not state a direction of the relationship between the IV and DV—does not state more or less simply there is a relationship

Nonparametric Statistics: analytical methods based upon non-continuous data—nominal and ordinal data

Non-Participant Observation: the researcher only observes and tries to remain outside the situation as much as possible

Non-Probability Sampling: sampling method where all of the individuals to be sampled do not have an equal probability of being included in the sample

Normal Distribution: when the mean, median and mode of the distribution are equal

Objective Grounded Theory: a more structured positivistic form of grounded theory

Observed Value (O): the actual value of the dependent variable in the data

One-Sample t-Test: see t-test to a population (see chart in eResources)

One-Shot Post-Implementation Design: a research design where no data is collected prior to implementation of the intervention—often used in program evaluation

One-Shot Pre-Post Implementation Design: a research design where the variable to be changed is measured prior to the program for each participant and then measured following the program to determine if difference has occurred—often used in program evaluation

One-Way ANOVA with two groups: a parametric statistical test using interval or ratio measurement to determine the amount of difference in the means of the dependent variable between independent groups—basic level of the Analysis of Variance with two independent samples/groups—(same as the independent sample/groups t-test) (see chart in eResources)

Online Survey: a survey using a questionnaire that is conducted on the Internet

Open Coding: in the objectivist grounded theory method of qualitative research, the first in the sequence of classification information that contains the major categories

Open-Ended Question: a type of question where the respondent can provide any response they want

Operational Definition: defining a construct in terms of how it is measured

Ordinal Measurement: a level of measurement based upon rank where the distances between the ranks is not equal (the magnitude of differences between ranks is unknown)

Outcome Evaluation: in program evaluation how well the program resolved the problems identified in the needs assessment and may include other factors associated with effects of the program (cost benefit)

Outliers: values in the distribution that are at the very ends of the distribution and can skew the distribution in one direction or the other

Oversampling: increasing the number of participants from a certain group in the population that is very small (small percent of the population) in order to be able to have data to utilize on that particular subgroup

Panel Design: a type of longitudinal design where the same individuals are studied over the entire course of the research—for example, select 200 individuals at age 1 and study each participant's health until they are age 40

Paradigm: a world view that organizes one's life and can change

Parallel Forms of the Measure: when two version of a scale are developed to measure the same thing

Parameter: term used for a measurement related to a population and is calculated based upon a sample from that population

Parametric Statistics: analytical methods based upon continuous data estimating population parameters using interval or ratio level data

Participant Observation: the researcher participates in the situation but at the same time records what is occurring

Pearson r: a statistical test using interval or ratio level measurement to determine if there is a linear relationship between two variables

Percent: the amount/number of things out of 100

Phenomenological Approach: a method of qualitative research that seeks to obtain the lived experiences of a particular situation/phenomenon, usually from a small number of individuals—emphasis is on the description of the phenomenon itself and not the individual to describe meaning

Phi Coefficient: a statistical measurement of the amount of relationship (association) between two categorical variables with only two levels (see chart in eResources)

Platykurtic Distribution: a distribution of values that is very flat and with most of the distribution having very similar frequencies

Population: all of the individuals which are the basis for the research and from which the sample (smaller subset of individuals) is selected for a research study

Positively Skewed Distribution: a skewed distribution that has the tail skewed to the right

Power: correctly rejecting the null—the probability of rejecting the null and saying that a difference exists when in fact (truth) it does exist

Predicted (P): the predicted value of the dependent variable that there is a difference (Experimental Hypothesis)

Predictive Designs: a type of research design used to determine the amount of relationship/change in a variable(s) (predicted) that can be related/attributed to another variable(s) (predictor)—the variables already exist and the researcher cannot introduce/manipulate these variables

Probability: how likely something is to occur—the total number of times that something can occur divided by the number of potential/probable outcomes—p value

Program Development Evaluation: in program evaluation research the determination of the best program to meet the problems identified in the needs assessment

Purposive Sampling: a method of non-probability sampling where the researcher specifically selects certain individuals to be in the sample that provide the best and most extensive information with regard to the question and serve the goals of the study

Qualitative Research: a research method to answer questions about a person, group or culture in-depth—intent is to single out and determine individuation—not to generalize to the population

Quantitative Research: a research method to gather evidence about variables from a sample that can be generalized to the population

Questionnaire: a questionnaire is the object or guideline used in surveying and typically consists of a number of specific questions related to the research inquiry

Quota Sampling: a non-probability sampling method where the population is divided into categories and a specific number of participants are non-randomly selected from each category

R^2: (adjusted) an estimate of the amount of variance attributed to a variable that could be used to predict the dependent variable with another new and different sample (in a new and different study)

Range: the distance or value between the lowest score and the highest score in a distribution

Ratio: the amount of a variable that is subsumed in a more inclusive variable—inclusive variable = gender, subsumed = Females and Males—ratio: there are 5 Females to 1 Male

Ratio Measurement: a level of measurement where the distances between each unit of measurement are equal (equal-interval scale) and there is a known zero (things CAN be compared using ratios)

Redundant Predictor: a predictor that accounts for the same variance as another predictor

Reflection: the action of recalling and unraveling the interaction between the researcher, the participants and the overall research process in an attempt to untangle and extract the subjectivity of the researcher

Regression—Backward Method: a parametric statistical method in a regression equation where the predictor variable with the smallest partial correlation coefficient with the predicted variable is removed from the equation and then the one with the next smallest is removed and so on

Regression—Multiple: a parametric statistical method using interval or ratio level measurement to test a hypothesized relationship between multiple IVs and one DV—used for prediction (see chart in eResources)

Regression—Simple Linear: a parametric statistical method using interval or ratio level measurement to test a hypothesized relationship between two variables—used for prediction (see chart in eResources)

Regression—Enter Method: a parametric statistical method in a regression equation when all of the predictor variables are entered into the equation at the same time

Regression—Forward Method: a parametric statistical method in a regression equation when the predictor variable with the largest correlation is entered into the prediction equation first, then the second largest and so on

Regression—Stepwise Method: a parametric statistical method in a regression equation when the forward and backward methods are combined; the regression equation is recalculated after each new predictor is entered into the equation with predictor variables that no longer contribute significantly to the explanation being removed

Rejection Level: value calculated from a statistical test that shows the probability of rejecting the null hypothesis—alpha level

Reliability: when the measure is consistent and the same results/score/outcome is found again and again—obtaining the same results every time

Replication: when the exact same research study is conducted by another researcher to see if the same results are obtained as in the first study

Researchable Question: a specific type of question that asks about the existence, amount of or characteristics of a variable or about the relationship between two or more variables and is stated in such a way that it can be tested with empirical research

Residual: the amount of error in a regression equation—the amount of difference between the values/scores and the regression line

Sample: the subset of the population actually studied and used to represent the population

Sampling: the method used to select individuals from the population to be participants in a research study

Sampling Bias: obtaining a non-representative sample—obtaining too much or too little of a variable than the amount in the population

Sampling Frame: individuals from the population that are actually available to be in the research and from which the sample is drawn—the sampling frame can be redefined as the population for the purposes of the research (for example only those individuals in the city that have cell phones)

Saturation: in qualitative research the point at which little or no new information is provided—when information becomes repetitious

Scale: a method to measure attributes of a variable using many questions or statements related to those attributes

Secondary data: research data that has been previously collected by someone else

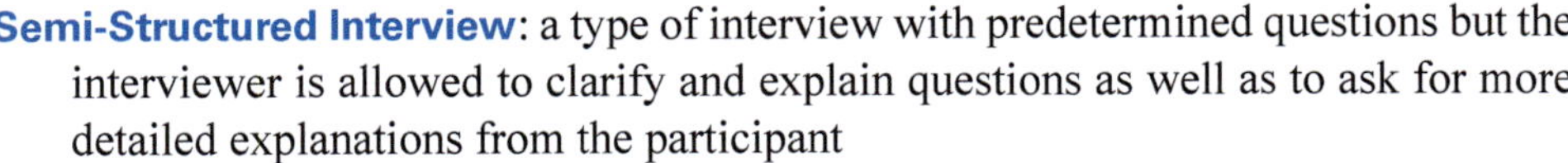

Semi-Structured Interview: a type of interview with predetermined questions but the interviewer is allowed to clarify and explain questions as well as to ask for more detailed explanations from the participant

Significant: see Statistically Significant

Simple Random Sampling: a sampling method where the individuals in the sample are selected at random from the population with each one having an equal probability of selection

Single Subject Design: A type of research design that measures the outcome of an intervention with one client, one couple or one family and is longitudinal (measurements over a period of time)

Skewed Distribution: when one side or tail of a distribution is much longer than the other side or tail of the distribution

Snowball Sample: a non-probability sampling method where the first participant in the research becomes a recruiter for the next participants and they in turn recruit participants and so on

Somer's d (see chart): a nonparametric statistical method using ordinal level measurement to predict a consequent condition (DV) from an antecedent condition (IV) using concordant and discordant pairs but only including ties from rows (antecedent) and not columns (consequent)

Spearman rho—Rank Order Coefficient: a statistical test using ordinal level measurement to determine if there is a linear relationship between two variables (see chart in eResources)

Split Half Reliability: taking all the items in a scale and dividing them into two parts and comparing the scores (answers) on one half to the other half to determine consistency

Stable Baseline: in single subject design where the occurrence of the target (behavior/attitude/problem) is relatively flat—not increasing, not decreasing, not cyclic and not erratic but rather constant across time

Standard Deviation: a measure of how things vary—a number that indicates the spread of the distribution and represents a defined distance along the base of the distribution curve—the square root of the variance

Standard Score: a score in units of standard deviation from the mean of the distribution (in a standardized distribution)

Standardized Distribution: setting the distribution to a standard normal distribution where the mean of the distribution is set to zero and the standard deviation is set to 1

Standardized Variable: a normally distributed variable that has a mean of μ and a standard deviation of σ

Statistic: term used for a measurement related to a sample

Statistical Regression: the amount of change that can occur in the results due to multiple sampling and measurement that leads to those measurements being closer to the average—a threat to internal validity

Statistically Significant: when a researcher decides that the outcome is unlikely to have occurred by chance—not occurring by chance—a "true" relationship

Strand: in mixed method design each method, qualitative and quantitative, is called a strand

Stratified Random Sampling: a sampling method that subdivides the population into "strata" from which the separate subsamples are randomly selected

Structured Interview: a type of interview in which every question is scripted and the interviewer is not allowed to deviate from the script to obtain answers to those specified questions

Summative Evaluation: in program evaluation determining how well the program is achieving the stated outcome

Survey: a set of questions to provide information relevant to the variables in the research study

Systematic Random Sampling: a sampling method that begins at a random position and then every nth entry from the population is selected for inclusion in the sample

***t*Test One Sample**: a parametric statistical test using interval or ratio level measurement to compare a sample to the population (see chart in eResources)

t-Test Paired—Matched Samples/Groups: a parametric statistical test using interval or ratio measurement with paired/matched groups to determine if there is a difference between groups—used in a pre-post design—same as a repeated measures ANOVA with only two groups (see chart in eResources)

***t*-Test—Two Independent Samples/Groups**: a parametric statistical test using interval or ratio level measurement to determine if there is a difference between two independent groups/samples (see chart in eResources)

Test-Retest Reliability: the degree to which the result of the measure following a short lapse of time is the same as the previous result—the correlation between the two measurements indicates the degree of reliability

Theory (Basic): applies to a myriad of situations—exhibiting breadth of explanation for individual and social interactions

Theory (Intervention): applicable to practice—may incorporate parts of various basic theories—used to explain more specific situations

Town Hall Meeting: a meeting where the community is invited to discuss any problems facing the community

Transcription Checking: in qualitative research, having a person outside the research study compare the transcription of the observation/interview with the original recording to identify mistakes and make corrections

Transferability: the ability of the results to extend beyond the sample of participants to the population (Qualitative Research and similar to generalizability in Quantitative Research)

Transplantability: the amount of similarity/difference evaluated a priori of factors (culture, clients, those delivering the program, etc.) to determine the potential success or failure of adopting a program in a new context (destination) that originated in another context (origin)

Trend Design: a type of longitudinal design where the sample selected from the population is always changing over the length of the entire data collection—census data

Two Group Pre-post Control Design: same as the one group pre-post design but with the addition of a group that does not receive the intervention

Type I Error: error in the researcher's decision saying there is a difference where there is no difference—reject the null when it is true—alpha error

Type II Error: error in the researcher's decision saying there is no difference where there is a difference—accept the null when it is not true—beta error

Unimodal Distribution: a frequency distribution with only one value having the highest frequency

Unstable Baseline: in single subject design when there is no pattern in the occurrence of the target (behavior/attitude/problem) prior to any intervention (erratic and non-predictive baseline—not increasing, not decreasing and not cyclic)

Unstructured Interview: a type of interview that allows the participants to recall and describe the experience in their own terms

Validity: the accuracy of the research measurements and the accuracy of those measurements to reflect the population

Variability: how values differ on a particular variable—the dispersion of the values on that variable

Variable: a construct that we can assign values/attributes to and use in research

Variance: the measure of the variability in the distribution—the sum of the square of the deviation from the mean of the distribution—the square of the standard deviation

Wilcoxon-Mann-Whitney U Test: a nonparametric statistical test using ordinal measurement to determine differences between two groups

Wilcoxon Signed Ranks Test: a nonparametric statistical test using ordinal level measurement to determine if there was a change after an intervention with two-matched or related groups (see chart in eResources)

x Variable: the predictor variable in a regression equation and plotted along the base—horizontal line—abscissa of the scatterplot

y Variable: the predicted variable in a regression equation and plotted along the side—vertical—ordinate of the scatterplot

Z Score: a score that has been transformed (standardized)—it can be used to determine how many standard deviations the score is from the mean in a standard normal distribution

Z Test: a statistical test that can be used if you know the mean and standard deviation of the population to determine if a particular sample is different from that population

REFERENCES AND ADDITIONAL READING

American Psychological Association. (2010). *Publication manual of the American Psychological Association* (6th ed.). Washington, DC: American Psychological Association.

Blalock, H. M. (1979). *Social statistics*. New York, NY: McGraw-Hill.

Bloom, M., Fisher, J., & Orme, J. (2003). *Evaluating practice: Guidelines for the accountable professional*. Boston, MA: Allyn & Bacon.

Charmaz, K. (2014). *Constructing grounded theory*. London: Sage.

Cresswell, J. W., & Cresswell, J. D. (2017). *Research design: Qualitative, quantitative and mixed methods approaches*. London: Sage.

Gibbons, J. D., & Chakraborti, S. (2010). *Nonparametric statistical inference*. Boca Raton, FL: Chapman Hall, CRC.

Gordon, R. A. (2012). *Applied statistics for the social and health sciences*. New York, NY: Routledge, Taylor & Francis.

Gordon, R. A. (2015). *Regression analysis for the social sciences*. New York, NY: Routledge, Taylor & Francis.

Grinnell, R. M., & Unrau, Y. A. (2005). *Social work research and evaluation: Quantitative and qualitative approaches*. New York, NY: Oxford University Press.

Hays, W. L. (1964). *Statistics for psychologists*. New York, NY: Holt, Rinehart and Winston.

Hersen, M., & Barlow, D. (1978). *Single case experimental designs: Strategies for studying behavior change*. Elmsford, NY: Pergamon Press.

Jayaratne, S., & Levy, R. (1979). *Empirical clinical practice*. New York, NY: Columbia University Press.

Jones, J. (1993). *Bad blood: The Tuskegee syphilis experiment* (Revised ed.). New York, NY: Free Press.

Kerlinger, F. N., & Lee, H. B. (2000). *Foundations of behavioral research*. Fort Worth, TX: Harcourt College Publishers.

Myers, L. S., Gamst, G., & Guerino, A. J. (2013). *Applied multivariate research: Design and interpretation*. London: Sage.

National Commission for the Protection of Human Subjects of Biomedical and Behavioral Research. (1979). *The Belmont Report*. Retrieved from www.hhs.gov/ohrp/regulations-and-policy/belmont-report/read-the-belmont-report/index.html

Patten, M. L., & Newhart, M. (2018). *Understanding research methods: An overview of the essentials*. New York, NY: Routledge, Taylor & Francis.

Patton, M. Q. (2014). *Qualitative research & evaluation methods: Integrating theory and practice*. London: Sage.

Royce, D. (1992). *Program evaluation: An introduction*. Chicago, IL: Nelson-Hall.

Royse, D. (2010). *Research methods in social work*. Belmont, CA: Brooks/Cole.

Royse, D., Thayer, B., & Padgett, D. (2015). *Program evaluation: An introduction to an evidence-based approach*. Belmont, CA: Cengage.

Rubin, A., & Babbie, K. (2017). *Research methods for social work*. Belmont, CA: Brooks/Cole.

Siegel, S., & Castellan, N. J. (1988). *Nonparametric statistics for the behavioral sciences*. New York, NY: McGraw-Hill.

Spitz, V. (2005). *Doctors from hell: The horrific account of Nazi experiments on humans*. Boulder, CO: Sentient Publications.

Tabachnick, B. G., & Fidell, L. S. (2007). *Using multivariate statistics*. Boston, MA: Allyn & Bacon.

World Health Organization. (2001). Declaration of Helsinki. *Bulletin of the World Health Organization*, *79*(4), 373–374. Retrieved from www.who.int/bulletin/archives/79%284%29373.pdf

Yegedis, B., & Weinbach, R. W. (2002). *Research methods for social workers*. Boston, MA: Allyn & Bacon.

INDEX